SACRAMENTO PUBLIC LIBRARY
828 "I" Street
Sacramento, CA 95814
11/17

WITHDRAWN
FROM THE COLLECTION OF
SACRAMENTO PUBLIC LIBRARY

D0975421

ALSO BY ROBERT W. MERRY

*Where They Stand: The American Presidents
in the Eyes of Voters and Historians*

*A Country of Vast Designs:
James K. Polk, the Mexican War
and the Conquest of the American Continent*

*Sands of Empire: Missionary Zeal,
American Foreign Policy, and the Hazards of Global Ambition*

*Taking on the World: Joseph and Stewart Alsop—
Guardians of the American Century*

Architect

of the

American Century

PRESIDENT McKINLEY

ROBERT W. MERRY

Simon & Schuster

New York   London   Toronto   Sydney   New Delhi

Simon & Schuster
1230 Avenue of the Americas
New York, NY 10020

Copyright © 2017 by Robert W. Merry

All rights reserved, including the right to reproduce this book or portions
thereof in any form whatsoever. For information address Simon & Schuster Subsidiary
Rights Department, 1230 Avenue of the Americas, New York, NY 10020.

First Simon & Schuster hardcover edition November 2017

SIMON & SCHUSTER and colophon are registered
trademarks of Simon & Schuster, Inc.

For information about special discounts for bulk purchases,
please contact Simon & Schuster Special Sales at
1-866-506-1949 or business@simonandschuster.com.

The Simon & Schuster Speakers Bureau can bring authors to your live event.
For more information or to book an event contact the Simon & Schuster Speakers
Bureau at 1-866-248-3049 or visit our website at www.simonspeakers.com.

Interior design by Joy O'Meara

Manufactured in the United States of America

1 3 5 7 9 10 8 6 4 2

Library of Congress Cataloging-in-Publication Data
Names: Merry, Robert W., 1946– author.
Title: President McKinley / Robert W. Merry.
Description: New York : Simon & Schuster, 2017. |
Includes bibliographical references and index.
Identifiers: LCCN 2016050943 (print) | LCCN 2016053191 (ebook) |
ISBN 9781451625448 (hardback) | ISBN 9781451625455 (trade paperback) |
ISBN 9781451625462 (ebook)
Subjects: LCSH: McKinley, William, 1843-1901. | Presidents—United States—Biography. |
BISAC: BIOGRAPHY & AUTOBIOGRAPHY / Presidents & Heads of State. |
HISTORY / United States / 19th Century. | HISTORY / United States / General.
Classification: LCC E711.6 .M54 2017 (print) | LCC E711.6 (ebook) | DDC 973.8/8092
[B]—dc23
LC record available at https://lccn.loc.gov/2016050943

ISBN 978-1-4516-2544-8
ISBN 978-1-4516-2546-2 (ebook)

To Maisie, Elliott, Genevieve, and Colton,
keeping the flame alive

— CONTENTS —

PRESIDENT
McKINLEY

The Mystery of William McKinley

President William McKinley arrived in Buffalo, New York, on the evening of September 4, 1901, intent on deflecting history with a speech. The Ohio politician's shiny and luxurious presidential train crawled into the city's Terrace Station at six-thirty that evening, and the presidential party moved quickly toward waiting carriages near the north gate of the Pan-American Exposition, an attention-grabbing extravaganza that opened its doors on May 20. It featured exhibits, spectacles, musical performances, athletic events, and more—most notably, displays of the latest technological wonders, including an X-ray machine and the startling advent of alternating current, allowing the efficient transmission of electricity through long-distance power lines. This promising advance brought enough power to Buffalo from Niagara Falls turbines, twenty-five miles away, to illuminate the entire exposition grounds in a nighttime display of electrical wizardry.

This was just the kind of marvel to capture the imagination of a nation on the move, pushing into the twentieth century as it had pushed westward across North America during the previous hundred years— with resolve, confidence, and disregard for accompanying hazards. Now, under McKinley, America was developing and harnessing technology like no other nation, generating unparalleled industrial expansion and wealth, moving beyond its continental confines and into the world. It wasn't surprising that Americans would flock to the Buffalo exposition—an estimated eight million or more over six months—to bask in their country's promise, or that Exposition leaders would designate a special day to honor the president. Neither was it surprising that McKinley would choose that day to summon support for a major policy departure for America—and for himself. The Pan-American Exposition represented a fitting convergence of the man, the event, and the era.

No development defined the era more clearly than the rise of America as a global power. This came about mostly through the brief, momentous war with imperial Spain two years earlier—"a splendid little war," as historian and diplomat John Hay called it. When it was over, Spain no longer possessed a colonial empire of any consequence, and America had planted its flag upon the soil of Cuba (as a temporary protectorate) and upon Puerto Rico, Guam, and the Philippines (as permanent possessions). For good measure, the country acquired Hawaii, one of the most strategic points on the globe, a kind of Gibraltar of the Pacific. In addition, the country was building a navy to rival the great navies of the world and demonstrating a capacity to deploy troops quickly and effectively to far-flung lands.

American economic and diplomatic power also surged. U.S. goods, both manufacturing and agricultural, were being gobbled up in overseas markets, and this burgeoning export trade promised ongoing U.S. prosperity. President McKinley was discovering, moreover, that this new military and economic might had rendered America a nation to be reckoned with. Just the year before the country had nudged the major European powers and Japan toward a collective policy in China—favorable to U.S. interests and conducive to regional stability—that most of those countries didn't particularly like.

As for the event, the Pan-American Exposition sought ostensibly to foster and celebrate a kind of diplomatic and economic brotherhood among the nations of the Americas. Indeed, when John Hay, as secretary of state, visited the Exposition the previous June, he titled his remarks "Brotherhood of the Nations of the Western World." But, as the *New York Times* noted, America's relations with its Western Hemisphere neighbors often reflected "unconcealed haughtiness mingled with something not unlike greed." And Hay's remarks, notwithstanding his title, seemed less a celebration of any kind of brotherhood than of American grandeur, reflected in his paean to "this grand and beautiful spectacle, never to be forgotten, a delight to the eyes, a comfort to every patriotic heart that during the coming Summer shall make the joyous pilgrimage to this enchanted scene."

Then there was the man, fifty-eight years old at the time of the Buffalo Exposition, now five months into his second presidential term. To his detractors, William McKinley seemed an unlikely figure to be presiding over the transformation of America. In this view, the affable, stolid, seemingly plodding McKinley hadn't really led America through the momentous developments of his presidency but rather had himself been manipulated by events beyond his control. And yet nobody could dispute his political popularity. His 1900 reelection margin exceeded the margin of all recent presidential victories. And even getting reelected at all marked a notable political achievement in an era with few two-term presidencies. Many in McKinley's day argued that his commanding position atop the country's political firmament testified indisputably to his political effectiveness and brilliance. But others dismissed that view as fanciful. They insisted on judging him as unequal to his deeds.

That was the mystery of William McKinley, which baffled many contemporaries as it would intrigue subsequent generations of historians and biographers. The wife of a prominent Ohio politician—alternately a McKinley ally and rival—referred to "the masks that he wore." A later historian of the period called him "a tantalizing enigma." The enigma was this: How did such a man manage to preside over such a national transformation? Or did he?

Short of stature, with broad shoulders and a large, expressive face, McKinley peered at the world through deep-socketed gray eyes that seemed almost luminescent. Kindly and sweet-tempered, he once invited into his closed carriage, during a downpour, a hostile reporter who had been attacking him in print throughout a congressional reelection campaign.

"Here, you put on this overcoat and get into that carriage," he told the rain-soaked journalist.

"I guess you don't know who I am," replied the surprised scribe. "I have been with you the whole campaign, giving it to you every time you spoke and I am going over to-night to rip you to pieces if I can."

"I know," said the congressman, "but you put on this coat and get inside so you can do a better job."

Such self-effacing solicitude, so natural in McKinley and rare in most high-powered men, led some to conclude this congenial politician lacked the cold instinct for audacious and functional leadership. Further, his intellect did not display an imaginative turn of mind given to bold thinking or creative vision. Rather, McKinley possessed an administrative cast of mind, focused on immediate decision-making imperatives. He was cautious, methodical, a master of incrementalism. Such traits contributed to the McKinley mystery. He never moved in a straight line, seldom declared where he wanted to take the country, somehow moved people and events from the shadows. He rarely twisted arms in efforts at political persuasion, never raised his voice in political cajolery, didn't visibly seek revenge. And yet he seemed always to outmaneuver his rivals and get his way. How did this happen?

It happened through some powerful yet opaque McKinley traits, most notably his ability to comprehend the intricacies of events as they unfolded and mesh them conceptually into effective decision making that moved the country in significant new directions. He had learned through a lifetime of politics that his quiet ways somehow translated into a commanding presence; his was a heavy quiet that could be exploited stealthily. Throughout his early days in the military, as a lawyer, and in politics, he could see that men responded to him and looked to him for leadership. Further, though a man of deep convictions, he developed a flexibility of mind that prevented dogma from thwarting opportunity. He struggled manfully to avoid the war with Spain, for example, but when that proved impossible he prosecuted it with a vigorous resolve to crush the Spanish Empire and kick it out of the Caribbean. Following the Spanish defeat, he hesitated on what to do with the Philippines but eventually concluded the only realistic course was acquisition of the entire archipelago. So he took it and never looked back.

And though a lifelong protectionist on trade matters—indeed, the country's leading advocate of high tariffs—he now saw that America's thrust into the world and its growing overseas trade rendered obsolete his old philosophical commitment to "ultra-protectionism." That was what he came to Buffalo to say, in terms so muscular and eloquent that nobody could miss the full import of his conversion.

As the presidential train pulled to a stop at Terrace Station, artillerymen from nearby Fort Porter set off a twenty-one-cannon salute so thunderous that it shattered several train windows and jolted nearly everyone in the vicinity, most particularly Ida McKinley. She swooned briefly from the sudden fright. Later, as McKinley led her to a waiting carriage, she experienced a "sensory overload" as the crowd roared, bells rang out, train whistles blasted, and bands struck up martial music. The solicitous husband placed a shawl over her shoulders, ushered her into the carriage, and spread a lap robe over her legs as four handsome bays pulled the vehicle toward the fairground.

McKinley remained always attentive to every nuance of Ida's health and mood. In fact, his constant attention to her was a hallmark of his public image. The press described her routinely as an "invalid," though her condition was more complicated than that word conveyed. She suffered from a series of interconnected maladies that at times restricted her mobility and left her psychologically brittle. On this occasion she revived quickly from the disorientation caused by all the noise and "smiled happily" from the carriage window as she passed onlookers. Hardly did it seem possible from her sprightly demeanor that just a few weeks before she had been hovering near death in San Francisco, fighting off an infection that had begun with a cut finger and spread through her blood. The nation had watched in rapt alarm as she nearly died, then finally entered a slow recovery. The president remained at her side through most of the ordeal, leaving her only when his presidential duties absolutely required it. He canceled the rest of what had been planned as an extensive Western tour and postponed his scheduled Buffalo visit from June to September. Thus was he now at the Pan-American Exposition.

After touring the 350-acre fairground, with its big red and yellow pavilions and 389-foot-high Electric Tower, the presidential entourage alighted at the nearby green-brick mansion of John Milburn, a broad-faced and clean-shaven Buffalo lawyer who served as Exposition chair-man. The congenial Milburn, an English immigrant, had offered the hospitality of his home during the presidential party's Buffalo stay.

The next morning, the president and Ida left the Milburn residence at around ten, escorted by twenty mounted police and twenty members of the U.S. signal corps. They headed by carriage to the Exposition structure called the Esplanade, where they were greeted by "probably the greatest crowd ever assembled there," as the *New York Times* speculated. Indeed, a record attendance of nearly 116,000 people flocked to the Exposition on this day. It wasn't surprising that the president's appearance would generate this kind of excitement. Intellectuals, commentators, and editorial writers may have argued over McKinley's civic contributions or his role in the events of his presidency, but among voters the president enjoyed a hearty sentiment of approval. To ordinary Americans, he seemed solid, competent, a product of Midwestern values absorbed during his Ohio youth and while representing his Ohio district in Congress and the entire state as governor. Voters took note of his exploits during the Civil War, when he entered the army as an eighteen-year-old private and ended the war as a brevet major, most of his promotions coming after feats of battlefield valor. They liked his unadorned political rhetoric heralding traditional mores and simple verities.

As he ascended the stand and reached the speaking podium, the president pulled from his coat pocket a speech produced by his own hand but with substantial research assistance from his loyal and highly competent secretary, George Cortelyou. As always, however, he had solicited advice from friends and colleagues on the fine points of expression. His theme, as so often in the past, was the upward trajectory of the human experience—and the imperative of maintaining it through unfettered economic energy. Expositions helped in that regard, he said, because they were "the timekeepers of progress. They record the world's advancement." And this particular Exposition, he added, illustrated "the progress of the human family in the Western Hemisphere."

The president then moved quickly to the state of global commerce, America's role in it, and the lessons to be learned from big advances in cross-border trade. The significance of these observations extended beyond McKinley's words and concepts. Since its inception, the Republican Party, McKinley's party, had been the party of protectionism: high tariffs not just for revenue but also to protect domestic enterprise from foreign competitors. This had been the philosophy also of the Republicans' antecedent party, the Whigs, and, before them, the Federalists. Thus did high-tariff principles go back to the beginning of the Republic—indeed, all the way to its first treasury secretary, Alexander Hamilton. And throughout the intervening decades no politician personified this outlook more solemnly than William McKinley. As chairman of the House Ways and Means Committee, he had shepherded through Congress in 1890 a high-tariff bill named after him. Upon becoming president, he promptly pushed through a new protectionism measure to overturn the more free-trade policies of Democratic president Grover Cleveland. But now he set out to move his party and his country in a new direction, more in keeping with America's new global position.

"Isolation is no longer possible or desirable," said the president, noting the powerful advances in the movement of goods, people, and information across wide distances. That had brought the world closer together, fostering more and more international trade. America, with its vast productive capacity, stood positioned to exploit this development like no other country. But this could happen only if Americans embraced a policy he called reciprocity: mutual trade agreements designed to reduce tariffs and enhance trade. "Reciprocity," he said, "is the natural outgrowth of our wonderful industrial development under the domestic policy now firmly established." Echoing a fundamental free-trade tenet, he added, "We must not repose in fancied security that we can forever sell everything and buy little or nothing." In other words, if the country wanted markets for its burgeoning products, it also would have to buy products from abroad. "The period of exclusiveness is past," said the president. "Reciprocity treaties are in harmony with the spirit of the times; measures of retaliation are not."

McKinley ended his speech by advocating a number of initiatives that together demonstrated a coherent view of how multiple elements of an expansionist program should be commingled. He wanted to bolster the U.S. Merchant Marine. "Next in advantage to having the thing to sell," he said, "is to have the conveyance to carry it to the buyer." He hailed the U.S. ambition to build a canal through the Central American isthmus, something he had been promoting with his usual quiet determination throughout his presidency. And he averred that the "construction of a Pacific cable cannot be longer postponed."

McKinley may not have been a man of vision in the vein of his contemporaries Theodore Roosevelt, Henry Cabot Lodge, and Alfred Thayer Mahan, all of whom perceived and promoted the American ascendancy long before events brought it into focus for others. But he was a man of perception who, once that focus emerged, knew how to formulate the vision and execute it. Under this concept, as applied by McKinley, America would push out on many related fronts: expanding global commerce and reducing barriers to it, augmenting naval power, controlling strategic points in the nearby Caribbean and far-off Asia, building a merchant marine, constructing and controlling an isthmian canal, enhancing cable communications around the world. As the *London Standard* would write of the Buffalo speech, "It is the utterance of a man who feels that he is at the head of a great nation, with vast ambitions and a new-born consciousness of strength."

McKinley's audience responded with particularly hearty applause to his call for reciprocity treaties, his advocacy of a Central American canal and a transpacific cable, and his warm words about Pan-American cooperation. After the speech, a number of people broke through the lines surrounding the podium to gather around the president, who avidly conducted an impromptu conversation with them for some fifteen minutes. This was a Secret Service nightmare: the president in close proximity to significant numbers of people who had not been properly scrutinized beforehand. As former attorney general John Griggs explained later, "I warned him against this very thing time and time again." But the president, he added, "insisted that the American people were too intelligent and too loyal to their country to do any harm to their Chief Executive." The next morning the president would sneak past his Secret Service detail to enjoy a solitary walk along Buffalo's leafy Delaware Avenue. And he repeatedly rebuffed suggestions from Cortelyou and others that he cancel a reception-line event at the Exposition's Temple of Music the day after the trade speech. "Why should I?" he responded. "No one would wish to hurt me." The president loved shaking hands with fellow citizens and developed a system of moving people along so efficiently that he could shake as many as fifty hands a minute.

Following the impromptu session with citizens, Mr. and Mrs. McKinley embarked upon a whirlwind of tightly orchestrated events and tours, including a review of U.S. troops at the Exposition stadium, a tour of horticultural exhibits, and visits to various national buildings representing such countries as Honduras, Mexico, Ecuador—and Puerto Rico, which McKinley had made a U.S. possession. The afternoon included a luncheon at the New York Pavilion, a brief rest opportunity, and then a reception at the Government Building, where the president shook hands for twenty minutes. The evening schedule included a fireworks display that occupied the president's attention until around nine. The next day's events included a boat tour below Niagara Falls and then the Temple of Music reception that Cortelyou had warned against.

Lurking in the shadows throughout the presidential visit and planning to join the receiving line at the Temple of Music was an obscure anarchist named Leon Czolgosz. While McKinley had made history through a lifetime of conscientious political toil, Czolgosz planned to make history through a single destructive act.

— 1 —

Ohio Roots

THE STAMP OF A BURGEONING STATE

The prominent Massachusetts minister and physician Manasseh Cutler captured the optimism of Americans at the dawn of their republic when he described the territory between Lake Erie and the Ohio River as "the garden of the world, the seat of wealth, and the *centre* of a great Empire." In these lands, he mused, "the arts and sciences [will] be planted; the seeds of virtue, happiness, and glory be firmly rooted and grow up to full maturity." It's worth noting that, when he wasn't ministering to his New England flock or tending to his patients, Cutler speculated in Western lands and dreamed of wealth, and no doubt there was some marketing hyperbole in his lyrical description of territory so far from American civilization. Indeed, that expanse struck most Easterners at the time as hopelessly inaccessible—on the far side of the merciless Appalachian Mountains, bordered on the north by British Canada and the south by Spanish Louisiana, peopled by hostile natives bent on protecting their homeland through whatever savage methods they could devise.

But Cutler understood the new republic's expansionist impulse. When he died in Massachusetts in 1823, those lands of his vision, now roughly the state of Ohio, boasted the country's fifth-largest population, with 581,434 residents. These were young and hearty folk—64 percent of them under the age of twenty-five—and by 1830 they had subdued nearly all the state's land suitable for cultivation. By midcentury Ohio led the nation in the production of corn, much of it transformed into whiskey and hogs for easy transport, and a decade later the state's population of 2,339,502 trailed only those of New York and Pennsylvania. As a later historian put it, "Ohio recapitulated the history of colonial encounter, conquest, and postcolonial development with breathtaking speed."

Ohio also developed its own political culture. One of the first imperatives of the new nation was to surmount that Appalachian barrier, push the Indians westward, and expand the country's territorial birthright to include those lands that had so beguiled the Reverend Mr. Cutler. Thus did Ohio's rise coincide with the rise of the nation. Unencumbered by entrenched interests and protected folkways, the pioneers of Ohio could shape their own brand of democracy. As the country entered the political struggle between Andrew Jackson's populist Democrats, committed to low taxes and limited government, and the governmental dynamism of Henry Clay's Whigs, Ohioans embraced elements of both.

Like the Jacksonians, they placed enormous faith in the collective wisdom of the people—"fully competent to govern themselves," as a prominent lawyer named Michael Baldwin put it in 1802, a year before statehood. He declared that the citizens constituted "the only proper judges of their own interest and their own concerns." Also like the Jacksonians, Ohioans insisted upon an equality of esteem for all citizens of whatever social or economic station. An early Methodist minister named John Sale expressed his appreciation for living "in a Country where there is so much of an Equallity & a Man is not thought to be great here because he possesses a little more of this Worlds rubbish than his Neighbor." But Ohioans also embraced elements of Clay's "American System" of public works and civic projects. A powerful commitment to commercial success took root, along with a devotion to both public and private endeavors designed to foster progress—canals, roads, bridges, schools, libraries, universities, newspapers.

Further, Ohio's central location and topography ensured that it became a magnet for various distinct population groups. Americans moved west generally in geographical bands that preserved the mores, folkways, and speech patterns of those in each migration. But in Ohio, Southerners flooded into the river valleys of the state's southern reaches, while New England Yankees settled the northeast corner and the lower Muskingum Valley. Settlers from Pennsylvania, New York, and New Jersey, mostly Scottish and Scotch Irish, clustered in the eastern and central portions of the state and the Miami Valley. Each group brought its own characteristics—dialect, outlook, politics, even barn architecture. Soon these cultural elements melded into a complex pastiche of politics reflecting multiple sensibilities of the broader country, contributing to Ohio as microcosm state.

It is noteworthy that, as the slavery issue gripped the nation, Ohio produced one of the country's most fervent warriors against human bondage in Joshua Giddings, and in Clement Vallandigham, one of its most fearless opponents of the North's eventual aggression against the wayward South. The state emerged as an outpost of antislavery sentiment and a pathway for runaway slaves seeking freedom via the famous Underground Railroad; but it also proved inhospitable to freed blacks desiring to settle there. When war broke out, however, Ohio's abhorrence of slavery and devotion to union won out. It sent more recruits per capita into the Northern army than any other state, placing 320,000 men into blue uniforms for the struggle.

One of those was William McKinley Jr., then barely eighteen, who worked as a schoolteacher and summertime postal clerk in Poland, a compact hamlet in Ohio's iron-manufacturing northeast. He was a winsome lad, short of stature but broad of shoulder, with a ready affability mixed with an earnest bearing. He traced his New World roots to David McKinley, "David the Weaver," who arrived in America early in the eighteenth century and settled in York, Pennsylvania, to ply his trade and seek his fortune. David McKinley's heritage extended back to a Scottish chieftain named Fionn laoch, translated as "fair-haired chief" and pronounced Fin-lay. With the "Mac" later added to denote "son of Fin-lay," the family name became McKinlay, subsequently changed to McKinley. Descendants of this early Fionn laoch migrated from Scotland to Ulster, Ireland, most likely in the seventeenth century, and became tenant farmers. From there they ventured across the Atlantic to America.

The American McKinleys eventually intermarried with folks of English ancestry and set out to exploit New World opportunities as best they could, subject to the vicissitudes of fate. David the Weaver purchased 316 acres of farmland along Pennsylvania's Susquehanna River, and one of his sons built upon his robust inheritance through extensive business activity. A second David McKinley, grandson of David the Weaver, fought in the American Revolution as a militia private and participated in a number of skirmishes. His son James, lacking even a meager education, gravitated to the foundry business and managed blast furnaces in the steel regions around New Lisbon (later Lisbon), Ohio. His son, William, born in 1807, carried on the trade at various Ohio locations.

This first William McKinley personified Ohio's devotion to hard toil, civic pride, and family fecundity. He was a broad-faced man with a square jaw, stern lips, and a taciturn demeanor. Though lacking even a modest formal education, he read when he could and kept three books constantly within reach: the Bible, Shakespeare, and Dante. But reading time was scarce. Foundry work required a strong back, multiple skills, and constant attention. To produce pig iron, he mined the ore, chopped and stacked the wood for the charcoal furnaces, burned the charcoal, manned the hot forges, and procured the finished product. Around 1830, with a partner, he rented a furnace at Niles and later joined a brother-in-law in leasing and purchasing furnaces at various times at Fairfield, New Wilmington, New Lisbon, and Niles, all Ohio towns.

In 1829 William McKinley married Nancy Allison, a solemn but caring woman who personified Ohio's commitment to simple verities and the Christian values of thrift, optimism, modesty, and hard work. She possessed abundant energy, organizational acumen, and a strong disposition to serve her community, particularly her Methodist church. The product of Scottish immigrants who settled initially in Pennsylvania, she was "a born gentlewoman," as a later biographer described her. This was reflected in a widely told story about her in later life, when she traveled to Columbus, Ohio, by train to visit her son, the governor of Ohio. A woman next to her struck up a conversation.

"Are you going to Columbus?"

"Yes."

"Do you have family there?"

"I have a son there."

She pushed her children to academic diligence and plenished the little family library with such volumes as Hume's *History of England*, Gibbon's *Decline and Fall*, and various Dickens novels. She subscribed to Horace Greeley's influential *Weekly Tribune*, which reinforced the family's aversion to slavery and embrace of Northern sentiments.

According to a report of the day, Niles contained "3 churches, 3 stores, 1 blast furnace, rolling mill and nail factory, 1 forge and grist mill and about 300 inhabitants." As William Sr. later recalled, "There wasn't much of a town there then. . . . No railroads, no canals, and terribly poor, wild country roads." William's income barely covered the necessities of the large family that soon emerged. The couple produced nine children, eight of whom survived into adulthood, and brought them up in a spacious but simple frame house on the town's main street, with part of the first floor set aside as a grocery store.

William Jr., born January 29, 1843, was the seventh child. He grew up in small-town isolation, the only regular outside communication coming via the stagecoach that traversed the dusty, rutted road to and from Pittsburgh. But young William's parents insisted that he and his siblings take full advantage of the local school, run by a teacher named Alva Sanford. The children were spiffed up each week for services and Sunday school at the local Methodist Episcopal church, where circuit-riding preachers cast their rugged eloquence and stern piety over the congregants. Along with religious instruction, they imparted a strong sense of duty, patriotism, and rectitude in human endeavors. Young William McKinley embraced all of it. Even as a small boy he accepted the challenging task of driving the family cows to and from pasture, a duty that in winter left his feet miserably cold. Decades later he remembered warding off the cold by pressing his feet into the soil where the cows had lain and enjoying the "pure *luxury*" of their leftover warmth.

When the lad was nine, his parents moved the family to Poland, in Mahoning County to the south. The father's business remained at Niles, some twenty miles away, which necessitated extended absences from his wife and children and long weekend commutes on horseback. But the new town offered greater educational opportunities, and young William enrolled in the Poland Seminary, founded in 1849 by an Allegheny College graduate named B. F. Lee. Through relentless fundraising, largely among civic-minded local Methodists, Lee managed to erect a three-story brick school and assemble a small staff of teachers and administrators. For William, the most important of these was an instructor named Miss E. M. Blakelee, who offered abundant encouragement to those willing to submit to her rigid authoritarianism.

At school and on nearby playgrounds, young William emerged as a popular lad, friendly in manner, who delighted in the various games and sports that occupied the town's boys. Neighborhood friends recalled that he excelled in competitive activities, and one noted, "Will is good at anything he goes at." But he insisted on fulfilling his studies before play on the theory that leisure time was more enjoyable without school obligations hanging over him. He maintained a neat appearance and always displayed gentlemanly manners, though he didn't look down on the rougher set. While he never indulged in swear words, he showed no disdain for those who did.

Within his family, he responded avidly to his strong-minded mother's moral entreaties and religious sensibilities. He demonstrated his piety at one of the stirring religious revivals that occasionally materialized on the outskirts of town, under huge tents erected for the occasion. People arrived in great numbers from surrounding environs to take in the "torrents of eloquence" flowing from the lips of the revival orators. At one camp meeting, a minister urged those wishing to "profess conversion" to step forward to the "mourner's bench" and unite with the church. Young William McKinley, just ten at the time and unprompted by family members, marched up to accept his savior. Nancy McKinley immediately concluded that the ministry would be an ideal calling for her son.

At school he thrived owing to a dutiful commitment to his studies and a natural intelligence. "It was seldom that his head was not in a book," one childhood acquaintance recalled. But there was a simplicity to his sturdy intellect. He could quickly get to the heart of a matter and distill it for ready comprehension, but seldom did he manifest flourishes of thought or flights of imagination. His was a literal and linear cast of mind. This served him well in the school discipline he most enjoyed: elocution. When it came time for "speaking pieces," as oratory was called, he stood ramrod straight and delivered his speeches with efficiency and pride.

He helped create a student group called the Everett Literary and Debating Society, a collection of young scholars who enjoyed public speaking and maintained a room at the academy set aside for the activity. The group raised money to buy a fancy carpet, a collection of classic literature and history books, and a large picture of Massachusetts senator Edward Everett, widely considered one of the greatest orators of the day. To protect the carpet, the boys left their muddy boots at the door and wore slippers purchased with society funds and kept on site for the purpose. Will McKinley was elected the society's first president.

As the slavery issue captured the national consciousness, generating intense political passions, there never was any doubt where the McKinley family stood. Mrs. McKinley told a biographer, "the McKinleys were very strong abolitionists, and William early imbibed very radical views regarding the enslavement of the colored race." The young man liked to linger and discuss politics with the rough-hewn men, many of them Democrats, who worked at the local tannery, and often the subject would be slavery. Though disagreements often were stark, young McKinley developed a style of argumentation that avoided animosity.

At seventeen, he completed his Poland Academy studies and entered Allegheny College in Meadville, Pennsylvania, about seventy-five miles to the northeast, to continue the education his parents considered vital to his future. His mother and sister Sarah loaned him money from their savings to pay for tuition and living expenses. At college he combined his characteristic bookishness with a zest for campus social life and also displayed his growing political agitation at Southern belligerency on the slavery issue. When a fellow student raised a glass to Jefferson Davis of Mississippi, an emerging leader of the Southern cause, McKinley replied that Davis was venturing toward treason, and he would gladly fight treason upon Southern soil if necessary. But he expressed himself in measured tones that minimized personal friction.

Increasingly, his peers respected him for his social grace even in hearty debate.

About a year into his college experience, McKinley contracted an illness, never fully identified, that sent him back to Poland for recuperation. Even with his health restored, though, a return to college proved impractical. An economic recession had curtailed his father's business and necessitated an income flow from all family members. McKinley settled into the town, pursued old friendships, and rekindled his close association with his devoted cousin, William McKinley Osborne, then working in a rolling mill. He landed jobs as postal clerk and teacher in the nearby Kerr school district. The school was some three miles from the McKinley home, and most days, when he wasn't "boarding around" (living temporarily with various families near the school), the young teacher walked the distance each morning and evening, scrambling over fences and scampering through neighbors' fields to save time. Years later he conceded, "Six miles would be a long walk for me now, I suppose, but it did not seem like much then." His teacher's salary was $25 a month.

Although this simple Poland life hardly matched the young man's ambitions, it seemed the only responsible course at the time. But it wasn't clear where his life was leading. Then fate intervened. With Abraham Lincoln's election in November 1860, the nation entered an ominous period of political agitation as Southern secession raised war tensions to a fevered pitch. One day at William Osborne's rolling mill, an elderly man rushed in and yelled, "They've fired on her! They've fired on her!" Upon hearing news of the Southern assault on the U.S. Army's Fort Sumter in South Carolina's Charleston Harbor, Osborne and his cousin knew instantly that the war speculation was over; actual war had arrived.

But the cousins weren't inclined to get caught up in the fervor that soon descended upon little Poland, even when they witnessed the scene that materialized at the Sparrow House tavern one June day shortly after the attack on Fort Sumter. People congregated from points near and far to raise a rousing call for the preservation of the Union and stir local lads into action. Flags and bunting festooned the boulevard, which was lined with teary-eyed women intently fluttering their fans and men and boys worked up into patriotic excitement. Rousing cheers rolled over the assemblage until the town's leading lawyer, Charles Glidden, ascended the front steps and called for silence, preparatory to an impassioned plea for Poland volunteers to join the regiments that Ohio soon would send into battle.

One by one the lads stepped up and signed on for what quickly became known as the Ohio Guards. Young women moved forward to pin red, white, and blue badges upon their chests, and in a few days, after drill practice at Poland, the young men were marched in formation to nearby Youngstown, where they would be mustered in and thence sent to Columbus for basic training. McKinley and Osborne, resisting the civic fever of the moment, resolved to think the matter over carefully, weighing family obligations against national imperatives. They watched the military drills at a nearby church green and followed the troops to Youngstown in a buggy to check out the situation and witness the unit's departure for Columbus. On the return trip, it became clear that there was only one course of action they could live with.

"Bill," said McKinley to his cousin, "we can't stay out of this war. We must get in." Osborne agreed and suggested they go immediately to inform their families. Nancy McKinley didn't protest. "Well, boys," she said, "if you think it is your duty to fight for your country, I think you ought to go." She was willing, she said, to place her son "into the hands of the good Lord." It turned out that when an angry Will McKinley had told his Southern college classmate that he would fight treason on Southern soil if necessary, he had meant it. The young man took pride in both his decision and his manner of arriving at it. "I came to a deliberative conclusion," he recalled, "and have never been sorry for it."

2

The Forge of War

TEST OF INTELLECT, LEADERSHIP, AND COURAGE

When young Will McKinley entered the U.S. military in June 1861, he harbored no expectation that it would transform his life. Like nearly all the provincial lads he encountered on his way to war, he didn't anticipate significant promotion, or any remuneration beyond the "paltry pittance of pay" that was the lot of the soldier, or any particular glory. Like them, he joined up simply to save the Union. And like them, he adjusted as best he could to the new military life and sought to come to terms with the mortal dangers he likely would soon encounter. The aim was to get on with it and return as soon as possible to the lives they knew before the war.

Upon making their decision to join up, McKinley and his cousin Bill Osborne set out for Camp Jackson (later Camp Chase) near Columbus. There Osborne learned a physical impairment precluded his service, and he returned home. McKinley was sworn into the army as a private on June 11. He had intended to sign on for three months, but those enlistments had been filled and only three-year commitments were available. When camp officers explained the situation, all would-be recruits save one opted for the longer service. The lone holdout was a divinity student eager to embrace his calling, but he later thought better of the matter and reversed his decision.

Military records described young McKinley thus: height five feet, seven inches; hair brown; eyes gray; complexion light. His occupation was listed as "student." He ended up in Company E of the Twenty-third Ohio Volunteer Infantry Regiment, led by an impressive array of officers pulled from Ohio's dynamic civilian society. Colonel William S. Rosecrans, a West Point graduate who had thrived as a businessman and inventor, soon would move on to an impressive wartime career as a general. Lieutenant Colonel Stanley Matthews would become a U.S. senator from Ohio after the war and serve on the U.S. Supreme Court. Major Rutherford B. Hayes would serve courageously during the war, sustain five war wounds, get promoted to general, and later become governor of Ohio and then U.S. president.

McKinley viewed Hayes particularly as a man to respect and emulate. He appreciated the officer's solemn reading of the Declaration of Independence to his recruits at camp, and he liked the way the major handled an episode in which some chagrined soldiers, including McKinley, resisted the weapons placed in their hands—clunky old muskets dating back to the War of 1812, converted to percussion caps from flints. They deserved better, protested the troops, and wouldn't accept these outmoded relics. The officers were aghast at such defiance, particularly since General John C. Frémont, the great pathfinder and former presidential candidate, was scheduled shortly to review the troops. At the entreaty of their officers, the troops agreed to accept the rifles, but only for the inspection.

McKinley later reported being awed by Frémont, "a great man to me" based on "the story of his wonderful adventures in the west." The private was thrilled during the review when the great man "pounded my chest and looked square into my eyes, and finally pronounced me fit to be a soldier."

But upon Frémont's departure, the matter of the rifles reemerged, and the standoff began to look ominous. Lieutenant Colonel Matthews warned his troops that the penalty for refusing to accept the old muskets would be a firing squad; he added firmly, "Depend on it." But Hayes took a different tack. Far from taking umbrage at the troops' defiance, he opted for persuasion over coercion. He explained with considerable patience that this was merely a training expedient and that proper weapons would be available soon. He was persuasive.

"From that very moment he had our respect and admiration," McKinley recalled years later.

Camp life quickly became a series of dull routines—3,000 troops sleeping on boards in 300 tents, regimented training, rotational guard duty, occasional passes for trips to Columbus to let off steam, frequent prayer meetings for those interested in religious renewal. McKinley regularly attended prayer sessions. "[They have] a good effect upon our brother soldiers, and are exerting a salutary influence," he explained in a letter to a Poland newspaper. To home he wrote, "It seems to be the determination of most, if not all, of our company, to preserve the good morals they brought with them, by avoiding the many temptations which necessarily surround them in Camp." This sentence doesn't seem credible. Perhaps the priggish young private didn't want his straitlaced family to know about the kinds of activities that inevitably emerged among young colts preparing for war, or perhaps the straitlaced lad himself had remained oblivious to what was going on around him. As for himself, the strongest drink he imbibed was lemonade, though he did develop a fondness for cigars. He spent much of his free time reading and following developments in the war and in politics, but he did receive visitors from home occasionally. He indulged his youthful romantic spirit by reading poems by Lord Byron.

He found that he took well to the hardships of military life. "I enjoyed sleeping on a rough board much better than I expected, with nought but an overcoat and a blanket to cover me," he wrote in a diary he maintained during this time. He was thoroughly imbued with the idealism of the cause, which he likened to the legacy of "our Revolutionary fathers." In a letter home he embraced the imperative "to hand down to posterity this government as free, as pure, and as spotless as our sires transmitted it to us."

In late July the training phase ended, and the Twenty-third Ohio trekked to Virginia to root out any guerrilla forces operating in the area. Traveling largely on foot, the troops bedded down at night upon the rough, cold ground and soon found themselves in unfamiliar mountainous terrain, far different from the flatlands of Ohio—"hills, high, such as I never witnessed before," as McKinley wrote in his diary. As the march drew the troops closer to guerrilla territory, McKinley's thoughts turned to the dangers of combat. "Tomorrow morning's sun," he confided to his diary, "will undoubtedly find me on a march. It may be I will never see the light of another day." Displaying his youthful earnestness and religious conviction, he went on:

> Should this be my fate I fall in a good cause and hope to fall in the arms of my blessed redeemer. This record I want to be left behind, that I not only fell as a soldier for my Country, but also as a Soldier of Jesus. . . . In this emergency let . . . my parents, brothers and sisters, and friends have their anxiety removed by the thought that I am in the discharge of my duty, that I am doing nothing but [that which] my revolutionary fathers before me have done, and also let them be consoled with the solacing thought that if we never meet again on earth, we will meet around God's throne in Heaven.

The Twenty-third Ohio finally made camp at Glenville, Virginia (later West Virginia), where no guerrilla activities were in evidence. The unit settled into a deadening routine of make-work activities, false alarms about enemy sightings, and sagging morale. McKinley retained his sense of humor in a letter home, writing about a sequence of events after a night patrol returned to camp with an exciting report that the enemy had been heard crossing a nearby bridge, their sabers clattering in the dark. The next night a young lieutenant led four men, including McKinley, into the wild to intercept the rebels. Hearing a noise in a dense thicket, the neophyte lieutenant thrust his bayonet into the brush—and apparently pierced a skunk, manifest in the "venomous smell [that] instantly issued from the bushes." Later, reaching the designated bridge, the troops secreted themselves in a nearby cornfield, their muskets cocked at the ready, and waited for the rebels. By dawn they had spied a lost calf and an itinerant hog. "We returned in the morning," wrote McKinley, "sleepy, tired, and not as full of romance as the night before."

Within a few weeks, however, both sides had amassed enough troops in the area that a set-piece battle seemed inevitable. It occurred on September 10, when Confederate general John Floyd crossed the Gauley River and positioned his sizable contingent on a plateau, not far from a place called Carnifex Ferry. The Twenty-third Ohio was given the job of attacking part of Floyd's force and driving it back south of the Gauley. The Union troops didn't manage to dislodge the intruders before nightfall, and McKinley's unit found itself at a river crossing it couldn't navigate because of devastating enemy fire. The men ended up crouching in water and mud as enemy bullets and cannonballs whizzed by overhead. When darkness came, they cautiously wended their way back to safety but found little comfort in their new surroundings. "With no blankets for a covering, no food to satisfy our almost starved bodies, we succeeded in procuring some straw which we laid upon," McKinley wrote in his diary.

In the meantime, Floyd realized the vulnerability of his position and got his troops back across the Gauley under cover of night. It wasn't much of a battle, but McKinley perceived value in the experience of facing enemy fire for the first time. "It gave us confidence in ourselves and faith in our commander," he wrote. "We learned that we could fight and whip the rebels on their own ground."

It wasn't until the next year, after the Twenty-third Ohio huddled in winter quarters for several months, that the regiment saw real action. In spring 1862 it was sent to Washington to help General George McClellan protect the national capital from Robert E. Lee's Army of Northern Virginia. This became particularly crucial after Northern defeats in August at Cedar Mountain and Second Manassas left both McClellan's force and Washington vulnerable to Confederate attack. McClellan quickly moved his army into a defensive position in Maryland to parry Lee's anticipated thrust into the North.

By this time, McKinley's military career had taken a significant upward turn, spurred by his superiors' perception that he possessed rare managerial skills. This got him assigned to the quartermaster corps, charged with distributing all nonweapon supplies, including food, clothing, blankets, and fodder for horses. And in April he was promoted to commissary sergeant. Hayes, now commander of the Twenty-third Ohio, took note of the young man who seemed able to keep things moving smoothly and quickly. The commander later recalled, "We soon found that in business, in executive ability, young McKinley was a man of rare capacity, of unusual and unsurpassed capacity, especially for a boy of his age."

He displayed more than executive ability on September 17, the single bloodiest day in American military history, when Lee's and McClellan's armies came together at Antietam Creek near Sharpsburg, Maryland. During the preceding days McClellan had enjoyed partial success in a number of smaller engagements, and now he launched an attack designed to cut off Lee's escape route. The battle began at dawn, described by McKinley later as "a lovely September day—an ideal Sunday morning." The fighting raged all day and into the night. Early that morning, the brigade of Colonel Eliakim Parker Scammon, including the Twenty-third Ohio, had taken an important bridge across Antietam Creek but later found itself pinned down on the far side of the creek. Worse, the men had begun the battle without breakfast and had had no access to food or water throughout the day. Famished and thirsty by midafternoon, the troops found their fighting ability waning ominously.

When Commissary Sergeant McKinley, posted two miles behind the lines, heard of the brigade's plight, he resolved to get sustenance to the beleaguered unit. He recruited a number of battle stragglers to help him load a wagon with provisions, including cooked meats, pork and beans, hardtack crackers, and barrels of water and coffee. He hitched the wagon to two horses and then asked for volunteers to help him get the wagon to Scammon's brigade. He got one affirmative response, from a young man named John Harvey. The two set off on a narrow road through a thick stretch of forest and into a dangerous clearing in the woods. Twice they encountered Union officers who ordered them back, one saying the enemy position was too well fortified to afford any chance of passage. But after the officers left, McKinley ignored their orders and kept going. When Scammon's regiment was almost in sight, Harvey remembered, McKinley "made one more appeal to me to run the blockade; he himself risking his life in taking the lead . . . and the horses going at full speed past the blockade." The back of the wagon was shot away by a cannonball, but within a few minutes they found themselves "safe in the midst of the half-famished regiment."

A cheer went up among the men, and one battlefield veteran exclaimed, "God bless the lad." Major James Comley, commanding the Twenty-third Ohio in the absence of Hayes (who was recuperating from a battlefield wound), promptly wrote a note to Hayes describing

McKinley's action and recommending that he be promoted to second lieutenant. McKinley himself shared the sentiment and issued an appeal to the regimental surgeon, Dr. Joseph Webb, who happened to be Hayes's brother-in-law. Demonstrating a high self-regard and robust ambition beneath his modest demeanor, McKinley asked Webb to intervene with Hayes in his behalf. Webb readily complied, writing to Hayes, "Our young friend, William McKinley, commissary sergeant, would be pleased of promotion, and would not object to your recommendation for same. Without wishing to interfere in this matter, it strikes me he is about the brightest chap spoken of for the place."

Hayes agreed. Convalescing in Ohio from his battlefield injury, he brought the matter up with Governor David Tod, who initiated actions to cite the resourceful sergeant for military valor and give him a battlefield promotion to second lieutenant. The newly minted officer got word of his elevation during a visit to Ohio on furlough and to perform some military recruiting duties. Visiting Hayes in Columbus on his way to Poland, he was given his letter of promotion. Years later he wrote to Hayes that that was "the proudest and happiest moment of my life."

He stopped off in Cleveland to visit a friend named Russell Hastings, a talented young captain also on recruiting duty. Hastings quickly learned that McKinley had sufficient funds to get home but not enough to get himself outfitted in a new officer's uniform.

"McKinley," said Hastings, "how would you like to go home to your mother in your second lieutenant's uniform, with your sword by your side? You ought to and you shall. Stay with me two or three days, and I will fit you out." Hastings later reported that the young man's eyes sparkled at the prospect. "What a proud boy he was when he donned his uniform," recalled Hastings. McKinley's sister Sarah reported that, later in Poland, her brother was "bubbling over with enthusiasm" at his new status. At a stopover at Gallipolis, Ohio, the young lieutenant had a photograph made of himself in his new uniform, standing erect, holding his military cap at his side. It presents the picture of a serious young man, hardly more than a boy, who appears self-possessed and ready for responsibility. Upon McKinley's return to his unit, Hayes wrote in his diary, "Our new second lieutenant, McKinley, returned to-day—an exceedingly bright, intelligent, and gentlemanly young officer. He promises to be one of the best." He speculated in a letter to his wife that the young officer could become one of the "generals of the next war."

Antietam changed McKinley's perception of the war, and war in general, but didn't seem to blunt his idealistic view of the conflict. Years later he spoke publicly of the "carnage" he witnessed, of "fallen comrades" and "our stricken comrades." He decried the losses, far greater in number and as a percentage of battlefield soldiers than anyone had anticipated—and certainly greater than other armies of recent European wars had suffered. But such reminiscences always came with references to the hallowed cause at the heart of the killing and the idealism of those who died to save the Union. Though sickened by numbingly routine scenes of death, he steeled himself for more of the same by concentrating on the tasks before him. He didn't seem to think much about his own mortality.

But McKinley's mother was developing stark fears about her son's wartime fate.

"William, I shall never see you again," she protested through tears, her arms around her boy as he prepared to leave Poland.

"Mother," he replied, "you will see me again. I shall come back to you alive and well."

Though ready for his new role, McKinley was glad he had served in the ranks and lamented in some ways the separation from his old comrades. He later viewed his first wartime year as "a formative period of my life, during which I learned much of men and facts." He added, "I have always been glad that I entered the service as a private, and served those months in that capacity."

About this time Hayes was given command of the First Brigade of the Second Kanawha Division, and one of his first actions was to appoint McKinley to the job of acting brigade quartermaster, with responsibility for supplying all brigade needs except weapons. McKinley served this role through most of the inactive winter months, during which the brigade camped at the falls of the great Kanawha River in what later became West Virginia. It was an opportunity to settle into his new officer's role, read up on war news and political developments, get to know his new commissioned comrades, develop his skills as a horseman, and grow a beard and mustache that turned out to be so thin and scraggly that they added hardly any years to his youthful appearance.

He also had more time for letters home. There wasn't much news to impart, as each day unfolded rather like the one before. "There is nothing new in camp, all being quiet," he wrote in spring 1863. "This is Sunday, and consequently have more time than usual, as I suspend all unnecessary business on that day." He reported a "fine dinner" earlier in the day: "Roast Chicken, Mashed Potatoes, Custard Pudding, Green Apple and Cherry pies, Bread and Butter, &c." He signed off, "My health is good and spirits fine. Love to all."

Serious combat activity resumed in late spring of 1863 when Hayes's unit was sent into Ohio to thwart the guerrilla cavalry exploits of the dashing rebel John Hunt Morgan. After successfully fulfilling that mission, Hayes's troops joined General George Crook's forces, charged with neutralizing rebel guerrilla activity between Richmond and the Virginia southwest. This was grueling work in harsh terrain infested with angry rebels. "We penetrated a country where guerrillas were abundant," McKinley recalled, "and where it was not an unusual thing for our men to be shot from underbrush—murdered in cold blood." A major battle ensued at Cloyd Mountain, where Union troops routed a Confederate contingent, though casualties were high. Afterward it was back to the grind of forced marches, incessant guerrilla fighting, deprivation of food and sleep. "Out of grub. . . . Live off the countryside," Hayes wrote in his diary. He described life in the field in stark language: "Stopped and ate, marched and ate, camped about dark and *ate all night*. We had marched almost continuously for about two months, fighting often, with little food and sleep, crossing three ranges of the Alleghenies four times, the ranges of the Blue Ridge twice, and marching several times all day and all night without sleeping." McKinley encountered difficulty fulfilling his quartermaster duties on available supplies.

No respite seemed likely when the Twenty-third Ohio was assigned to Virginia's Shenandoah Valley to counter the exploits of Confederate General Jubal Early, who was using the valley to stage raids into

Maryland and Pennsylvania. Through faulty reconnaissance, General Crook's force found itself surrounded by Early's troops near Winchester. The commander ordered a withdrawal, with Hayes's brigade providing cover from behind a stone wall. As Hayes began his own retreat, he suddenly remembered that no one had delivered word to Colonel William Brown, whose regiment had been positioned in reserve in a nearby orchard. The colonel and his regiment faced almost certain annihilation by advancing enemy troops if he didn't quickly join the retreat.

Looking for someone to deliver a retreat order, Hayes spotted McKinley. Pointing to the stranded regiment, he asked the young lieutenant to carry the order to Brown. Scarcely had he completed his request before McKinley wheeled his bobtailed horse around and headed toward Brown's unit at a gallop. Even as he made his request, Hayes figured the messenger's chances of survival were negligible. Nearby officers shared that perception. "None of us expected to see him again," recalled Russell Hastings. McKinley spurred his chestnut mare through a harrowing patch of land with bullets flying and shells exploding everywhere. He galloped through open fields, over fences, through ditches. Once an exploding shell generated so much dust and smoke that the young horseman disappeared from sight. But the mists cleared, and there he was, approaching his destination.

McKinley drew up to Brown and delivered the order to retreat, then added, "I suppose you would have gone to the rear without orders."

"I was concluding I would retire without waiting any longer for orders," replied Brown. "I am now ready to go wherever you shall lead, but, Lieutenant, I 'pintedly' believe I ought to give those fellows a volley or two before I go."

"Then up and at them as quickly as possible."

Brown's regiment administered a punishing volley, followed by rattling musket fire, then slowly worked its way back to safety, with McKinley helping guide the beleaguered brigade along the way. When he reached Hayes to report his mission accomplished, the commander exclaimed with wonder mixed with affection, "I never expected to see you in life again."

Later that day the retreating troops, pursuing safety from Early's formidable force, passed through Winchester, where many Union sympathizers watched in solemn silence. One pro-Union Quaker woman known to the troops stood at her doorway with tears streaming down her cheeks. The passing troops didn't want to console her for fear of agitating her Confederate neighbors, but McKinley offered soothing words in a low voice: "Don't worry, my dear madam, we are not hurt as much as it seems, and we shall be back here again in a few days."

At nightfall, as the troops passed a battery of artillery left behind by retreating soldiers, McKinley asked Hayes for permission to retrieve the armaments. When the skeptical commander replied that it would take too much exertion and time, McKinley suggested the Twenty-third Ohio would provide sufficient manpower to get the job done.

"Well, McKinley," replied Hayes, "ask them." McKinley promptly went to his old E Company compatriots and collected enough volunteers to haul the guns back to the artillery captain who had left them behind in the haste of retreat. According to one witness, the captain "cried like a baby."

A week after the battle, McKinley was promoted to captain (some eighteen months after his promotion to first lieutenant), and General Crook sought to get the efficient young officer into his command. Hayes didn't want to lose him but could hardly refuse the general's request, and so William McKinley, at age twenty-one, became acting adjutant general of Crook's army, the unit's leading administrative officer.

By this time things began to change in the Shenandoah, where the wily and relentless General Phil Sheridan was put in charge of all nearby troops and ordered to destroy Early's force, as well as the Shenandoah Valley itself as a source of supplies for Confederate forces. General Early still had plenty of fight in him, though, and with a superior force he accosted Crook's army in early September near Berryville, Virginia. But Crook and Hayes maneuvered themselves adroitly. "We whipped them," Hayes recalled. McKinley's job as a general's staff officer during the encounter was to act as a high-grade messenger, darting through the battlefield carrying new or revised orders. It was hazardous work; McKinley once had his horse shot from under him.

Two weeks later the two armies clashed at Opequon Creek, and Sheridan logged his first big Shenandoah triumph, though the early indications didn't look good for the Union men. At one point, McKinley was ordered to ride toward a contingent of troops on a distant hillside to determine if they were blue or gray. Russell Hastings remembered, "Away went McKinley, accompanied by his orderly, down the hill, through a cornfield, over an open field, getting closer and closer to this body of cavalry. Soon he was seen to halt, hesitate a moment and then turn and ride rapidly away, toward his command. Now there was no need to question who these troopers were, as a heavy carbine fire was opened upon McKinley, and his orderly was seen to reel and fall from his saddle."

Also during this battle, McKinley was sent to deliver verbal orders to General Isaac Duval to move his Second Division to the right of Sheridan's main force. Duval promptly asked, "By what route shall I move my command?"

McKinley had not been told what orders to convey on Duval's route. Hesitating, he looked around and replied, "I would go up this creek." Duval grew queasy in the absence of specific orders; he didn't want to make a faulty decision and later take the blame.

"I will not budge without definite orders," he insisted. McKinley knew there was no time for any such explicit instructions. He quickly concluded he must ignore rank.

"This is a case of great emergency, General," he declared. "I order you, by command of General Crook, to move your command up this ravine to a position on the right of the army."

The general complied.

The young captain's judgment was confirmed when the First Division commander, choosing his own route to the same point on the battlefield, arrived a half hour after Duval's unit was firmly in place. But McKinley could have been in serious trouble if things had gone awry after he issued his demand in the name of General Crook but without any specific instruction from the general.

Sheridan spent October—"brown October," as it became known—devastating the entire Shenandoah Valley, burning barns, fields, crops, and many farmhouses. "This valley will feed and forage no more rebel armies," declared Hayes in a letter to his wife. But Jubal Early hadn't given up, and on October 19 he unleashed a surprise attack at Cedar

Creek that nearly overran the Union forces before they could be rallied by Sheridan, who had returned from a Washington conference the day before and was now twenty miles away in Winchester. As soon as he gleaned the seriousness of the situation, Sheridan rushed to the battlefront in one of the most storied rides of the Civil War, covering the last twelve miles at full gallop atop his legendary black stallion, Rienzi.

As he neared the battlefield, he ran into young McKinley, returning from an assignment to move an artillery battery to a more advantageous position. The captain took the general to Crook's headquarters, and the top officers promptly repaired to a nearby red barn, where Sheridan gave orders for a major charge. McKinley later recalled, "Then it was suggested that Sheridan should ride down the lines of the disheartened troops." His overcoat was pulled off, his epaulettes placed upon his shoulders, and he set out to rally his army. The subsequent charge reversed the battlefield fortunes and destroyed Early's army and his ability to wage war in the Shenandoah. By destroying the primary supply source for most of Lee's army, Sheridan's victory put a squeeze on the entire Southern military effort.

This dramatic turnaround bolstered President Lincoln's political standing and contributed to his solid reelection victory two weeks later. The officers and men of General Crook's army cast their votes in the field and had them collected by election judges going wagon to wagon as the column was on the march. An ambulance served as an election booth, and ballots were tossed into an empty candle box. By this time McKinley had been promoted to brevet major for "gallant and meritorious service in West Virginia and the Shenandoah Valley."

With Early's army neutralized and the Shenandoah subdued, Sheridan's valley campaign ended, and Crook's army went quietly into winter quarters near Winchester. It was a cold winter, "colder than any huckleberry pudding I know of," as Hayes put it. But warm clothing arrived soon, and turkeys were issued on Thanksgiving Day "at the rate of a pound to a man." By the time spring arrived, it was clear that the North would be victorious and that the officers and men of the Shenandoah would face no more harrowing exploits to test the fates.

THE CIVIL WAR transformed young William McKinley much as his father's white-hot forges transformed crude iron ore into ingots of pig iron ready for more sophisticated uses. He went to war as an unseasoned teenager with only a vague sense of who he was or what he would do with his life. He left the army an adult who had been severely tested in questions of intellect, administrative ability, leadership, and courage. He had passed these tests and demonstrated that men gravitated naturally to his side—and that many older men were drawn into roles of solicitous mentorship. As Hayes said of the young man, "I did literally and in fact know him like a book and love him like a brother." For McKinley, the questions that bedevil many young men seeking a start in life—What is my worth? What can I accomplish? How far can I go?—had now been answered. There didn't seem to be any need to place limits on his ambitions or plans.

Yet this new confidence and sense of self settled upon him softly, without ostentation or bravado. It meshed with a simplicity of temperament to produce a demeanor of heavy quiet. He learned the power of mystique, of leaving unsaid that which didn't need explicit expression, of keeping people guessing as to his intentions or motives. If this led some to underestimate his intellect or resolve, he didn't seem bothered by it. Thus emerged some of the enigmatic elements of his persona—a congenial and easygoing demeanor shrouding an increasingly restless ambition.

Upon entering the army, he received valuable counsel from an old veteran who took the young recruit under his wing. "Now, William," he had said, ". . . you can easily make yourself so valuable to your superior that he cannot get along without you. Do little things not exactly under your supervision. Be conscientious in all your duties, and be faithful, and it will not be long until your superior officer will consider you an indispensable assistant." McKinley embraced that advice, and it fueled a military rise that would help define him in later life. In discussing the war afterward, he seldom talked about his own experiences and never about his exploits of bravery. His focus was the meaning of the war, the sanctity of the Union, the evil of slavery, sometimes the joys of camaraderie. Yet everyone knew, even as he rose in American politics and gained national recognition, that the rank he attained in the war remained a point of pride. Asked once, after he had become U.S. president-elect following stints as a successful lawyer, a prominent congressman, and a big-state governor, how he wished to be addressed, he replied, "Call me Major. I earned that. I am not so sure of the rest."

3

Life and Work

PROFESSIONAL SUCCESS, PERSONAL ANGUISH

On August 28, 1865, barely a month after leaving the military, Will McKinley sat down at his parents' home in Poland, Ohio, and crafted a letter to his army friend Russell Hastings. In a pensive but lighthearted mood, McKinley wrote, "How are my old fellows this blessed morning? I imagine I see you in a large rocking chair at home nursing your feet." His imagination had free rein also with regard to himself. "I dream of lands, tenements and hereditaments," he wrote, "and wake up [to] think I am an heir. Isn't that strange?" He revealed that he was "getting along much better than I expected. Poland is very tame, but I have banished myself." He had become "once more a 'rustic youth,' wrapped in the mysteries of law. 'The solemnities of the marriage contract' [and] the old customs of the Saxons & Danes are continually flitting through my brain."

Having survived war's carnage, McKinley set his sights on a legal career. By year's end he had entered a training regimen in the firm of Charles E. Glidden, the same lawyer who had led the rousing rally at Poland back in June 1861 to get young men into the Union army. McKinley studied under Glidden's tutelage for a year. Then, at the urging of his sister Anna, he enrolled in the Albany Law School in New

York. An old friend from his Poland Seminary days, Robert L. Walker, loaned him money for the academic pursuit.

At Albany McKinley shared rooms with another aspiring lawyer, George Arrel, who later described his roommate as a dogged fellow given to studying until one or two in the morning. He showed no interest in athletics or physical activity but enjoyed the theater and good company. He was a "jolly" companion, "always good-natured and looked at the bright side of everything." He "despised vulgarity" but avoided quarrels and evinced a quiet determination that commanded respect. He made no secret of his ambition: to become a member of Congress like his wartime mentor, Rutherford Hayes, who had captured a House seat for Ohio in 1864.

While at Albany McKinley sent Hayes a letter revealing his interest in the law. The congressman, remembering McKinley's organizational talents, replied that he would have recommended a career in railroading or some other industrial enterprise. "A man in any of our western towns with half your wit ought to be independent at forty in business," wrote Hayes. "As a lawyer, a man sacrifices independence to ambition which is a bad bargain at the best." He added, "However, you have decided for the present your profession, so I must hush." McKinley carefully preserved the letter but discarded the advice.

After a year at Albany, McKinley returned to Ohio and passed his bar examination in March 1867. He settled in Canton, seat of Stark County, where his sister Anna had become a schoolteacher. Located about sixty miles south of Cleveland, Canton boasted a growing population that had hit 5,000 by war's end. It was surrounded by rich agricultural lands and enjoyed close proximity to coal mines that fueled industrial expansion in the area. McKinley saw abundant prospects for financial betterment, and besides it was a charming and congenial place to live.

He rented office space in a building just off Market Street, the main city thoroughfare, and hung out his shingle as attorney at law. Soon his personal solidity and winning temperament gained attention and a smattering of clients. George Belden, a prominent lawyer and former judge whose office was in the same building, reacted with interest when McKinley inquired about joining Belden's firm. "Do you know a young man by the name of McKinley (brother of our Miss McKinley), recently admitted to the Bar?" Belden asked his law partner, Joseph Frease. "Inquire as to this man McKinley, so that you can let me know all about him."

Shortly thereafter Belden sauntered into McKinley's office late one afternoon and dropped upon his desk a sheaf of papers. He wasn't feeling well, he said, and likely wouldn't be able to undertake a case scheduled for trial the next morning. He wanted McKinley to take over. The young man protested that he didn't have sufficient experience for such an assignment and couldn't possibly prepare in the short time before trial.

"If you don't try this case, it won't be tried," said Belden, and walked out.

McKinley pored over the material throughout the night and appeared in court the next morning. He won the case—but was taken aback to see Belden watching the proceeding from a seat under the balcony at the rear of the courtroom. A few days later Belden entered McKinley's office and handed him twenty-five dollars for his efforts.

"I can't take so much," protested the conscientious young lawyer. "What I did wasn't worth it, and, besides, I only took the case because you insisted."

"It's all right, Mac," replied Belden airily, "I got a hundred." Then he added, "Now, the fact of the matter is, Frease has just been elected to the bench and I'm looking for another partner." McKinley accepted on the spot, and his career took off.

Avoiding courtroom flamboyance, McKinley employed plain language and sturdy logic that cut through the complexities of his cases and deciphered their essential elements. William Day, another Canton lawyer and later a judge, said McKinley possessed "the same power of epigrammatic expression" that served him later in politics. Displaying courtesy and fairness, combined with his consistently thorough preparation, he impressed both judges and juries. Charles Fairbanks, a senator from Indiana and later vice president, once said McKinley's impressive bearing, always powerfully erect and self-assured, gave him the look of a statesman.

To cement himself to the community, he plunged into civic and fraternal activities—and always seemed to rise to leadership positions in whatever realm he entered. Taking an active part in veterans' organizations, he displayed proudly the bronze badge of the Grand Army of the Republic and the red, white, and blue ribbon of the Loyal Legion. He joined the Knights of Pythias and the local Masonic lodge, eventually becoming a Masonic Knight Templar. He became active in the local YMCA, rising to president. He joined the First Methodist Church and became superintendent of its Sunday school. He aligned himself with the county Republican committee and rose to its chairmanship. Through such activities he acquired a warm following of adherents who saw him as a town pillar and referred to him fondly as "the Major."

When Rutherford Hayes ran for governor the year of McKinley's Canton arrival, the Major campaigned vigorously for his erstwhile commander and helped him carry Stark County on his way to a narrow statewide victory. In the process McKinley earned a reputation as an effective campaigner and also gained an ear in the governor's office on patronage matters of interest to Canton's political elite. The next year he energetically supported the presidential campaign of General Ulysses Grant, organizing Grant clubs, spearheading rallies, and earnestly praising his candidate at demonstrations. He cheered Grant's 1868 presidential victory and enjoyed the attention his political activities brought. The local paper, the *Evening Repository*, adopted him as a political favorite.

The following year McKinley received the Republican nomination for county prosecuting attorney, an honor widely considered merely ceremonial since the office had been a Democratic fiefdom for years. But the *Repository* endorsed him as "a good lawyer and a fine orator," and the Major's relentless campaigning carried the day against a complacent opponent who hadn't perceived the force of McKinley's political persona. As prosecutor, McKinley went after illicit liquor sales, particularly in the town of Alliance, where saloons routinely served alcohol to underage boys from nearby Mount Union College. When McKinley sought reelection in 1871, his Democratic opponent avoided complacency and won—by just 143 votes.

McKinley's law practice flourished under Belden and expanded further when the senior partner retired shortly after the Major entered the partnership. This opened the way for him to take on some of the county's most important and lucrative cases, and by the mid-1870s he was earning a solid income of nearly $10,000 a year. He bought a small frame house near the city center and socked away savings equal to his annual income. William Sr. was impressed. "I am pleased to hear that your business is good," he wrote to his son.

In just four years young McKinley had carved out an impressive station for himself—not rich but financially secure, highly respected as a community leader, blessed with abundant friends, recognized as a man of notable political talents. His short, bulky frame cut an imposing figure, and people responded avidly to his personal traits—a broad, handsome face featuring candescent gray eyes (he long since had lost the scraggly beard); a deep, resonating voice; a ready smile and hearty laugh that betokened warmth and confidence; moral rectitude devoid of sanctimony. Townsfolk perceived another characteristic that stirred confidence: a natural caution leading him to ruminate on a problem before action. In Ohio's rough-hewn nineteenth-century society, a favorite word describing impressive figures was "manly," meaning a willingness to confront tough decisions and take the consequences. McKinley was manly but never rash.

He also never tried to be what he wasn't. He joined others in laughing at himself after a slightly embarrassing social episode during his law school days when, upon tasting ice-cream for the first time, he expressed concern that his hostess had somehow allowed the custard to freeze. "You know," he said later in recounting the incident, "I was a simple country boy." In Canton, the simple country boy was gaining a degree of sophistication, which he always managed, however, to keep encased in a demeanor of good humor and naturalness. Behind that pleasant exterior was a sturdy ambition, invisible except to his closest and most discerning friends.

Canton proved so hospitable to Will and Anna McKinley that soon other family members were moving there also. Anna refurbished her brother's frame house for the subsequent arrival of their parents, and brother Abner settled there around the same time with his new bride. The senior McKinley, a relentless foe of idleness, bought a blast furnace in Michigan to satisfy his appetite for hard work, while Nancy devoted herself to the Methodist Church. Her irrepressible nature, organizational efficiency, and pleasant manner soon captured attention, and townsfolk began referring to her affectionately as "Mother McKinley." The family arrival cemented Will's satisfaction with his Canton life. The only thing missing was a wife and family.

Enter Ida Saxton, the belle of Canton and leading light of one of the town's premier families. Her grandfather, a Pennsylvania printer named John Saxton, arrived soon after service in the War of 1812 and quickly perceived an opportunity in local newspapering. He transported a printing press from the East by oxen and in 1815 established the *Ohio Repository* as a weekly paper. He gave it a strong liberal voice—abolitionist, champion of the underdog—and recruited the best talent he could find. One reporter was Joseph Medill, later co-owner and editor of the *Chicago Tribune*; a close family friend was Horace Greeley of the *New York Tribune*.

Although the newspaper thrived and remained in the family for decades, Ida's father, James Saxton, ventured into other pursuits—merchandising, banking, mining—and built considerably upon the family fortune. Ida, the first of three children, grew up in luxury and ease in the town's largest home, with three live-in servants. She took avidly to education, which her father ensured was as good as could be obtained, including a local private school, boarding schools in New York and Cleveland, and the Brooke Hall Female Seminary at Media, Pennsylvania. Believing that women could perform in business as effectively as men, James Saxton insisted that his daughter's education be "more practical than ornamental," as he put it in a letter to a school mistress. As Ida got older he had her working in his Stark County Bank, first as teller and eventually as manager when he was away tending to his other enterprises. She thrived in all roles assigned to her.

At Brooke Hall, she embraced the school's emphasis on developing physical strength through strenuous hikes and multiple-mile walks. Unlike others in Ohio society (including the elder McKinleys), she saw no harm in dancing or card games, and she loved shopping, opera, theater, and concerts. Accomplished at the piano and the leading student in any class, she also was a natural leader of other young women, sometimes leading them in what one contemporary called "mischievous" directions. But she never directed her sharp wit against her peers or lapsed from her natural congeniality.

Ida presented a figure and persona that turned heads: petite, fit, self-assured, full of wholesome laughter, with rosy cheeks, large deep-blue eyes, and abundant chestnut-colored hair. As a local reporter put it, whether she was engaging in political conversation, playing cards, walking briskly through town, or questioning prominent speakers on lecture tours, Ida Saxton "left the stamp of her personality." She certainly left her mark at her father's bank, where her increasing responsibilities caused some in town to cast a jaundiced eye. But one local reporter wrote, "Through all the flutter that her presence caused . . . Miss Saxton preserved a businesslike calm. She worked diligently and learned the business thoroughly."

Beset by many suitors jockeying for sessions in the Saxton parlor, she learned to combine coquettish banter with a certain dexterous reserve. Eventually she set her sights on a young lawyer from Maryland named John Wright. When it was revealed that he had fought on the Confederate side during the war, James Saxton manifested considerable chagrin, but it didn't bother Ida. Soon the two were seen together frequently at picnics and dances, and it was generally assumed that they would marry upon her return from a scheduled European tour during the latter half of 1869. Shortly before her departure, she and Wright were enjoying the signature dish of a nearby lakeside inn, creamed chicken on waffles, when Anna McKinley approached to introduce her brother, the lawyer. The encounter didn't seem to leave much of an impression on Ida, but Will McKinley was struck by what he saw—first, her somewhat unladylike zest in devouring her chicken on waffles; then, her beauty, charm, and piquant personality. He lodged every detail in his memory, to be recalled later at the slightest provocation.

Ida's European trip unfolded as so many others of the time: rising at around six each morning to devour guidebooks on the day's tour; tensions with the chaperone; getting her ears pierced and drinking wine for the first time; shock at the hardships of peasant life on the Continent; new musings on the meaning of life. But arriving at Geneva on September 25, she learned that her life would not be what she had anticipated. A letter from home informed her that John Wright had died—of meningitis, she later learned. Her sister Mary, known as Pina, who was traveling with her, wrote home the next morning, "Ida looked pale and feels very badly. She did not eat any breakfast. . . . It was a fearful shock to her." Struggling to ward off depression, she continued with the tour but without much enthusiasm. "How different things [will] look when I get home," she wrote shortly before sailing for New York on December 9.

Back in Canton, she threw herself into bank responsibilities and renewed her position as leading lady of the town's eligible young set. She encountered McKinley again when he entered the bank to complete some business with James Saxton, and she discerned that her father favored this serious young man. She found herself warming to him too. He impressed her particularly as the local YMCA president when he eloquently introduced Horace Greeley at an event sponsored by the organization. Soon they were seen together around town and at the famous dance parties frequently held in the third-floor ballroom of what became known as "Saxton House."

By fall 1870 he had overcome his fear of rejection and proposed marriage during a buggy ride outside Canton. She accepted. When he sought James Saxton's blessing, the father exclaimed with misty eyes, "You are the only man I have ever known to whom I would entrust my daughter." Others, though, considered it an unlikely match. On one side was a sober, excessively polite, somewhat prudish lawyer who kept his emotions always in check. On the other was an impulsive, witty, flirtatious young woman with an appetite for adventure and rollicking times. But he was thoroughly captivated by her lively wholesomeness, expansive intellect, and underlying sound judgment, and she appreciated his rectitude, kind regard for others, and smoldering ambition. Physically, they combined into a lovely couple that gained notice when they walked into a room.

"It is now settled that Miss Saxton and I will unite our fortunes," McKinley wrote to Hayes and his wife, Lucy, expressing hopes they would attend the wedding. "I think I am doing a good thing. Miss S— is everything I could hope for." The wedding took place on January 25 in the newly constructed Stone Presbyterian Church. Nearly 1,000 guests witnessed Ida stroll down the aisle in an ivory satin gown, with bridesmaids wearing dresses described by the *Repository* as "faultless in taste and exceedingly rich and beautiful." McKinley stretched his finances to give her a ring of California gold, with diamonds around a ruby. After the ceremony and lavish reception at Saxton House, the couple boarded a ten o'clock eastbound train for a three-week honeymoon in New York and other major cities. Upon hearing McKinley talk extensively of his political plans, Ida became convinced her husband would someday become president of the United States.

Will and Ida settled into a wood-frame house, just twelve blocks from Saxton House, purchased for them by James Saxton for $7,800. There they began an idyllic life. On Christmas Day Ida gave birth to a baby girl they named Catherine, after Ida's mother. They called her Katie. In fall 1872 it seemed the fates continued to smile upon the seemingly favored couple: Ida learned she was once again pregnant.

Then the fates stopped smiling. A series of developments—some related, some not—cast a pall upon Will and Ida. First, Ida learned that her mother, probably her closest friend, was dying of a mysterious and painful disease (probably cancer) that would claim her before the birth of Ida's second child. Wracked by anxiety, Ida struggled through her pregnancy. Her sister noted that her "nervous system was nearly wrecked." She apparently also suffered a blow to her immune system. It is impossible to know if these developments affected the health of the second child, but little Ida, born April 1, 1873, was "sickly" from birth and died of cholera within five months. This dealt another powerful blow to the psychological health of the mother.

It seems that around this time Ida also suffered a serious accident, possibly a fall from a carriage, that damaged her lower spine and affected her ability to walk. For months she was frequently bedridden, and McKinley often had to carry her to a waiting carriage for any trips they wished to undertake. She subsequently gained some mobility but never was able to walk long distances or carry on any serious exercise routines of the kind she had so loved in earlier times. On top of this, she began experiencing neurological fits described as "paroxysms" or "convulsions." Her doctors knew what family members steadfastly kept shrouded in secrecy: she had epilepsy, considered at the time a psychiatric disorder, a form of insanity. Many epileptics of the day were shunted away in horrendous institutions, but McKinley had no intention of letting that be his wife's fate. He resolved to nurture her through life and through the matrix of maladies that had descended upon her with such menace.

Saxton invited Will and Ida, with daughter Katie, to move in with him at Saxton House, and six months of rest there brought about a welcome recuperation for Ida—although, as her sister later noted, she "never entirely recovered." Saxton also assisted McKinley financially by retaining him for legal work and referring friends to him. He invited McKinley into Canton commercial real estate ventures that provided a modest but steady supplemental income.

Slowly the young family returned to something approaching a normal life, although punctured by Ida's intermittent seizures and other physical and psychological difficulties. By spring 1874 Ida was able to venture out to social events around town, and Will once again accepted out-of-town legal cases and pursued his political activities. But Ida was riddled with fears that daughter Katie remained vulnerable, as little Ida had been. Abner McKinley told a friend, "She would sit for hours in a darkened room, holding Katie on her lap, weeping in silence." She seldom let Katie out of her sight.

Then in June 1875 the fates delivered another blow. Katie developed scarlet fever and died on June 25. Ida nearly died herself of a broken heart. An early McKinley biographer learned from sister Pina that "the black pall of grief" led to another nervous breakdown. She refused to eat and slipped into ennui and despair. "Ida would have died," a friend said later, ". . . but William would just not let her go." The husband never let up on his solicitousness toward his troubled wife and never showed impatience or frustration. Slowly, he coaxed her out of her despair and fostered in her a renewed "interest in existence." He even offered to discard his political ambitions.

"If you would suffer by the circumstances surrounding me in a competition for public station," he wrote to her, "I will devote my ambition to success in private life." She summarily rejected such a course with the idea of devoting her nurturing impulses now to his budding political career. "I have no fear that your choice in life will leave you as you are in the things that make you dear to me," she replied. Thus, while he continued to devote himself to her health and comfort, he also salved his own grief through political activity, with the idea of getting elected to Congress the following year, the same year Hayes planned to run for president.

McKinley's reputation in his district centered on his personal qualities far more than on his political views. When the avidly pro-McKinley *Alliance Record* listed nine reasons why he should get the Republican nomination for Congress in 1876, none focused on issues. Rather, the paper extolled his "spotless record," his "good service for the party," and his Civil War exploits—and argued that Stark County deserved the seat because, after all, it hadn't sent a man to Congress in eighteen years. To the extent that McKinley's views were considered, he was known as a party loyalist who would never stray from fundamental Republican doctrines, particularly high tariffs to protect U.S. manufacturers from foreign competition.

Further, while hospitable to the interests of business, he also was known as a friend of labor, a reputation buttressed by a celebrated court case early in the campaign year. Coal miners in the Tuscarawas Valley went on strike in March, and when mine owners sought to bring in strikebreaking outside labor, violence erupted near the Stark County town of Massillon. The result was substantial property damage and many injuries. One mine operator was beaten nearly to death. The local sheriff appealed for help to Governor Hayes, who sent in a unit of militia to quell the violence. Twenty-three miners were arrested.

When local public opinion went heavily against the miners and no lawyers in the area would represent them in criminal court, McKinley volunteered for the job. Going against two of the area's most celebrated barristers, he won acquittals for all the defendants save one. When the miners got up a collection to pay the legal fee, McKinley waived it in recognition of the financial hardship they had sustained during the strike. It was a brilliant political stroke in a district evenly divided between Democrats and Republicans. First, the much-publicized trial brought him recognition throughout the Seventeenth District. Second, he managed to assuage antiminer sentiment with the argument that all citizens deserve fair representation at trial while also generating widespread support from miners and the broader contingent of the district's working classes. That contributed to his victory margin in November of some 3,300 votes.

Hayes also triumphed in the presidential race, but not before the election threw the country into a constitutional crisis of serious proportions. Democrat Samuel J. Tilden captured 51 percent of the popular vote to 48 percent for Hayes. Tilden also outpolled Hayes in the Electoral College, 184 to 165, putting him just one vote shy of the presidency. But Republicans alleged that Democratic officials in three Southern states—Florida, Louisiana, and South Carolina—had suppressed the black vote through intimidation. They challenged the Democratic victories in those states (as well as a single electoral vote in Oregon for different reasons). If those challenges could be upheld, Hayes would squeeze out a one-vote Electoral College triumph. This spawned a deadlock that continued for weeks, until congressional leaders created a fifteen-man commission of legislators and Supreme Court justices to settle the matter. It did, in Hayes's favor. Congress ultimately validated that outcome on the basis of a deal in which Hayes agreed to withdraw remaining federal troops from the South and effectively end Reconstruction in exchange for the votes of Southern Democrats.

The 1876 outcome, viewed by many at the time and later as a stolen election, turned out to be a turning point suffused with irony. Republicans had used antiblack discrimination as a basis for challenging presidential vote totals in the South and then sealed the deal by ending Reconstruction and turning back to the South much greater leeway in managing the region's race relations. This inevitably meant more widespread antiblack discrimination. For a dozen years, lingering Civil War passions had dominated national politics, reflected in the penchant among Northern politicians to "wave the bloody shirt," emphasizing what many Northerners considered the South's profound civic transgressions leading to and during the war. Southern politicians responded with equal asperity, and there didn't seem to be much hope for any lessening in interregional acrimony.

Then McKinley's mentor, in a move born of political necessity, sacrificed the protection of Southern blacks in favor of fostering greater prospects for healing the wounds of war among the nation's whites. As far as is known, McKinley never commented on this fearsome trade-off, either publicly or in private letters or conversation. While he took pride in his lifelong antislavery convictions and his wartime part in saving the Union and emancipating black Americans, he seemed to accept widespread racial prejudice as an inevitable fact of life that would direct the course of national politics long into the future. The result was a kind of patronizing attitude toward African Americans—lamenting their tragic fate and cheering them on as they struggled against it but offering little in the way of political action aimed at ameliorating their condition.

And of course the young congressman-elect was elated to have his friend and mentor entering the White House, however he got there, just as he himself was taking his place in Washington. The friendship of the two men deepened as McKinley stood ready in Congress to assist the president in every way possible. Hayes reciprocated by avidly accepting McKinley's patronage suggestions and inviting him frequently to the White House for casual dinners and official occasions.

Ida played no serious role in her husband's congressional campaign, appearing at only one political event. When William settled in at Washington's Ebbitt House, just two blocks from the White House, Ida was in Philadelphia, under the care of a leading neurologist of the day, Silas Weir Mitchell. During her stay, she proudly revealed to a friend, her husband wrote her three letters a day. By the end of 1877 Ida's condition had improved sufficiently that she could join her husband in Washington during congressional sessions and take on a modest, but highly guarded, social routine. She loved going to the White House, and Rutherford and Lucy Hayes developed a special fondness for her.

As a congressional back-bencher, McKinley concentrated on consolidating his political standing in his Seventeenth District. His political persona wasn't much different from the image he had projected as a litigation lawyer. Covering a McKinley appearance shortly after his election, the *Warren Chronicle* said he was "one of the best political stumpers in the state": "His manner of presenting the matter in discussion is clear, logical and forcible."

But keeping the seat proved challenging. Whenever Democrats gained dominance in the state legislature, they sought political advantage by recasting congressional districts to throw Republican incumbents on the defensive. Thus, when McKinley faced the voters again in 1878, three of his district counties had been replaced by other counties more heavily populated by Democrats. He still won, though his victory margin declined to just 1,234 votes. "The Victory in the District, was a very gratifying one to me personally," he wrote to Hayes, "and besides it was a grand triumph for just principles."

The old district was restored in time for the next election, but McKinley encountered serious political adversity when he sought a fourth term in 1882. Three problems converged into a daunting challenge. First, Columbiana County argued that Stark County had held the seat long enough, and it was time now for Columbiana to carry the district banner to Washington. Then a local judge named Peter A. Laubie, from Columbiana, alleged that McKinley, in seeking a clear path to the 1880 nomination, had promised that he wouldn't run in 1882, thus making way for Laubie and Columbiana County. Finally, 1882 turned out to be a big Democratic year. In Ohio, Democratic voters outnumbered Republicans by 19,000 votes in congressional elections. Nationally, the Democratic wave was even more stark; the party gained seventy House seats that year.

The Laubie allegation proved particularly nettlesome, as it undermined McKinley's reputation for rectitude and bolstered those in the party who wished to get him out of the way to further their own ambitions. An example was an anonymous party man from Mahoning County quoted in the *New York Times*. "The trouble with McKinley," he said, "is that he has not grown as we believed he would, and has not made the mark nor won the influence in Congress that was promised in the start. . . . He has not attempted to go toward the front, but seems to have been overshadowed by younger members and men with less natural promise." Recognizing the delicacy of the Laubie challenge, McKinley crafted a counterstrategy with carefully timed responses, first from his friends, then from his own pen, and finally an orchestrated riposte from all the district newspapers that favored his reelection.

Through it all, McKinley sought to maintain a statesmanlike pose, avoiding angry expressions or harsh counterattacks. He revealed to his brother Abner that in responding to a letter from Laubie demanding to know if he denied making the promise, "I was disposed to be a little caustic, but my better judgment advised me against it."

In the end he captured the nomination without difficulty, but the general election proved more troublesome. The initial vote count gave him a victory of just eight votes, and he headed to Washington as an incumbent. But well into his new term, a review panel dominated by Democrats awarded the seat to his opponent. So he returned to Canton a defeated politician. On top of that, the Democratic legislature once again reconstituted his district, giving Democrats an estimated registration advantage of some 900 votes.

McKinley's natural optimism asserted itself as he reviewed the new district, encompassing counties that he barely knew and where his reputation was only dimly known. "I believe we can carry it," he wrote to his former law partner and close friend, Allan Carnes. To another friend, John Pollock, he wrote that he didn't anticipate the kind of difficulty he had encountered in 1882. "There will be nothing in the canvass to revive it, except as my enemies may desire to do it, and if they do, there can be no better time than the present for my friends to show their strength." He carried the new district by 2,000 votes and obtained a new lease on his congressional seat.

DURING HIS YEARS as a congressman, McKinley had gained strength as a politician. Elected initially on the basis of his personal qualities and his record as civic leader, he now also possessed abundant skills in the arts of political maneuver and campaign management, reflected in the Laubie episode. Though tough-minded and unsentimental as a political tactician, he managed to keep these traits shrouded behind his image as a man of character who remained above the fray and apart from the petty machinations of politics.

Meanwhile, he faced the challenge of balancing his career with the demands and needs of his wife, whose health and mental equilibrium seemed to be in a state of constant fluctuation. As he wrote to Abner in January 1882, "Ida is growing stronger and better. She was five days without any fainting attacks and they have been less frequent on other days. I am very busy." He showered her with loving letters whenever they were apart, with salutations such as "My own precious darling,"

"My precious love," and "My precious wife." In Canton, he worked from an office in their third-floor living quarters at Saxton House, with Ida never far away. His attentiveness never slackened. Now, at the start of his fourth full House term, he could indeed conclude that he had fashioned a balance that could meld his marriage and his political career. The lingering question was where that career would take him.

4

The Ohio Republicans

A CLASH OF TEMPERAMENT AND AMBITION

In early 1885 an aspiring Ohio politician and Civil War veteran named Robert Kennedy heard rumors that Congressman McKinley opposed his candidacy for the Republican gubernatorial nomination in favor of rival Joseph Foraker. When Kennedy wrote to McKinley seeking clarification, McKinley responded immediately. But it was a delicate business. While he genuinely intended to remain neutral, he didn't want to strike a disingenuous pose. "I am neither 'an active friend of Judge Foraker,' nor bitterly opposed to you," wrote McKinley. "I never permit an occasion to pass without speaking well of you and expressing my admiration for your services in war and your zeal and services for the party." Thus, should Kennedy get the nomination, "you will have no more faithful ally in your campaign and one who will do more proportionate to his ability than I will."

But here McKinley felt a need to interject a note of realism about Foraker, who had run for governor two years earlier and acquitted himself well despite an ultimate general election defeat: "I had thought that if Foraker wanted the nomination he would likely get it by reason of his splendid campaign." True, he lost the election, "but I have never heard it charged to him and there is a good feeling for him in this election, while here you also have many friends."

McKinley's carefully calibrated diplomacy reflected his political persona, always intent on avoiding unnecessary animosities and willing to work with anyone on any political matter so long as their interests aligned. But there was a deeper imperative in McKinley's determination to keep intraparty relations as smooth as possible. Ohio politics resided on a knife's edge of parity between Republicans and Democrats, with political sentiment so closely divided that neither party could afford to let slip its cohesion or unity of purpose.

This party parity stemmed from intertwined economic and demographic developments. After becoming an agricultural powerhouse in the first half of the nineteenth century, Ohio turned its attention to the industrial challenge. With Great Lakes access to the north, the robust Ohio River east and south, and multiple other rivers and canals, Ohio enjoyed a transportation bonanza. Further, its central location rendered it a natural crossroads for burgeoning railroad lines, both east-west and north-south. All this, coupled with the development of vast seams of coal in thirty-two eastern and southern counties, spurred a manufacturing explosion. By 1872 Ohio produced five million tons of coal annually; within fourteen years production doubled. This led to the development of coal-fired open-hearth furnaces for steel production, and by 1892 Ohio ranked second among all states, behind Pennsylvania, in the manufacture of steel. Inevitably, new manufacturing uses for the steel soon emerged.

In Cincinnati Cyrus McCormick invented the reaper and Obed Hussey developed the farm mower. Cleveland became an industrial behemoth as well as an oil hub. Columbus became the "Buggy Capital of the World," while the National Cash Register Company turned Dayton into a center of new technology. By century's end, Ohio had plunged into chemicals, automobile and rubber manufacturing, soap products, and pharmaceuticals.

All this required labor, and laborers poured in from overseas. In the twenty years beginning in 1870, Ohio's population grew by a million people, to 3,672,329. The greatest influx was from Germany, and by 1870 half of all foreign-born Ohioans were Germans. But the wave included growing numbers of Irish and immigrants from southern and eastern Europe—Italians, Slavs, Croats, Poles—who were mostly

Catholic and less inclined than the Germans to assimilate smoothly into the prevailing Anglo-Saxon culture. Before long these immigrants represented significant population segments in the industrial cities of Cleveland, Youngstown, Akron, Dayton, and Toledo.

McKinley's Republican Party largely represented native-born Ohioans, mostly British and German in provenance, Protestant, middle class, residents of small country towns. As the party that had destroyed slavery, the GOP projected a reformist ethos focused on improving the American character through material and moral progress. The greatest vehicle of material progress, in the Republican view, was the protective tariff. Moral betterment was promoted through the temperance movement against alcohol consumption, the promotion of public education, and (to a limited extent, given the political realities of the day) a concern about civil rights for black Americans.

The Ohio Republican Party, in short, was the party of middle-class respectability, crisply represented by Rutherford and Lucy Hayes, from the small Ohio town of Fremont. Lucy's refusal to serve alcohol in the White House got her the nickname "Lemonade Lucy." Her zeal for missionary and reform movements got her recruited to the presidency of the influential Woman's Home Missionary Society. These were quintessential Ohio Republicans. Novelist Brand Whitlock noted that among such people it was "inconceivable that any self-respecting person should be a Democrat."

But many Ohioans were, including large numbers of the new immigrants as well as rural populists with Southern roots and sensibilities. More laissez-faire on cultural matters and suspicious of reform movements, they also favored inflationary economic policies (free silver coinage or greenback issuance) and opposed government intervention into the lives of citizens. They certainly didn't want anyone to take away their alcohol.

Ohio's political parity rendered it imperative that each party consolidate its base, meaning minority segments with splinter-issue passions had to be accommodated. Republicans needed to assuage the temperance movement so it wouldn't split off into a one-issue protest party and undermine Republican prospects. But that meant few Democrats could be lured to the GOP in close elections. Democrats had to conciliate populist dissidents demanding soft-money policies to aid debtors and slam elites. That meant, likewise, that few Republicans would rally to the Democrats. The result was a precarious political environment for politicians of both parties. McKinley's mercurial Seventeenth District was a case in point.

Thus it wasn't surprising that both parties cherished internal harmony. Yet Ohio Republicans were headed toward a rift that would roil party councils for years. It would be a schism not of ideology but of personal temperament and political ambition involving primarily four large figures: three rising politicians with finely honed political skills and an old salt of a pol who had navigated the shoals of history for more than three decades and who now, in his declining years, held fast to his political station and ultimate ambition.

The old salt was John Sherman, a lanky, rustic-looking man with a closely cropped beard and fiery pale-blue eyes. Though widely known as the brother of Civil War General William Tecumseh Sherman, he was a man of mark in his own right. Born in 1823, he cast his first presidential vote for that political titan of the misty past, Henry Clay, founder of the Whig Party. From a family of prominent landowners and jurists in Connecticut and Ohio, Sherman grew up in privilege but showed a rebellious streak. As a boy he habitually got into fights and was expelled from school for punching a teacher. Still in his teens, he set out on his own and became a lawyer at twenty-one.

He thrived, though the rebellious impulse never fully dissipated. Outraged by the slaveholder grip on 1850s America, he ran for Congress and won. He served six years in the House, then sixteen in the Senate. Beginning in 1877 he served four years as Treasury secretary under Hayes, then returned to the Senate. He played pivotal roles in the slavery issue before the war, in the government's efforts to finance the war, in Reconstruction after the war, in currency issues, civil service reform, tariff policy. He served as chairman of the House Ways and Means Committee, the Senate Finance Committee, and the Senate Foreign Relations Committee. Throughout these assignments and endeavors, his organizational skill and leadership capacity propelled him to the forefront of American politics.

Now he hungered for the presidency. The Republican nominating conventions of 1880 and 1884 had seen squibs of support for him, but these bids had fizzled. He would be sixty-five in 1888, so that had to be his year. But Sherman had liabilities. He lacked magnetism and rhetorical flair. Worse, he displayed a distant, unfriendly manner. They called him "the Ohio icicle" based upon a frosty persona visible in his thin, unsmiling lips and abrupt nature. Increasingly self-absorbed, he returned to the Senate, after his stint at Treasury, insisting that the body waive its traditional rules and restore him to his previous seniority, including his Finance Committee chairmanship. When his successor as chairman, Justin Morrill of Vermont, refused to yield, Sherman responded in "bad grace," as one journalist put it. Colleagues respected him but didn't much like him, and voters greeted his standoffishness with wariness.

Then there was Joseph Benson Foraker, known as Ben, born three years after McKinley, the son of an Ohio farmer and miller. His early life paralleled McKinley's: brought up in the Methodist Episcopal Church; manifested what one teacher called an "aptitude for declamation"; early and fervent adherent of the fledgling Republican Party; army sergeant at sixteen and brevet captain by war's end. He saw extensive action at Chickamauga and Missionary Ridge, then marched with General Sherman through Georgia.

After the war he received a bachelor's degree from Cornell University, moved to Cincinnati, married a congressman's daughter, and entered the law. In his thirties he enjoyed legal and social prominence fueled in part by his imposing persona; he was tall, well-proportioned, with a large, droopy mustache, and "a voice like a fire-alarm," as the *Washington Post* described it. He also seemed at times somewhat imperious, and some felt he displayed his ambition a bit too nakedly.

He craved political success, but when he captured his party's nomination for a local judgeship, he lost the general election to a Democratic rival. Two years later, nominated for county solicitor, he lost again. But in 1879 he was elected to the Cincinnati Superior Court, and then a big break arrived in 1883 when the state's two-term Republican governor, Charles Foster, designated him to be the party's next gubernatorial candidate. Foster needed a stand-in in a year when a Republican split—a result of Foster's controversial effort to regulate liquor distribution—undermined party prospects. "The Republicans are demoralized," the Democratic *Cincinnati Enquirer* crowed, adding that the party's leaders "determined to sacrifice as little as possible so they sacrificed Foraker." But his exemplary campaign gave Foraker a statewide profile and much goodwill among prominent Republicans, reflected in McKinley's carefully phrased letter to Robert Kennedy. In a letter to Foraker after the election, McKinley wrote, "No candidate for Governor ever made a more brilliant canvas, and the friends you made will stick to you through life."

That sentiment was shared by Ohio's third major GOP figure, Marcus Alonzo Hanna of Cleveland, one of the state's most successful industrialists. His grandfather established himself as a New Lisbon farmer and grocer in 1814, and Mark's father, Leonard, expanded the business into a broad network of merchandising enterprises. Young Mark grew up in considerable luxury. "The table was abundant, the food well-cooked, the linen of excellent quality, and the children well-clothed," wrote one biographer. A schoolmate remembered young Hanna as "a pleasant, wholesome fellow, clean of tongue and with more polish of manners than many of his playmates."

The family fortune was devastated when Leonard and his brothers invested $200,000 in a canal project that failed. When Mark was fifteen, members of the extended family migrated to Cleveland and set out to reestablish their financial standing in the wholesale grocery business. Then they got into Great Lakes shipping to deliver goods to emerging transit points in Wisconsin and Minnesota. After his schooling, young Mark set about to learn the business and eventually moved into executive positions. In 1864 he married Augusta Rhodes, whose father, a strong Democrat, had extensive coal and iron interests. Daniel Rhodes initially tried to keep the two love-struck youngsters apart because he despised Hanna's politics, but on the wedding day he finally came around.

"It's all over now, Mark," he said to his new son-in-law, "but a month ago I would liked to have seen you at the bottom of Lake Erie."

Now he said he wanted the young couple to move into his Cleveland mansion and Mark to take over his business. Mark demurred. He hungered for success in the emerging oil-refining business. But when his refinery burned down, as his father-in-law had predicted, he concluded the Rhodes company and the Rhodes mansion constituted his best option for financial recovery.

"Your money is gone now, Mark," said the father-in-law when he heard about the fire, "and I'm damned glad of it."

Hanna turned out to be a business visionary of rare brilliance. With more and more coal being shipped to more and more blast furnaces turning out more and more iron and steel, Rhodes & Co. was positioned to expand its enterprise. But Hanna perceived that he could expand far more quickly, and with far less capital investment, by creating a sales agency, brokering deals among mining companies, iron and steel producers, and manufacturers. Thus the company took a cut in a large proportion of the burgeoning transactions that kept the industrial expansion humming. Rhodes & Co. still mined coal and ran blast furnaces, and it invested in other companies that did also, but that became a foundation for building the sales agency business and cementing long-term brokerage relationships. Later, by investing in railroad companies, developing a shipping line, and getting into shipbuilding, Hanna expanded his company's reach throughout the Great Lakes region.

Soon Rhodes & Co. (later Hanna & Co.) was one of the great industrial enterprises of the nation, and Hanna was one of the richest men in Ohio. His complex network of contractual relationships required a solid reputation, and Hanna's business persona was one of "absolute accuracy, honesty and integrity," recalled his corporate lawyer, Andrew Squire. "His early business associates were his late business associates." When economic downturns undercut the value of his contracts, he never sought to wriggle out of his obligations.

Hanna expanded his business interests to include a city transit line, a local newspaper, and a downtown theater. The transit line and theater thrived, but the newspaper, the *Cleveland Herald*, lost money. Worse, in attempting to lure away star reporters from a competitor, the *Cleveland Leader*, Hanna ran afoul of *Leader* owner Edwin Cowles. The outraged Cowles unleashed a newspaper attack on Hanna so vitriolic that it damaged his reputation for the rest of his life. Cowles's newspaper consistently portrayed Hanna as heartless, greedy, obsessed with self-aggrandizement. When Hanna finally decided to sell his paper, including major assets to Cowles, the triumphant publisher celebrated with an editorial that described Hanna as a picture of fair-mindedness and rectitude. But others picked up the Cowles cudgel as Hanna gained statewide and national attention.

Hanna seldom paid much heed to the attacks. A jaunty fellow with luminous brown eyes and a generosity of spirit, he loved to mix with interesting people, including the actors and musicians who performed at his theater and Republican politicians dedicated to business interests. "Mr. Hanna wanted company all the time," recalled Elmer Dover, a political associate. "He was always drawn to men who did things, who accomplished things."

Increasingly he was drawn to Republican politicians. He saw business as the vehicle of prosperity and prosperity as the goal of politics, and thus he fancied political figures who equated business success with the national interest. With more leisure now and plenty of money, he established himself as a Republican political operative, a man who could funnel cash to favored politicians, lend his well-honed organizational acumen to political campaigns, and muster the various talents needed for a smooth-running political operation. His ultimate goal: to usher an Ohio man into the White House.

The fourth man in the vortex of Ohio Republican competition was William McKinley. The criticism of that anonymous observer in the *New York Times* contained an element of truth, for he hadn't quite emerged as a truly potent leader either in Congress or in Ohio. But within Republican circles, both in Washington and at home, he was gaining notice and respect for his congenial disposition and professional solidity. For several years running he was a regular on the Resolutions Committee of state Republican conventions. As keynote speaker at the 1880 state convention, he stirred a hearty response with a rousing testimonial to John Sherman. Also in 1880, he was elected as an Ohio delegate to the Republican National Convention.

And in Congress he was positioned for advancement through his membership on the high-profile Ways and Means Committee, which had jurisdiction over the hot tariff issue. When a friend wrote to say he had heard McKinley would relinquish his Ways and Means seat to become chairman of Judiciary, the congressman scotched the rumor. "A place on [Ways and Means] is of far more value to my district, and has more to do with its material interest than any other committee," he wrote. What's more, he was emerging as the committee's leading voice for protectionism, the panel protégé of Chairman William ("Pig Iron") Kelley of Pennsylvania, himself a vigorous advocate of high tariffs.

Inevitably McKinley's unyielding high-tariff advocacy, coupled with his often elaborate earnestness, stirred some free-trade adherents to ridicule. Journalist Ida Tarbell would write that McKinley had "an advantage . . . which few of his colleagues enjoyed, —that of believing with childlike faith that all he claimed for protection was true." But among the Major's Republican colleagues in Congress, and increasingly among protectionist leaders and voters around the country, his sober genuineness on the issue generated respect and admiration. Clearly protectionism represented his ticket to national attention.

THE STORY OF the momentous interaction among these four men begins in 1884, when Sherman went up against the popular and flamboyant James G. Blaine, known as the Plumed Knight of Maine, for the GOP presidential nomination. Ohio Republicans were split on the matter, but without rancor. Most Blaine men embraced Sherman as their second choice, while Sherman's adherents designated Blaine their backup candidate. McKinley was a Blaine man, while Hanna and Foraker favored Sherman.

The state convention that year elected McKinley its permanent chairman, and the Canton congressman responded with a highly partisan speech. "The difference between the Republican and Democratic party," he declared, "is this—the Republican party never made a promise which it has not kept, and the Democratic party never made a promise which it has kept." When floor nominations opened for at-large delegates to the national convention, Foraker nabbed the first slot, given the stature he had gained from his recent gubernatorial campaign. Other names then emerged from the floor.

When McKinley's name was called out, the Major, from his chairman's podium, politely demurred based on promises to other candidates that he wouldn't let his name go forward while their fate remained undetermined. Given the man's growing popularity, the delegates wouldn't hear of it. Pandemonium ensued as motions were made and voted on to give McKinley the slot by acclamation while the chairman banged his gavel and declared the actions out of order. Ultimately the delegates overwhelmed the chairman, who reluctantly accepted the outcome. Hanna, drawing on support from Sherman delegates and others who appreciated his party benefactions, also garnered an at-large slot and became a national convention delegate.

At the national convention, held in Chicago, Blaine won the nomination on the fourth ballot, while Sherman never garnered any appreciable support beyond his partial tally from the Ohio delegation. McKinley added to his political luster by serving as chairman of the Resolutions Committee and, at one crucial point, executing a deft parliamentary maneuver that thwarted the Sherman forces from interrupting a roll-call vote that favored Blaine. Though no one knew it at the time, the big development was Hanna's opportunity to get to know McKinley and Foraker. He appreciated both but developed an emotional, almost sycophantic attachment to Foraker.

"Among the few pleasures I found at the convention," Hanna wrote to Foraker just before leaving Chicago, "was meeting and working with you." He added, "I hear nothing but praise for you on all sides, all of which I heartily endorse and will hope to be considered among your sincere friends." Returning to Cleveland, he wrote again: "I assure you, my dear fellow, that it will not be my fault if our acquaintance does not ripen, for I shall certainly *go for you* whenever you are within reach."

In succeeding months, Hanna showered Foraker with solicitousness, inviting him and his wife to Cleveland for extended weekends, expressing fealty to his gubernatorial ambitions, assuring him that he sought no rewards for his dedication. He projected just two ambitions: to help get Foraker into the governor's office and Sherman into the White House. For his part, Foraker expressed appreciation for Hanna's support but maintained a certain distance. He rarely accepted Hanna's proffered hospitality in Cleveland and never responded in kind to his effusive tone.

When Foraker was elected governor in late 1885, with considerable financial and organizational help from Hanna, the Cleveland industrialist assumed he would be consulted on significant patronage jobs. It didn't happen. When Foraker passed over Hanna's candidate for the lucrative position of state oil inspector in favor of McKinley's candidate, Louis Smithnight, Hanna uncharacteristically assumed a martyr pose. "The Major is never behind hand with his claims," he wrote to Foraker. "I tell him he 'wants the earth' and it looks as if I was getting about where I generally do in politics—left with only my reputation of being a good fellow, always accomodating [*sic*], etc., etc."

The episode didn't diminish Hanna's devotion to Foraker. "I told McKinley," the industrialist wrote in the same letter, "that I only cared for *you* in this matter." When Foraker was inaugurated, Hanna sent him another letter: "I tell you my dear friend I felt proud when you stood before the people of this great State, its chosen executive. . . . I feel that you will mount the ladder rapidly and I will always be glad to stand at the *bottom* to help keep it from *slipping*."

Meanwhile tensions emerged between Foraker and Sherman. Always alert to potential threats from rivals, the venerable senator recoiled when Republican newspapers began touting Foraker as a possible vice presidential candidate in 1888. Sherman's people quickly grasped that Foraker's vice presidential ambitions, if he had any, would undermine his support for Sherman's presidential bid, given that the Constitution prohibited men from the same state from running for president and vice president on the same ticket. As the well-spoken and attractive Foraker gained national attention within Republican ranks, Sherman's men even speculated that Foraker might actually covet the presidency.

Irritations mounted when the Sherman forces sought a state convention resolution declaring party unity on behalf of the senator's presidential candidacy. One aim was to smoke out Foraker. If he opposed the resolution, he would reveal his true colors. The governor took the bait, justifying his opposition by arguing that it could harm Sherman's standing by exposing fissures within the Ohio GOP left over from the 1884 Sherman-Blaine rivalry. "I am keeping out of the fight," Foraker wrote to Hanna, "rather because I do not want to fight Sherman and I cannot conscientiously or consistently fight for him in this respect."

Relations deteriorated further when Foraker took umbrage at being excluded from a secret meeting in Canton at which Sherman's top men discussed campaign strategy. Both men were embarrassed when the *Cleveland Plain Dealer* revealed the meeting and played up the Sherman-Foraker feud. More tensions emerged when the *Cincinnati Commercial Gazette*, a stalwart Republican paper, blasted Foraker for withholding his full support from Sherman and presented a Sherman interpretation of the feud that Foraker considered distorted. In a letter to Sherman, Foraker suggested the senator's actions constituted a "strain" upon their friendship, and he told a Sherman partisan that the senator's correspondence had left him "very mad."

Foraker seemed bent on having it both ways: maintaining his relationship with Sherman in the early phase of his presidential campaign while keeping his options open should the senator fade along the way. Given Sherman's temperament and ambition, he would never accept that. Realizing the tensions could harm their careers, both men sought to rise above the squabble as Foraker won reelection and Sherman got his party's endorsement. But the tensions were never far from the surface.

Hanna struggled to remain neutral, working assiduously for Sherman's presidential bid, even getting designated the senator's campaign manager and personal representative at the nominating convention, while also supporting Foraker whenever he could. But once reelected, the governor rebuffed Hanna once again on his renewed effort to get his man appointed oil inspector—or, barring that, to get him a secondary position. When Hanna suggested obliquely that perhaps Foraker's home city of Cincinnati and surrounding Hamilton County were getting an outsized share of the governor's patronage, Foraker shot back, "No one will make any headway for himself by talking about Hamilton county having more than her share, for that is exceedingly unjust." Nevertheless Hanna continued to emphasize his special regard for the governor. "How glad I am," he wrote Foraker at one point, "that I don't know enough to be a governor or even President. . . . Consider me in this matter only as to how I can help you."

It was getting increasingly difficult for Hanna to remain neutral, however. When Foraker heard rumors that he wouldn't be called upon to make Sherman's nominating speech at the Republicans' national convention in Chicago, he seethed. After being excluded from Sherman's strategy sessions, Foraker complained to Hanna. "I am wholly ignorant as to Mr. Sherman's plans and wishes, hopes and prospects," he wrote on May 10. Hanna implored the senator to invite Foraker to a forthcoming Washington meeting of Sherman managers. Sherman did so, but Foraker was unable to attend. He assured the senator, though, that upon being briefed on the campaign plans by Hanna or former governor Foster he would cooperate fully. He already had warned Sherman that the Blaine movement in Ohio "seems to be developing so strongly that I am getting somewhat uneasy." Blaine remained officially out of the race, however, and Ohio was coming around to a unified front in behalf of Sherman.

Corporate business kept Hanna on the road throughout the weeks before the convention, and thus he couldn't get to Columbus to brief the governor on Sherman's campaign strategy. Foraker's anger exploded onto a letter he dashed off to Hanna on May 25, protesting not only the industrialist's absence from Columbus but also a change in Foraker's assignment of rooms at the Sherman headquarters hotel, the Grand Pacific, during the Chicago convention. After quoting from several letters assuring him he would be briefed by Hanna, Foraker wrote,

With these letters before me, I was surprised to receive your letter in which you do not speak of any arrangement having been made according to which you were to see me, or of any information with which you were charged with the duty of imparting to me, or of any plan in accordance with which we are to work or of any organization of the delegation that had been determined upon or suggested, but which is chiefly an assignment of reasons why I should surrender the rooms in the vicinity of our headquarters that I have had engaged for more than three months. . . .

These letters appear . . . "out of joint" with one another, and . . . satisfy me that the so-called "fool-friends" are not all killed off yet, as I supposed, and induce me to say that I prefer to retain my rooms.

Hanna replied meekly that the suite assignment had been motivated only by a concern for Foraker's comfort and convenience. "They will be left as they were," he assured Foraker. But Foraker then said no, he would accept the change after all. Hanna patiently replied that he would reverse course yet again and take care of it. He never suggested to Foraker or anyone else how he felt to be addressed by the governor as if he were hired help who needed stern correction rather than the loyal benefactor that he had been for four years. Hanna sought to end his reply on a jaunty note: "Adieu, until we meet on the battlefield and my Ohio comes out victorious."

As the convention's June 19 opening session approached, Hanna told reporters that Sherman would garner 300 delegates in early balloting and build from there to the nomination. "The Sherman men have probably the best organized working force on the ground," declared McKinley's hometown paper, the *Evening Repository*. "They . . . confidently claim their three hundred or more certain delegates will receive additions on every ballot." Still, the ghost of James G. Blaine hovered over the convention like a thundercloud, threatening a bolt of political lightning at any moment. Despite Blaine's disavowal of interest in the nomination and his removal to the distant shores of Scotland, Blaine partisans worked furiously behind the scenes to generate a sudden Blaine rally at just the right moment.

Beyond Sherman and Blaine stood numerous "favorite son" aspirants—Walter Gresham of Illinois, Benjamin Harrison of Indiana, Chauncey Depew of New York, Russell Alger of Michigan, William Allison of Iowa—hoping a convention deadlock might open the way for them. Fueling this hope was a perception that even Sherman's supporters weren't sure they liked him very much. "Sherman won't do; he's too cold," one skeptic remarked to an Ohio delegate. When rumors filtered through the convention that Sherman's Ohio support was shallow, Sherman partisans saw Foraker as the rumormonger. Foraker denied it, but some of his convention behavior—particularly his seconding speech for Sherman, which seemed designed primarily to stir his own convention enthusiasts—generated skepticism. The *Repository* wrote that the demonstration following Foraker's speech seemed to be "more of a Foraker boom than a Sherman boom."

When the balloting began on Friday, June 22, Sherman pulled 229 votes, more than double the tally of his nearest competitor, Gresham of Illinois. On the second ballot, the senator's vote crept up to 249, still a far cry from the 300 predicted by Hanna and even further from the 417 needed for nomination. Worse, aside from Ohio and Pennsylvania, Sherman's support came almost entirely from the solidly Democratic South, which provided almost no general election support to Republicans. Sherman needed a broader display of support to avoid the decline now presaged by the third ballot, which was taken just before adjournment for the day, when his tally dropped to 244.

By nightfall some Ohio delegates were concluding that, if Ohio wanted to send a president to Washington, it would have to be someone other than Sherman. A self-appointed delegation of five Ohio men went to see McKinley at the Grand Pacific suite of the former general Green B. Raum, who ran the Sherman literary bureau. With hats in hand, they paced the floor before a seated McKinley and importuned him to embrace their effort to build a fire of support for him. One witness later characterized the entreaty: "Everything is arranged. . . . It will not start in Ohio. You need not say a single word. You cannot stop it, either. . . . You owe it to the state, you can't hold the state solid for Sherman."

McKinley rose from his chair and with friendly but firm demeanor pronounced his utter opposition. One petitioner said it would be done anyway. "It must not be," replied McKinley. When they protested further, the Major showed them to the door as he declared, "It shall never be so. If you do that I will rise in the convention and denounce it."

When the balloting resumed the next morning, Sherman slipped further. He now had 235 votes, just nineteen more than Indiana's former senator Harrison. But Harrison's number remained far short of the nomination number, and many delegates felt the convention needed a new face—perhaps McKinley's. When a Connecticut delegate called McKinley's name from the floor, the congressman climbed upon a chair and interrupted the roll call with his stentorian voice:

Mr. President and Gentlemen of the Convention: I am here as one of the chosen representatives of my State. I am here by resolution of the Republican State Convention, passed without a single dissenting voice, commanding me to cast my vote for John Sherman for President, and to use every worthy endeavor for his nomination. I accepted the trust because my heart and judgment were in accord with the letter and spirit and purpose of that resolution. It has pleased certain delegates to cast their votes for me for President. I am not insensible to the honor they would do me, but in the presence of the duty resting upon me I can not remain silent with honor. I can not, consistently with the wish of the State whose credentials I bear, and which has trusted me; I can not with honorable fidelity to John Sherman, who has trusted me in his cause and with his confidence; I can not, consistently with my own views of personal integrity, consent, or seem to consent, to permit my name to be used as a candidate before this Convention. I would not respect myself if I could find it in my heart to do so, or permit to be done that which could even be ground for any one to suspect that I wavered in my loyalty to Ohio, or my devotion to the chief of her choice and the chief of mine. I do not request—I demand, that no delegate who would not cast reflection upon me shall cast a ballot for me.

It proved to be one of the most dramatic moments of the convention. No one questioned McKinley's sincerity or suspected a double game of any kind. But the Major's selfless action raised his stature instantly in the convention, and many attendees concluded that he might be an attractive candidate if Sherman could be persuaded to yield. After the senator's vote total declined to 224 on the fifth ballot, even Hanna began to wonder if Sherman should hold on. Late on Saturday, he wired Sherman that a sudden move to Blaine seemed imminent: "Many of your best friends say that the only way to prevent a Blaine nomination is to wire me to announce your withdrawal and let McKinley come in. . . . I do not advise this and it should only be done as a last resort." Later in the day, Hanna put a little more starch into his reporting: "The Blaine move is to be made on the next ballot. We think McKinley the only man who can defeat him. . . . I regret the situation but fear I am right."

Sherman couldn't bring himself to relinquish his lifelong presidential ambition, however, and Hanna set about to keep his delegation together. McKinley remained ironclad in his Sherman support, even going to the New Jersey delegation after midnight to thwart plans there to place his name in nomination. "To accept a nomination, if one were possible, under these circumstances, would inevitably lead to my defeat," he told the delegation chairman. Drawing out his words for emphasis, he added, "*And . . . it . . . ought . . . to . . . lead . . . to . . . my . . . defeat!*" The chairman said he would honor the congressman's wishes.

Meanwhile Foraker took a different tack. On Saturday he stated through the Associated Press that he had been "faithful and true to Mr. Sherman" and could not "be accused of unfaithfulness or treachery." But the senator's case had become "hopeless," and he now supported Blaine. Although Foraker later disavowed the statement, it unleashed shock and dismay throughout the Sherman forces as their convention standing withered. Murat Halstead, the influential editor of the *Cincinnati Commercial Gazette* and a McKinley admirer, wired to Sherman, "The Ohio delegation is already broken." Blaine couldn't be stopped, he added, unless Sherman withdrew in favor of McKinley. "Give us a word, and we believe we can pull McKinley through." It didn't take long for Sherman to wire his response: "Let my name stand. I prefer defeat to retreat."

Then word arrived from Scotland that Blaine absolutely renounced any candidacy irrespective of what the delegates did. Without the Plumed Knight exercising his magnetic pull, the dynamics of the convention changed in ways that could have posed a renewed opportunity for Sherman. A new round of negotiations might have pulled a favorite-son delegation or two to his banner, reversing his decline and boosting him to victory. But that wasn't possible now because Ohio's own governor had abandoned him, and the senator's position within the Ohio delegation had become untenable. When voting resumed on Monday, Harrison crept up to 231 votes on the sixth ballot and captured the prize with 544 on the eighth.

THE DRAMATIC EVENTS of Chicago in June 1888 divided Ohio Republicans into two factions and destroyed the state party's internal harmony. On one side were the Sherman partisans who stayed with the fight to the end and took pride in their political fidelity. This group included Sherman, McKinley, former governor Foster, a jaunty congressman named Benjamin Butterworth, and that rising master of political organization, Mark Hanna. Nobody personified this group's political ethos more distinctly than McKinley, who stood on a chair to renounce presidential ambition at the very moment when the office may have been coming his way. "Guided by a fine sense of honor," wrote Halstead in the *Commercial Gazette*, "he has made no mistake, and has done his duty thoroughly."

On the other side was Foraker, who never again would be able to work with his former comrades. He probably was never as devious or treacherous as his most bitter critics alleged, but he had allowed his actions to place upon him a stamp of opprobrium. Given his brilliance and resourcefulness, he was destined to play a major role in Ohio politics, forging alliances as needed and projecting power throughout the state well into the next century. But the cloud of controversy would hover over him for the remainder of his career, curtailing his range of maneuver.

As for Hanna, his devotion to Foraker was torn asunder upon the rocks of disillusion. A Cleveland lawyer named James Dempsey, who knew Hanna well, once said of him, "Mr. Hanna despised treachery. I think his greatest characteristic was his fidelity to friends." Hanna himself liked to say, "I stand by my friends, whether they deserve it or not." Foraker didn't stand by his friend and forfeited Hanna's friendship in the bargain. For that, Foraker would pay a price. He said years later that he never again had a political ally as closely associated with him as Hanna.

The disruption of the Hanna-Foraker alliance led inevitably to a Hanna-McKinley combine. If Sherman couldn't make it to the presidency and Foraker wasn't worthy of it, then Hanna would devote his considerable skills and resources to the career of William McKinley, a man on the rise, with all the talents, ambitions, and virtues that Hanna was looking for. Besides, McKinley wasn't the kind of man who would treat him like a hired hand. If Hanna seemed at times given to a kind of political hero worship, McKinley would make an ideal hero.

The Major was becoming a man of stature, hailed for his strong character, devotion to Republican ideals, and quiet magnetism. And he had good reason to believe that, by renouncing a path to the White House, he quite possibly had opened up a wider avenue later toward the same destination. As his mentor and friend Rutherford Hayes wrote to him following the convention, "You gained gloriously. The test was a severe one, but you stood it manfully. . . . A better crown than to have been nominated." He added a fragment of sound advice for future reference: "Men in political life must be ambitious. But the surest path to the White House is his who never allows his ambition . . . [to] stand in the way of any duty, large or small."

5

Steadfast Protectionist

"IN THE TIME OF DARKEST DEFEAT, VICTORY MAY BE NEAREST"

B ack in 1877, at the beginning of William McKinley's career as
an Ohio congressman, he received a bit of advice from the man
he admired most. "To achieve success," said Rutherford Hayes,
who himself had just achieved his country's highest level of political
success, "you must not make a speech on every motion offered or every
bill introduced. You must confine yourself to one thing in particular.
Become a specialist." Then he turned specific: "Why not choose the
tariff?"

It was good advice, and the new congressman embraced it. A man
of conventional sensibilities, McKinley wasn't the type to blaze new
trails in pursuit of success. His inclination was to follow the counsel
and example of men who already had paved the way. Because such men
often perceived him as a worthy protégé, he never lacked for advice on
how to reach attainment. But no one influenced him more powerfully
than Hayes—leaving aside, of course, the younger man's early rejection
of a lucrative industrial career in favor of the law and public service.

As for the tariff, it was an ideal area of concentration for the young
congressman, who possessed a highly absorbent mind but not a facile

one. His was a stolid intellect, without imagination but with a potent capacity for mastering masses of intricate detail. Further, he tended to view public policy in simple, binary terms—the right way to do things and the wrong way. For him, the right tariff policy was protectionism. High tariffs, he once said on the House floor, helped shape America as a country "without a superior in industrial arts, without an equal in commercial prosperity, with a sound financial system, with an over-flowing Treasury, blessed at home and at peace with all mankind."

By the late 1880s, McKinley had become a leading congressional expert on the country's multifarious tariff structure, which at one point encompassed some 1,524 separate tariffs on as many items, including iron and steel products, wool and woolens, various paint products, wallpaper, crockery, cutlery, glass and glassware, linens, soaps, starch, sugar, and many more. McKinley knew them all, and so now, some twelve years after embracing Hayes's wise counsel, he was reaping the benefit of his years-long tariff preoccupation.

But McKinley faced a difficult challenge in balancing his political endeavors with a delicate personal life weighted down by the needs and whims of the truly sad woman who was his wife. Ida McKinley long since had abandoned hope of capturing the kind of life that seemed in prospect when she was a vibrant young woman of stunning beauty, sharp intellect, and scintillating persona. Now she was brittle and sedentary, preoccupied with small matters of everyday existence, embroidering or crocheting for hours as she sat in her wooden, ornately carved rocking chair.

Over the years the McKinleys came to expect both good times and bad in regard to Ida's health. Sometimes there would be no seizures for extended periods, and her strength would return sufficiently for short walks or longer carriage rides. McKinley even took her on two trips to California, much to her delight. But only rarely was she allowed to travel alone from Washington to Canton; more often her lack of physical strength and prospects for seizures necessitated that she travel with a watchful companion.

She dealt with her plight by clinging to her husband and demanding as much attention and affection as he could possibly give. In Washington, during late-night strategy sessions in the Major's Ebbitt House study, across the hall from the couple's residential suite, she frequently summoned him on trivial pretexts. He always interrupted the discussion, accepting his colleagues' raised eyebrows as the price to be paid for the balance he sought in his life. He knew her best health came at times of serenity, and the key to her serenity was himself.

When they were apart, he showered her with expressions of love. If congressional business kept him on the Hill late at night, he always got a message to her. Once he informed her that he would probably sleep in his office and added, "I hope you will not worry about me, but have a good night's rest & I will try & breakfast with you in the morning. . . . God bless & keep you. Accept a heart full of love and a thousand kisses." When he could not monitor her health during times apart, he became anxious. "My darling wife," he wrote at one point, "I am quite solicitous to know how you are. The telephone is out of order. I hope you are feeling better. Please send me a line saying how you feel. Accept a heart full of love."

He sent her multiple communications a day when they were apart. When he was traveling by rail she could predict the arrival time of telegrams based on when he was scheduled to reach his destination or change trains. Asked by a friend what the Major could possibly convey to her in these multiple wire messages, she replied tartly, "He can say he loves me." There was some validity in his feeling that he could ward off her attacks and intermittent infections by keeping her tranquil. On a camping trip near Waynesburg, Pennsylvania, she became distraught over the exuberant yelling of small boys nearby and had to retreat to her tent with a severe headache. On another occasion, when McKinley mentioned in passing an attractive woman he had seen at President Garfield's funeral, she flew into a fit of jealousy so intense that it led to a serious epileptic seizure.

Some of McKinley's friends suspected his attentiveness was largely defensive, designed to prevent episodes of unpleasantness. But no one questioned the depth or tenderness of his love. He once told the wife of a political friend that, when he first met Ida, she was "the most beautiful girl you ever saw." Recognizing that others may not see this fading invalid in the same way, he added, "She is still beautiful to me now."

In mid-July 1888, while McKinley was attending a House session, an aide approached with a telegram reporting that Ida, in Canton, had contracted a serious infection and was unconscious with fever. He rushed from the floor and caught the next train home. When he got there, he plunged into a carriage waiting to whisk him to Saxton House. Dashing up three flights of winding stairs, he tenderly took her hand and whispered, "Ida, it is I." He sat up with her all night, receiving intermittent warnings from a doctor that if her fever didn't break soon she likely would die. The next morning she regained consciousness and managed a wan smile and the words "I knew you would come." Though the fever had broken, it left her in a weakened state for months.

The distraught husband took a leave of absence from his House duties and refrained from political activities that fall, except for a desultory but successful reelection effort. By year's end, when Congress convened again, she was able to travel to Washington when he resumed his House routines. But he stayed glued to the Ebbitt House except when duties required his presence on the House floor. Those wishing to confer with him on governmental matters had to travel down Pennsylvania Avenue to see him. When word spread about his solicitous regard for his troubled wife, a reporter came around to interview the couple. The result was a *Home Magazine* article, reprinted in newspapers across the country, that praised McKinley for "his entire consecration to his invalid wife." It was the first time Ida was portrayed in print as an invalid, and it gave the nation a glimpse of an intriguing public servant who juggled official duties tirelessly with loving ministrations to a tragic spouse.

Despite his devotion to Ida, McKinley had no intention of abandoning or even slackening his political ambition. When he received an unsolicited offer to become attorney for a big railroad company at an annual salary of $25,000, he turned it down despite knowing that the job would have provided lifetime financial security and bolstered efforts to support Ida's expansive needs. He told a friend that he was motivated by the thought that he was "serving the country a little." But of course he didn't shun such an opportunity merely for the life of a congressman. He harbored a higher ambition.

His higher ambition was the presidency. He never said so, of course, preferring to keep his aspirations shrouded behind the veil of his characteristic taciturnity, just as he kept so much of his thinking concealed from others. But as early as his honeymoon his bride became convinced that he would someday be president. Even allowing for the starry regard nurtured by young love, it seems likely that the magnitude of his ambition was revealed during the couple's intimate conversations about their future together. Of course, he had watched his great mentor, Rud Hayes, reach the White House just as he was beginning his own career precisely as Hayes had begun his: by capturing a U.S. House seat for Ohio. And Hayes certainly encouraged his protégé's White House ambitions, as reflected in the older man's letter to the younger man after McKinley pushed aside the presidential boomlet at the 1888 convention. Then there was Mark Hanna. Everyone knew his big goal was to usher an Ohio Republican into the White House, and it wasn't difficult to see just which Ohio Republican he had in mind. McKinley's increasingly intimate association with Hanna left little doubt about his ultimate political objective.

But in early 1889 he directed his ambition to a lesser prize: the House speakership, a constitutional office that could bring wide national attention. "I am doing no soliciting," he wrote to Hayes. "If I am successful the selection will come in an honorable and self-respecting way." But by summer he had dropped the coyness, and soon political observers discerned his seriousness in Hanna's Washington presence. As Theodore Burton, a congressman from Cleveland, put it, "No one except those who were close to him ever knew how anxious Mr. McKinley was for an office when he went after it."

His principal competitor was Thomas B. Reed of Maine, a mountain of a man with a placid face and high-pitched voice that accentuated a harpoon wit often wielded in behalf of an acidic cynicism. Highly cultivated and intellectually gifted, he became fluent in French after age forty and "read heavily and happily in French." He maintained his diary in French, "for practice." Loathing cant and sham, Reed cast a haughty eye upon his Democratic opponents and also some errant Republicans, but he did so with a verve and wry acuity that riveted audiences whenever he merely cleared his throat to speak. Once, after devastating an opponent in House debate, he cast his countenance across the floor and said, "Having embedded that fly in the liquid amber of my remarks, I will proceed." McKinley once observed with a smile, "Everybody enjoys Reed's sarcastic comments and keen wit, except the fellow who is the subject of his satire."

The two men presented two different leadership styles: McKinley, the sweet-tempered adjudicator, always looking for common ground; Reed, the polemical bruiser who employed the force of words to delineate issues and keep opponents on the defensive. Reed considered McKinley "a man of little scope." But when he outpolled the Ohioan in the Republican conference, the new speaker promptly elevated his erstwhile opponent to the chairmanship of the Ways and Means Committee. This was a plum assignment. Following the 1888 elections, Republicans controlled both houses of Congress for the first time since 1875 and also had their man, Benjamin Harrison, in the White House. Thus the GOP was positioned to dominate national policy, and the first order of business was an overhaul of the nation's tariff policy. The man to lead that effort was Chairman McKinley, who crafted a strongly protectionist measure in his committee and sent it to the House floor.

Hovering over the tariff debate of 1890 was the nation's tariff history going back to its first revenue law, fashioned in 1789 by George Washington's Treasury secretary, Alexander Hamilton. From that time forward, the tariff issue drove a wedge through the American body politic. On one side were the Federalists and later the Whigs—Hamilton and Henry Clay prominent among them—who wanted the federal government to build up the nation through public works such as roads, bridges, and canals. High tariffs would pay for these civic programs and, when fashioned to protect specific industries from foreign competitors, could also foster expansive enterprise in the new nation. On the other side were the anti-Federalists and later Democrats—Thomas Jefferson, Andrew Jackson, James Polk—who opposed such levels of government intrusion into the private economy and favored keeping tax levels as low as possible so the people themselves could build up the nation from below. These competing philosophies represented one of the country's most persistent political fault lines.

Hamilton's original tariff bill imposed an average taxation level of only about 8.5 percent on imported goods, and Hamilton argued that any protection encompassed in those duties should be discontinued as soon as protected industries established themselves in the American economy. But Northeastern industrialists argued that protection should be substantial and permanent to ensure national prosperity.

The industrialists prevailed in the 1820s with passage of two hearty tariff laws. Particularly controversial was an 1828 bill, quickly labeled the "Tariff of Abominations" by Southern opponents, that slapped high duties on iron, molasses, distilled spirits, flax, and various finished goods. A boon to Northern producers, it pinched Southerners in two ways—first, by raising prices on necessities the South didn't produce, and, second, by crimping the importation of British goods and thus reducing Britain's ability to purchase Southern cotton. The Tariff of Abominations, enacted during the John Quincy Adams presidency, generated severe sectional tensions that culminated in an ominous constitutional standoff during the subsequent Jackson administration. Jackson threatened to invade South Carolina if it made good its threat to "nullify" the tariff law by declaring that it didn't apply to that state. South Carolina backed down, and a compromise of sorts was reached, including some modest tariff reductions, but the issue continued to stir political tensions throughout the country. Whereas before the 1820s, average tariff rates fluctuated generally between 16 and 26 percent, afterward the levies typically reached 50 percent, then hovered around 35 percent following the Jackson compromise.

James Polk, running for president in 1844, crafted a new concept designed to assuage Southern planters as well as Northern industrialists. Polk proposed legislation based on two principles: first, tariff rates should not exceed levels needed to run the government on an economically sound basis; second, within that range the government could acceptably impose targeted duties to benefit specific industries in need of protection. Polk's bill, typically viewed as a "free trade" measure, passed Congress in 1846 and served as the country's fiscal bedrock through the 1850s, with average tariff rates running generally between 20 and 28 percent.

The protectionist forces were never fully subdued, however, and in 1859 Justin Morrill, a House Whig from Vermont, teamed up with that irrepressible Ohioan, John Sherman, now Ways and Means chairman, to craft legislation designed to get the nation back on a protectionist path. Although it passed the House, it languished in the Senate—until Southern secession took much of the opposition out of the picture. When the war came, necessitating as much revenue as the government could raise, even stern opponents of the Morrill bill changed their tune. The *New York Evening Post*, which had attacked Morrill's handiwork as "a booby of a bill" and the "blunder of the age," now argued that wartime imperatives required free-traders to work with protectionists. "War is an exceptional state," said the paper, "and demands extraordinary measures." After the war, promised the *Post*, it would go back to being a free-trade paper.

But the war generated a huge debt, and the country couldn't very quickly get back to being a free-trade nation. Besides, the Republicans, as the party of industrial expansion, maintained their dominant position in American politics by nurturing their electoral base—including the industrial states, where protectionist sentiment ran high. During this time tariff rates hovered well over 40 percent. Then a new problem emerged: the tariffs were generating too much revenue, and federal coffers were overflowing with excess funds that government officials didn't know what to do with. The Democratic answer was simple: reduce tariff levels. Republicans couldn't go along with that, given their fiscal philosophy and industrial constituency, so they struggled to find other means of addressing the problem.

After New York Democrat Grover Cleveland, a free-trade man, was elected president in 1884, he pushed the Democratic-controlled House to fashion a bill patterned after the Polk legislation of the 1840s. The man who stepped up to the task was Democrat Roger Q. Mills, a rugged-looking Texan with a bushy mustache and deep-set eyes, who served as Ways and Means chairman in the Democratic House. Mills, as ardent a free-trader as could be found in Congress, believed that raw materials should be duty-free and taxes on manufactured items should be reduced substantially. The Mills bill, which cleared the House in July 1888, did both. In the Republican-controlled Senate it encountered a withering attack led by Senator Nelson Aldrich of Rhode Island, whose devotion to his wool, cotton, and sugar constituents only partly explained his protectionist zeal. The rest could be attributed to sheer ideology.

The Senate summarily discarded the Mills bill in favor of a substitute put forth by a prominent Finance Committee member named William Allison, a Republican loyalist from Iowa. Allison removed many items from Mills's free list, restored high tariff rates on numerous imports, and sought to address the revenue surplus in part by eliminating or lowering internal excise taxes on whiskey, tobacco, and other domestic products. The bill also reduced import duties on sugar, which couldn't be produced sufficiently at home to meet domestic demand. Besides, Aldrich offered the novel argument that higher tariffs on other items would reduce revenues further by inducing foreign producers to curtail imports. The Allison bill cleared the Senate and went to the House, where it languished in the Ways and Means Committee without any prospect for reaching the floor.

That was the state of play through the 1888 presidential election: two very different bills representing two different fiscal philosophies represented by the two parties. When Republicans emerged triumphant in the election they quickly invoked the sanctity of voter sentiment. "The people have spoken," said McKinley on the House floor as he began the fight for his Ways and Means bill, patterned after the earlier Allison measure. "If any one thing was settled by the election of 1888 it was that the [Republican] protective policy . . . should be secured."

The McKinley bill sought to address about $10 million of the country's annual $60 million surplus by eliminating domestic excise taxes on tobacco and alcohol. But the chairman sought to maintain or raise tariff rates on other items sufficiently to preclude any importation of these goods, including woolens, higher grade cottons, cotton knits, linens, stockings, earthen and china ware, and all iron, steel, and metal products. McKinley dismissed the opposition view that these duties would expand the nettlesome surplus. Echoing Aldrich, he argued that when tariffs are placed high enough, "you diminish importations and to that extent diminish the revenue." This was particularly true, he argued, in the case of tin plate, used in the burgeoning canning industry but not manufactured to any appreciable degree in the United States. McKinley's aim was to raise the rates on tin plate high enough to throttle the import flow and create from scratch a domestic industry.

McKinley's bill also placed duties for the first time on wheat and other agricultural items to address a robust global increase in agricultural production, much of it with cheap labor. Thus the U.S. farmer, said the chairman, must direct his "care and concern" to preserving "his home market, for he must of necessity be driven from the foreign one." Canada, for example, exported about $25 million in agricultural products to the United States. By erecting trade barriers, the country could ensure that that $25 million would come from domestic sources instead. Who could say, asked McKinley, "that $25,000,000 of additional demand for American agricultural products will not inure to the benefit of the American farmer . . . and give to the farmer confidence and increased ability to lift the mortgages from his lands?" (Applause.)

But the McKinley bill took a different tack on sugar—an article, McKinley said, "of universal family use," around which a powerful trust had emerged through the protection of the sugar tariff. To help consumers and thwart the trust (and pick up House votes), McKinley proposed the elimination of all sugar duties, accompanied by a "bounty" of two cents a pound for domestic producers who otherwise would be harmed by reduced prices wrought by the tariff elimination. Since seven-eighths of the sugar consumed by Americans was imported, eliminating the tariff would take a big chunk out of the budget surplus—nearly $56 million, according to official estimates, offset by the bounty cost of $8 million. Not surprisingly, the bounty idea stirred an instant backlash. The Ways and Means minority report said it proved "that the whole [tariff] system is a system of discrimination between the various productive industries of the country, a system which imposes charges upon some for the support of others and disregards every principle of justice and equality in distributing the burdens of taxation." But the bounty idea prevailed.

McKinley dismissed opposition warnings that high tariffs would curtail U.S. exports as other countries put up retaliatory barriers. "We place no tax or burden or restraint upon American products going out of the country," insisted the chairman, citing statistics showing that U.S. exports increased under protectionist policies and declined during free-trade periods. "This bill is an American bill. It is made for the American people and American interests." (Applause.)

But that crusty Texan Roger Mills dismissed the view that market constrictions could generate prosperity. America's ingenuity of enterprise was creating surpluses "in all branches of our industries," he noted, including agriculture, mining, forestry, and more. The Democrats wanted to foster international trade so these surplus products could be sold in world markets in exchange for other nations' excess products or raw materials. But Republican barriers to imports, argued Mills, inevitably induced other nations to impose their own barriers against American goods. "There are people all over the world who need our meat and bread," said Mills, "and the only reason for depression is because governments have thrown obstructions in the way between the producer and consumer."

What Republicans didn't understand, argued Mills, was that international trade was like any other human transaction: to get something, you must give something. So it is with the foreigner who wants to sell his products: "Let in his cottons, woolens, wool, ores, coal, pig-iron, fruits, sugar, coffee, tea—let all these things come into the country, because when you do that something has to go out to pay for them. . . . That will create a demand for that American product."

Thus did Mills counter the protectionists' static economic analysis, in which a gain for foreign producers would necessarily entail a loss for American manufacturers and farmers. He urged instead a dynamic view of global market expansion that benefits importers and exporters alike. By way of illustration, he traced the import levels and domestic production of pig iron. The statistics proved, said Mills, that when imports increased, so did domestic production; when imports declined, domestic production declined also. "The Republicans tell us that when importation starts up production starts down. It is not true."

But McKinley had the votes. His bill, encompassing nearly 4,000 separate items, cleared the House on a 164–142 tally on May 21 and went to the Senate, where it fell under the sway of the redoubtable Senator Aldrich, bent on shaping the final product to his particular liking. The Senate attached some 496 amendments but also embraced the thinking of James G. Blaine, now Harrison's secretary of state. Blaine felt that Republican protectionism had gone too far, as he made clear in the Senate one day when he encountered some GOP members in the vice president's office just off the Senate floor. "I think the bill is an infamy and an outrage," he stormed. "It is the most shameful measure ever proposed to a civilized people. Go on with it and it will carry our party to perdition." Then he thrust his fist upon his new beaver hat, which was lying upon a nearby table, with such force as to "smash it flatter than a pancake," according to one newspaper account. He hurled the misshapen hat against the wall for added emphasis.

In calmer moments Blaine proposed a policy innovation designed to blunt the full force of McKinley's tall tariffs. Called "reciprocity," the Blaine concept, in its final Senate form, would permit the president to impose tariffs on certain South American products that were destined for the free list if those countries imposed tariffs on particular U.S. goods. The idea was to retain fundamental Republican protectionism while allowing negotiated free-trade exceptions that clearly could benefit the United States. Though McKinley had reacted frostily to the idea when Blaine proposed it during House deliberations, he now warmed to it and lent his considerable authority to its deliberation. It was part of the measure that passed the Senate on September 11 and went to a joint House-Senate conference committee.

The bill that emerged from conference addressed two imperatives for Republicans, one economic and the other political—the budget surplus and the push from industrial interests for ever greater protection. The surplus quickly faded, though increased federal spending under Harrison contributed to that result. And the party had assuaged the agitations of businessmen who wanted to close off American markets as thoroughly as possible. The measure was distinctive in four particulars: its expansive farm duties, the novel sugar bounty, the tariff to protect a hardly existent tin plate industry, and the reciprocity principle. A pleased President Harrison signed the measure into law on October 1, barely a month before the midterm elections.

Though McKinley would hint later that the tariff-writing effort got a bit out of control in the Senate, the final measure unquestionably reflected his view that protectionism was the key to American prosperity and greatness. In his House speech, he drew a stark distinction between protectionist America and free-trade Britain. The total value of U.S. imports and exports increased by 62 percent between 1870 and 1889, said McKinley, while Britain's trade increased by only 25 percent over the same period. Further, Britain's proportion of global trade had fallen from 27 percent in 1830 to just 21 percent in 1880; during that time America's share of global trade increased from 3.7 to 11.5 percent. "We lead all nations in agriculture," McKinley declared, "we lead all nations in mining, and we lead all nations in manufacturing. These are the trophies which we bring after twenty-nine years of a protective tariff. Can another system furnish such evidences of prosperity?"

Perhaps not. But critics quickly pointed out that there wasn't much evidence of a cause-and-effect relationship between protectionism and American prosperity. Senator John B. Allen of Washington argued that many other factors also contributed to America's expanding growth. The country's history showed, he said, that "prosperity and adversity have come alternately under both a high and a low tariff."

Allen had a point. America was a young and frisky nation, rich in rivers, coastlines, fertile soil, and minerals; populated by a vibrant and expansionist people; powerfully positioned across the North American midsection and facing two oceans. Its destiny seemed well established irrespective of fiscal policies at any particular time, and hence the great 1890 tariff debate probably didn't carry the significance many attributed to it. But it did generate potent political passions, and the reaction against the McKinley tariff was swift and severe. Opponents predicted big increases in the price of household necessities, and clever tradesmen exploited the opportunity to raise prices even before the tariff act could have any real impact. Given that Americans seemed evenly divided between protectionist and free-trade sentiments, any bill moving so far in either direction was destined to kick up fierce agitation.

One result was that McKinley, though nationally known now, wasn't known favorably in all quarters. By the time he got back to Canton to campaign for reelection, his district had become a hotbed of controversy over his tariff law. Also contributing to his vulnerability—and to that of Republicans throughout the nation—was an economic recession that hit in mid-1890. And Democrats in the Ohio legislature challenged the Major further with yet another redistricting thrust that added heavily Democratic Holmes County to his district for the first time. Gleeful Democrats figured the new district contained some 3,000 more Democrats than Republicans.

When the ballots were counted, the veteran Canton congressman lost his seat by 303 votes. It was a bad night for Republicans everywhere. McKinley's party lost eighty-five House seats around the country, while Democrats picked up two Senate seats. Naturally the election would be viewed widely as a stern repudiation of the McKinley tariff. As reports coming into McKinley's campaign headquarters revealed the magnitude of the defeat, the Major sat in a dimly lit office, puffing on a cigar and reflecting upon the results. In walked his good friend George Frease, *Repository* editor. Frease looked around at the disheveled office, with discarded papers, brochures, buttons, and posters surrounding the solitary political figure languishing in defeat.

"It's all over," said the editor.

McKinley said nothing.

"What am I to say in the paper?" asked Frease.

McKinley turned his gaze upward to reveal a pensive expression. Then his congenital optimism asserted itself. "In the time of darkest defeat," he said, "victory may be nearest."

After further rumination, it was determined that McKinley would draft the editorial to be published in the next day's paper. It began, "Protection was never stronger than it is at this hour. And it will grow in strength and in the hearts of the people." The editorial argued that the elections had been decided "upon a false issue"—the ploy of free-traders and retailers to raise prices and charge it upon the McKinley bill. "But the people who have been duped will not forget. Nor will the friends of protection lower their flag."

McKinley certainly had no intention of lowering his own flag of protectionism. Nor was he the kind of man to retreat into any pathos of defeat. When Mark Hanna wrote to express encouragement, the Major wrote back, "I agree with you that defeat under the circumstances was for the best. . . . There is no occasion for alarm. We must take no backward step." As he put it in the *Repository* editorial, penned in the midst of adversity, "Reason will be enthroned and none will suffer so much as those who have participated in misguiding a trusting people. Keep up your courage. Strengthen your organizations and be ready for the great battle in Ohio in 1891, and the still greater one in 1892."

6

Four Years in Columbus

THE COMFORT OF RICH AND POWERFUL FRIENDS

McKinley wasted no time in projecting publicly the attitude he had struck anonymously in his *Repository* editorial. Early in 1891, after former president Cleveland gave a speech at Columbus extolling the virtues of free trade, McKinley attacked the Democratic tendency to exalt "cheap goods from abroad above good wages at home." He characterized the previous Democratic free-trade period as a time "when cheap foreign goods . . . destroyed our manufactories, checked our mining, suspended our public works and private enterprises, sent our workingmen from work to idleness . . . surrendered our markets to the foreigner . . . and diminished domestic production and domestic employment." Clearly the Republicans' electoral defeat of 1890 wasn't going to intimidate this protectionist warrior.

But he wasn't sure what political avenue to pursue in waging the fight. He contemplated a run for Ohio governor, confident the nomination could be obtained without a fuss. But the governorship didn't seem particularly alluring given that it lacked a veto power and other tools of political leverage. Also he would face a formidable opponent in Democratic incumbent James E. Campbell, whose political standing had soared in 1889 when he stifled Governor Foraker's third-term bid. Losing to Campbell could upend McKinley's presidential plans. Perhaps a return to Congress after a proper interval, he mused, would be the better ticket. "I should be quite content," he told reporters anxious to divine his intentions, "to look after my personal affairs, which have suffered of course by my long absence from my business and my clients."

Still, the governorship conferred national stature and constituted a sturdy springboard to higher office. He listened respectfully when a delegation of Ohio Republicans argued that only he could unite Ohio's Sherman and Foraker factions. Still pondering the question, he showed up unannounced at Foraker's Cincinnati home to inquire whether the former governor would nominate him for governor at the state GOP convention if he decided to run. When Foraker said yes, the Major entered the race.

Foraker rose to the occasion. At the GOP's June convention at Columbus, he declared that every Republican in the state knew and loved McKinley, whereas every Democrat "fears him." No man had ever been nominated for Ohio governor "who . . . was such a distinctively national and international character." Enthusiastic delegates promptly nominated the Major by acclamation.

He kicked off his campaign at his birthplace town of Niles, where GOP partisans had erected a huge tin arch across the central thoroughfare emblazoned with the words "Protection is Prosperity." Tin was placed everywhere as a tribute to the industry expected to rise on the wings of McKinley's big tariff on foreign tin plate. The campaign garnered national attention as a barometer of Republicans' ability to rebound from their 1890 devastation, particularly given Campbell's unrelenting attack on the McKinley tariff.

But Campbell also pressed for expansive silver coinage, thus forcing McKinley to deal with the flammable currency issue. This put him in a delicate position, as he had flirted with inflationist sentiments early in his career and even now embraced "bimetallism" as a defensible middle ground. He also had supported the ill-conceived 1890 Sherman Silver Purchase Act, which sought to expand the money supply through the federal purchase of $50 million worth of silver annually. Unfortunately it had spawned an ominous outflow of gold to foreign lands, as investors sought to redeem silver notes for gold. Even John Sherman, who never truly embraced the concept despite his sponsorship, now favored its repeal. All this placed McKinley at odds with the hard-money Eastern GOP establishment, hardly a favorable stance for any GOP presidential aspirant. He scrambled to get himself more conventionally positioned. "We cannot gamble with anything so sacred as money," he declared at Niles, "which is the standard and measure of all values."

The McKinley campaign enjoyed abundant financial support from Mark Hanna, who augmented his own considerable contributions by raising funds from generous Republican donors from multiple states. The money was to be used in part to meet McKinley's personal expenses during the campaign, a common practice at the time. "I am a thousand times obliged to you for your letter with enclosure," the Major wrote to Hanna. Two weeks later he asked Hanna to send all further contributions directly to the party committee. "I have sufficient to defray my personal expenses," he reported.

But Hanna wasn't around for other campaign duties because he was busy trying to save Sherman's Senate seat from Foraker, now bent on upending his rival when the Ohio legislature convened in January 1892 with an early duty of filling that seat. The Sherman and Foraker forces worked furiously to secure commitments from prospective legislators during the political season by offering campaign support. After the legislative elections, they cajoled and pressured Republican legislators right up to the day of balloting. Inevitably the battle intensified the state's Republican rift. Even before Foraker made his move, Hanna had publicly scorned his former political ally. "Foraker has been a very heavy load for some time," he said in New York in March 1890. "Politically I am done with him."

Now Hanna spared no effort in behalf of Sherman, whose support among state Republicans was broad but desultory. He organized efforts in all key districts, particularly around Cleveland, applied pressure where needed, and distributed campaign funds copiously in an effort to round up Sherman commitments among legislators and prospective legislators. Meanwhile the beleaguered senator defied convention by leaving Washington and installing himself at Columbus to assist personally in his own cause. "The situation was bad, almost desperate,"

recalled a Sherman loyalist. Hanna was outraged when three legislators who had committed to Sherman disappeared amid rumors that
they planned to reappear on election day and vote for Foraker. Hanna
tracked them down and forced them back into line with an austere
firmness. But the situation remained fluid—and very dangerous for
Sherman. In the end, the venerable senator managed to squeeze out
enough votes for victory. He promptly credited Hanna. "I feel that
without you I would have been beaten," Sherman wrote to his benefactor. "You have been a true friend, liberal, earnest and sincere, without
any personal selfish motive."

In the meantime, Hanna's other favorite politician also emerged
victorious. McKinley outpolled Campbell in November by 21,511
votes in a year with few notable Republican triumphs. He would go
to Columbus, cement his standing as a statewide political leader, and
acquire the executive experience that would bolster his future White
House run. Thomas Reed wrote, "I am much rejoiced over your victory
which is the only bright spot in the last elections."

Early in 1892 the McKinleys moved into Columbus's ornate Chittenden Hotel, facing the Capitol Building. When the Chittenden
burned down some months later, the couple moved into the equally
plush and well-situated Neil House, where they enjoyed a spacious
apartment that included office, parlor, bedroom, dining room, store
room, and maid's quarters. In both locations, the couple settled into
a comfortable routine. The Major enjoyed his wood-paneled executive
chamber and avidly embraced his daytime schedule of appointments,
political negotiations, and decision making. He fashioned serious initiatives designed to overhaul the state's unequal tax system, improve
safety for railroad workers, and rejuvenate Ohio's deteriorating canal
network. He also pushed for a more equitable redistricting regimen,
ensuring that the party with the most votes would capture most of the
state's congressional seats. Over the next two years, the heavily Republican legislature approved all of the governor's major initiatives.

During the evenings of his governorship, McKinley would sit with
Ida as she crocheted the dozens of slippers that she delighted in distributing to friends, acquaintances, and anybody in need that she might
hear about. Occupying his favorite chair nearby, the governor would

read papers, draft speeches, and chew on the end of an ever-present cigar. Occasionally, recalled Charlie Bawsel, McKinley's chief executive clerk, he would read aloud from partially prepared speeches, and Ida would nod her approval here and there as her fingers fluttered over her crochet work. Sometimes the governor would retreat to his office to receive lawmakers and other officials intent on discussing pressing governmental matters. "But a conference must be of the most pressing nature," recalled Bawsel, "to detain him long from Mrs. McKinley's side." The governor's evenings belonged "wholly to her. This, the little lady insists upon."

He demonstrated his devotion further with a morning and afternoon ritual that became famous in Columbus. Upon reaching the capitol steps each morning after striding through the government plaza from his hotel residence, the governor would turn and doff his hat toward her hotel window across the way. She would respond by waving a handkerchief. Precisely at three o'clock each afternoon, he would step outside and repeat the gesture, acknowledged again with her handkerchief wave. It was such a touching scene that government employees, hotel guests, and tourists often positioned themselves around the plaza to witness it. Indeed the local expectation surrounding the gesture stirred one newspaper wag and later politician, Warren Harding, to express suspicions that the gubernatorial ritual took place even when Ida was out of town.

Ida's health entered a phase of improvement during this time, though that did not diminish her tendency toward peevishness. At one point, when she proudly traveled on her own from Canton to Columbus, she neglected to notify Bawsel to have someone pick her up at the train station. Blaming Bawsel, she became quite "huffy." She also became indignant when Bawsel neglected to notice a new gown she was wearing. But she always perked up at any prospect for travel, and a delighted McKinley took her on numerous trips across the country as he pursued political duties and speaking engagements. When he attended the 1892 Republican National Convention at Minneapolis, she stayed with a cousin in Chicago and attended the World's Fair, which she pronounced "the greatest exhibition the world has ever witnessed."

At Minneapolis, McKinley emerged as one of his party's most formidable leaders, chosen by delegates as the convention's permanent chairman. Hanna, though not a delegate, showed up and positioned himself to exploit any McKinley boomlet that might arise as delegates struggled with what to do about their incumbent president, Harrison, who clearly was unpopular around the country. But Harrison had the votes for renomination, and the convention unenthusiastically accepted his inevitability. McKinley objected when the Ohio delegation cast all but one of its votes for him, but there wasn't much he could do about it. Ultimately he received 182 first-ballot votes to Harrison's 535 and 183 for Blaine. The governor was particularly glad to be off the ticket because he suspected that 1892 was going to be just as treacherous for Republicans as 1890 had been.

He was right. Although the party picked up thirty-eight House seats (offsetting the eighty-five-seat loss of 1890), it lost nine Senate seats, and former president Cleveland engineered a White House return with a plurality of 372,639 votes over Harrison. McKinley had been wise to bide his time on the presidential front. He gained added national stature during the 1892 campaign year even as his party floundered.

Then came a development that threatened to destroy his political career. In February 1893, as McKinley was traveling to New York City to pick up Ida from medical treatment and deliver a banquet speech, he received an urgent telegram from his office during a train stop at Dunkirk, New York. The wire reported that McKinley's old friend, Robert L. Walker, the Youngstown industrialist and McKinley benefactor, was facing bankruptcy. The Major had cosigned various Walker loans amounting to $17,000, largely because Walker had helped finance his law studies at Albany a quarter century before and had contributed $2,000 to each of McKinley's congressional campaigns. McKinley felt beholden to the man and believed his financial standing to be rock solid.

What he didn't know was that Walker had got himself hopelessly overextended in his business ventures as a severe economic downturn began gathering momentum in 1892. When the beleaguered entrepreneur had asked McKinley to sign various routine loan extensions, they actually had been notes in blank that Walker had then inflated into massive liabilities, undertaken in a desperate effort to save his businesses and personal fortune. For McKinley, it now appeared, the exposure might be $100,000 or more, far beyond his assets.

Getting the news of Walker's imminent bankruptcy on a Thursday, the governor promptly canceled his speech and asked Abner McKinley to fetch Ida from New York and escort her back to Ohio, where a crisis-management effort would soon ensue. He then booked train passage to Youngstown, where he intended to issue stern words to Walker and assess the magnitude of his own liability. Reaching Walker's residence on Friday, amid newspaper accounts of the fiasco, he found the fallen entrepreneur in such a state of anguish that McKinley's famous compassion prevailed over his anger. Instead of berating Walker as he had intended, he offered words of solace.

"Have courage, Robert, have courage," said the aggrieved victim to the man whose fraudulent behavior could likely destroy his political career. "Everything will come out all right."

But with newspapers now furiously following the story, he had little time for compassion. On Friday evening he issued a statement designed to get ahead of the headlines and assure voters that he would never shirk his financial obligations. "I will pay every note of Mr. Walker's on which I am endorser," he said. "I must understand the situation before I can rest for my whole future, politically and financially, is involved in this." Then he rushed to Cleveland to consult with a close friend and political patron named Myron Herrick, a wealthy lawyer and entrepreneur whom Hanna had drawn into Ohio politics and the McKinley circle. While the governor was en route to Cleveland, Herrick summoned Ida by wire to his Cleveland mansion. "Do not worry over the Walker matter," he added to soothe her concerns. "Your husband has friends who will see that every obligation bearing his name will be paid and no stain will blot his fair name." The problem, however, was that having his friends pay off his debts could in itself constitute a bit of a stain.

At stake was a political career carefully nurtured over many years to position the Major for a presidential pursuit. The governor, now fifty years old, could address the financial crisis without much exertion by abandoning politics and becoming a railroad lawyer or joining a prestigious law firm in New York or Chicago. Many such opportunities would open up, and he expressed a willingness to pursue that course if necessary. But there would be no return to the political world he loved so thoroughly, and he wished to avoid that fate if possible. Beyond that, it wasn't clear how voters would assess the implications of his apparent bad judgment in signing what amounted to blank checks to a swindler.

On Saturday, Herman Henry Kohlsaat, a wealthy Chicago businessman, newspaper publisher, and devoted McKinley confidant, spotted a newspaper article on the governor's predicament. He wired his friend: "Have just read of your misfortune. My purse is open to you. . . . Will meet you anywhere you say in Ohio." McKinley asked Kohlsaat to take an overnight train to Cleveland. When he arrived at nine the next morning, McKinley greeted him at the train station with downcast demeanor and a look of crisis about him—"pale and wan, with dark rings under his eyes," as Kohlsaat later recalled. The governor placed his hand upon his friend's shoulder but was too beset with emotion to speak. His eyes welled up with tears. Kohlsaat asked about the magnitude of the debt.

"I don't know," replied the governor, in obvious bewilderment. It soon transpired that he was on the hook for about $130,000—"in excess of anything I dreamed of," McKinley told his friends.

Others appeared at the Herrick residence to join the crisis-management deliberations, among them William Day of Canton, the prominent lawyer and wise counselor; wartime buddy Russell Hastings; and John Tod, wealthy son of a former Ohio governor. Hanna was delayed by business but came when he could. Ida arrived on Saturday, more composed than some participants had expected. Addressing the assembled men in the Herricks' ground-floor parlor, she announced her resolve to liquidate her jewelry and inheritance assets, worth an estimated $75,000, to help defray the debt. When she was urged to abandon that idea, she became curt.

"My husband has done everything for me all my life," she snapped. "Do you mean to deny me the privilege of doing as I please with my own property to help him now?"

McKinley, always averse to tense situations (and perhaps averse to her suggestion), took Ida upstairs for a private talk. In their absence, Tod expressed strenuous objections to tapping into her wealth.

"Because McKinley has made a fool of himself, why should Mrs. McKinley be a pauper?" Tod demanded.

"Because," replied Kohlsaat with equal asperity, "if McKinley is to stay in politics he must show clean hands and not be open to the charge he has put his property in his wife's name."

Kohlsaat's rejoinder got to the heart of the matter: the imperative of saving McKinley's political career. The weekend session in Cleveland yielded an agreement that Herrick, Day, Kohlsaat, and Hanna would place McKinley's assets into a trust and begin acquiring his outstanding obligations. At Ida's insistence, a separate trust was established, under Hanna's supervision, for her assets, although Hanna indicated he wouldn't let them slip into the financial vortex except as a last resort. Under the arrangement, McKinley was to have no knowledge of the workings of the trusts.

He was profoundly touched by his friends' generosity. In a February 23 letter to the Herricks, he wrote that he and Ida "shall never forget your tender and loving hospitality." He said his mail was overflowing with sympathy "and the most earnest protest against Mrs. McKinley turning over her property." Three days later, after hearing from Kohlsaat about Chicago efforts to raise money for the trust fund, he wrote to his Chicago friend, "The pen will not—can not speak what is in my heart this morning, your letter is so full of personal sweetness. . . . Did ever man and wife have such friends and how can we ever repay them?" He reported that his mail was "abounding with kindness," as well as offers of material assistance.

But, hearing that his friends were raising funds to retire his debts outright, the governor objected strenuously. On March 14 he wrote to the designated trustees, insisting that no contributions from friends and supporters should be used to cancel his debts. While he accepted the idea of the fund consolidating his obligations and spreading out the repayment schedule, he insisted he must remain on the hook for eventual full repayment: "I cannot for a moment entertain the suggestion of having my debts paid in the way proposed . . . so long as I have health to earn money."

McKinley's friends had other ideas. They spread out through the Midwest in search of fund contributions, fortified with a Herrick-produced form letter lauding McKinley's contribution to his country. The money flowed in: $40,000 from Chicago alone; $10,000 from Philadelphia. Charles P. Taft, owner of the *Cincinnati Times*, gave $1,000. John Hay, the literary figure and former Lincoln secretary, gave $2,000, as did steel magnate Henry Clay Frick. Contributors of $5,000 included industrialists George Pullman and Philip Armour, as well as Hanna, Herrick, and Kohlsaat. The Illinois Steel Company contributed $10,000. The voluble and compelling Herrick got the banks holding McKinley's notes to discount the amounts by 10 percent as a contribution to the cause. By early summer the full amount was raised and the debt canceled. In keeping with his insistence that he should not escape his obligations, McKinley sent Herrick an amount from every paycheck throughout the remainder of his life to pay down the debt, now in the hands of his asset trustees.

McKinley's financial fiasco and its outcome represented a dual re-flection upon the man. As the story unfolded in newspapers across the country, he looked foolish and weak, a politician who couldn't manage his own financial affairs, let alone the country's. Beyond that, his need to avail himself of the comfort of rich friends—with large financial stakes in government actions—generated the view among some that he was a puppet of plutocrats. Yet it was remarkable that this debacle didn't seem to blight the governor's career as many had anticipated. His opponents and detractors naturally seized upon it—and would continue to do so for years. But the tale of financial woe didn't seem to penetrate his general popularity with Ohio voters or later with the national constituency he sought to build for his presidential quest. His image as a man of rectitude and quiet wisdom seemed to fortify him politically. This was reflected in the outpouring of support, includ-ing financial support, that flowed into Canton and Columbus. Some 5,000 donations came in from ordinary citizens across the nation, and while McKinley returned all those delivered to him, his trustees even-tually gave up trying to "stem the flood of spontaneous generosity," as a McKinley biographer later put it. Somehow McKinley's plight gener-ated extensive sympathy and a desire to protect him for future leader-ship.

By summer the storm had passed, and McKinley plunged into his next political adventures: a second gubernatorial term and preparations for an 1896 presidential run. But now the political landscape was entirely changed by economic hard times that hit with a fearsome force. It began in the farm sector, where a real estate boom had drawn in thousands of Eastern investors beguiled by low interest rates and prospects for quick wealth. A $200 investment in Western land had been known to return $2,000 in a few months, historian John D. Hicks reports, adding, "Small wonder that money descended like a flood upon those who made it their business to place loans in the West!" Then came the drought of 1887, and the bubble burst. Farmers couldn't produce sufficient crops to pay the mortgage; money dried up; banks and their borrowers went under. In drought-stricken Kansas, half the state's Western farmers pulled up stakes and fled.

The Western farm bust soon undermined the industrial sector, particularly the railroad industry, and panic swept the country. Railroads had been expanding on borrowed money and now couldn't cover the debt service as farm shipments dried up. As railroads declined, so did the rest of industrial America and the big-city Eastern banks. One result was falling stock prices, which precipitated a run on gold supplies as holders of securities cashed out of the market in exchange for gold. By spring the Treasury's gold reserve had dropped below $100 million, considered a minimum confidence level. By year's end, about the time of McKinley's reelection, some 500 banks had failed, more than five times the annual average of the previous five years, and a record 15,242 U.S. companies went bankrupt. Unemployment soared.

Though tragic for the nation, these developments buoyed Republican prospects as voters blamed Democratic policies for the calamity. McKinley captured his party's gubernatorial nomination for a second term—again by acclamation—and defeated his Democratic opponent, Lawrence Neal, by some 81,000 votes. Meanwhile Republicans ended up with 111 legislative seats to just 27 for the Democrats. Confident he spoke for his state's collective electorate, McKinley declared in his inaugural address, "The best government always is that one which best looks after its own, and which is in closest hear-touch with the highest aspirations of the people."

But with the nation's economic travail continuing throughout McKinley's second term, the governor faced major civic disruptions in the form of labor strikes and threats of mob rule. In April 1894 the United Mine Workers called on coal miners to walk off their jobs in what one Ohio publication called "one of the greatest strikes, in point of numbers, in the history of any country." Some 200,000 miners went on strike in Ohio alone, along with many others in Pennsylvania, Indiana, Illinois, and elsewhere. Civic tensions ran high, and the action devastated the regional economy as the strikes shut down railroads and factories fueled by coal. Normal commerce ceased. At the request of local sheriffs, McKinley sent out militia troops—some 3,000 in all—to restore and maintain order during the job action. Later in the year he deployed troops to protect train service during a railroad strike. When labor representatives suggested the governor's actions could harm him politically, he replied, "I do not care if my political career is not twenty-four hours long, these outrages must stop if it takes every soldier in Ohio."

As soon as the strikes were settled and order was restored, he turned his attention to getting funds and provisions distributed to areas where miners were suffering serious financial deprivation due to the strike. The *Cincinnati Enquirer* wrote, "Praise for the prompt action of Governor McKinley is on every tongue among the distressed. . . . Every detail of the relief work is under the general supervision of the governor." Reflecting both his natural inclinations and his political acumen, McKinley combined toughness in the face of disruption with compassion for those caught up in the struggle.

The governor's national stature was growing, reflected in the requests he received for campaign appearances for Republican candidates during the 1894 midterm elections. He agreed to make forty-six set speeches in the seven weeks before the elections but ended up delivering 371 addresses of various lengths as towns and cities flooded Republican National Committee headquarters with requests as soon as they learned the governor would be in their vicinity. Though he traveled 12,000 miles through seventeen states, he "seemed tireless," wrote journalist Samuel G. McClure, who traveled with McKinley. "Every State committee in the Mississippi valley and beyond it apparently took it for granted that the gallant champion of 'patriotism, protection and prosperity' could not be over-worked." With McKinley leading the way, the GOP picked up 120 House seats in 1894 and six in the Senate.

The governor relinquished his executive duties in January 1896 amid an outpouring of affection and expectation about his future. He and Ida now anticipated their return to Canton and a calm life in a nice home on a tree-lined street. The sensation of going home was heightened when McKinley leased the very house on North Market Avenue in which he and Ida had begun their marriage. Though it harbored dark ghosts, it also called forth stirring memories of wonderful days before the onset of the tragedies that had deflected their lives. The place needed work, but both felt elation at being back at the point of their origin and also at the prospect of trading years of hotel life for residence in an actual home.

They arrived in Canton on January 24, 1896, a day before their silver wedding anniversary, and settled into their new home in time for a two-day fete to mark their twenty-five years of marriage. It was to be no minor affair; 1,000 invitations had been sent out. The house featured a main-floor office for the Major and, across the hall, a parlor for Ida. Both rooms were festooned with artifacts and mementos illustrating their lives and passions and giving a sense of their narrative to the many visitors—friends, acquaintances, and strangers—who would be passing through as McKinley pursued his presidential aims. The Major's office featured law books, prints with Civil War battle scenes, an engraving of Hayes with Lincoln and Grant, and a leather chaise, "which we prize very much," McKinley said in a letter. Ida's parlor featured family pictures, including one of little Katie before her death. Though only the Major and Ida lived there, the dining-room table was always set for twelve in anticipation of the many guests, personal and political, who would be mustered through in the coming months of campaign activity.

Ida's health had taken a turn for the worse during the final months in Columbus. "Mrs. McKinley is not getting on as well as I wish," McKinley wrote to his wife's New York doctor, who treated her with a flow of medications. "She has her attacks, and I hope when I come down to New York to be able to see you." In addition to the attacks, she was experiencing an involuntary loss of muscle control, described by Charlie Bawsel as "a dropsical trouble." To counter the muscle loss and bolster her up, she often was bound in bandages.

McKinley continued to devote abundant time and attention to his troubled wife even as he thrust himself into the maelstrom of presidential politics. By his lights, he had balanced successfully Ida's needs with his political endeavors for more than two decades, and there was no reason to think he couldn't continue to do so as the political prize he had coveted for most of his adult life came into view. Things were slipping into place, including the economic dislocation that was undermining the opposition party as the campaign year began. John Sherman, noting the Democrats' declining fortunes, saw bright prospects for McKinley in 1896. "The recent elections," he wrote to Los Angeles editor Harrison Gray Otis, "have cleared the political sky and I believe fairly opened the way for the nomination of Maj. McKinley. He will be heartily supported from Ohio and, I trust, be nominated and elected."

7

The Major versus the Bosses

"I AM AFRAID WE MUST COUNT ON THEIR HOSTILITY"

I n May 1895, Governor McKinley issued a crucial political assignment to his top lieutenant, Mark Hanna. The task was to travel to New York, meet with the big Northeastern GOP bosses, and seek their support for McKinley's presidential nomination. These men wielded patronage power that translated into huge party leverage. Capable of delivering big blocs of delegates to GOP national conventions, they often held the balance of power in nomination battles.

First among them was New York's former senator Thomas Platt, a man so inarticulate and listless that nobody could figure out how he dominated his state's politics. But somehow he did, largely through uncanny wiles and a relentless determination. "Almost a full score of succeeding Legislatures obeyed every indication of his will," wrote a contemporary journalist, "and no Republican committee or convention in any part of the State considered itself superior to his judgment." A political ally once observed that, while he couldn't turn back time or produce a three-year-old steer in a minute, "there is little else he can not do if he has the nerve." Tom Platt seldom lacked nerve.

Then there was U.S. Senator Matthew Quay of Pennsylvania, son of a minister. Even Platt deferred to Quay on political strategy. The

Pennsylvanian was a true scholar who had amassed an expansive library and read Cicero and other classical writers in Latin. So commanding was he in state politics that he seldom felt a need to speak in public. His tool for dominating the Pennsylvania Republican Party was deft and forceful backroom maneuvering, seasoned by a sardonic wit. When the naïve Benjamin Harrison ventured that Providence had made him president, Quay noted dismissively that a bigger factor was a phalanx of political bosses willing "to approach the gates of the penitentiary to make him president."

Other important Northeastern bosses included Rhode Island's Aldrich, who made a fortune in railways, banking, oil, and electricity before entering the Senate and amassing power as easily as he previously had amassed wealth; Joseph H. Manley of Maine, a close associate of the Plumed Knight, James G. Blaine, and chairman of the Republican National Committee's executive body; and James S. Clarkson of Iowa, who had attended every Republican National Convention since 1876. Hanna met with these men over dinner at the lavish Fifth Avenue Hotel, then rushed back to Ohio to report the results to McKinley, who was staying with Myron Herrick in Cleveland. Herrick drove the governor to Hanna's majestic home on Lake Erie for dinner and a conference.

Following the meal, the industrialist led McKinley, Herrick, and Herman Kohlsaat into what he called his "den," where he passed out cigars and settled into an overstuffed chair. To Herrick, he seemed "as keen as a razor blade" as he indulged in some bragging for getting into and out of New York without alerting reporters. Then he turned to McKinley.

"Now, Major, it's all over but the shouting," he said. "You can get both New York and Pennsylvania, but there are certain conditions." He evinced no discomfort with the conditions.

"What are they?" asked the governor.

"Quay wants the patronage of Pennsylvania, Aldrich of New England, Manley of Maine," replied Hanna, adding that Platt desired a bigger reward.

"They want a promise that you will appoint Tom Platt Secretary of the Treasury," said Hanna, "and they want it in writing." It seems that

Platt thought he had secured a similar commitment from Harrison eight years earlier, but the payoff had never materialized. Hence the demand for a promissory note.

McKinley stared ahead for a time, puffing on his cigar. Then he rose from his chair, paced the room a few moments, and turned to Hanna.

"Mark," he said, "there are some things in this world that come too high. If I were to accept the nomination on those terms, the place would be worth nothing to me, and less to the people. If those are the terms, I am out of it."

"Not so fast," replied Hanna. "I meant that on these terms the nomination would be settled immediately, but that does not mean that their terms have got to be accepted. There is a strong sentiment for you all over the country, and while it would be hard to lick those fellows if they oppose you, damned hard, I believe we can do it."

McKinley's countenance brightened. He stared into the void for a few seconds, apparently lost in thought. Then he said, "How would this do for a slogan: 'The Bosses Against the People'?" The three men agreed it would define the nomination battle nicely. Upon further rumination it was modified to "The People Against the Bosses."

That conversation in Hanna's den became an inflection point for the 1896 presidential campaign. Nearly all political analysts considered McKinley the early frontrunner for the Republican nomination, but now he would have to roll over the party bosses to get the prize. Worse, the influential political figures who met with Hanna in New York surely would fan out across the country to get other state party leaders to consolidate their grip on their states' delegate-selection process, withhold delegates from McKinley, and thus deter his nomination. Then they could pool their power and broker a convention outcome more to their liking, getting a nominee who would play their game and pay their price. It would be an arduous six-month campaign as state parties went through the process—in county, district, and finally state conventions—of selecting delegates to the national convention in St. Louis in June.

McKinley brought some political strengths to the battle. First among them was Hanna, whose devotion to McKinley's political success was so intense that he resigned his position as head of Hanna &

Co. in January 1895 and turned the business over to his brother. After twenty-eight years of furious business activity, he now would direct his energies almost entirely to the McKinley effort. In spring 1895 the McKinley campaign set up its headquarters in Cleveland's downtown Perry-Payne Building, and Hanna took command of every detail. The *Washington Post* called him "the John the Baptist of the McKinley Presidential movement." He was working for the governor, said the paper, "out of pure devotion" and desired nothing in exchange. This made him "a terror to the opposition" because "he is as shrewd and clever as the best of them."

Although by this time Hanna's talents were well understood throughout the country, he remained haunted by a lingering reputation for ruthlessness, greed, and even moral laxity—residues from the unrelenting attacks upon him by Edwin Cowles's *Cleveland Leader* and later by the *Cleveland Press*, which sought to build up its circulation by tearing down the city's elites. In some ways he was an easy mark. Big, brash, quick of thought, slow to forgive, he attacked the game of business, and later the game of politics, with a zest for competition and a passion for winning. He also displayed a capacity for taking charge of any enterprise with which he became associated. Cleveland lawyer Andrew Squire said "he loved to be a leader." Lifelong friend A. B. Hough pronounced, "Whatever he went into was all Hanna."

Full of life, he brought a jaunty enthusiasm to his dealings with all, from the most powerful to the lowliest. When he owned the Cleveland Electric Railroad, he had 900 men on the road—and knew most of them by name. He would linger next to his motormen and chat with them along the route, often sitting on stools that the motormen kept nearby for the purpose. Throughout his ownership, he never experienced a strike or walkout. At one point, as he prepared for a European trip, another Cleveland railroad company faced a strike threat, and Hanna feared his men might walk out in sympathy. He called together about forty for a talk.

"Boys," he said, "I have been preparing to go to Europe for a little rest. It looks as if there will be trouble on the other road, however, and I would like to know before I go away if you are likely to be drawn into it." If so, he said, he would cancel the trip. "If you are satisfied with your wages and your treatment and agree to keep at work I will go." His men assured him it would be safe to go, and they remained on the job even as the other line suffered a strike.

He brought the same directness of expression and dealings to his political activities, along with an open generosity toward those who aligned with him. A Cleveland lawyer named Dan Reynolds told the story of a financial crisis in a local GOP campaign committee around 1886, when the committee found itself in debt to the tune of $1,250 after an election season. Fanning out in search of willing donors, party officials came up empty and congregated at GOP headquarters to review their plight. In walked Hanna, who promptly discerned the long faces.

"It looks pretty blue in here," he said in his lively manner. "What is the matter?" When told, he sat down at the table and wrote a check for the full amount. "There," he said, handing over the check, "pay your debts and look cheerful."

In 1884, when a feed merchant named David Kimberly declared his support for both Hanna and Cowles as delegates to the next GOP national convention, Cowles called him in and said he wouldn't accept his support if he also supported Hanna. "You can't serve two masters," said Cowles, hinting that his newspaper would oppose Kimberly's planned bid for Cuyahoga County treasurer if he aligned himself with Hanna as well as with himself. When the man sheepishly went to Hanna to explain his predicament, the industrialist brushed it off. "Go ahead and do what you can for Cowles," he said, "and after he is out of the way, do the best you can for me." Later, during Kimberly's campaign for treasurer, he received three anonymous donations totaling $1,200, along with a note saying that if he won the election he could pay the amount back, but if he lost the loans would be forgiven and the benefactor would remain nameless. He later learned it was Hanna. "He was the biggest hearted man I never knew," said Kimberly.

Hanna's many friends and associates knew well this side of him, but his public persona continued to suffer from the lingering reputation wrought by Cowles, the *Cleveland Press*, and now increasingly by anti-McKinley Democratic newspapers. But while his personal qualities stirred controversy, nobody questioned his professional and political

shrewdness. As McKinley's nomination battle unfolded, that shrewdness produced another asset for the governor: strong support throughout the South, which never voted Republican in general elections but
provided a large pool of delegates at GOP conventions, many of them
blacks and white liberals. Upon relinquishing his corporate position,
Hanna rented a palatial home in Thomasville, Georgia, and invited
McKinley and Ida down for an extended visit under the guise of offering them a warm respite from the Northern winter and surcease from
political obligations. The real purpose was to introduce the governor
to well-placed Republican politicians who came through in a steady
stream of glad-handing. Greeting these Southern bigwigs in Hanna's
comfortable sun parlor, the earnest and amiable McKinley quietly captured substantial numbers of delegates throughout the region. As Tom
Platt later lamented, "He had the South practically solid before some
of us awakened."

McKinley's Thomasville success reflected his sympathetic persona
at middle age. The years had expanded his girth and given him a broad
face that looked as if it had been chiseled and polished from a block of
granite. The deep-set eyes and wooly eyebrows highlighted a countenance that was at once alert and kindly. He had a fastidious look about
him—his Prince Albert coat "never wrinkled," the young journalist
William Allen White observed, "his white vest front never broken."
Fastidious also in manner, he presented himself with what seemed like
a studied correctness, "sweet, but not cloying," as White put it, "gentle
but . . . carefully calculated." For White and others given to elaborate
and sometimes cynical judgments, these traits made McKinley seem
"unreal." In a similar vein, Edwin Godkin, influential editor of *The
Nation* and the *New York Evening Post*, assessed McKinley's oratory
harshly. "Whether you plunge into it, or skim over it," wrote Godkin,
"the sense of touching something wooden is unmistakable."

But McKinley's carefully modulated persona impressed those engaged in the political game, both friend and foe, who saw behind his
pleasant façade a shrewd politician with finely honed powers of observation and analysis. John Hay, whose long career as a writer, diplomat, and presidential secretary lent credence to his assessments of men,
praised McKinley's "unusual qualities, extraordinary ability and force

of character." The quiet confidence he had cultivated in the crucible of war now translated into a subtle kind of leadership, always formal but also accessible and never troublesome. His reputation for loyalty and trustworthiness drew men to him, while his even-tempered affability kept them attached. His gubernatorial stenographer, Opha Moore, witnessed only one flash of anger during his four years as governor, when a visitor told an off-color joke. "I wish that fellow would stay away from here," he said afterward with disgust.

The electorate developed a perception that McKinley's public image closely matched his private behavior. Stories of his devotion to his troubled wife, whose infirmities were now generally well known publicly, though not in detail, contributed to his image as a very human politician. Voters sensed that what they read and heard of the man was his actual self, and what they read and heard gave comfort. He may have seemed unreal or wooden to intellectuals such as White and Godkin, but out in the country people appreciated his dignity, integrity, and sound judgment. This fortified his campaign strategy of going after the bosses.

But the bosses didn't intend to bow down to McKinley. Platt was "angry and astounded" when the governor rejected the bosses' deal, according to newspaper reports. Congregating a dinner meeting of "wrathy" state-party bigwigs in July to discuss the nettlesome front-runner, he announced plans to insert former New York governor Levi Morton into the presidential race as his state's favorite son. Quay was mulling a presidential run himself to consolidate Pennsylvania's delegate bloc and deny state support to the Ohio man. They encouraged other state leaders to follow suit. Hay, increasingly a McKinley loyalist, wrote to Hanna, "I am afraid we must count on their hostility."

Soon various leaders announced their candidacies for president. Few were national figures capable of pulling delegates from outside their states, but by consolidating their states' delegate pools they could position themselves for a possible emergence in a brokered convention. These men included William Bradley in Kentucky, candidate for governor that year; that reliable Iowa protectionist, Senator William Allison (sponsored by state boss James Clarkson); a former senator from Nebraska named Charles Manderson; Minnesota senator Cushman K.

Davis; and the venerable Shelby Cullom of Illinois, now sixty-six years old, former longtime governor, senator for the past twelve years, and the unchallenged leader of Illinois Republican politics.

Then there was the bulky and sardonic House speaker Thomas Reed, who did have a national following and entered the race with every intention of giving McKinley and the bosses a hearty challenge. His strategy was to consolidate the New England delegations—Maine, Massachusetts, New Hampshire, Vermont, and Rhode Island—and build from there. The wild card was former president Benjamin Harrison, now approaching sixty-two, who could command the Indiana delegation and enjoyed national stature. But he had fallen in love with a fetching widow twenty-four years his junior, and many speculated that would keep him out of the race.

But this favorite son "combine" wasn't McKinley's only problem. Closer to home was the pesky Ben Foraker, who engineered a potent comeback at the 1895 Ohio GOP convention in Zanesville, where he wrested control of the state apparatus from Hanna and McKinley. The convention nominated Foraker's man, Asa Bushnell, for governor and endorsed Foraker himself for the next open U.S. Senate seat. Foraker's former private secretary, Charles Kurtz, became state party chairman, supplanting McKinley's man, Charles Dick, whose bid for state auditor was rebuffed. Foraker avoided a nasty public clash by accepting a convention endorsement of McKinley for president, but the convention outcome "shocked us a good deal," recalled Charles Dick later, noting that it made McKinley look weak in his own state just as his presidential bid was getting under way.

THE CAMPAIGN YEAR began with a number of political realities. The Republicans were the governing party, the Democrats the dissident voice. The GOP had held the presidency for twenty-eight of the previous thirty-six years, and Republicans generally believed they determined the national destiny. After all, the party was hardly past its infancy when it won a great sectional war, saved the Union, ended slavery, and knitted the country back together as best as it could be done. It had fostered the great postwar industrial expansion, provided land for railroad lines and state universities, promoted the construction of roads, bridges, and canals. As Thomas Reed put it, "Progress is the essence of Republicanism."

Indeed Republicans were the progressive party, comfortable with the application of federal power in behalf of major national goals: protecting the voting rights of blacks, curbing antitrust abuses, bolstering domestic industry through intrusive and complex tariff schedules. All this outraged Democrats, who harked back to the states' rights and strict construction ideals of Jefferson and Jackson. "The Democratic party can not, will not, dare not, leave the high road of constitutional obligation, of governmental limitations," declared Michigan congressman John L. Chipman on the House floor in 1890. "The paternal idea of ruling men is the autocratic idea."

But now the settled politics of the postwar era was challenged by a new wave of political anger swelling across the nation. It began with the recession in the Western farm sector, which seemed to have no end, and ballooned into a national movement when the Panic of 1893 brought on the great economic cataclysm of President Cleveland's second term. By the end of his tenure, some 15,000 businesses had gone under, along with 600 banks and seventy-four railroads. Unemployment remained high for years, approaching or exceeding 15 percent.

These economic woes soon generated powerful political currents. In the rural West and South, where millions could barely subsist as money evaporated and farms went idle, people saw the crisis as one of financial liquidity. The reason they couldn't get loans to tide them over, they believed, was because heartless Eastern money men were hoarding the nation's money for their own purposes. And the Republicans' tariff barriers slammed them further by placing higher prices on necessities they could hardly afford in the first place while constricting foreign markets for their goods. "The farmers of the West," declared Georgia's Democratic representative Henry G. Turner on the House floor, "have mortgaged their lands to the East," the dominant region in a Republican Party that "has made the laws under which all the trusts that oppress [my constituents] have had their origin . . . that has devised our bad fiscal system, that outlawed silver, that has contracted the currency to the verge of bankruptcy."

Thus there emerged throughout the South and West a full-throated, populist cry for the free coinage of silver to expand the money supply and ease the plight of hapless farmers and other rural folk. Easterners naturally viewed this as an irresponsible call for the debasement of the nation's currency. A new political fault line had opened up in the land.

With his tariff preoccupation and penchant for consistency, the stolid-minded McKinley resisted the idea of adjusting his campaign to address this development. In August 1895 he met with a number of campaign advisers—including former governors William Merriam of Minnesota and Michigan's Russell Alger—at Hanna's Cleveland home. The question was what should be the principal issue of the forthcoming campaign. McKinley, noting the political devastation recently visited upon Democrats, urged an ongoing embrace of protectionism as the primary antidote to the nation's economic travails. Republicans were united on that issue, he argued, but seriously divided on currency matters. Favoring party coalescence over unnecessary disruptions, he preferred his traditional studied ambiguity on the high-voltage currency issue.

Others weren't so sure. Hanna, steeped in the arcana of finance and the principles of hard currency, favored a GOP commitment to a single gold standard, "and he was anxious and willing to lend his aid to the furtherance of this policy," Merriam recalled. But the campaign executive wasn't about to resist his boss's wishes, particularly with others present. He expressed his views gently and then retreated. The campaign would hew to the candidate's signature embrace of protectionism under the slogan "The Advance Agent of Prosperity." Hanna would wait for later opportunities to press the currency matter.

Meanwhile, as the campaign year began, so did the war of attrition over delegate selection. The South remained relatively solid, despite desperate measures by Platt and his allies to help local officials break up McKinley's Southern organizations. They funneled abundant cash into those contests, fostered ploys such as calling "snap" conventions at the county level to catch the McKinley men flat-footed and roll over them. But as the process unfolded, Hanna's Thomasville strategy held up. Reed managed to get only fourteen and a half delegates from Georgia, Louisiana, North Carolina, Virginia, and Texas. Morton picked up one delegate from Alabama and two from Florida, while Quay captured two in Georgia and one in Mississippi and divided a Louisiana slot with Allison, who cadged another three in Texas. Against McKinley's far more robust pickings in the region, these didn't amount to much. Some Northern states also slipped into line, including Wisconsin in mid-March and Oregon three weeks later.

But the governor could get the nomination only by generating a sense of his own inevitability. To do that he needed to demonstrate that he could bust up at least a couple of the Northern favorite-son organizations. He snapped into action when he got word on February 4 that Harrison had told Indiana's GOP chairman, John Gowdy, that he wouldn't run. That evening, as Charles Dick was eating dinner at his home in Akron, the phone rang. It was McKinley, calling from Canton.

"Can you come down here at once?" he asked. "I want to talk with you." Dick got the first train out of Akron, arriving at Canton around nine.

"I want you to go and see Gowdy, with Mr. Hanna's consent," said the governor, "and take up the Indiana situation." Dick got the first train for Cleveland the next morning and conferred with Hanna, who warned him to operate by stealth. "Don't stir up . . . speculations of the newspapers," said the industrialist. Dick rushed to Indianapolis and enlisted Gowdy's support in an effort to canvass state party officials and pull local leaders to the McKinley cause. By the time he left, Indiana was in the bag, and hardly anyone knew the effort had been orchestrated at McKinley headquarters.

One big question facing the campaign was whether to go for delegates in the highly controlled states of New York and Pennsylvania, where Platt and Quay ruled supreme. There were opportunities to pull in a few antimachine delegates there, but McKinley supporters in both states feared that, if they took on the machines in their states, their rebellious efforts might be repudiated by the McKinley campaign in order to mollify the powerful bosses. At a Canton strategy meeting, McKinley suggested they wave off their supporters in those hostile states on the theory that the few delegates available there weren't worth the hassle.

"No," said Hanna, "we shall get a delegate wherever we can."

It was a sound judgment. Though the New York and Pennsylvania pickings remained slim, the effort placed Platt and Quay on the defensive and undermined their argument that their favorite-son strategy would destroy McKinley's candidacy. Meanwhile McKinley's popularity proved nettlesome for other potential favorite sons. In Minnesota in late March, Cushman Davis abandoned his candidacy after three of the state's five district conventions refused to endorse him. That gave Minnesota to McKinley. Around the same time Manderson's Nebraska effort also collapsed.

But McKinley still needed delegates, and the best place to get them, Hanna concluded, was Illinois, which might ensure McKinley's nomination victory if he could capture it. As the *Washington Post* explained, referring to the McKinley men, "If they can capture the State they think they will have delegates enough to hold firm against any combination of the wicked plotters—Platt, Quay, Clarkson, et al. If they fail to capture it the combined opposition will have strong intrenchments from which to go out and make the fighting." The man they chose to lead the fight was Charles G. Dawes, just twenty-nine when he approached Hanna to offer his services to McKinley. Kohlsaat was there when they met. After the young man's departure, Hanna looked at Kohlsaat and, contemplating the man's youthful appearance and lack of political experience, said, "He doesn't *look* much, does he?"

"Any man who will work for nothing and pay his own expenses looks good to me," replied the publisher.

For his part, Dawes had found his candidate. "McKinley seems to be the coming man," he wrote in his diary.

The rangy Dawes was a fresh-faced young man with bright eyes and a ready smile who projected a self-confidence beyond his years. As it turned out, he was not only a brilliant man of multiple talents but also one to stir the heart of William McKinley, twenty-eight years his senior. The governor developed with the younger man what became the closest thing in McKinley's life to a father-son relationship. Dawes's actual father was a prosperous Marietta, Ohio, lumber dealer who rose to the rank of general during the Civil War and served a term in the U.S. House. Upon graduation from Marietta College, young Dawes moved to Lincoln, Nebraska, where he got into business and entered the law. He specialized in railroad-rate cases, became a bank director, and made serious money with a utility company investment in La-Crosse, Wisconsin. Preoccupied with the complexities of the currency issue, he mastered them sufficiently to write a book on the subject. He also was an accomplished musician, the composer of musical scores that earned national popularity.

In January 1895, seeking to maneuver through the recession, he bought the Northwestern Gas Light and Coke Company in Evanston, Illinois, and moved his young family to Chicago. A master of organization and time management in the mold of Hanna, he combined his business responsibilities with a tireless commitment to McKinley's Illinois effort. As the young operative wrote in his diary, "Cullom is furious at McKinley's 'invasion' of Illinois, which he considers his own particular and personal property."

Dawes fanned out through the state, making contacts, identifying McKinley sympathizers, organizing local efforts in behalf of the governor. He encountered plenty of McKinley support but also a widespread fear of bucking the well-entrenched senator. "It is McKinley against the field," wrote Dawes, "against the bosses, against everything that the bosses can bring to bear." The Cullom forces organized a number of snap conventions in crucial districts to outmaneuver Dawes before he could marshal sufficient strength to threaten the senator. "It is not fighting fair," wrote Dawes in his diary. He organized an "indignation meeting" to protest the tactics.

Slowly Dawes's relentless efforts paid off. He went after Cullom in his own district, picking off various counties in late March. "We have them beaten in Logan County," he wrote to McKinley on March 19, two days before Logan Republicans voted in convention to "instruct" delegates to vote for McKinley. By March 29 two more counties in Cullom's district had endorsed the Ohio man. Three days later, the full district convention rebuffed its native senator and instructed delegates to vote for McKinley. Amid rumors that Cullom had ended his campaign, the senator wired a friendly delegate, "I have not withdrawn, and do not intend to withdraw." Three days later he wrote to a friend, "I do not hesitate to say to you that appearances indicate that the Governor will be nominated." But Cullom still wanted to be positioned should a convention deadlock materialize. If that happened, he added, "I believe now that my chances are not the worst."

Thus the battle would come down to the state GOP convention on April 30 in Springfield. No one doubted that McKinley would garner a big bloc of delegates, particularly after April 23, when three district conventions voted to instruct for him, while a fourth endorsed his candidacy without instructions. But the question was whether his forces would seek a state convention resolution instructing at-large delegates to vote for the governor at the national convention in St. Louis. At a Canton meeting with McKinley and Hanna, Dawes got the go-ahead to push for instructions.

When the young political director arrived in Springfield with elaborate procedural plans on how to get the favored convention outcome, he encountered a cluster of state party pros, McKinley men but bent on upending Dawes's plans in favor of their own personal interests. At a crucial meeting Chicago mayor George Swift attacked Dawes directly, questioning his maturity and knowledge of Illinois politics. He urged that all tactical decisions be postponed several days. The articulate and self-assured Dawes rose to his feet and issued a fifteen-minute rebuttal, explaining with considerable rigor why his approach was necessary. "It was a question of my life or death as a political manager," Dawes recalled later. He prevailed.

Then, a day before the Illinois convention was set to begin, a political detonation occurred 750 miles to the east that had a potent impact on events in Springfield. Vermont Republicans, meeting in convention at Montpelier, surprised everyone by voting "in a perfect furor of enthusiasm" to endorse McKinley's candidacy over that of Thomas Reed, who had been considered New England's dominant politician. The McKinley forces emerged in the final days, Vermont senator Redfield Proctor told reporters, like "a tidal wave, ground swell, cyclone, avalanche, you can take your choice of expression." This followed a dramatic development in New Hampshire in which the state convention adopted a resolution that mentioned both Reed and McKinley with equal favor. These twin New England actions seemed to spell the demise of the Reed candidacy.

That provided a big boost to Dawes's Illinois push. Until the final vote, the outcome was unclear, although Dawes never doubted it. A series of *Washington Post* headlines between April 28 and May 1 tells the story: "Cullom Forces Well Organized"; "Cullom Gains Ground"; "Cullom Hopes to Win"; "Cullom Bowled Over." The convention gave McKinley four instructed at-large delegates along with the twenty district delegates already instructed. In addition, the governor clearly would get most of the uninstructed delegates.

The governor was thrilled—and brimming with pride toward his young protégé. He wrote to Dawes:

My Dear Mr. Dawes:

I can not close the day without sending you a message of appreciation and congratulation. There is nothing in all of this long campaign so signal and significant as the triumph at Springfield.

I can not find words to express my admiration for your high qualities of leadership. You have won exceptional honor. You had long ago won my heart. . . .

My concern has been about you all week lest under the great strain you would break down. I pray you take care of yourself and now get a good rest, you have earned it. I hope you can run over here—bring your wife and we will have a restful time. How relieved you must feel!

Accept my heartfelt thanks and tell all of your associates how grateful I am at their unselfish devotion. Please convey to Mrs. Dawes and the children the sincere regard of Mrs. McKinley and myself, and believe me,

Faithfully yours

The Illinois outcome sent a clear signal of McKinley's commanding position in the nomination fight. Ohio congressman Charles H. Grosvenor, a close McKinley ally who made a name for himself by calculating the governor's delegate totals at various points throughout the spring, now said his candidate had 488 committed delegates, with another sixty in the "likely" category. With 456 convention votes needed for nomination, it appeared that McKinley couldn't lose. Stated

Grosvenor, "Everybody who has knowledge enough to be significant and candor enough to be manly knows that this contest is over."

One politician who fit Grosvenor's definition of significant and manly was Pennsylvania's Matthew Quay, who issued a statement on May 19 that he planned to meet with McKinley in Canton as soon as he could escape his Senate duties. The announcement "set the tongues of statesmen a-wagging," as one newspaper reported. Quay was beset by reporters demanding to know why he wanted to meet with his presidential adversary.

"Well, you see," replied Quay, lighting a fresh cigar and displaying the smile of a sly politician, "there has been a great deal of talk about McKinley being unsound on the money question, and it occurred that it would not be a bad idea for me to run over to Canton and ask him about it. . . . That is my sole object in going."

But the announcement raised a big question about the solidarity of the bosses. On May 22 Quay took a train to Canton, where McKinley met him at the station in his modest family carriage. The two men lunched together at the governor's home, and then McKinley drove him back to the station for his return trip. Reporters observed plenty of cordiality and warmth in the demeanor of both men. Later that afternoon, McKinley took a train to Cleveland for consultations with Hanna. Neither man would discuss publicly the nature of the conversation, but within a week Quay said outside the Senate chamber, "Maj. McKinley is sound on the money question." Soon the papers were reporting that, while Quay officially remained a presidential candidate (because of political commitments he had made), he now would be working with Hanna to smooth the way for McKinley's nomination— and to get whatever he could for himself in return for hoisting his surrender flag. Given the Ohioan's commanding position, it wouldn't be much.

Whatever the details of McKinley's private accommodation with Quay, it represented a victory for his brand of politics. He had begun the nomination fight by rejecting the demands of the Eastern bosses, including Quay, with a sense of principle that helped define his candidacy. The story got into the public consciousness when the *Washington Post* revealed its outlines in a March 26 article that received wide attention. The reporter got many of the details wrong, but he captured the gist. The tale shows, he wrote, "that the big three of the Republican Party—Quay, Platt, and Clarkson—hoped to find McKinley as putty in their hands. When they failed, they vowed war on him." Already by late March, the reporter noted, their war was sputtering. "And over in the Ohio city by the lake, one Mark Hanna is laughing in his sleeve."

8

St. Louis Triumph

TAKING COMMAND OF THE NATIONAL PARTY

On Sunday, June 7, 1896, nine days before the scheduled start of the Republican National Convention in St. Louis, Herman Kohlsaat traveled to Canton and lingered for eight hours at the McKinleys' North Market home. He spent much of that time urging the governor to take a political stand his friend considered distasteful. Kohlsaat was a sound-currency man who wanted the country's money to be backed by a single gold standard. He wanted the Republican platform to embrace that standard and explicitly reject the movement for free and unlimited silver coinage.

The Chicago newspaperman had been mildly problematical during Charles Dawes's campaign to collect Illinois convention delegates. Kohlsaat's *Chicago Times-Herald* had supported McKinley avidly but also had promoted the gold standard with such zeal that it created confusion about the candidate's true currency stance. When Mark Hanna was asked who represented McKinley on the money issue, himself or the *Times-Herald*, the industrialist often replied, "Kohlsaat is a crank and does not represent anybody but himself." These comments inevitably got back to Kohlsaat, and the two men, though friends for years, stopped talking because of the frictions over currency.

Whatever Kohlsaat said during his Canton visit, McKinley wasn't buying it. He retorted that 90 percent of his correspondence and visitors cautioned that a strong gold plank would spell his general election defeat. One alarmist was the prominent party man Whitelaw Reid, owner and publisher of the *New York Tribune*, who had run for vice president with Benjamin Harrison during Harrison's unsuccessful 1892 reelection bid. "If a gold plank is adopted," the often officious Reid had warned McKinley during a recent Canton visit, "we will not carry a State west of the Mississippi." Reid's *Tribune* echoed that view in an editorial: "There is no occasion to maintain that the words 'Gold Standard' must of necessity be used, because the present standard is that, and everybody knows it." The aim was to avoid the word *gold* in the platform and thus keep the political waters calm. As Edwin Godkin's *Nation* magazine put it, McKinley was less a silver man than a "silverish man," meaning he "wishes to be considered 'friendly to silver'—just friendly enough to get the votes of the silver men, but not friendly enough to lose those of the gold men."

Besides, McKinley still didn't think the currency controversy could possibly supplant protectionism as the campaign's leading issue. While he acknowledged that Western and Southern passions over money would have to be managed during the convention, he told Kohlsaat that those passions would dissipate within a month—so long as he didn't exacerbate the situation by fostering a strong gold plank.

This outlook reflected McKinley's tendency to view political events in static terms—seeing things as they were and assuming they would continue in the same vein. Dynamic thinking wasn't his forte. Though deft in responding to events as they unfolded, he lacked an instinct for anticipating them, much less shaping them. Thus, as the convention loomed, he didn't see the potency of the silver issue. Indeed he didn't want to see it. If he embraced gold as a push-back on the rising silver sentiment, it would amount to an acknowledgment that the money issue was now the campaign centerpiece. Once again Godkin got it right. "The fight that the McKinley men are making at St. Louis," explained *The Nation*, "is not so much against the gold standard as it is against giving precedence to the gold standard as an issue."

A few days after his Canton visit, Kohlsaat got a telegram from a

Chicago friend named Alexander Revel, who had traveled to St. Louis for the convention. "If you want to see the word 'gold' in the plank," wrote Revel, "you should come down here." Kohlsaat quickly caught an overnight train to St. Louis, arriving at ten on the morning of Friday, June 12. He went straight to McKinley's Southern Hotel headquarters, where a number of McKinley's friends were vigorously engaged in fashioning a currency plank. Kohlsaat promptly inserted himself into the deliberations.

Those deliberations unfolded against a backdrop of America's long and often unsuccessful effort to maintain equilibrium between the demand for money and its supply, an effort that extended back to the controversy unleashed by Hamilton's First Bank of the United States, designed to give the economy sufficient liquidity, maintain currency stability, and ensure economic efficiency. Jefferson and his Republican allies attacked the bank as a dangerous concentration of financial power, and its charter lapsed in 1811. But the War of 1812 revealed the need for a central banking authority. State banks in the Northeast, where the war was unpopular, hoarded the country's meager reserves of specie (gold and silver), forcing banks in other regions to rely on printed money. The result was a menacing wave of inflation and considerable economic dislocation. Thus the Second Bank of the United States was established in 1816—and immediately slipped into corruption as its officials speculated in the bank's stock and fostered venal practices by its branch members. When new bank leaders sought to clean up the mess by foreclosing on overdue mortgages and redeeming overextended notes from state banks, they triggered the Panic of 1819. Banks failed, prices collapsed, unemployment soared.

President Andrew Jackson, a sound-money man who hated all concentrations of power, killed the national bank with a series of bold and highly controversial political maneuvers in the 1830s. But the state banks he fostered couldn't always maintain the needed balance between money demand and money supply, and that proved disastrous when the Panic of 1837 ravaged the U.S. economy for nearly seven years. An anguished call rose up for rescinding Jackson's last executive action, his Specie Circular, designed to curb a dangerous inflationary wave sweeping the country in conjunction with wild land speculations in the West. Jackson's answer was to require purchases of government property to be transacted in gold or silver.

But when the threat of inflation suddenly gave way to the threat of falling prices, or deflation, Jackson's protégé and chosen successor, New York's Martin Van Buren, couldn't see that the Specie Circular was precisely the wrong medicine when the country desperately needed liquidity. In the name of a sound currency, he clung to Jackson's old policy even as it deepened the Panic and destroyed his presidency in the 1840 elections.

Something similar was happening now, in the 1890s, when a deflationary cycle emerged after the Western land-price bubble burst and surging grain production devastated farm prices. As the silverites saw it, declining prices meant there weren't enough dollars to accommodate the demand for goods. In farm regions, they argued, the money supply hadn't kept up with the burgeoning production of wheat and other agricultural products. The answer was to expand the money supply through the coinage of silver. As a fiery young Democratic congressman from Nebraska, William Jennings Bryan, declared in 1893, "Mr. Speaker; if metallic money is sound money, then we who insist upon a base broad enough to support a currency redeemable in coin on demand, are the real friends of sound money." On the other hand, he added, "If all the currency is built upon the small basis of gold those who hold the gold will be the masters of the situation."

Gold advocates countered the call for more liquidity by noting that the nation's money supply had increased by 240 percent since 1860 and 104 percent since 1872, much faster than the rise in population. They pointed out further that global gold production had increased substantially in previous years, bolstering the money supply throughout the world. In a series of explanations entitled "The Free Coinage Catechism," Godkin's *Nation* argued that the price of wheat, for example, reflected the supply-and-demand ratio on wheat itself and had nothing to do with any money-supply shortage, which was nonexistent anyway. An artificial increase in money, argued the magazine, would merely unleash a wave of inflation, and the wheat farmer's added revenue from higher wheat prices would be offset by higher prices on everything he had to buy to live and produce. Thus "the farmer would be relatively no better off than he was before."

All this established the framework for a political drama about to unfold at the Republican convention. As those McKinley associates grappled with the issue at the Southern Hotel, their basis of discussion was a document crafted in Canton by McKinley and others and hand-carried by Hanna to St. Louis the previous Wednesday. A copy was delivered to Senator Foraker as well, who was slated to be on the convention's platform-writing Resolutions Committee and thus would be well positioned to get the governor's favored language into the final document.

The crucial elements of the McKinley draft stated that the party favored sound money "unreservedly" and opposed any effort "to debase our currency or disturb our credit." The party had been responsible for resuming specie payments in 1879, after Civil War greenbacks had flooded the country, and since then had "kept every dollar as good as gold." It was committed to "maintaining all the money of the United States, whether gold, silver or paper, at par with the best money of the world." It had no objection to silver so long as it could be maintained at parity with gold and if other major trading countries would enter into an international bimetallism agreement based on an equality of value between the two metals. Until then, "it is the plain duty of the United States to maintain our present standard, and we are therefore opposed under existing conditions to the free and unlimited coinage of silver at [a ratio of] sixteen to one."

Given his previous conversation with McKinley, Kohlsaat considered the language much stronger than he had anticipated. It appears that the governor had stiffened his gold commitment after Kohlsaat's departure. Others sensed the same thing. The *New York Sun*, after talking with an anonymous inside source, reported that "the drift at present is toward a very much better money plank than was anticipated two or three weeks ago." The paper added, with a touch of malice, that "Mr. McKinley has been screwed up [by his friends] to a stronger idea on the money question." It isn't clear how McKinley reached acceptance of this draft wordage, but it seems his aim was to balance the political pressures from both Western silver men and Eastern gold interests. His model was language crafted by the Ohio state party and the Indiana GOP convention. Both were seen as political "straddles"— supporting the principle of a sound currency while avoiding any specific mention of gold.

While McKinley's friends in St. Louis—including William Osborne, Myron Herrick, and Senator Redfield Proctor of Vermont—favored the Eastern position, they weren't sure it would be politically prudent to reflect that sentiment in the platform with explicit language, including the word *gold*. At Hanna's request, on Thursday these men set about to refine the language by scrutinizing every sentence, clause, and word. Hanna was in and out of these sessions, as his broader managerial duties called him away intermittently. But he seemed to favor the McKinley straddle.

In truth, he strongly favored the gold standard and believed the wave of angry Western populism had to be met with a stern political counterforce. But his job was to get McKinley nominated, and it was crucial that he keep his candidate out of any crossfire between the two emotional currency factions. Better, he believed, to let the pro-gold sentiment build among delegates before aligning McKinley with the gold forces. In the meantime, he would stay in the shadows and certainly keep his candidate there.

On Friday some new people joined the St. Louis discussion group: Kohlsaat; Henry C. Payne of Wisconsin, a Milwaukee machine politician who served as a Republican committeeman from his state; former Minnesota governor William Merriam; and Melville E. Stone of Chicago, head of the Associated Press and a close McKinley friend. When Kohlsaat saw the latest draft on Friday morning, he noticed that the word *gold* had been inserted between *existing* and *standard*, thus binding the party to the principle that "the existing *gold* standard must be maintained." But the crucial word had been crossed out in the typewritten draft, signifying that the group hadn't yet agreed to go the distance. When Kohlsaat asked about it, Hanna said the word had been excised because of strong objections from Indiana, Michigan, Iowa, Nebraska, and other states west of the Mississippi, where McKinley delegates were needed for the nomination.

When Kohlsaat ventured that avoiding the word was "cowardice," Hanna exploded.

"Damn you, Herman," he declared, "haven't you any compromise in your make-up?"

"Not on this issue, Mark," replied Kohlsaat.

"Well," said Hanna, "I have no more time to waste on a damned crank." And he left the room.

The conferees debated the matter for the next five hours, finally reaching agreement at three o'clock in favor of the explicit gold commitment. They sent for Hanna and informed him of the decision. The campaign manager looked straight at Kohlsaat.

"Are you satisfied now, you damned crank?" he asked.

"Yes," replied Kohlsaat. "I don't like the promise to send a commission to Europe to work for bimetallism, but will stand for it."

As the exhausted group was breaking up, Hanna called Kohlsaat into his room. Clasping the newspaperman's hands in both of his, he said, "You probably have noticed I have dropped you entirely for a couple of months. Well, I want to tell you I am just as strong a goldman as you are, but if I had been as outspoken as you we would not have gotten the votes for McKinley, but I want you to know I love you just as much as ever." The friendship continued for years.

Later on Friday, Herrick wired the draft to McKinley, who by now was convinced of the need for a strong statement. He wired back his approval via the telegraph machine in his Canton study. But Hanna wasn't ready to reveal the status of things before he could assess convention sentiment, and that would take a couple days as delegates arrived in St. Louis. Among them were two particularly important Easterners with fervent pro-gold convictions: New York's Thomas Platt and Massachusetts senator Henry Cabot Lodge, a brilliant but haughty Yankee with a romantic vision of America's destiny and a streak of "dauntless intolerance," as one observer admiringly put it. Lodge arrived bent on forcing the word *gold* into the currency plank by whatever means necessary.

On Monday he marched into Hanna's office and, without any preliminary greeting despite its being the first time the two men had met, announced, "Mr. Hanna, I insist on a positive declaration for a gold-standard plank in the platform." Hanna looked up from his desk.

"Who the hell are you?" he demanded.

"Senator Henry Cabot Lodge, of Massachusetts."

"Well, Senator Henry Cabot Lodge, of Massachusetts," said Hanna, "you can go plumb to hell. You have nothing to say about it."

"All right, sir," said Lodge, unfazed, "I will make my fight on the floor of the convention." And he departed.

It was precisely what Hanna wanted: convention rumors that the Eastern gold men were marshaling their forces to take over the drafting of the currency plank. When Hanna's quiet delegate soundings revealed widespread convention support for a firm gold plank, the campaign manager decided it was time to drop his secrecy tactic. He sent Merriam to deliver the final McKinley draft to Platt, while Kohlsaat showed a copy to Lodge. The senator evinced surprise. "Why, that plank is all right," he declared, then suggested a couple of minor improvements that were readily accepted. Merriam, a member of the Resolutions Committee, delivered a copy to Foraker, who had become chairman of the platform-writing panel, ensuring his influence over the final language.

As word seeped out about the strong gold plank, many concluded McKinley and Hanna had been rolled on the issue. The *Washington Post*, which had been predicting for days that the currency plank would be a straddle, now presented a totally different picture. "Hanna Yields to Lodge," declared a *Post* headline. It wasn't true, but it served Hanna nicely. The Western silver men might not like where the convention was going, but they couldn't blame the man in Canton, who was widely viewed as more sympathetic to their interests than the convention seemed to be. Hanna later wrote to a friend, "The whole thing was managed in order to succeed in *getting what we got*, and that was my only interest."

What induced McKinley to move from his rigid support for the gold-plank "straddle," as reflected in his intransigent response to Kohlsaat, to his final acceptance of the strong gold position? No one ever knew, because he never explained it. Once again the mysterious politician managed to position himself—and, in this instance, his party—where they needed to be for maximum political effectiveness. The governor wasn't quite prepared to embrace the gold standard as his centerpiece position in the general election, but now he could do so if political circumstances should require it, which they would. Once again he managed to preserve his flexibility on a hazardous issue while remaining entirely out of the political crossfire.

WITH THE CURRENCY plank settled and hardly any doubt about the nominee, the St. Louis meeting figured to be a convention of rare serenity and good feeling, though many no doubt would lament the lack of the usual dramatics. In the days preceding the first gavel, other candidates maneuvered to accommodate reality. On June 8 Shelby Cullom abandoned his presidential ambition in favor of McKinley. "There's no use keeping up your holler when the thing's settled," he said. Matthew Quay's situation was more complicated. Given that he already had accepted McKinley's inevitability, it was natural for him to withdraw. But in entering the combine of bosses the previous year, he had promised to keep fighting to the end, and he didn't want to renege on his commitment. Mr. Quay, wrote the *Washington Post*, "is in a somewhat embarrassing position."

His close collaborator, Thomas Platt, faced no such dilemma. Having established his battle lines, he would never retreat. He intended to fly the Levi Morton flag into the nomination balloting and be positioned for any eventuality that could undermine McKinley's standing with delegates. Unfortunately for him, nothing seemed likely to upend McKinley except a raucous convention split over the currency plank, and Hanna had deftly eliminated that threat. So Platt's defiance was mostly for show, although it occurred to him that perhaps a respectable Morton showing could get the vice presidential nod for the New Yorker, which could enhance Platt's control over New York patronage.

That left Thomas Reed. Although his plan to capture New England was bruised, he entered the convention with enough delegates to be a factor should lightning strike. But then his top campaign official, Joseph Manley, arrived in St. Louis and declared McKinley the winner. "In my judgment the convention will nominate Gov. McKinley on the first ballot," he said in a statement. "It is useless to attempt to deny that this will be the result." It was a stunning statement from a man who owed his devotion to Reed. Around the convention hotels, folks were even more stunned to learn that Manley had neglected to tell Reed about his planned statement but for some reason had alerted Hanna. When reporters told Reed of Manley's prediction, he exclaimed, "No, sir; it is not true! Manley would have made no such statement." Many figured that Manley's action would cost Reed half his delegates.

As the convention's first day approached, the only anticipated drama centered on credentials, the vice presidential selection, and the response of Western silver men when the gold plank was ratified by delegates. Beyond that, the proceedings had the appearance of a coronation—hardly dramatic but satisfying to party men who liked the idea of a united GOP heading into the general election.

This was apparent as the National Committee set about resolving credential disputes prior to the first gavel. By June 12 the committee had acted on seventy-two disputed delegates and settled sixty-two in McKinley's favor. This stirred the irascible Platt to declare that, if the committee seated twelve anti-Platt delegates claiming convention slots from New York, he would bolt with his remaining delegates. "This is a riot of excess," declared Platt, "and must be stopped."

Hanna, suspecting a bluff, laughed it off. "I cannot sacrifice old friends in order to conciliate old enemies," he said. That response emboldened New York's pro-McKinley forces to challenge Platt at a preconvention delegation meeting, where McKinley ended up with seventeen New York delegates to Morton's fifty-five. The Credentials Committee signified its McKinley devotion by approving the credentialing actions of the National Committee, and Platt promptly announced that he wouldn't bolt the convention after all.

Throughout the morning of June 16, the great Convention Auditorium in downtown St. Louis came to life as delegates, party notables, and guests made their way into the hall and mingled as the convention's noon starting time approached. Erected at a cost of $70,000 specifically for the convention, it was slated for demolition by October 1. Built of wood, its exterior covered with what one newspaper described as "a compound of dirty gray plaster," the structure was designed to hold some 14,000 bent-cane chairs, including 924 for delegates directly in front of the speaker's stand. The place was festooned with red, white, and blue bunting, and huge paintings of party luminaries graced the walls: Abraham Lincoln above the speaker's platform and Civil War notables Grant, Sherman, Sheridan, Farragut, and Meade situated prominently around the vast hall.

At 12:20, after some difficulty getting silence, party chairman Thomas Carter gaveled the eleventh Republican National Convention to order and led it through routine business before introducing temporary chairman Charles Fairbanks of Indiana. Delivering the keynote address, Fairbanks lauded "honest currency laws," castigated Democrats for lowering McKinley tariff levels during the Cleveland years, and warned of the "evil effects" of free silver coinage. His words were greeted warmly but without enthusiasm. Indeed the lack of buoyancy among delegates stirred Hanna to declare, "There will be enthusiasm in the convention tomorrow if I have to hire every 'rooter' in St. Louis."

The next day Hanna had reason for enthusiasm when a procedural vote tested McKinley's convention strength against that of his opponents. The governor pulled 568½ votes to only 339½ for the combined opposition, which signified the governor likely would have a hundred delegates to spare on his way to the nomination two days hence.

That same day a poignant scene unfolded in the Resolutions Committee after it approved the McKinley gold plank on a 40–11 vote. A collection of Western delegates rose to announce they couldn't accept the policy and would leave the convention if the gold plank prevailed on the floor. They were led by Henry Teller of Colorado, a Republican since Lincoln's day, a twenty-year Senate veteran, and a man of immense national stature. Joining him were young senator Fred Dubois of Idaho; senator Frank Cannon of Utah, known as the "Utah Maverick"; and representative Charles Hartman of Montana. They presented a series of resolutions that would be distilled into a substitute free-silver plank for convention-floor consideration.

Senator Lodge spoke for many on the gold side when he praised the silver men in tender words, suggesting he felt something approaching personal bereavement at the possible loss of such valued party colleagues. But there wasn't much the majority could do, insisted Lodge, except let their errant colleagues depart in peace and sympathy as the majority worked its will through the normal processes of deliberation.

Resolutions Committee chairman Foraker presented the platform to the convention the next morning and received a raucous ovation when he came to the gold plank. Upon completion of his presentation, all eyes turned to Teller, a gaunt figure with a long face accentuated by a high forehead and white beard. As the clerk read the substitute plank, he stood dispassionately, his hair the color of the metal he cherished, the weight of his sixty-six years visible in his stooped shoulders. Then he stepped to the podium amid hearty cheers of respect even from those who vehemently disagreed with him. He drew a long, deep breath, stood silent for a moment, then spoke in a halting voice, almost whispering. Slowly his intonation gained timbre as he ascended to a passionate delivery that lasted nearly forty minutes. There was hardly a fidget among the 12,000 or so attendees.

He could not depart the party he had loved so well, said Teller, "without heart burnings and a feeling that no man can appreciate who has not endured it. And yet I cannot, before my country and my God, agree to that provision that shall put upon this country a gold standard." Tears were seen in the eyes of some Western delegates as Teller added that he and his silver colleagues "take this step, not in anger, not in pique, not because we dislike the nominee . . . but because our consciences require as honest men that we should make this sacrifice."

Teller then watched as delegates voted on his substitute plank—and downed it 105½ to 818½. When Utah's wavy-haired Senator Cannon later addressed the assemblage, he made the mistake of attacking Republicans as "once the redeemer of the people, but now about to become their oppressor." Instantly the kindliness of the crowd evaporated. Hisses and cries of "Go! Go!" swept the floor. Sufficient order was restored for Cannon to finish, and then with a heavy countenance Teller led his flock out of the hall and the Republican Party, some twenty-five men walking single-file like a procession of ducks, including the entire Colorado, Nevada, and Idaho delegations. Tears welled up in many eyes, including Teller's. It was all high drama but not particularly significant in political terms. As the *Washington Post* opined, "Had it not been for the personality and prominence of Senator Teller, it is doubtful whether the occurrence of the much-advertised bolt would have produced more than a minimum sensation."

Back in Canton, McKinley was awakened by an early-morning phone call from Hanna, who delivered a forecast of the day's events and plenty of optimism. McKinley quickly shaved and dressed, then descended the stairs to his office, humming the Scottish air "Bannockburn." He displayed a buoyant mood throughout the day as streams of relatives, neighbors, and reporters passed through the house, to be flooded with the governor's favorite stories from past conventions. He delivered a brief tutorial to his nieces on the nomination process, and when his mother arrived with sisters Helen and Sarah, he jumped up from his front-porch seat to greet them enthusiastically.

Lunch was served around two, and Ida sat next to the Cincinnati newspaperman and close family friend Murat Halstead, who detected a certain "pensive" element in her mood. After listening to her digressions, Halstead concluded she was ambivalent about "the Presidential business," as he wrote later. "Of course, she wants her husband to win now, but she would rather he had not been drawn into the stream of events that is bearing him on to higher destinies, for the tendency of the great office will be to absorb the Major's attention, so that she can hardly, however great his devotion, have all the time in his society she would fondly claim."

When a congratulatory telegram arrived that made reference to two passages of Scripture, one of the luncheon guests suggested a Bible be brought in so they could scrutinize the citation. When one gentleman at the table suggested jocularly that the Major likely didn't have time to acquaint himself with the book's inside, Ida flashed her displeasure: "He does, indeed, know the inside of his Bible—no man better, I assure you, and I speak that which I do know."

It was thought that the nominating speeches and roll calls would begin late and go into the night, but shortly after lunch word arrived via long-distance telephone and wire services that the nominating speeches were about to begin. The Major seated himself in a heavy armchair next to his desk, pad and pen in hand, and took up the telephone receiver that an assistant had dialed in to the convention hall. From that location he followed every word and vote for the next several hours.

Across the hall, Ida and a number of other women, friends and relatives, awaited news from the governor's study. At one point McKinley left his post, walked across to the parlor, and asked in a jocular tone, "Are you young ladies getting anxious about this affair?" When they said yes, the Major assured them all would be well, then returned to his big chair. At 3:21, when Foraker pronounced the name of William

McKinley during his nominating speech, the auditorium erupted in a "veritable Niagara" of wild cheers and yells that lasted nearly half an hour. Listening on McKinley's office telephone, it "was like a storm at sea, with wild, fitful shrieks of wind," Halstead recalled later. When order finally was restored, the deft orator Foraker said with a sly tone, "You seem to have heard of him before." That rekindled the torrent of applause.

Later, when someone sought a reading on how long the Quay demonstration lasted in comparison to McKinley's, the always even-handed governor cut him off. "No, no!" he said. "Do not ask that question."

The room fell silent when the roll call began, the only sound some low, absent-minded humming and whistling on the part of the Major. Then were heard the words "Alabama, eighteen for McKinley." As the process continued, it took on a herky-jerky quality as vote challenges followed some roll-call responses, delaying the proceedings. But the Major sat patiently, with hardly a change in countenance, and recorded results on his pad as the votes came in. When Ohio's forty-six votes were recorded for McKinley, he passed beyond the needed 447, and the nomination was his. He got up from his chair, walked across the hall to the waiting ladies, and informed them of the result. Bending down to his seated wife and mother, he kissed each in turn as the younger woman beamed her pleasure and the older one whispered a motherly sentiment in his ear.

Immediately the whole of Canton went "stark, gloriously mad," as Halstead put it. The big alarm gong at city hall rang out the news, and some 15,000 happy citizens formed up in front of the courthouse for the prearranged parade, led by three companies of militia. With bands playing and drums sounding, the throng marched up North Market Street toward the McKinley home. Even before it could get there, the streets became a panorama of flags, festoons, and decorations of all kinds. The parade group, joined by thousands of others, made its way to the McKinley front lawn, eager for a speech. To thunderous cheers, the governor stepped to the porch and expressed his feelings with his usual subdued graciousness. "There is nothing more gratifying or honorable to any man than to have the regard and esteem of his fellow-townsmen," he said, "and in this I have been peculiarly blessed."

Back in St. Louis, the balloting continued, with McKinley getting a final total of 661½ votes, to 84½ for Reed, 61½ for Quay, and 58 for Morton. Then weary delegates faced the task of selecting a vice presidential running mate who could balance the ticket and give it added luster. It seemed that those who wanted the job weren't entirely acceptable to the McKinley camp, while those considered acceptable didn't want it. The obvious candidate was Reed, who had emerged as a national force and a master politician, if perhaps a bit cynical for some. But Reed absolutely disavowed any interest. "Under no circumstances," his man, Joseph Manley, told reporters. "You cannot make that too emphatic." Kentucky's governor Bradley, yearning for the nod, didn't pass muster at McKinley headquarters, and Hanna certainly wouldn't reward Platt by accepting New York's Morton. Besides, that would slam the anti-Platt forces who had clustered so faithfully around McKinley.

An unlikely choice, but McKinley's, was Garret Hobart of New Jersey, longtime state legislator, party official at both the state and national levels, and successful businessman in banking and railroads. McKinley genuinely liked the man, but he liked also that Hobart could represent the crucial Northeast without being involved in any internecine party squabbles such as those that festered in New York and Pennsylvania. Given that he hadn't risen to the upper levels of politics, his emergence was a surprise to some convention people. But it wasn't a surprise to Hobart. "I knew from the first," he told reporters shortly after the convention, "that my nomination was certain." Once again McKinley and Hanna got what they wanted.

9

The Victor

SOUND MONEY, PROTECTIONISM, AND PATRIOTISM

By the time McKinley captured the Republican nomination, young Charles Dawes felt certain he knew who would become the Democrats' standard bearer. The governor's opponent, he told McKinley and Hanna, would be Nebraska's William Jennings Bryan, the "boy orator of the Platte," as he was known, just thirty-six years old, a former two-term congressman and now a $30-a-week political commentator for the *Omaha World Herald*. But there was a proviso: Dawes's prediction would hold, he said, only if the silver-tongued Bryan could get himself to the rostrum for a major speech at the Democrats' Chicago convention in July. Even with the proviso, it was an audacious prediction.

To McKinley and Hanna, wizened veterans of political wars, it was more than audacious. It was so preposterous as to become a running joke among the three congenial friends.

"It will be Dick Bland," growled Hanna whenever Dawes ventured his prediction. McKinley, who considered Richard Parks Bland of Missouri a personal friend, agreed the likely winner would be the ten-term House veteran who had lost his seat two years earlier in the Democratic debacle. A serious-minded farmer widely appreciated for his quiet but immutable convictions, Bland was known affectionately as "Silver Dick" in honor of his lifelong fealty to free silver.

There was a certain logic in the Bland prediction because it reflected a judgment that the Democratic Party was about to be conquered by the free-silver fervor sweeping the South and West. Many leading "Gold Democrats," including President Cleveland, believed it was still possible for their party's "stable currency" elements to prevail over the silver agitators at the Chicago convention. But McKinley, Hanna, and Dawes knew otherwise.

Nothing captured this reality more starkly than the fate of John Carlisle, Cleveland's distinguished-looking Treasury secretary, when he announced his candidacy for the Democratic nomination as a "sound money" man backed by Cleveland and his cabinet. Carlisle's name went forward on March 16. Two days later the press quoted numerous political professionals saying Carlisle couldn't carry a single Southern delegation, much less the convention. A prominent Northern party man said the Treasury secretary "would be the weakest nominee whom the Democrats could name." On April 5, Carlisle quietly departed the race.

But Bland faced opposition from other silver advocates, including former Iowa governor Horace Boies, a handsome, white-haired populist and ex-Republican. Former Massachusetts governor William Eustis Russell wanted the nod, although his party's state convention in Boston hadn't demonstrated much enthusiasm for him. Ohio Democrats put forth John R. McLean, owner and publisher of the *Cincinnati Enquirer*, a fiery free-silver paper. Some Democrats even suggested the party should turn to Colorado's senator Henry Teller, now that he had bolted the GOP in St. Louis. Here and there could be heard a lonely voice for Bryan, though few considered him presidential timber. Clearly Bland seemed to have the most unobstructed path.

But Dawes knew the full depth of Bryan's oratorical flair. The two men had enjoyed a cordial friendship during their years together as young lawyers in Lincoln, Nebraska. They had gone to the same church, lived on the same street, worked in the same downtown building. They competed in the courtroom and at a discussion society called the Round Table. Bryan's intemperance of thought struck Dawes as hopelessly naïve, even dangerous, but he appreciated Bryan's force of personality and soaring eloquence. If he could get to that podium, Dawes was convinced, Bryan would sweep the convention. He was no ordinary politician.

The son of a Methodist father and a Baptist mother, the precocious Bryan rejected the religions of both parents at age fourteen and got himself baptized as a Presbyterian, thus demonstrating a streak of independence that would become familiar to the country. Reared in Illinois, where his father was a state circuit judge, he was home-schooled until age ten, weaned on the Bible and McGuffey's Readers. He was graduated as valedictorian from Illinois College and earned a law degree at Chicago's Union Law College. After his two House terms, he made an unsuccessful bid for the U.S. Senate from Nebraska, then accepted a position as a columnist for the free-silver *Omaha World Herald* in order to keep his name before Nebraska voters—and perhaps gain some national notice with his fiery commentary.

At the Democrats' Chicago convention, it didn't take long for the party to sweep away the old establishment by embracing a platform that respectable Republicans, and even some Democrats, considered radical. It demanded the free and unlimited coinage of silver and gold at the ratio of 16 to 1, denounced the protective tariff, advocated governmental regulation of trusts and railroads, called for enlarged powers for the Interstate Commerce Commission, and blasted the Supreme Court's ruling that a federal income tax was unconstitutional. The aroused delegates even rejected a motion to commend the presidential service of Grover Cleveland, the only Democratic president since James Buchanan's pre–Civil War tenure.

Meanwhile the irrepressible Bryan was wheedling a speaking slot on the convention's key evening program, positioned behind four speeches that turned out to be either lackluster or discordant. First came South Carolina's unkempt "Pitchfork Ben" Tillman, looking like a "train robber," as one journalist put it. He stirred waves of hisses with a rabid appeal to sectionalism. Then there was New York senator David B. Hill, whose competent but staid speech wailed against the platform and implored delegates to respect the party's "old Democrats . . . who have grown gray in its service." After that the delegates suffered through two speeches notable for their hollowness.

Then came Bryan. Having fortified his vocal cords by sucking on a lemon and calculated with perfect pitch the tenor of the moment, he both captured and amplified the political crosscurrents roiling the consciousness of farmers, miners, merchants, laborers, and rural folk everywhere. His theme was equality of human value. Why should Eastern businessmen, he demanded, be placed on a higher plane of esteem than ordinary citizens?

The man who is employed for wages is as much a business man as his employer . . . the farmer who goes forth in the morning and toils all day—who begins in the spring and toils all summer—and who by the application of brain and muscle to the natural resources of the country creates wealth, is as much a business man as the man who goes upon the board of trade and bets upon the price of grain. The miners who go down a thousand feet into the earth . . . and bring forth from their hiding places the precious metals to be poured into the channels of trade are as much business men as the few financial magnates who, in a back room, corner the money of the world.

The floor and galleries exploded in applause as the hall fluttered with white handkerchiefs waving furiously. It was time, said Bryan, for the great mass of Americans to take control of the nation's politics. "We have petitioned, and our petitions have been scorned; we have entreated, and our entreaties have been disregarded; we have begged, and they have mocked when our calamity came. We beg no longer; we entreat no more; we petition no more. We defy them!"

From the gallery, a man shouted, "Go after them, Willie!" Another yelled, "Give it to them, Bill!"

He went after Republicans in declaring, "If protection has slain its thousands, the gold standard has slain its tens of thousands." He set up his audience perfectly for the final defiant demand: "You shall not press down upon the brow of labor this crown of thorns, you shall not crucify mankind upon a cross of gold." Then Bryan fluttered his fingers down the sides of his head, as if to suggest the trickle of blood, and stretched out his arms into the image of a cross.

The convention went wild with cheers and applause that lasted half an hour. The next night, the Nebraskan captured the Democratic nomination on the fifth ballot, after Bland's standing dissipated steadily through the first four votes. Dawes had seen it coming.

But McKinley had missed the populist wave's full force. On June 20, he greeted well-wishers in Canton with a stout defense of protection but didn't mention the currency issue. He later spoke of the necessity of a sound dollar but without much elaboration or apparent conviction. Godkin's *Nation*, ever vigilant for signs of weakness on currency matters, wondered about McKinley's backbone should he be elected: "McKinley's character is so vague, and so little forecast of what he is likely to do can be got either from his career or from his language, that a good deal of uncertainty must mark the first year or two of his administration."

This concern wasn't entirely misplaced. Meeting with friends at his Canton home shortly after the St. Louis convention, the governor pushed aside a suggestion that the money issue would dominate the campaign. "I am a Tariff man, standing on a Tariff platform," he said. "This money matter is unduly prominent. In thirty days you won't hear anything about it." The Major's friend William Day replied, "In my opinion, in thirty days you won't hear of anything else."

William Jennings Bryan would ensure that Judge Day was right. Further, it wasn't clear McKinley and his men were prepared to fight on that unfamiliar battlefield. Hanna, who would manage McKinley's canvass as the newly installed chairman of the Republican National Committee, had fashioned a traditional campaign relying on surrogate speakers to tout the GOP candidate throughout the summer, then building up to big torchlight parades and rallies as the November election approached. McKinley too had looked forward to a light campaign schedule during the summer.

Now that wouldn't suffice, as Hanna quickly perceived. He canceled a scheduled August cruise along the New England coast and wrote to McKinley, "The Chicago convention has changed everything." He foresaw "work and hard work from the start" and viewed the situation in the West as "quite alarming. . . . With this communistic spirit abroad the cry of 'free silver' will be catching." Early Midwest soundings indicated free-silver sentiment was welling up in Iowa, Indiana, Michigan, Illinois, even Ohio. Traditional Republican farmers appeared poised to abandon the party in favor of what one Iowa political manager called "the free silver craze [which] has taken the form of an epidemic."

It boiled down to the calculus of presidential map and math. Republicans had dominated presidential politics through most of the decades since 1860 by capturing New England, the Northeast, most of the Midwest, and much of the West. Democrats dominated the Solid South and border states. But Democrats had won the presidency under Cleveland in 1884 and 1892 by capturing traditionally Republican states in the Northeast, Midwest, and Far West: California, New York, New Jersey, Connecticut, Wisconsin, Michigan, and Illinois. Now Bryan seemed poised to seize traditional Republican strongholds in the West, including Colorado, Kansas, Nebraska, the Dakotas, Wyoming, and the new states of Washington, Idaho, and Utah. Thus it was imperative that McKinley rebuff Bryan's Midwest onslaught and prevent any electoral erosion in that crucial region.

That in turn would require an entirely new kind of campaign. It wouldn't be enough simply to stir the faithful with military bands, torchlight parades, and massive rallies—the traditional approach to a presidential campaign. The currency issue had scrambled the nation's political fault lines to such an extent that it wasn't clear who the faithful were. That created an imperative to educate voters on the fundamentals of currency policy and persuade them that the only sound course was sound money. Hanna had to get the message out that the Democrats' inflationist silver embrace would erode the savings of ordinary Americans, disturb delicate financial markets, upend the nation's economy, and undercut prosperity everywhere.

Hanna quickly created a new organizational structure, with him "in the saddle," as he put it. Rather than leading the state party organizations loosely, as in the past, he would be the field marshal, directing state parties closely on strategy and execution. He set up a dual headquarters structure, in New York and Chicago, to address key geographic challenges quickly and efficiently. When he saw he must devote most of his time to New York fundraising, he installed Dawes as head of the Chicago operation.

Dawes introduced modern accounting methods and chose business professionals as his associates over political hacks. "No contract is made by this Committee without my approval," he assured McKinley on August 1, "and no contract is let without . . . competitive bids." Dawes helped create a Traveling Men's Bureau, a Speakers' Bureau, and a Literary Bureau, all charged with pursuing the campaign's educational mission. He reported to McKinley that the operation was running smoothly and morale was high. "There has not been the slightest trace of any friction among the members of the Committee," he wrote.

With the New York office handling fundraising, Chicago took on the educational role, pursued primarily through the distribution of pamphlets, brochures, posters, buttons, and favorable newspaper articles, sent out in more than a dozen languages. Eventually Dawes oversaw the distribution of some 100 million pieces of literature into a country of about 15 million voters. The New York office sent out 20 million more into the Northeast. One particularly popular pamphlet turned out to be a forty-page piece explaining the silver question in easily digestible, conversational prose.

The Chicago operation hired 100 employees to produce these materials and ship them out every day in railroad cars. Some 275 separate messages were tailored to specific regions and audiences—farmers, military veterans, first-time voters, ranchers, store owners, laborers—reached through a distribution chain that began with state GOP committees and extended through county and precinct offices. When Hanna discovered that some state and local committees weren't always snappy in distributing materials, he got the Chicago operation to devise ways of sending materials directly to voters. Staffers also sent masses of materials to newspapers for reprinting or distribution inside the paper. Some of these were sent out in the form of plates that allowed small papers to save money by eliminating stages of the printing process. Eventually the newspaper-distribution program reached nearly 3 million people every week.

All this was new. And it required more money than any presidential campaign had ever raised or spent. The printing budget for the Literary Department turned out to be close to half a million dollars. Some $900,000 was distributed through the state GOP committees, while the Chicago organizational budget was $274,000. The New York operation consumed nearly $1.6 million, while Chicago spent more than

$1.9 million. Altogether the campaign expended $3,562,325.59, more than double Harrison's 1892 spending.

But Hanna's early efforts at fundraising proved disappointing as Northeastern industrialists held back, "scared . . . so blue" by the threat of Bryan, as John Hay wrote his friend Henry Adams, "that they think they had better keep what they have got left in their pockets against the evil day." Besides, the industrialists weren't sure what to make of the seemingly parochial and often laconic McKinley, whose political base had been small Midwestern towns. In August, Dawes reported to McKinley his concern "that we are mistaken in assuming that we are going to have more funds than in 1892." While interest was high among businessmen, he explained, "it is more difficult for them to spare the money" in economic hard times.

The relentless Hanna set out to convince industrial money men that both he and his candidate were serious and bent on stemming Bryan's populist tide. He warned the titans of banking, insurance, railroads, oil, and other industries that it wouldn't be sufficient now for him to go hat in hand to various small industries protected by Republican tariff policies and get the usual modest contributions. Turning back the ominous free-silver threat required big money. Ultimately he proved persuasive. John D. Rockefeller's Standard Oil Company gave $250,000, while Rockefeller himself contributed another $2,500. Banker J. P. Morgan also gave $250,000, and $174,000 came in from a number of railroad companies. Chicago meatpacking enterprises gave $40,000, and the New York Life Insurance Company, traditionally favorable to Democrats, donated $50,000.

By crafting his educational campaign and building his fundraising juggernaut, Hanna transformed American politics. Now the parties would move beyond efforts merely to stir party stalwarts with dramatic late-campaign rallies and parades. The aim would be to build the base by expanding the ranks of the faithful through political education. At a time when significant immigration was bringing new voters into the political process, the Hanna innovations would become crucial to maintaining party leverage in an increasingly dynamic political environment.

Bryan meanwhile developed his own plan to maximize his limited campaign budget (about a tenth of McKinley's) by crisscrossing the nation via railroad and casting his eloquence over countryside and cityscape from the platforms of trains. He set out from Lincoln on August 7 on his way to New York City, where he planned to kick off his campaign at Madison Square Garden, and immediately his dynamism and stamina could be seen. His journal entries captured the program's grueling nature: Lincoln to Chicago, 555 miles; Chicago to New York, 913 miles; New York to Buffalo, 440 miles; Buffalo to Erie and return, 176 miles; Buffalo to Toledo, 84 miles; short trips around Upper Red Hook, New York, 100 miles. The Lincoln–New York trip included speeches at Omaha; Des Moines; the Iowa towns of Grinnell, Iowa City, and West Liberty; Chicago; the Ohio towns of Mansfield, Lima, Alliance, and Orrville; and Pittsburgh. He even stopped at Canton to deliver a speech in which he acknowledged his opponent's "high character and personal worth," while also slyly urging Cantonites to keep "your distinguished citizen among you as a townsman still."

Bryan set for himself a campaign regimen that ultimately would encompass, he later calculated, 570 speeches and 18,000 miles of travel in twenty-nine states. He spoke an average of 80,000 words a day, and on one mid-October day made twenty-three speeches, the first at Muskegon, Michigan, at seven in the morning and the last at midnight in Lansing. He later booked thirty Chicago addresses in three days with the aim, one newspaper speculated, of placing "himself practically in personal contact to the extent of sight and hearing of the entire population of . . . Chicago."

This campaign frenzy, coupled with the populist surge unleashed by Bryan's charismatic persona, generated serious nervousness among McKinley men.

"You've got to stump or we'll be defeated," Hanna told McKinley at one strategy session.

"You know I have the greatest respect for your wishes," the governor replied, "but I cannot take the stump against that man." He knew Ida couldn't hold up under the strain; he didn't want to leave her; and his instincts warned against competing with Bryan on his own turf.

But Hanna wouldn't give up. Myron Herrick, visiting the industrialist in Cleveland, found him "scared to death" over Bryan's kinetic campaign. "We have got to get McKinley out on the road to meet this thing," Hanna told him. Herrick dutifully traveled to Canton to press the case for a stump tour.

"Don't you remember that I announced I would not under any circumstances go on a speech-making tour?" replied McKinley, insisting that a course alteration now would give an appearance of weakness. "I might just as well put up a trapeze on my front lawn and compete with some professional athlete as go out speaking against Bryan."

Evincing a degree of self-awareness while gigging at Bryan, he added, "I have to think when I speak." He didn't consider himself well suited to Bryan's kind of political showmanship, which would simply escalate if he sought to compete with it. "If I took a whole train, Bryan would take a sleeper," said the Major. "If I took a sleeper, Bryan would take a chair car. If I took a chair car, he would ride a freight train. I can't outdo him, and I am not going to try."

Instead he developed a different concept for connecting with the electorate and conveying his message. Rather than going to the voters, he would invite the voters to come to him. This wasn't altogether novel. Benjamin Harrison had welcomed a number of delegations to his Indianapolis home during his 1888 campaign, and McKinley himself had received numerous well-wishers after getting the Republican nomination in June. Word went out that he would welcome Americans from anywhere in the country who wished to see him at Canton and hear his plans for the nation.

The response was greater than anyone had anticipated. Streams of visitors made their way to Canton's North Market Avenue to show support and see the candidate in his own environment. It turned out that the "Front Porch" campaign, as it was called, also allowed McKinley to control his message by managing the exchanges with delegation leaders.

When a letter arrived at Canton or campaign headquarters announcing that a delegation of farmers, cigar makers, merchants, or churchmen wanted to visit on a particular day, the campaign sent a letter back asking the delegation spokesman to visit Canton beforehand to discuss the matter. At these meetings, McKinley asked what the spokesman intended to say. If the answer was vague, McKinley said something like, "That will hardly do." He requested a letter ten days or so before the event with the proposed remarks written out. Sometimes, if they weren't quite right, the governor edited them before sending them back.

On one occasion, a delegation spokesman arrived with his proposed address already written. "Just read it to me," said McKinley. After hearing it, the governor sought a complete rewrite—but with his characteristic diplomatic sensitivity. "My friend," he said, "that is a splendid speech, a magnificent speech; no one could have gotten up a better one. But this is not quite the occasion for such a speech. There are occasions when that would be just the right thing. It is sound and sober from your standpoint, but I have to look at it from the party's standpoint." He counseled the man on how to make his speech just right for a Front Porch exchange.

Employing such techniques, McKinley manipulated his image and message as delegations of every civic stripe arrived at the Canton train station, marched down Main Street to an elaborate plaster arch constructed for the occasion, then waited until summoned to the McKinley Front Porch. Brass bands and cheering locals escorted them along their way, and the town was festooned with patriotic bunting. At a nearby tent, visitors were offered two glasses of beer and a sandwich (for "wets") or a cup of coffee and two sandwiches (for "drys").

As each delegation approached his house, McKinley remained inside, then emerged with dramatic flair to cheers from the assembled. Often Ida would come onto the porch or wave her greeting from behind a window. As the spokesman uttered his remarks, McKinley listened intently, "like a child looking at Santa Claus," his Canton friend Harry Frease later recalled. Then the candidate climbed upon a chair to deliver his own well-tailored remarks, often memorized, always including an expression of delight in welcoming such valued guests to his home. Afterward he invited them up to shake hands and enjoy a glass of lemonade.

The Front Porch strategy was a tremendous success. Between mid-June and Election Day, McKinley welcomed some 750,000 Americans in hundreds of delegations from thirty states. In the process, he unleashed a steady stream of carefully calibrated campaign oratory that was covered every day by newspapers throughout the country. And he never had to leave Ida or drag her along on any campaign hurly-burly.

McKinley used these sessions to draw a stark contrast between Bryan's inflationist agenda and what he hailed as his own, more responsible sound-currency commitment. He attacked the "new experiment" proposed by Democrats that would "debase our currency and further weaken, if not wholly destroy, public confidence." Warming to the attack, he ventured in late July to actually utter the word *gold*, though he always returned quickly to his cherished tariff issue: "That which we call money, my fellow-citizens, and with which values are measured and settlements made must be as true as the bushel which measures the grain of the farmer and as honest as the hours of labor which the man who toils is required to give. [Loud applause] . . . Our currency to-day is good—all of it, as good as gold—and it is the unfaltering determination of the Republican Party to so keep and maintain it forever. [Cheers]."

Even *The Nation* was impressed, although it expressed its satisfaction with a wry qualification. The candidate inserted gold into his rhetoric, said the magazine, "in a somewhat furtive way . . . hastening to take a good pull at the tariff to steady his nerves."

What *The Nation* missed was that McKinley was weaving together three separate threads—currency, protection, and patriotism—into a seamless political vision. The connection may have been artificial, but the result was effective. The Bryan Democrats, he said in August, believed in not only *free* trade but also *free* silver, putting the two together as equal evils. "Having diminished our business they now seek to diminish the value of our money. Having cut wages in two, they want to cut the money in which wages are paid in two." On the money issue, he lauded the Democratic Party's Grover Cleveland wing, which was "patriotically striving for the public honor, and is opposed to free silver." The Bryanites, on the other hand, "are devoted to this un-American and destructive policy, and were chiefly instrumental in putting upon the statute books tariff legislation which has destroyed American manufacturing, checked our foreign trade, and reduced the demand for the labor of American workingmen."

This was harsh rhetoric, employing terms such as *un-American* and suggesting that Republicans had a corner on patriotism. But McKinley genuinely despised Bryan's divisive class-driven politics. "My countrymen," he asserted to a delegation of black Americans from Cleveland, "the most un-American of all appeals observable in this campaign is the one which seeks to array labor against capital, employer against employee. [Applause] It is most unpatriotic, and is fraught with the greatest peril to all concerned. We are all political equals here—equal in privilege and opportunity, depending upon each other, and the prosperity of the one is the prosperity of the other. [Great cheering]."

As the campaign progressed, Bryan captured the nomination of the country's leading alternative party, the People's Party, known as Populists, which embraced an agenda similar to the Democratic platform and Bryan's rhetoric. Facing a decision whether to embrace Bryan's candidacy or go with their own nominee, the Populists chose Bryan at their July convention in St. Louis. But they complicated matters by selecting a different vice presidential nominee, Georgia's Tom Watson, more attuned to Populist thinking than Bryan's running mate, the wealthy industrialist Arthur Sewall of Maine. That created an awkward voting situation quickly dubbed the "twin-tailed ticket," which became even more awkward when Watson sought to get Sewell off the Democratic ballot so he could run with Bryan on both tickets. Although Bryan needed Populist votes to win, he didn't enjoy the attacks on his Democratic running mate or the ballot-box confusion. He was pleased, however, when he got still another splinter-party nod, that of the National Silver Party, which could pull votes in the Far West.

Thus Bryan became a triple nominee with bright prospects throughout the South and West. But he was anathema in New England and the Northeast, where he was denounced by major Democratic newspapers in New York, Baltimore, Philadelphia, and other cities. The *New York World* wrote, "Lunacy having dictated the platform, it was perhaps natural that hysteria should evolve the candidate."

Meanwhile a contingent of angry "Gold Democrats" convened a convention at Indianapolis and created yet another party ticket dedicated to siphoning off Democratic votes from Bryan even if that helped McKinley. They gave their presidential nomination to seventy-nine-year-old Illinois senator John M. Palmer, whose qualifications probably didn't include his age. The vice presidential selection was a more youthful Kentuckian named Simon Bolivar Buckner, only seventy-three. Hanna, always alert to political opportunity, slipped increments of cash to the Palmer campaign in the closely contested states of Delaware, Virginia, West Virginia, and Kentucky. Palmer reciprocated by declaring toward the end of the campaign, "I promise you, my fellow Democrats, I will not consider it any great fault if you decide next Tuesday to cast your ballots for William McKinley."

As the campaign moved into its final weeks, Hanna sent out prominent Republicans to stump for McKinley and whip up a final wave of enthusiasm. One was the ambitious New Yorker Theodore Roosevelt, head of the New York City Police Commission and former U.S. Civil Service commissioner in the Harrison administration. Roosevelt, famous as a reformer in Platt-dominated New York, also was gaining notice for his tendency toward outrageous pronouncements encased in amusing language. In a mid-October speech in Chicago, he "minced no words," the *Washington Post* reported, in attacking Bryan, along with Illinois governor John Altgeld, a fiery progressive and tireless warrior in behalf of free silver. Altgeld had won the permanent enmity of the nation's propertied interests by freeing the last prisoners accused of throwing bombs at the Chicago Haymarket riots of 1886. Roosevelt declared that Bryan deserved "the contemptuous pity always felt for the small man unexpectedly thrust into a big place." The Nebraskan, he added, didn't look well in a lion's skin, but that wasn't his fault. The blame rested with "those who put the skin on him," including Altgeld.

In Altgeld's case we see all too clearly the jaws and hide of the wolf through the fleecy covering. Mr. Altgeld is a much more dangerous man than Mr. Bryan. He is much slyer, much more intelligent, much less silly, much more free from all the restraints of some public morality. The one is unscrupulous from vanity, the other from calculation. The one plans wholesale repudiation with a light heart and bubbling eloquence, because he lacks intelligence and is intoxicated by hope of power; the other would connive at wholesale murder, and would justify it by elaborate and cunning sophistry for reasons known only to his own tortuous soul.

Roosevelt's remarks, reported the *Post*, "brought cheers from his Republican hearers." They were the words of a man bent on employing distinctively stark rhetoric and dramatic gestures to gain notice and propel his career upward. Whether they converted anyone to the Republican cause was an open question, but they certainly brought attention to Theodore Roosevelt.

AS ELECTION DAY approached, everyone knew the outcome would be determined in the Midwest, particularly Indiana, Illinois, Michigan, Iowa, and Ohio. But few felt sure where these states would come down. Predictions and counterpredictions punctuated campaign coverage, and a late-campaign *Washington Post* review identified fifteen states as "doubtful."

But Hanna remained confident. Responding to rumors that anxious party officials in Indiana, Michigan, and Minnesota had pleaded for a quick infusion of resources from national headquarters, he told reporters, "I want people to feel apprehensive. The more frightened Republicans and sound money Democrats become in these States the greater will be the majority for McKinley."

Privately he wrote to Harrison, "The outlook is generally encouraging, and I feel there is no doubt of our success." He even returned an unneeded campaign contribution at the end of October. Another boon to the campaign—and to America's wheat growers—arrived when wheat prices unexpectedly spiked due to shortages in India, Russia, and Australia. This seemed to negate Bryan's persistent argument that low wheat prices reflected a shortage of currency tied to the restrictive gold standard. By October 20 wheat prices in Chicago hit nearly 80 cents a bushel, up more than 30 percent in a matter of months. "What has happened to this 'law' under which silver and wheat must go arm in arm?" asked the *Chicago Tribune*, a Republican paper. "What agency has dared to separate those whom Altgeld and Bryan have joined together in the unholy bonds of rotten money?"

As the free-silver frenzy visibly waned in October, McKinley happily turned his attention to the broader economic themes that had always animated him: protective tariffs, prosperity, factory orders, the confluence of interests between working men and their bosses. Around the country vast rallies of political enthusiasm unfolded. Late on November 2, as the campaign reached its culmination, a vast Canton congregation erupted into wild cheers, sprightly band music, fireworks, and waving American flags. McKinley, seeing the flags, said, "Glorious old banner it is. So long as we carry it in our hands and have what typifies it in our hearts the Republic and our splendid free institutions will be forever secure." The next morning he rose early to vote at a country store four blocks from his home and then receive a morning visit from Hanna. He appeared serene throughout the day. "I never saw him look better," said a visiting friend from Akron. At nightfall he sat down in an easy chair in his study, puffed his cigars, and marked returns on a sheet of paper as they came in from across the country via telephone and telegraph. It soon became clear that his victory was secure. "The feeling here beggars description," Hanna wired from Cleveland, where he had returned to vote and monitor the election results. "You are elected to the highest office of the land by a people who always loved and respected you."

The victory was sweeping. McKinley captured 271 electoral votes to Bryan's 176. The Ohioan dominated all of the Northeast and New England, as expected, but also swept the battleground states of the upper Midwest: Minnesota, Iowa, Wisconsin, Illinois, Michigan, Indiana, and Ohio. He captured a plurality of 464,000 votes in eighty-five crucial Midwestern cities, the same cities that had given Cleveland a 162,000-vote advantage just four years earlier. McKinley's Illinois victory margin was 141,537 votes, 69,913 of them coming from Cook County (including Chicago). His 7,107,822 popular votes exceeded Bryan's total by nearly 600,000.

When Herman Kohlsaat rang the McKinley home from Chicago just after midnight to congratulate his friend, the call was answered by McKinley's nephew, James McKinley, who had difficulty locating his uncle. He finally returned to the phone to report that he had found the president-elect in a bedroom, kneeling in prayer with his wife and mother. All he could hear was the eighty-seven-year-old Nancy McKinley saying of her son, "Oh, God, keep him humble."

MCKINLEY'S 1896 VICTORY, and the manner of his obtaining it, altered American politics for a generation. The transformation came not only through Hanna's new educational style of campaigning and the expansive fundraising techniques devised to finance it. The systematic approach to blanketing the nation with campaign literature, broken down for targeted demographic groups, had never before been executed on such a scale. One Hanna biographer later described it as an "attempt . . . gradually to wind up public opinion until it was charged with energy and confidence." This required a series of communication efforts coordinated and timed for maximum cumulative effect by Election Day.

Beyond that, the clash of ideas unleashed by the campaign also set the nation upon a new course. The Republican Party, having prevailed as the country's governing institution by winning the Civil War, ending slavery, stitching the country back together, and setting in motion the industrial expansion of the latter half of the nineteenth century, was losing much of its political force by century's end. New civic angers, sensibilities, impulses, and concerns were coming to the fore, more focused on class consciousness, economic disparities, and perceived industrial abuses. Bryan had mustered these sentiments into a great political wave that threatened for a time to wash over the nation.

But McKinley, the stolid-minded politician focused on old verities and the adhesive power of representative democracy, had diverted that wave and taken leadership of the country under a banner of unity, focused on the intertwined interests of farmers, laborers, miners, industrialists, urbanites, rural folk, blacks, whites. In projecting his political vision, he sometimes seemed naïve, even simple-minded. But nobody doubted his sincerity, and that lent appeal and vigor to his leadership. He managed to pull disparate voters to his side through his preoccupation with prosperity born of economic growth. It was the right message when the national economy had been reeling for years under Democratic leadership. The Republican Party that McKinley shaped in 1896 would cohere as a political entity and survive as the country's dominant political force for most of the next three and a half decades.

10

Building a Cabinet

"AND THERE ARE IDIOTS WHO THINK
MARK HANNA WILL RUN HIM"

On November 12, 1896, President-elect McKinley sat down at his desk to craft a letter to the man whose selfless devotion over many years had guided his path to the presidency. His aim in writing to Hanna was twofold: first, to express deep appreciation; second, to lure his Cleveland friend into the McKinley Cabinet. In pursuing the first aim, the governor found his emotions welling up. "Your unfaltering and increasing friendship through more than twenty years," he wrote, "has been to me an encouragement and a source of strength which I am sure you have never realized, but which I have constantly felt and for which I thank you from the bottom of my heart." Recollecting all those years of loyalty and friendship "fill me with emotions too deep for pen to portray."

Then to business: "I want you as one of my chief associates in the conduct of the government." Acknowledging Hanna's expressed misgivings about joining the Cabinet, he described the call to Washington as an imperative of patriotism. "I want you to take this tender under the most serious consideration and to permit no previous expressed convictions to deter you from the performance of a great public duty."

Hanna had no intention of acceding to McKinley's plea. For one thing, he didn't like the appearance of it—the perception that he was getting a high-profile job in return for his political devotion. He wanted his dedication to McKinley to be seen strictly as a product of principle. This was particularly important in light of the increasingly vicious attacks from some Democratic newspapers, notably William Randolph Hearst's *New York Journal*, which had endorsed Bryan as a circulation ploy. Hearst cynically suspended his pro-gold convictions so the *Journal* could become New York's only major pro-Bryan paper and thus corral that readership. He then shamelessly pushed Bryan's candidacy in his news columns by portraying McKinley as an empty-headed front man manipulated by the oafish, misanthropic Hanna, ravenous for power and money. Hearst's cartoonist Homer Davenport, whose savage pen brought him fame and wealth through widespread syndication, devastated Hanna by drawing him as a corpulent human monster with a malevolent grin and dollar signs plastered all over his expensive suits. Hanna sought to dismiss the attacks as a burden he must bear for his political success in a partisan-press era. But friends knew the depth of his pain. Coming across one particularly ghoulish caricature of himself while breakfasting with a companion, he passed it across the table with the words, "That hurts."

Beyond that, despite his boundless respect for McKinley, Hanna didn't want to remain in the man's shadow. Throughout most of his life, in building his business with his distinctive talents and drive, he had been his own man. Then, in pursuing his dream of getting an Ohioan into the presidential mansion, he had suspended his independence of identity. Now he hankered to become his own man again. That probably meant a return to industrial pursuits. It certainly precluded a job as governmental hired hand, however elevated.

But Hanna harbored a secret ambition for a government position that could satisfy his desire for independence. He revealed it one day in January 1892, four years before McKinley's election, to his corporate lawyer, James Dempsey. "Jim," said Hanna, "there is one thing I should like to have but it is the thing I never can get."

"What is it?"

"I would rather be a Senator in Congress than have any other office on earth."

When Dempsey suggested the ambition wasn't unrealistic if Hanna set his mind to it, the Cleveland man replied, "Jim, I could no more be elected to the Senate than I could fly."

But now, with his enhanced political standing, Hanna could entertain the idea more hopefully. Ben Foraker was scheduled to become Ohio's junior senator early in 1897, so that seat wasn't in play. But John Sherman's term would expire in two years, and that might be a possibility if Sherman, now seventy-three, decided to retire. Beyond that, Hanna couldn't help speculating about a possible scenario that could speed things up: What if McKinley offered Sherman a place in his Cabinet as, say, secretary of state, thus inducing him to abandon his Senate seat in March? It was an enticing thought.

In the meantime, McKinley turned his attention to the Cabinet-making challenge with a full understanding that his recruitment for top governmental jobs could determine his level of success as president. When reporters asked the governor's cousin and confidant, William Osborne, if the president-elect had commenced building his Cabinet, Osborne replied, "I guess that is about the only thing agitating his mind nowadays." It was a task replete with myriad political pressures and demands that were sometimes intertwined, often in conflict. The New York challenge became particularly nettlesome when Tom Platt suggested that his machine would accept a pro-tariff merchant named Cornelius Bliss to fill the Cabinet's New York slot. Bliss, a broad-faced man with fluffy side whiskers, had served for years as treasurer of the national Republican Party and proved himself an effective political fundraiser. He was aligned with New York's reform elements but always managed to work amicably with all factions. By pronouncing Bliss acceptable, Platt hoped to preserve his influence with McKinley, despite his aggressive opposition during the nomination campaign, by making it easy for the governor to accept his recommendation.

But that infuriated New York's antimachine agitators, particularly *New York Tribune* publisher Whitelaw Reid, whose brilliance and influence were sometimes undermined by his self-importance and tendency to go on at tiresome length in expressing his views. Hearing of Platt's Bliss ploy, Reid wrote McKinley a ten-page letter imploring him to resist. He quoted the worst things said about McKinley by Platt's henchmen during the nomination battle—that he was "unsafe and erratic, not firm but impressionable . . . [had] no fixed opinions . . . [was] turned and twisted by every changing wind"—and suggested that, if McKinley succumbed to Platt's pressure, it would "confirm him in his theory" of the governor's character. "To yield," warned the publisher, ". . . is to show that you fear him."

McKinley agreed it was dangerous to placate a man such as Platt. Hanna also had advised the governor before he met with a Platt emissary: "They must not *dictate*." But the governor didn't particularly like Reid's suggestion that a Bliss appointment would demonstrate his own character defects. Besides, he liked Bliss and considered him a pretty good solution to the New York conundrum. Unfortunately it became moot when efforts to sound out Bliss for attorney general or navy secretary yielded a negative response—necessitated, he said, by his wife's faltering health. The result was that Platt put forth a number of New York favorites, many unacceptable to McKinley, and the New York situation became a festering problem.

In the meantime the governor busied himself with two of the most prestigious Cabinet positions: Treasury and State. For Treasury he wanted his old House colleague, Nelson Dingley Jr. of Maine, chairman of the Ways and Means Committee. Dingley had gained national prominence and captured McKinley's heart with his strong high-tariff advocacy. The governor invited Dingley to Canton on December 3 for lunch and a job offer, but three weeks later the congressman informed the president-elect that serious health problems prohibited his acceptance of such a demanding position.

As for the State portfolio, even before McKinley could take serious steps toward filling the slot, various newspapers revealed Hanna's Senate ambitions in articles fueled by anonymous figures described variously as "a close friend of Chairman Hanna" or "a gentleman who is as much in the confidence of McKinley and Hanna as any one." This clearly was an orchestrated effort to send up trial balloons to assess the reaction from various quarters. As one of these anonymous sources said, referring to Hanna, "He is not ready yet to begin his career in national politics by entering the Cabinet, but prefers rather to enter the Senate." During a Washington visit, Hanna encountered William Osborne and reiterated his Senate desire. Osborne promptly wrote to

McKinley, "Mr. Hanna has his heart set on going to the Senate." It seems McKinley sanctioned these maneuverings on Hanna's behalf while avoiding any assurances that he would pursue John Sherman for State.

Thus in early December, after consultations with McKinley, Hanna traveled to Washington to meet with Sherman. He was authorized to ask, he said, whether the senator would accept the State Department position if offered. Within two weeks Hanna got a reply: "After full reflection," wrote Sherman, "I have made up my mind to say 'yes.'" The senator asked for a quick decision from McKinley and offered to support Hanna's senatorial aims upon his resignation. "I feel under deep obligation to you for your assistance from years ago and will avail myself of any opportunity to do you a kindness."

In the meantime McKinley pursued his own leading choice for the State portfolio: Iowa's venerable senator William Allison, known as "the sage old pilot of the Senate." It was said that the worst epithet ever hurled at the genial, soft-spoken Allison was "the Old Fox," denoting his ability to outmaneuver the opposition with just the right argument at just the right time. McKinley appreciated his probing intellect and diplomatic skill, not to mention his strong protectionist leanings. But in late December Allison signaled through various friends that he would not take a Cabinet position.

That cleared the way for more serious consideration of the Hanna-Sherman concept. A big question was what the Foraker machine would do with the Senate vacancy. Ohio governor Asa Bushnell, a Foraker man, never seemed inclined to accommodate the Sherman-McKinley-Hanna wing of the party. As early as November, Hanna outlined the plan to Foraker and solicited his help in urging Bushnell to appoint him. The wily politician remained noncommittal. He later said he did not consider Hanna "very well endowed" for the Senate. He didn't even credit Hanna for McKinley's presidential victory, which he suggested was inevitable. It wasn't clear whether these views were genuine or merely cover for underlying political interests.

In any event, McKinley undertook the task of assessing rumors that Sherman's age was eroding his mental acuity. Recalling recent sessions with the senator and getting favorable reports from Sherman friends, he concluded he needn't worry about the man's mental capacity. It was a hasty conclusion based on insufficient evidence—and influenced, perhaps, by his underlying desire to satisfy Hanna's fervent senatorial ambition. Having embraced the idea, though, the governor turned defensive at any suggestion that he had misjudged the matter. He stubbornly wrote to *Chicago Tribune* editor Joseph Medill, "The stories regarding Senator Sherman's 'mental decay' are without foundation and the cheap inventions of . . . evil-disposed or mistaken people. When I saw him last I was convinced . . . of his perfect health, physically and mentally." All the same, he determined to name a strong and trusted man as assistant secretary if Sherman should become secretary. He had in mind his Canton friend Judge William Day.

McKinley offered the job to Sherman on January 4. A day later, Sherman wrote to McKinley, "I have concluded to accept your tender of the portfolio of Secretary of State, and will heartily do all I can to make your administration a success." He suggested that "Hanna is above all others entitled to friendly consideration" as his successor, and he predicted that Bushnell would react favorably if McKinley made his desires known.

Hanna didn't take any chances. He wrote to McKinley on January 13, the day before Sherman's decision was announced, asking him to write to Bushnell quickly so the governor wouldn't have time to ponder other options. In the meantime, Sherman wrote to Bushnell urging "serious and favorable consideration" of Hanna and hinting that any party discord over the matter could harm all Ohio Republicans, including Bushnell when he faced reelection later in the year. He also indicated that McKinley "[would] be much gratified by this compliment to Hanna, to whom he largely attributes his great success in the Presidential election."

But it wasn't clear Bushnell would comply. A prominent Republican from Cleveland told reporters on January 14 that he understood "from a good source" that the Foraker forces anticipated a confrontation on the succession question. "Foraker is determined to prevent Hanna from going to the Senate," he said, "and the fight is going to be a bitter one." By late January the press was reporting that Bushnell had decided to give the post to Ohio attorney general Asa Jones, a Foraker loyalist. Bushnell told Hanna at a political banquet that he could offer no encouragement and wouldn't make a decision until Sherman had actually resigned his seat after McKinley's inauguration. That left Hanna in an agitated state of suspension. But the political pressure on Bushnell—from national Republicans, the Ohio party, and business-men throughout the country—proved too much for the governor to buck, and on February 21 he announced he would appoint Hanna to the Sherman seat. "So strong was the storm," reported the *Washington Post*, "so unanimous was the opinion in favor of Hanna, that the For-aker machine had to bow to the inevitable."

In the meantime McKinley occupied himself with the rest of the Cabinet. After Dingley turned down the Treasury Department, Her-man Kohlsaat called from Chicago. "I have a Secretary of the Treasury for you," he said.

"Who is it?"

"Lyman J. Gage, president of the First National Bank." He was born penniless, got his first bank job at fifteen, and now was widely admired throughout the Midwest.

McKinley asked Dawes to interview Gage about his tariff views and political outlook, and the young entrepreneur reported back that, while the banker opposed tariff rates so high that they fostered trusts and monopolies, he embraced the general protectionist principle and acknowledged that the government's revenue shortfall necessitated higher tariffs. He was a solid gold man. And he was a Republican, though he had voted for Cleveland in 1884 against James G. Blaine, whom he considered unsavory. When word of the Dawes-Gage conver-sation leaked to the press prematurely, causing embarrassment, Gage deftly issued a statement saying he had not received any Cabinet offer, that he would accept one if offered, and that he would feel "no sense of disappointment or chagrin" if no offer came. McKinley liked the way he handled the matter and invited Gage to Canton in late January to offer him the Treasury job. Gage readily accepted.

From the beginning of his deliberations, McKinley wanted to give the War Department to his friend Russell Alger, former Michigan gov-ernor and 1888 candidate for the GOP presidential nomination. A lawyer and wealthy lumber merchant, Alger also had risen to brevet general during the Civil War. He had been a stalwart McKinley man from the start. But there were two drawbacks. His relations with Sherman had been strained since Sherman accused Alger's presidential campaign of buying Southern delegates at the 1888 GOP convention, and he was dogged by accusations that he had vacated his command at a crucial juncture during the war. Alger defended his war record and insisted his command absence stemmed merely from his having missed a train.

Alger moved decisively to patch up his association with Sherman, visiting him for an hour and eliciting Sherman's statement that "it would be very gratifying to him personally" to have Alger in the Cabinet. Later, when reporters asked about his frictions with Sherman, he brushed it off with the words, "Oh, there is nothing in that. . . . Senator Sherman told Senator Burrows to say to Mr. McKinley that it would gratify him exceedingly to see me in the Cabinet."

But for good measure Alger got other friends, including New Hampshire's Senator William Chandler and Vermont's Senator Proctor, to endorse his War Department candidacy. As for the Civil War matter, McKinley decided to let it go, despite an inquiry report that concluded, "There is nothing in the files of the War Department which relieves this serious cloud upon an otherwise excellent and brilliant military career." He considered it too far in the past and too isolated a matter to be disqualifying. On January 29 Alger accepted the post.

McKinley dangled the Interior Department before Joseph McKenna of California, a federal judge who had served four terms in the U.S. House. A bright and conscientious legislator and jurist, McKenna had impressed McKinley during their days together in Congress, and the governor pushed hard to overcome McKenna's concern that giving up his lifetime tenure on the bench would erode his meager finances. He sent Melville Stone to San Francisco for two days of cajolery and later got Los Angeles newspaperman Harrison Gray Otis to press further on the matter.

McKenna finally agreed to visit Canton for a discussion. Over lunch, McKinley said jocularly, "Well, judge, they have been pretty busy with your name lately for a cabinet post."

"Yes, governor, but I don't believe you realize what you are doing."

McKenna felt obliged to reveal that he was a Catholic, which could raise concerns among some about his having jurisdiction over Indian education. But the governor's plan for McKenna would obviate that concern.

"The place I want you for, judge," said McKinley, "has nothing to do with Indian Missions. I want you for Attorney-General."

McKenna was stunned. "Oh, I was misinformed," he said, and accepted on the spot. It was a late change in thinking on the part of McKinley, who had been pressured by Platt to give the Justice Department to John McCook of New York, a prominent corporate lawyer and civic leader. But Hanna disliked McCook, and McKinley decided to offer the New Yorker the Interior Department instead.

For the Navy position, the president-elect had only one candidate: John D. Long of Massachusetts, a Harvard-trained corporate lawyer with a probing intellect and courtly demeanor. A former governor and congressman, he collected friends and admirers wherever he went. One described him as "probably the most popular man in public life in Massachusetts." Stoop-shouldered and gentle, he suffered from intermittent emotional strains. But Long avidly embraced the civic challenge.

For the Agriculture Department, McKinley turned to James "Tama Jim" Wilson (nicknamed for his home county in Iowa), a Scottish-born farmer and agricultural educator who had served in state politics and the U.S. House. Imposing and well-spoken, Wilson was a font of the latest political news and gossip from throughout the West. McKinley also slated a Cabinet position for Maryland's James Gary, a prominent party official from Baltimore and a successful textile executive, whose name had been put forth by numerous Southern interests. But he held back on naming a specific place for Gary pending a final communication with the man he wanted most, Hanna, still waiting to hear about his Senate prospects. He sent Hanna a poignant letter:

It has been my dearest wish . . . to have you accept a place in my Cabinet. . . . I have always hoped and so stated to you at every convenient opportunity that you would yet conclude to accept the Postmaster-Generalship. . . . I have reluctantly concluded that I can not induce you to take this or any other Cabinet position. You know how deeply I regret this determination and how highly I appreciate your life-long devotion to me. You have said that if you could not enter the Senate, you would not enter public life at all. No one, I am sure, is more desirous of your success than myself, and . . . I predict for you a most distinguished and satisfactory career in that greatest of parliamentary bodies.

In light of Hanna's reluctance, McKinley would tender the postmaster job to Gary. Thus, with only Interior still open, McKinley faced two challenges: what to do about New York and what to do about Roosevelt, who seemed out of control much of the time but whose friends wanted him to become assistant navy secretary. The New York conundrum began with Whitelaw Reid, who had been angling for a major position, preferably the State Department; barring that, navy secretary; barring that, ambassador to Great Britain. But Platt hated Reid, whom he considered a sanctimonious meddler alienated from the real world. While McKinley didn't feel any particular need to placate Platt, he had no interest in infuriating him. Besides, though he appreciated Reid's intellect and loyalty, the man talked too much, didn't know his place, and couldn't protect a secret.

The challenge was to bypass Reid without destroying a valuable political friendship. The solution came through a collaboration of intrigue between the governor and Reid's longtime friend, John Hay, who wanted the Court of St. James for himself and had impressed McKinley increasingly with his tact, loyalty, and judgment, not to mention his generous financial contributions. For weeks Hay had encouraged Reid's ambitions in letters to the publisher in Phoenix, where he had gone for relief from severe asthma. But when Reid's prospects narrowed down to nothing, Hay, with McKinley's consent, got Reid's father-in-law, Ogden Mills, to travel to Phoenix to break the news. Hay then drafted a letter for McKinley to send to Reid, designed to put the best possible light on the rejection. "I have ceased thinking of Reid," Hay wrote to McKinley. "He thinks enough about himself for two."

The letter emphasized how valuable Reid was to McKinley and how fervently he wished to employ the publisher's manifold talents. But, alas, he wouldn't risk jeopardizing the man's faltering health. "I feel that

I must reluctantly forego for the present what would have been a great personal pleasure, in the hope that in the future things shall so come about as to make it possible, without fear of injury to your health, that I shall be able to avail myself in some way of your splendid talent and patriotic self-sacrifice." Reid responded amicably but couldn't resist stating that his much-improved health was "certainly better than when I was doing the work that you have distinguished with such praise." But the matter was settled, and McKinley promptly tendered the British ambassadorship to a delighted John Hay.

Things went awry with McKinley's effort to get a New York man in the Cabinet when McCook announced that the only job he wanted was attorney general. With inauguration day approaching, McKinley faced the prospect that he wouldn't be able to assuage Platt, whose New York influence expanded with his recent election to the U.S. Senate. Platt now demanded the appointment of lawyer Stewart Woodford, a former federal prosecutor, who was unacceptable to McKinley.

But the governor had a reserve plan. He had never accepted Cornelius Bliss's early rejection of a Cabinet post, and he sent a string of associates, including Hanna, to plead with Bliss. Platt also weighed in. It worked, although Bliss remained sadly ambivalent even after accepting the Interior post. When a friend offered congratulations, he replied, "I need your sympathy more than your congratulations." But for McKinley it was a signal triumph—and just in time. The Bliss acceptance came a day before the presidential inauguration.

The final assemblage was this: State, Sherman of Ohio; Treasury, Gage of Illinois; War, Alger of Michigan; Navy, Long of Massachusetts; Agriculture, Wilson of Iowa; Interior, Bliss of New York; attorney general, McKenna of California; postmaster general, Gary of Maryland. It encompassed the geographic balance McKinley wanted, with representatives from New England, the Far West, the Midwest, New York, and the South. (While Maryland wasn't quite a Southern state, the Gary designation won approval throughout the region.) Further, most of those named not only were well known to the incoming president but were good friends, including Sherman, Alger, Long, Wilson, and McKenna. He managed to satisfy New York reformers without antagonizing the Platt machine. And all the Cabinet members were men of substantial stature in the eyes of the public, though of course their true abilities would become known only through performance in office.

McKinley enhanced his reputation as an effective executive with the manner in which he went about building his Cabinet. He was a master at tossing out names to assess the reaction of party stalwarts while carefully shrouding his own thinking, then inviting candidates to Canton for interviews or rejecting them based on what he heard. He fulfilled the task with a dispassionate tough-mindedness, demonstrated in his dealings with Reid and McCook. He also ignored the counsel of numerous friends, including Hanna, in rejecting Henry Clay Payne of Wisconsin, a former railroad lobbyist and lumber dealer, when Wisconsin's progressive elements declared him anathema. Hanna had told the governor, "[You may] wipe out every obligation that you feel toward me, and I'll ask no further favors of you, if you'll only put Henry Payne in the Cabinet." McKinley remained unmoved.

Many encountering McKinley for the first time discovered a man far more informed and decisive than they had expected. "I never met a man in my life with whom I was so favorably impressed by a day's acquaintance," said Lyman Gage. Hay, who called McKinley "the Majah" and had supported him financially and otherwise, expected chaos at McKinley's bustling house when invited to Canton for lunch toward the end of the Front Porch campaign. "But he met me at the station," reported Hay to his friend Henry Adams, "gave me meat, and . . . took me upstairs and talked for two hours as calmly and serenely as if we were summer boarders in Beverly at a loss for means to kill time." He was particularly struck by McKinley's inscrutable visage. "It is a genuine Italian ecclesiastical face of the fifteenth century. And there are idiots who think Mark Hanna will run him!"

The final vexing personnel question was what to do about Roosevelt, full of intellectual energy, physical vigor, and often uncontrollable bustle. His tendency to venture into the outrageous was evident in his unrestrained rhetorical attack on William Jennings Bryan and John Altgeld during the previous fall. But his many friends, who adored him for his kinetic force and affectionate ways, unleashed a whirlwind of lobbying in behalf of his desire to become John Long's assistant at the Navy Department. They included Henry Cabot Lodge, John Hay,

Tom Reed, and Maria Storer, a wealthy Washington hostess whose husband, Bellamy, had helped save McKinley from his financial crisis during his gubernatorial days. When many of the same people had pressured Blaine to name Roosevelt his assistant during Blaine's tenure as secretary of state, Blaine had rejected the idea out of hand. "My real trouble in regard to Mr. Roosevelt," he wrote a friend, "is that I fear he lacks the repose and patient endurance required in an Assistant Secretary."

McKinley shared that view. "I want peace," he told Maria Storer, "and I am told that your friend Theodore . . . is always getting into rows with everybody." To William Howard Taft, a young federal appeals court judge who joined the Roosevelt chorus, he elaborated, "The truth is, Will, Roosevelt is always in such a state of mind." But Roosevelt's legions of friends overwhelmed McKinley's skepticism, as did Roosevelt's well-earned reputation as a genuine naval expert based on his authoritative book on naval strategies during the War of 1812. McKinley eventually succumbed to Maria Storer's plea that he give Roosevelt "a chance to prove he can be peaceful."

DURING THIS CABINETMAKING, with reporters following every move, the world got its first expansive look at the private McKinley—the dedicated family man who attended church every Sunday with his wife and mother, who surrounded himself with members of his extended family, who loved taking his "invalid" wife on carriage rides into the country and doted on her whenever he wasn't focused on pressing civic matters. When Ida traveled to Chicago to stay with a cousin and shop at Marshall Field & Co., he wrote her daily. "Everything is going on pleasantly here," he reported on her first day away, "but you are greatly missed I assure you. I hope you will keep well & come back greatly benefited and have that part of your wardrobe provided which was your special mission." A family friend told a reporter that "since Mrs. McKinley is in Chicago he behaves like a new bridegroom separated for the first time from his bride." He went to Chicago himself shortly before Christmas with a resolve "to find rest and change, and . . . to do as little as possible and be as quiet as he can," the *Washington Post* reported. On their last day in Chicago, a crowd of 4,000 well-wishers surrounded the McKinley carriage in front of Marshall Field's and refused to let them move on until the president-elect had shaken several hundred hands. On Christmas Day, back in Canton, the couple dined, according to tradition, with his mother at her modest home.

By the end of the year Ida was feeling so healthy and sprightly that she organized a dinner dance for a hundred guests at Saxton House. Ostensibly to honor two McKinley nieces, the event took on wider significance as a display of her ability to serve as first lady. It featured orchestra music, card games, a ten-thirty supper, and postsupper dancing. The *Repository* reported that "an old-fashioned cotillion was danced by Mr. and Mrs. McKinley," and younger guests "were delighted with the graceful ease with which Mrs. McKinley was able to go through the figure."

On March 1, the day of the McKinleys' departure for Washington, leaden skies brought rain showers before the clouds parted for an auspicious afternoon of bright sunshine. The Major entered his breakfast room at eight o'clock in a lighthearted mood, according to press reports. That night he and Ida entrained for the Washington journey amid upbeat band music and tumultuous cheers from townsfolk, with bonfires throughout the city lighting the night sky. The couple slept on the train and arrived in Washington the next morning refreshed and expectant. They were whisked by carriage directly to their old haunt from congressional days, the Ebbitt House.

That night they were invited to the White House for an informal dinner, though Ida was unable to attend due to fatigue. McKinley arrived at 7:30 and was greeted by the outgoing president in the Red Parlor. Following a "suitable repast" that was "exceedingly simple and in good taste," as one newspaper reported, the president-elect returned to the Ebbitt at around ten. Mrs. Cleveland, upon hearing of Ida's infirmity, sent over a large bouquet of flowers.

The next day was a time of repose and ceremony. When a delegation representing McKinley's college Greek fraternity, Sigma Alpha Epsilon, arrived to present the president-elect with a ceremonial medallion, he was delighted to see Postmaster General William Wilson, an old House colleague from the other party. With his characteristic bonhomie, the governor clasped Wilson's hand warmly and said, "I have not seen you since the storm of last November. Come over by the window where I can see you plainly and make sure you look as you did in the good old days when you were on one side and I on another." At midmorning McKinley and Cleveland went through the customary exchange of courtesy visits, first McKinley appearing at the White House, then Cleveland visiting the McKinleys at the Ebbitt. Neither visit lasted more than a few minutes, as the exchange was merely ceremonial.

The real ceremony was scheduled for the next day, March 4, as the nation honored what had become the greatest ritual of democracy the world over: the inauguration of America's next national leader and military commander.

11

Inauguration Day

LOOMING CHALLENGES OF NATION AND WORLD

President-elect McKinley rose from bed at six on the morning of March 4 and greeted his wife with a jaunty reminder, though she needed none, that this would be her first day as the country's first lady. Around six-thirty he opened the door of his Ebbitt House suite to say good morning to his loyal bodyguards, Daugherty and Gardner. A porter arrived with an armful of wood, and soon a fire was crackling on the sitting-room grate. The hotel prepared a special breakfast of quail on toast, broiled chicken, porterhouse steaks, Spanish omelets, dry toast, hot rolls, wheat muffins, tea, and coffee. The governor took breakfast in his private dining chamber, but Ida ate hers in bed on the counsel of her husband, who wanted her to conserve her energy for the coming inaugural activities.

Thus did the fifty-four-year-old Ohioan begin the day that would see him become the twenty-fifth U.S. president. If weather is augury, the day was auspicious. "Not a cloud cast its shadow over any part of the inaugural proceedings," reported the *New York Times*. For nearly a week the city had filled up with all manner of citizenry—political bigwigs, Republican loyalists, office seekers, ordinary folks hankering for a glimpse of history. Railroad companies estimated that they had brought into the city some 225,000 visitors, and the Baltimore and Ohio line laid down fourteen miles of temporary track to handle excess rail cars. The city's hotels were filled to capacity, and one reporter determined through inquiries at various establishments that they had turned down as many people as they could accommodate. He speculated that the rest found lodgings at boardinghouses or merely alighted wherever they could.

On the way back to his suite after breakfast, McKinley greeted well-wishers in the hotel lobby, then saw his mother making her way through the crowd. He bent down to kiss her and inquired after her health "in the most affectionate terms." At nine-thirty a local barber named Clarence Chaplin arrived with a basin of warm water and fluffy towels to shave the president-elect. Afterward McKinley donned a new suit made entirely of American-grown wool. Shortly past ten he greeted the Senate committee, including Senator Sherman, assigned to escort him to the White House in Sherman's luxurious carriage. The crowds outside were so thick that the carriage could scarcely move, but McKinley's mounted escort—the Ohio National Guard's vaunted Troop A, eighty men atop coal-black chargers—slowly opened the way.

At the White House McKinley received greetings from President Cleveland in the Blue Room. The two men entered Cleveland's presidential carriage, with its four-in-hand team of sorrel horses, and seated themselves according to protocol, with the president-elect on the president's left. To cheers from the crowd, the carriage driver maneuvered the vehicle into the procession scheduled to move up Pennsylvania Avenue to the Capitol. Included in the procession, in addition to Ohio's Troop A, were mounted police, military units, martial bands, the Cleveland Cabinet, and top military leaders. "The ring of nearly 2,000 iron hoofs on the asphalt filled the still air," reported the *Washington Post*. The *New York Times* noted that "Major McKinley was removing his hat constantly in response to the cheering" along the way.

Reaching the Capitol, the presidential carriage stopped before the large bronze doors near the Senate chamber. The two men made their way to the vice president's room, to be greeted by the incoming vice president, Garret Hobart, and others. McKinley asked if Ida had reached the building and been seated in the gallery. Assured that she was well situated, he relaxed, sat down, and chatted amiably with the assembled dignitaries. At 12:18, Cleveland and McKinley walked up the green-carpeted aisle of the Senate chamber, filled with senators, House members, Cabinet officers, and foreign ambassadors. Then Hobart was sworn in and delivered a brief address filled with patriotic pieties and promises to embrace his new duties with humble solemnity. Taking his assigned seat next to Cleveland, McKinley scanned the gallery, spotted Ida, and smiled warmly.

When the Senate chamber ceremony ended at 12:45, those inside were directed through the Capitol's east entrance to the temporary inauguration platform. In the lead was Ida, leaning heavily on the arm of McKinley's newly named private secretary, J. Addison Porter. She wore a purple gown with heavy wraps about her shoulders and a gray aigrette in her snugly fitted bonnet. Then came other members of the president's family, Supreme Court justices, the president and president-elect, members of Congress, ambassadors, state governors, and Cabinet officials. More than 40,000 spectators jammed the Capitol's east grounds to witness the spectacle.

The crowd grew quiet as Chief Justice Melville Fuller and McKinley stepped forward for the brief oath, with McKinley's hand upon a large, gilt-edged Bible, affirming that he would "preserve, protect and defend" the Constitution. Then the new president kissed the Bible, removed his overcoat, and stepped to the lectern to deliver his inaugural address.

Reading from his handwritten text in a strong voice, he said the current "depression in business and distress among the people" required a strict spending regimen along with increased tariff rates. He vowed to call a special congressional session to address tariff-revenue needs and also promised to protect "the credit of the Government, [and] the integrity of its currency." He extolled America's commitment to freedom and equality of rights but acknowledged that the commitment had not always been maintained fully, particularly with regard to black Americans. "Lynchings," he declared, "must not be tolerated." He took a swipe at trusts and monopolies, noting the GOP's opposition to "all combinations of capital organized in trusts, or otherwise, to control arbitrarily the condition of trade among our citizens." He promised "a firm and dignified foreign policy" that disavowed "wars of conquest" and "the temptation of territorial aggression."

McKinley's prose reflected the man—sturdy, direct, devoid of rhetorical flourishes, employing no more words than necessary. Following the speech, the president attended a Capitol luncheon with government dignitaries, and then he and Cleveland returned to the presidential carriage for the ride back down Pennsylvania Avenue—this time with the former president sitting to the left of his successor. Then came a long and boisterous parade past the presidential reviewing stand in front of the White House, an evening dinner-dance at the lavishly decorated Pension Building, and a fireworks demonstration that the *Times* called "one of the biggest displays of the kind ever witnessed here." Ida emerged from the White House for the evening festivities in a gown of silver and white brocade lined with pale blue satin, with a high neck of soft laces and long sleeves finished with lace frills.

The McKinleys reached the Pension Building at 8:40 and moved slowly through the crowd to a private antechamber, where the first couple received special guests, including Mark and Charlotte Hanna and various Cabinet officials. A bit later they appeared on a second-floor balcony to wave to the 5,000 celebrants below. Following about an hour on the balcony, the couple repaired to a private supper room, decorated with masses of American Beauty roses (Ida's favorite), for an intimate meal with close friends. They left the building at 11:30 via the Fourth Street exit and were back at the White House by 11:40. "Shortly after," reported the *Times*, "all the lights [at the presidential mansion] were extinguished."

IT WAS A burgeoning nation, full of zest and optimism, that bestowed the mantle of leadership upon William McKinley on that crisp March day. Not even the 1893 Panic, which still dampened commerce, could seriously erode the American sense of opportunity. The U.S. population had nearly doubled since 1870, to 75 million, with fully two-thirds of the increase coming from native births, the rest from immigration. The industrial era was generating an economic bustle in America that was recognized throughout the world as a rare phenomenon. When Democratic critics chided Republicans during the Harrison administration for fostering the nation's first billion-dollar budget, Tom Reed dismissed the disparagement with characteristic disdain. "Yes," he said, "but this is a billion dollar country!"

The billion-dollar country outpaced all others in steel production, in its timber harvest, in meatpacking, and in the mining of silver, gold, iron, and coal. This fervor of production was pushing America into the world in search of markets. In the thirty-six years leading to McKinley's inauguration, exports tripled, and the country's trade activity now surpassed that of all other nations save Great Britain. What's more, America led the way in the development of life-transforming inventions, including the internal combustion engine, incandescent light, the telephone, steam-powered ocean vessels, moving pictures, radio telegraphy, the phonograph, and more.

America had been from its inception a nation of vast designs, driven by an impulse to consolidate its position across the North American midsection—purchasing the vast Louisiana expanse in 1803, negotiating possession of Florida in 1819, annexing Texas in 1845, acquiring much of Oregon Territory in 1846, and conquering lands in 1848 that would become its southwestern domain. "For nearly three centuries," wrote historian Frederick Jackson Turner in 1893, "the dominant fact in American life has been expansion."

Now, having cemented its existence in the carnage of civil war, the country faced the question of where its expansionist spirit would lead it. Turner, whose analysis of this spirit had brought him national fame, didn't foresee any slackening in America's outward push. "That these energies of expansion will no longer operate would be a rash prediction," he wrote. "The demands for a vigorous foreign policy, for an interoceanic canal . . . and for the extension of American influence to outlying islands and adjoining countries, are indications that the movement will continue."

Whatever course America pursued, and whatever McKinley's national plans might be, nothing took precedence over the need to attack what the *Washington Post* called the country's "industrial distress and financial embarrassment." No one was surprised that the new president's central economic aim would be restoring the McKinley tariffs, which had averaged nearly 50 percent on finished and semifinished imports.

That had been shaved to 42 percent during the second Cleveland administration by the so-called Wilson-Gorman bill, and McKinley believed no economic resurgence could happen until his rates once again prevailed through adoption of something approaching the House-passed Dingley bill of 1895. Besides, the economic downturn had produced a federal budget deficit of 70 million dollars, which also required attention. McKinley's answer was a big increase in import taxes.

But it wasn't clear the Senate would go along. Although Republicans held forty-six seats in the coming session to the Democrats' thirty-four, independent pro-silver elements commanded ten seats. Thus silver Republicans could bolt their party and hold up any tariff bill to get concessions on the currency issue. Godkin's *Nation* speculated that the only way McKinley could get the needed tariff votes was by "doing something for silver." Godkin viewed that as more harmful to the economy than insufficient tariffs, and the danger was punctuated when the silver forces disdained the November election results. "The victory for gold," declared A. J. Warner of the American Bimetallic Union, "is a victory of trusts and syndicated wealth, brought about by corruption and coercion, and not a victory of the people, or for the people, and it cannot last."

But an economic rebound could blunt the silver push, and business developments suggested it might be happening. In November railroads reported significant cargo increases for grain and cotton and also a rise in passenger traffic. A boom was developing in the Indiana energy belt, and idle plants were resuming operations in a number of states. Analysts attributed this in part to a new economic certainty born of McKinley's settled views on protectionism and sound currency. Further, U.S. banks were acquiring large amounts of gold, much of it hoarded during the campaign season as Americans sought protection from the anticipated currency devaluation if William Jennings Bryan were elected. In addition, global gold production was increasing, particularly in the U.S. territory of Alaska but also in Australia, Russia, Mexico, and China.

These pools of capital fueled corporate investment that promised to boost the economy. "No one now doubts that the brighter day is dawning," asserted R. G. Dun & Co., a market analyst, in November.

Two months later it reported that pig iron output grew 12 percent in December and nearly 42 percent since October 1. Coke production increased nearly 89 percent in just three months, while wool sales were moving upward. "Money markets," said Dun, "feel a steady increase in demand for commercial and manufacturing loans."

Business confidence also swelled on news of McKinley's commitment, declared in his inaugural speech, to pursue an international monetary conference designed to get the major industrial nations, now adhering to a strict gold standard, to embrace a responsible bimetallic regimen that would allow for the monetization of silver, along with gold, while ensuring that doing so wouldn't constitute a currency devaluation. Even before his inauguration, McKinley had endorsed the efforts of a special commission under Colorado's Republican senator Edward Wolcott, a strong silver man, to assess prospects for such a conference in various European capitals. Though no doubt sincere, McKinley's approach constituted a shrewd political maneuver. It allowed him to keep the bimetallism issue at bay while the commission's efforts were pending and posed in the meantime little likelihood that European governments would force the issue by embracing the concept.

On his major domestic initiatives—high tariffs but with a nod to reciprocity, sound money with an embrace of bimetallism under international agreement, a clamp on federal spending while recognizing it was a billion-dollar country—McKinley felt comfortably aligned with voter sentiment. On foreign policy, however, voter sentiment wasn't easily discerned because those issues hadn't been aired with any depth during the campaign. And yet the country stood at the threshold of some momentous developments that would shape its global identity in the twentieth century.

First among these was Cuba, the long sliver of an island that stood sentinel over the Caribbean and Gulf of Mexico, two bodies of water that America considered within its sphere of influence. But Spain held on to this Antilles jewel with a tenacity born of its lingering disappointment at having lost its vast global empire—including Mexico and extensive colonies throughout Central and South America—in the nineteenth century. Now all it had left to show for its former glory were

Cuba and Puerto Rico in the Americas, and the Philippines and a few small islands in Asia.

And Cuba was threatened by an insurgency that began in February 1895 with the aim of ripping this "ever faithful isle," as it was called in Madrid, from Spanish dominion and giving it sovereign independence. Spain almost lost the island during an earlier rebellion, from 1868 to 1878, that claimed almost 260,000 lives on both sides. But eventually a new government in Madrid, product of a Spanish revolution that replaced the old absolute monarchy with a constitutional structure, negotiated a settlement with the Cuban insurgency that granted amnesty to its leaders and offered concessions on some grievances. Now the same leaders were back in the fight with a fearsome resolve.

They executed a "scorched earth" strategy of burning croplands and destroying food supplies in hopes that Spain would abandon the fight out of compassion for starving Cubans or perhaps America would intervene to assuage the human misery unfolding just ninety miles from its Florida tip. The rebels controlled the countryside throughout Cuba's impoverished eastern half and pushed westward toward the capital of Havana, causing havoc in population areas dominated by Spanish-born Cubans known as *peninsulares*—mostly military officers, Catholic clerics, and governmental officials—who held sway over Cuba's civic life and remained loyal to Madrid. Spain had nearly 200,000 troops on the island, but they were proving ineffective in thwarting the attack-and-run tactics of the insurgency's 40,000 nimble and brutal guerrilla warriors.

Responding to repeated setbacks, Madrid sent in another 50,000 troops in February 1896 and named General Valeriano Weyler y Nicolau as Cuba's governor and military leader. Weyler fashioned a strategy designed to push the rebels out of the island's more developed western and central regions and force them back into the eastern portions, where they could be systematically eliminated. He split Cuba into military zones, divided by north-south combat barriers of fences, trenches, and soldiers. Then he sought to seal off the zones to rebel activity one by one, pushing the rebels farther and farther east.

It didn't work. Though rebel activity declined, it continued to disrupt the lives of the island's main population areas and thwart Weyler's plan to isolate the rebels. Weyler then made a fateful decision. He established a network of "concentration zones," called *reconcentrados*—towns and localities completely under government control—and forced some 400,000 rural peasants into these militarized camps. The idea was to isolate potential rebel sympathizers and dry up the supplies, intelligence, and manpower that had been flowing to the insurgency. Unfortunately the Spanish military lacked the capacity to provide food and basic human necessities in these camps, and they soon became death traps. By the beginning of 1897 tens of thousands had died from disease and starvation.

The American people and their political leaders watched this unfolding conflict with growing unease trending toward outrage at the brutality of Weyler, who was becoming known as "the butcher." Having such chaos gathering force nearby, and at a location of such crucial strategic significance, naturally raised concerns among American leaders. There also was a trade connection focused primarily on one commodity: sugar. The U.S. Sugar Trust, a consortium of eight major refiners with a big corner on Cuban sugar production, profited wildly when the McKinley tariff bill removed all import duties on sugar. Trade soared. U.S. imports from Cuba, mostly sugar, exceeded those from all other nations except Britain and Germany. Fully 87 percent of Cuba's total exports went to the United States. When the Wilson-Gorman bill eliminated the duty-free policy, it devastated the Cuban economy—and contributed to the turmoil that spawned the insurgency. It was easy to see that Cuba's fate and America's interests were inextricably linked.

Further, the United States had become a staging area for the insurgency. Operating mostly out of Miami and New York City, rebel leaders, many of them naturalized U.S. citizens, raised money and churned out masses of propaganda designed to tilt the burgeoning North American nation toward recognition of the insurgents as legitimate belligerents. Rebel sympathizers in New York, known as the New York Junta, became particularly effective as propagandists whipping up American sympathy for the Cuban rebels. The Junta, in collaboration with its Miami counterpart, also outfitted ships to transport supplies, money, and men to the revolution. Responding to Spanish protests, U.S. officials sought to intercept these "filibustering" vessels, but some got through nonetheless. Of seventy-one missions launched from American shores, only twenty-seven made it to Cuba, but that still rankled Madrid. What's more, when Spanish officials captured these pro-rebel adventurers, they threw them into hellish prisons, where one of them died, and this generated further tensions between Spain and the United States.

President Cleveland harbored little sympathy for the Cuban rebels, whose brutal tactics he disdained. He labeled them "rascally Cubans" and set his policy toward the avoidance of involvement beyond protecting U.S. citizens and property. But popular support for the revolution mushroomed, and in early 1896 Congress passed a resolution, by lopsided margins in both houses, recognizing the rights of belligerency of both sides and declaring that the United States should acknowledge "the independence of Cuba." The issue generated a surge of political emotion, but Cleveland ignored the resolution and the gathering political sentiment behind it. He issued a statement asserting, "The only action now proper is to continue to hold responsible for injuries to American citizens the only government which, so far as appears, has and maintains authority in Cuba." The insurgency simply lacked the standing to merit recognition, he insisted.

After the McKinley election, pro-rebel legislators sought to pressure Cleveland with yet another resolution declaring America on the side of the Cuban rebellion, but it fizzled after Secretary of State Richard Olney warned that, even if the resolution were to pass over a White House veto, Cleveland would ignore it as an unconstitutional encroachment upon the president's foreign policy prerogatives. At the same time, Prime Minister Antonio Cánovas del Castillo of Spain put forth a plan for Cuban autonomy and economic concessions if the rebels would quit the fight. The rebels rejected it, but the action further dampened congressional sentiment for a pro-rebel resolution in the final weeks of the Cleveland administration.

As he prepared for inauguration day, McKinley didn't relish the prospect of inheriting this incendiary situation. His focus had always been domestic matters, as attested by the fact that he seldom mentioned Cuba during his Front Porch campaign. Now he feared war would upend his domestic agenda. Besides, he had seen enough war in his youth to dispel any romantic notions about it. "I have been through one war," he once said. "I have seen the dead piled up; and I do not want to see another."

Whether he could avert hostilities with Spain remained questionable. McKinley told Hay in the months before the inauguration that he hoped a negotiated end to the rebellion could emerge before he took office. He let congressional leaders know that he opposed any resolution on Cuba that would tie his hands and publicly lauded the Cleveland administration for avoiding actions that could "create an immediate ugly situation for the new administration." During his pre-inauguration dinner with Cleveland at the White House, he told his host, "Mr. President, if I can only get out of office at the end of my term, with the knowledge that I have done what lay in my power to avert this terrible calamity, with the success that has crowned your patience . . . I shall be the happiest man in the world."

IN THE MEANTIME other foreign developments suggested that the Cuban crisis eventually would be pulled into a broader context of American strategic imperatives and global ambitions. America's burgeoning economic might was raising inevitable questions about the military power required to protect its commercial interests, and that in turn posed questions about what kind of navy the country would need. A new era was emerging that would test the limits of American expansionism.

One test could be seen in the North Pacific. The Sandwich Islands, now known as Hawaii, was an idyllic Polynesian kingdom that for decades had served as a magnet for Americans—first, traders seeking supplies and respite from weeks at sea; then missionaries worried over the fate of pagan souls; then whaling expeditions; and, finally, sugar interests. By the 1840s, at the height of the whaling era, five-sixths of all ships calling at Hawaii flew the Stars and Stripes, and the sons and daughters of missionaries were becoming increasingly embedded into Hawaii's social elite, sometimes through marriage and childbearing. In 1842 the John Tyler administration declared, with an audacity reminiscent of the Monroe Doctrine, that while America had no designs on the islands it would not accept any other nation acquiring or dominating them.

The U.S.-Hawaiian relationship deepened during the Grant administration with a reciprocity agreement that eliminated duties on various trade items between the two countries. Although America wanted to establish a naval base on the strategically located Pearl River as part of the agreement, Hawaii's King Kalakaua wouldn't cede territorial sovereignty. But he promised he wouldn't grant any "port, harbor, or territory" to any other power, thus ensuring that America would enjoy unmatched influence over the islands and be supreme in "the intimacy of our relations," as Cleveland later expressed it. Though the free-trade reciprocity agreement affected many trade items—mostly agricultural staples from Hawaii and farm implements, animals, lumber, and tobacco from America—the big item was, once again, sugar.

Exporting duty-free sugar into the United States, Hawaii substantially expanded its market share just as demand was exploding through the advent of the U.S. canning industry. Soon nearly all Hawaiian sugar went to the United States, and it amounted to an eighth of all sugar consumed by the country. American sugar magnates rushed to the islands to exploit the free-trade opportunity with the most modern methods and technology. When reciprocity began in 1876, sugar production in the islands jumped 50 percent. By 1881 production was nearly 47,000 tons; three years later, 71,000 tons; in 1890, 130,000 tons. "Plantations became so mechanized," one historian noted, "that they were akin to factories." Profit margins for some plantations reached 50 percent in good years.

Inevitably the money flowing into the islands via the sugar trade generated political power and transformed Hawaii's civic culture. The establishment became fractured. Wealthy white businessmen, although a small proportion of the population, now demanded more influence and privilege within the governmental structure. Native populations encountered increasing difficulty in maintaining their small farms and social position. Old customs and folkways began to wither.

Then came large numbers of Japanese workers to toil on the sugar plantations—nearly 30,000 immigrants between 1885 and 1894, brought in for three-year stints under carefully crafted agreements worked out with the Japanese government. About half remained in Hawaii afterward, however, and this further undermined the islands' old Polynesian culture. Hawaii's population at the time of McKinley's inauguration was about 109,000, with about a third native Polynesians.

Growing tensions within the polity culminated in a new Hawaiian constitution, forced upon King Kalakaua by the increasingly aggressive white establishment, largely merchants, lawyers, clerks, and artisans, who mustered a militia that the king found threatening. The so-called Bayonet Constitution tilted power and prerogative toward the whites and away from native Hawaiians. The king struggled under the new charter to maintain peace between these population groups until his death in January 1891.

His successor was his sister, Queen Liliuokalani, fifty-two at her coronation. A graceful woman of refined tastes and good education, Queen Lil, as she was called in America, also displayed a tendency toward naïveté in assessing people in her official circle. Far more than her brother, she revered Polynesian culture (though she married a Caucasian) and hated the Bayonet Constitution's restraints on royal power. She chafed under it for two years before moving in January 1893 to replace it with a new charter by royal decree. Meanwhile economic turmoil ensued with passage in America of the McKinley tariff, with its duty-free policy toward all imported sugar and generous bounty for domestic sugar producers. That ended the Hawaiian sugar boom—until the Wilson-Gorman bill restored the status quo ante, demonstrating once again the far-reaching impact of U.S. tariff policies.

The white establishment responded to the queen's unconstitutional actions by mounting a rebellion and requesting troops from the USS *Boston*, which happened to be moored off Honolulu. The *Boston*'s commanding officer, Gilbert Wiltse, sent troops ashore, ostensibly to protect American lives and property, but royalists grew nervous when the troops bypassed American residential areas and stationed themselves near the Government Building. This intimidation compelled Queen Liliuokalani to abdicate her throne, thus ending the 1,600-year-old kingdom.

In the middle of all this was U.S. minister to Hawaii John Stevens, a strong advocate for U.S. annexation of Hawaii. Just about everything he did during the constitutional crisis was improper. He made it clear from the beginning that he would not support the queen, though he was accredited to her government, and wouldn't even offer assurances of neutrality. That rendered the troop landing all the more intimidating. He quietly emboldened rebel elements with promises of support. When the rebels pronounced the creation of a provisional government, he quickly extended U.S. recognition, though the provisional entity lacked many elements of a functioning government. He later declared a U.S. protectorate over Hawaii and charged *Boston* forces with the job of defending it.

The new government slowly took root and promptly sent a delegation to Washington to pursue annexation. It arrived on February 3 and eleven days later signed an annexation treaty with Secretary of State John W. Foster. President Harrison promptly sent it to the Senate, where an informal poll of members revealed only lukewarm support. The prevailing attitude in Washington seemed to be that there was no need to hurry the matter.

A month later, five days after Cleveland's second inauguration, on March 4, the Democratic president withdrew the annexation treaty—for "the purpose of reexamination"—before it could even be debated. Cleveland opposed American expansionism generally, and in this particular instance he wanted the government to "stop and look and think," as he put it to Carl Schurz, a leading anti-imperialist of the day. He didn't like the reports he was getting about Minister Stevens, and he particularly recoiled at the thought of his country disregarding native Hawaiian sentiment in pursuing annexation. He sent a retired Georgia congressman named James Blount to investigate the situation and pick up the pieces.

Blount filed a report excoriating Stevens and extolling the queen. This killed annexation as a viable congressional option and raised prospects for a restoration initiative, pushed with considerable energy by Cleveland's secretary of state, Walter Gresham, a preachy moralist outraged by America's involvement in the Hawaiian coup. But it soon became clear that any such action would be disastrous. The provisional government was by now well entrenched; the queen seemed increasingly erratic; and Cleveland had no stomach for military actions that could spill significant quantities of blood. In frustration, the president shoved the issue back to Congress and washed his hands of it.

But it wouldn't go away, and Gresham's pious approach generated partisan emotions on the matter. Republicans now decried the lost opportunity to acquire Hawaii, while Democrats defended the president. The issue took on added intensity with reports that Japan was pursuing claims to the islands based on the growing numbers of Japanese living there. The retired Hawaiian postmaster general, H. G. Whitney, arriving in Seattle on September 4, 1896, reported rising island sentiment for U.S. annexation because of the "growing Japanese trouble," as the *Washington Post* described it. Whitney said Hawaii's Japanese residents now numbered 25,000, about a quarter of the archipelago's population, and they were arriving at a rate of about 3,000 a year. Meanwhile Germany, building a powerful navy to rival Britain's and casting about for colonies, was hovering about the islands with obvious imperial designs.

Two months later, following McKinley's election, former secretary of state John Foster stopped off in Chicago en route from Honolulu to Washington and told reporters that the Hawaiian provisional government would initiate another annexation bid as soon as McKinley was president. He added that "the ultimate fate of the islands, if they are not annexed by the United States, will be annexation by some of the other great powers." Hawaiians, he said, were too divided by class, race, faction, and national identity to govern themselves. By inauguration day McKinley knew that the issue would soon land on his desk.

He knew also that the question would become intertwined with the powerful strategic advocacy of Alfred Thayer Mahan, who had jolted the American consciousness and world capitals with his daring 1890 treatise, *The Influence of Sea Power upon History, 1660–1783*. If Frederick Jackson Turner was the analyst of American expansionism, Mahan was its prophet, heralding the dawn of American Empire and celebrating sea power as the agency of U.S. greatness. His book has been called "probably the most influential work on naval strategy ever written," and throughout the nineteenth century only Harriet Beecher Stowe's *Uncle Tom's Cabin* had more immediate political impact on the country than Mahan's volume.

He was born in 1840, the son of a professor at the U.S. Military Academy at West Point, and early on was beguiled by the romance of the sea. Graduating from the Naval Academy at Annapolis, he saw some Civil War action and then pursued a conventional naval career of sea duty interspersed with shore responsibilities. Reaching the rank of captain at midcareer, he found he didn't much like sea duty. What's more, he wasn't very good at it. A number of ships under his command were involved in collisions, and his rebellious nature, often in protest of perceived wrongs that others considered petty, rankled his superiors. His career was sputtering.

Then he got a job as instructor at the navy's new Naval War College at Newport, Rhode Island. Attacking the subject of military history, and particularly naval history, he produced numerous books and scores of magazine articles that cemented his reputation as the greatest military strategist of the day. His intellectual epiphany was the story of Hannibal, the Carthaginian general forced to invade Rome by land— over the Alps, with elephants, cut off from supplies and information, almost guaranteed to fail—because Rome had gained complete dominance over the Mediterranean. From there he crafted his thesis that naval power is requisite to national expansion, and expansion is requisite to national survival.

His thesis took on added force with the advent of ironclad, steam-powered warships that needed coaling stations in order to ply the waters of the world, protect commercial interests, and keep potential enemies far from home shores. That meant that any great power in the coming century would need to command territory in far-flung regions in order to keep its ships fired up. Great-power status required a great navy and an imperial impulse.

A sterling case in point was Hawaii, situated in the middle of the North Pacific, far from any other commanding sites and hence positioned to dominate a vast expanse of the globe, both sea and land. Any hostile nation that wanted to attack the U.S. West Coast would have to launch the assault from Hawaii, the only truly viable coaling station on the attack route. Thus, by annexing Hawaii America could project its defensive perimeter out into the Pacific, far from its continental shores. But without Hawaii America was vulnerable to any power capable of launching an attack from those strategically located islands. The same was true in reverse. With Hawaii, America could project power far into Asia; any nation that got Hawaii could thwart such U.S. power projection. Thus could Hawaii be seen, wrote Mahan, as "a position powerfully influencing the commercial and military control of the Pacific, and especially of the Northern Pacific, in which the United States, geographically, has the strongest right to assert herself."

That location would be even more vital, wrote Mahan, if the United States built a canal across the Central American isthmus, which he strongly advocated. It would have to be protected on both sides of the isthmus, and Hawaii would be crucial in protecting the Pacific side. But it couldn't be done without big battleships capable of going up against hostile battleships on the high seas. America was building such a deep-water navy, partly spurred by Mahan's earnest advocacy. Underlying the project was a growing awareness in Washington that America was emerging as a global power almost by default, positioning itself inexorably to contend with the world's most powerful nations. That beguiling Central American canal idea was raising questions also, for example, about how it would be protected on the Atlantic side, particularly with Spain's mismanagement of Cuba raising prospects that other European powers could move in to exploit the chaos and seize the strategically located island. The Mahan vision was getting increasingly difficult to resist.

McKinley hadn't given much thought to such matters by the time of his inauguration on the sunny March day that unfolded so smoothly and seemed such an augury of good times. But geopolitical forces were gathering even as he stood on that East Capitol platform and uttered his conviction that "peace is preferable to war in almost every contingency." Nobody could foresee just what contingencies might emerge to test the limits of that thesis.

— 12 —

Taking Charge

THE LEADERSHIP OF ATTRITION

Throughout his career, McKinley nurtured a reputation for holding no grudges and seeking no political revenge. "Never keep books in politics," he advised his friend, Indiana senator Charles W. Fairbanks, meaning don't catalogue the slings and arrows of civic life with the aim of getting even. Better to let it slide and keep foes in mind for future alliances when interests might converge. Still, being human he was susceptible at times to ignoring his own counsel. As Charles Emory Smith, who became a Cabinet member under McKinley, saw it, the president, "with all his equanimity of temper and . . . beauty of disposition, was keenly sensitive to deceptive pretense and justly indignant at malign hostility."

So it was natural that the new president developed a pique toward Illinois senator Shelby Cullom, who had questioned McKinley's integrity in selecting administration officials. "He is hunting for men who are utterly and entirely subservient to him," wrote the Republican senator to a friend, "and a man who has any independence of character has not much show if [the president] knows him to be such." The letter's recipient passed the senator's words on to McKinley, who displayed a certain frostiness when Cullom arrived at the White House one day to press for patronage favors. Sensing the hostility, the senator turned a bit aggressive himself, dismissing one office seeker favored by McKinley as a "jackass."

Without a word, McKinley rummaged through some papers on his desk, pulled out the offending letter, and handed it to Cullom. There ensued a "general overhauling" between the two men, with Cullom complaining about the president's longtime aloofness toward him.

The president softened his tone. "What do you want?" he asked.

When Cullom listed his desired patronage positions, the president granted them all. "The quarrel ended in a love feast," wrote a McKinley biographer. But having granted the favors and patched up the feud, McKinley never thereafter seemed inclined to grant Cullom's wishes on anything. "I always yielded," recalled Cullom later; "in fact, it was impossible to resist him."

Cullom's experience reflected a reality of the McKinley persona: behind his famous magnanimity and bonhomie lurked a resolve to get what he wanted. Many McKinley adversaries missed this powerful trait. They cleaved to a deprecatory notion that the president was a leaf in the wind, blown hither and thither by random gusts of political sentiment or by the latest entreaty from any persistent friend, most notably Mark Hanna. The nation's citizenry meanwhile viewed him as a uniformly kind and thoughtful figure, full of dignity and sympathy for his fellow human beings; always with a carnation in his lapel, which he would remove in an instant whenever he encountered a small child who might like to have it.

Neither of these versions captured the fullness of the man. His closest associates knew he seldom gave as much as he got in any friendship or political alliance. The convivial demeanor masked a calculating political operative who could casually discard people when they no longer had value (while maintaining a florid cordiality toward them) and who sent out subtle signals about lines of intimacy that shouldn't be crossed. "I don't think that McKinley ever let anything stand in the way of his own advancement," his good friend Charles Dick once said, speculating that the Major's sense of personal destiny could be attributed to the acclaim and attentions he had enjoyed since his Civil War days. "He had been petted and flattered until he felt that all the fruit on the tree was his," said Dick, no doubt recalling a previous observation by Benjamin Butterworth, an Ohio congressman who revered Hanna but harbored a wariness toward McKinley. "Why, if McKinley and I were walking through an orchard which had only one bearing tree," Butterworth told a newspaperman, "and that tree had but two apples, he would pick both, put one in his pocket, take a bite out of the other, and then calmly turn to me and ask: 'Ben, do you like apples?'"

These contradictions suggest that McKinley was more complex than many, both friends and foes, perceived. It was Julia Foraker, wife of the Ohio senator and a shrewd political analyst, who wrote in her memoir of "the masks that he wore" in building and projecting his public image. The masks weren't necessarily phony; he *was* kind, patient, dignified, thoughtful, and congenial. But they concealed other traits: his occasional ruthlessness; his desire for distance from people; his unbending resolve; his penchant for operating by attrition, patiently nudging events incrementally to the desired goal, whatever the opposition. Few McKinley intimates understood the man in all of his dimensions.

One who did was Elihu Root, another later McKinley Cabinet member, who perceived that the president's stoic demeanor, his skill as a listener, his reluctance to project any force of personality were tools employed in getting people to do his bidding without quite realizing it. "He had a way of handling men so that they thought his ideas were their own," said Root. "He cared nothing about the credit, but McKinley *always had his way.*"

These traits were all on display at Cabinet meetings in the new administration. The Cabinet met Tuesdays and Fridays at eleven in the rundown White House Cabinet Room. The president usually opened these sessions with an anecdote or story to bring some mirth to the proceedings and loosen up the discussion. No one doubted that McKinley was in charge. "His pre-eminence in the council was unchallenged," wrote Smith. But often the president would withhold his own judgment as he elicited the thoughts of others in order to secure their unvarnished views. And he proved adept at summing up the attitudes of his counselors so the discussion could proceed without misunderstanding. Once he arrived at a decision, he announced it with finality and never looked back, though his pace of decision making struck many as slow and often roundabout.

McKinley early established a resolve to end the congressional supremacy that had marked the government since Reconstruction. That searing episode had clipped presidential power, and since the Grant administration some twenty years earlier no president had managed to serve two successive terms. McKinley knew that presidential success required presidential force, and he worked quietly to reverse the power differential he had inherited from Cleveland, whose agenda was modest and who had accepted the prevailing congressional preeminence.

Foremost among his methods was an effort to maintain consistently cordial relations with influential members of Congress who could thwart or boost his initiatives. Neither Harrison nor Cleveland had devoted much effort toward congressional relations. "This is the first time in eight years," reported the *Washington Post*, "that a President has deliberately sought to treat the Senate with respect."

Never too busy to meet with members who wished to see him, he often called them to the White House for extended conversations on major legislation. Throughout his fourteen years in Congress he had forged harmonious friendships with most key legislators, and he leveraged those connections assiduously in behalf of his agenda. Most often, though, he eschewed strong tactics of cajolery or pressure, relying instead on his time-tested technique of asking questions and listening patiently as his visitors mused aloud about the dynamics of an issue—and as he subtly nudged their thinking to the desired result. But he never hesitated to introduce patronage matters as a sly inducement to getting votes in Congress. And though he seldom employed his veto pen (he vetoed only fourteen bills throughout his presidency), he found that the mere threat of a veto, if used sparingly and deftly, could tip the scales in delicate circumstances and help propel legislation. The result of McKinley's focus on Congress and his approach to congressional dealings was a significant sway over that branch of government. "We have never had a president," conceded Senator Cullom, "who had more influence with Congress than Mr. McKinley."

The new president moved quickly to establish cordial relations with the press, which Cleveland had kept at arm's length. One reporter suggested that newsgathering during the Cleveland years had been akin to "the fashion in which highwaymen rob a stage coach." McKinley sought to eliminate any feeling among reporters that they must pilfer White House information in order to keep readers informed about presidential policymaking. Though he granted few formal interviews and didn't meet with reporters en masse, his top White House staffers, J. Addison Porter and George B. Cortelyou, briefed reporters daily on events and developments. He set aside part of the White House reception room as a journalistic work area, quickly dubbed "Newspaper Row," and insisted that reporters should receive quickly any new presidential speech, message, or communication, along with briefings on inside developments. The aim was to ensure that the American people received a steady flow of White House news—and a strong sense of the president's governmental command. One newsman from the McKinley era later wrote, "While apparently not courting publicity, [he] contrived to put out, by various shrewd processes of indirection, whatever news would best serve the . . . administration." Thus did he enhance his political standing with voters—and his ability to sway Congress.

McKinley also stepped up presidential travel and gave far more public speeches than his predecessors. The aim, as a British diplomat explained after discussing the matter with him, was "to carry out what he considered an important function of his office, viz: that the President and the people should be brought closely together." This burnished his public image and further bolstered his influence with Congress. After his March 4 inauguration in 1897, he delivered thirty-seven public addresses or short remarks during the remainder of that year, seventy-four in 1898, and 108 in 1899. He went on forty speaking tours during his presidency, prompting one academic to write, "No President . . . ever did half as much traveling through the United States." Much of this travel was carefully calculated to sway public opinion on looming congressional initiatives or political deadlocks.

Finally, the president created an unprecedented number of volunteer commissions to study pending issues and report back to the White House with analysis and recommendations. This helped him set the terms of debate and build momentum for action. Further, he displayed a penchant for naming prominent members of Congress to these commissions to demonstrate his regard for that branch of government and gain leverage in subsequent legislative debates. He also liked to place prominent academics on his commissions to highlight expertise and establish commission authority.

None of this was done with any bombast, philosophical musings about managerial principles, or elaborate rationales on why things weren't what they ought to be. Never did he reveal to his Cabinet or friends any underlying outlook on how best to manage a government or accumulate political power. He simply executed his high office in ways designed to maximize his governmental leverage.

THE WORKING QUARTERS at the White House in those days provided little in the way of convenience or efficiency. Indeed the building, a relic of the eighteenth century, displayed signs of decay everywhere: peeling paint and wallpaper, discolored closets, sagging floors, threadbare carpets, faded draperies. Though Congress ignored the need for a major restoration, it had bestirred itself to install some modern amenities, including electricity, steam heating, bathtubs, telephones, even an elevator, which, however, was frequently out of service. The mansion was considered a public building, and sightseers were allowed to mill about its corridors and rooms until two o'clock each day. The place teemed also with office seekers, a bane to presidents since the republic's early days.

At the east side of the mansion's north entrance was a rickety stairway that led to the second-floor executive offices and a long hallway lined with wooden chairs for waiting petitioners. Two offices at the north end of the executive suite housed presidential clerks and typists—numbering, at the beginning of McKinley's presidency, just six (one of whom handled Ida's correspondence). Across the hall was the president's office, the Cabinet Room, and an office for his secretary, along with an oval-shaped library. The presidential office, though spacious, was so unprotected from throngs of tourists and office seekers that McKinley soon turned it into a waiting area and retreated to the Cabinet chamber, where he established himself at the head of the long conference table. He had the space outfitted with stationery, pens, inkwells, and a blotter and positioned before it a comfortable carved-oak swivel chair that served for years as his station of work and for receiving visitors. The room featured a large brass chandelier directly above the president's head, a rolltop rosewood desk, and a marble-topped table dating back to Lincoln's occupancy. A few presidential portraits on the faded walls hinted at the chamber's rich history.

Proceedings and activities in those offices soon revealed limitations of some staff members and Cabinet officials. One problem was Addison Porter, a kind of presidential staff chief overseeing the clerks and typists, organizing the president's schedule, and representing him to the public and to White House visitors. He was a Connecticut newspaper editor and Yale graduate whose family wealth outshone his record of achievement. Porter initially wanted to be ambassador to Italy. Somehow the secretarial slot emerged during a Canton conversation with McKinley, who evidently felt—erroneously, as it turned out—that this Eastern Yalie would bring dignity to his presidential offices.

Effete, foppish, puffed up, and erratic, Porter turned out to be the kind of person McKinley had never liked. A leading journalist of the day, John Russell Young, said that, if encountered in a drawing room, "he would impress you as a poet who had in earlier years written upon spring and the falling leaves and had suffered . . . brooding on the mysteries of the universe." Unfortunately this temperament was ill-suited for maintaining a smooth routine even in McKinley's small executive setting. Yet McKinley's kindliness merged with a tendency of avoidance in messy personnel matters, and nothing was done about the problem.

Fortunately in the wings was young George Cortelyou, who had been retained after serving as Cleveland's stenographer. McKinley made him chief executive clerk, and he soon brought a snap to White House operations. A stern-looking man with a square face featuring penetrating dark eyes and a well-groomed dark mustache, Cortelyou took command of the president's office needs, drafting letters, taking the president's dictation in flawless shorthand, ushering important visitors quickly to the Cabinet Room while time-wasters languished upon the hallway chairs. He also dealt with the press, much to the delight of White House reporters. "I want to tell you how much newspaper men with whom I have talked appreciate your courtesy and value the assistance you give them," one editor wrote. Cortelyou essentially expropriated Porter's job while the unsuspecting secretary soothed himself with the notion that his worth to the president could never be truly challenged by a mere clerk. But Porter's significance faded steadily over time.

As for the Cabinet, attention quickly turned to Secretary of State Sherman, whose declining energy and faltering memory had sapped his judgment and spawned a growing irascibility. Early in his tenure, Sherman described his government's Hawaiian policy to the Japanese minister—and not only got it wrong but stirred questions of U.S. good faith when the administration took a far different tack. He sent to his British counterpart an incendiary letter regarding treaty matters between the two countries that stirred outrage at home and abroad. A London newspaper characterized it as "an explosion of bad manners," while Godkin's *Nation* called Sherman's antics "a mixture of deceit and slang-whanging." During the summer, Sherman gave a series of interviews while on vacation that proved so diplomatically rancorous that William Day, the assistant secretary installed by McKinley to keep matters at State in hand, had to rush back to Washington from his own vacation to clean up the mess. The *Columbus Dispatch* reported, "The chaotic condition of affairs in the Department of State, which has for some time been apparent to the general public, has reached such serious proportions as to cause grave apprehensions to the administration." Some papers inevitably attacked the man who had installed Sherman in the first place. "This is a heavy price to pay for the presence of Mark Hanna in the United States Senate," declared Hearst's anti-McKinley *New York Journal*.

To all outward appearances, McKinley ignored the problem, giving rise to the customary aspersions about his head-in-sand insensibility and habitual inertness. Of course he comprehended the problem fully and viewed himself as dealing with it through his normal decision-making processes of attrition and incrementalism. Whether such glacial approaches could serve his presidency—and the nation—in the face of this kind of crisis remained an open question that soon would be applied to other looming difficulties. But McKinley felt he had filled the void in the meantime with the temperate and astute Assistant Secretary Day. As the *Columbus Dispatch* explained it, "Judge Day will become Secretary of State, so far as it is possible for him to be so without a specific appointment." The paper speculated that after the Ohio senatorial election in early 1898, when Hanna would make a bid for a full senatorial term, McKinley may "then perhaps apply a more radical remedy."

Other Cabinet members also displayed limitations. Despite War Secretary Alger's impressive background in the military, business, and politics, he proved defensive in his dealings with colleagues and seemed a bit of a *poseur*. Competent enough in normal circumstances, he turned bewildered and ineffectual when confronted with difficult or complex problems. When Alger was named to the war post the *Brooklyn Eagle* editorialized, "We tremble to contemplate the outcome of a war conducted under his direction."

Postmaster General James Gary, sixty-three at McKinley's inauguration, seemed beset by ill health, which stirred speculation that his tenure would be short. And Navy Secretary John Long, courtly and sound of judgment, also was slowed a bit by infirmities, though his health seemed to improve during the administration's early months. Still, he needed occasional days off to preserve his stamina and never left his post without fears of what his impulsive assistant secretary, Theodore Roosevelt, would do in his absence. "He is so enthusiastic and loyal," wrote Long in his diary, "that he is in certain respects invaluable; yet I lack confidence in his good judgment and discretion." McKinley, though, developed a fondness for the voluble Roosevelt and his often amusing *pronunciamentos* on matters large and small. Among the president's frequent guests for his afternoon buggy rides around Washington were Day and Roosevelt.

Another favorite turned out to be John Hay, the new ambassador to London, who showered the president with letters notable for three things: a self-effacing tone that seemed tinny from the pen of so accomplished a man; an obsequious quality that could make some men cringe but seemed to strike the president as entirely genuine; and a flow of news, anecdote, gossip, and insight that added up to highly valuable and satisfying information. Complimenting McKinley on his inaugural address, Hay called it "perfect . . . exactly right in what it says and what it does not say . . . a masterpiece from beginning to end." The previous December he had sent the president-elect a gold ring containing a few hairs from the head of George Washington. He wrote, "It is my confident hope and belief that your administration may be not less glorious and the memory of it as spotless, as that of Washington." (He neglected to mention he had given a similar ring to Rutherford Hayes twenty years earlier.) Stopping off at New York on his way to London, Hay wrote of his assignment, "I know the place is far beyond my merits"—despite, he noted in passing, "all the approval your appointment of me has received here and in England." McKinley soon discovered that, along with the letters, he would receive from Hay consistently high-quality work focused intently on the president's highest priorities.

Hay faced a big challenge in patching up U.S.-British relations following a tense standoff between the two countries during the Cleveland years. In 1895, with a navy that writer Rudyard Kipling considered "as unprotected as a jellyfish," the United States audaciously thrust a sword of belligerence at Great Britain, then involved in a dispute with Venezuela over the jungle border between that country and British Guiana. Cleveland intervened on the side of Venezuela, generating serious friction between the two Anglo-Saxon nations. Although the crisis passed without conflict, the episode left the relationship strained.

The president named young Charles Dawes to the high-profile job of comptroller of the currency. Dawes, whose devotion and loyalty to McKinley were boundless, retained his high station in the president's esteem and affection, while his elegant wife, Caro, stirred in Ida a loving regard reserved for a very few. The McKinleys emphasized to Charles and Caro Dawes that they were welcome at the White House at any time and included them in nearly all formal social events. The president avidly sought Dawes's counsel on matters of state and delighted in their rambling discussions on political developments and the people involved in them.

MCKINLEY ASSUMED THE presidency with a clear sense of his premier priority: establishing a Republican-style tariff policy that could meet the country's revenue needs and boost economic growth. Other immediate goals included a push for an international agreement establishing bimetallism in the industrial world (as promised in the GOP's St. Louis platform), annexation of Hawaii, negotiations with Britain and Canada over a number of border and environmental issues, legislation to solidify the country's currency and banking laws, and ending the war in Cuba while somehow avoiding hostilities with Spain.

McKinley initiated his tariff campaign just two days after his inauguration, when he called Congress into an "extra session" to begin March 15. On that date he issued a message to Congress laying out the need to attack the deficit financing of the Cleveland years and end "the remarkable spectacle" of the country's growing public debt "to meet the ordinary outlays incident upon even an economical and prudent administration of the government." The country hadn't seen a budget surplus since the fiscal year that ended on June 30, 1892, said the president, and the previous three fiscal years had produced a combined deficit of nearly $138 million. "Ample revenues must be supplied," said McKinley, not only to halt deficits, pay for legitimate federal activities, and liquidate the national debt but also for all the protectionist purposes he had extolled throughout his career: "to preserve the home market . . . ; to revive and increase manufactures; to relieve and encourage agriculture; . . . and to render to labor in every field of useful occupation the liberal wages and adequate rewards to which skill and industry are justly entitled."

But McKinley's trade philosophy had evolved since he had slumped in his chair at campaign headquarters that November night in 1890 and insisted that his tariff bill from earlier in the year hadn't caused that day's GOP shellacking. There didn't seem to be much limit back then on his desire for ever greater protection for American manufacturers supplying goods to American consumers. But now he could see that America's burgeoning industrialism was outstripping American consumer demand, and prosperity in the postdepression era that would define his presidency would require an active American pursuit of foreign markets. Excessive trade barriers would thwart that development and curtail the country's growth potential. That's why, in his inaugural address, he had touted the "reciprocity principle" in his 1890 bill aimed at "the opening up of new markets for the products of our country, by granting concessions to the products of other lands." It was never clear how these new sensibilities on trade evolved in McKinley's thinking or precisely what spawned them. But the president clearly saw a dawning era with America playing a big role in global trade, nurtured and protected by a powerful navy fueled from U.S. coaling stations around the world. Though not a man of vision, he was a man of perception who saw clearly the major developments of his time.

And that's why McKinley looked with favor upon the bill that emerged in the House Ways and Means Committee under Chairman Nelson Dingley, who also believed that a more moderate approach would serve the country better in the new industrial era of global markets. Throughout the previous winter, his committee, with roughly the same membership, had carved out a measure notable for setting tariff rates that were closer to those of the Democrats' 1894 Wilson-Gorman bill than those of the McKinley measure. As Dingley wrote to a political ally, George Tichenor, "We expect to cut really all our duties considerably below those of the act of 1890." Dingley took his bill to the House floor just four days after Congress convened its special session and pressed successfully for a floor debate lasting only nine legislative days.

On the surface, the House discourse unfolded along the lines of all previous tariff debates. "Free-trade tariffs have always brought calamity to our country," declared Tennessee's Republican representative Henry R. Gibson. Whenever the experiment has been tried, "hard times have been the invariable result." Retorted Democrat Joseph W. Bailey of Texas, "I warn you now that if this bill fails . . . to bring the prosperity which the Republicans have promised, you will not live long enough to obtain a patient audience with the American people upon the absurd proposition that you can make them prosperous by increasing their taxes."

But behind this familiar rhetoric was a subtly shifting debate. Ida Tarbell, a contemporary journalist who studied the tariff issue closely and despised the traditional Republican protectionism, wrote later that the Dingley bill, which cleared the House pretty much as Dingley had crafted it, "was a fairly good protectionist measure, certainly a real improvement on the McKinley Bill. There were fewer prohibitive rates [designed to halt entirely any importation of particular goods], less contradiction, and less quackery." Dingley and McKinley weren't alone among Republicans now favoring greater moderation on rates. They were joined by Rhode Island's Nelson Aldrich, the imperious chairman of the tax-writing Senate Finance Committee. "Industrial conditions in this country," declared Aldrich, ". . . do not demand a return to the rates imposed by the act of 1890." That sentiment guided his committee's actions on the bill, which generally imposed a downward pressure on rates, particularly for chemicals, earthenware, glass, metals, and certain wool products.

But Aldrich, as commanding a figure as he was, lost control of the measure on the Senate floor. Free-silver Republicans, as Godkin's *Nation* had warned, held the balance of power in the chamber and felt no particular loyalty to the party establishment. These senators, whose constituents included Western wool growers and also some Eastern wool manufacturers, set an inflated price for their support on the bill. Taking their cue from the defiant National Association of Wool Manufacturers, they demanded high enough tariff rates to kill all wool imports. More moderate senators argued that such trade barriers would stir ongoing political opposition, and thus tariff policy on woolens would continue to fluctuate, generating policy uncertainty and economic havoc. But the radicals ignored such entreaties and pushed rates on clothing and combing wool to 1890 levels, while rates on carpet wool, which had no foreign competition, reached unprecedented levels.

The Senate version cleared the chamber on July 7 with some 872 amendments pushing up rates favored by a host of interests, which couldn't be ignored so long as the wool lobbies received the full measure of their demands. A subsequent conference committee continued the splurge, boosting rates even further. Traditional free-traders were outraged when Congress approved a conference report that embraced the highest trade duties ever seen in the country. Tarbell, who hated the McKinley bill as a sop to trusts and industrial elites, considered the final Dingley product "more oppressive" than the discredited 1890 legislation.

But the political response across the land turned out to be surprisingly mild. Given the four-year depression that had gripped the nation under a Democratic administration, the voters were ready for an antidote, even one that had been discredited in previous times. Besides, the issue had lost some of its sting in the face of the emotion-laden free-silver cause. Perhaps most significant, the new president enjoyed enough trust and popularity across the country to generate a feeling that he ought to be given a chance to prove what he could do for the country.

Just before four on the afternoon of July 24, McKinley received Nelson Dingley in the Cabinet Room, along with Representative Alva Hager of Iowa, chairman of the House Enrolled Bills Committee, who clasped the formal Dingley document in his hand. Seated with several Cabinet members, the president rose and greeted his visitors, then reclaimed his oak chair to sign the measure, which Porter had placed before him. Though the president had a number of pens at hand, Dingley pulled out a dainty stylus and asked that it be used for the occasion. McKinley readily complied, though he jocularly commented on its small size. Then, dipping it deeply into the inkwell, he appended his signature, inquired as to the date, and then affixed that upon the parchment as well.

"It is just four minutes past four o'clock," remarked Attorney General McKenna, glancing at the clock on the mantel.

McKinley stood and extended warm congratulations to the Maine congressman, who acknowledged the compliment and then departed with Hager.

Though the president harbored some disappointment at many of the law's high duties, he took satisfaction at achieving his first big presidential objective within five months of taking office. And he consoled himself with the view that the measure, by restoring the concept of reciprocity, gave him an opportunity to negotiate trade pacts that would reduce mutual tariffs and open up new international markets to U.S. farmers and manufacturers. The Dingley Act gave the president three avenues of reciprocal negotiation: he could bargain with European countries to get executive agreements on artworks, liquor, wine, and other small items; he could pursue agreements with Latin American nations on tea, vanilla beans, and tonka beans; and he could cut tariff rates on major items by up to 20 percent for five years (in exchange for equal reductions for U.S. goods), so long as those agreements could be reached within two years. They would be subject to congressional approval.

McKinley quickly demonstrated his seriousness on reciprocal trade deals by opening up discussions with the French ambassador on a possible agreement with that nation. He responded to reports that the State Department lacked the resources to act aggressively on the matter by appointing a respected diplomat, John A. Kasson, to a new position of special commissioner, with plenary powers, to pursue trade pacts wherever possible. Kasson, a former Ways and Means Committee member in the House who later served as minister to both Austria and Germany, soon demonstrated his seriousness in pursuing his mission.

Observing the tariff bill's emergence from across the Atlantic, the *London Standard*'s editor concluded the legislation's "ultra-protectionism" would guarantee Britain's continued supremacy in the overseas carrying trade. He foresaw for America political and economic havoc in the form of "further deficits, gold shipments, a fatiguing succession of strikes and panics and fanatics as political saviors." It didn't turn out that way. The country's devastating deflationary spiral that had begun in 1891 had turned around, with raw-material prices reaching their lowest point in 1896 and manufacturing goods beginning a steady rise in value about a year later. This turnaround unleashed a spurt of economic activity, with mining, manufacturing, and farming all contributing potent spurts of productivity and growth. Not even high tariffs could dampen this surge of economic activity. "Wealth of all descriptions began to increase in an unheard of way," wrote Tarbell. Commercial interests quickly credited the president with these favorable portents, and McKinley naturally took pride in what he viewed as the vindication of his decades-long protectionist embrace, though evidence was scant that the new tariffs actually had any impact on the economic rebound. The "business men of both parties not only express satisfaction with the situation," New York's John McCook wrote to the president, "but rightly attribute the results accomplished, to the manner in which you have been able to . . . carry through what was practically an adverse Senate, the tariff legislation."

— 13 —

White House Life

FAMILY, CRONIES, CIGARS, AND POLICY

At a White House reception during McKinley's first presidential year, he walked up to Ida as guests congregated around her and bowed with elaborate courtliness. Then he pronounced in a tone audible to all, "Madam, your party is a great success!" It was a touching gesture—and a phony one. In fact as the date for the event had approached, with much to be done to ensure a social triumph, Ida's health and stamina had collapsed, and she was forced to her bed for rest and serenity. Jennie Hobart, wife of the vice president and one of Ida's most devoted new friends, suggested that the party be postponed, but McKinley wouldn't hear of it. He took command, setting the menu, handling invitations, bringing in entertainment, even selecting flower arrangements. The party was a success, but it wasn't Ida's party.

McKinley's devotion to his wife's comfort and tranquility never slackened as the burdens of the presidency descended upon him. But now he felt a need also to burnish her image as a first lady performing the traditional functions of that prominent role. If that meant putting up an occasional false front, given that she was not always able to perform the role, then he was willing to do so. Jennie Hobart explained that the president took "no end of pains to give her the lion's share of the credit, even when none was due."

The peculiar nature of Ida's condition, which beset her intermittently with various maladies between periods of relative health and calm, made it possible for McKinley to showcase her best times, when the word *invalid* seemed overblown. This confused the public and even some reporters, who had conjured an image of a frail woman confined to a wheelchair and needing constant care. During her first week in the White House, when reporters heard she had gone to a local hospital, they instantly concluded she had been rushed there because of her infirmities. In truth she went simply to visit Russell Hastings, the Major's friend since Civil War days, who was being treated for a fractured leg. At a New York dinner in April, as she was conversing with dignitaries, the mayor's wife suddenly swooned and slumped to the floor. Based on fragmentary information, some reporters rushed into print with the story that it was the first lady who had swooned. Corrections followed the next day.

But if her good days could be made to appear almost normal, the bad days always returned soon enough in the form of exhaustion, muscle fatigue, debilitating headaches, and those sudden seizures that couldn't be explained. The president and family members sought to ensure that the first lady, just forty-nine when she entered the White House, would be defined by the good times. Particularly acute was the need to maintain a shroud of secrecy around Ida's epilepsy. The public wouldn't understand, it was assumed, and would view her as mentally impaired or perhaps even insane.

Ida's family and the White House staff endeavored to accommodate her special needs and remained always ready to snap into action at the first sign of trouble. Charlie Bawsel, the family aide during McKinley's gubernatorial days, visited in May and wrote to his wife with a knowing hint, "Mrs. McKinley had one of her headaches, and you know what that means for those around her." Particularly troublesome for the president was the White House social protocol that required the first lady to be seated at table away from her husband. At an early dinner at the mansion, with Ida positioned across the table from McKinley, the ever-alert Jennie Hobart noticed the president was "anxious to the point of distraction and never took his eyes from her" because of his fear that she may have an epileptic episode.

"Could it possibly offend anyone," the president asked Mrs. Hobart, "for me to have my wife sit beside me?" He feared that strangers seated next to her would suffer embarrassment in the event of an unexpected seizure. Mrs. Hobart assured the president that White House protocol was his domain, and he could change it at will. He did so, and of course some social critics complained that such arbitrariness rendered protocol "a difficult task," as one magazine put it. But most people understood. McKinley was more accommodating in the matter of having the president escort the highest ranking female guest into the dining hall at formal dinners, while the first lady would be escorted behind him by the highest ranking man. The president escorted Ida at his first White House dinner, but it generated so much social confusion that he quickly reverted to the accepted practice. Besides, in these instances—as in receiving lines, which were organized along a similar pattern—he was never too far away under protocol practices to step in if necessary.

McKinley never knew when he would need to step in. During an autumn trip to Massachusetts, Ida seemed in her best health as she greeted friends and strangers during multiple social occasions. She caused a stir by saving a young boy from serious injury or possible death in Pittsfield. As the McKinleys traveled rapidly through town in an open carriage, a number of boys leaped upon the side of the vehicle to get a close-up glimpse of the president. When one began to lose his grip Ida reached down with a thrust of energy, grabbed the lad, and pulled him to safety. One newspaper reported, "He would have fallen under the wheels had it not been for her."

But shortly afterward, during a lunch at the Stockbridge, Massachusetts, home of prominent lawyer Joseph Choate, Ida had one of her seizures. Her face became contorted, and she emitted a kind of hissing sound. The president calmly rose from his seat, walked around the table, and placed a large napkin over her head and face. He then returned to his seat, explaining matter-of-factly, "My dear wife is sometimes afflicted with seizures." The conversation continued and after a few minutes the president once again rose, walked to Ida, and removed the napkin. "Mrs. McKinley," recalled Choate's daughter, "was herself again." This was McKinley's standard response in such circumstances, a ritual routinely accepted—and kept secret—by presidential intimates and even casual friends.

Even in good times, Ida lacked stamina. She could walk down a flight of stairs with the aid of her ever-present cane, but she could not make it upstairs. In the White House, when the temperamental elevator didn't function, the Major would carry her to the second floor. She maintained her place in receiving lines as long as she could, but a chair was always placed strategically behind her, and she frequently retreated to it as her strength waned. At Jennie Hobart's suggestion, she kept a bouquet of flowers in her lap to fend off endless handshaking. She delighted in afternoon drives with her husband, gave luncheons for the wives of diplomats and members of Congress, traveled on presidential trips. But in all of these ventures she needed to pace herself lest the physical burden become too much. More often she kept busy with her ongoing passion for crocheting and knitting slippers, which bolstered many philanthropic causes when she gave them to charities, which then sold them at inflated prices to finance their good works.

The impact of the first lady's infirmity on her temperament also remained intermittent. On rare occasions, she could seem to be almost the charming and lighthearted Ida of her youth, and her "cleverness and wit was given free play," as one doctor noted. She delighted in doing impersonations of prominent people, with an uncanny sense of intonation and dialect. Her wit occasionally was seasoned with just a hint of indelicacy. "When I put Mr. McKinley to bed," she told a Cabinet wife, "I go to bed with him." The Major delighted in the jauntiness that came with her good times. "I'm tremendously glad," he told an interviewer, "that I married a woman with a sense of humor."

What's more, Ida often displayed a candid casualness about her fate. "I always forget that I cannot walk until someone reminds me of it," she once told reporters. Without any hint of self-consciousness, she spoke of her "lameness." She never seemed embarrassed in public settings when limping to a waiting carriage or availing herself of a wheelchair. Nor did she react with umbrage when a lifelong friend named Mary Logan wrote publicly—and provocatively—that some details of Ida's infirmity "can never be told."

But there were also those less endearing traits that accompanied her infirmities—the brittleness, the childlike insouciance, the tendency toward strong opinions on petty matters. Although she relied on young nieces and other relatives who served as White House social assistants, she complained about their youthful socializing. "Young people are always on the go, always out, always coming in late," she grumbled to a friend. She loved card games but hated to lose, and her devoted husband adopted a tactic of booting the game for her peace of mind. Assisting one female friend into her chair at a card table, the Major whispered into her ear, "Mrs. McKinley always wins." A constant concern for McKinley was the "jealous suspicions" displayed by Ida whenever he paid the slightest attention to an attractive woman in social situations. He normally maintained a cool reserve to dampen prospects for embarrassing scenes.

Ida adjusted her life to diminish the likelihood of headaches and anxieties. She avoided the color yellow in her clothing and in White House decor because it unsettled her. She loved blue because she found it soothing. She read magazine articles but avoided books, aside from poetry, because the expanse of words on the page taxed her mental stamina and brought on headaches. She set a fashion trend by wearing small bonnets because they caused less pressure on her head and hence fewer headaches. She wore her hair loosely in what was known as a "shingle bob," which became popular among women who had no idea why the first lady opted for such a hairdo. She took a bedroom facing north to avoid the afternoon sun, another headache source. And she took sedatives before social events to diminish prospects for seizures at such occasions. (None occurred during her White House years.)

Such tactics, combined with the solicitous ministrations of family, friends, and staff, enabled Ida to project the image of a traditional first lady—and, at times, actually perform the role in something approaching a normal way. She demonstrated firmness in serving wine at White House social functions despite persistent criticism from temperance agitators. She introduced afterdinner entertainment to the executive mansion and brought popular music to social events, including ragtime, to which guests danced the cakewalk and two-step. It was inconceivable to both herself and her husband that she should forfeit such a role or relinquish the national standing it conferred. The American people, never fully understanding Ida's enfeeblement, developed an affection for the woman who seemed heroic in serving her husband and nation.

McKinley helped maintain this equilibrium by doting on her as much as possible within the context of his presidential duties. He breakfasted with her every morning at 8:30, devoted his lunches to her whenever he could, and played cards with her into the evenings when social obligations didn't intervene. When he planned to work late, which he did often, he soothed her to sleep by reading aloud from the Bible before returning to his office.

He also devoted time and attention to the medications sent to her by an absentee New York doctor named J. N. Bishop, who attempted to calibrate the proper medicine based on letters from the president regarding Ida's latest symptoms. It was a questionable medical approach and reflected poorly on both doctor and husband. "I have decided to make a change in her medicine," the doctor wrote to McKinley during the 1896 campaign, "and this change I hope, will help her to control and overcome the attacks that you tell me trouble her." But Bishop often felt he wasn't getting sufficient information to make his calibrations. "Pardon me for saying," he wrote at another time, "that I feel I am treating her under a good many disadvantages, one of which is the lack of information that I have before me in regard to her physical and nervous condition." He explained that some medications work for a time but then lose effectiveness and must be changed. McKinley often wanted continuation of medicines that had worked in the past, even when Ida's condition worsened. Early in his presidency, he wired Bishop, "Bottle of medicine just received, not the same as the one preceding, please send the old medicine." The doctor's assistant replied that actually it was the same but he would "forward another supply, as you request, and trust that it may be satisfactory." The exchange reflected the inherent ineffectiveness of long-distance treatments—and perhaps also the futility in thinking such medications could improve Ida's condition.

AS MCKINLEY SOUGHT to meld his complex personal life with his presidential duties, it helped that he had no hobbies that pulled him away from the White House. "The president has taken a notion to horseback riding," reported the *Washington Post* early in his presidency, and he even borrowed a mount from Nelson Miles, the army's commanding general. But he soon gave it up in favor of walks and carriage rides, which afforded greater opportunity for conversation and also for taking Ida along. He didn't play golf, though he told an interviewer, with characteristic diplomacy, that he supposed it "was a very good game for the people that liked it." Never had he developed a zest for fishing or hunting, but he did like croquet, which kept him at the White House and near Ida.

He spent abundant time with family members who flocked to the executive mansion for extended periods, and he attended services every Sunday at the Metropolitan Methodist Episcopal Church on C Street. Since Ida disliked going out on Sunday mornings, the president often attended church alone, occupying Ulysses Grant's old pew.

Besides his family and matters of state, McKinley's only real passion was politics and the men embroiled in the game. He loved to sit back with cronies over cigars and exchange stories from the colorful past or probe the intricacies of looming political battles. After one intimate White House dinner for Cabinet members, he brought out a box of Cubans made to fit the tastes of the emperor of Austria, "who likes his cigars long, fat, and strong," reported the *Washington Post*. Fully eight inches long and an inch and a half in diameter, they cost two dollars apiece. But they burned down so slowly that the men had consumed only about half the cigars when they were called to rejoin the ladies.

The elements of McKinley's life came together particularly during his many travels outside Washington for speeches, ceremonial appearances, and vacations. Ida always traveled with him, along with numerous family members and government officials, and he could easily combine his attention to her with socializing, crony conversations, and work. In the spring he traveled to New York to help dedicate the Grant Monument and then to Philadelphia, where he extolled the virtues of George Washington before the Society of the Cincinnati. In June he addressed the Philadelphia Manufacturers Club, where he urged patience as he struggled to steer the country toward more prosperous times. "The distrust of the present will not be relieved by a distrust of the future," he declared, to applause. "A patriot makes a better citizen than a pessimist."

Also in June the president traveled to Nashville to give a speech at the Tennessee Centennial Exposition, and in early July he enjoyed a brief respite at Canton, including attendance with Mother McKinley at services of the First Methodist Episcopal Church. In late July he began a six-week working vacation that took him to Vermont, New York, Pennsylvania, and back to Canton. Along the way he visited the Lake Placid, New York, grave of abolitionist John Brown, a martyr to some and a villain to others; thus did the president demonstrate the strong antislavery sentiments he had absorbed at his mother's knee. He also spent a few days on Lake Erie aboard Hanna's luxurious yacht. The McKinleys returned to the White House in mid-September but within ten days were off again on the Massachusetts trip.

DESPITE HIS PERIPATETIC ways, the president pressed ahead with his 1897 initiatives, in particular (aside from the tariff) bimetallism and Hawaii. In mid-April he named three envoys to represent the United States in a proposed conference to fashion a mutual commitment of major industrial nations to "a fixity of relative value between Gold and Silver as money," as John Hay described it in a memo. McKinley demonstrated his seriousness by putting the commission under the leadership of Colorado's Republican senator Edward Wolcott, a convivial and eloquent orator characterized by the pro-gold *Times* of London as having "an almost religious view of the relations between gold and silver." The president also named pro-silver Democrat Adlai Stevenson, former congressman and vice president during Cleveland's second term, and Charles J. Paine of Massachusetts, a wealthy industrialist and noted yachtsman who was known as a sound-money man but who supported bimetallism when it was embraced by major European powers.

Wolcott had traveled to Europe the previous fall in a quasi-official capacity to assess interest in bimetallism and had returned with optimistic reports, though London's *Times* speculated that he might have "mistaken personal courtesies for evidence of sympathy with [his] object." The paper expressed skepticism about his "temperament of an enthusiast." With no plenipotentiary powers to negotiate outcomes, the commission set out to persuade foreign governments to participate in the proposed international monetary conference. The commission would score a success if it got Britain, France, and Germany to embrace a bimetallism conference. A truly big win would be getting Britain to resume silver coinage in the mints of India (which had discontinued silver coinage some time earlier) and persuading the Bank of England to keep a portion of its reserves in silver.

At McKinley's urging, the commission stopped first in Paris, where it was expected the French would seek to tie bimetallism to a demand for lower tariffs on French goods. But the president had insisted that the commission's work must be regarded as "entirely separable and distinct" from tariff policy. That created complications, exacerbated by French desires to hold back until it was clear whether Britain would be on board. But Wolcott persisted, and the result was a conditional understanding by mid-June: the two countries would open their mints to free silver coinage at a ratio with gold of 15½ to 1 if other nations, particularly Britain and Germany, followed suit and if Congress and the French Parliament approved.

Next stop was London, where the ever-diligent Hay already was on the case and where the House of Commons previously had expressed an interest in pursuing a multination bimetallism regimen. Hay asked Lord Salisbury, the venerable and compelling prime minister, if that resolution still expressed the government's sentiments. "He answered," Hay reported to Washington on May 20, "without hesitation in the affirmative." Salisbury also said Britain certainly would send delegates to a bimetallism conference if it could be organized. But when asked if Britain would reopen the Indian mints, Salisbury couldn't offer unbridled encouragement. There was "a considerable division" in Parliament, he said, and even the cabinet was "not entirely of one mind" on the matter. Interviewing other cabinet officials and opposition leaders in Parliament, as well as top journalists, Hay discovered deep feelings on the subject. The editor of the *Times* said there was "absolutely no possibility of any cooperation of England in the establishment of bimetallism."

But upon the commission's arrival in early July Hay pressed ahead, buoyed by Wolcott's congenital optimism. He got the commissioners an audience with Queen Victoria at Windsor Castle and a session with the full British cabinet. At a later high-level meeting, with the French ambassador present, Salisbury asked the Americans and French to collect their thoughts into a memo so he could study them in detail. In a letter to McKinley dated July 16, Hay said the British now seemed to understand that the Americans and French were united on the issue and took it seriously. He anticipated that Britain soon would demonstrate its own seriousness. Hay also reported that Wolcott made "an admirable impression. His whole heart is in the work, but his manner is refined and conciliatory." In his own back-channel letter to McKinley, Wolcott waxed optimistic. "The whole situation," he wrote on August 6, "is most promising and marks a distinct advance since my last letter."

The next day the British announced an extended delay on the issue while the government consulted with officials in India. And on October 11 Hay got word from Chancellor of the Exchequer Sir Michael Hicks Beach that the Indian government was "dead against" any silver coinage and remained intent on pursuing a strict gold standard. Further, the Bank of England announced its adherence to gold. Hicks Beach told him, Hay reported to McKinley, "that whatever might be the personal wishes of the members of the Government they could do nothing else, in face of the unanimous opposition of the business world and of the Indian government."

That killed any prospect for an international bimetallism agreement. Although some pro-silver legislators felt McKinley could have put himself forward more forcefully on the issue, the episode reflected his inclination to nudge events along from behind the scenes. No one close to the issue questioned his commitment to the party's bimetallism platform pledge. He pulled to the effort serious men with well-known sympathies for the silver cause. He kept himself thoroughly informed on developments through back-channel reports from Hay, Wolcott, and his ambassador to France, Horace Porter. At crucial points he issued directives on how his people should proceed.

But when the effort fizzled, he wasted no time on laments. Already he had urged Congress to create a commission to tighten the nation's domestic monetary system, and the House quickly responded with a bill, though it languished in the Senate through the special session. Meanwhile, with the price of silver falling and no prospect for shoring it up with an international agreement, the president moved inexorably toward a commitment to gold. Burgeoning global commerce rendered it imperative that America coordinate its policies with those of other big trading nations, which were moving toward a gold basis. As the president said in Cincinnati on October 30, "It should be our settled purpose to open trade wherever we can" and to "strengthen the weak places in our financial system." One weak place was the ambiguity on monetary policy, which McKinley now set about to address. He was assisted in the effort by a spike in global gold production, from $205 million in 1896 to an estimated $240 million in 1897—and a further estimated rise to $300 million by 1900, according to the director of the U.S. Mint. That would let McKinley pursue a gold policy without fear of constricting commerce.

ALTHOUGH MCKINLEY'S VIEWS on Hawaii congealed early, he sought in typical fashion to shroud his outlook. "Of course I have my ideas about Hawaii," he told a representative from the islands, "but consider that it is best at the present time not to make known what my policy is." In fact he agreed with Mahan, Roosevelt, and Lodge that acquisition of Hawaii represented a geopolitical imperative, though their martial tub-thumping left him cold. He intended to reverse Cleveland's general hands-off policy and bring about the annexation.

Within a week of his inauguration, he discussed the issue with former secretary of state John Foster, the country's leading diplomatic "handyman," as Chauncey Depew called him, and Maine's Republican senator William P. Frye, a leading annexation advocate. The president expressed sympathy for their views but said he wouldn't pursue the issue while the tariff bill was pending. Frye reported the conversation to Hawaiian envoy Francis Hatch, whose job was to bring about annexation as quickly as possible. Hatch promptly advised his government, "We ought not to take any chance of antagonizing Pres. McKinley, or giving him any idea that we are arranging a programme for him."

But wheels were turning. When Hatch's wife paid a courtesy call on Ida, McKinley showed up to extend his respects. Shortly thereafter, Hanna appeared at Hatch's residence to offer assurances that annexation would be pursued in due course. He asked Hatch to visit him after talking to the president, although Hatch had had no hint of any presidential summons. Sure enough, the invitation soon arrived, and McKinley received Hatch, along with his colleague William O. Smith.

The president seemed totally engaged as he peppered his guests with questions, demonstrating a detailed understanding of the issue and a sympathy toward his visitors' aims. While emphasizing that domestic matters such as the tariff must come first, he expressed "a great interest" in Hawaii and added, "As soon as some of the pressure is off, I hope to have an opportunity to take this matter up." The president asked if Honolulu preferred an annexation treaty, which would need a two-thirds vote of the Senate for ratification, or a legislative approach, which would require only a simple majority of both houses. The Hawaiians said it didn't matter to them, so long as it could be done quickly. The president replied, "I don't know but what I may come to that."

Hatch immediately went to the Arlington Hotel to see Hanna, who reiterated the administration's interest in annexation and launched into a highly informed discussion of the political intricacies surrounding the issue. Hatch reported to Honolulu that Hanna would be highly valuable when the time came, but "unfortunately, he is going to be the judge of that point." The envoy equated Hanna's interest with a strong presidential desire for annexation. He wrote to his government, "Everything is coming along very nicely here."

For McKinley, the issue was being handled precisely as he preferred—largely through backroom maneuverings. He knew House Speaker Reed vehemently opposed annexation—and American expansionism in general—and he needed Reed's parliamentary dexterity on the tariff bill. So why complicate the tariff effort by raising Reed's ire unnecessarily on annexation? The Hawaiians too, with assurances of McKinley's ultimate support, felt comfortable with the pace of things.

But suddenly Japan emerged as a complication. The European Hawaiians had risked bloodshed and their own safety in wresting civic dominance from the native population. Now the islands' growing Japanese population, under the protective patronage of Tokyo, was threatening to upend their cherished oligarchy, not to mention their dream of U.S. annexation. Japan demanded that Hawaii's native Japanese be granted voting rights as a protection against governmental and civic abuse. This would overwhelm white dominance, and the threat increased every month as more Japanese were brought in by profit-seeking immigration companies. Japanese voting-age males now numbered 18,156, compared to 17,663 Chinese (who weren't agitating for the franchise), 13,148 native Hawaiians, and 8,275 whites. In January 1897, Hawaiian president Sanford Dole informed Hatch in Washington that "the Japanese are still piling in." Hatch concluded, "A stand must be taken somewhere or abandon the country to Japan."

That also occupied the mind of Japan's impetuous foreign minister, Count Okuma Shigenobu, a Meiji politician much in sympathy with his country's rising wave of jingoist fervor. Okuma felt the Western powers had exploited and slighted Japan long enough, and the country should demonstrate its strength and resolve—particularly, as he saw it, in enforcing the terms of Japan's 1886 immigration treaty with Hawaii. Tensions mounted between Japan and Hawaii when the Honolulu government rejected hundreds of migrants who arrived on Hawaiian soil, according to Hawaiian officials, without having been appropriately vetted. Japan heightened tensions further by announcing in January that it was sending its biggest warship to Honolulu.

McKinley's Navy Department responded by developing a plan for a possible war with Japan. On April 2 Secretary Long ordered the armored cruiser *Philadelphia* and two smaller warships, under the command of Admiral Lester Beardslee, to Hawaii. News reports, based largely on dispatches from the U.S. consul general at Honolulu, Ellis Mills, informed the American public that Japan's "peaceful invasion" of Hawaii threatened to pull the islands out of America's sphere of influence.

In April Okuma ordered Japan's ambassador at Washington, Hoshi Toru, to inform Secretary of State Sherman that Japan opposed any U.S. annexation of Hawaii because it would undermine Japanese interests in the islands. This was highly provocative, but Sherman apparently missed its significance and neglected to inform the president. When it finally did sink in that Japan considered its Hawaiian interests superior to American interests, it became clear that the issue had reached a new level of intensity.

Navy Secretary Long quickly concluded the crisis necessitated quick annexation. Administration officials also concluded they must fortify the U.S. military presence around the islands. Illinois representative Robert Hitt, chairman of the House Foreign Affairs Committee, held hearings that produced a consensus, according to the *Chicago Tribune*, that the "invasion of the Asiatics can be stopped only by immediate annexation." And McKinley asked Roosevelt to identify all warships that could be sent quickly to Hawaii. The assistant navy secretary ordered Admiral Beardslee, now at Hawaii with four combat ships, to remain there indefinitely.

Tensions heated up in late April and into May with three developments. First, Hawaii angered Japan by rejecting more immigrant workers brought in by the immigration agencies. Then McKinley signaled his thinking on Hawaii by filling the post of minister there with Harold M. Sewall, who was quickly slammed by Godkin's anti-expansionist *Nation* as "a Jingo and annexationist." Sewall, son of the Democrats' 1896 vice presidential candidate, promptly confirmed Godkin's characterization by revealing that he got the post following "a full avowal to the President of my belief that annexation was the only course for the United States to pursue." The president asked Sewall for a quick report on the Hawaiian situation upon his arrival there. Finally, aboard the Japanese warship *Naniwa*, when it arrived at Honolulu, was a special emissary, Akiyama Masanosuke, who declared that Hawaii's rejection of Japanese immigrant workers violated an 1871 Hawaiian-Japanese treaty. He vowed to investigate the matter and hinted his inquiry could spawn indemnity demands.

This latter development greatly unsettled Washington. Hawaii predictably would reject any indemnity claims, which could give Japan a cause for coercion. The crisis seemed to be gathering urgency. William Day at State asked John Foster to draft an annexation treaty, which he did quickly by dusting off the 1893 document he had fashioned for President Harrison, later annulled by Cleveland. When he handed Day the proposed agreement, rolled up for easy grasp, Day lifted it aloft and declared, "And that little roll can change the destiny of a nation." McKinley wasn't ready yet for altering destiny, but he kept the document within easy reach in anticipation of the right moment for action.

The president's measured approach inevitably irritated the feverish Roosevelt, who delivered a speech at the Naval War College on June 2 that included the word *war* sixty-two times and extolled the virtues of martial zeal. "All the great masterful races have been fighting races," he declared, "and the minute that a race loses the hard fighting virtues, then . . . it has lost its proud right to stand as the equal of the best." He said a strong military was necessary to fend off wars that inevitably beset the weak. In a letter to Mahan, Roosevelt dashed off what he would do "if I had my way": annex Hawaii "tomorrow" or establish a protectorate; build the Nicaraguan Canal "at once"; build a dozen new battleships and send enough of them to Hawaii "to hoist our flag over the island, leaving all details for after action"; and push Spain out of Cuba "tomorrow."

McKinley would never embrace Roosevelt's impetuosity, of course, but he was coming around to the New Yorker's vision of America in the twentieth century. "I suspect that Roosevelt is right," he told his friend Lemuel Ely Quigg, a New York congressman, "and the only difference between him and me is that mine is the greater responsibility."

His responsibility took on greater urgency on June 7 when the administration received three disturbing dispatches from Honolulu that reported Japanese demands on Hawaii, sent by Okuma in Tokyo: indemnities for the rejected immigrants; guarantees that future immigrants would not be turned away; extensive Japanese rights throughout the islands, including voting rights; and a requirement that Hawaii respond to the demands immediately. On June 8 Sherman forwarded the dispatches to the president with a terse note, reflecting that he hadn't lost his critical faculties on this one: "Respectfully submitted to the President. This paper and the two enclosed are of extreme importance."

Washington developments unfolded rapidly. On June 8, after meeting with Roosevelt and others, McKinley decided to get the treaty signed and sent to the Senate for ratification. On June 10, Long cabled Admiral Beardslee, "Watch carefully the situation. If Japanese openly resort to force, such as military occupation or seizure of public buildings, confer with Minister and authorities, land a suitable force, and announce officially provisional assumption of protectorate pending ratification of treaty of annexation." On June 16, after McKinley and Sherman returned from their Nashville trip, Sherman and the Hawaiian diplomatic commissioners signed the treaty. In sending the treaty to the Senate, McKinley wrote that annexation, "despite successive denials and postponements, has been merely a question of time." It was "not a change," he emphasized. "It is a consummation." On the same day Sherman told Japan's minister Hoshi that the annexation language abrogated terms of past treaties between Japan and Hawaii, though he didn't anticipate any loss of rights for Hawaiian citizens and residents. On June 17, Hoshi recommended to Okuma that Japan send a fleet to Hawaii "for the purpose of occupying the islands by force." Okuma replied, "It is too late."

Okuma was right. Unless Japan wanted war with the United States, it would have to accept the inevitable. On three occasions during the tensions Japan asked for support from Great Britain, which disavowed any vital interest in the matter. Japan then sent three further protests to the U.S. government, with an escalation in forcefulness of expression, protesting against any harm annexation could bring to Hawaii's Japanese residents. Responding to each, Sherman dismissed Japanese concerns so airily that *The Nation* was moved to write, "The sum and substance of the whole correspondence is that we snap our fingers at Japan." The magazine added there was "no such thing as a right to annex a country, and that Japan, if its interests are affected, has just as much right to prevent our annexing as we have to annex."

True, but the exercise of that anti-annexation right would bring war, and Japan wasn't prepared for war. By sending his annexation treaty to the Senate, knowing full well that the matter couldn't be settled in the chamber for months and probably not at all in 1897, McKinley signaled that the United States *was* prepared for war. For good measure, the administration leaked to the press the substance of Admiral Beardslee's orders in the event of Japanese provocations. The *Washington Post* headline told the story: "TO HOIST OUR FLAG; How Japan's Interference in Hawaii Will Be Checked; Instruction Sent to Beardslee; The Islands to Be Seized at Once if Any Aggressive Action Is Attempted."

On July 15, the Senate Foreign Relations Committee reported the annexation treaty to the Senate floor without amendment. The vote was 6 to 2. Already measures had been introduced in both houses for annexation through legislation rather than through treaty, as a hedge against the possibility that the treaty could run into trouble in the Senate. It was understood that the annexation treaty would slide over to the next session of Congress, set to begin in December. In the meantime, in late July Japan accepted an offer from Hawaii to enter into arbitration to settle all disputes between the two countries regarding indemnity claims and Japanese rights on the islands. American officials had urged the Hawaiian government to settle those outstanding matters as Congress grappled with annexation. By fall Japan's aggressiveness began to wane, and by year's end it had relaxed its strident immigration policies and withdrawn its protests on assurances that the United States would ensure that legitimate indemnity claims would be honored.

It would take many months before annexation would be complete, but U.S. actions on the matter throughout 1897 represented a significant departure in foreign policy. Though the acquisition process was often messy and, to some, morally questionable, the country had stripped away any regard for international niceties in its pursuit of its first overseas colony. It is noteworthy that, during this delicate time (prior to his first Annual Message in December), McKinley never hailed the Hawaiian acquisition in public statements or speeches. There is no record that even within the councils of government he extolled the strategic significance of annexation in the kinds of stirring words that fell from the lips and the pens of Roosevelt, Mahan, and Lodge. But as his comment to Quigg attests, he saw the Hawaiian opportunity in precisely the same terms. And he leveraged his own wiles and the full powers of his office to bring it about, risking diplomatic censure and even war. The same expansionist zeal that had driven the explosive development of Ohio early in the nineteenth century and the inexorable conquest of the North American continent over subsequent decades now animated this son of Ohio at the dawn of the new century. For McKinley, this spirit clearly was more a matter of instinct than philosophy, but that didn't lessen its significance as a force of history.

Probably no nation understood the underlying significance of McKinley's actions more crisply than Great Britain, the world's most powerful and extensive empire. The *Times* of London suggested this would not be an isolated policy initiative. "Will America pursue the colonizing course upon which she has now entered?" asked the paper. "President McKinley tries hard to represent the case as wholly exceptional, but the forces tending in an opposite direction are very strong." Added Britain's ambassador to Washington, Sir Julian Pauncefote, in a dispatch to London, "The most important act of the present administration, involving a change of policy as regards the acquisition of territory outside the Union, has just been consummated by President McKinley."

— 14 —

Cuba

"THE STILLNESS OF DEATH AND THE
SILENCE OF DESOLATION"

I n April 1897, during a presidential trip to New York, McKinley met with the legendary Carl Schurz in the president's Manhattan hotel suite. Schurz had stirred the American imagination with his extraordinary life: youthful partisan in the 1848 Prussian Revolution; wounded in that rebellion and banished from his native land; Civil War service in his adopted country as U.S. minister to Spain and Union field general; postwar Wisconsin senator and Hays administration cabinet official; and now one of the country's most implacable foes of American imperialism. John Hay considered him a kind of "wonderful land pirate, bold, quick, brilliant, and reckless."

In his earnest way, Schurz expressed concerns to McKinley over rumors that the president might nominate a strong annexationist as minister to Hawaii. The president dismissed the concern. "Ah, you may be sure," said McKinley, as the two men shook hands, "there will be no jingo nonsense under my Administration. You need not borrow any trouble on that account."

Not surprisingly, Schurz recoiled when McKinley later gave the Hawaii portfolio to the feisty imperialist Harold Sewall. And he was astonished on June 17 when the president sent his Hawaiian annexation treaty to the Senate for ratification. The next time the two men met, Schurz pressed McKinley on the matter, getting increasingly emphatic as he sensed that the president didn't seem to recall the previous conversation.

"Yes, yes, I remember now," the president finally said. "You are opposed to that annexation, aren't you?" He sought to assuage the Prussian with assurances that the treaty wouldn't get Senate consideration during the current session and would be fully debated before any votes were taken. Schurz wasn't assuaged. He thought the president lacked either a sense of direction or a commitment to forthrightness. More likely, the two men held different views on what the foreswearing of any "jingo nonsense" meant. For Schurz it meant opposition to any kind of expansionism, even peaceful annexation; for McKinley it meant pursuing his emerging expansionist agenda in a measured and responsible way, without rabid rhetoric or reckless adventurism. But the president also wanted to buy time as he sought to move events systematically toward his goals with as little friction as possible. Anticipating Schurz's opposition, he sought to delay that eventuality until he could fortify himself on the issue. Of course, when it became clear that incrementalism couldn't counter Japan's diplomatic belligerence, McKinley quickly produced an annexation treaty to get the Japanese to back off. He could be bold when necessary.

But his instinct for incremental decision making took on immense urgency in another foreign policy challenge that threatened to burst into a full-blown crisis. That was the war in Cuba between the island's Spanish overlords and its insurgent forces.

Almost from inauguration day, McKinley found himself in a political box on the issue. He wished to avoid war with Spain while pursuing a delicate diplomacy aimed at getting the fading Spanish Empire out of the Caribbean. If feasible at all, this would require time and flexibility. But Congress, increasingly anti-Spain and pro-insurgency, threatened actions that could deprive the president of both time and flexibility, and popular sentiment was moving in tandem with Congress. Meanwhile the business community, a key McKinley constituency, opposed any actions that might upend the country's incipient economic recovery.

At the foundation of the president's thinking was a subtle shift in outlook between himself and his predecessor. Cleveland, sympathetic to Spain and averse to those "rascally Cubans," favored Spain's continued possession of Cuba, albeit under a system that granted to the island a significant degree of autonomy. This was not surprising given Cleveland's general anti-expansionist sentiments. If America harbored no serious ambition to expand its regional influence, then the best prospect for regional stability rested with the status quo. After all, an insurgent victory could generate a power vacuum that might lure to the region other European nations more threatening to U.S. interests than the hollow Spanish Empire.

McKinley, on the other hand, sympathized with the rebels more than with their Spanish rulers. In part this reflected the humanitarianism that undergirded his family's abolitionist convictions before the Civil War. Beyond that, the new president questioned whether autonomy could succeed, although he didn't rule it out and would support it if the warring factions could agree on an autonomous structure. But he didn't think that could happen, given Spain's apparent inability to crush the rebellion within any realistic time frame. Hence the insurgents would shun autonomy in favor of full independence as the war sapped Spain's financial health and political stability. In the meantime the conflict threatened growing chaos near American shores, with U.S. citizens increasingly abused and U.S. interests challenged. That was becoming untenable for America.

Further, McKinley believed America could fill any Caribbean power vacuum, preserving the Monroe Doctrine and meshing the country's expanded regional influence with his other global ambitions: a canal through the isthmus of Central America, the acquisition of Hawaii, a growing merchant marine, expanding naval fleets with coaling stations around the world, and reciprocal trade agreements generating markets for American products. Spanish Cuba didn't figure into this vision.

Neither did war with Spain. In his cautious way, McKinley focused initially on side issues that nettled U.S.-Spanish relations. One was the fate of U.S. citizens languishing in Cuban jails. Alabama's Democratic senator John Morgan insisted Cuban prisons were "crowded" with Americans forced into intolerable conditions, "without a place to lie down or a bench to sit upon, and with all of the inconveniences that it is possible to conceive of." But Maine's Republican senator Eugene Hale declared that only twelve U.S. citizens were incarcerated in Cuba, three or four of whom were expected to be released soon. No one knew what the precise number was or the circumstances of their arrests.

Most troublesome was the case of Ricardo Ruiz, a Cuban dentist who had become a naturalized U.S. citizen in 1880 but had lived in Cuba continuously since then. Arrested and charged with blowing up a train in the rebel cause, he had been placed in solitary confinement, where he died from brain injuries that Spanish authorities insisted were self-inflicted. His death generated sensational coverage in U.S. newspapers, much of it pointing accusatory fingers at Spanish officials. On March 9, Ruiz's widow arrived in Washington with her five children to seek help in securing financial redress from the Cuban government. Since Cleveland had agreed to a joint Spanish-American commission to investigate the death, McKinley used it as the impetus to send a commissioner to Cuba who also could investigate the broader Cuban situation. This served two hallmark McKinley purposes: methodical information gathering and resistance to pressure for quick action.

Another vexing issue was the filibustering operations by Cuban partisans—notably, the so-called New York Junta—seeking to ship money, manpower, and weapons to Cuban insurgents from American soil. Both Cleveland and McKinley had embraced the principle, constantly pressed by Madrid, that the United States had a responsibility to interdict such missions, and most were thwarted. But for Spain, caught in a bloody war it couldn't seem to win, America's antifilibustering efforts never seemed sufficient. In early April, Secretary of State Sherman issued a statement saying that U.S. citizens "pursuing lawful occupations in a lawful way" could expect full U.S. protection. But those who, "under cover of American nationality, engage in hostilities against Spain must accept the consequences of their own acts." At the same time, the administration urged Spain to protect American property and investments from destruction and confiscation brought on by the war.

In late April, McKinley appointed William J. Calhoun of Illinois as commissioner to Cuba to investigate the Ruiz death and "make a very comprehensive inquiry into the condition of affairs on the island," as the *Washington Post* reported. Calhoun, a square-faced trial lawyer with a tidy white mustache, had known McKinley since their days together at Ohio's Poland Seminary. He left Washington on May 8 for a month-long stay in Cuba, and McKinley hoped his inquiry would freeze U.S. political activity on the issue. But New Hampshire's Republican senator Jacob Gallinger introduced a resolution calling on the president to protest the anticipated execution of General Juan Ríus Rivera, a captured rebel leader whose fate was foreshadowed with characteristic anti-Spanish umbrage by Hearst's pro-insurgent *New York Journal.* "It is time," the senator exclaimed, "that this war is ended, it is time that the great nation of Spain should be given to understand that this is the close of the nineteenth century, and that war should be fought upon a higher plane than that of butchery, of crime, and of rapine."

Leading the opposition was the round-faced, white-haired George F. Hoar, Republican of Massachusetts, whose courtly demeanor and outward conviviality gave way to pugnacity and spitefulness whenever he became aroused in political discourse, which was often. Hoar relished his role as one of the Senate's most impassioned anti-imperialists.

"Now, what have we here?" he asked, then answered, "In the first place we have a statement of what we think Spain is going to do, and that is all. It is a prophecy, a guess, a prediction—"

"It is a fact," interjected William Allen, Populist from Nebraska. Hoar ignored him and continued: "A surmise, a conjecture; what we suppose she is going to do; not a fact, but a prophecy."

Mr. ALLEN: Does the Senator from Massachusetts profess himself to be so ignorant as not—

Mr. HOAR: I do not yield to that kind of an interruption.

Mr. ALLEN: As not to know that there is an intention on the part of the Spanish Government to summarily destroy this man's life?

Mr. HOAR: It is prophecy; and the Senator from Nebraska, when he has a little more experience, will, perhaps, discover what he does not seem to have learned, that prophecy is not an exact science, and that no event which has not happened can be accurately described as a fact.

Ignoring Hoar's lecturing tone, the Senate passed Gallinger's resolution unanimously, with Hoar and Maine's pro-Spain Eugene Hale abstaining. Then Alabama's Senator Morgan introduced a resolution declaring that "a condition of public war exists between the government of Spain and the government proclaimed" and pledging America's "strict neutrality between the contending parties." This was a backdoor effort to get America into a war with Spain, in the view of the scholarly Alvey A. Adee, second assistant secretary of state. In a memorandum to Secretary Sherman, promptly forwarded to McKinley, Adee wrote, "A 'recognition of belligerency'—as the issuance of a formal proclamation of neutrality is generally styled—is not a middle course,—it would rather be a stepping stone to intervention." That's because it would impose more severe obligations of neutrality than the country faced under its prevailing bystander stance, in which the Cuban insurgency was viewed as merely an internal Spanish matter. This new position, argued Adee, would give Spain rights of search and interdiction on the high seas in order to enforce America's stated neutrality. That in turn "could scarcely fail to provoke a *casus belli* which would precipitate . . . [an] offensive and defensive alliance with the Cuban insurgents."

That's precisely what McKinley wished to avoid. But the Senate on May 20 approved Morgan's resolution, 41–14, with eighteen members of McKinley's own party voting aye. In the debate before the vote, McKinley's allies argued that the Senate should stand aside pending Calhoun's report. But a particularly telling argument came from Maryland's Democratic senator Arthur Gorman, who said he supported the measure only because the administration wasn't adequately protecting American citizens and diplomatic officials in Cuba from the war's lethal chaos. When he referred to "their failure," Senator Hale interjected, "Failure by whom?"

"Failure by the executive branch of the government: by the President of the United States and the Secretary of State," Gorman replied.

McKinley immediately saw a dual threat. One was the resolution itself, which reflected a potentially troublesome current of popular sentiment. But he knew it would be thwarted in the House when it encountered the massive bulk and boulder-like tenacity of Speaker Reed, who despised foreign adventurism and dominated House procedures.

The president knew Morgan's resolution would die a quiet death in Reed's chamber.

But he perceived far more political danger in allegations that he wasn't protecting Americans caught in the Cuban vortex. Even before the Morgan vote, McKinley instructed the State Department to solicit telegraphic reports from top consular officials throughout Cuba. These later formed the basis for a May 17 presidential message to Congress revealing that between 600 and 800 American citizens on the island "are in a state of destitution, suffering for want of food and medicines." McKinley asked Congress to appropriate $50,000 to assist the beleaguered Americans, and the Senate voted the appropriation unanimously within eighteen minutes of receiving the president's message. The House followed suit a few days later. "The policy of the Administration in reference to Cuba," opined Whitelaw Reid's *New York Tribune*, "is not likely to be criticized, as was that of its predecessor, on the score of vacillation or indifference to the rights of American citizens."

On June 8, Calhoun returned from Cuba and promptly reported to Judge Day and the president. On the Ruiz matter, Calhoun said the precise cause of the dentist's demise probably would never be learned, but Spanish authorities had detained him illegally and therefore were responsible for his death. In an extensive memorandum, Calhoun explored all aspects of the war, including its devastating effect on U.S. trade and investment, the havoc unleashed by General Valeriano Weyler's pitiless *reconcentrados* policy, and prospects for a palatable outcome. Traveling from Havana to Matanzas, Calhoun had encountered areas of total destruction. "Every house had been burned," he wrote, "banana trees cut down, cane fields swept with fire, and everything in the shape of food destroyed." He saw "children with swollen limbs and extended abdomens," caused, he was told, "by a want of sufficient food." The entire island was "wrapped in the stillness of death and the silence of desolation."

Calhoun bolstered McKinley's suspicion that the insurgents likely wouldn't accept anything less than full independence and that Weyler couldn't produce a military victory. But the propertied classes, fearing a dire fate if the masses upended the traditional power structure, would fight independence with relentless ferocity. It wasn't clear precisely what outcome McKinley wanted, but he now embraced fully the idea that Spain had to end the war as quickly as possible and that America was justified, based on national interest and humanitarian principles, in pressuring Spain to change policy and negotiate a settlement with the rebels. He issued a diplomatic note, delivered to Spain's U.S. ambassador, Enrique Dupuy de Lôme, protesting Weyler's "uncivilized and inhumane" policies "in the name of the American people and . . . common humanity" and demanding that Spain conduct its war under "military codes of civilization."

The president then turned his attention to two crucial personnel matters: what to do about Cleveland's consul to Havana, Fitzhugh Lee, and whom to send to Madrid as U.S. minister to Spain. Lee, a plainspoken former Confederate brigadier whose bloodlines connected him to the famous Lees of Virginia, made little effort to hide his pro-insurgent views. Madrid harbored a strong antipathy to the man that exceeded only barely the antipathy felt by President Cleveland, who viewed his reports as dogmatic and slanted. A rotund figure who habituated Havana boulevards and salons in white linen suits and Panama hats, Lee relished his role in the thick of an unstable diplomatic situation. Cleveland urged McKinley to fire the consul, but the new president feared Madrid would interpret such a move as weakness. Besides, unlike Cleveland, he appreciated Lee's blunt assessments from the war-torn island.

Selecting a minister proved more daunting. "What am I going to do about the Spanish mission?" the president asked during a March conversation with John Hay and Henry White, an experienced diplomat who had served at U.S. legations in Vienna and London. Extending his hands outward in frustration, he declared, "I must have a trained diplomatist there." The president asked White to take the post, but he declined, citing personal reasons. Former secretary of state John Foster also declined.

The president faced a deadline in formulating his policy toward Spain, which meant he needed his own minister in place relatively soon. He told his friend Seth Low, president of Columbia University, that he was "desirous to adopt every possible measure to bring about a change" in Spanish-American relations before the December start of the next congressional session, when lawmakers would demand a coherent and aggressive strategy on Cuba. He urged the Madrid portfolio upon Low, but he demurred. So did prominent lawyers Elihu Root of New York and Jacob Cox of Ohio. The president even considered Whitelaw Reid, whose selection would enrage Tom Platt. But Reid wasn't interested.

The president finally settled upon Stewart Woodford, sixty-one, of New York, the man he previously rejected when Platt put forth his name for a Cabinet post. But Woodford seemed a good fit for the Madrid mission. He had maintained amicable relations with all New York factions through a career that had included brief stints as a U.S. congressman and his state's lieutenant governor, as well as a six-year tenure as a U.S. attorney. Conscientious and well-spoken, the bald-headed Woodford cut a notable figure, with bushy white eyebrows and droopy white whiskers that gave him a kindly but sad-eyed appearance. McKinley found him to be competent in executing his delicate portfolio but also a bit defensive in needing constantly to clarify his actions at length. On June 16 Woodford wired his response to McKinley's job offer: "You have done me great honor. I accept and will try to justify your choice." Hurrying to Washington, he received detailed instructions from McKinley, along with a request that he send the president intermittent back-channel missives to keep him well apprised of unfolding developments. Recognizing the extreme difficulty of his mission, Woodford wrote to the president on his way to Madrid, "I remember your personal injunctions to be patient, courteous, kind and firm. I will try to carry out your wishes. But I cannot too deeply impress upon your mind my serious apprehension that my efforts will fail."

He arrived in Spain on September 1 to find civic chaos, accentuated by the August 8 assassination of Prime Minister Antonio Cánovas del Castillo. Though the assassin was an anarchist with no apparent tie to the Cuban conflagration, his act deepened the country's sense of crisis. Spain was governed by an oligarchy of wealth that dominated local governments, the legislative Cortes, and the ruling cabinet. Atop that structure sat the monarch, Austrian-born Maria Cristina, the Hapsburg widow of King Alfonso XII. She served as queen regent, occupying the throne until her son, Alfonso XIII, reached the age of sixteen in 1902. In the meantime the queen regent sought to maintain peace between the governing Conservatives, strong-willed nationalists who viewed victory in Cuba as a matter of Spanish honor, and the reform-minded Liberals, more inclined to seek a negotiated settlement through some kind of autonomy. Prime Minister Cánovas had shown no intention of softening his bellicose approach after installing the brutal General Weyler as head of the Cuban effort and fostering the cruel tactics that had caused so much anguish and anger in America. Cánovas's inflexibility was reflected in a brusque response to McKinley's diplomatic note, issued just four days before his assassination.

The queen regent favored the Conservatives in hopes they would bring about a military victory—and also with the knowledge that her aroused public was in no mood to give up the fight or bow to American pressure. Indeed a show of weakness in the face of adversity could stir the proud nation to revolution and even upend the monarchy. Maria Cristina tied her government's fate, and her son's, to the cause of war. She installed Cánovas's war secretary, General Marcelo Azcárraga Palermo, as the new prime minister and kept the Liberals at bay. Hannis Taylor, Woodford's predecessor in Madrid, told his replacement that "popular feeling [throughout the country] is very bitter against the United States" and that the queen regent struggled with "the quandary of not wishing to offend us and yet trying to keep in touch with the local popular feeling."

Woodford perceived her quandary when he presented his credentials to the queen on September 13. "I read it in her face and manner," he wrote to the president, adding that she carried herself with a "pleasant and agreeable" demeanor. Five days later Woodford spent three hours with Spain's foreign minister, Carlos Manuel O'Donnell y Abreu, the duke of Tetuan. The minister read aloud to the duke extensive passages from his letter of instruction, crafted by McKinley himself before Woodford's Washington departure. Immediately the foreign minister could see that his country now faced a new and more threatening United States.

In friendly but firm tones, the McKinley document outlined America's dark concern about a nearby conflict that brought to the United States "a degree of injury and suffering which can not longer be ignored." Thus Spain must seek an end to the war as quickly as practicable by crafting "proposals of settlement honorable to herself and just to her Cuban colony and to mankind." The president issued a veiled threat by suggesting that, if his efforts to foster peace proved fruitless, he would face "an early decision as to the course of action which the time and the transcendent emergency may demand." That could mean, at the least, U.S. recognition of the insurgency's belligerency rights. Woodford told Tetuan that McKinley wanted a response and evidence of Spanish compliance by November 1.

The minister reported to Washington that the duke was "courteous and temperate" in the discussion and afterward demonstrated unfailing cordiality toward him. But the man seemed "deceived" about the likely success of Weyler's Cuban offensive and Dupuy de Lôme's Washington diplomacy. Woodford wrote to the president, "I felt compelled to assure him, frankly and so plainly that there could be no misunderstanding, that my government could not stand idly by during any further indefinite time, but that Spain must convince us . . . that she could and would put the war in the way of prompt and certain settlement or devise some way by which the good offices of the United States could be exerted to that end."

Studying the meaning of McKinley's statement, Spanish officials took heart in the fact that the president had made no financial demands to indemnify Americans harmed by the war, not even Ricardo Ruiz's family. (Woodford wisely had chosen not to complicate his diplomacy at that point with such demands.) The Americans had couched their position in courteous language and had refrained from any stark ultimatum. A government consensus emerged that Spain could keep America at bay without sacrificing national honor—and buy time for military success—if it could fashion a minimally acquiescent response.

In the meantime Woodford concluded he could soothe the diplomatic situation and place his country in a favorable light by releasing the essence of the McKinley statement to the press. He was taken aback when both McKinley and Tetuan rejected the idea, particularly since he already had provided a summary to a *New York Journal* reporter who had been dogging him. McKinley wasn't pleased, as he wanted to preserve his freedom of action if Spain rejected his diplomatic formula. Spanish officials were so nettled by the leak they threatened to expel the *Journal* reporter from the country. Silenced publicly, Woodford provided private briefings to Western diplomats in Madrid in an effort to fend off any anxiety in major capitals over U.S.-Spanish tensions. In long conversations with the ministers from Britain, Russia, Germany, and France, he outlined the American position in extensive detail, emphasizing that America had no interest in acquiring Cuba. Then he listed the health hazards posed to Americans, particularly of yellow fever, by the unsanitary conditions in war-torn Cuba; described the consequences of the sugar trade interruption and other commercial blockages; and detailed the enormous losses suffered by U.S. citizens "in their persons and property," amounting to "very great sums."

He pointed out that Cuba, with a population of less than 1.8 million, had fielded an insurgency force of probably fewer than 40,000 men, and yet Spain couldn't suppress the rebellion with an army of more than 200,000 trained soldiers and an expenditure of some $300 million. Thus, he argued, Spain "cannot crush the rebellion within any reasonable time." He carefully avoided any detailed suggestion of how peace should be restored but emphasized that America stood ready to extend its good offices toward a true system of autonomy (akin to Canada in the British Commonwealth) or, failing that, Cuban independence.

Woodford's disquisitions contributed to a growing feeling in Europe that Cuba's fate belonged to Spain and the United States. On September 23 the *Washington Post* reported that, among European capitals, only Vienna would oppose U.S. intervention in Cuba (presumably because of the queen regent's Hapsburg heritage). "Spain," contended the *Post*, "has little to hope from European powers if the United States should interfere in behalf of Cuba." Hay reported from London that British prime minister Lord Salisbury asserted no British interests in Cuba "except commercial ones, and . . . he would look with favor on any policy that would restore tranquility and some measure of prosperity to Cuba."

In late September came a powerful development: the queen regent boldly responded to the American pressure by asking Práxedes Mateo Sagasta, leader of the Liberals, to form a government. This meant a new policy based on a June 24 Liberal manifesto advocating a division between the counterinsurgency campaign and efforts to fashion a new Cuban government under a substantial grant of autonomy. "Senor Sagasta is a very shrewd politician," Woodford informed Washington. "I . . . think that he has really come to believe that civilized methods of warfare and quite liberal autonomy are the only possible methods by which Spain can retain . . . a hold on Cuba."

Sagasta installed as minister of colonies a prominent Liberal figure named Segismundo Moret y Prendergast, an England-educated foreign policy expert—"honest and earnest," as Woodford described him— who had advocated Cuban autonomy since 1891. Had Spain embraced his reform proposals before the war's outbreak, claimed the manifesto, the country "would have averted the disasters and prevented the horrors of the present insurrection." Woodford attributed the change to McKinley's carefully calibrated actions. "I have reason to know," he wrote the president, "that the Queen Regent was told [by European leaders] that the demands of our Government were so moderate and our cause so just that the public opinion of Europe would hardly justify continuance of the policy and methods of the warfare in Cuba."

Wasting no time in recalling Weyler, Sagasta replaced him with General Ramón Blanco y Erenas, a veteran military man whose star had dimmed after his unsuccessful efforts to put down a separate insurrection in the Philippines. But Blanco's mandate in Cuba was not to quash the rebellion, as Weyler had failed to do, but to soften the military effort in ways designed to bolster the pursuit of autonomy. On October 6 Sagasta committed his government to pursuing such a system even as the military effort continued. McKinley endorsed the new policy by sending to Madrid a private cable saying, "President McKinley will endeavor to induce the insurgents to accept autonomy, and if they refuse he will do his utmost to put an end to agitations, and to prevent filibustering, as he believes now that Capt. Gen. Weyler is recalled, Congress will support this policy."

But Sagasta and Maria Cristina were walking a treacherous path, caught between the rising American power and crosscurrents of nationalist opposition in both Spain and Cuba. As the *Washington Post* editorialized, "Senor Sagasta . . . must be controlled by the prevailing sentiment in Spain. This is anti-American to the last degree." The paper described the Spanish as "a hot-blooded, sensitive race" who believed the United States had "given aid and comfort to the insurgents, and that any efforts which we may now put forth to end the war are purely in the interest of the Cubans." In Cuba, meanwhile, the Spanish elite—the creditor class of some 350,000 islanders, which owned nine-tenths of Cuban property—feared that under autonomy it would be swept away by the island's 1.15 million non-Spanish Cubans, many of them abjectly poor and uneducated. "They believe," reported the *Post*, "that they will have to struggle for the maintenance of society and civilization, and the prospect appalls and maddens them." Riots in the streets of Havana and attacks on Liberal newspapers gave testament to these fears.

In mid-October, the Cuban insurgents rejected autonomy, which enraged Spain's Conservative elements. One newspaper urged "energetic action to crush the rebellion by force of arms." But the Liberal government pressed on in hopes that its system of autonomy, when finally crafted and announced, would gain majority support. Later that month Sagasta's ministry replied to the McKinley communication with a 1,000-word statement, expressed in gracious language, that accepted the friendly U.S. offices in the effort to end the Cuban war, cited Weyler's recall as evidence of good faith, and promised a complete home-rule government in Cuba. But the statement turned the tables a bit in urging the United States to step up its antifilibustering efforts as a demonstration of its own good faith. Woodford, writing to McKinley, called the response "a great moral victory" obtained through the president's "firmness and courage." In a subsequent note, the minister expressed satisfaction that the Spanish ministry had acted quickly enough that McKinley could incorporate these positive developments into his Annual Message to Congress in early December.

But as details of the Sagasta plan emerged, it stirred discontent in both Spain and Cuba. In a series of letters to the president, Woodford reported that Spanish public opinion had settled into "acquiescent, but not enthusiastic, approval"; then that it had become "still acquiescent, but even less cordial than last week"; and then that it seemed "to grow less and less cordial toward the United States." Austria's ambassador to Madrid described Sagasta's government as precarious and said "elements now in opposition would be strong if they could be consolidated."

Nevertheless Sagasta and the queen regent continued their push for amicable relations with the United States. Woodford reported that in receiving him and his wife, Maria Cristina had asked anxiously about McKinley's view of her reforms. "She then added," wrote Woodford, "that she hoped my President would be pleased." He continued, "I believe that she is sensible and is honestly trying to do the best she can under most difficult circumstances."

Meanwhile Fitzhugh Lee reported from Havana that opposition to Sagasta's reforms had congealed into a local defense organization composed of businessmen and the managerial classes. "Not an autonomist in their ranks," wrote Lee, "and with the firemen, who are armed too, number some 25,000 men." He added, "I am not certain whether they can be kept under control of the Palace authorities." Suggesting this civic anger soon could be turned against vulnerable U.S. citizens and diplomats, Lee recommended that McKinley send a warship or two to Havana to protect Americans if necessary. "My scouts . . . report," he wrote the following week, "that nothing would result from the presence of our ships, and that they would be received in the spirit they were sent, viz., as messenger of peace and protection to life and property."

AS 1897 NEARED its end, McKinley certainly understood the implications of his calculated but perilous actions in inserting the United States into Spain's colonial crisis. In doing so, he may have unleashed a course of events that could end the Cuban war, establish a new status for that troubled island, and cement an ongoing peaceful association between America and the fading Iberian power. But it also could place his country on an inexorable path to war. Woodford, from his vantage in Madrid, suggested the question of war or peace for America hinged now upon "the success or failure of the [Spanish] Cabinet program in Cuba." McKinley, in his usual reticent way, never responded to that thought. But he commanded little or no control over events in Cuba, and hence the path upon which he had set his country may have been beyond his control as well.

Still, McKinley didn't succumb to discouragement or alter his usual calibrated incrementalism. He viewed executive decision making as akin to a vast chessboard upon which he would move the pieces slowly and deliberately, after careful rumination on how one move could affect subsequent moves, both his own and his opponent's. He defended this approach in a conversation with a prominent congressman, who recounted the president's words to the *Chicago Tribune* under a grant of anonymity: "I know that the people of this country from one end to the other are getting impatient because we do not move faster, but I am convinced that prosperity is here and that war is the only thing which will prevent its continuance. It would be easy to free Cuba by a war, but to do it without one, to satisfy the people, and keep us in the high road to prosperity, is a thing which cannot be done in a day. That is the problem which confronts us, and we must solve it slowly but surely."

McKinley held fast to the idea that America under his leadership could effectuate a happy solution to the Cuban carnage without being drawn into a war with Spain. But his actions since summer signaled unmistakably that he was prepared for war if the peaceful approach failed to produce the speedy outcome he had demanded in the name of his country. As *Collier's Weekly* summed up the president's message to Spain, it was "tantamount to saying, Make peace in Cuba yourself, or we shall feel constrained to make it for you."

15

Year-End Assessment

CHALLENGES IN OHIO, THE NATION, AND THE WORLD

O n September 2, 1897, thirty-six years after the start of the Civil War, President and Mrs. McKinley traveled to Fremont, Ohio, for a reunion of old soldiers from the Twenty-third Ohio Volunteer Infantry Regiment. The president joined some eighty-one other veterans of the Twenty-third in celebrating its Civil War exploits. Fremont was, of course, the home town of Rutherford Hayes, and the day's events included a "touching scene" at the Hayes gravesite, where the "visibly affected" president delivered a few emotional remarks about his beloved commander and mentor, who died in 1893. But the celebrants devoted the day mostly to rousing activities that included two cannon salutes, martial music, an afternoon bonfire, a military review, evening fireworks, and invigorating speeches reflecting the sturdy patriotism of the day. The president, wrote the *Washington Post*, "is very fond of these boys in blue and takes no pains to conceal it."

McKinley drew laughter during his brief speech by declaring, "My comrades, the memories of the war are sweeter than service in the war." He praised his regiment but noted that Ohio produced 200 infantry regiments, "and there were two million men and upward just like you from all of the Northern States and Territories of the Union, who were willing to do and die for the government and for the flag. [Cheers]." The president extolled the national unity he saw in the country some three decades after war's end. "Today," he said, drawing more cheers, "instead of having sectional divisions beneath this flag, we have none . . . and the men who fought for this flag and the men who opposed it . . . are now forever united in faith and friendship for its defense."

The unity idea was a frequent motif of presidential speechmaking, and people clearly enjoyed hearing it, however overblown it might have been. In McKinley's Annual Message three months later, he returned to the theme, heralding "the growing feeling of fraternal regard and unification of all sections of our country, the incompleteness of which has too long delayed realization of the highest blessings of the Union." Clearly the president wanted to bury the "bloody shirt" that had enflamed sectional passions for decades. But he knew that unity and social harmony also required good times and a sense that American prosperity was widely shared. He devoted elements of his Annual Message to these themes.

The document, delivered to Congress on December 6 at the start of the new legislative session, touted the president's success in getting his tariff bill enacted, though he acknowledged the new trade policy hadn't yet eliminated the government's budget deficiency, which stood at $42 million. Time would reveal the legislation's ultimate impact, argued the president, but "the people, satisfied with its operation and results thus far, are in no mind to withhold from it a fair trial." In the meantime he promised a serious effort to enact comprehensive currency legislation establishing a functional relationship among gold, silver, and paper currency. He said the government had an "obvious duty" to redeem future greenbacks only in gold, though he stopped short of endorsing Treasury secretary Gage's call to retire greenbacks altogether. This could contract the money supply, he feared, and crush the economic recovery. In truth, though McKinley recognized the ultimate need for a broad currency regimen, he liked the country's monetary situation at the end of 1897, with new gold discoveries boosting money supply. He wished to avoid any premature solution that could prove harmful.

The president devoted the greatest portion of his message to his efforts to end the war in Cuba. He defended America's legitimate interest in Cuban affairs extending back to the 1823 Monroe Doctrine and said America couldn't sit by while Spain pursued a war policy that was "not civilized warfare [but] extermination." He had addressed his "first duty," which was to American citizens in Cuba, by effecting the release of twenty-two imprisoned Americans and pushing the $50,000 appropriation to aid U.S. citizens caught up in the conflict.

While saying he wanted a peaceful solution "just and honorable alike to Spain and to the Cuban people," the president emphasized that Spain had no leeway for delaying a settlement. "The supposition of an indefinite prolongation of the war is denied," he declared. He disavowed any American interest in Cuban annexation. "That, by our code of morality, would be criminal aggression." But he sought to maintain his own freedom of action by opposing any U.S. recognition of Cuban independence ("impracticable and indefensible") or of belligerency rights for Cuban insurgents ("unwise, and therefore inadmissible").

Essentially the president urged patience upon Americans and their congressional representatives as he continued his delicate efforts to nudge events toward an agreeable solution. Enumerating the actions Spain already had taken in response to his pressure tactics—removing Weyler, ending the *reconcentrados* program, accepting the principle of home rule—he promised his government "will abate none of its efforts to bring about by peaceful agencies a peace which shall be honorable and enduring." But, he added by way of warning, should America feel a need to "intervene with force," it would come only when the necessity "will be so clear so to command the support and approval of the civilized world."

Turning to Hawaii, McKinley noted that the annexation treaty had been ratified unanimously by the Republic of Hawaii "and only awaits the favorable action of the American Senate." The "logic of events" rendered annexation "the natural result of the strengthening ties that bind us to those Islands." It was "gratifying" that Japan had retreated from its previous complaints and now evinced "confidence in the uprightness of this Government, and in the sincerity of its purpose to deal with all possible ulterior questions in the broadest spirit of friendliness." He

avoided any flourishes of expression on the islands' strategic significance or potential role in American expansionism.

But he did hail a number of initiatives designed to expand America's
global reach and commerce: a canal across Central America serving as
a "great highway of trade between the Atlantic and Pacific"; the push
for reciprocal trade agreements; enlargement of the country's merchant
marine to address an inadequacy "humiliating to the national pride";
and the "great increase of the Navy . . . justified by the requirements
for national defense."

The president declared his commitment to the Civil Service legislation enacted in 1883, the so-called Pendleton Act, to chip away at
the country's traditional "spoils system," which entailed the hiring and
firing of federal personnel based on political patronage. Like his predecessors going back to Chester A. Arthur in the 1880s, McKinley found
himself caught between reformers such as Carl Schurz, who wanted a
professional workforce untainted by political barter, and "spoilsmen"
such as presidential allies Mark Hanna and Charles Grosvenor, who
wanted to maximize the political leverage of governmental hiring.

In June 1897, McKinley had shown his hand by moving to protect
a large number of federal employees from arbitrary removal, thus ir-
ritating some of his closest friends but delighting reform factions. The
Chicago Tribune declared, "Any doubts which might have existed about
President McKinley's fidelity to civil service reform must vanish now."
Godkin's *Nation*, always wary of McKinley's intentions, gushed, "President McKinley deserves and will receive the heartiest praise of good
citizens, without distinction of party." It was smart politics, expanding
his support base among reform elements often uncomfortable with his
tendencies toward political realism.

Although McKinley's Annual Message didn't highlight growing signs
of prosperity, newspapers peppered readers with encouraging reports.
According to the *Pittsburgh Dispatch*, iron merchants were responding
to growing demand for their products by encouraging producers to
prepare for the fall trade "with a degree of confidence greater than that
which marked the outset of any season for several years." London's *Pall
Mall Gazette* said the American iron and steel industry was gaining
global dominance, and the causes of America's favorable position were

"permanent, and everything points to the United States remaining the cheapest steel-producing country in the world." Meanwhile textile manufacturers throughout New England and the Mid-Atlantic region started reopening mills, rehiring workers, and restoring prerecession wage levels. Wheat prices, a key index of farm belt prosperity, hit a dollar a bushel in August. U.S. wheat exports through Philadelphia, already the largest on record, "will reach figures in excess of what has been the most sanguine expectation of shippers," said the *Washington Post*, which reported also that New York banks were issuing business loans in greater volume than had been seen in years. The country's "general condition to-day," announced the *Philadelphia Inquirer*, "is more satisfactory than it has been for four years and bids fair to grow steadily better."

Of course, these trends didn't impress ardently anti-McKinley Democrats. The *St. Louis Republic* refused to attribute any of the economic good news to McKinley, whom it deemed "one of the weakest characters" ever to reach the White House. But the president knew the economic rebound, coupled with his steady brand of leadership, would enhance his political standing, and that of his party, as the country moved into an election year.

ON THE MORNING of December 2, 1897, in Canton, Mother McKinley, eighty-eight years old, awoke to find she couldn't speak. Fearing she had suffered a stroke, she went to the room of her daughter Helen to express her concern in hand signals. She seemed to Helen to be fully in possession of her mental and physical faculties. But in the early afternoon she sank into semiconsciousness. Abner McKinley, visiting from New York, wired the president of their mother's condition and promised an update at five o'clock. McKinley didn't wait for the update. "Tell mother I will be there," he wired back and took the next train to Canton. When McKinley's father had died five years earlier, it had been a difficult time for the son. But William Sr. had never exercised the kind of impact on the younger William that Nancy had.

He arrived at his mother's bedside at ten o'clock the next morning and remained with her for a day before returning to Washington for presidential duties. Disposing of immediate White House business in twenty-four hours, the president rushed back to Canton with Ida and a retinue of relatives and servants. He found his mother still alive and capable of recognizing family members. But soon she lapsed into a coma-like condition. "The President is almost constantly at the bedside," reported the *New York Times*, "refusing to be relieved by others and to take the rest and exercise he needs." Three days later, she displayed a brief interval of consciousness, but then, just after two o'clock in the morning, she died, with all of her children and many other relatives standing around her bed.

The funeral took place two days later at Canton's First Methodist Episcopal Church amid a constant rainstorm. The president, sitting in the first pew directly before the pulpit, "gave no outward evidence of his sorrow," reported the *Times*. The service began with the chant "Still, Still with Thee" and included the hymns "Jesus, Lover of My Soul" and "Lead, Kindly Light." The Rev. C. E. Manchester's eulogy included the statement, "It is not given to many to have such grace of life, such perfection of character as crowned her."

Following the funeral, a crowd of 3,000 braved the elements in a procession to the gravesite at the West Lawn Cemetery near the center of town. Following remarks that were "very short and simple," Mother McKinley was lowered into the grave by pallbearers. That evening the president and Ida boarded an overnight train for Washington and the crush of presidential duties. He knew that he would be thrust immediately into a political maelstrom that could undermine his political standing in the country. The old feud within the Ohio Republican Party had reemerged like an abscess, and Mark Hanna's political fate hung in the balance.

The story began with intrigues precedent to the Republican state convention in Toledo in June. Hanna's senatorial appointment was set to expire when a new legislature, to be elected in November 1897, would convene in January to fill that senatorial slot for the remainder of John Sherman's term, scheduled to expire in January 1899, and for the subsequent six-year term. Hanna wanted both terms as a crowning affirmation of his political stature. A defeat would represent not only a crushing termination of his political career but also a symbolic blow to McKinley, whose public image depended significantly upon his ability to dominate Ohio politics. McKinley and Hanna reasoned that a strong party endorsement from Toledo would position Hanna to command the needed legislative votes—so long as Republicans retained their majority status in the November elections.

In the weeks leading to the convention, newspaper reports suggested some Hanna enemies, invariably tied to Senator Foraker, wanted to impede his election. The plan apparently was to urge county Democrats to elect Foraker delegations to the state convention so they could pass a rousing endorsement for Asa Bushnell's reelection as governor but thwart any endorsement for Hanna. The man behind this plan was said to be Cleveland mayor Robert McKisson, a leading Foraker-Bushnell confidant, who reportedly wanted to become Ohio's lieutenant governor as part of the plan.

All this was brought into the open by Ohio congressman Clifton Beach, who told reporters in late April that "Mark Hanna is in grave danger of defeat for the Senate" because of political maneuverings in Cuyahoga County, surrounding Cleveland. "If McKisson should declare himself one way or the other Hanna might be more certain of election," said Beach, "but McKisson is too sly for that. He is going to keep still and do his fighting on the quiet until the time comes to stab Hanna."

"Does Hanna realize the gravity of the situation?" a reporter asked Beach.

"He certainly does, but he is not talking."

The tireless Hanna promptly went to work in Cuyahoga County and corralled 65 percent of the delegates. "This means the overthrow of Mayor McKisson's control of the county machine," asserted the *Washington Post*. "It goes without saying the Cuyahoga County delegation to Toledo will be unanimously for Hanna." Hanna publicly dismissed the significance of the Cuyahoga intrigues. "I suppose they need something of that kind to warm up their blood," he said.

But tensions mounted on the eve of the convention when Hanna's forces announced plans to give the state GOP campaign chairmanship to Charles Dick, Hanna's talented campaign chief, over Charles Kurtz, a Foraker stalwart and Hanna nemesis who served as state party chairman. Hanna felt he needed a loyal man running the party campaigns as he pursued his senatorial bid, and he couldn't trust Kurtz. But Bushnell argued that the party's gubernatorial candidate had always named campaign chairmen, and he intended to fight for that party courtesy. With battle lines drawn, Foraker openly promoted Kurtz's candidacy with the full force of his influence, while the McKinley administration was "freely quoted as favoring Dick," the *Post* reported.

When the Toledo convention convened on June 22, the cunning Hanna quickly took control of the proceedings. But he sought to ease tensions by suggesting Dick would withdraw his candidacy if Kurtz would do the same, thus paving the way for a compromise campaign chairman. Kurtz promptly rejected the idea. When the balloting commenced, Dick won 2 to 1, and the convention unanimously endorsed Hanna's senatorial candidacy. For good measure, the Hanna forces replaced Kurtz as state party chairman with a Hanna friend named George Nash. Signifying the desire of many party officials to bridge the chasm between the two warring factions, the convention also endorsed Bushnell's reelection bid without dissent. But the chasm remained.

Still, with his party endorsement and ties to the increasingly popular McKinley, Hanna appeared headed to victory in January. At a party rally kicking off the Ohio campaign in mid-September, Foraker even praised the incumbent senator, saying Ohio could not afford to lose his leadership or tamper with the McKinley administration's national standing. Besides, Republicans enjoyed a 30,000-vote edge over Democrats in party registration. Yet a feeling emerged within both parties that somehow the Republicans could lose legislative seats in November. Chairman Daniel McConville of the state Democratic Party told reporters on October 30, "Our position has greatly improved within the last week, and we have every reason to feel confident." McKinley wrote to Hanna, "I sympathize with you in the hard work you have before you. Be of good courage, I am sure you must win." The president announced he had invited Hanna to join him in Canton during his scheduled visit there to vote. While administration officials took pains to persuade the press that the Canton meeting wasn't intended to have any political significance, no one believed it. As the *Washington Post* reported, "There was quite a smile on the face of Chairman Nash, of the Republican State Committee, this afternoon when this remark was repeated to him."

When the first votes were counted in November, it became clear the Republicans had taken a drubbing in Hamilton County, surrounding Cincinnati; Democrats registered gains in numerous regions of the state, including McKinley's own Stark County. It appeared initially that Hanna might go down, although Governor Bushnell captured an easy reelection victory. But final returns gave Republicans a five-vote legislative majority for a balloting that combined the votes of both houses. Though Democrats held a two-vote majority in the Senate, the GOP enjoyed a seven-vote advantage in the House. "Am just home and hasten to tell you how relieved I am with the latest Ohio news," McKinley wrote to Hanna. "You measured up to the requirement of the situation to the delight of your friends and the disappointment of your foes."

The congratulatory words proved premature. "The Foraker men have knives up their sleeves," wrote the *Washington Post*. Rumors filtered through Columbus that the anti-Hanna forces would put up McKisson or Kurtz for the short term and push Bushnell for the subsequent six-year term. On November 9, press reports said Dick had surveyed every Republican member-elect of the next General Assembly and discovered that fully thirty of them wouldn't pledge their votes to Hanna. C. V. Harris, secretary of the state Democratic Party, told reporters, "We have decided to throw the Democratic vote . . . to Gov. Bushnell, on condition that he can get votes enough from the Republican side of the House to elect him. . . . The deal is all arranged."

Then, on November 10, came a remarkable broadside in a newspaper interview. "The days of Hanna's bossism are over," declared Kurtz. "The people here are against him, and that settles it." He was asked if he felt at all bound by the party's unanimous resolution for Hanna at the Toledo convention. "That meant nothing," he replied. "It was adopted by a convention controlled by the paid agents of Mr. Hanna." Asked if dissident Republicans would need Democratic votes to unseat Hanna, Kurz answered, "There are a number of Republicans in the new Legislature that cannot be bulldozed or bought for Mr. Hanna, amply sufficient to secure his defeat."

The interview continued in a similar vein. Kurtz expressed no concerns about the impact of a Hanna defeat on President McKinley because the president "is weary of Hanna posing as his political creator."

Bushnell was "treated like a dog" by Hanna after Toledo. Hanna's defeat would please nearly all Republicans, "who are kept dancing in attendance upon him for any favor they may desire."

Foraker revealed that same day that he had no intention of helping Hanna through the coming travail that his longtime allies were engineering. "So far as I can now foresee," he said, "I shall not have anything to do with the matter." The senator raised eyebrows when he abruptly canceled a New York trip and rushed to Ohio. Bushnell meanwhile testily declined to say anything but "I do not care to talk on the subject."

Following all this from Washington, McKinley became alarmed and implored friends to do all they could to bolster Hanna's cause. When Charles Grosvenor called at the White House one morning for a chat, the president found he didn't have sufficient time to debrief the congressman on Ohio developments as much as he wanted. He asked Grosvenor to return for lunch and retained him on the subject until after three o'clock.

Throughout the remainder of November and into December, Ohio's political percolation over Hanna's fate intensified. The *Washington Post*, which led most other papers on the story, reported on November 13, based on background interviews with Foraker intimates, that behind the senator's coy silence lurked a ferocious combatant bent on getting rid of Hanna once and for all. "Along the whole line of Foraker men," reported the paper, "the word has gone forth that Mr. Hanna is to receive his political quietus, if it can be accomplished through their instrumentality." Rising from the depth of the intraparty rivalry going back to 1888 came all the accumulated venom that Ohio party officials had managed to keep under control for years. Every slight inflicted by Hanna as he emerged as a party power now rose to the surface.

But the battle was about more than just Hanna's fate. Political analysts began spinning scenarios on the broader implications of a victory for the Foraker forces. First, Hanna's patronage power would disintegrate and government jobs formerly controlled by him would fall under the sway of Foraker. Next, Bushnell would go after the long senatorial term in hopes of further strengthening the Foraker faction. A fill-in candidate would be put up for the short term. Third, these developments would strengthen Foraker's political position so power-fully that he likely could position himself to run for president—against McKinley in 1900 if his rival faltered in the meantime; if not, in 1904.

On December 1 a Democratic state senator from Columbus named Pugh reiterated that legislative Democrats were seeking to combine with GOP dissidents to defeat Hanna with a GOP alternative candi-date. "I have had an extensive correspondence with the Democratic members . . . on this subject," said Pugh. "They all feel . . . that we, as Democrats, should do all that is possible to defeat Mr. Hanna." He said that if just three Republicans joined united Democrats on this maneuver, Hanna would be broken. If true, this was a remarkable de-velopment because no one had believed that any significant number of legislative Democrats would ever vote for a Republican.

In Washington, emotions ran high. A December 19 dispatch in the *St. Louis Republic* reported that Vice President Hobart summoned Foraker to a Capitol Hill meeting with top congressional Republicans and expressed concern about what the senator's friends were doing. Said the vice president, "Senator Foraker, Mr. Hanna must be returned to the Senate. . . . And now on behalf of Senator Hanna and the party at large, I ask you to call these friends off."

Foraker unleashed a strong peroration disavowing any involve-ment in the fight and refusing to interfere in the legitimate political activities of his associates. "I have not attained to that position in bossism," he intoned, "where I can telegraph my friends to put their private feelings in their pocket at a word from me." According to the *Republic*, Hobart then threatened Foraker with a concerted campaign to destroy Foraker's reelection prospects, whereupon Foraker issued his own threat. "I will in turn guarantee," he said, "that there will not be a single Republican Congressman elected in Ohio next fall, and that President McKinley will not receive the vote of the Ohio delega-tion nor any considerable part of it in the next Republican National Convention."

At the White House, McKinley's alarm intensified. After reading an article in a Cincinnati newspaper suggesting a state senator named J. L. Carpenter might bolt the Hanna cause, he asked Grosvenor to get him back in line. After Grosvenor complied, Carpenter sent a testy letter to

McKinley saying he never contemplated voting for anyone but Hanna. A similar letter from state representative J. J. Snider to Hanna allies in Ohio was promptly forwarded to McKinley to assuage his concerns.

By January 1, just eleven days before the balloting, things looked bad for Hanna. In the legislature were seventy-five Republicans, sixty-five Democrats, and five pro-silver "Fusionist" Republicans. When House Republicans caucused on matters related to the organization of the chamber—elections for House speaker and lesser offices, among other things—ten Republicans and Fusionists didn't show up. That seemed to signal a Democratic victory in House organizational matters. In the Senate a single Republican boycotted the party caucus, suggesting Democrats likely would dominate that chamber as well.

Two days later, the auguries proved true, as Kurtz Republicans joined the opposition to give control of both houses to the Democrats. "Unless there is a material change in the political situation in Ohio within the next twenty-four hours," predicted the *Post*, "Senator Hanna is defeated." The paper added that the outcome "has stunned the Republicans of the State, and telegrams of earnest protest and threatened vengeance have been pouring in upon the nine Republican members of the House who joined the combine to defeat Senator Hanna." Some defectors were threatened with personal violence if they dared show their faces publicly.

Following the furious efforts to corral wavering legislators, political and journalistic vote counters concluded on January 4 that Hanna needed at least three House votes to secure the seventy-three joint ballots he needed for election. Hanna, in Columbus, worked the holdouts assiduously. A Cincinnati banker named J. G. Schmidlapp wrote McKinley that he had called on Hanna and sensed that the ordeal "is wearing on him." He added, "My heart really bled for him in the position he has been unfortunately placed in." McKinley promptly wrote Hanna, "I cannot tell you how much I feel for you under the great strain you are subjected to. . . . I need not tell you . . . how anxious I am that you shall be returned to the Senate."

As the January 12 vote neared, it appeared that the political atmosphere in Columbus was beginning to shift toward Hanna. A gathering wave of anger now rose up against the Bushnell-Kurtz offensive, which was faulted for needlessly driving a wedge through the state party. The *New York Press* described developments with a certain asperity, claiming the "voters of Ohio arose against the conspirators. They held mass meetings all over the State, they burned the traitors in effigy, warned them with letters and telegrams that their political judgment day was come, and on the day that Bushnell . . . was inaugurated as Governor shamed him beyond all precedent." Indeed Bushnell's second inauguration turned out to be a bust—or "frost," as it was quickly dubbed. Fearing he might incite an angry civic protest, the governor refrained from riding in the inaugural procession, which was a failure anyway as only one political organization joined in. The parade was mostly military units, whose soldiers shattered custom by refusing to salute the governor as they marched by his reviewing stand. During this time Hanna supporters flocked to the capital by the thousands to attend an enormous rally for their candidate.

The Bushnell-Kurtz forces were experiencing difficulty in finding a candidate equally acceptable to Democrats, maverick Republicans, and Fusionists. Democrats, caucusing all night in an effort to find an acceptable free-silver man, rejected both Bushnell and Kurtz before finally summoning McKisson. The Cleveland mayor, according to those present, promised if elected to embrace the free-silver platform plank approved at the Democrats' 1896 Chicago convention. That inevitably rankled some wavering Republicans.

But when the ballot was taken, McKisson failed to get enough Democrats to augment the seven Republicans who ultimately bolted their party to thwart Hanna. The result was that Hanna, though beleaguered and battered, squeezed out a one-vote victory. McKinley was elated when he got Hanna's telegram: "God reigns and the Republican Party still lives."

Inevitably Hanna's foes cried foul, tossing out allegations that he had purchased the election through underhanded payments to wavering legislators. Legislative Democrats impaneled a special investigative committee, comprising all Democrats save a single Republican who declined to participate in what he considered a loaded inquiry. It concluded that laws were broken and sent a damning report to the U.S. Senate, which undertook its own investigation, pursued by a committee dominated this time by Republicans. It exonerated Hanna. The public at large never knew what to make of the allegations, which dogged Hanna for the remainder of his life and beyond, although no substantive proof of wrongdoing ever surfaced.

In any event, the battle and its outcome generated plenty of excitement among Republicans, and even some Democrats outraged by the Bushnell-Kurtz ambush. Newspapers throughout the country issued commentary on what the *St. Louis Globe-Democrat* called "one of the most sensational senatorial contests ever waged anywhere in the country." Many papers took on a scolding tone. The *Brooklyn Daily Eagle* intoned, "Believers in fair play in politics and in good faith in dealings between man and man must regret that there has been treachery in Ohio." The *New York Mail and Express* added, "There has never been in the history of American politics . . . another conspiracy to defeat the will of the people so utterly without principle, so wholly founded in jealous malignity and so marked by the personal ambitions of small men." But however treacherous Hanna's opponents might have been, observed Whitelaw Reid's *Tribune,* the episode left Ohio's Republican Party "in a maimed and enfeebled condition," though it expected the party ultimately to gain strength from the ordeal.

The *Tribune* had it about right. For years Ohio Republicans, fixated behind the scenes on the ongoing internecine battles between the two tenacious party factions, had labored sedulously to keep the feuding from exploding into public view. The aim was to outmaneuver the opposition, not destroy it. All that changed with the Bushnell-Kurtz assault on Hanna, designed to shatter the party's McKinley wing, leaving it wounded upon the floor of politics, humiliated and moribund. The anti-Hanna faction had placed an all-or-nothing bet and lost. Had the vote gone the other way, it would have been a devastating blow to McKinley, sapping his civic standing, disturbing his political base, and snatching away much of his Ohio patronage power. It might even have set back his prospects for reelection. But now, in the wake of the Ohio imbroglio, the McKinley-Hanna combine appeared invincible, ready for the next battle, a political force to be reckoned with. As the *Tribune* put it, "The difficult task of reuniting Ohio Republicans in an impregnable majority will test . . . [Hanna's] wisdom, patriotism and magnanimity. And yet the advantage of position which was his in the struggle so hardly won is still his in even greater degree in the hour of victory."

16

America and Spain

A CLASH OF INTERESTS AND A TEST OF WILLS

On Saturday, January 15, 1898, in Madrid, Minister Woodford presented his young daughters to the queen regent. After
the customary desultory exchange, as the Woodford family
began to back away toward the door, Maria Cristina asked the minister
to remain. He quickly perceived that she harbored a serious agenda.
She asked if the conversation could be kept secret from all but herself,
Woodford, President McKinley, and her colonial minister, Moret y
Prendergast. Woodford said yes, except that the exchange would have
to become known to his trusted private secretary.

Nodding her assent, the queen pronounced her commitment to
peace for her unhappy land and credited McKinley with wanting peace
also. She expressed appreciation for the president's efforts to help end
hostilities.

"I have done all that you have asked or suggested," said the queen,
citing the change in ministries, the promise of autonomy, and General
Blanco's softer war strategy, designed to relieve the suffering in Cuba.
"The suffering is horrible and makes me sick at heart," she said, add-
ing she would "persevere in these paths to the end." But if President
McKinley was her friend, he should help her by taking two actions.

First, issue a proclamation calling on U.S. citizens to stop supporting the Cuban rebels; second, break up the New York Junta, the rebel venture operating out of Manhattan.

Recognizing immediately the delicacy of his position, Woodford explained that his government was "a representative popular government and our Executive must in very large degree do what the majority of our citizens . . . wish and decree." He said Americans wanted their executive to stop the war at once.

The queen interrupted: "The president can do this, and if he does it the people in your country will stop giving money, and the insurgents will know that they cannot get help; and their chiefs will accept autonomy and surrender; and this will stop the war; and the rebellion will be over and I shall have peace."

Woodford noted respectfully that a recent rebellion within Blanco's army raised questions about his ability to crush the rebels. And recurrent rumors about antigovernment conspiracies in Madrid further undermined her regime's credibility. Drawing herself up and looking "every inch a Queen," Maria Cristina said, "I will crush any conspiracy in Spain." But in the meantime she wanted the president to give her initiatives a chance to succeed. She asked if Woodford, as her friend, would ask McKinley to accede to her wishes. "I am sure from what I am told that he will listen to you."

Woodford thanked her for her good opinion and said he would relay the conversation to the president in detail. But he wouldn't advise him on what to do. The president, he said, "will certainly do what he shall . . . think right and just towards Spain and Cuba and the United States."

The monarch dismissed the envoy with a cordial but "very sad" demeanor.

The next day, Colonial Minister Moret described to Woodford the pressures on his government from fiery conservatives demanding, among other things, Weyler's reinstatement.

"General Weyler will never be allowed to land in Cuba again," Woodford shot back. He emphasized that there was "no possible retreat" from the Liberal government's chosen path. "Any weakness would now be fatal," he warned.

"There will be no weakness," replied Moret. But he reiterated the queen's entreaty that McKinley stop the Junta and other rebel assistance from U.S. soil. The guerrillas would fight on unless subdued militarily. That's why McKinley must quash the Junta.

Woodford promptly sent McKinley a long back-channel letter revealing the desperation of Maria Cristina and her ministry. He warned that the conversations themselves could bring down the Liberal government and perhaps even the dynasty if word leaked out that the two had "violated Spanish traditions and offended Spanish pride" with personal entreaties to a foreign power. The conversations revealed the vise that gripped the queen and her ministry. As long as there was a chance that Blanco's military measures, combined with the autonomy offer, could secure peace, the ministry was probably safe. But McKinley had made clear that, if that policy faltered, America would intervene unless Spain surrendered Cuba. If the queen did that, however, a revolution likely would rend her nation and destroy her son's dynasty.

"If they fail," wrote Woodford, "and have to choose between war with us or the overthrow of the dynasty they will try to save the dynasty." That's why they so earnestly had beseeched Washington to stop the Junta—to enhance their ability to reach a Cuban accord and escape the vise.

But the vise already had tightened before Woodford's conversations, when thousands of conservative Cubans, mostly Spanish born, stormed Havana newspapers that had criticized the Spanish Army in Cuba and its leaders. They smashed windows, destroyed printing presses, and filled the streets of Havana with chants of "Viva Spain!," "Viva the king!," "Viva Weyler!," and "Down with autonomy!" Key figures in Prime Minister Sagasta's government, including Moret, viewed the riots as part of a broader plot to unleash civic tensions in Madrid and force the queen to cast aside the Sagasta ministry. Some "Carlist" agitators even wanted to upend the dynasty altogether and replace it with a far more autocratic monarchy harking back to a competing family line.

The Havana agitation died down, but Fitzhugh Lee advised his government that the volatility there could ignite further disruptions, including anti-American riots. American relief efforts to help starving Cubans were arousing anger among Havana and Madrid conservatives who viewed the assistance as a "pretext . . . to interfere in Cuban affairs" and "widen the breach between the Cuban peasantry and the Spaniards," as the *Washington Post* reported. But Lee also perceived a growing realization among Spanish Cubans, as he wrote to Judge Day, "that U.S. intermediation for peace is the only resort left." He recommended that Washington step back and "let matters progress in that direction rather than for the U.S. to insist upon being heard at once."

That fit McKinley's inclination precisely. He had established America's position, and Madrid had responded with a credible program. Now the burden rested upon the queen and her ministry to make it work. The president would watch and wait.

In the meantime McKinley became increasingly comfortable with the powers of his office. Particularly in the matter of patronage did he adopt a sharper tone than most people had seen before, reacting to petty disputes or rivalries in matters involving government jobs. "Those persons who have presumed that nothing could disturb the President's fine poise," reported the *St. Louis Globe-Democrat*, "have learned that he possesses the power to condemn unsparingly bickerings and spitefulness of contestants in his party." The paper said the president had taken to dismissing from his presence those wishing to air grievances against others and that he insisted that state factions resolve patronage disputes before bringing requests to him.

But true to his strong sense of loyalty, McKinley sometimes suspended formalities when close friends were involved. When Russell Hastings sought consideration for a nephew, then struggling through the Naval Academy at Annapolis, the president sent the matter to Navy Secretary Long, who informed the president that young Hastings was among eleven midshipmen designated for dismissal. The president's scruples didn't preclude him from intervening in behalf of the lad. "I desire to thank you for the efforts in behalf of my nephew Russell," wrote Hastings to McKinley, "which—through him—I am informed have come to a successful issue."

The president accepted the complaint of Public Buildings Commissioner Theodore Bingham that White House receptions had become far too raucous and overcrowded, with so many gate-crashers squeezing into the mansion that comfort and social enjoyment were impossible.

Bingham, a taut-faced fusspot with a meticulously waxed mustache, proposed a series of exclusive receptions, with guests carefully screened, beginning with a function on January 19. "For the first time in twenty years," reported the *Post*, "the invited guests . . . were received and entertained in comfort, owing to the absence of the multitude which heretofore has . . . turned what is supposed to be a dignified and agreeable function into a most unpleasant and promiscuous crush." But then the officious Bingham, in a memorandum to McKinley elaborating on his plans, described the interlopers of past receptions as "vulgar mobs" made up of "butchers, cabmen, market and grocery clerks, and the scum of the city." McKinley immediately shut down Bingham's program and returned to "vulgar mob" receptions. He would never be party to Bingham's brand of snobbery.

As 1898 commenced, Ida's health entered a period of stability, and she responded by placing a greater stamp upon White House life. She now had the stamina to frequently attend theatrical comedies from the presidential box at various Washington playhouses, and she delighted in the laughter they generated. "There is enough trouble in the world," she once said, "without seeing sad plays and reading sad books." In January she organized a debutante ball for her niece Mary Barber and the next month presided over an elaborate reception for the diplomatic corps. She set a precedent by inviting a stream of actors to the mansion for extended conversations about their craft, and she asked one performer to deliver a number of character monologues by playwrights Ian Maclaren and J. M. Barrie in the Blue Room. She still took pains to pace herself, however, by such methods as presenting herself in receiving lines while seated in a throne-like blue velvet chair.

It wasn't clear what caused her physical improvement. One factor may have been the White House physician, Captain Leonard Wood, who sought to reduce Ida's stress level through a kind of conversation therapy. While encouraging Ida to expand her White House activity, he also sought to soothe away anxieties caused by her fuller schedule. Wood's friend Herman Hagedorn described it as an "elixir of ambition and assurance," and Ida seemed to respond to what the *New York Times* later described as the doctor's "tenderness toward his patient." Meanwhile McKinley continued to provide Ida with medications prescribed by Dr. Bishop in New York; around this time he sent Bishop a $250 check for more bromides.

The president remained, as the *New York Times* put it, "not more devoted to his public duties than he was to the welfare of his wife." But no less devoted, either, and he spent long days and many evenings poring over papers and engaging men of power on pressing matters of state. His aim was to render decisions with a deft sense of timing designed to exploit opportunities for action at moments of maximum leverage.

In late January 1898 the president traveled to New York to deliver a major address to the National Association of Manufacturers at the posh Waldorf-Astoria Hotel. Speaking before 1,000 industrial and financial titans, he declared that all outstanding U.S. bonds should be paid in gold. The timing was significant as the Senate was about to vote on a resolution by Colorado's Senator Teller, that staunch silver advocate, declaring that the payment of outstanding bonds in standard silver dollars would not violate the public faith or undermine the public credit. The president countered that view:

> *The money of the United States is and must forever be unquestioned and unassailable. . . . Nothing should ever tempt us—nothing ever will tempt us—to scale down the sacred debt of the nation through a legal technicality. Whatever may be the language of the contract, the United States will discharge all of its obligations in the currency recognized as the best throughout the civilized world. . . . Nor will we ever consent that the wages of labor or its frugal savings shall be scaled down by permitting payment in dollars of less value than the dollars accepted as the best in every enlightened nation of the earth.*

The president could not have been clearer: he was declaring his party to be the gold-standard party. His embrace of gold—and, perhaps more significant, the timing of it—offered a telling insight into his instinct for parsing the complexities of political challenges and wending his way through political thickets. Though he had flirted with modest soft-money concepts early in his career, he had bowed to Republican orthodoxy in time for his presidential run—while keeping a wary eye on the dangers represented by the free-silver craze. But then in his presidential bid he had crushed the free-silver candidacy of its most compelling advocate. Since then the promise of better economic times had blunted the silver movement, while the growing flow of gold into federal vaults provided much-needed liquidity. The timing was perfect for a bold leadership thrust on the issue, and the president seized it.

At the *Nation*, Godkin was delighted. For more than thirty years, he wrote, both parties had been "rent in the same manner" over the currency issue—split between hard-currency and soft-currency advocates. But now the Democrats, under William Jennings Bryan, had declared their colors. "The Democratic Party," wrote Godkin, "now stands for nothing else under the sun than a depreciated currency." And McKinley was placing the Republicans in clear opposition to that. "The main purpose," Godkin explained, "is to bring the supporters of the gold standard and of the national honor upon a common platform, to arm them with a common purpose, to drive all cowards out of their skulking-places, and compel them to take one side or the other." Now the division would be between the two parties, not within each.

IN EARLY JANUARY 1898, Senate Foreign Relations Committee chairman Cushman K. Davis, Republican of Minnesota, announced plans to call up the president's Hawaii annexation treaty in executive session and ask the Senate to debate it daily until it could be disposed of. To Davis, a senator since 1887 and his state's governor before that, Hawaii represented more than just a commercial way station or even a crucial naval outpost. He agreed with Alfred Thayer Mahan that America must follow Britain's example and attain global power through a "step-by-step" acquisition of key strategic points around the globe. He wanted the United States to join Britain in an Anglo-Saxon, world-dominating alliance, and Hawaii would be the first step toward that end.

It wasn't clear that Davis had the sixty Senate votes needed for ratification. In the eighty-eight-seat chamber, Republicans held forty-seven seats to thirty-four for the Democrats, with Populists holding seven seats. It was assumed that nearly all Republicans, including silver Republicans, would vote aye, possibly excepting Justin Morrill of Vermont and certainly the cantankerous Richard Pettigrew of South

Dakota. The Populists would split on annexation, and the Democrats would mostly oppose it. But Democratic leaders declined to make Hawaii a party issue, which likely meant some Democrats would straggle in as aye votes. Whether there would be enough remained unclear.

McKinley's ratification hopes began to fade when three Republicans from beet sugar states—John Thurston of Nebraska, John Gear of Iowa, and John Spooner of Wisconsin—announced their opposition. Thurston argued that the islands, some 2,000 miles from U.S. shores, would constitute a national burden more than a strength. But insiders knew what really motivated the three: fears that U.S. acquisition of a vast sugar empire would thwart development of the nascent beet sugar industry in their states.

During the closed sessions, Davis issued a fervent call for ratification on both commercial and military grounds. It was evident, he said, "that the opening of the new century which is now so near, must mark the opening of a new condition of affairs in the far east." Those vast markets were coveted by every European power, he said, and if America stood aside, those powers soon would control the entire Asian seaboard. Hawaii would give America leverage to compete with those countries commercially and to thwart their military ambitions. If America didn't take the islands, they would fall under the sway of Britain, Japan, Germany, or Russia.

Delaware's Democratic senator George Gray posed a question much on the minds of many senators—and reflecting the country's prevailing racial and ethnic sentiments. "In case the islands should be annexed," he asked, "is it the policy to have them admitted as a State of the Union with their present mixed population?"

"Such I do not believe to be the purpose of any one," replied Davis. "I, myself, freely admit that the population of Hawaii is not such at the present time as would be desirable in an American State."

As the closed-session debate continued, ratification chances dimmed further. The McKinley-Davis forces seemed stuck at fifty-six votes, and the *Post* reported that "the President has been appealed to in order that the influence of the administration may be exerted." Of course another option would be to seek annexation through a joint resolution, which would require only a bare majority of both congressional houses. The problem there was the anti-imperialist House poo-bah, Speaker Reed, described by friends as implacably opposed to Hawaiian acquisition. It wasn't clear how far he would go in trying to kill the legislation in his House fiefdom.

Then an important visitor arrived on American shores: Sanford B. Dole, president of Hawaii. He debarked in San Francisco in mid-January and became officially a guest of the United States upon reaching Chicago on January 22. The son of Hawaiian missionaries, the U.S.-educated Dole had become a lawyer in Boston and then practiced law in Honolulu before entering politics. Though not a planter, he was connected by blood to major figures in both sugar and pineapples. His gentle temperament was reflected in his soft eyes and placid face, accentuated by a billowy white beard that flowed to his chest. But behind that demeanor was a tendency toward occasional mood swings and emotional agitations. He had been a leader of the so-called Bayonet Revolution that created a new Hawaiian Constitution in 1887 and in the later rebellion that deposed Queen Liliuokalani in 1893. Like most Hawaiian whites, he fervently wanted to attach his island republic to the United States.

Arriving in Washington with his wife on January 26, Dole was greeted at the train depot by Secretary of State Sherman, who escorted the couple to the majestic Arlington Hotel for an afternoon rest. Later they received an official visit from McKinley. Ushered into Dole's suite and announced by Hawaii's minister Francis Hatch, the president stepped up to Dole and said, "I welcome you to the United States and to its Capital, and hope your stay in this country will be very pleasant." After further pleasantries, the two men retreated to a corner of the room for an intimate fifteen-minute chat.

A week later the president and first lady honored President and Mrs. Dole with an elaborate state reception attended by nearly 3,000 guests, including most of the diplomatic corps, Cabinet secretaries, members of Congress, and Supreme Court justices, along with their wives, and many more who were uninvited but had "the position to awe their way in," as the *Washington Evening Star* put it. It seems Commissioner Bingham's plan for more stringent gatekeeping already had gone by the wayside. The elaborate decorations included a "profusion of ferns and palms [that] made a beautiful background for the hand-somely gowned women and uniformed men," reported the *Post*, which added that Ida wore "a very becoming gown of black velvet, with Duchess Lace garniture."

Upon his return to Hawaii in early March, Dole publicly expressed confidence that the U.S. Congress would embrace annexation, most likely in a joint resolution. Asked about his impression of McKinley, he said it was "extremely favorable. I found him to be an unassuming, frank, and sterling man. He seems to have heart and soul in the annexation treaty."

Back in Washington, as it became clear that the votes weren't there for treaty ratification, annexation supporters turned their attention to Thomas Reed and a plan to circumvent his opposition with a parliamentary maneuver. The idea was to attach the language to a Senate appropriations bill, thus forcing it onto the House floor through a kind of legislative back door. But on February 6, the speaker announced his support for annexation. Two weeks later pro-treaty Senate leaders decided to abandon the treaty and prepare a joint resolution. On March 16, Davis's Foreign Relations Committee approved resolution language, along with an extensive written memorandum justifying the resolution approach, complete with an exhaustive description of the circumstances surrounding the 1845 Texas annexation through joint resolution. The process would take a bit longer, but chances of success seemed high.

McKinley watched all this from the White House with intense interest. "The President is anxious about Hawaii," wrote presidential secretary George Cortelyou in his diary. He quoted McKinley as saying late one evening, "We need Hawaii just as much and a good deal more than we did California. It is manifest destiny." In equating the Hawaiian acquisition with the country's westward expansion across North America, McKinley identified himself as an overseas expansionist—in other words, an imperialist.

This was reflected in his interest in an American-dominated canal through Central America, most likely through Nicaragua. He initiated a quiet quest for information through his preferred data-gathering method, a special investigative commission. Under congressional authority granted to him in June 1897, he appointed a commission under the chairmanship of Rear Admiral John G. Walker. In January 1898 the commission traveled to Nicaragua and other Latin American countries to determine the canal's feasibility and prospects for engaging with Central American governments on the matter. But there was a snag—the so-called Clayton-Bulwer Treaty between the United States and Britain, which committed both countries to joint control of any isthmian canal and precluded either from any unilateral construction project. The United States repeatedly had sought to revise the 1850 treaty, but Britain consistently had rejected the idea.

Not surprisingly, the anti-imperialist Godkin saw no problem with this. If the canal were strictly a commercial enterprise, he wrote in the *Nation*, why worry about joint control or neutral management? Only if it were seen as a vehicle of imperialism would it matter that America dominate the waterway. But Godkin's views were a tough sell in a country increasingly beguiled by the notion of American expansionism. Americans wanted the canal, and they wanted to own it.

Of more immediate concern to McKinley in early 1898 were signs that his wait-and-watch approach to Spanish diplomacy was facing severe tests. On January 20, Spain's minister to Washington, Dupuy de Lôme, called on William Day at the State Department and unleashed a brazen challenge to the United States. Nothing kept the Cuban insurrection alive, he said, except the pro-rebel attitude of the American people. He praised McKinley for his "courage" in resisting that dangerous outlook, but the insurgents were propelled by hopes that the president ultimately would bend to public pressure and give them official U.S. recognition and support.

The minister attacked Fitzhugh Lee for predicting the failure of autonomy and advocating U.S. annexation of Cuba. He complained that Navy Secretary Long's planned fleet maneuvers near Cuba could lead to clashes with Spanish vessels in the vicinity. He decried a recent House floor speech by Robert Hitt of Illinois, chairman of the Foreign Affairs Committee, which he defensively (and erroneously) viewed as a warning of possible U.S. intervention. All this, he said, belied U.S. assurances that the new Spanish policy would be given a chance to succeed. Then came the clincher: if America truly wanted Spain to succeed, it must curtail the New York Junta. "The unfriendly attitude of the United States keeps things alive," said Dupuy. But even in the face of that, he expected Spain to have the Cuban situation firmly in hand by May 1. This turned out to be a diplomatic gaffe that McKinley quickly would exploit.

Day asked what would be the Spanish response if General Lee asked for U.S. ships to protect U.S. citizens and property in Havana. That would be regarded as incipient intervention and an unfriendly act, replied Dupuy.

"This, if sent to protect our Consul and American rights and interests?" Day pressed, a bit incredulous.

"Yes," replied the minister.

Four days later Day summoned Dupuy back to the State Department for a briefing on the president's response to his complaints. Ignoring the minister's more provocative allegations, the president merely said he continued to hold firm on the policies outlined in his December Annual Message, that he still wished to give Spain "a fair opportunity" to test its autonomy scheme, and that he didn't see any reason for contentions in the meantime. As to the matter of his sending a naval vessel to Havana, the president believed that the discontinuance of friendly U.S. naval visits, adopted in the Cleveland administration, had been unfortunate, and he saw no reason why U.S. ships shouldn't visit the ports of Cuba in a friendly way—particularly given Dupuy's prediction, unwisely tendered, that peace was near at hand.

"It is the purpose of the President," said Day, "to resume these visits, and that very soon."

Dupuy allowed as how he also thought the discontinuance of friendly naval visits had been a mistake, thus acceding implicitly to McKinley's decision. Day said McKinley wouldn't hesitate to send U.S. vessels to protect American lives and property whenever necessary, but he felt it preferable to send the vessels as a routine action, unrelated to any necessity, and he had "now determined upon that course." The minister had no choice but to accept the decision. He then reported Spain's interest in sending a commissioner to Washington to explore reciprocal trade agreements related to Cuban goods. The idea, it seemed, was to find areas of agreement between the two countries as they continued to grapple with the nettlesome Cuban matter.

After the session, Day rushed to the White House to brief the president, who promptly summoned Navy Secretary Long. He ordered Long to send the battleship *Maine*, at Key West, Florida, to Havana for a routine friendly visit and to inform General Lee that it would be coming. Later that afternoon Day summoned Dupuy back to the State Department and apprised him of the president's decision. The minister's complaints and contentions of January 20 had backfired. The president shunned them in signaling unmistakably that the burden of peace rested with Spain, not the United States. Then he upped the ante by ordering a battleship into Spanish colonial territory.

The next morning at eleven, the 324-foot, 6,682-ton *Maine*, with her four 10-inch guns and half-dozen 6-inch guns, "came gliding into [Havana] harbor as easily and smoothly as possible," Lee reported to Day. The ship, under the command of Captain Charles Sigsbee, "was a beautiful sight," added Lee, ". . . and has greatly relieved (by her presence) the Americans here." Sigsbee received a cordial welcoming visit from a representative of Vice Admiral José Pastor, the Spanish captain of the port, as well as an officer from the Spanish flagship in the harbor. Spanish forts surrounding the harbor fired salutes, "and all the ceremonies called for by naval etiquette had been observed," reported the *Washington Post*. Although Lee described palace authorities as "rattled" by the arrival, no anti-American incidents or unrest emerged. For good measure, though, Spanish authorities reinforced police protection around the consulate.

McKinley continued to believe things were moving in the right direction, as he sought to emphasize in casual conversation with Dupuy de Lôme at a White House diplomatic reception on January 26. When the men were ushered into the State Dining Room for coffee and cigars, the president motioned for Dupuy to join him at a small table. Between puffs on his cigar the president said, "I see that we have only good news." With Congress at least temporarily subdued on the Cuban question and Spain seemingly intent on complying with U.S. requirements, he told Dupuy, "you have no occasion to be other than satisfied and confident." Despite Dupuy's concerns about American public opinion, he told his government that the president's words represented a "sincere declaration" of his patience.

But in the Spanish capital Woodford could see that public opinion was "still very much excited," although Moret and other officials exhibited extreme cordiality and seemed genuinely anxious to consummate the proposed commercial treaty among Spain, Cuba, and the United States as a demonstration of goodwill.

Then came an abrupt change in the tenor of Spanish diplomacy. On February 3, a messenger delivered to Woodford the Spanish government's official reply to McKinley's December 20 note outlining U.S. policy toward Cuba and Spain. Written by Foreign Minister Pío Gullón e Iglesias, the reply dripped with dismissive language that essentially told the United States to butt out. America's mere proximity to Cuba gave it no right of intervention or even diplomatic pressure, said the statement, and Spain recognized no U.S. prerogative to prescribe a termination time for Spain's Cuban war. Besides, American refusal to deal with the New York Junta contributed to the war's longevity far more than anything else. Spain took umbrage at U.S. "hints of a change of conduct," implying possible military intervention, and it would continue its "firm resolution" to preserve its sovereignty over Cuba "at every hazard."

In a conversation with Moret, Woodford called the Spanish government's reply "a serious mistake." He then wrote McKinley that Spanish authorities had become pessimistic about their ability to suppress the rebellion in any timely way either through autonomy or arms. A respected *New York Herald* reporter told him that the Spanish ministry felt it had agreed to all the concessions it could possibly make without endangering its own power and the ruling dynasty. "They will do no more," said the reporter, "and will fight if what they have done does not secure our neutrality."

Then on February 9, Dupuy de Lôme informed his boss, the Spanish foreign minister, that Hearst's aggressively pro-Junta *New York Journal* shortly would publish a letter he had written to a friend in Havana with "expressions humiliating to the President." His position as minister to Washington, he said, was about to become "untenable." True enough, publication of the letter set off a political firestorm in America that would test the diplomatic mettle of both countries. It seems a clerk at the Spanish embassy in Washington had seen the letter when it lay unopened and unguarded in an out-basket. He informed Junta officials, who alerted allies at the Havana post office to intercept it there when it arrived. It was sent to Junta officials in America, who spent several weeks authenticating it before leaking it to Hearst's *Journal.* The story hit the streets of New York like a bomb explosion, then reverberated throughout an incensed America.

No one could figure out what had possessed Dupuy to violate diplomatic etiquette so egregiously or to act so recklessly in sending his letter through regular mail channels. Written shortly after release of McKinley's Annual Message in December, Dupuy's letter decried the president's "natural and inevitable coarseness" in repeating newspaper criticisms of General Weyler. It also labeled McKinley as "weak and catering to the rabble, and besides a low politician who desires to leave a door open behind himself while keeping on good terms with the jingoes of his party."

Worse, Dupuy invited his friend to "agitate" the matter of a reciprocal trade agreement between Spain and the United States, but "only for effect" because he was bent on using the trade negotiations "to make a propaganda among the Senators and others in opposition to the junta." In other words, he certified his own government's hypocrisy in its seemingly solemn diplomatic efforts in behalf of a bilateral trade treaty. It was difficult to see how the two countries could carry on any kind of serious discussions on any topic if Spain stood exposed as merely going through the motions for ulterior purposes.

Characteristically McKinley reacted dispassionately to the insult, declining to respond publicly and assuming his diplomats would handle it appropriately. But U.S.-Spanish tensions intensified when Madrid sought to finesse the matter by casually accepting Dupuy's resignation and declaring the matter closed—all before any Spanish official had given Woodford the courtesy of an audience so that he could demand, as would be customary in such circumstances, Dupuy's recall. When Woodford finally did see Gullón e Iglesias, the minister of state airily informed him that Dupuy's resignation had been "asked and accepted." This was untrue. The government had taken no action indicating censure of Dupuy and in fact had accepted his resignation in a letter praising his conduct as minister in Washington.

With Americans seething with indignation, Judge Day at the State

Department put the matter in perspective with a statement: "The Spanish government will be expected to disclaim all responsibility for the utterances of the recent Spanish Minister. If Minister Woodford's dispatches indicate that this disclaimer has been made, the incident is closed. If not, it is still open."

In Madrid, Woodford expressed his government's chagrin in a letter to Gullón and the next day received Colonial Minister Moret, his closest associate at the Spanish court. Moret expressed deep regret and sought Woodford's counsel on what the Spanish government should do. The American minister unloaded on Moret, decrying Gullón's misrepresentation and saying his letter gave him "an open door for correcting the possible mistake." The letter "left to your Queen and to her Ministers to decide . . . what . . . she as a lady and you as gentlemen ought to do." But he added that, if Spain sought to avoid a full diplomatic corrective, he would resign his post and return to America, "stating why I do it." He added, "I cannot remain accredited to a Sovereign or have official relations with a Ministry who could attempt to [avoid] the duty of a just explanation by pleading or suggesting the technicalities of diplomacy."

Not surprisingly, Madrid quickly issued an apologetic statement, disavowing any sympathy for Dupuy's unfortunate words and committing Spain to Cuban autonomy and to trade reciprocity. In a letter to McKinley, Woodford said the Spanish note "was not all that I could have wished, but it was much more than we could reasonably expect, considering the excited state of popular and even official feeling here." It seemed that Spain simply couldn't extricate itself from the political, military, and diplomatic vise in which it was locked. The *Nation*, noting Dupuy's reference to "poor Spain" in his offending letter, suggested those two words constituted "the best comment one can make on the spectacle of a nation of such a splendid past, fallen on such evil days."

17

Path to War

"HISTORY IS BEING MADE AT A RAPID RATE"

A s darkness descended upon Havana on the evening of February 15, 1898, dense clouds shrouded the evening sky. In the sultry and still air, the USS *Maine* barely tugged at her anchor. A quiet descended over the ship after bugler C. H. Newton, following the 9 p.m. two-bells signal from the ship's clock, played "Taps," signifying lights out. At about 9:30 Lieutenant John Blandin, watch officer, ambled along the port quarterdeck, positioned himself near a ten-inch turret, and cast his gaze across the placid water to the city lights. He laughed mildly when Lieutenant John Hood approached and asked with mock sternness if he was asleep.

"No," replied Blandin, "I'm on watch."

Suddenly a deafening boom rocked the ship as a fiery blast ripped through its hull. Three hundred yards away on the harbor pier, an evening stroller named Frank Weinheimer, visiting from New York City, heard a crunching sound. He turned toward the *Maine* as a "terrible roar" shattered the night. Immense shards of steel, cement chunks, and wood splinters shot up and out in all directions. "It looked as though the whole inside of the ship had been blown out," recalled Weinheimer.

Aboard the *Maine*, Commander Sigsbee was completing a letter to his wife when he was jolted by a "bursting, rending, crashing sound or roar of immense volume." The vessel shook, then listed to port. He rushed to the main deck, where billows of smoke impaired breathing. Light from a fire amidships revealed wreckage everywhere. The *Maine*'s two stacks had collapsed, its bow shattered into a mass of twisted metal. He could see that his ship shortly would rest on the harbor floor, and the "white forms" he saw bobbing on the water would multiply. Within an hour, with waves flowing across the poop deck, Sigsbee managed to get some survivors off the ship and onto a gig. He and the other survivors found refuge aboard a nearby U.S. steamer called the *City of Washington* and a Spanish man-of-war, the *Alfonso*. Sigsbee ended up on the *City of Washington*.

After ensuring that his wounded men and officers were being well tended, Sigsbee descended to the captain's cabin to write a report to Navy Secretary Long: "Maine blown up in Havana Harbor at nine forty tonight and destroyed. Many wounded and doubtless more killed or drowned. Wounded and others on board Spanish man of war and Ward Line steamer." It was approaching 1 a.m. on February 16 when Sigsbee's cable reached Washington, via Key West. A Navy courier delivered it to Long's residence, where his daughter, just returning from a social outing, woke up her father to give him the news. After consultations with hurriedly summoned naval subordinates, Long sent an officer to inform McKinley. The president, awakened by White House staff, emerged from his bedroom in a dressing gown. After reading the note, he muttered in a tone of bewilderment, "The *Maine* blown up! The *Maine* blown up!" When McKinley later appeared for breakfast, Myron Herrick, visiting from Cleveland, chided him for being late and for the stern look upon his face.

THE STERN LOOK betokened not just the president's anguish at the carnage. The *Maine* disaster would transform the political and diplomatic landscape. Whatever its cause, it threatened to fuel the fires of U.S. war agitation, engulf McKinley's leadership of incrementalism, and upend his carefully crafted plan to end the war in Cuba and expel Spain from the Caribbean while avoiding hostilities with that beleaguered country. As news reports pegged the possible death toll at 250 or more (it eventually hit 266), members of Congress rushed to condemn Spain as either the perpetrator or an abettor of those who committed the crime. The notion that it could have been an accident seemed inconceivable to many, and their ire wasn't assuaged by expressions from Madrid decrying the explosion and offering official condolences.

McKinley sought to counter this attitude. He approved Long's decision to convene a naval board of inquiry and labored to keep the nation tranquil until it issued its report. Throughout the day of February 16, he summoned Cabinet members and numerous congressional leaders to urge calm and patience. "My duty is plain," he told his friend from Indiana, Senator Fairbanks. "We must learn the truth and endeavor, if possible, to fix the responsibility. The country can afford to withhold its judgment . . . until the truth is known." The White House issued a "semi-official statement" saying the president doubted the *Maine's* destruction resulted from an overt act. Cabinet officials, emerging from a hurriedly called White House meeting, told reporters the same thing. "Every representative of the President," said the *Washington Post*, "has thus far been sedulously careful to say nothing that could in any way connect the Spanish government in the remotest degree with the disaster."

But the agitators weren't mollified. The president's own assistant naval secretary, Theodore Roosevelt, wrote to a friend, "Being a Jingo . . . I would give anything if President McKinley would order the fleet to Havana tomorrow." He privately attributed the *Maine* disaster to "an act of dirty treachery on the part of the Spaniards." New York's influential newspapers, particularly Hearst's *Journal* and Joseph Pulitzer's *World*, embraced that view as well. Told by his night editor that the *Maine* explosion would make page 1, along with "other big news," Hearst shot back, "There is not any other big news. Please spread the story all over the page." Soon Hearst and Pulitzer were competing to determine whose paper could be the more bellicose—and sell more papers in the process. On the evening of February 17, the *Journal* emblazoned a headline across its front page that read, "WAR! SURE! MAINE DESTROYED BY SPANISH; THIS PROVED ABSOLUTELY BY DISCOVERY OF THE TORPEDO HOLE." There had been no such discovery, but that mattered little to Hearst.

Many in Congress took their cue from the newspaper magnate. Illinois senator William Mason, a Republican, even speculated that the facts were "being concealed from the people . . . [and] members of Congress." Was there not a "danger," he asked, that the navy, "in investigating itself, will be . . . finding a state of facts that does not exist?" Five days later Nebraska's Allen sought to resurrect the hoary notion of U.S. recognition of rebel belligerency rights, almost sure to lead to war. Allen's effort generated a spirited debate. "Calmness, silence, patience are necessary," declared Nebraska's Thurston, ". . . for the safe and peaceful and successful prosecution of the inquiry." Thurston's judgment prevailed, which pleased McKinley. A Cabinet secretary told reporters, on condition of anonymity, that the president "will not be jingoed into war, or act in anticipation of events which may never occur."

But in the interim McKinley contemplated the various scenarios that could emerge, including the possibility that navy divers would see that the explosion came from outside the ship and thus conclude it was not an accident. On February 26, the Cabinet explored two possible U.S. actions if that happened. One would be to demand an indemnity from Spain; the other would be war. Problems with the first included strong opposition from an agitated American public. Also Spain likely would "seek to delay, to arbitrate, or . . . absolutely refuse to entertain the proposition, thus throwing the burden of the first overt act upon the United States," as a State Department memo put it. Given that McKinley would not wish to be the aggressor, it was suggested that any indemnity demand be accompanied by an extensive statement of U.S. grievances stemming from the war, a catalogue of humanitarian abuses caused by it, and an announcement of U.S. recognition of Cuban independence. This might mollify some pro-war elements in the United States while forcing Spain to make the first move if it considered rebel recognition a *casus belli*.

From Madrid, meanwhile, Woodford reported an inconsistency of behavior that bordered on the bizarre—probably reflecting the crosscurrents of pressure buffeting the queen's ministry. The queen regent, in a private conversation with Woodford, once again pleaded for McKinley to quash the Cuban Junta. The same entreaty came in a subsequent Woodford conversation with Moret y Prendergast and Gullón e Iglesias. But in a gesture of friendship the Spanish ministers also said Madrid was prepared to move quickly on a commercial treaty and on an indemnity payment to the family of the deceased dentist Ricardo Ruiz.

Then came a three-pronged Spanish complaint from Moret to Woodford. The colonial minister accused a U.S. naval officer named "Brownsfield" of landing his ship, the *Brooklyn*, at the Dominican Republic to assist rebel filibusters there. According to the report, the *Brooklyn* commander had with him the young son of a martyred rebel leader, Calixto García. Moret then accused Consul Lee of maintaining ties to the rebels and privately advocating U.S. annexation of Cuba. Some firebrand officials in Madrid, he warned, wanted to expel Lee from Havana to demonstrate Spanish pride. "Moret believes," Woodford reported to McKinley, "that General Lee's home and Legation are the centres of sympathy for the insurrection" and that through his influence "the insurrection is helped and autonomy retarded." Moret also reported that Spanish officials in Cuba likely would banish offending U.S. newspapermen, including reporters for the *Journal* and *World*.

Regarding the reporters, Woodford said he had "absolutely no suggestion to make." It was Spain's affair. He conveyed the other complaints to Washington, where officials promptly went public with Spain's push against Lee. There was some truth in Madrid's suggestion that Lee indiscreetly had signaled his sympathy for the Cuban rebels. But McKinley was in no mood to entertain such a challenge. After consulting with Day and Long, he issued a statement asserting, "The President will not consider the recall of Gen. Lee. He has borne himself throughout this crisis with judgment, fidelity, and courage, to the President's entire satisfaction." Two days later the White House told reporters of Madrid's allegation of naval support for Cuban filibustering operations under the command of Captain Arent S. Crowninshield (not "Brownsfield," as Spanish officials mistakenly had identified him). Press dispatches revealed that during Crowninshield's benign mission to the Dominican Republic he had been accompanied by his own son, not García's son. "There was not, of course, the slightest foundation for this assertion," reported the *Post*.

It was a major diplomatic humiliation for Madrid—first, having McKinley brusquely reject its desire for Lee's recall, then having its accusation against a respected U.S. naval officer exposed as flimsy and reckless. "Moret is sincerely grateful for the prompt and satisfactory explanation of the Crowninshield incident," Woodford wrote to McKinley. "[He] accepts your judgment with regard to Consul General Lee."

But such atmospherics went only so far in helping McKinley press his delicate game of persuading Madrid to give up Cuba while avoiding any public demand that it do so. Even a hint that that was his aim would elicit an angry Spanish rebuke. At the same time, an appearance of presidential irresolution could stimulate more jingoist sentiment at home and undermine U.S. efforts to pressure Spain to make conciliatory actions in Cuba. He needed a display of resolve that wouldn't be provocative to Spain.

On March 7 the president summoned top congressional leaders, along with War Secretary Alger and Navy Secretary Long, for an extended discussion in his private White House library. He emphasized the need for military preparations in case war became unavoidable and confirmed unofficial reports that Spain was seeking to purchase warships on the global market. Turning to Joe Cannon, chairman of the House Appropriations Committee, he asked for a major supplemental appropriation for national defense. After some discussion, the appropriate amount was pegged at $50 million. When Cannon that afternoon slipped a special appropriations bill into the House hopper, reporters flashed the news across the country and around the world. The response was electric. Within two days, both houses of Congress had passed the bill unanimously. As Nelson Dingley explained to reporters, the president had been engaged in military spending with the expectation of subsequent congressional support. "We now propose to place ample funds at [his] disposal," he said.

Ample, indeed. Woodford reported to McKinley that Spanish officials were "simply stunned" at the news. "To appropriate fifty millions out of money in the treasury, without borrowing a cent, demonstrates wealth and power," wrote the minister, adding the lack of restrictions on the funds "demonstrates entire confidence in you by all parties." Woodford pointed out that Spanish officials also feared the appropriation would encourage the rebels to persevere, thus dooming autonomy. Their concerns deepened when the U.S. government immediately earmarked part of the $50 million to purchase two Brazilian cruisers under construction in England that Spain had hoped to obtain.

But Spain had no money. Its debt burden exceeded $400 million, and annual debt-service costs absorbed some $65 million of an annual budget of between $150 million and $160 million. Meanwhile Blanco was spending some $8 million a month on his war effort. "There can be no question," argued *The Nation*, "that Spain is financially embarrassed." Not sufficiently embarrassed, though, to entertain the idea of selling Cuba to the insurgents, who on March 1 offered to pay Spain up to $200 million for the withdrawal of its troops and recognition of Cuban independence. Spain consistently rebuffed intermittent offers on the part of the United States and various European powers to foster the purchase of the island. Godkin's *Nation* captured the underlying sentiment: "The Spanish people are as patriotic a race as ever lived. The impulse of a splendid past is still upon them. . . . Threatened bankruptcy, certain defeat in the long run, will not for a moment deter that proud nation from fighting for its honor."

AS THE PRESIDENT waited for the results of the naval inquiry, conducted aboard the lighthouse tender *Mangrove* anchored in Havana Harbor, he filled his days and nights with activity related to Spain and Cuba, often quickly delegating less pressing matters to subordinates or casting them aside altogether. He cajoled members of Congress, pushed for contingency war plans, managed the extensive correspondence from Woodford, pursued unexpected opportunities such as the purchase of the Brazilian cruisers, and devoted long hours to rambling strategy sessions with his most trusted advisers. After dining with Ida and devoting his early evenings to her, he often returned to his Cabinet Room table for further toil until eleven o'clock or later. Secretary George Cortelyou noted in his diary that the president often appeared "careworn" and "haggard," though he remained always "very gentle and considerate." Occasionally he escaped the White House for an afternoon walk around Lafayette Park or a buggy ride with Ida or Judge Day.

The president had managed to foster a political calm in Washington pending the naval commission report, but it was a brittle calm. Senator

Chandler of New Hampshire on March 8 declared in an interview that war with Spain was inevitable, and the risk of such a war was "one of the plainest dictates of policy and humanity." Then Vermont's Redfield Proctor, a close McKinley friend and one of the Senate's most respected members, rendered an anguished portrayal of Cuban suffering, based on a recent tour of the island. During a March 17 Senate floor speech, which transfixed his colleagues, the senator said he had expected his visit to confirm his belief that the stories of Cuban devastation had been overblown. Now he knew they weren't.

The horrors of the *reconcentrados* policy, said Proctor, defied comprehension for anyone who had not seen them. "Torn from their homes, with foul earth, foul air, foul water, and foul food or none," said Proctor, "what wonder that one half have died and that one quarter of the living are so diseased that they cannot be saved." People were perishing in the streets from starvation, and often they were "found dead about the markets in the morning, where they had crawled, hoping to get some stray bits of food from the early hucksters." These were people, he explained, who had been "independent and self-supporting before Weyler's order." Blanco's touted efforts to end Weyler's brutality had been a sham, said Proctor; he had talked with many businessmen who had been early opponents of the insurrection, and not one now saw any hope for Spanish-ruled Cuba.

Though Proctor spoke without belligerence and avoided any policy advocacy, his stark picture generated powerful impressions throughout the country. "The speech will undoubtedly arouse great sympathy for the Cuban people," said Senator Cullom, "for . . . it is evident that Senator Proctor speaks the truth." Ben Foraker added, "It may stir this country to action; at least, I hope it will."

These pressures coincided with a White House briefing in which naval board members informed McKinley that they believed the *Maine* disaster had been no internal accident. Knowing this would inflame congressional passions further, McKinley redoubled his efforts to squeeze Madrid into ending the war at whatever cost. On March 22 Woodford delivered to Moret a blunt warning: unless Madrid reached some kind of agreement with the Cuban rebels "within a very few days," the president would submit the whole question of U.S.-Spain relations to Congress. This was essentially a threat of war, as McKinley had been holding at bay the war-hungry Congress. After Woodford informed Washington that Foreign Minister Gullón wished to speak with him, Day cabled the U.S. minister: "The President approves your statement to the Minister for the colonies. . . . He will await your telegram after your interview" with Gullón.

The next day Woodford repeated the warning to the foreign minister, with particular emphasis on the words "within a very few days." When Gullón professed to be "surprised" at the apparent change in U.S. thinking, Woodford countered that the only change was Washington's realization that Cuban autonomy had failed and Spain could not subdue the rebels or lure them into a settlement. Gullón said he would submit the matter to the Council of Ministers and report back by eight o'clock that evening.

After discussion with the Council, Gullón told Woodford that Spanish officials would consider further concessions, though it wasn't clear how significant they were. Gullón said Spain would empower the Cuban Congress to negotiate a peace with the rebels after it reconvened on May 4. To foster the negotiation, Spain would agree to an interim cease-fire, "provided the United States can secure the acceptance and enforcement of like immediate truce by the insurgents." Woodford reported that an intense struggle within the Spanish cabinet ultimately produced the concessions, but only after the queen intervened.

This development thrilled the U.S. minister. "Truce and negotiations in Cuba," he wrote the president, "mean, in my respectful judgment, that the Spanish flag is to quit Cuba." McKinley and Day disagreed. This seemed like another delaying tactic, and they thought Woodford missed the significance of Spain's carefully phrased proviso that Madrid couldn't cede its governmental responsibilities to the Cuban Congress. Late into the evening of March 25, Day produced a long cable to Woodford clarifying the Washington position. It read as if it had been dashed off, perhaps with a bit of frustration. He sent it off at midnight:

> *The President's desire is for peace. He cannot look upon the suffering and starvation in Cuba save with horror. The concentration of men,*

women and children in the fortified towns and permitting them to
starve is unbearable. . . . There has been no relief to the starving ex-
cept such as the American people have supplied. The reconcentration
order has not been practically superseded. . . . For your own guidance
the President suggests that if Spain will revoke the concentration order
and maintain the people until they can support themselves and offer to
the Cubans full self-government with reasonable indemnity, the Presi-
dent will gladly assist in its consummation. If Spain should invite the
United States to mediate for peace and the insurgents would make like
request, the President might undertake such office of friendship.

The message was clear. McKinley fully embraced the humanitarian impulse that had driven so much of the congressional agitation. Vague
promises of future actions wouldn't serve. The president required immediate action, with timetables for results.

Woodford didn't quite get the president's intent. He wired Day, "Do
the words 'full self government' mean actual recognition of independence, or is nominal Spanish sovereignty over Cuba still permissible?"
Day's response: "Full self Government with indemnity would mean
Cuban Independence." The assistant secretary also wired a fuller rendition of what the president wanted: first, armistice until October 1,
initiated by Spain, with negotiations in the meantime between Spain
and the insurgents through the friendly offices of the president; second, immediate and full revocation of the *reconcentrados* order and full
Spanish cooperation in U.S. relief efforts; third, if peace terms proved
elusive through October 1, McKinley could arbitrate a settlement. Day
said McKinley also would seek rebel acquiescence in the final plan but
only if Madrid requested such an action.

Woodford presented these terms to Spanish officials, who promised
to respond by Tuesday, March 31. But on Tuesday they asked for two
more days. Day shot a cable to Woodford: "It is of the utmost importance that the conference be not postponed beyond next Thursday and
definite results then reached. Feeling here is intense."

Indeed feeling reached a fever pitch in Washington after release of
the naval inquiry conclusion that the *Maine* had been destroyed by
an external explosive, meaning foul play rather than an accidental in-

ternal combustion. (Subsequent inquiries questioned this conclusion, and most experts now consider the matter indeterminate.) The board of inquiry found that discipline aboard ship had been "excellent" and all orders and safety regulations had been strictly observed. The configuration of the hull, with outside bottom plating "bent inward" and a portion doubled back upon itself, "could in court's opinion have been produced only by explosion of a mine under bottom of ship," a report summary put it. Though the report didn't identify the perpetrators, it suggested "a grave responsibility appears to rest upon the Spanish Government," as the *Maine* had relied upon Spain for "the security and protection of a friendly port."

The report reached the White House early on the morning of March 25, a Friday. The president brought in Day and Long to join him in poring over the extensive text and appendices in the Cabinet Room, then convened that day's regular Cabinet meeting, which lasted through most of the afternoon. After briefing the Cabinet on the report, McKinley sought help in crafting the language of his message to Congress, which was to accompany the report summary on Monday. He spent most of Saturday working on his message text with Judge Day and pondering the test of wills he soon would face with both Congress and the Spanish ministry.

In his cover document to Congress, McKinley avoided any hint of patriotic fervor. He called the *Maine* disaster an "appalling calamity" that generated "an intense excitement" that in less controlled nations might have led to "hasty acts of blind resentment." But, he asserted, this spirit soon gave way to "the calmer processes of reason" and a resolve to ascertain the facts. After summarizing those facts, as interpreted by the board of inquiry, McKinley revealed that he had communicated to Spain the board's findings and America's view of the situation. He concluded, "I do not permit myself to doubt that the sense of justice of the Spanish nation will dictate a course of action suggested by honor. . . . It will be the duty of the Executive to advise the Congress of the result, and in the meantime deliberate consideration is invoked."

This bland approach proved highly provocative. With 266 patriotic servicemen in their graves or lost forever in the waters of Havana, most Americans wanted something more stirring. Beyond that, many disdained the notion of a president ceding leadership to Congress on what probably constituted the nation's most severe crisis since the Civil War. "It is to speak moderately," suggested the *New York Times*, "to say that the general tone of comment on the message was one of disappointment." In the House, Minority Leader Joseph Bailey of Texas introduced a resolution recognizing Cuban independence. Democrats rallied solidly behind the measure, and it appeared that a scattering of Republican mavericks might join them to hand McKinley a devastating political defeat. In the end, with Speaker Reed's parliamentary dexterity and a promise from McKinley of a major new Cuban policy, disaster was averted.

In the Senate, that Democratic hawk John Morgan of Alabama introduced a resolution declaring war on Spain based on "the succession of events which have occurred in the Island of Cuba, notably the starving and imprisonment of American citizens." The *Maine* disaster didn't even have to figure into it, he said. Vice President Hobart, on an afternoon ride with McKinley, warned the president that he was losing his influence over the Republican-controlled Senate. The president seemed stunned. "Say no more," he said, and fell silent.

Two days later—a day of "grave anxiety," in Cortelyou's words—Woodford reported Madrid's response to McKinley's proposal. Prime Minister Sagasta said he would submit the *Maine* issue to arbitration, fully revoke the *reconcentrado* policy, and set aside a large sum of money for a Cuban relief program. He also would submit future peace discussions to Cuba's insular parliament and would cease hostilities until the parliament convened on May 4. But to preserve its national pride Spain would accept a cease-fire only if the rebels asked for it. Without an armistice through October 1, as McKinley had proposed, there would be no prospect to arbitrate a solution in the fall. The response, Woodford told the president, "was a sorrow to me for I have worked hard for peace." In typical fashion, Sagasta didn't reject McKinley's armistice proposal outright. He suggested further negotiations pending the return of his legislative Cortes in a few weeks. As the *Washington Post* put it, "Spain's only hope now lies in delay."

McKinley couldn't afford delay. He found himself caught between congressional agitation and Spanish intransigence. With his cherished incrementalism in decision making lying in shambles, he risked losing control of his own government. It was time for the kind of boldness he normally sought to avoid. Even before Madrid's disappointing response, McKinley called to the White House a stream of influential Republican legislators and promised a new direction, though he remained vague on the details. As the *Washington Post* explained, "Anxiety for prompt action, while ill-concealed, is curbed in the belief that the President will . . . announce that he has decided to delay no longer, and make recommendations upon which Congress can act." Congress continued to percolate with expressions of bellicosity toward Spain and irritation toward McKinley, but Republican leaders of both houses managed to curb any threatening legislative action.

The president did enjoy scattered support around the country. The *Louisville Courier-Journal* said the president had "risen above politics in his treatment of the Cuban question." And the *Baltimore Sun* appreciated his effort to lead "a patient and forbearing nation keeping its temper under control in spite of sore provocation." But plenty of public sentiment matched the anger of a group of Richmond, Virginia, agitators who drew a large crowd by hanging and burning the president in effigy—and adding an effigy of Mark Hanna for good measure.

The problem facing McKinley, even after he managed to subdue congressional restlessness with his promise of a new direction, was a psychological difficulty relinquishing his hope of getting Spain out of Cuba without war. From the beginning, he had known precisely what he wanted to accomplish, and he never veered from that goal or slackened the ponderous resolve he brought to it. But perhaps he had been naïve in thinking war threats could intimidate Spain into abandoning its cherished Cuban colony before his own constituency forced him into an actual war. In any event, now he was stuck with the results of that ploy, and he was having difficulty coming to terms with it.

The president's self-promoting friend, Herman Kohlsaat, described an incident at the White House during this time of struggle. At an evening piano recital in the Blue Room, the president asked Kohlsaat to join him in the Red Room. The president sat down on a large crimson-brocade lounge, rested his head on his hands, with his elbows on his knees, and poured out his heart at Ida's recent decline of health and his own tribulations with a Congress bent on war. "The Spanish fleet is in Cuban waters," sighed the president, "and we haven't enough ammunition on the Atlantic seacoast to fire a salute." Secretary Long also perceived the effects of stress and lack of sleep. The president, he wrote in his diary, "has shown a good deal of weariness and nervous strain."

But the logic of the situation was pointing the way. He would ask Congress for authority to intervene militarily to end the war and effect Cuban independence. He set about drafting his message—while also maintaining hopes that new developments might block the path to war. Sagasta played on McKinley's hopes by accepting an initiative from Germany to have Pope Leo XIII serve as a mediator between Spain and the United States. When the pope proposed an armistice during the coming rainy season, to prepare the way for Cuban independence in the autumn, Madrid evinced interest. Woodford, whose initial pessimism about prospects for peace long since had given way to starry visions of diplomatic success, waxed enthusiastic in his correspondence with the president. "If conditions at Washington will enable you to give me the necessary time," he wrote, "I am sure that before next October I will get peace in Cuba."

But Judge Day smelled a rat. The proposal crafted by Spain in response to the pope's entreaty, he wrote to Woodford, "is not armistice." It was merely an invitation to the insurgents to lay down their arms while the autonomy government in Havana determined "what expansion if any of the decreed home rule scheme is needed or practicable." Embracing Day's interpretation, McKinley set April 6 as the day for sending his message to Congress. As that day dawned, expectations ran high in Washington. A crowd of 10,000 gathered at the Capitol in hopes of catching a glimpse of history. Cortelyou wrote in his diary, "History is being made at a rapid rate."

But around noon a dispatch arrived at the White House from Consul Lee, who requested a delay so he could get vulnerable Americans out of Cuba before the president's message inflamed anti-U.S. passions in Havana. Present in the Cabinet Room when Lee's dispatch arrived were McKinley's new attorney general, John Griggs (Joseph McKenna had gone to the Supreme Court), Alger, Long, and Day. The president sent for three top members from both House and Senate so he could inform them of his dilemma. They came promptly, but in the interim Secretary Long suggested that the president probably should send the message despite Lee's concerns, lest the delay send a false signal of presidential irresolution. McKinley raised his hand.

"I will not do it," he announced. ". . . I will not do such a thing if it will endanger the life of an American citizen in Cuba." When the members arrived, the president told them he would deliver his message five days later, on Monday, April 11.

Not surprisingly, news of the delay generated great disappointment throughout Washington, along with some skepticism. The always impatient Roosevelt privately suggested the president's backbone was "as soft as a chocolate éclair." When the Senate went into executive session to hear from Minnesota's Cushman Davis, Foreign Relations Committee chairman William Chandler of New Hampshire questioned him closely: "Does the Senator from Minnesota know that a message has really been prepared?"

"Yes," replied Davis.

"Did the Senator see the message?"

"Yes."

"Did the Senator read the message?"

"Yes."

"And is the message one for which we can afford to wait?"

"Yes."

That satisfied Chandler and his colleagues, and official Washington settled in for the wait.

On April 6, McKinley received a communication from the ambassadors of six European nations appealing for a peaceful settlement of differences between the United States and Spain. The president replied diplomatically that Washington recognized "the good will which has prompted the friendly communication" and anticipated that the European powers likewise would appreciate America's resolve "to fulfill a duty to humanity by ending a situation, the indefinite prolongation of which has become insufferable."

As the time for McKinley's congressional message neared, Madrid grew increasingly desperate. The queen regent on April 9 invited the ambassadors of the major European powers to offer their counsel on

Spain's course. When they advocated an armistice she pounced on it as cover for another effort to placate the menacing Americans with an armistice plan. For good measure, her government informed Pope Leo of her action in order to solicit his good offices, and he obligingly praised the decision. But like nearly all Spanish actions, the armistice was hedged, designed to give General Banco leeway to place conditions on its terms and duration.

McKinley had had enough. When Spain's new minister to Washington, Luis Polo de Bernabé, sought American acceptance of the armistice plan and a further postponement of the president's message, the president and his Cabinet agreed there could be no delay. McKinley decided to simply append the final Spanish concessions and requests to his message in order that Congress could consider them as it desired. The Cabinet drew up a memorandum to this effect, which Day read to Polo later in the afternoon.

On April 9 Fitzhugh Lee left Havana, along with some 300 other Americans eager to be out of danger. Two days later McKinley sent to Congress a 7,000-word "war message," laying out Cuba's recent tangled history, clarifying his own actions in light of that history, and reiterating his views of the matter as outlined in his December Annual Message, including his rationale for opposing recognition of either Cuban belligerency rights or "any particular government in Cuba." He identified two modes of intervention: as an impartial neutral or as the active ally of one party or the other. He opted for the first intervention mode.

He justified "neutral intervention" on four grounds: first, to serve the cause of humanity in stopping the "barbarities, bloodshed, starvation, and horrible miseries" that blighted the island; second, to protect and indemnify American citizens beset by the chaos of the Cuban war; third, to stop the war's devastation to U.S. commerce; and, fourth, to terminate the violence and instability so close to U.S. shores that posed a constant threat to the country's well-being, prosperity, and tranquility. The *Maine* explosion, he said, represented a distilled example of this constant threat. He saw no prospect of Spain's bringing peace to the island: "I ask the Congress to authorize and empower the President to take measures to secure a full and final termination of hostilities between the government of Spain and the people of Cuba, and to secure in the island the establishment of a stable government capable of maintaining order and observing its international obligations, insuring peace and tranquility and the security of its citizens as well as our own, and to use the military and naval forces of the United States as may be necessary for these purposes."

Typically the president's message contained no soaring rhetoric, and Secretary Long considered its conclusion to be "somewhat indefinite and hardly a *sequitur* from the argument which precedes it." For members of Congress who wanted stirring patriotic language and recognition of Cuban independence, it generated waves of anger. "The message has caused great discontent in Congress," reported the *New York Times*. Ben Foraker told the paper, "I have no patience with the message," and Missouri's Democratic representative Alexander Dockery called it "anemic."

Even as McKinley set his country upon a one-way path to war, he couldn't bring himself to embrace the idiom of war. As he had told Carl Schurz, he didn't want any "jingo nonsense" in his administration. But many wondered if his incremental leadership style and rhetorical blandness were equal to the kind of enveloping challenge he now faced. The question unsettled many in Washington, but McKinley showed no inclination to alter his course. He would manage events and developments as they came his way with a conviction that his judgment and maneuverability would carry him through. But the barrage of criticism often pained him. The day after the war message was sent up, Cortelyou entered the Cabinet Room with a passel of letters and telegrams.

"Mr. President," he said, "I have some communications for you bearing upon the message. Here is a particularly good one from Ex-Attorney General Garland." Augustus Garland, an old friend of the president's, was a Democrat, and McKinley seemed prepared for an expression of disapproval. A look of "deep concern and sorrow" spread across the president's face.

"Is he for us?" he asked. Upon reading it, he discovered Garland agreed completely with his course. His face brightened. "That is a beautiful letter of congratulations," he said, "and I appreciate it deeply."

Despite the many expressions of opprobrium he received, the president continued his practice of reading large numbers of the letters addressed to him as a means of assessing public opinion.

Once the dust settled and Congress took up the issue, McKinley was back in a more comfortable political mode, working with congressional members in a long series of small, behind-the-scenes actions designed to nudge events in his direction. In the House on April 13, Democrats pushed a resolution to recognize the Cuban Republic, but Republicans beat it back on a vote of 150 to 190. The chamber then gave lopsided approval to a resolution McKinley fancied, authorizing and directing him to intervene to end the war and foster a stable and independent Cuban government, using U.S. military force as needed. It demanded that Spain "at once relinquish its authority and government in the island of Cuba and withdraw its land and naval forces from Cuba and Cuban waters."

The Senate proved more troublesome, as some eleven Republicans, including Foraker, joined Democrats in approving an amendment from Indiana's David Turpie recognizing the Cuban Republic "as the true and lawful government of that island." Another amendment, by Colorado's Senator Teller, disavowed any U.S. domination of Cuba following hostilities. When the Senate approved its resolution with both amendments, McKinley accepted Teller's language but hinted he might veto the final conference report if it contained the Turpie amendment. After much legislative arm-twisting and some private McKinley cajolery, the House stripped out Turpie. On April 19, McKinley's favored version also passed the Senate.

Employing listless rhetoric and subtle persuasion, the president had got what he wanted. And now, as he no doubt knew, he also would get a war. On Wednesday, April 20, McKinley signed the resolution, and John Sherman sent an ultimatum to the Spanish government, to be delivered through Luis Polo in Washington and Woodford in Madrid. The Spanish minister promptly requested his passport and departed for home. As McKinley was about to sign the resolution, with Cabinet and congressional dignitaries standing by, Maine's Republican senator William Frye asked how much time the ultimatum allowed before a reply was required.

"Until Saturday," replied the president, looking up from his parchment and fixing his gaze upon the strongly anti-Spain senator. ". . . I suppose you would like to give them only fifteen minutes." The senator nodded with a smile. Senator Stephen Elkins of West Virginia mused,

"This is a historic occasion; you are virtually signing the declaration of War, Mr. President."

Indeed, he was. When word of the ultimatum reached Madrid the next day, Spain broke off diplomatic relations with the United States and informed Woodford of the action before he could deliver his official communication. Woodford left the same day. On April 25 McKinley asked Congress for a formal declaration of war. Then he sought to take a nap but was unable to sleep in the quiet of the house. He wandered down the hall in his dressing gown and discovered houseguests Russell Hastings and Webb Hayes, son of the former president, in the state bedchamber. He stretched out on a sofa as they chatted and soon drifted off to sleep. At around four he was awakened by the White House doorkeeper with news that Congress had passed its resolution, which declared that the war actually had begun with Spain's actions of April 21. It now was back for his signature. McKinley sent for Attorney General Griggs and had Hayes arrange a table. Vice President Hobart and Hayes provided pens, Hayes adding an inkwell. Sitting in a bedroom in his dressing gown, the president signed his first name with one pen, then his last name with the other. He gave Hayes one of the pens and the inkwell as souvenirs. William McKinley, through his ponderous, step-by-step leadership, had become a war president.

Short of stature but broad of shoulder, with luminescent gray-blue eyes and a ready smile, William McKinley pulled men to his side through a heavy quiet that was commanding. Generous-spirited and congenial, he mystified his opponents by always getting his way without resorting to overt tools of leadership. He left his nation, and even the world, far different from what they were when he assumed office.

The president's parents, William Sr. and Nancy, represented sturdy Ohio values of hard toil, thrift, modesty, education—and family fecundity. They produced nine children, eight of whom survived into adulthood. The elder McKinley managed blast furnaces in Niles, Ohio, where the family settled into a simple frame house, with part of the first floor set aside as a grocery store. "There wasn't much of a town there then," recalled the father.

When his college education was cut short by a mysterious illness, young McKinley became a postal clerk and school teacher in Poland, Ohio. At age eighteen he entered the Civil War as a private and ended it as a brevet major, with most of his promotions coming after battlefield heroics. His commanding officer, the future president Rutherford Hayes, described the young man as "exceedingly bright . . . and gentlemanly. . . . He promises to be one of the best."

Rutherford Hayes, upon learning that young McKinley planned to become a lawyer and enter politics, counseled that he should choose a more lucrative industrial career. The young man carefully preserved the letter but discarded the advice.

7

8

After clerking with a prominent Poland, Ohio, lawyer and studying at Albany Law School in New York, McKinley moved to Canton, Ohio, a burgeoning town near abundant coal mines and surrounded by ric farmlands. He soon emerged as a prominent local barriste and civic leader.

At first sight, McKinley was smitten by Ida Saxton, petite, lively daughter of Canton's richest industrialist. She had grown up in splendor in what was known as "Saxton House" and soon demonstrated serious business acumen as manager of her father's Canton bank. William and Ida were married in January 1871 and soon had two daughters, including Katie, shown here at age four. It was a storybook romance.

The young McKinleys settled into a spacious Market Avenue home purchased for them by Ida's father. Then fate crushed the sprightly Ida with a series of tragedies and maladies. When both daughters died before age five, Ida never recovered from the psychological blow. She developed epilepsy and other ailments. A carriage accident drained her stamina and impaired her mobility. She became sedentary and brittle. McKinley's devotion to her would become a hallmark of his political persona.

Throughout his political rise, McKinley interacted with the era's three other giants of Ohio politics: Marcus Hanna, rich industrialist and political operator who became McKinley's great benefactor; John Sherman, the state's political colossus who became President McKinley's secretary of state after age had sapped his abilities; and Joseph Benson Foraker, an occasional McKinley ally but more often a rival for position and power. In the end, McKinley and Hanna thoroughly outmaneuvered Foraker.

17

In his 1896 presidential bid, McKinley shunned campaign travel in favor of his famous "front porch" strategy, inviting Americans to visit his Canton home for oratory and refreshments. The candidate received some 750,000 Americans in hundreds of delegations from thirty states for tightly controlled and orchestrated political exchanges that were widely covered by reporters from across the nation. McKinley used the sessions to blast the soft-money "free silver" policies of his fiery opponent, William Jennings Bryan of Nebraska.

In his inaugural address, the new president promised "a firm and dignified foreign policy" that disavowed "wars of conquest" and "the temptation of territorial aggression." It was a commitment soon honored in the breach, as a persistent and bloody anti-Spanish insurgency in colonial Cuba strained U.S.-Spanish relations to the breaking point. In his speech, the president also vowed to increase tariff rates and maintain a hard-currency monetary policy.

McKinley lacked the bold imagination of the era's greatest exponents of U.S. expansionism: Massachusetts senator Henry Cabot Lodge, brilliant, haughty Yankee with a romantic vision of America's destiny; Theodore Roosevelt, assistant naval secretary, full of bustle and dreams of American greatness; and Alfred Thayer Mahan, persistent advocate of sea power as the agency of U.S. global power. Events soon nudged the president in the direction of these men's national ambitions.

When the USS *Maine*, sent to Cuba by McKinley to protect Americans threatened by the chaos of insurrection, blew up in Havana harbor, war became inevitable. McKinley long since had concluded Spain must leave Cuba, either peacefully or through U.S. military pressure. Within weeks of war's declaration, Commodore (later Admiral) George Dewey destroyed Spain's Pacific fleet at Manila, thus becoming an instant national hero. Shortly thereafter, the War Department under Russell Alger captured Cuba's second-largest city, Santiago, but poor management of the war effort cost Alger his reputation and his job.

25

John Hay, McKinley's ambassador to Britain and then secretary of state, performed brilliantly in both roles. He cemented the "Special Relationship" with the British during his ambassadorial tenure and later ended the Western carve-up of China with his "Open Door" policy of equal treatment for countries seeking trade and economic development in the Middle Kingdom. The president called Hay's behavior in office "handsome."

Elihu Root, a leading New York lawyer, was taken aback when asked to become war secretary. "I know nothing about war," he said. But McKinley's intermediary said the president wanted "a lawyer to direct the government of these Spanish islands, and you are the lawyer he wants." Beguiled by the logic, Root took the job, to McKinley's "great satisfaction." It proved to be a smart move by the president.

McKinley's expansionist policies, particularly his decision to take the whole of the Philippines as a U.S. colony, generated a powerful anti-imperialist movement. Carl Schurz (above left), leading intellectual and activist of his day, railed against the policies of his former friend. House Speaker Thomas Reed (above right), called "the Czar" by friend and foe, quit his post in frustration at his inability to blunt the president's expansionism. Another leading anti-imperialist was Mark Twain, who directed a blistering assault at the president.

Spanish-American hostilities ceased just after 4 p.m. on August 12, 1898, when U.S. Secretary of state William Day and French ambassador to the United States Jules Cambon (representing Spain) signed a "protocol" setting the terms of the American victory, with McKinley looking on. As McKinley protégé and devotee Charles Dawes wrote, "The President has had his way as usual." The terms were stark: Spain lost nearly its entire overseas empire, while America became a global power to be reckoned with.

After America acquired the Philippines in Asia, McKinley sent to the islands the highly regarded federal judge William Howard Taft with a mandate to build democratic institutions and foster a program of local Filipino "autonomy," but not independence. Taft's policy of firm tolerance ultimately meshed with U.S. military efforts against a persistent anti-American insurgency. When the insurrection leader, Emilio Aguinaldo, was captured in a bold U.S. action in March 1901, it marked the beginning of the end of his movement.

When war broke out, Lieutenant Colonel Theodore Roosevelt found glory and fame in leading his troops on a hazardous assault upon the San Juan Heights just outside Santiago. That led to a successful bid to become New York governor and a frenzied movement at the 1900 Republican convention to make him McKinley's vice presidential candidate. McKinley remained neutral on the matter but welcomed the impetuous younger man after the convention swept him onto the ticket. In succeeding McKinley, Roosevelt never gave him credit for his many presidential accomplishments.

McKinley and Ida traveled to Buffalo in September 1901 for the heralded Pan-American Exposition, where the president planned to deflect history by announcing a new trade initiative. The next day, while in a receiving line, he was shot by an obscure anarchist named Leon Czolgosz. He died on September 14, 1901. Among his last words: "It is God's way. His will, not ours, be done."

34

When McKinley was shot and placed upon a chair, he exclaimed to his secretary, George Cortelyou, "My wife—be careful, Cortelyou, how you tell her—oh, be careful." The president's solicitousness toward his lifelong companion, who could be brittle and difficult due to her infirmities and psychological challenges, became the stuff of legend in Washington and around the country. She died on May 26, 1907, at age fifty-nine.

Victory at Sea

THE EMERGENCE OF SERENDIPITOUS IMPERIALISM

President McKinley didn't wait for Congress to declare war on Spain before setting in motion critical elements of his military strategy. On April 22 he ordered a blockade of Cuba by the Atlantic squadron under Commodore William Sampson. And on April 24 he authorized Navy Secretary Long to wire an order to Commodore George Dewey, commander of the navy's Asiatic fleet at Hong Kong. Dewey, sixty, had been preparing for this war since his arrival in Asia the previous December; in fact he had been waiting throughout most of his forty-year career for an opportunity to demonstrate his mettle as a high-level combat officer. Thus he was ready for Long's cable, which the *New York Times* described as "remarkable for terseness, conciseness, and comprehensiveness." It read: "Dewey, Hongkong, China: War has commenced between the United States and Spain. Proceed at once to Philippine Islands. Commence operations at once, particularly against the Spanish fleet. You must capture vessels or destroy. Use utmost endeavors. LONG."

The story behind Dewey's assignment to Asia demonstrated the war thinking that gripped parts of official Washington, including the White House, long before McKinley's peace efforts fizzled. At the center of this particular intrigue was the navy's irrepressible bureaucratic busybody, Theodore Roosevelt, whose officious ways had stirred Long to muse that "the best fellow in the world—and with splendid capacities—is worse than no use if he lack a cool head and careful discretion." On September 27, with Long out of the office on holiday, Roosevelt intercepted a letter to his boss from Senator Chandler touting Commodore John Adams Howell for the Asiatic command. Bad idea, thought Roosevelt, who considered Dewey a far better choice. Though Howell had gained fame as an inventor of innovative naval weapons, Roosevelt considered him unequal to the assignment, particularly if the United States went to war. In seeking to get Chandler to withdraw his recommendation, Roosevelt readily conceded Howell's "great inventive capacity" but characterized him as "irresolute and . . . extremely afraid of responsibility"—two characteristics Roosevelt considered particularly odious. The assistant secretary hoped his well-known expansionism would carry weight with Chandler, himself a leading Senate expansionist. It didn't work.

When Chandler rebuffed Roosevelt's entreaty, the assistant secretary summoned Dewey to his office, motioned him to a chair, handed him a cigar, and lit it. "Do you know any Senators?" he asked.

The commodore said he had a longtime family connection to Redfield Proctor from his home state of Vermont. This was ideal. In addition to his cordial friendship with McKinley, Proctor was a rich businessman with tentacles of influence throughout the Republican Party and within the administration. Whereas Chandler had joined the congressional push to hasten a war with Spain over McKinley's objections, Proctor always honored his friendship with McKinley. Even in delivering his eloquent and influential report to the Senate on the depredations he had witnessed in Cuba, he took care to avoid any expressions that could possibly unsettle the president.

When Dewey approached Proctor, the senator seemed "delighted" to help and promptly called at the White House to put the case before McKinley, who already had been entreated by Roosevelt on the same matter. Commodore Dewey, said Proctor, "is the man you want." The president nodded his assent and promised to press the matter "right away" with Long.

"Here," said Proctor, sliding a slip of paper across the table, "write it down, Mr. President."

The commander-in-chief complied, writing in pencil, "Long, appoint Dewey command Asiatic Squadron." Proctor picked up the powerful sheet.

"You'll never regret this, Mr. President," he said, then proceeded to Long's office to present his fait accompli. Long wasn't amused to have his decision-making prerogative yanked from him on such an important personnel matter. He went along but communicated his displeasure to Dewey with a retaliatory belittlement. He refused to bestow the promotion in rank that normally would go with such an assignment.

"I am glad to appoint you, *Commodore* Dewey," said Long to the naval officer, emphasizing his rank, "but you won't go as a rear admiral. You will go as a commodore." He paused to let the implications sink in, then added, "Perhaps you used too much political influence." When Dewey protested that others also had employed political influence, the secretary cut him off. "You are in error, Commodore," he said.

Only later did Roosevelt deliver to Long the Chandler letter revealing that the secretary himself had been in error. The gentlemanly Long acknowledged as much in a letter to Dewey but didn't reverse what the commodore considered a "little pinpricking slight."

Adding to the intrigue of the matter was the question of why Roosevelt had selected this particular officer as the best man for Asia. Dewey had demonstrated distinctive gallantry as a young Civil War officer under the command of the legendary David Farragut, then settled in to an unremarkable career that interspersed various shipboard and overseas duties with intermittent Washington assignments. In 1889, after eight years at sea, he returned to Washington for a series of increasingly important desk jobs, culminating in his rank of commodore and the presidency of the Board of Inspection and Survey, responsible for inspecting and approving all new warships. In this capacity the dutiful Dewey learned a great deal about the navy's latest warship technology.

Yet it appeared that his career was nearing its end. He lamented to a friend in 1894 that the peacetime navy offered "little opportunity for a naval man to distinguish himself" and predicted he would be "known in history . . . as 'George Dewey who entered the Navy at a

certain date and retired as Rear Admiral at the age limit!' " In the meantime, Dewey, a widower for many years, enjoyed his Washington life.
Fastidious in dress and manner, with closely cropped white hair and a
well-manicured mustache, he cut a notable figure in social Washington
and derived particular pleasure in hanging out at the prestigious Metropolitan Club on H Street, where Roosevelt also was a member.

The young assistant secretary took a shine to the veteran naval
officer. Although Dewey demonstrated no particular expansionist vision of the kind that animated Roosevelt and his friends Henry Cabot
Lodge and Alfred Thayer Mahan, the commodore projected an air of
decisiveness and dependability that Roosevelt appreciated. The assistant secretary often dined with Dewey at their club and invited him
along for horseback rides through Rock Creek Park. It was natural for
the power-conscious Roosevelt, always bent on getting his own men
in key positions, to identify Dewey as precisely the right man for Asia.
In a pattern that was becoming familiar at the Navy Department, the
meddlesome Roosevelt overstepped his authority in conducting his
Dewey intrigue but was proved correct on the merits.

THE MCKINLEY ADMINISTRATION'S preparation for the coming
naval war had been in progress throughout the president's efforts to
reach his goals without war. Mahan's geostrategic analyses may have
captured with clarity and eloquence the path to national greatness
through the projection of sea power, but the country had been pursuing that path almost by instinct, seemingly part of an inexorable
pursuit of its manifest destiny as an imperial dominion. By early 1896,
as McKinley busied himself with his presidential campaign, the U.S.
House was appropriating money for four new battleships and fifteen
torpedo boats, the former "to carry the heaviest armor and most powerful ordnance . . . and to have the highest practicable speed for vessels
of their class," as a congressional report put it. When the appropriation
measure reached the Senate, that chamber moved to keep the building
program apace with new technological developments. It supplanted
some torpedo boats with "torpedo boat catchers," designed to destroy
enemy torpedo boats that posed serious threats to battleships. The
great maritime powers of the time—Great Britain, France, Germany,

and Russia—were rushing to build such vessels, and America's decision to follow suit reflected the country's global ambition.

In the meantime the U.S. naval fleet consisted of four battleships of the first class, two of the second class, and forty-eight other ships, including armored cruisers, torpedo boats, and other assorted vessels. "I have all Navy in good shape," wrote Roosevelt in his diary, perhaps taking a bit more personal credit than was warranted. But the auguries were good. The new battleship *Iowa* passed its trials with an impressive top speed of seventeen knots, a shade more than the contract called for.

Long's Navy Department moved early in 1898 to prepare its fleets for prospective battle. It shipped tons of ammunition to the Asiatic squadron, ordered all ships to remain fully coaled up, and consolidated most of its Atlantic fleet at Key West, Florida, and its Asiatic fleet at Hong Kong. It scoured the globe for ship-buying opportunities of the kind that had brought the two prospective Brazilian ships into the U.S. fold. It also ordered all combat ships to be painted black to obscure their profiles at sea and render them more elusive targets. In January and February, Washington naval officials ordered Dewey to retain men whose enlistments had expired and, in the event of war, to contain the Spanish fleet in Asia and attack the Philippines. One of these orders was dispatched by Roosevelt, again when Long was out of town, but the instruction reflected naval policy that had been developed beforehand.

Closer to home, Long organized his Atlantic fleet into two flotillas. One was the North Atlantic squadron under the command of Commodore Sampson, with twenty-four ships of various sizes and missions. Sampson's flagship would be the armored cruiser *New York*, and the squadron would operate out of Key West, ready for offensive actions against Cuba in event of war. The other was the smaller but highly maneuverable "Flying Squadron" of five powerful ships under Commodore Winfield Scott Schley: the armored cruiser *Brooklyn* (Schley's flagship), the battleships *Massachusetts* and *Texas*, and the cruisers *Columbia* and *Minneapolis*. Operating out of Hampton Roads, Virginia, the Flying Squadron was to stand ready for quick action at any point along the Atlantic Coast to rebuff Spanish attacks upon the homeland—attacks the Spanish fleet almost assuredly lacked the range to pull off. Roosevelt thought this fleet was placed at Hampton Roads merely to assuage the "hysterical anxiety by the Northeast and its representatives in Congress."

Sampson and Schley were as different in background and temperament as two men in the same navy could be. The ascetic-looking Sampson—tall, slender, stoop-shouldered, with deep-set eyes under thick black eyebrows—was a man of modesty, coolness, and deliberation. He once taught chemistry at Annapolis, and journalist Richard Harding Davis said the fifty-nine-year-old Sampson looked like a "calm and scholarly professor of mathematics." He grew up poor in upstate New York, the son of a day laborer, and pursued whatever meager opportunities for education he could find until he managed to get to the Naval Academy, where he graduated first in his class. He saw combat at the Southern blockade during the Civil War and had a ship sink under him. Recently he had commanded the ultramodern battleship *Iowa* and served as president of the naval board of inquiry on the sinking of the *Maine*.

Schley, just four months older than Sampson, grew up in relative comfort near Frederick, Maryland, and embraced life with a fun-loving spirit and glad-handing openness that were alien to Sampson. At Annapolis he graduated near the bottom of his class, reflecting a tendency to place "pleasure and holidays in higher esteem than plodding study," as he put it. Though he too served with distinction during the Civil War and had some high-profile assignments afterward, he had displayed what some naval officials considered bad judgment during an 1891 naval tour in which he allowed sailors to go ashore in Chile during a time of tension there. The result was a melee, with two sailors killed. In contrast to Sampson's quiet ways, Schley displayed a talent for self-promotion and collecting friends and followers through his ready wit and unfailing charm.

While the navy seemed prepared for war, many harbored concerns about the army. "If the Army were one-tenth as ready as the Navy," Roosevelt wrote a friend, "we would fix that whole business in six weeks." Allowing for the usual Roosevelt hyperbole, there was some truth in his observation. The army's commanding general, Nelson A. Miles, had been warning his civilian superiors for years about the service's manpower and equipment deficiencies and the "unguarded condition of our coast." In a November 1895 message to Congress, Miles reported that the "entire Gulf coast and all the great cities of the Atlantic coast northward to Philadelphia are entirely without modern guns." The general believed the army's enlisted strength should equate to at least one soldier for every 2,000 citizens. That meant a minimum strength of some 38,000 enlisted men, whereas the army numbered only about 25,000.

Miles, fifty-nine when war broke out, boasted a military career that spanned thirty-seven years. At the start of the Civil War, the twenty-two-year-old farm boy enlisted in the Union army and rose from private to brevet major general by war's end. Wounded four times, he received the Medal of Honor for gallantry at Chancellorsville. After the war, he became a Regular Army colonel but rose again through his bold actions in the Indian wars of the Great Plains. Broad-faced and handsome, Miles stirred respect and affection from his troops and the press but often feuded with fellow officers. Roosevelt called him a "brave peacock." Though he possessed courage in abundance, he wasn't particularly endowed with vision or imagination.

SUCH WAS THE state of the U.S. military in April 1898 when war began. By then McKinley was organizing his team and his White House working quarters for the coming challenge. An upstairs office next to the Cabinet Room was converted into a "War Room," with fifteen telephone lines and twenty telegraph machines. The walls displayed maps used to trace troop and ship locations throughout the Caribbean and in Asia. Captain Benjamin Montgomery became the president's telegrapher, and "an expert Western Union operator" named Smithers also was assigned to the room. Soon thousands of secret cables were passing through daily, including outgoing administration orders for warship and army unit movements and incoming reports on activity at sea and in the field. The president enhanced his command over the army, and demonstrated his bureaucratic cunning, by promoting Henry C. Corbin, fifty-six, to brigadier general and nominating him for adjutant general. In that capacity the hulking, brilliant Corbin became a kind of unofficial chief of staff to the president, exercising immense power and giving the president significant leverage over Alger and Miles.

"The President appears to be cheerful," Cortelyou wrote in his diary, "and . . . notes with the greatest interest every matter having the slightest bearing on the pending situation." On April 22 McKinley joined Secretary Long on the longest walk he had taken since becoming president and felt, he told the secretary, much refreshed from it. But as war pressures mounted, the president became more inclined to show displeasure to subordinates. When Corbin embarrassed him by congratulating two military officials on their promotions before McKinley had sent their names to the Senate, he gave the adjutant a serious dressing down—and didn't seem the least bit remorseful about his uncharacteristic harshness. "It's a good plan to call some people down now and then," he told Hastings and Cortelyou. "We all need to be called down once in a while."

More serious was the matter of the Cabinet. Cortelyou considered it "a good working Cabinet but in some respects not a strong one." Some members lacked force and a grounding in "the mighty epochs of human history or . . . international affairs." He considered William Day to be a conspicuous exception to that critique. Long felt McKinley had "made a mistake" in putting four men into his Cabinet who seemed too old or infirm for their jobs, "cripples," as he called them—Sherman, Gary, Alger, and himself. Postmaster-General Gary resigned on April 21, the day war began. And Long reported to his diary that he himself had been feeling much more healthy and fit in recent weeks.

But the Sherman problem was becoming acute. Long wrote that the secretary of state had become "of little use in the Cabinet; now and then a flash of his old strength, but generally quiet, retiring, and silent." He also was developing a tendency toward peevishness as his mental capacity declined. Hay in London heard that a "crisis was precipitated by a lapse of memory in a conversation with the Austrian Minister of so serious a nature that the President had to [act] without an instant's delay." On April 22 McKinley sat down with Sherman to ask, in his typically gentle manner, for his resignation. Two days later, at a Cabinet meeting, the secretary reluctantly announced his departure. The president prevailed upon Day to accept the position, but only through the duration of the war and with the proviso that he could name his first assistant. He appointed John Bassett Moore, a bearded, stocky law professor at Columbia University and former State Department official who was considered the country's leading scholar of international law. The country embraced Day's elevation. "Judge Day," declared the *Louisville Commercial*, "has developed qualities that entitle him to a place among American statesmen of the first rank." McKinley finally now had a strong team at State.

That left War Secretary Alger, who didn't seem up to the war challenge. Young Charles Dawes speculated that he might be "endangering his position . . . by his actions and unwise talk." Alger complained frequently that his "prerogatives are being encroached upon," Dawes wrote in his journal, adding wryly that, fortunately for the war effort, there was some truth in his complaint. Long took a similar view. "At present it seems as if the Army were ready for nothing at all," he wrote in his diary after an April 20 military meeting with the president. It was clear that Alger had not brought to the army the kind of war preparations that Long and Roosevelt had executed in the navy. But McKinley concluded that replacing Alger would be too disruptive at such a critical time.

On April 22 Congress authorized a call for volunteers and followed up four days later with legislation to increase the regular forces to 62,527 men for the war's duration. Though the War Department insisted that a volunteer force of 60,000 would be sufficient, McKinley on April 23 called for 125,000 volunteers to serve for two years or until war's end. (He later was to add another call for 75,000 men to cover all possible contingencies.) War-planning sessions yielded the decision that Cuba would be invaded, but not until after Sampson could destroy the Spanish Atlantic fleet—and probably also not until after the summer rainy season, when yellow fever and malaria would be rampant. Miles argued that this would give him the time required to drill and equip his troops in the United States. He told the president that he didn't have enough ammunition "to last an army of 70,000 men in one hour's serious battle." McKinley accepted that argument with the idea that, in the meantime, the blockade would curtail Spanish efforts to further fortify the island, and the army would send a force of 5,000 men to Cuba's southern coast to supply arms to rebel forces under General Máximo Gómez. On April 29 Miles ordered Brigadier General William R. Shafter, the Fifth Corps commander, to assemble the 5,000-man force at Tampa, Florida, and prepare for the Cuban expedition.

But then Spain's Admiral Pascual Cervera left the Cape Verde islands with his Atlantic fleet and disappeared into the ocean expanse. Facing the looming danger of a sudden appearance of Cervera's warships, including four armored cruisers and three destroyers, McKinley postponed the Cuban expedition. In the meantime, the mustering of troops at Tampa continued at a pace that outran the camp's capacity. By the end of May, the Tampa camp encompassed some 17,000 troops. One of them was Theodore Roosevelt, whose jumble of piquant traits included a powerful sense of patriotism and a veneration of courage as a necessity of virtue. The vigorous Roosevelt resigned his naval job, joined the army, got himself commissioned as a lieutenant colonel, helped organize the U.S. Volunteer Cavalry, and became the unit's second in command under his friend Colonel Leonard Wood. The unit, recruited mostly by Roosevelt, included western rustics he had met during his turbulent ranching experience and eastern aristocrats from his prep school and Harvard days. The proud officer had his fawn-colored uniform specially made by Brooks Brothers.

Roosevelt quickly became incensed with the lack of organization at Tampa. He wrote to Lodge, "No words could describe to you the confusion and lack of system and the general mismanagement of affairs here." Shafter was forced to concede to Washington, "The place was overestimated and its capacities are exceeded."

As the army struggled with the Tampa mess, McKinley turned his attention to war finances. Reporting to Congress that the previous $50 million appropriation was approaching exhaustion, he asked for a series of tax increases—mostly excise taxes on beer and tobacco and a stamp tax on legal instruments, stock transfers, bank checks, and the like—designed to raise some $100 million. Both houses quickly passed the legislation, which was designed to finance the war for the next year or so.

The president also nominated eleven men to the rank of major general, including four from civilian life and two Southerners whose designation was calculated in part to symbolize America's post–Civil War unity. One of the Southerners was Alabama's representative Joseph H.

Wheeler, known as "Fighting Joe" from his days as a dashing Confederate cavalry officer, when he rose to the rank of major general. After the war he became a lawyer and represented his Alabama district in Congress for most of the next seventeen years. Like many Southerners, the sixty-one-year-old Wheeler loved the idea of putting on the uniform of his once and current country. The other Southerner was Fitzhugh Lee, whose blunt pronouncements as U.S. consul in Havana had given him considerable national stature.

ON THE EVENING of May 1, rumors began filtering into Washington of a significant U.S. naval victory in the Philippines. The next day's newspapers provided sketchy reports, mostly from Madrid via London, of serious Spanish devastation. The *New York Times* cautioned, "While it is quite clear that the Spanish squadron has suffered a crushing defeat, the dispatches leave in doubt the intensely interesting question whether the American squadron has suffered material damage." Nevertheless Washington erupted into what the *Times* called "wild rejoicing." Newsboys rushed to the streets to hawk extras in violation of an ordinance forbidding them from calling aloud their wares after 8 p.m., but police stood by benignly. At the White House, noted Cortelyou, the news of Dewey's action "was a source of the greatest satisfaction to the President and others who had gathered here."

The next day the *Times* reported that the cable from the Philippines to Hong Kong had been cut, which meant that official military reports from Dewey wouldn't be forthcoming for several days, since Dewey would have to dispatch the information by ship to Hong Kong. Slowly a narrative of the battle emerged and then reached full focus with Dewey's preliminary dispatches on May 7.

Dewey had set out for the Philippines from Mirs Bay, near Hong Kong, on April 27 with nine ships, including six fighting vessels with 1,611 crewmen. Four of those were protected cruisers, meaning their decks were fortified with steel armor, although their sides were not. His fighting ships' fifty-three heavy guns included ten potent eight-inch breech-loading cannon. Dewey's intelligence indicated that Admiral Patricio Montojo would be waiting for him in Philippine waters, most likely in Subic Bay. Arriving off Subic on the afternoon of April 30, the commodore sent in three ships to probe the whereabouts of Montojo. He wasn't there, which meant he must be in Manila Bay. Dewey, who considered this a better combat location for his squadron, was elated. "Now we have them!" he exclaimed to one of his officers.

Under cover of darkness Dewey navigated his ships through the Manila harbor entrance, with lights covered and gun crews ready to return fire from nearby hills. Though he knew the harbor and entrance would be mined, he calculated that the risk of a hit was slim enough to justify proceeding. As it happened, his ships encountered no mines that posed serious danger, and the shore batteries didn't seem to be anticipating a night entry. Only his last vessels drew fire, and that was limited to just three ill-directed rounds that inflicted no damage. It appeared that Montojo's officers had been literally asleep on the job. The Spanish admiral had positioned his seven fighting ships—two unprotected cruisers and five gunboats—in a crescent formation stretching east to west. He had only thirty-seven heavy guns and none larger than 6.3 inches.

At dawn Dewey maneuvered his ships into position to cruise past the Spanish squadron, with Montojo's ships facing his portside guns. At 5:40 a.m. Dewey's flagship, the protected cruiser *Olympia*, positioned itself in front of the enemy fleet at a range of about 5,000 yards. A seemingly relaxed Dewey turned to his commander, Captain Charles Gridley.

"You may fire when you are ready, Gridley," he said.

The first shot exploded from the flagship's forward turret, signaling to the rest of the squadron that the battle was on. Dewey's ships passed in front of the enemy vessels, delivering devastating fire. Then they executed a "countermarch," bringing their starboard guns into play. In all, the Americans executed the firing maneuver five times, three westward runs and two to the east. During the fighting, two of Montojo's cruisers charged at the *Olympia*, but both were repelled under a barrage of debilitating fire from the Americans. The *Reina Cristina*, Montojo's flagship, sustained fearsome firepower, with one shell killing twenty men at once and another killing or disabling nine. The *Reina Cristina* soon sank, shortly after Montojo managed to get himself aboard another ship.

At 7:35 Dewey received a report from Gridley that he interpreted as indicating his squadron was running out of ammunition. "It was a most anxious moment for me," he wrote later, explaining that he didn't realize how much damage his ships had delivered to the enemy and feared a disparity in ammunition supply could turn the tide of battle. But he soon learned that the report had been garbled. He had plenty of ammunition, and as the smoke cleared he could see the devastation visited upon Montojo's fleet. "Some of them were perceived to be on fire," Dewey wrote later, "and others were seeking protection behind Cavite Point." Confident of victory, the commodore ordered breakfast for his men, then returned to the fray to finish the job.

The tally of Spanish destruction and death was startling. All eight of Montojo's warships had been sunk or disabled. Some 161 Spaniards had been killed and another 210 wounded. Dewey sustained no serious damage to his vessels and no deaths; nine men had been wounded.

The next day Dewey warned Spanish officials that if another shot was fired at his ships from Manila batteries, he would destroy the city. Word came back that the garrison guns would remain silent so long as his ships didn't position themselves to bomb Manila. "From the moment that the captain-general accepted my terms," Dewey wrote, "the city was virtually surrendered, and I was in control of the situation." He quickly occupied the Cavite garrison, which had been abandoned by Spanish forces, and demanded that local authorities provide access to the stocks of coal needed to keep his ships stoked for action. Then he neutralized all shore batteries along the bay's entry route. When Spanish officials denied him access to the telegraphic cable, he had it cut so it could not be used to his detriment. Dewey now controlled the bay and could take the city at any time. Lacking the troops to occupy it, however, he settled in to his territorial command and requested a contingent of army troops to subdue Manila.

Instantly George Dewey was a hero in America. Manufacturers rushed to place his visage on products as inducements to sales and to bring out new ones aimed at exploiting the patriotic fervor unleashed by his victory. A new chewing gum was dubbed "Dewey Chewies." The commodore was celebrated in song and verse, his portrait emblazoned on "badges, banners, lithographs, and transparencies," according to one historian, as well as "paperweights, pitchers, cups, plates, butter dishes, shaving mugs, teething rings, and rattles." Official Washington unleashed its own display of enthusiasm. Roosevelt wired a message to Dewey: "Every American is your debtor." John Hay wrote to praise the "mingled wisdom and daring" of his audacious Manila Bay entrance. Publicly Hay captured the national pride unleashed by this unassuming sailor: "It is these quiet, gentlemanly Americans," he told the London press, ". . . who may be depended upon to surprise the world when the opportunity of making history comes in the line of duty." Senator Proctor took to crowing just a bit in a letter to McKinley, highlighting his own wisdom in pushing Dewey for the Asiatic command. "We may run him against you for President," wrote the senator. If McKinley was taken aback at such a ribbing, he didn't show it. He quickly promoted Dewey to rear admiral and told the nation, "The magnitude of this victory can hardly be measured by the ordinary standards of naval warfare."

Within days of Dewey's victory, General Miles brought forth a plan to send 5,000 troops to Manila to secure the city and eliminate the danger posed to Dewey's ships from a possible Spanish campaign to retake Manila and its mounted guns. McKinley responded quickly, and soon troops were mustering at San Francisco under Major General Wesley Merritt, the army's second-ranking officer, who was to command a jurisdiction called "the Department of the Pacific," including the entire Philippine archipelago. By month's end, Merritt's projected troop strength had ballooned to 15,000, three times what Dewey had requested.

This increase in forces occurred against a backdrop of tensions between Merritt and Miles over the mission of the Philippine operation and the kinds of troops needed for its accomplishment. Merritt saw the mission as subduing the entire archipelago and thus wanted large numbers of well-trained regular troops, as opposed to less experienced volunteers. This was necessary, he argued, to meet the challenge of "conquering a territory 7,000 miles from our base, defended by a regularly trained and acclimated army of from 10,000 to 25,000 men, and inhabited by people, the majority of whom will regard us with the intense hatred born of race and religion." Miles disputed Merritt's estimate of enemy strength and his definition of the mission. "The force ordered at this time is not expected to carry on a war to conquer extensive territory," he wrote to Merritt, but rather to create "a strong garrison to command the harbor of Manila, and to relieve the . . . fleet under Admiral Dewey with the least possible delay."

The troop strength matter was settled when Merritt was given a few more regulars, as well as the Tenth Pennsylvania militia command, touted as a particularly effective volunteer unit. That brought Merritt's troop strength to 20,000, a remarkable number reflecting America's new willingness to project power into the world. As for the precise nature of the mission, that resided with the president, and he remained characteristically coy on the question.

But although the president wasn't inclined toward any expansive pronouncements, he fully meant to exploit the Dewey victory boldly. In a letter to Alger, he revealed his intention to subdue all of the Philippines, at least for the time being, under an American military government. Not only should U.S. forces bring about the "acquisition and control of the bay," he wrote, but they should also become "an arm of occupation to the Philippines for the twofold purpose of completing the reduction of Spanish power in that quarter and of giving order and security to the islands while in the possession of the United States." That left to the future the eventual political disposition of the islands, a question McKinley wasn't yet prepared to answer.

Nevertheless Dewey's triumph had consequences well beyond anything anyone had contemplated during America's growing fixation with the agonies of Cuba. It brought forth a kind of serendipitous imperialism—the acquisition almost by accident of strategic territory in far-flung regions of the world, the result of actions by people who had other ends in mind and who hadn't contemplated what they would do with such rewards of victory. The president, it was said, began his education on the Philippines by tearing a small map from a schoolbook, and when a government official arrived with more detailed charts he received them avidly while acknowledging his limited knowledge. "It is evident," he said, "that I must learn a great deal of geography in this war." But the logic of victory was generating its own impetus, as well as study requirements, and soon official Washington and the country at large embraced with growing comfort the mantle of imperialism. As Henry Cabot Lodge wrote to Roosevelt, "Unless I am utterly and profoundly mistaken, the administration is now fully committed to the large policy that we both desire."

19

The Caribbean War

"WHAT YOU WENT TO SANTIAGO FOR WAS THE SPANISH ARMY"

On Monday, May 2, President McKinley convened a joint Cabinet-military meeting at the White House to draw up expansive new plans to take the war to Spain's Cuba. The concept of a modest expedition of 5,000 men to join rebel leader Máximo Gómez now gave way to a strategy of establishing a Cuban beachhead near Havana, probably at Mariel, and then pouring in some 50,000 troops for a march on the Cuban capital, Spain's pivot of power in the Western Hemisphere. General Shafter's regulars at Tampa would serve as vanguard, capturing and fortifying the beachhead, and then volunteer forces would follow as quickly as they could be trained and transported through Tampa. There wouldn't be much interaction with rebel forces, whose fighting capacity and spirit increasingly were viewed as less robust than previously thought. When War Secretary Alger was asked how quickly he could get his troops in place for the mission, he replied that he needed three weeks.

It was a rash answer, and Navy Secretary Long knew it. Four days later, at the regular Friday Cabinet meeting, Long emphasized his readiness to transport army troops to a Cuban invasion. He presented a letter previously sent to Alger "stating that the Navy is ready to convoy any force of forty or fifty thousand men to Cuba, and urging the War Department to take active steps," as Long described it in his diary. Not surprisingly, Alger took offense. The army, he said, could handle its end of the war without naval interference. The wily Long responded good-naturedly that his intent was simply to counter any impression "that there is any delay on our part."

No doubt Long truly wished to dispel any concerns about naval delays. But in doing so he also placed a spotlight on Alger, "the most active of all members of the Cabinet for war," as Long described him. For two months, the navy secretary added in a diary entry, Alger had insisted that he could get his army ready in ten days, "whereas, in fact, not a volunteer has left his state, and in my judgment there has been a striking lack of preparation and promptness."

In fact Alger didn't have anything approaching an adequate army. As a leading trade publication called the *Army and Navy Journal* put it, "To invade Cuba requires an army, and whoever may be held responsible for the result, the fact remains that we have no army. We have some excellent raw material for one, that is all." The problem was that Alger hadn't given his boss a realistic picture of just how long it would take to muster in and train the volunteer force. Long's aim at the May 6 Cabinet meeting was to force into the open Alger's lack of readiness.

It was not what McKinley wanted to hear. He faced military, diplomatic, and political imperatives for an aggressive and speedy war. For one thing, delay could introduce into the region power ambiguities, which might in turn lure European nations bent on exploiting the chaos and getting a Caribbean foothold. Beyond that, the navy couldn't maintain an effective Cuban blockade indefinitely. Hurricane season would arrive in late summer, and in the meantime the arduous maritime task of sealing off the island imposed serious wear and tear on Long's ships. Also, given that the president certainly didn't want to launch an invasion during the dangerous, yellow fever–infested rainy season, he felt a need for hurried action before the onset of the rains. Finally, Dewey's Manila victory had diminished Washington's concerns about initiating the invasion with Admiral Cervera's whereabouts unknown, although U.S. planners certainly didn't want to take any fool-hardy chances with the vulnerable transport operation.

With all this in mind, the president needed Caribbean victories quickly to force Madrid into a war settlement. The longer it took, the greater the expenditure in blood, treasure, and American prestige—and the greater the political danger facing McKinley at home. The American people had wanted this war, had practically forced the president into it as he expended valuable political capital in seeking to get the desired result without war. That approach had left an impression among many that he was an inert president, insufficiently engaged and aggressive when the country's honor and interests were threatened. He could hardly afford to have that image attach to him now as a war president. And he knew also that nothing saps a president's political standing more quickly than voter perceptions of military ineptitude or an appearance that he got the country into a war he couldn't win. Thus delay was his enemy, along with the Spanish military and yellow fever. He needed, as the *Washington Post* put it, "a short, sharp, conclusive, and immediate campaign."

On May 9, General Shafter in Tampa received orders to "seize and hold Mariel or most important point on north coast of Cuba and where territory is ample to land and deploy Army." At the same time, Washington ordered the army to move volunteer forces at Camp Chickamauga, Georgia, and other locations in the South to Tampa for incorporation into the invasion force. These troop movements were to proceed "without delay."

But delays proved unavoidable. First, the army scheduled its Cuban landing without giving the navy enough notice so its chartered convoy ships could be brought into position for the massive and complex transport operation. Long was outraged. "Our ships are all ready," he complained in his diary, "but we must at least have notice when and where they are wanted." He protested to McKinley, who authorized a delay until May 16. On May 13 word reached Washington that Cervera's fleet had been sighted near Martinique, in the eastern Caribbean. Alger seized upon the report to press for another delay, thus receiving still more time to get the sputtering troop movement operation in shape. Roosevelt, working to outfit his Rough Riders, poured his frustration into his diary: "The blunders [and] delays of the ordnance bureau surpass belief. They express us stuff we don't need and send us the rifles by slow freight! There is no head, no energy, no intelligence . . . in the War Dept." Concerned about the lack of ammunition and water, Miles urged McKinley to put off the Cuba attack and instead invade Puerto Rico, an easier target. McKinley rejected the notion.

Then came word on May 19 that Cervera, seeking to evade Sampson's nearby fleet, had led his squadron into the harbor of Santiago de Cuba, the island's second largest city, with some 30,000 inhabitants, located in the southeast. This gave America a stunning military opportunity. If Sampson could bottle up Cervera's ships within the harbor, and if Shafter could initiate a successful land offensive against the city, Santiago could be the locus of a dazzling U.S. dual victory on land and sea. The city lay isolated from the Spanish main force, defended by 10,000 or so Spanish regulars but cut off from the sea by the U.S. blockade and from the land by surrounding insurgent forces. The aim would be to overwhelm Santiago's Spanish defenders and take control of the harbor's commanding heights, thus allowing Sampson's mine sweepers to clear the harbor for an American entry that would culminate in the destruction of Cervera's aged and poorly outfitted warships. Then, bypassing Havana, U.S. forces could capture Puerto Rico as an added inducement to Spanish capitulation—and perhaps as a later indemnity prize. The plan had the added advantage of requiring fewer volunteer troops, which weren't fully ready anyway.

On May 26 McKinley convened a White House war council to explore prospects for a new strategy. Present were Alger, Long, Miles, and the navy's top brass. They didn't take long to embrace the new plan. Miles detailed the concept in a series of memos that added new initiatives, including the seizure of most of the island's deep-water ports, providing masses of materiel to the rebels through those ports, and initiating a U.S. Army march across the island to destroy Spanish outposts throughout the countryside. McKinley, drawing perhaps on his long-past Civil War experiences as well as his inherent sound judgment, promptly rejected these superfluous add-ons while approving the fundamental strategy.

During this period, the strains of McKinley's job began to show once again, "the color having faded from his cheeks and the rings being once more noticeable about his eyes," as Cortelyou observed in his diary. In addition to the momentous decisions facing him, he found himself mediating disputes among war leaders, a task he found distasteful. Cortelyou wondered if Alger had "risen to the full measure of success thus far in these trying times" and noted that "there are many who doubt whether he will do so in the remaining days of the war." Long, he added, "moves along quietly," but often seemed to lack decisiveness and "nerve."

McKinley appeared to revive, though, when relaxing with friends, particularly Myron Herrick and his wife when they visited from Cleveland. After a late-May visit, with much casual conversation and poetry reading between the two couples, Cortelyou observed, "The President looked exceeding well to-night" when he stopped by late for a final war briefing. He also read letters from parents of servicemen begging him to keep their sons away from Cuba during the coming rainy season.

McKinley continued his attentiveness toward Ida, whose health went through a period of significant revival during this time. "Now she can almost walk alone," wrote Cortelyou. In fact her solicitousness toward her husband sometimes seemed to exceed his toward her. During a New York visit, when a cousin reported from Washington that the president seemed "very tired and worn out," she immediately wired him an admonition, "Do not expose yourself or work too hard." She demanded a direct telephone connection between her Manhattan hotel and the White House so she could bypass central exchanges and diminish the risk of their conversations being picked up by nosy operators in league with anti-McKinley newspapers. But his own attentiveness never wavered. When she arrived at her New York hotel, there was his usual telegram of greeting waiting for her. And he continued to interrupt serious matters of state when the White House maid tapped on his door to say Mrs. McKinley wished to see him. As McKinley's secretary Porter explained, "No matter how busy he may be, nor how deeply engaged in any subject, he invariably drops everything on the instant and goes into their own apartments." But he made up for the interruptions by working regularly late into the night, usually well past eleven o'clock and sometimes past midnight.

ON MAY 31, Adjutant General Corbin, acting under presidential instruction, sent orders to Shafter, commander of the Fifth Corps being organized at Tampa, to land a force near Santiago de Cuba and "capture or destroy the garrison there," then assist Sampson in destroying the Spanish fleet. In many ways, Shafter, then sixty-three, seemed an unlikely choice for the command. A tower of corpulence who tipped the scales at more than 300 pounds and suffered from gout, he had difficulty just getting atop a horse—and quickly would wear down the animal in any event. With his lumbering walk, fleshy face, and weary-eyed gaze, he gave off an appearance of passivity. But he could be blustery, enjoyed a reputation for blunt honesty, and cared not a whit for political intrigues. Besides, he had been in line for promotion, and that's how things were done in the army at that time. Both Miles and Corbin wanted him for the job, and McKinley went along with his generals.

But the massive challenge of preparing 50,000 troops or more for an amphibious assault on Cuba proved too much for Shafter. The result was a mess of chaos and wasted motion. Colonel Wood described it as "confusion, confusion, confusion. War! Why it is an advertisement to foreigners of our absolutely unprepared condition." General Miles, arriving on June 1, discovered 300 railroad cars loaded with war materiel along the roads around Tampa. But the invoices had been lost, so officers were forced to "hunt from car to car to ascertain whether they contain clothing, grain, balloon material, horse equipments, ammunition, siege guns, commissary stores, etc." While his volunteer troops were "suffering for clothing," fifteen cars of uniforms languished on a railroad siding miles from the encampment. When Roosevelt brought in his Rough Riders after an arduous four-day ride from Texas, he discovered "a perfect welter of confusion . . . an almost inextricable tangle." His troops were forced to buy food from local shops with their own money, as commissary operations had been overwhelmed by the numbers of arriving troops, up to five regiments a day.

McKinley followed all this "most earnestly and intently" from his War Room. "Only once in a while," wrote Cortelyou, "does he show any temper." But his patience was wearing thin. Through Alger and

Corbin, he sent numerous wires to Shafter asking for status reports on when the army would be off and urging quick action. Twice in early June Miles and Shafter assured Washington that the expedition would leave on June 7. When that day unfolded without reports of a departure, McKinley and his War Department lost patience. At 7:50 p.m. Corbin wired Shafter that the president wanted him to proceed even if it meant transporting as few as 10,000 men. An hour later, Alger preempted the previous order. "Since telegraphing you an hour since," declared the war secretary, "the President directs you to sail at once with what force you have already."

By the next afternoon Shafter had a 17,000-man advance force aboard thirty-five ships, along with 959 horses and 1,336 mules, 112 six-mule wagons, eighty-one escort wagons, and masses of armaments of every purpose and description. Given the haste and shortage of ships, not all the desired equipment could be taken. Some cavalry troops, including Roosevelt's, even had to leave their horses behind. But the convoy finally was headed out of Tampa Bay, into the Gulf of Mexico, and toward Cuba. Then the general received an urgent message from Washington: "Wait until you get further orders before you sail. Answer quick." It seems that U.S. vessels had spotted two Spanish men-of-war in the St. Nicholas Channel, off the northeastern coast of Cuba. With prospects seemingly high that the transport operation could be attacked, Washington ordered a delay until Sampson could reinforce the naval escort. "We mean to start this expedition as soon as convoy is strong enough," the assistant naval secretary, Charles Allen, cabled an agitated Sampson, who didn't believe any Spanish warships were in the vicinity.

Sampson was right. It turned out the sightings actually had been U.S. warships mistakenly identified as Spanish. This "ghost squadron" caused a six-day delay. Meanwhile thousands of troops languished aboard overcrowded ships in subtropical heat with barely sufficient comfort and provisions. Roosevelt reported to a friend from his anchored transport ship that "the interminable delays and the vacillation and utter absence of efficient organization are really discouraging."

Finally, on June 14, the convoy set off, and five days later it reached its destination on Cuba's southern coast. On June 20 Sampson sent his chief of staff, Captain French Chadwick, to see Shafter and discuss landing and battle plans. The shipboard conference produced an apparent misunderstanding of serious proportions. Chadwick anticipated that Shafter would attack Spain's hillside forts at the mouth of the harbor so Sampson could clear mines, enter the harbor, and destroy the Spanish fleet. Based on the conversation, he thought Shafter agreed with this plan. But Shafter already had opted to march his army inland to Santiago, bypassing the areas of greatest support to Sampson's squadron, and attacking the city from the east. The direct route to the mouth of the harbor, in Shafter's view, posed too many obstacles of terrain and undergrowth, and hence he would face a large risk that he would get bogged down under withering fire from the surrounding heights. And with the yellow fever season approaching, he favored what he considered the fastest route to a Spanish surrender.

Based on conversations with rebel leaders, Shafter decided to land his army at a small coastal hamlet called Daiquiri, following a series of planned feints and bombardments designed to ease the way for the landing. As soon as he had sufficient troops at Daiquiri, about 6,000 men, Shafter sent a contingent of soldiers toward the coastal town of Siboney to the west. Dislodging about 600 Spanish troops there without much fight, the Americans added a new landing area. Shafter pulled together the regular forces of General Henry Lawton with volunteers under General Wheeler, the wizened Alabamian later described by Roosevelt as "a regular gamecock." They were ordered to advance toward the town of Las Guasimas on a reconnaissance mission. Hungry for glory, Wheeler maneuvered his troops ahead of Lawton's, then attacked the town's Spanish defenders. Apparently forgetting in his exuberance where he was, the former Confederate general yelled after the retreating Spaniards, "We've got the damn Yankees on the run!"

The skirmish, with Roosevelt's Rough Riders participating, had cost the Americans sixteen killed and fifty-two wounded. But it left U.S. forces in command of Las Guasimas, cleared the road to Santiago, and positioned the Americans for a march on the city. The Spanish general in charge, Arsenio Linares, had intended to retreat from Las Guasimas when the Americans arrived, but his withdrawal proved to be less orderly than he had planned. Over the next week Shafter sought to position and supply his troops for the coming assault against the San

Juan Heights, seven miles ahead, a formidable Spanish line of defense protected by well-entrenched troops under Linares. Shafter fashioned a simple plan of attack that reflected his particular turn of mind. He would take the heights with a frontal assault while General Lawton, with an infantry division and light artillery battery, would capture the enemy redoubt at El Caney, six miles north of Santiago.

On June 30 the operation commenced, with Shafter's troops marching all day toward the heights and getting to within a mile of the ridge. At daybreak the next morning Lawton began his assault on the Spanish position at El Caney, which proved highly fortified and resistant to American fire. Throughout the morning, Lawton pummeled El Caney, to little effect. This led to delays in the planned assault on the heights, which was supposed to commence only after El Caney had been taken. It was another Shafter blunder, since El Caney could have been sealed off with a much smaller force, thus making available a large portion of Lawton's infantry and artillery units for the main assault on San Juan Heights.

Meanwhile the Americans began an artillery attack on the heights at 8 a.m. as infantry and unmounted cavalry soldiers pressed forward for a ground assault. The road leading to the battle area soon filled up with American soldiers caught in an ominous crunch. From the tallest peaks of the heights, San Juan Hill and Kettle Hill, came withering enemy fire, while the exposed U.S. advance force was frozen in place by more American soldiers pressing forward from the rear. "The situation was desperate," wrote *New York Herald* reporter Richard Harding Davis. "Our troops could not retreat. . . . There was only one thing they could do—go forward and take the San Juan hills by assault."

When Roosevelt's Rough Riders, anchoring the right flank of the American line, received orders to attack at about 1 p.m., the impetuous New Yorker leaped upon his mount, Little Texas, and rode back and forth among his men, exhorting them to push forward through the barrage of enemy fire raining down upon them. Soon Roosevelt's little regiment was so far ahead of the rest of the attack force that Davis, watching from a distance, concluded that "someone had made an awful and terrible mistake." A foreign military observer called the assault "very gallant, but very foolish."

But the Rough Riders kept going, and soon other units charged forward through waist-high grass to join the assault as Roosevelt's men reached the top of Kettle Hill. Lieutenant John Pershing's Tenth Cavalry, made up of well-trained black troops, joined the Kettle Hill attack, while Brigadier General Jacob Kent's First Infantry Division moved up nearby San Juan Hill. Enemy defenders quickly abandoned both hills, and by 2 p.m. the Americans commanded the San Juan Heights, looking down upon Santiago de Cuba. With Davis poised to capture in prose the Rough Rider charge in all of its foolhardy glory, Roosevelt soon would become one of the country's leading military heroes, a man to beguile the imagination of a galvanized nation.

In Washington, President McKinley received news of the battle in progress before he had finished breakfast. When Cabinet members arrived for the regular Friday meeting, the president briefed them on the state of the battle, as conveyed through the clicking telegraph machines in the nearby War Room. Such was the excitement and anticipation that the Cabinet was unable to consider any matters beyond the Santiago situation. Just before midnight the War Department received Shafter's battle report from Siboney: "Had a very heavy engagement today, which lasted from 8 a.m. till sundown. We have carried their outer works and are now in possession of them. There is now about three-quarters of a mile of open between my lines and the city. By morning troops will be intrenched and considerable augmentation of forces will be there." He added that Lawton had captured El Caney at 4 p.m. Casualties, he said, would exceed 400, mostly wounded. They ended up being 225 Americans killed and 1,384 wounded. Spanish casualties included 215 dead and 376 wounded.

At 2 a.m., with McKinley sitting up in anticipation of further reports, Shafter sent a cable that introduced an ominous note into the White House vigil. It said simply, "I fear I have underestimated today's casualties. A large and thoroughly equipped hospital ship should be sent here at once to care for the wounded." Then he fell silent for the next thirty-four hours, leaving his war secretary and president in the dark on his precise circumstances. Disturbing rumors about Shafter's predicament began circulating around Washington in late afternoon, and at 1 a.m. Alger finally fired off a demand for information: "We are awaiting with intense anxiety tidings of yesterday."

McKinley stayed up past 4 a.m. awaiting a reply; when none came he finally went to bed.

Then, around noon on Sunday, July 3, Shafter sent a cable that left official Washington filled with foreboding. He said he could not conquer Santiago with available forces and likely would withdraw his troops to an outer perimeter five miles back, where rail lines would facilitate his supply operation. He expressed sorrow at his casualty rate and concerns about illnesses that had overtaken generals Wheeler and Samuel Young. Indeed, he added, he wasn't feeling very well himself, though he remained in command. Although McKinley and his Washington advisers could only speculate at what was going on, the truth was that Shafter, having barely eked out his San Juan Heights victory, promptly lost his nerve. Wracked by fever and enervated by the exertions of command, he succumbed to fits of anxiety over all that could possibly go wrong in his theater of war.

This was a potential disaster. How could it be, McKinley wondered, that a small city of some 30,000 inhabitants and 10,000 defenders, totally cut off from the outside world, reduced to a state of near starvation, couldn't be subdued by 17,000 well-armed American troops that stood poised on the high ground surrounding the city? If Shafter got himself bogged down five miles away and Santiago held out, the entire strategy was at risk. Spain would not capitulate, yellow fever would ravage the troops, and McKinley would take on the appearance of a wartime incompetent. The dejected president sat with his war advisers through much of Sunday pondering what to do. Washington, so far from the action, couldn't take responsibility for the safety of the troops. The decision would have to rest with Shafter. The general was promised quick reinforcements if he would remain in place, and Alger warned him of the negative impact on the national mood if he pulled back.

As if he hadn't injected enough woe into White House councils, Shafter sent an early-afternoon cable on Sunday reporting that Cervera had bolted from Santiago harbor with his entire fleet and made good his escape. Apparently unmindful of the strategic disaster this represented, he expressed satisfaction that the admiral's big naval guns were no longer in position to menace his troops. Fortunately, though not surprisingly, Shafter had fired off his message without knowing what he was talking about. Cervera had in fact attempted an escape, but the outcome had not been as Shafter reported. Official word arrived at Washington from Sampson: "The fleet under my command offers the nation as a Fourth of July present the whole of Cervera's fleet. It attempted to escape at 9:30 this morning. At 2 the last ship, the *Cristobal Colon*, had run ashore 75 miles west of Santiago and hauled down her colors. The *Infanta Maria Teresa*, *Oquendo*, and *Vizcaya* were forced ashore, burned, and blown up within 20 miles of Santiago. The *Furor* and *Pluton* destroyed within 4 miles of the port."

Sampson didn't mention in his report that, when Cervera made his break, Sampson himself had been in conference with Shafter at Siboney and hence the man in charge was his old rival, Commodore Schley, commanding his flagship, the *Brooklyn*. Rushing back aboard his own flagship, the *New York*, Sampson missed most of the battle but got to the scene in time to join the chase for the *Cristobal Colon*. As he passed the harbor entrance, Sampson ordered the big battleships, the *Iowa* and the *Indiana*, to resume their positions off the harbor entrance to prevent two remaining Spanish ships at Santiago from leaving the harbor and menacing U.S. transport vessels at Siboney. The Sampson report struck a discordant note with some in the navy who felt that he sought to take undue credit for a victory that more properly belonged to Schley. This issue, along with some questions about a key Schley maneuver during the battle, would intensify the Sampson-Schley antagonism in coming months and create something of a national spectacle.

But in the immediate afterglow of victory, the nation rejoiced. The *New York Times* said the news was received at Washington "like splendid sunlight bursting through low-hanging clouds." McKinley promptly released to the public his message to Sampson: "You have the gratitude and congratulations of the whole American people. Convey to your noble officers and crews, through whose valor new honors have been added to the Americans, the grateful thanks and appreciation of the Nation."

The *Times* added that the victory was particularly welcome given the "discouraged tone" of Shafter's message of the day before, which the White House had released to the public after striking out the general's suggestion that he might withdraw his troops from his hard-won perimeter. "When . . . General Shafter from his invalid's couch admitted the hopelessness of the fight he was waging and called for help," wrote the *Times*, "the somber side of the war for the first time showed itself."

But now even Shafter could see that the Schley-Sampson victory changed the calculus of military power around Santiago. Before dawn he demanded the surrender of Santiago, and the next day he cabled Washington, "I shall hold my present position." After entering into negotiations with General José Toral (Linares had been wounded in battle), Shafter informed Washington that he expected an unconditional surrender soon. To buck up the general—and curtail his repeated references to his ill health—McKinley got Alger and Corbin to cable him a message expressing "sorrow and anxiety" about his infirmity and suggesting, "[You] must determine whether your condition is such as to require you to relinquish command." That was the end of Shafter's health complaints.

But not the end of his questionable judgment. On July 8 he wired the War Department recommending that the United States accept Toral's terms of surrender, which included U.S. permission that his troops repair to another Cuban location with their equipment and weapons. Shafter argued that many of Toral's troops would disperse into the countryside, thus preventing widespread bloodshed by obviating the need for an attack on the city and protecting his troops from a likely onslaught of yellow fever. McKinley was incredulous. He asked Corbin to draft a response, then edited it heavily and had it sent out over Corbin's signature. Noting that Shafter had predicted an unconditional surrender, the message went on, "Under these circumstances, your message recommending that Spanish troops be permitted to evacuate and proceed without molestation . . . is a great surprise and is not approved." After reflection McKinley concluded the message had been inadequate, so he fostered a follow-up communication with a more direct repudiation: "What you went to Santiago for was the Spanish army. If you allow it to evacuate with its arms you must meet it somewhere else. This is not war."

There followed days of give-and-take between Shafter and Toral, with Washington closely following the discussions and keeping Shafter within McKinley's strict parameters. When General Miles arrived at Siboney to offer on-site guidance, he quickly embraced Shafter's soft approach and joined in recommending acceptance of another Toral offer that couldn't pass muster at Washington. McKinley correctly saw that Toral was stalling in hopes that delay would bolster his bargaining position. But he had to respond when Miles reported on July 13 that there had been a hundred cases of yellow fever in the command "and the opinion of the surgeon [is] that it will spread rapidly."

The president promptly called a Cabinet meeting, with top military officials present, to discuss the situation. The nearly three-hour session revealed growing impatience within the administration and a consensus that Shafter and Miles were being bluffed by the Spanish general. It was agreed that the generals should be instructed to attack Santiago with full force "unless in your judgment an assault would fail." They also formulated plans to remove troops to high ground as soon as Santiago was captured. Even before getting the word, Miles and Shafter could see the direction of things. They gave Toral twenty-four hours to capitulate or face a naval bombardment of the city. That led to two days of further negotiations, culminating in Toral's capitulation on July 17. An offer from McKinley to transport Toral's troops home to Spain helped ease the way for the settlement. The Spanish officers also were allowed to keep their sidearms as a final U.S. concession.

With Santiago subdued, Miles took an army to conquer Puerto Rico, the small Caribbean archipelago whose main island, encompassing 5,320 square miles, was less than a tenth the size of Cuba. Miles accomplished his mission in two weeks following a July 25 landing at Guánica. The general brought the main island under his control except for the capital city of San Juan, which remained isolated and unthreatening. There were few casualties, and unlike Shafter, Miles managed his troop transport and supply challenges with smooth efficiency. But few newspapermen covered the campaign, and Americans reacted with a kind of ho-hum pride following the more stunning victories in the Philippines and Cuba.

FEW EPISODES IN McKinley's career reflected more distinctly the man's political and managerial style than his leadership of the war effort. Never inclined toward bombast or overt take-charge exhibitions, he displayed his normal indirect methods of management—listening more than talking, delegating to subordinates the execution of major decisions, soliciting opinions and advice from many sources while keeping his own counsel until it came time for decision making. Nor did he allow himself to get waylaid by the minutiae of the war enterprise.

Yet no one in Washington maintained a more detailed understanding of the big issues emanating from the war, and no one deflected him from his chosen path. "He is the strong man of the Cabinet, the dominating force," wrote Cortelyou, who probably occupied the position of closest vantage over the president's behavior. While McKinley carefully sought the views of his top military leaders, particularly Long and Alger, he also made clear that he would be the final arbiter on major decisions—and often on their execution as well. "No orders of importance were issued, from either the War or Navy Department, without his full knowledge and approval," wrote Charles Sumner Olcott, an early biographer who conducted extensive interviews with McKinley associates, "and these were often revised by him."

As usual, he fixed his attention on the large goals emerging from the challenges that descended upon him. He never displayed the Roosevelt-Mahan-Lodge zeal in behalf of American sea power—and certainly never talked in their idiom of national grandeur. Yet when the war he sought to avoid became inevitable, he quickly employed that new navy to insert American power into faraway Asia and the nearby Caribbean in ways never before seen. Perceiving clearly the political and military dangers in a protracted war, he moved aggressively to pummel the enemy and thus end the conflict as quickly and decisively as possible.

Now, with four major victories within three months, he faced the question of what kind of peace he wished to fashion—and what kind of America would emerge from those victories. For the short term, everyone knew what would happen: Spain would sue for peace, and America would exact a heavy price that would severely curtail the Iberian nation's global reach. For the longer term, it wasn't so clear, but few expected America to retreat to its position of old upon the North American continent. A British commentator named Henry Norman, writing in the *London Chronicle*, foresaw a new fate for George Washington's famous admonition to his nation, "Avoid foreign entanglements." This warning, said Norman, now "ceases to be the compass of the statesman and becomes the curio of the historian." Whether McKinley shared that view remained, at this point, an open question. But a hint emerged from a scrap of paper upon which the president scribbled, "While we are conducting war and until its conclusion, we must keep all we get; when the war is over we must keep what we want."

20

End of Hostilities

"THE PRESIDENT HAS HAD HIS WAY AS USUAL"

Around noon on July 26, 1898, Secretary of State Day got word that French ambassador Jules Cambon wished to meet with him and President McKinley as soon as possible. Day called the president, who set an afternoon meeting for three-thirty. Cambon arrived at the appointed hour with his assistant, Eugene Thiebault, and was ushered into the White House library. He informed the president that he came not representing France but as a special envoy of her majesty, the queen regent of Spain. He had a communication from Spain's Foreign Office, he said, and with the president's indulgence Thiebault would read it. McKinley nodded his assent.

The document began with typical cloying diplomatic language about Spain's war motivation being "the vindication of her prestige, her honor, her name," even in the face of "such uneven strife" as that presented by America's military might. But finally it got to the point: "Spain is prepared to spare Cuba from the continuation of the horrors of war if the United States are on their part likewise disposed." After the reading, Cambon praised America's brilliant military triumph and suggested the country's "glory and honor" couldn't rise higher through continued struggle. He called on McKinley to grant Spain "liberal and honorable terms."

McKinley expressed interest in pursuing peace and said he would consult his Cabinet and others and report back in a few days. Perceiving an ambiguity in the statement, Day asked whether Spain wanted to settle merely the Cuban matter or all points of dispute (meaning, most significantly, the disposition of the Philippines). Cambon said he thought it was the latter, and McKinley indicated that would be a requirement. Upon Cambon's departure, McKinley authorized Cortelyou to inform the newspapers of Spain's peace overture, thus locking Madrid into the process it had commenced.

That night the president scribbled out his terms on a piece of paper for future reference. There was a certain diplomatic audacity in what he wrote, as it required that Spain relinquish both Cuba and Puerto Rico as conditions of the United States merely entering into talks. "This requirement," wrote the president, "will admit of no negotiation." The matter of the Philippines, he added, could be settled through peace talks.

Over the next four days McKinley presided over Cabinet discussions at the White House and aboard a lighthouse tender during a Potomac cruise. He called Attorney General Griggs back from vacation. He discussed the matter with numerous members of Congress and summoned the thoughts of John Hay and other U.S. diplomats. Throughout the discussions, he kept his own thinking to himself. While he encountered extensive agreement that Spain should give up Cuba and Puerto Rico, the Philippines generated some dispute. Among Cabinet members, Griggs, Bliss, and Wilson favored U.S. possession of the entire archipelago, while Long, Day, and Gage advocated the acquisition merely of the port of Manila. Alger offered no firm advocacy, and the new postmaster general, Charles Emory Smith, mostly remained silent.

Throughout the discussions, McKinley goaded both sides, drawing out arguments and ensuring that all considerations got equal treatment. He chided the secretary of state for his limited view of the Philippine opportunity. "Judge Day only wants a hitching post," he said. But he also ribbed Agriculture Secretary Wilson for his expansionist zeal, saying "Yes, you Scotch favor keeping everything—including the Sabbath." When Day pointed out that the president hadn't put to a vote his call for confining the country's Philippine ambitions to a Manila naval base, the president quipped, "No, I was afraid it would be carried."

Employing such dexterous banter the president kept the discussion going, and his own thinking obscure, through various iterations of the reply. An early version called for America to get merely a naval station at Manila and another at the Ladrone Islands (later the Marianas) in the western Pacific. But ultimately the Cabinet agreed to leave the Philippine question to the peace negotiators.

Thus the final version demanded, first, that Spain relinquish Cuban sovereignty and evacuate the island immediately; second, that in lieu of a pecuniary indemnity Spain must grant to the United States Puerto Rico and all surrounding islands as recompense for its "losses and expenses . . . incident to the war" and also an island in the Ladrones to be selected by the United States; third, the United States would occupy and hold Manila, city and harbor, pending the final settlement, "which shall determine the control, disposition, and government of the Philippines."

That was precisely what McKinley wanted, as reflected in his scribbled note of July 26. When Cortelyou remarked that the final version represented an impressive collaboration, McKinley smiled knowingly, pulled from his pocket his earlier note, and handed it to the secretary. "The final changes in that document were largely his own," wrote Cortelyou later. Charles Dawes, following the deliberations closely, added, "The President has had his way as usual."

But it wasn't clear he would have his way with Madrid. On Saturday, July 30, the White House sent word to Cambon that the president would see him that afternoon at two. When the minister and his secretary appeared, McKinley asked Day to read the U.S. response. Upon hearing it, Cambon said he had expected a more magnanimous reply. After all, the United States had never expressed concerns about Spanish rule over Puerto Rico.

The president replied that he wouldn't entertain any discussion leading to modifications. Puerto Rico would have to be relinquished.

Cambon said he thought Spanish officials might accept the loss of Cuba and Puerto Rico, as well as their smaller West Indies islands. But McKinley's expansive demands would raise suspicions in Madrid that the United States wanted all of the Philippines.

The president, projecting a transparently insincere coyness, said the fate of the Philippines would depend upon the treaty to be negotiated by the two countries' commissioners and ratified by their legislatures. The ambassador responded by reading the paragraph on the Philippines.

"These are very harsh terms," he said.

McKinley asked: In what particulars?

Replied Cambon: They might lead to U.S. acquisition of the full archipelago.

No, replied the president, the terms don't say that; it would be left to the negotiators.

Cambon's skepticism was well-placed. After all, the U.S. commissioners would be under the president's sway, while Spain's commissioners would not be negotiating from a position of strength. But McKinley was genuinely conflicted on the question. He wanted more time to ponder it, more information to bolster his thinking, and full flexibility of decision making. His approach gave him all three.

Four days later the same four men met again in the White House library at 3:45. Cambon said Madrid considered the president's terms "very severe." He asked if Puerto Rico could be substituted by some other island. "To this," wrote Day later, "the President promptly answered that it could not be." Cambon said Spanish officials feared the United States would insist upon taking the entire Philippine archipelago. While Madrid would cede some territory there, he said, Spain felt its suzerainty "should not be interfered with."

The president responded that he would yield nothing. That led to discussions on how many commissioners should be named on each side (the president recommended five) and the venue of negotiations (he argued for Washington, while Cambon suggested a neutral location, perhaps Paris, would be more appropriate). McKinley said he would get back to Cambon on those matters later in the day.

That night he sent Day to Cambon's residence to say he still wished for five commissioners on each side, but Paris would be acceptable as the locus of negotiations. He emphasized, though, that Spanish acceptance of his terms meant an immediate evacuation of Cuba and Puerto Rico—no postponement pending the outcome of the negotiations.

Cambon once again expressed chagrin at the American intransigence but said he understood the terms and would convey them to Madrid.

MEANWHILE DEVELOPMENTS WERE brewing around Santiago de Cuba that threatened to destroy McKinley's bargaining position vis-à-vis Spain. Shafter's army was wilting under the strain of tropical disease, particularly malaria, and soon it would be ravaged by yellow fever. Washington had instructed the general to get his troops to higher and safer ground immediately after the fall of Santiago, but Shafter had dawdled in complying, and now his army was so enervated that any effort to march his men overland would prove disastrous. The only solution, in the view of Shafter's officers, was to transport the army by ship to some location on the American East Coast. Shafter and his officers decided to convey this sentiment to Washington via the press. Accordingly on August 4 newspapers across America bannered an Associated Press story that sent shock waves through the nation and rocked official Washington:

> Santiago de Cuba, August 3, 5:30 p.m. (delayed in transmission).—Summoned by Major General Shafter, a meeting was held here this morning at headquarters, and, in the presence of every commanding and medical officer of the 5th Army Corps. General Shafter read a cable message from Secretary Alger, ordering him . . . to move the army into the interior, to San Luis, where it is healthier.
>
> As a result of the conference, General Shafter will insist upon the immediate withdrawal of the army north within two weeks.
>
> As an explanation of the situation, the following letter from Colonel Theodore Roosevelt, commanding the 1st Volunteer Cavalry, to General Shafter, was handed by the latter to the correspondent here of the Associated Press for publication:
>
> "Sir—In a meeting of the general and medical officers called by you at the palace this morning we were all, as you know, unanimous in the view of what should be done with the army. To keep us here, in the opinion of every officer commanding

a division or a brigade, will simply involve the destruction of thousands."

Roosevelt's letter, reflecting his famous vivid expressiveness, explained that yellow fever had not yet appeared in his regiment, but malaria was rampant, and "the whole command is so weakened and shattered as to be ripe for dying like sheep when a real yellow fever epidemic . . . strikes us as it is bound to if we stay here." The AP story also reprinted a "round robin" letter, signed by Shafter's top officers, expressing the same sentiments and a similar warning from the army's medical corps.

These letters, delivered via the public press, constituted military insubordination on a grand scale. Further, by signaling the depleted state of the U.S. Army at Santiago, the correspondence could have encouraged Spain to stiffen its bargaining position—or even send its remaining forces on the island, still substantial, to Santiago to seek a reversal of the American victory.

Looking back, the administration always had intended to force the Santiago surrender as soon as possible and then get U.S. troops quickly to high ground to avoid the yellow fever pestilence. That's why McKinley had become increasingly frustrated with Shafter's glacial pace of action—first, in departing Tampa, then in forcing a Spanish surrender after he had taken the San Juan Heights. And now, in the wake of the surrender, Shafter continued his lassitude, devoting more attention to the disposition of his Spanish prisoners than he did to his own troops. His cables to Washington had been full of assurances. Few cases of yellow fever had emerged; the cases that had emerged were mild; and the situation seemed "somewhat improving."

What he didn't say, if indeed he even knew, was that his troops had been increasingly devastated by malaria, far less deadly than yellow fever but capable of weakening the troops and rendering them dangerously vulnerable when yellow fever arrived with the rainy season. In ignoring Washington's order to get his men to safer territory, Shafter had debilitated his army. It didn't help that the general's dysfunctional quartermaster corps had not adequately fed or clothed the troops, nor had the medical corps adequately tended to them.

By late July Shafter began to recognize his army faced a humiliating doom. On August 2 he cabled Washington that he was ready to transport the troops home. This was stunning news to McKinley, who had been given no knowledge of the condition of Shafter's troops. The transports weren't readily available, nor were the coastal rest sites completed. The president called in Surgeon General George Sternberg, who assured him that the plan to march the troops to higher ground remained sound. The result was a stern order to Shafter to follow the initial plan.

Shafter was in a pickle. He couldn't follow orders because his negligence had preempted the feasibility of doing so. He couldn't own up to the situation because it would expose his ineptitude and irresponsible lack of candor in communicating with his superiors. He took the cowardly path of turning the dilemma over to his officers, who promulgated the round robin and Roosevelt letters.

For McKinley, learning of the situation for the first time through the newspapers, the news seemed calamitous. Seeing his entire peace strategy now at risk, he became "very much agitated and indignant," Alger wrote later. Already he had demonstrated his displeasure at news reports of the hideous fate of sick and wounded soldiers being moved from Cuba to New York aboard two transport ships, the *Seneca* and the *Concho*, without sufficient food and little medical attention. A *New York Times* editorial asked if the army's medical department actually intended "to kill off our sick and wounded soldiers by shipping them from point to point on unfit transports, without physicians, without medical supplies, and with nothing but beans, bacon, and hard tack for food." An indignant McKinley pummeled Alger with "many searching questions" and promptly ordered an investigation into the matter.

Secretary Alger sought to explain the scandal publicly by noting difficulties faced by his army in Cuba: high surfs made landing of supplies difficult; so many people wanted out that the ships inevitably became overcrowded; the captains never informed higher authorities that they lacked sufficient water. The *New York Times* punctured Alger's high-surf excuse by stating that the two transports left Santiago after it had surrendered, easing the way for the loading and unloading of ships within the harbor. The *Times* added that "no mere wholesale denial or disclaimer of responsibility either by Gen. Shafter or the Secretary of War will satisfy the public indignation." Cortelyou considered Alger's statement "lame" and decried his opportunistic maneuverings. He constantly tried to take the sting out of the president's communications to Shafter and other errant officers, wrote the secretary, and he was quick to issue self-serving statements to the press. After McKinley's *Seneca-Concho* investigation order, Alger rushed to waiting reporters outside the White House and conveyed "the impression . . . that *he* had ordered the investigation." Cortelyou feared the War Department would become "one of the few blots on the brilliant record made in the conduct of the war."

Though McKinley didn't seem inclined to blame Alger for the army's dysfunction, he had lost his patience with Shafter. In a letter to the general he said the round robin letter "makes the situation one of great difficulty. No soldier reading that report if ordered to Santiago but will feel that he is marching to certain death." The big question, though, was what Madrid would do with the information.

The answer came on August 9 when Cambon and Thiebault called at the White House to deliver the Spanish response to the president's August 5 position. It became clear that Spain had no desire to continue the war—but still wished to negotiate McKinley's demands. The language of Spain's response was vague as to the disposition of the Philippines, and it asserted evacuation of Cuba and Puerto Rico couldn't take place until approved by the Spanish legislature.

The president stood firm. "I demanded of Spain the cession and consequently the immediate evacuation of the islands of Cuba and Porto Rico," he declared to Cambon. "Instead of a categorical acceptance, as was expected, the Spanish Government addresses me a note in which it invokes the necessity of obtaining the approbation of the Cortes. I can not lend myself to entering into these considerations of domestic government."

Cambon suggested translations may have contributed to some misunderstanding, and it was natural for Madrid to want to express regret at the loss of its colonies. He was confident, he said, that Spain intended a "full and unqualified acceptance" of the president's terms.

If that were true, replied McKinley, his government would draft a "protocol" clarifying the U.S. position, setting forth a time for the negotiations to begin, and establishing a timetable for the evacuation of Cuba and Puerto Rico. If Madrid signed the document, that would answer the question.

That night State officials drafted the protocol and submitted it to McKinley for his approval, which he gave after some minor tinkering with the language. The next day the document was presented to Cambon, who sent it to Madrid with an admonition that McKinley remained unmovable and "Spain will have nothing more to expect from a conqueror resolved to procure all the profit possible from the advantages it has obtained." On August 12 the French minister reported back that he had been authorized by Madrid to sign the protocol on behalf of the Spanish government. At four o'clock that afternoon, Cambon and Thiebault reappeared at the White House for a signing ceremony in the Cabinet Room. Present were the French diplomats, the president, Secretary Day, and various invited officials from the State Department, the White House, and the military.

"Mr. Ambassador," said Day to Cambon, "the papers are ready." The president stood at the far end of the Cabinet table as Cambon and Day seated themselves across from each other at the other end. In turn the two men affixed their signatures to the four copies of the protocol. When that was completed, three other officials were admitted into the room—Secretary Alger, General Corbin, and naval official Charles Allen—as McKinley extended to Cambon his hand and a warm expression of appreciation for the good offices of the ambassador and his nation in facilitating the end of hostilities. He invited the French diplomat to remain while he signed a presidential proclamation suspending U.S. military action. Moments later, Day turned to the large globe in the corner and said to Cortelyou, "Let's see what we get by this."

WHAT THE UNITED States got was added to another strategic prize acquired on July 7, at the height of the Santiago siege. On that date the Hawaiian Islands came under the U.S. flag through a joint congressional resolution introduced initially in the House on May 4 by Nevada's Democratic representative Francis G. Newlands. There was no doubt that Newlands's resolution would pass the House handily if brought to a vote, but standing athwart the resolution's legislative path was that physical and political Goliath, Speaker Reed, who for months had vacillated between demonstrations of acrimony toward annexation and promises of cooperation. Now he seemed inclined toward acrimony. "Speaker Reed," reported the *Washington Post*, "has always been and is now opposed to annexation, and if no action is taken in the House it will be due to his powerful and antagonistic influence."

McKinley had no intention of making it easy for the speaker to buck his annexation plan. On May 11 he summoned to the White House all members of the House and Senate foreign policy panels to urge prompt action. In conjunction with the visit, Cortelyou delivered to the Washington press corps a full briefing on just how much the president wanted Hawaii. The next day the House Foreign Affairs Committee cleared the annexation measure 10–4, along with other enabling resolutions, and sent them into the clutches of Reed, who held sole discretion on whether they would get to a floor vote. When Foreign Affairs Chairman Robert Hitt urged Reed to speed them along, the speaker responded with a dismissive coyness.

Finally, on May 23, following an informal canvass showing overwhelming House support for annexation, Reed announced he would let the resolutions proceed to the floor calendar, where they would compete with other crucial legislation for floor consideration before the looming congressional adjournment. But as the days unfolded it became clear that Reed still hadn't abandoned hope of killing the resolutions—if he could shroud his involvement behind legislative legerdemain. For two weeks annexation proponents waited for their measures to reach the floor, and constantly the resolutions fell behind other bills. Finally it became clear that Joe Cannon, chairman of the House Appropriations Committee and a fervent annexation foe, was working stealthily with Reed to crowd the calendar with appropriations conference reports and squeeze out annexation. Reported the *Post*, "Just where the friends of annexation are going to have an opportunity to bring up their resolutions this week is not apparent now."

It was all too much for Ohio's representative Charles Grosvenor, the McKinley loyalist and a man of both force and wiles. On June 8 he rose on the House floor to force the issue into the open through parliamentary maneuvers aimed at requiring the Rules Committee to put annexation onto the floor schedule. He accused the leadership of perpetuating "a continuing order to obstruct the passage of the Hawaiian resolutions." Iowa's representative John Lacey, "retorted with much vigor" declaring: "The gentleman should be ashamed to make such an accusation." But in exposing to public knowledge the House leaders' sly obstructions, Grosvenor flustered Reed and his allies. Two days later word filtered through Congress that the president shortly would submit to lawmakers a special message calling for immediate annexation as a military necessity, prompted by the wartime need to ship men and materiel to the Philippines and also to discourage adversarial nations—notably Japan and Germany—from seeking military advantage in the islands while America was pinned down in its war with Spain.

That broke the logjam. The next day a vote was scheduled, and on June 16 the House passed the resolutions 210–92. Reed vacated the House chamber during the vote and had a colleague announce, to cheers from Democrats, that he would have voted no had he been there. Then the resolutions went to the Senate, where opponents declared their intention to kill them through endless debate right up to the time of adjournment. When a test vote engineered by Foreign Relations Committee chairman Cushman Davis demonstrated overwhelming annexation support, the opposition effort to thwart a vote fizzled.

But annexation opponents had their days of debate. California's Democratic senator Stephen White summed up anti-imperialist anxieties when he declared, "If we consummate this scheme we will be told we must have the Philippines, because Hawaii is not worth much unless we can have something else to use it for. And when we have annexed the Philippines we must have something else. So we will extend our action around the globe and enter upon an imperialistic policy." Hoar of Massachusetts added that America could gain great world stature "if we come out of this war without entering upon the fatal folly of retaining far distant possessions."

When annexation proponents forced a roll call vote on the issue on July 6, it passed 42–21. Cortelyou, upon receiving the engrossed resolutions at the White House, took them immediately to the Cabinet Room, where McKinley had mustered a few signing witnesses, including Ida, assistant White House doorkeeper Alonzo Stewart, a couple military officials, and the president's old friend from Canton, George Frease. At 7 p.m. the president turned the primary annexation resolution into law by affixing the words "Approved, July 7, 1898. William McKinley." According to the *Post*, he remarked that with the annexation of Hawaii the nation had entered upon "a new era which would be productive of great benefit."

FIVE WEEKS LATER, with the signing of the protocol with Spain and the accumulation of territories in the Caribbean and Asia, the president freely displayed his felicity at the turn of events under his leadership. Cortelyou noticed that he seemed particularly "genial and pleasant" as he conversed with Cambon after the signing. He had every reason to believe this represented the zenith of his career, just as it represented for America a new era of global consequence. But in politics, as in life, nothing stays the same for long, and McKinley soon found himself grappling with an issue that threatened to undermine his political standing and his party's. The army's war performance was coming under withering condemnation from Democrats, editorialists, civic notables, and citizens across the nation.

After the sobering revelations of the round robin and Roosevelt letters, all agreed that the army must evacuate its Cuban troops as quickly as possible and get them to a transfer camp—called Camp Wikoff, in honor of an officer killed at Santiago—hurriedly being prepared at Montauk, Long Island. Inevitably the army couldn't get the camp into shape in time for the thousands of troops arriving from Santiago. The result was another scandal of army incompetence, with the first waves of troops finding insufficient tents, beds, clothing, food, doctors, and medicines. Compounding the embarrassment were widespread reports of ongoing supply problems and medical inadequacies at four other major domestic bases—in Georgia, Virginia, and Florida—that had served nearly 165,000 enlistees since the spring. By mid-August the army faced a medical crisis as typhoid fever ravaged the men of those camps. Ultimately nearly 2,500 officers and men died of typhus and other diseases, while combat deaths throughout the war numbered only 281.

Alger's army managed to flood the needed supplies into Camp Wikoff, and by early September the situation had stabilized. Alabama's indefatigable General Wheeler, placed in charge of Wikoff, proved particularly resourceful in cutting bureaucratic red tape. But the damage had been done, and few Americans now believed the army could do anything right. A doctor from a New York State volunteer regiment, asked about the condition of his troops at Wikoff, replied, "Forty of our men are dead through the ravages of battle and disease; five have lost their reason, seventy are wounded, and 400 are physical wrecks. . . . There are not 150 men in our whole regiment who are fit for camp duty." The *New York Times* reported that even former army apologists now attacked the military and its leaders: "The general opinion is that 'red tape' is killing men at Montauk, and that the man at the head of the War Department is so incompetent to do the cutting that the situation must continue . . . until the last possible victim is dead or a new head is found to grapple with the problem." Suspicions of illegal profiteering and favoritism abounded.

The situation was exacerbated by Alger's clumsy response to these multiple lapses. Never acknowledging the magnitude of the problems nor issuing any public apology to the nation or his troops, he offered instead bland excuses. "The Secretary of War cannot be supposed to be everywhere and give his personal attention to every detail," he exclaimed to reporters at one point—"petulantly," as the *Times* reported. The president sympathized with Alger's complaint that he couldn't oversee everything in an army that had ballooned from about 25,000 troops to more than 260,000 in some three months. To Cortelyou he dismissed some of the criticism as "unreasonable and unwarranted" and argued that "the Secy could not be responsible for many of the conditions at Santiago and other places." But he knew this festering problem soon would attach to him if he didn't move on it. As the *New York Evening Post* put it, "Alger is responsible for Algerism, but McKinley is responsible for Alger."

To deflect the barrage of criticism and ensure his own control over events, the president initiated two actions. One was a visit to Camp Wikoff. The other was a decision to establish an investigative commission charged with establishing the facts of the matter. McKinley arrived at Wikoff on September 3, along with Alger, Vice President Hobart, and other dignitaries, and spent five hours in the camp. He interviewed officers, talked with soldiers, inspected tent quarters, and generally showed his regard for troop welfare. He spent an hour and a half in the hospital wards, interviewing medical officials and offering soothing words to wounded and ill soldiers.

"I'm sorry to see you so sick," he told one stricken sergeant. "I hope you are getting better." At frequent intervals he would exclaim, "How sorry I am to see these brave fellows in such a condition." But he also expressed his view that camp management had reached a creditable degree of efficiency, asserting, "I think I never saw a handsomer camp." Widespread press reports of the president's visit were highly favorable, isolating him from most of the national ire directed at Alger and the army.

Meanwhile McKinley used Agriculture Secretary James Wilson as an intermediary to inform Alger of his intention to appoint an investigative commission. Wilson also said the president wanted Alger himself to ask for the commission, to demonstrate his good faith in the controversy. Alger initially resisted the idea. "He told me he is having army officers do that work," Wilson reported to the president. But Wilson persisted, and Alger ultimately gave way when Wilson "pointed out the weight that would attach to a report from men not in army life placing responsibility where it properly belongs."

Alger made the request in a September 8 letter to the president, and McKinley's subsequent announcement generated widespread support throughout the country. To head the commission, the president named Grenville M. Dodge of Iowa, a Union general in the Civil War and pioneer of the Union Pacific Railroad. Assembling commission members at the White House on September 26, the president told them, "If there have been wrongs committed, the wrongdoers must not escape conviction and punishment." By giving the commission several months to report its findings, the president managed to quell the national outrage, at least for a time, so he could concentrate on other matters—notably, the negotiations with Spain, a replacement for Day at the State Department, mounting difficulties in the Philippines, and the coming November elections.

With the shooting war with Spain over, Day's commitment to his State duties also expired. But McKinley had one last assignment for his longtime Canton friend: to chair the five-man commission that would negotiate final terms with Spain. Day accepted, with the proviso that, once the negotiations were completed, he would escape the Washington hubbub and return to his quiet life in Ohio.

The president knew precisely the man he wanted for Day's replacement: John Hay. In mid-August he offered the ambassador the job via telegram. The ambassador replied with his usual false modesty: "The place is beyond my ambition. I cannot but feel it is beyond my strength and ability." But a week later he reported that Queen Victoria herself had wired Arthur Balfour, who was running the British Foreign Office, asking him to convey her congratulations to Hay. "This is—I am told—a very unusual kindness and compliment," wrote Hay, adding, "It makes me very humble to be the recipient of so much undeserved praise and confidence."

It was in fact much deserved. In his brief London tenure, Hay had cemented a friendship between two nations that only three years earlier had faced off ominously over the Venezuelan border dispute. Now Balfour was declaring that "between English-speaking peoples war is impossible." Joseph Chamberlain, British colonial secretary, went further in concept and eloquence. "There is a powerful and generous nation," he said, "speaking our language, bred of our race, and having interests identical with ours. . . . At the present time these two great nations understand each other better than they ever have done, since over a century ago they were separated by the blunder of a British government." Hay worked assiduously to foster that sentiment among Britons and articulated its significance in his own eloquent prose. He spoke of "a peace between us and a friendly regard—a peace growing more firm and solid as the years go by, and a friendship which, I am sure, the vast majority of both peoples hope and trust may last forever." The new amity between the two nations, forged during McKinley's presidency through Hay's elegant diplomacy, would prove to be a development of global significance.

To replace Hay at London McKinley chose the seventy-two-year-old Senator Hoar of Massachusetts. One rationale for the offer, according to speculation, was to get his strong anti-expansionist voice out of the Senate. But Hoar declined, citing health and age considerations. When the president indicated he might consider Whitelaw Reid, New York boss Tom Platt quickly weighed in with a twenty-two-page letter begging McKinley to choose someone other than the priggish antimachine newspaperman. He eventually selected Joseph Choate, a leading New York City trial lawyer with strong Republican ties and a wide following among Eastern establishment figures.

As a consolation to Reid, McKinley asked him to join the U.S. peace commission. Reid avidly accepted. Then the president corralled three sitting senators—Republicans Cushman Davis of Minnesota and William Frye of Maine and Democrat George Gray of Delaware. Of the five, Day steered a middle course, philosophically committed to expansion but wary of going too far. Gray had opposed Hawaiian annexation and seemed uncomfortable with any overseas acquisitions. Davis and Frye were strong advocates of taking all of the Philippines, while Reid seemed inclined in that direction. In placing three senators on the commission McKinley ignored concerns of some that it violated the separation-of-powers principle. "Permit me to respectfully remind you," wrote New Hampshire Senator Chandler in a heartfelt protest to the president, "that you cannot constitutionally appoint Senators as Peace Commissioners." It was "an important principle of republican liberty" that the three branches of government "should be kept unmingled." But McKinley brushed aside such objections without much regard to what he considered mere constitutional niceties. As usual, he put his focus on directing events in his stealthy way and getting the outcome he wanted. In doing so, he signaled to discerning observers that he intended to exercise the full powers of the presidency even in the face of congressional complaints.

As the president looked ahead to the coming elections, he had reason to think his party might buck the traditional tendency of voters to slam the majority party in midterm balloting. The economy was in greater shape than it had been in years. Prices were solid, the iron trades healthy, business failures down, cereal exports up. Perhaps most important, for the first time in the nation's history total exports were double the value of imports, and even manufacturing exports exceeded manufacturing imports. Soaring gold production boosted investment capital for both farmers and manufacturers. All this translated into jobs and solid wages. What's more, the patriotic fervor unleashed by the war and its triumphant outcome seemed to buoy voter sentiment toward the majority party.

But McKinley wasn't inclined to leave anything to chance. When he accepted a speaking invitation at an Omaha peace celebration in October, Republicans showered him with pleas to add other appearances where closely contested campaigns were unfolding. He accepted many of them—"not making political speeches," he said, "but discussing current events connected with the administration." But of course any presidential appearance during the heat of an election autumn constituted a political event. One McKinley biographer portrayed this as "a significant departure from accepted political practice that became a precedent for the traveling White House of twentieth-century campaigns." Once again the president didn't feel constrained by precedent or what he considered outmoded political etiquette. He was in politics to win.

When the votes were counted, Democrats gained twenty-nine seats, eight of those coming from splinter parties. Republican losses, held to twenty-one, constituted a respectable showing for a party in power between presidential elections. Besides, Republicans picked up seven Senate seats while Democrats lost eight. The results, though mixed, reflected high voter esteem for McKinley and his party halfway through the president's term.

21

Empire

"THE SINGLE CONSIDERATION OF DUTY AND HUMANITY"

In late September 1898 President McKinley received an information bonanza with the arrival in Washington of General Francis V. Greene, who had traveled from the Philippines to deliver a message from Admiral Dewey. A round-faced man with a salt-and-pepper mustache and a demeanor of crisp seriousness, the forty-nine-year-old Greene had become a successful New York businessman following a sixteen-year army career that included stints as a West Point professor and a military attaché in Russia. Reentering the army after the *Maine* explosion, he had landed in the Philippines with some 3,550 troops following Dewey's naval victory.

McKinley avidly solicited Greene's firsthand observations because for weeks the president had been struggling with the Philippine conundrum, the last remaining momentous issue emanating from the victory over Spain. The fate of Cuba, Puerto Rico, and Guam had been essentially settled, thanks to the president's dogged insistence that disposition of those matters must precede peace talks. Of course, the Paris negotiations inevitably would generate nettlesome points of contention as Spain sought to squeeze whatever advantage it could from its reduced global position. But the president had secured the desired outcome in the Caribbean and the Ladrones.

The Philippine archipelago was something else entirely. McKinley didn't know what he wanted there. More important, he didn't know enough about the islands to know what he should want. He consulted the chief of the navy's Bureau of Equipment, Commander R. B. Bradford, who had visited the islands years earlier. Bradford warned that it would be difficult to hold Manila as a naval base without commanding the entire island of Luzon, and holding Luzon would be difficult if other powers took possession of nearby islands, which seemed inevitable if the United States left them out there for the picking. That seemed to argue for taking the entire archipelago, but McKinley needed to assess what military and civic challenges that would entail and what kinds of commercial opportunities would ensue. Besides, he couldn't ignore the political dangers at home at a time of growing anti-imperialist fervor.

Dewey's message via Greene didn't help much in answering McKinley's questions. The president had asked the admiral which island should be acquired if he confined his demand to a single landform. Dewey selected Luzon, since it contained Subic Bay, highly favorable for a naval base and coaling station and also a point of strategic command over Manila. By the time Dewey got his reply to McKinley, however, the answer had become obvious. The admiral also offered "a few random bits of data on climate, resources and trade" that didn't add up to much. Nor did McKinley find particular value in Dewey's bland observation that Luzon's inhabitants were far more capable of self-government than the Cubans. It was beginning to appear that, for all his tactical brilliance in battle, the admiral possessed a leaden, incurious mind.

But Greene's mind was facile and restless, and he had devoted his six weeks in Asia to an exhaustive study of the archipelago, including its people, climate, mineral wealth, agriculture, commerce, economics, politics, and the implications of recent developments since the native insurgency had begun in 1896 under a fiery and articulate young leader named Emilio Aguinaldo. The president consulted with Greene numerous times over several days and received from the general a comprehensive written report that pulled together much of the information McKinley needed for sound decision making.

Greene estimated the Philippine population at between 7 million and 9 million, with a significant proportion of those—about 3.4 million—living on Luzon. There were some thirty separate races, each speaking a different dialect, though fully five-sixths of the Christian population (about 6 million people) belonged to two tribes, the Tagalog and the Visayans. These dominant tribes seemed to be "industrious and hardworking," although there had been "occasional evidences of deceit and untruthfulness in their dealings" with U.S. officials. Most Filipinos worked in agriculture and demonstrated little inclination or ability in manufacturing, the arts, or mining. In the few major cities (Manila, Cebu, Iloilo), there were "many thousands" of educated, propertied natives, including merchants, lawyers, doctors, and priests.

For centuries the Spanish ran the Philippines largely as a trading center, connecting the New World with far Asia. This meant their central aim was to dominate Manila and lesser port cities on the islands of Luzon, Panay, and Negros, while the Catholic order became the primary Spanish influence in the countryside. Spanish officials largely ignored the islands' vast agricultural and mining resources until the nineteenth century's Industrial Revolution spawned efforts to develop Philippine raw materials for export and create Philippine markets for finished goods. This unsettled the archipelago's civic equilibrium as Spain first opened up society with administrative reforms, then pulled back severely with the arrival of the infamous General Valeriano Weyler, the same iron-fisted leader who later generated so much brutality and civic unrest in Cuba.

In Greene's view, if Philippine society could be stabilized and Western technology and knowhow brought to bear, the United States could exploit rich opportunities in the mining of gold, coal, oil, and sulfur, as well as in harvesting rice, corn, hemp, sugar, tobacco, coffee, cotton, and cocoa. Upgrades in transportation could spur greater internal commerce and foster trade with many logical markets throughout Asia and the Americas. "With these islands in our possession and the construction of railroads in the interior of Luzon," wrote Greene, "it is probable that an enormous extension could be given this commerce, nearly all of which would come to the United States."

But such a path was strewn with difficulties, reflected in the recent history of the islands, which Greene summarized (though McKinley already knew much of this background). Like Spanish rule in Cuba, the Philippine version had been autocratic and incompetent. "The natives have no place in the government," wrote Greene, except for clerks in the public offices in Manila and petty positions in the villages. Also decisions at those levels could be nullified at whim by the imperious governor-general, whose arbitrary decision making "is shown in the hundreds of executions for alleged political offences" from 1895 through 1897, as well as thousands of deportations and imprisonments. Moreover Greene revealed widespread reports "that pecuniary dishonesty and corruption exist throughout the whole body of Spanish office holders."

All this led to Aguinaldo's vigorous independence movement beginning in August 1896. Born poor and without prospects around 1869, this mixed-blood peasant defied the odds of life. Spanish authorities didn't even allow men of his station to tuck their shirts into their trousers, a means of marking their lowly status. Mark Twain, emerging as a fiery leader of America's anti-imperialist forces, was to write of Aguinaldo, "Grandson of a Chinaman, a race held in aversion out there—one handicap. Son of a peasant vegetable-peddler—another. Not fluent in the tongue of the masters of the country . . . another. Allowed but a mean and meager schooling by the masters of the land—another. 'Denied the remotest semblance of equality' with the master race—another. Barefoot by compulsion, and not even allowed any authority over the southern extension of his own shirt—certainly another."

Slight of build ("short but well-knit," as the *New York Tribune* described him), with a smooth face and languid eyes, Aguinaldo soon demonstrated a rare ability to inspire men with his organizational skill, fervent idealism, and lyrical expressiveness. His decisions and actions were "slow and deliberate," said the *Tribune*, adding that this trait "may be a sign of depth and breadth of mental caliber." He never seemed ruffled or agitated in either victory or adversity, which was all the more remarkable given that he was only twenty-seven when he emerged as the leader of the Philippine insurrection, commanding a force of 30,000. His resolve was reflected in how he dealt with a political rival, Andrés Bonifacio. Outmaneuvering Bonifacio, Aguinaldo got himself named president of the revolutionary government in early 1897. Then, not content with that victory, the new president ordered the arrest and trial of Bonifacio on trumped-up treason charges. He was executed on May 10, 1897.

In reviewing Aguinaldo's insurgency, Greene said the rebel force "can hardly be called an army," but it nonetheless proved highly effective as a vexatious guerrilla operation against 25,000 of the best regulars Spain could send to the islands and numerous native militias under Spanish command. Aguinaldo captured nearly 3,000 militia troops during June and July 1896 while also constantly harassing Spanish forces in the trenches, "keeping them up at night and wearing them out with fatigue." Surrounding Manila, Aguinaldo cut off supplies to the city and forced the citizens, including Spanish troops, to subsist on horse and buffalo meat. Capturing Manila's water works, he cut off its water supply. Spanish forces lost some 150 officers and 2,500 men, killed and wounded, over a ten-month period, while Aguinaldo's forces, despite heavier losses, pressed the fight relentlessly, capturing more and more territory surrounding Manila.

Finally, the Spanish governor-general, Fernando Primo de Rivera, entered into an agreement with Aguinaldo whereby the rebel leader and his associates would leave the country in exchange for $800,000 and numerous civic reforms, including press freedom, Philippine representation in the Spanish Cortes, secularization of the much-despised monastic orders, and a general amnesty for all insurgents. Moving to Hong Kong, Aguinaldo distributed half of the $800,000 to his fighters but retained the rest as a "trust fund" pending evidence that Primo would live up to the bargain. He didn't, and Aguinaldo initiated plans for resuming the fight.

That was the state of play on April 25, 1898, when the United States declared war on Spain (retroactive to April 21). Immediately the relationship between Aguinaldo and McKinley's government took on a serious aspect—as well as multiple complications. On April 24 Aguinaldo, traveling through Singapore, met with U.S. consul E. Spencer Pratt and offered to resume his fight in conjunction with the U.S. Navy's looming Philippine action. Pratt telegraphed this news to Dewey in Hong Kong, who asked that Aguinaldo rendezvous with the

Americans there. Aguinaldo rushed to the British treaty port but arrived just after Dewey's departure for his epochal Philippine mission.

The Pratt-Aguinaldo meeting soon became engulfed in controversy. According to Aguinaldo, Pratt courted him with "honeyed phrases" and promised U.S. support for Philippine independence. Pratt denied that he had issued any such commitment, which of course he had no authority to do. No one would ever know for sure which version was correct, but for years the dispute would unsettle U.S. relations with the renewed Philippine insurgency.

In any event, U.S. naval officials transported Aguinaldo and seventeen other revolutionary chiefs to Manila Bay, where they landed at Cavite, about thirteen miles south of the capital, and soon began outfitting a new rebel force with guns, ammunition, and other materiel, much of it obtained from the Americans. By this time Dewey had destroyed the Spanish fleet and taken control of Manila Bay, but he knew American forces must occupy the city to protect his fleet from shore batteries and force a Spanish surrender. Aguinaldo could help by attacking the Spanish military in the regions surrounding Manila. Dewey met with the rebel leader on May 19 and offered encouragement, as well as the weapons. Aguinaldo once again insisted that the American had extended U.S. support for Philippine independence. Dewey denied it. But an informal alliance had been forged.

In a few weeks Aguinaldo's renewed force was attacking the Spanish authority. "They were very successful," wrote Greene in his memo to McKinley, "the native militia in Spanish service capitulating with their arms in nearly every case without serious resistance." Other militia units retreated into Manila, allowing Aguinaldo to gain sway over more and more surrounding countryside. "The situation is very grave," reported a Spanish army officer named Augusti, who warned that Manila soon could fall to the rebels. He said the "white population of the suburbs, fearing they will be massacred by the rebels," had entered fortified areas of Manila, even though they were vulnerable to an anticipated U.S. naval bombardment. They preferred bombardment to massacre, he explained.

On June 23 Aguinaldo issued a proclamation declaring a new "revolutionary" government in the islands, with himself as revolutionary president—the "personification of the Philippine people"—with a tenure lasting "until the revolution triumphs." Greene characterized Aguinaldo's civic structure as "a Dictatorship of the familiar South American type," although he allowed that Aguinaldo insisted his ultimate aim was a true republic.

In the meantime, McKinley grappled with the internal squabbling between generals Nelson Miles and Wesley Merritt over how big a force should be sent to the Philippines. He settled the matter, as we have seen, by ordering 20,000 troops there under Merritt, though he purposely remained vague on the mission. Soon Merritt had an advance contingent of 11,000 troops at Cavite, ready to take the capital. Spain had 15,000 men inside the city, along with 50,000 to 70,000 civilians. And Aguinaldo's Army of Liberation boasted between 13,000 and 15,000 men surrounding the city.

It was a delicate military and diplomatic situation. Merritt's orders, direct from McKinley, were to occupy Manila without letting the insurgents in. But it wasn't clear how he could do that with Aguinaldo's forces surrounding the land perimeter of the city and its suburbs. Prospects for success increased when General Greene entered into a negotiation with one of his Spanish counterparts whereby the Spanish abandoned a portion of their left wing, permitting Greene's troops to take a position adjacent to Manila Bay. Thus the Americans could supply their troops from the sea and protect the supply route with Dewey's big guns. It appeared that the Spaniards would rather deal with the Americans than with Aguinaldo, which didn't surprise Greene. As he wrote to McKinley, "The Spanish officials have intense fear of the Insurgents; and the latter hate them, as well as the friars, with a virulence that can hardly be described."

The Spanish at Manila now were in a hopeless position—hemmed in by hate-filled rebels, with Americans besetting them also from the sea and from their enclave at the Spaniards' left flank. But when the new governor-general asked Madrid for permission to surrender, his superiors promptly dismissed him. His replacement cleverly entered into negotiations with Dewey, through the Belgian consul. He suggested that, if the Americans attacked, he would hold out only so long as he must to avoid besmirching his honor. Accordingly on August 13

Merritt's forces attacked two Spanish positions near the beach, inducing a surrender not only of those positions but of the entire city.

Hearing of the American attack, Aguinaldo's forces rushed into the suburbs and were stopped from entering the city by a phalanx of American forces. Now the Americans and the insurgents faced each other along an extended line around Manila. But Merritt and Dewey had fulfilled their mission of taking the city while keeping the insurgents out. Spain's economic hub in Asia had been seized, her regional position destroyed. All this occurred a day after Secretary Day and Ambassador Cambon signed the Protocol ending the Spanish-American War, news of which had not yet reached Manila.

Six weeks later, as McKinley studied Greene's memorandum and discussed it extensively with the general, some fundamentals came into focus. One was that Spain's Philippine sovereignty could never be restored; the ethnic and political animosities were simply too intense. That was the one point on which nearly all Filipinos agreed. Any effort in that direction would unleash a catastrophic civic upheaval—and likely lure other Western powers into the region.

Beyond that, Greene favored a certain circumspection toward Aguinaldo. "He is not devoid of ability" as a guerrilla fighter, wrote Greene, but educated Filipinos in the major cities viewed him as "lacking in ability to be at the head of affairs." These urban opinion leaders would align with Aguinaldo or anyone else to destroy the Spanish imperium, but afterward they favored "the support of some strong nation for many years" as a necessary transition to independence. Greene urged the president to view Aguinaldo's movement as largely a Tagalog phenomenon, lacking significant support not only from the urban intelligentsia but also from the Visayan tribe of the central islands, which had remained aloof from the insurrection.

Finally, Greene argued that the islands' abundant economic opportunities couldn't be exploited effectively without a central governing entity ensuring unfettered internal trade. A subdivided archipelago, he suggested, would be hampered by a tangle of tariffs, commercial inefficiency, and economic stagnation.

Reading and rereading Greene's report, talking with him extensively, and pursuing other avenues of inquiry, McKinley concluded

America must take all of the Philippines. Commander Bradford had crystallized the military folly in a partial acquisition that couldn't easily be defended from major powers swooping down to grab other available land parcels. Greene's point about the commercial necessity of a united archipelago resonated with the president. Then there was the civic disruption sure to emerge from any lingering power vacuum, with local tribes and groups in fierce competition for position and power and with ambitious nations—Germany and Japan in particular—interjecting themselves into the mess and spreading even more chaos. The president remained mindful of the intense hatreds that had emerged among various groups during the dysfunctional Spanish rule. And he felt a responsibility, having essentially kicked Spain out of the Philippines, to stabilize the archipelago as quickly as possible to minimize the bloodshed of transition. Also, as he told a group of Methodists visiting the White House in November 1899, he felt a humanitarian obligation to educate the Filipinos and to "uplift and civilize" them.

But McKinley was in no hurry to reveal his thinking. He foresaw a dual danger of hostilities with Aguinaldo's Tagalog insurgents and heightened anti-expansionist fervor at home. Most ominously, the two could feed off each other—the rebels pressing their fight in hopes of sapping McKinley's political standing in America, and annexation opponents in America getting more agitated and numerous as the war lingered. Given that intertwined threat, he would bide his time and move stealthily, reverting to his tried-and-true leadership of incrementalism. Certainly this could lead to swipes that once again he was demonstrating his characteristic indecisiveness and cowardice. But that was nothing new, and he long since had learned to ignore such attacks.

In the meantime he would press his resolve to establish U.S. sovereignty over the full archipelago even if that meant war with Aguinaldo. The president articulated this resolve in responding to a communication from Dewey and Merritt, who asked, "Is Government willing to use all means to make the natives submit to the authority of the United States?" The query arrived in Washington on August 17, and the president's response, delivered through General Corbin, went out the same day: "The President directs that there must be no joint occupation with the insurgents." The army must preserve peace, protect property, and maintain stability in the islands, said Corbin: "The insurgents and all others must recognize the military occupation and authority of the United States and the cessation of hostilities proclaimed by the President. Use whatever means in your judgment are necessary to this end."

AS THE PRESIDENT grappled with the Philippine question, he turned his attention also to the peace negotiations with Spain that shortly would commence in Paris. On September 15 he met with his peace commissioners for three and a half hours, then lunched privately with its chairman, Judge Day. At the next day's Cabinet meeting, Day resigned as secretary of state and received from the president a memorandum of instruction. It said Spain's departure from Cuba and the Caribbean was an "imperative necessity" justifying the stark terms of the Protocol. The Philippines, however, "stand upon a different basis" because there was no particular imperative, from the U.S. standpoint, that Spain leave Asia. On the other hand, "the presence and success of our arms at Manila imposes upon us obligations which we cannot disregard." Thus did the president signal the direction of his thinking.

The president emphasized to Day that he wanted frequent and timely cables on all significant developments as the negotiations proceeded. The cables should go directly to him and not be sent through the State Department, though the new secretary of state, John Hay, certainly would be kept informed. By late September, with Day established in Paris, the judge began sending chatty memos to the president filled with updates, gossip, observations, and explanations—just what the president wanted and knew he would get from his longtime Canton friend.

In addition McKinley dropped a "hint" to Commissioner Whitelaw Reid that he would welcome private letters from Paris. He knew the newspaperman's pronounced vanity would stir him to file long, discursive memos filled with great orotundity as well as piquant observations. Despite Reid's self-importance, he was a man of considerable intellect and sharp insight.

The big question before the commissioners, of course, was the Philippines. McKinley wasn't prepared to reveal his full thinking on that subject, but he wanted his negotiators to follow the same avenues of inquiry that he had pursued. Thus in early October he sent to Paris copies of General Greene's report—"valuable notes and memoranda," as Hay described the document in a cover memo. At McKinley's instruction, Hay also sent memos related to an incident at the White House concerning a visit there by two men who presented themselves as representatives of Aguinaldo's declared government in the Philippines. The men, Felipe Agoncillo and Sixto Lopez, on their way to Paris to try to influence the peace negotiations, called on October 1, 1898, at 10:15 a.m. With State Department official Alvey Adee as interpreter, the president received them and inquired as to their purpose. Agoncillo said they wished to lay before the president, on behalf of Aguinaldo and the Filipino people, a statement of the political situation in the Philippines for U.S. consideration in pursuing a negotiated peace.

McKinley carefully explained that he would be pleased to listen but only with the understanding that they were private Philippine citizens and not representatives of Aguinaldo or any political entity within the islands. Accepting the distinction, Agoncillo launched into a brief disquisition on the travails of the Filipino people and the importance of independence.

McKinley interjected to ask if Agoncillo would make his communication informally and in writing to Adee. He promised to read the statement and give it due consideration. Agoncillo accepted the invitation, whereupon the president instructed Adee to emphasize once again the terms under which he had consented to receive them.

McKinley considered it crucial to convey to his peace negotiators that nothing had passed between these men and the United States that could be construed as U.S. recognition of any Aguinaldo government or official standing within the Philippines. As Hay wrote to the U.S. commissioners, "Following his purpose of not receiving these gentlemen as envoys or recognizing in any way the character of their mission, the President does not propose to commend them to you." He once again touted "the careful and elaborate memoranda submitted by General Greene." Clearly the president wanted to nudge his negotiators toward his own thinking without revealing the substance of it. Indeed when the *Chicago Tribune's* Joseph Medill visited the president at the

White House and suggested he should state "directly and openly" his intention to acquire all of the Philippines, McKinley "expressed some annoyance."

By October 5 the U.S. negotiators saw what kind of intransigence they could expect from their Spanish counterparts. Day wrote to the president, "You would be astounded at the ingenuity and persistence with which our opponents undertake to enlarge the meaning of these clear articles." First, the Spaniards demanded that the Americans accept, before any further discussions commenced, the principle of "status quo" in the Philippines—meaning restoration of full Spanish authority. The Americans rejected that out of hand as outside the spirit of the Protocol, which stipulated it was a matter for negotiation. The Spanish commissioners acquiesced with a "conciliatory" tone that led Day to conclude the demand was more a test than a serious proposal.

Then the Spanish commissioners threw a wrench into the discussions by demanding that the United States assume the large Cuban debt, "the expense," Day wrote to McKinley, "of years of Spanish misrule, and . . . of its barbarous persecution of the people of Cuba." Debt goes with sovereignty, insisted the Spanish, to which the Americans replied that the United States had never asked for sovereignty in Cuba and the Protocol didn't address the question. After getting clearance from the president, Hay wrote to Day, "We are still free to regard it as acceptance in trust for people of Cuba without express obligations in treaty." A historical survey indicated that there was no serious precedence in international law for the idea that debt inevitably goes with sovereignty.

But the nettlesome issue consumed the negotiators through much of October and generated fear on the part of some American negotiators that the discussions could break down. "I hope we shall be able to get a treaty," Day wrote to McKinley on October 23, "but am a little pessimistic about it." Two days later McKinley rendered a final decision on the debt question, and Hay wired Day, "The President directs me to say that under no circumstances will the Government of the United States assume any part of what is known as the Cuban debt."

Later that night Reid met with his longtime Spanish friend, the ambassador to Paris Fernando León y Castillo. When Reid informed

Castillo of the president's decision, "he seemed almost to break down," Reid informed the president in a back-channel letter. "It is cruel, cruel, most cruel," the despondent ambassador moaned. He urged that the matter be put aside pending a determination on whether the United States would grant some concession elsewhere. If that wasn't possible, said Castillo, the Spanish commissioners would be completely repudiated at home, and the negotiations would break down. Upon leaving, he sighed, "My old friend, pray God that you and your country may never have to submit to the lot of the vanquished!"

Having determined his position on the Cuban debt, McKinley now turned his attention decisively to the Philippines. And not a moment too soon. Admiral Dewey on October 18 sent a dispatch to Navy Secretary Long urging quick action to avert a looming crisis in the islands. "Spanish authority has been completely destroyed in Luzon," he wrote, "and general anarchy prevails [outside] the city and Bay of Manila. Strongly probable that Islands to the south will fall into same state soon. Disturbing reports have been received of inhuman cruelty practiced on religious and civil authorities."

On October 25, the same day as the president's Cuban debt decision, he sent a letter to Day. "I am greatly pleased with the progress you are making and the manner in which you are presenting the American case," he wrote by way of preamble. As the commission neared serious consideration of the Philippine question, he would like to get the commissioners' sentiments on the issue. Then, dropping his own coyness, he added, "There is a very general feeling that the United States, whatever it might prefer . . . is in a situation where it cannot let go. The interdependency of the several islands, their close relations with Luzon, the very grave problem of what will become of the part we do not take, are receiving the thoughtful consideration of the people, and it is my judgment that the well-considered opinion of the majority would be that duty requires we should take the archipelago."

The commissioners quickly responded to the president's request, starting with Day, whose outlook McKinley already knew. Day felt the country "shall be embarrassed in a peremptory demand for the entire group" because the Protocol left the final disposition to negotiation. "There is little room for negotiation," he wrote, "when one party demands at the outset all that is to be negotiated about." He wanted just Luzon and perhaps a few other strategic islands. Senators Frye and Davis, joined by Reid, favored taking the full archipelago, with a payment to Spain for the islands if necessary. Senator George Gray favored "moderation, restraint and reason in victory" over being a "ruthless conqueror," though precisely what he would take remained vague.

But the president already had crafted his policy, as he made clear in an October 28 instruction sent to the commissioners through Hay. "Grave as are the responsibilities and unforeseen as are the difficulties which are before us," he wrote, "the President can see but one plain path of duty—the acceptance of the archipelago." Spain must be extricated from the Philippines; no other power could be allowed in; that left the United States, motivated "by the single consideration of duty and humanity."

McKinley argued for basing his Philippine claim upon the right of conquest, but the commissioners unanimously countered that that could not be sustained with any diplomatic propriety because Manila didn't fall until after the Protocol was signed. "I wish to submit to your careful consideration," wrote Day to his boss, "that we should not take the untenable ground that Spain should cede the islands because of any right of conquest, great or small, achieved after the Protocol was executed." If no treaty emerged, he added, the United States could proceed with military operations that would trigger a true definition of conquest. But of course a successful negotiation was far preferable, and thus a different approach would be necessary. In the end, the U.S. commissioners based their claim on the requirement of an indemnity to be paid by Spain to cover America's costs in prosecuting a war forced upon it by the Iberian nation. But the president also responded favorably to Senator Frye's suggestion that a substantial payment to Spain could ease the way for a final settlement. If the commissioners thought the United States should pay "a reasonable sum of money to cover peace improvements which are fairly chargeable to us under established precedents," wrote Hay to Paris, the president "will give cheerful concurrence."

When the Americans issued their formal demand for the Philippine archipelago on October 31, the Spanish representatives responded with a barrage of objections and requests for delay as they mustered further arguments for why the demand couldn't be justified, violated the terms of the Protocol, reflected poorly on America, and so on. They evinced a reluctance to even consider such harsh terms lest they be pilloried in Madrid and their careers destroyed. "Yesterday everybody was predicting that we would get no treaty," Reid wrote the president on November 15.

McKinley stood firm but sought to break down Spanish resistance by authorizing a $20 million payment to accompany the Philippine cession. Reid began to get a sense of brighter prospects. "I think & know from inside news from Madrid," he wrote the president, ". . . that the Queen Regent is now convinced that nothing can be gained by contending either for the debt or for the Philippines & that she is anxious to accept the inevitable & end the agony." The Spanish government receded on November 28. Twelve days later the commissioners signed the final treaty, corresponding largely to the terms of the Protocol and McKinley's subsequent instructions on the Philippines. The president got all he wanted: the Philippines, Puerto Rico, Guam; Spain out of Cuba and the Caribbean, with no debt assumed by the United States. All this for $20 million pulled out of a growing U.S. Treasury. It still needed Senate ratification, but the outcome, however contingent, represented a signal achievement.

THROUGHOUT HIS CAREER, William McKinley had displayed a tendency to view events through a prism of idealism and thus sometimes distort reality with language that didn't quite reflect the world as it really was. In hailing the country's great military victory over Spain and its acquisition of new, far-flung territories, he resisted the reality that America had embarked upon an imperial venture. Certainly he wasn't naïve about the intentions of Emilio Aguinaldo, capable of mustering an army of 30,000 combatants in the cause of Philippine independence. Yet in issuing a proclamation on America's vast new role in the archipelago, he talked of "benevolent assimilation" and promised that America would demonstrate that "we come, not as invaders or conquerors, but as friends." A short time later, in a Boston speech, he proclaimed, "Our concern was not for territory or trade or empire, but for the people whose interests and destiny, without our willing it, had been put in our hands."

But of course territory, trade, and empire all emerged from the war's outcome, and many Americans thrilled to the idea that their country now was pursuing its destiny far beyond its North American boundaries. Why, after all, had the United States built its powerful navy over the previous several years, including years of McKinley's presidency? As the *Philadelphia Press* crowed after Dewey's Manila Bay victory, "Sea power counts and in the world's wide work it is the first and last thing which does count." The paper noted that fourteen years earlier, a Naval Board of Experts had recommended eighteen battleships. "The report was laughed at. Does any one laugh now?"

Mahan and Lodge and Roosevelt knew what it was all about. It was about projecting power into the world for purposes of trade and wealth and national prestige around the globe. And, yes, there was an element of helping less developed peoples, but ultimately it was about power. McKinley knew that also, but he couldn't quite bring himself to say it. Perhaps McKinley's cousin and lifelong friend William Osborne captured the reality in a way the president couldn't express. McKinley's recent tour of speeches on the results of victory, Osborne said, were "a triumphant march of what they call Imperialism." He touted his cousin's presidency as a "history making Administration."

It was indeed history-making. Godkin's *Nation* noted that McKinley's installation of a military governor in the Philippines "initiates the first experiment which this nation has ever tried in the control of a territory at a great remove from our shores." The magazine said the country had hardly even begun to contemplate the implications of such a revolutionary experiment. Carl Schurz, the great anti-imperialist, took a dim view of it all and warned McKinley of widespread opposition in the country to the annexation of far-away lands. "I . . . predict," he wrote, "that this popular feeling against such political entanglements by the proposed annexations will very much grow in intensity as the burdens which the imperialistic policy will put upon us, become more apparent to the public mind."

Whatever currents of opposition might emerge in America or in the acquired territories, McKinley had set his course. And he moved now, in his slow and deliberate but very stubborn way, to execute the policies he had established for himself and his country.

22

War's Aftermath

RATIFICATION, BAD BEEF, AND AN
OMINOUS NEW CONFLICT

Ida McKinley was sitting in the White House Red Room on May 6, 1899, when a contingent of guests arrived for one of those ceremonial visits that marked a significant part of Ida's daily routine. This particular group included a New York teenager named Pauline Robinson, tied to the rich and influential DuPont family of Delaware; another New York debutante, Miss Lee; and the wife and daughter of Washington's Episcopal bishop. When introduced to the first lady, Miss Robinson executed a perfect "Dodworth curtsy" and perceived that Mrs. McKinley seemed to like "pomp and flattery." As the first lady, dressed in blue, her favorite color, put down her knitting to receive the guests, she noted "with evident pride" that she had knitted 4,000 pairs of slippers, including one that fetched $300 at a charity fair the previous year. "Look here," she said, opening a bag of yarn and presenting a photo of the president she kept always with her during such labors, "I am never idle, and this is a great incentive to work."

In conversing with her guests, the first lady seemed particularly enamored of Pauline. "My dear," she entreated her, "draw your chair up closer to me." When the young woman said it was a privilege to meet her, Ida brushed aside the flattery.

"My dear, wait till you meet the President—then I shall consider you to have been truly honored." She launched into a series of highly entertaining and favorable stories about "the Major." Miss Lee, who seemed to have heard some of these stories, repeatedly said, "Oh, I have heard about that." Ida, becoming visibly irritated at the idea that her anecdotes were not fresh, turned to Pauline and addressed her in a confidential tone: "There is no use in telling Miss Lee anything. She knows it all."

As if by magic, the president appeared and sought to take the sting out of Ida's petulance. He presented her with a bouquet of her favorite flowers, lilies of the valley, which she received with evident delight. But when the president sought diplomatically to terminate the visit so she could attend a scheduled meeting with a Lutheran minister, Ida once again turned peevish. "That makes no difference to me," she snapped. "Does it to you?"

Well, replied the president, seeking to soothe his wife with a bit of repartee, perhaps Lutherans didn't matter, but he certainly liked Methodists and Episcopalians. Ida was not amused. "What about Presbyterians?!" she barked. That was, of course, her own denomination.

"Why my dear," replied the president, "of *course* I like Presbyterians." That seemed to mollify her, and she rose for her next appointment. Before departing, she turned to Miss Robinson and handed her the bouquet of flowers she had just received. The stunned young lady later wrote in a letter home, "Everyone seemed to think that was an unusual thing for Mrs. McKinley to do."

That small incident reflected a central reality of William McKinley's life: however preoccupied he might become with affairs of state or burdens of war, Ida always commanded a significant share of his attention. And sometimes this attention went beyond his well-known tender solicitude and extended to warding off the occasional displays of pique and querulousness that could lead to tense and embarrassing moments. McKinley usually could humor Ida with lighthearted banter mixed with a touch of firmness, but it was never clear what form her moods would take or what might trigger a tantrum. It wasn't merely a matter of avoiding embarrassment. More important was McKinley's ability to present to the nation a true first lady, performing the tasks and responsibilities traditionally associated with that role. Thus the president could never relax his resolve to buoy his wife's moods and maintain her contentment with notes of devotion, affectionate attention, and lilies of the valley.

Given this imperative and Ida's need for travel and leisure time with him, McKinley regretted his inability to break away for significant vacation time during 1898, and he planned now to reverse that. He also anticipated significant travel for speeches touting his record and promoting his agenda. Sojourning south in December for eleven public appearances in Georgia, Alabama, and South Carolina, he hailed what he considered a new national spirit of post–Civil War unity, fostered by the patriotism of the recent war. "Sectional lines no longer mar the map of the United States," he declared in Atlanta, to great applause. "Sectional feeling no longer holds back the love we bear each other." Clearly he remained committed to burying the bloody shirt.

With the war over, McKinley also picked up the pace of White House socializing. At a small January 8 dinner, the president and Treasury Secretary Gage led others in singing Methodist hymns. Mark Hanna seemed to enjoy the music but didn't join in. In early 1899 the McKinleys held five evening receptions, one drawing nearly 8,000 visitors, and in mid-January the president and Ida entertained the Washington diplomatic corps at a lavish White House dinner. Later that month Lyman and Cornelia Gage entertained the president and Ida at an evening repast that the *Washington Post* called "one of the most beautifully appointed dinners ever served in Washington." The Gages' oval table was festooned with Farleyense ferns and, yes, lilies of the valley.

But tasks of state never receded far from the president's mind. After two years as president, he had developed a distaste for government officials preoccupied with their own worth. "How these men try to magnify the importance of their work," he complained to Cortelyou, later praising the modesty of a particular government official. "We hear a great deal about him," said the president, "but not from him." Clearly the admonitions of Mother McKinley remained lodged in his consciousness.

Even with war's end, McKinley anticipated many challenges in 1899. Looming large was the need to secure Senate ratification of the

Paris peace accord. McKinley knew that the rising crescendo of anti-imperialist sentiment could rattle his effort to get the required two-thirds vote, and events in the Philippines could rattle it even more. Aside from that, national politics soon would be roiled by the coming report of McKinley's Dodge Commission investigating army incompetence and possible corruption.

When the president sent the Paris treaty to the Senate on January 4, the *Washington Post* predicted that perhaps seventy of the Senate's ninety senators would vote aye. But military developments in the Philippines, mixed with political developments at home, threatened the president's policy. The Philippine story begins with the new U.S. military governor, sixty-year-old General Elwell S. Otis, a rotund fellow with muttonchop whiskers dominating an otherwise bland face. He possessed an impressive résumé: decorated for his Civil War and Indian conflict service; a Harvard law degree; founder of the army's staff academy at Leavenworth, Kansas. But after replacing Wesley Merritt on August 29, 1898, Otis confirmed his reputation as a managerial fusspot obsessed with minute details. Always in motion, he seldom moved forward. General Arthur MacArthur, who served under him, viewed him as "a locomotive bottomside up on the tracks, with its wheels revolving at full speed." Further, his pomposity often led to careless decision making.

Otis proved adept at cleaning up a squalid, dysfunctional Manila left by the Spanish, with garbage piling up, disease rampant, and inhabitants starving. In keeping with McKinley's humanitarian view of American interventionism, U.S. forces organized police and garbage collection operations, built health facilities, immunized children, established military courts, and reopened schools. But Otis adopted an arrogant attitude toward Aguinaldo and his insurgent forces, echoed in his troops' bigoted view of the indigenous people and frequent abusive behavior toward them. Otis actually felt a need to issue an order forbidding his troops from using the word *nigger* and other derogatory terms when referring to Filipinos in their presence.

But Aguinaldo quickly discerned that the American general didn't take seriously either his military capabilities or his political resolve. It would never be known if a more conciliatory approach could have averted hostilities, given the gulf between American and insurgent aims—McKinley believing his country had acquired sovereignty over the Philippines through war and negotiation; Aguinaldo insisting he spoke for the Filipino people in declaring his country's independence, forming his government, and assuming the role of revolutionary president. But Otis's approach, largely approved by Washington officials with little appreciation for the delicate nature of the situation, exacerbated tensions in the islands.

On September 8 Otis issued an ultimatum to Aguinaldo (approved by the president) ordering him, "respectfully," to remove his troops from Manila, including its suburbs. If the insurgent leader didn't comply within a week, declared Otis, "I shall be obliged to resort to forcible action, and . . . my Government will hold you responsible for any unfortunate consequences that may ensue." Aguinaldo pleaded with Otis to remove the incendiary language calculated to humiliate the Filipinos. In a second letter, Otis toned down the wording a bit, but not much, and he refused to withdraw the first ultimatum (simply leaving Aguinaldo free to ignore it). The insurgent leader removed his troops, and Otis quickly concluded that Aguinaldo would be a soft touch. "Affairs much more satisfactory," he wired Washington on September 15, Aguinaldo's deadline day for compliance. "Manila quiet and business progressing favorably. No difficulty anticipated."

Later, when Otis got reports of a possible massacre of remaining Spaniards at Iloilo on Panay island, he sought authorization from Washington to send a contingent of troops there under General Marcus Miller. Permission was granted—but only if the Spanish could be rescued without violence. "It is most important," wrote Corbin to Otis, "that there be no conflict with the insurgents." When Miller arrived, the Spaniards already had left, but he landed troops anyway, generating bitterness in equal measure among Philippine insurgents and American anti-imperialists. Meanwhile Washington was getting the jitters over increasing prospects for violence. Corbin wired stern instructions to Otis: "The President considers it of first importance that a conflict brought on by you be avoided at this time if possible." Then, demonstrating Washington's naïveté, Corbin asked, "Can not Miller get into communication with insurgents, giving them President's proclamation and . . . assuring them that while [the United States] will assert its sovereignty, that its purpose is to give them a good government and security in their personal rights."

He was referring to McKinley's notable "benevolent assimilation" proclamation of December 21, in which the president declared U.S. sovereignty over the Philippines. The military authority maintained by the United States in the city and harbor of Manila, stated the president, "is to be extended with all possible dispatch to the whole of the ceded territory." But the president sought to assure Filipinos, asserting, "We come, not as invaders or conquerors, but as friends, to protect the natives in their homes, in their employments, and in their personal and religious rights." Those cooperating with this new military authority, "either by active aid or by honest submission," would receive the reward of American support and protection. "All others will be brought within the lawful rule we have assumed, with firmness if need be, but without severity so far as may be possible."

McKinley crafted this language to reassure Filipinos of America's amity and cooperation. That's why Corbin thought the proclamation could be used to placate rebel anxieties at Panay. But many in the Philippines viewed it as inimical to everything they wanted for their country. Even Otis feared certain passages could prove incendiary, so he made the remarkable decision of toning down certain passages before forwarding the document to Aguinaldo. It was a serious lapse in judgment. Worse, he inadvertently sent to General Miller at Panay the original version without informing him that it had been edited. When Miller passed it along to an Iloilo rebel leader, he promptly sent it to Aguinaldo, who quickly concluded the Americans were playing some kind of double game.

Miller eventually left Iloilo, but Otis's splenetic approach and Aguinaldo's suspicion and anger contributed to tensions already well established by the military situation on Luzon, with America controlling Manila and its suburbs and Aguinaldo's 30,000-strong force dominating the countryside. As one observant soldier put it, "I believe it only a matter of time when there will be a clash, for the two armies' outposts are within a mile or two of each other, and a single shot from either side would precipitate a general engagement."

Back in Washington, it wasn't surprising that this unstable situation would agitate many senators already uncomfortable with the breadth of McKinley's Philippine policy—and particularly the Iloilo misadventure. A floor debate on January 11 revealed serious reservations based on questions of diplomatic and constitutional propriety. Democratic senator Augustus Bacon of Georgia introduced a resolution disclaiming any U.S. intent "to exercise sovereignty, jurisdiction, or control over said islands" beyond the time when the Filipinos could organize a government (presumably under Aguinaldo). A resolution by Nebraska's Populist senator William Allen declared that any military action against the Filipino insurgency would be "an act of war unwarranted on the part of the President and the exercise of Constitutional powers vested exclusively in Congress," which had never authorized any such war against Filipinos.

Undergirding both resolutions was the conviction that the United States had no right under the Constitution or international law to annex the Philippines. But Ben Foraker vehemently disagreed. "Among the powers of nationality," declared the Ohioan, "are the powers to make war and to make treaties." Implicit in those powers was "the power to acquire territory by conquest or otherwise and to inherit all the consequences that may accrue through war."

On January 25, Cushman Davis, one of the U.S. peace commissioners and chairman of the Senate Foreign Relations Committee, urged ratification of the peace treaty to forestall "continued uncertainty, renewed encouragement to the insurgent Filipinos . . . and a prolongation of the state of war with much of its horrors," as the *New York Times* characterized his remarks. He seemed confident of victory, the paper reported, but added that President McKinley, following his normal routine of poring over newspaper reports and talking extensively with senators of both parties, had concluded that ratification might face difficulty.

The president was right. On February 1, the *Washington Post* reported that "the lack of sufficient votes is very evident," and senatorial vote counters said the president remained two votes shy of success. When further resolutions emerged attacking the president's Philippine policy and foreswearing any U.S. interest in annexing the Philippines, some Republicans urged acceptance of one of these resolutions to ease the way for ratification. The president opposed that approach and even seemed to join some senators who would let the treaty die before allowing a Senate minority to dictate policy. As McKinley viewed it, he had surveyed his Philippine options thoroughly and had reached a sound conclusion based on logic. He hadn't set out to turn America into an Asian colonial power; the war had done that. But now, responding to events as they unfolded, he would pursue steadfastly the only policy that made sense to him. The president worked the issue assiduously, lobbying wayward senators and dangling patronage and other favors in an effort to cadge votes.

To bolster his political standing further, he announced creation of yet another commission, this one to study the Philippine situation and formulate policy options. He named to the group Charles Denby, a Democrat and former minister to China; Dean C. Worcester, a University of Michigan zoologist who had traveled extensively through the islands; and Cornell University president Jacob Gould Schurman. When he asked Schurman to head the group, the academician initially demurred, saying he opposed U.S. dominance over the archipelago.

"Oh . . . that need not trouble you," McKinley assured him. "I didn't want the Philippine Islands, either." That's why, he said, he crafted protocol language that left his options open. But "in the end there was no alternative." Somehow Schurman accepted this as reassurance and took the position. The commission left for Manila on January 31.

AT AROUND 11:30 on the evening of Saturday, February 4, McKinley sat at his Cabinet Room table, dictating to Cortelyou passages for a forthcoming Boston speech. A White House aide interrupted to deliver a dispatch received earlier that day by the *New York Sun*. The paper's Manila correspondent reported that Aguinaldo's insurgents had initiated a general assault on U.S. forces in the Philippine capital; that U.S. forces had driven the Filipinos back with heavy losses to the insurgents; and that action continued. The president silently read it several times, then placed it on his table, leaned back in his chair, and mused, "It is always the unexpected that happens. . . . How foolish those people are. This means the ratification of the treaty; the people will understand now."

At 8:05 the next morning he got official word from Dewey and later in the day a status report from Otis. The general said the insurgents had attacked U.S. outer lines with a large force, then renewed the attack several times through the night. By 4 a.m. the entire U.S. line managed to repulse the attack, push the insurgents back beyond their previous position, and capture several villages and defense works. "We are still driving enemy and think we will punish him severely," wrote Otis. He later reported that fifty-nine U.S. servicemen had died in battle, along with 3,000 Filipinos. It wasn't clear to later historians which side actually precipitated the battle, though the first shot likely had been fired by an American soldier. But the long face-off perimeter between the two armies was inherently unstable, and a conflict probably was inevitable. Certainly the McKinley administration hadn't wanted a shooting war at that time.

But the war was on. It introduced new complexities into the Philippine situation and also threatened the president's political standing if he couldn't bring it to a quick conclusion. Given Aguinaldo's troop strength of 30,000 and his demonstrated military capacity, a short war didn't seem likely.

The events around Manila seemed to push the Senate vote toward a favorable outcome, helped along by a treaty endorsement from the country's leading Democrat, William Jennings Bryan. But it was a near thing. On February 5, before news of the battle had sunk into the national consciousness, the *New York Times* ran the headline "Hangs Upon a Thread: Fate of Peace Treaty Still a Matter of Doubt." The next day, with the vote scheduled for 3 p.m., the paper suggested the final two votes would almost certainly emerge, though they hadn't yet been definitively identified. The Senate revealed its sentiment when it voted down an amendment seeking to place the Philippines on the same path toward independence granted to Cuba. Then came the ratification vote. First South Carolina's Democratic senator John McLaurin announced his support, perhaps induced by patronage promises. Then Democrat Samuel McEnery of Louisiana offered his vote in exchange for a Senate roll call on his resolution declaring that U.S. Philippine policy "is not intended to incorporate the inhabitants of the Philippine Islands into citizenship of the United States." (The measure passed the Senate but died in the House.) Finally, Republican John Jones of Nevada switched from nay to aye after the initial roll call.

The result was fifty-seven votes for ratification, one more than needed. Henry Cabot Lodge, a fierce treaty advocate, slumped in his Senate chair with relief. "It was the closest, hardest fight I have ever known," he told Roosevelt, "and probably we shall not see another in our time where there was so much at stake." Lodge's Massachusetts colleague, the great anti-interventionist George Hoar, rushed to the White House the next morning to mend fences. When Lodge showed up and found the miscreant seated before the president, "with a beaming smile on his Pickwickian face," the great interventionist could hardly believe it. "Only a few hours before," Lodge's friend Henry Adams fumed, "in the full belief that his single vote was going to defeat and ruin the administration, Hoar had voted against the treaty, and there he was, slobbering the President with assurances of his admiration . . . and distilling over him the oil of his sanctimony."

But McKinley, true to his studied magnanimity, let pass Hoar's rebellion out of a friendship that extended back many years and was distilled in an exchange some months earlier when the president encountered Hoar at a social function. The president asked what kind of mood his friend was in.

"Pretty pugnacious, I confess, Mr. President," replied Hoar.

"I shall always love you, whatever you do," said the president, taking his friend's hand and showing a bit of mist in his eyes. But behind the mist, and the sincerity it betokened, was a calculation, no doubt, of the next time he would need Hoar's vote.

MCKINLEY'S DODGE COMMISSION had served its early purpose well, lancing the boil of national outrage at reports of army mistreatment of America's soldiers and getting the president's party past the November elections with as little damage as possible. For more than two months, beginning in late September, the commissioners conducted 109 meetings and probed every aspect of the army's wartime record (leaving aside only policy and strategic matters). They interviewed Secretary Alger along with all the major army bureau chiefs and other well-placed officers. They talked with scores of lesser officers, enlisted men, medical personnel, and charity workers. They pursued information in Chicago, Detroit, Harrisburg, Cincinnati, Boston, New York, Philadelphia, and Tampa.

What emerged was a narrative not much different from what the country already knew. Many problems were "the inevitable consequences of tropical campaigning and hasty mobilization," as one historian later put it. Distribution difficulties stemmed from the effort to move so many men and so much materiel so quickly with so little functional infrastructure. The Medical Department, lacking prestige within the service, found itself slighted by top authorities, bereft of the supplies and materials needed to perform adequately. Incompetence undermined the Quartermaster Department, responsible for shipping medical supplies. Field commanders ignored sanitation instructions and often belittled medical personnel who tried to enforce them. In short order the Hospital Corps increased in number from just 791 personnel to nearly 6,000—still half of what was needed. Such a frenzied buildup generated inevitable administrative chaos.

It appeared the Dodge report would give the president what he had asked for: a basis for placing responsibility where it belonged and for taking appropriate action. Also, Grenville Dodge and his colleagues weren't uncovering evidence of illegality or corruption. The scandal seemed contained, the narrative politically manageable.

Then the army's commanding general, Nelson Miles, ripped up the narrative and injected into the controversy an incendiary new element. On December 21, he told the commission that defective food had been "one of the serious causes of so much sickness and distress on the part of the troops." The problem, he said, was that the army's commissary general, Charles Eagan, had supplanted the traditional approach of maintaining beef on the hoof with newfangled canned and refrigerated beef products. These products, Miles declared, contained "some serious defect" that sickened large numbers of troops. The next day he went further in an interview with Hearst's intemperate *New York Journal*, which introduced its sensational story with the headline "Miles Makes Grave Charges against the Administration—Poisons Used in Beef Made the Soldiers Ill—Tons of Bad Meat Sent to Troops in Porto Rico—These Charges, He Declares, Contain Only a Few of the Facts Which [He] Has Gathered."

Now the story had a focus that it previously had lacked. This suggested not only malfeasance on a grand scale but also an unconscionable insensitivity toward the health and well-being of the soldiers sent into harm's way in behalf of their country. An outraged Alger became particularly sympathetic toward General Eagan, who was struck, said Alger, "with the suddenness and sharpness of a blow from an assassin's knife out of the dark."

Behind the Miles allegation was a series of petty controversies, irritations, and perceived slights that ballooned into a seething antipathy for Alger, McKinley, and most of his subordinate generals. After leading a contingent of reinforcements to Cuba to assist General Shafter outside Santiago, Miles took umbrage at a cable sent by Alger to Shafter clarifying that Miles would not supersede Shafter's authority. Why this should rile the general was mystifying, since Miles and Alger had worked out the arrangement before his departure. The general again took umbrage following his quick victory against the Spanish in Puerto Rico. He wanted to arrange a surrender and Spanish evacuation of San Juan but received orders to remain in place pending the outcome of the Paris peace talks. So consumed with his own ego was Miles that he couldn't see the diplomatic necessity in McKinley's stand-pat order following the signing of the armistice protocol.

During his Puerto Rican campaign, Miles went public with his animosities in an interview with a friendly *Kansas City Star* reporter. He accused Alger of neutralizing his authority in Santiago, rejecting his program for containing yellow fever, publicly distorting his communications, and withholding crucial naval vessels from his Puerto Rican landing operation. Arriving in New York in September, he touted his own strategic brilliance to reporters and asserted credit for the victories in both Santiago and Puerto Rico. The *Washington Post* captured Miles in a headline: "Gen. Nelson A. Miles: Makes Up in Ambition What He Lacks in Modesty."

In going after Alger, Miles chose an easy target. The secretary had seen his national standing decline sharply with the army incompetence scandals. Many reporters, intent on keeping the story alive, adopted Miles as the good guy who fought to protect his troops from the failings of Alger and also of Adjutant General Corbin, whose increasing power in the White House rankled Miles. An example centered on a plan to have returning troops from Puerto Rico and Santiago veterans from Montauk parade through New York in a celebratory demonstration. McKinley approved the plan contingent upon the troops being certified as physically fit. An exchange of telegrams revealed that most army officers involved, including Miles, considered the thing impractical, and the president withdrew his approval. That led to newspaper reports that a vindictive Corbin had canceled the parade to thwart public recognition of Miles. After talking with Miles in October, General Shafter warned Corbin that he was "wild with suppressed rage . . . breathing vengeance on the Department."

Miles had first taken an interest in the beef matter in June, when he heard reports in Tampa that the troops were grumbling about the preserved meat. After his return from Puerto Rico he surveyed regimental commanders and received widespread condemnation of the canned beef. Yet at this point nobody had suggested the meat was tainted or contained poisons. That came from a longtime friend of Miles named William Daly, a Pittsburgh physician serving with Miles as a volunteer surgeon. Daly told Miles the meat had tasted of boric and salicylic acids, unsafe chemicals sometimes used to preserve meat. He later said he had tested the meat chemically and discovered acid traces. That was the sole basis for Miles's allegation that the meat was poisonous.

Unquestionably the canned meat product was unsavory. Roosevelt said the troops wouldn't touch the stuff unless very hungry. "At the best," he said, "it was tasteless; at the worst, it was nauseating." The Dodge Commission later would conclude that tropical temperatures produced liquefaction of the meat's fat, thus making it "unpalatable," as the Associated Press put it. "Most of the beef, though," added the news service, "is found to have been satisfactory for emergency use, where fresh beef or beef on the hoof could not be procured." There certainly was no evidence of actual taint. Even McKinley's Cabinet tasted the product and found it "in perfect condition, wholesome and sweet." And the AP said the statements of chemical treatment made by Miles and Daly were "not borne out by the chemical experts" who testified before the Dodge Commission.

But before the commission could reach that conclusion, the Miles allegation generated plenty of baneful consequences. Stung and incensed, Eagan requested an opportunity to testify in rebuttal before the commissioners and took the occasion to attack Miles as a liar "with as black a heart as the man who blew up the Maine possessed." He added for emphasis, "I wish to force the lie back into his throat, covered with the contents of a camp latrine." The *Washington Times* reported that, although Eagan's words were "the words of violence and heat—the phrases of mad passion—they were read with calmness and without any display of feeling."

But they generated plenty of feeling in the army hierarchy, which recommended a court-martial to try Eagan for his intemperate attack on a superior officer. Typically McKinley deliberated on the matter carefully before formulating his response. On January 17 he consulted with Alger and Corbin in a meeting "long in duration," then informed his Cabinet that the court-martial would proceed. Eagan was charged with conduct "unbecoming of an officer and a gentleman and . . . prejudicial to good order and military discipline."

Eagan's sensational outburst and his subsequent trial kept the "embalmed beef" scandal percolating in the national consciousness for weeks and served further to undermine Alger's standing with his countrymen. Then McKinley, determined to stay ahead of the story, created yet another investigative panel, a military court of inquiry, to investigate Miles's grimy allegations. That kept the story alive for another two months.

Testifying before the "beef court," Miles quickly retreated from his most incendiary allegations of corruption and fraud and walked back many of his harshest remarks to reporters. In late April the court rejected any suggestion that the army's canned or refrigerated beef contained harmful preservative chemicals. It was nutritious food, said the court—adding, though, that it should not have been used in the tropics on such a large scale without sufficient experimentation beforehand. That, said the court, was a "colossal error." But it discerned no ulterior motive in Eagan's effort to feed the troops. As for Miles, it said he had "no sufficient justification" for his allegations and demonstrated particularly bad judgment in not reporting his suspicions immediately upon developing them, as soldiers continued to eat the allegedly tainted meat for weeks in the meantime.

In late January Eagan was found guilty of charges that carried a penalty of dismissal from the army. McKinley commuted that sentence to suspension from duty for six years, the remainder of the time prior to Eagan's scheduled retirement. Under the president's commutation, he would be reinstated in time to retire with regular rank and pay.

That finally ended the sensational beef controversy for the country—but not for Alger, whose political standing continued to plummet. "The honor of the army has been soiled," declared the *New York Times*. Later, when Alger appeared with the president at a Boston event, his name elicited hisses from the audience. The president's cousin, William Osborne, writing from London, said nearly everyone he talked to deprecated Alger. He urged the president to "clear the atmosphere of this army criticism immediately."

In late March Alger traveled to Cuba for a three-week fact-finding tour to escape the firestorm and bolster his national image. It didn't work, in part because upon his return he announced plans to run for senator from Michigan in the fall. That would place McKinley in a delicate position should an intraparty battle emerge for the post, as seemed likely. It also aligned Alger with Michigan's governor Hazen Pingree, a fiery populist and harsh McKinley critic. This proved troublesome when Alger told reporters that "Gov. Pingree is for President McKinley first, last, and all the time." Asked about it, Pingree responded with characteristic sarcasm and scorn:

> *The question whether I am for McKinley lies with the President, not with me. If Gen. Alger knows that President McKinley is opposed to territorial expansion, and is not an advocate of the murders and the destruction being visited upon the innocent Filipinos, he has a right to say that I am for McKinley. If Gen. Alger is informed that McKinley is opposed to trusts and . . . in favor of legislation to restrict and suppress them, then I am closer to the opinions of McKinley than has generally been believed. If Gen. Alger is assured that President McKinley is not in touch and sympathy with the disreputable political methods of Mark Hanna and his friends, and deprecates such leadership, then I am for McKinley.*

The next Day Alger told reporters that, sure, he may have disagreed with some administration policies, but Treasury Secretary Gage did the same in putting forth a currency plan that was rejected by the president. This was a gross violation of Cabinet protocol, which held that members should never reveal the positions of their colleagues in private Cabinet discussions.

Such behavior was untenable, as many newspaper commentators understood. "Why," asked the *New York Times*, "does the President keep Alger in the place in which he has displayed an incompetence so abysmal, a spirit so small?" From across the Atlantic, the *Times* of London intoned, "Mr. Alger is a burden which no President, no party, would carry voluntarily. . . . He imperils Mr. McKinley's renomination and re-election." Many papers expressed puzzlement at McKinley's lassitude in the face of such an internal crisis. The *New York Times* speculated, charitably, that the "kindliness of [McKinley's] heart probably has resolved to stand by Alger all the more tenaciously because of the open manifestation of aversion for him."

But the president's heart was becoming less kindly by the day. Each evening Cortelyou showed him that day's press coverage, with the "demand for a change" becoming practically unanimous. Cortelyou noted in his diary that the president continued to treat Alger "with every courtesy—too much, many think—and the evidently strained relations are made as bearable as the situation can warrant." But behind the scenes the president was dealing with the situation in his own way. He had "several rather trying interviews" with Alger in early July and finally got him to resign, effective the following January 2—nearly six months away. The president withheld this information, however, in hopes he could get Alger out sooner. On July 18, responding to Cortelyou's disparagement of Alger, the president looked at his secretary a few moments, then said quietly, "Something will come to a head tomorrow."

The next morning McKinley invited his secretary on a walk through the White House grounds. "Well," said the president, "he has over and left it with me. . . . It is to take effect at my pleasure." He claimed the culminating interview with Alger had been "brief and devoid of any embarrassing features."

The deed was done. The president that afternoon drafted a brief message to accompany Alger's resignation notice, then sought comments from Hay, Long, and Cortelyou. When they all approved, the president placed it in the drawer of his Cabinet Room table and told Cortelyou, "I'll leave that there to-night and you will know where it is if anything happens to me to-night."

To replace Alger McKinley quickly set his sights on Elihu Root, the high-powered New York attorney known for his quick mind, moderate reformism, probity, and professional loyalty. He was a slender, stern-looking man with a shock of thick hair covering his forehead and thin lips that could erase his austere countenance instantly by forming into what Hay called a "frank and murderous smile." Root had no background in military matters, and nobody was clamoring for the New Yorker's elevation, not even Tom Platt, because nobody saw the value he could bring to such a position. But McKinley, who had consulted with Root shortly after his inauguration and had offered him the Spanish mission in 1897, knew what he wanted. His novel and creative thinking was manifest in a telephone exchange between Root and a presidential messenger, Congressman Lemuel Quigg.

"The President directs me to say to you that he wishes you to take the position of Secretary of War," said Quigg.

"Thank the President for me," replied Root, "but say that it is quite absurd, I know nothing about war, I know nothing about the army."

Quigg asked Root to hold the phone while he consulted with McKinley. Returning, he said, "President McKinley directs me to say that he is not looking for any one who knows anything about the army; he has got to have a lawyer to direct the government of these Spanish islands, and you are the lawyer he wants."

Beguiled by the logic and the challenge of leadership, Root accepted, and the president expressed to Cortelyou his "great satisfaction." In constructing his initial Cabinet in early 1897, the president's performance had been not much above mediocre. Now he had a Cabinet as strong as any in recent memory.

23

Aguinaldo

INTERTWINED MILITARY AND POLITICAL DANGERS

On April 19, 1899, rumors began circulating in New York City that House Speaker Thomas B. Reed, that irrepressible bulk of political will and guile, had taken a $50,000-a-year position with a prestigious Manhattan law firm and soon would resign his House seat. Asked about it by reporters, Reed dismissed the question with his characteristic gruffness. "I would rather not talk on that subject," he growled. "In fact, I have not given the matter any consideration as yet." Then he headed off on a three-month European vacation.

The speaker's reply wasn't entirely truthful, and the reporters knew it. He did in fact intend to abandon his speakership and join the firm of Simpson, Thatcher & Barnum. The next day many newspapers treated the rumors as fact. "Speaker Reed's withdrawal from public life," announced the *Washington Post*, "will be, beyond doubt, the most important and far-reaching incident which has occurred in political circles for a long time." The paper called Reed "a clear and forcible speaker, a sharp and ready debater, a parliamentarian unexcelled, and a man whose tremendous force of character dominated the House."

The *Post* speculated that sixty-year-old "Czar Reed," as he was known, felt frustrated as a presidential aspirant and thus would abandon politics for money. "He is a man who loves the good things of life and chafes if he has them not."

This interpretation, correct as far as it went, missed a significant element. Reed's beloved Republican Party had taken a turn he could neither abide nor forestall. He fumed at McKinley's imperialism and fumed even more at the position it placed him in—charged with maintaining party unity in behalf of the president's agenda and yet aghast at his foreign policy. The annexation of Hawaii was bad enough, and he had done what he could to undermine that errant action without precipitating a public rupture with the president. But now, truly enraged at McKinley's Philippine policy, he took to directing his acerbic wit indirectly at his nemesis. In mock opposition to a large appropriation for a Philadelphia museum, he said, referring to a Philippine tribe, "This seems like a great waste of money. We could buy 150,000 naked Sulus with that."

Though he liked the idea of increasing his wealth, Reed wrote to a friend, that wasn't his primary motivation. "Had I stayed," he explained, "I must have been as Speaker always in a false position," either promoting policies that repelled him or directing his power as speaker against those who had given him the power. Either course was untenable for a man of Reed's principle.

Just a decade before, when Reed had bested McKinley in the run for speaker, he had dismissed his rival as "a man of little scope"—"sly" perhaps but "above his level." He certainly lacked Reed's intellectual depth and devastating wit. The Major was a Mason who attended church regularly and listened respectfully to nearly all who approached him, even Democrats. To Reed, he seemed to operate in a bubble of blandness.

And yet now he was president of the United States, the country's dominant political figure, moving it in directions that Reed couldn't abide. The mystery of William McKinley was perhaps most mystifying of all to Thomas Reed. But if the speaker didn't understand McKinley and his rise, McKinley understood Reed all too well as a powerful figure who, at any moment, might direct his powers to thwart the presidential agenda. McKinley never spoke ill of Reed, but his view of the man was reflected in the fact that he had set foot in the White House only once during McKinley's two years there. Rumors actually filtered through Washington that the White House might recruit an opponent for the speakership at the next Congress. Thus it wasn't surprising that Reed would decide to steal away from Washington.

But opposition to the president's expansionism wouldn't recede with Reed's retreat. Industrialist Andrew Carnegie, who had helped get McKinley out of his financial jam during his gubernatorial days, now helped underwrite the anti-expansionist activities of Carl Schurz and Mark Twain. He closed a letter to the president by identifying himself as "Your friend personally; but the bitterest enemy you have officially, as far as I know." Schurz attacked relentlessly in national magazines and at meetings and rallies around the country. The peace treaty with Spain, he declared, had "half a dozen bloody wars in its belly" and constituted "an open and brutal declaration of war against our allies, the Filipinos, who struggled for freedom and independence from foreign rule."

These men were not alone. In transforming America from a con-tained land power into a global empire, McKinley had stirred a ro-bust opposition movement that included former presidents Harrison and Cleveland, current prominent politicians William Jennings Bryan and George Hoar, reform-minded thinkers such as Edwin Godkin and Samuel Francis Adams, college presidents and academics, labor leaders, prominent clergymen, and famous writers Twain, William Dean How-ells, Edgar Lee Masters, and Ambrose Bierce. "It would be no mean task," writes historian Robert L. Beisner, "to think of another issue that has united such a collection of Democrats and Republicans, progres-sives and conservatives, party stalwarts and independents, businessmen and labor-union chiefs."

It wasn't simply humanitarian impulses that propelled these oppo-nents of empire. Racial attitudes played a part for some. Schurz, for example, feared a massive influx of "Spanish-Americans, with all the mixture of Indian and negro blood, and Malays and other unspeakable Asiatics, by the tens of millions!" But the main arguments were that America had no business subjugating other peoples, that the impera-tives of imperialism would undermine democracy at home, and that the price in blood and treasure was higher than America should impose upon its citizens. As Senator Hoar expressed it, "There has never been a republic yet in history that acquired dominion over another nation that did not rule it selfishly and oppressively." California's Democratic Senator Stephen White declared that "the carrying out of the expansion question will prove disastrous to the republic."

McKinley knew he must get ahead of these arguments with his own reassuring Philippine policy rationale. It wasn't that the anti-imperialists were sweeping the country with their polemics. Most Americans embraced the idea of American greatness, and in those times that usually meant expansion, colonies, global trade, and a big navy with coaling stations around the world. McKinley was delivering on that. But the anti-imperialists could erode his political standing, particularly if U.S. forces in the Philippines got bogged down in a costly struggle, with growing casualty reports and no discernible victory in sight. Then his political fortunes would fall abruptly, and he knew it.

He chose as his vehicle of communication a February 16 address before a dinner of Boston's Home Market Club. Ten days earlier, as he worked on the speech and read passages to young Charles Dawes, the president seemed to Dawes "much troubled." Later, accompanying Mrs. McKinley and others to the theater, Dawes heard from General Corbin that the president had been shaken by Filipino casualty reports after the battle around Manila. Sinking into McKinley's consciousness, wrote Dawes in his diary, was the "enormous responsibilities now resting upon him and his country." The president's Boston speech was designed to clarify his policy and capture the imperatives of colonial responsibility undertaken "in the name of human progress and civilization."

The president and his party left Washington for Boston at 5:25 p.m. on February 15 and made it to Jersey City by 11:40 that night. The presidential car then was placed upon a float and transported to New York's Harlem River station, where it was attached to a Boston-bound train. Among those in the presidential party were secretaries Alger, Long, and Bliss, Postmaster General Smith, Representative Grosvenor, Cortelyou, and two White House doorkeepers. The party reached Boston at 10:02 the next morning, and the president was greeted by cheering crowds at the station and along the streets to the Hotel Touraine, where a cavalry battery delivered a twenty-one-gun salute. The procession was marred a bit by jeers directed at Alger: "Yah, yah, yah, beef, beef, beef!" yelled some in the crowd. The president spent the afternoon "in quietude" until escorted to the Mechanics' Hall at 4:15 for the Home Market Club reception and dinner. Nearly 2,000 were served at the dinner, making it "the largest banquet ever arranged in this country," said the *Washington Post*. Another 3,800 spectators filled the hall balconies.

When the time came to deliver his remarks, the president stood upon a bunting-draped dais under a wall of more bunting, with huge pictures of George Washington, Abraham Lincoln, and William McKinley, each labeled "Liberator." That coincided neatly with the president's message.

He began with a brief rendition of the war and its aftermath, emphasizing the "universal and hearty commendation" that greeted the decisions and actions leading to victory. But wars generate their own logic, often unforeseen and uncontrollable, and America's late war entrusted to the country the lands of Cuba, Puerto Rico, and the Philippines. "It is a trust we have not sought," said the president. "It is a trust from which we will not flinch."

Acknowledging the opposition to the Philippine cession, the president outlined the options facing him and the country at the end of hostilities. He dismissed the idea of giving the islands back to Spain with the words, "No true American consents to that." Requiring Spain to transfer them to some other power or powers would have been "a weak evasion of duty." The idea that the archipelago could have been "tossed into the arena of contention or the strife of nations; or . . . [been] left to the anarchy and chaos of no protectorate at all," said the president, was "too shameful to be considered."

That left U.S. acquisition, undertaken in behalf of "the welfare and happiness and the rights of the inhabitants of the Philippine Islands. [Great and long-continued applause.]" True, the people there had not given their consent to this acquisition, but how could they in the heat of a war and the chaos of its aftermath? He continued:

> *Every present obligation has been met and fulfilled in the expulsion of Spanish sovereignty from their islands; and while the war that destroyed it was in progress we could not ask their views. Nor can we now*

*ask their consent. Indeed, can any one tell me in what form it could
be marshaled and ascertained until peace and order, so necessary to the
reign of reason, shall be secured and established? [Applause.] . . . It is
not a good time for the liberator to submit important questions concerning liberty and government to the liberated while they are engaged
in shooting down their rescuers. [Applause and cheering.]*

Here's where McKinley showed the iron resolve normally kept
shrouded behind his countenance of magnanimity. Having explained
how the stark forces of reality had imposed upon America the unsolicited duty of receivership, the president made clear there would be no
turning back, no wavering, and no hand-wringing. "Grave problems
come in the life of a nation," said McKinley, "however much men may
seek to avoid them. They come without our seeking,—why, we do not
know, and it is not always given us to know,—but the generation on
which they are forced cannot avoid the responsibility of honestly striving for their solution."

The solution was twofold: convey to the Filipinos through word
and deed that America's intentions were benevolent; and crush the
rebellion that was thwarting America's uplifting mission. Ultimately,
said the president, the task of determining the Philippine future would
fall to Congress, "the voice, the conscience, and the judgment of the
American people." But in the meantime the job resided with him as
commander-in-chief. He concluded:

*Until Congress shall direct otherwise, it will be the duty of the Execu-
tive to possess and hold the Philippines, giving to the people thereof
peace and order and beneficent government; affording them every opportunity to prosecute their lawful pursuits; encouraging them in thrift
and industry; making them feel and know that we are their friends,
not their enemies, that their good is our aim, that their welfare is our
welfare, but that neither their aspirations nor ours can be realized until
our authority is acknowledged and unquestioned. [Loud and enthusiastic applause.] . . .*

*I cannot bound my vision by the blood-stained trenches around
Manila,—where every red drop, whether from the veins of an Ameri-*

can soldier or a misguided Filipino, is anguish to my heart,—but by
the broad range of future years, when that group of islands, under the
impulse of the year just past, shall have become the gems and glories of
those tropical seas. [*Prolonged applause.*]

As he did so often, the president wrapped himself in his country's
flag. Patriotism dripped from his words. But he added a new element
to the American story: the idea that the nation was venturing into the
world not for conquest or exploitation but to lift up less civilized peoples and foster productive and healthy nations where none before had
existed. There was a certain patronizing tone in these passages, even
a condescension. Perhaps that was inevitable in a world dominated
by Western power, technology, mobility, and wealth, and when most
other regions untended by Western colonialism seemed backward and
helpless by comparison. And the president's particular brand of idealistic expansionism certainly lent itself to allegations of hypocrisy, given
the exploitation that inevitably accompanied most colonial enterprises,
as Senator Hoar had noted. Indeed the anti-imperialists savaged the
speech, none more vociferously than Godkin in *The Nation*. "There
was not a spark of initiative or leadership in it," said the magazine,
portraying McKinley as "one of those rare public speakers who are able
to take a good deal of humbug in such a way as to make their average
hearers think it excellent sense and exactly their idea."

Perhaps Godkin's underlying complaint was that public sentiment coincided largely with the president's vision and not the anti-
expansionist thinking of his magazine. It was clear, in any event, that
the Boston speech gave much of the country precisely what it wanted:
an agreeable rationale for America's bold new venture into the world.
The anti-imperialists would continue their agitations, but the country's
majority sentiment favored the expansionist surge—so long as it was
executed smoothly and at an acceptable cost.

IN THE PHILIPPINES, meanwhile, Aguinaldo saw his job as raising
the cost. After his initial defeats outside Manila in early February, he
began massing troops twelve miles north for a counterattack before
Otis received reinforcements scheduled to arrive soon under General

Henry Lawton. "If Regular troops enroute were here," reported Otis, "could probably end war, or all active opposition, in twenty days." But it soon became clear that Aguinaldo posed a more serious threat to Otis's forces than the general realized. "Situation in Manila critical," he wired Lawton. "Your early arrival necessary."

Even before Lawton's arrival, Otis managed to dislodge rebel troops when they became most threatening. On March 6, after an insurgent ambush on U.S. forces near the Manila reservoir, the Americans scattered the insurgents. The next day, the *Post* reported that a series of rapid U.S. advances, followed by flank movements, resulted in the enemy being "completely routed." The paper added, "The rebels bolted at the first sign of the advance, but they separated into small bodies whenever the [cover] afforded opportunities, and kept up a running fire."

This was significant, reflecting a pattern that soon defined the war. Aguinaldo's troops would mass here or there, inflict whatever damage they could, then scramble before Otis could attack. The Filipinos were no match for the Americans in firepower or arms accuracy, and America's superior weaponry inflicted heavy losses upon the enemy whenever Otis managed to engage. But often he couldn't engage because Aguinaldo's troops simply disappeared into the jungle. They displayed remarkable agility in darting from place to place, avoiding decisive set-piece battles, and preserving themselves for future small-scale attacks. Thus did Aguinaldo settle in for a long war.

Otis, focusing on minutiae as usual and lacking a big-picture vision, missed the significance of the Aguinaldo strategy. Early in the war, after a U.S. unit charged a Philippine sniper field and found it vacant, the general reported that the enemy had "skulked back to their homes disguised as civilians" and suggested such behavior betokened a lack of resolve that would render the insurgents ineffective fighters.

The general didn't know his enemy. As General Arthur MacArthur moved north on Luzon and the Filipinos evaporated before him, Otis thought things were going well. The casualty ratio overwhelmingly favored the Americans, and Aguinaldo's troops couldn't stop them or even inflict serious losses. In late March, when MacArthur reached Malolos, site of Aguinaldo's provisional government, he expected "desperate resistance" from the Philippine forces. But Aguinaldo just faded away with his government and command structure before MacArthur could enter the city. Otis, sensing victory, wired Washington, "Present indications denote insurgent government in perilous condition; its army defeated, discouraged and scattered. Insurgents returning to their homes in cities and villages between here and points north."

Once again Otis got it wrong. Clinging to a strategic concept fast losing its plausibility, he couldn't see that Aguinaldo's chief aim was to avoid debilitating set-piece battles and preserve his army for future assaults designed to enervate U.S. forces over time. Part of the problem was a misconception of Philippine society and the inhabitants' view of the U.S. arrival. The idea, shared by most Washington officials, including McKinley, was that Aguinaldo represented a small minority of Tagalog people and that most other Filipinos would embrace the U.S. presence as soon as they perceived McKinley's promised benevolence. Then they would assist in bringing down the insurgency. No doubt this described many Filipinos who wanted the U.S. civic project to proceed in earnest as soon as possible. But this view underestimated Aguinaldo's support and also missed the capacity of his forces to intimidate countryside inhabitants into providing insurgents with food, supplies, and safe shelter as they scampered here and there before the advancing Americans.

Meanwhile the president's Philippine Commission under Jacob Schurman had arrived in Manila and begun extensive fact-finding efforts. On April 4 it issued a proclamation designed to clarify to Filipinos the American policy. It promised "an enlightened system of government" providing "the largest measure of home rule and the amplest liberty consonant with the supreme ends of government and compatible with those obligations which the United States has assumed toward the civilized nations of the world." It also made clear, though, that the United States would enforce its Philippine sovereignty. Commission interviews with Philippine elites convinced the commissioners that "Filipinos in general incapable of self government," as Schurman put it in a memo to Hay. "Masses ignorant and the few capable are without experience, except Spanish misgovernment."

In late April MacArthur surrounded Aguinaldo's army at the leader's new makeshift capital, Calumpit, and delivered a debilitating blow. In four hours of fighting, his troops took the town, moved beyond it, crossed the important Rio Grande River in a brilliant maneuver, and routed a large Philippine force under General Antonio Luna. But Aguinaldo scrambled to a nearby railhead and escaped with a large force. Meanwhile Lawton pushed the enemy north and west and entrenched himself comfortably at Angat, east of Calumpit.

Fighting ceased with the onset of the rainy season in May, and both sides assessed their positions. For McKinley, a big question was how many troops were needed to finish the job once the dry season returned. By late April, 7,000 regulars were on their way to Luzon, with another 8,000 scheduled for departure shortly. With volunteers returning home as their enlistments expired, Otis would have some 30,000 troops, mostly regulars. "This is believed at the War Department to meet all of the needs of the summer season," reported the *Washington Post*.

But by May 7 MacArthur realized an insurgent force of 7,000 men had dug in at Bacolor, within artillery distance of his troops. This seemed to suggest that more troops would be needed when fighting resumed. Otis's army could sweep large swaths of territory with ease but lacked sufficient strength to hold captured lands. At a June 2 Cabinet meeting, it was determined that, while Otis's 30,000 men would suffice for the summer, a reassessment would be required in the fall.

Around the same time, Schurman bundled up his thoughts into a long telegram whose transmission cost, Hay wryly suggested to the president, could perhaps have been used to buy off Aguinaldo and get him back to Hong Kong. Schurman dismissed the idea of a quick Philippine victory. Insurgent leaders, he warned, planned guerrilla warfare, with both active and passive resistance designed to enervate the U.S. effort "and win by dividing American opinion, of which they keep well informed." Further, he argued that Aguinaldo's cadre had instilled in the uneducated rank and file a stark view of U.S. perfidy, reflected in the fate of America's native Indians at Anglo-Saxon hands. "Masses ignorant," he wrote, "amazingly credulous with childish grasp of actual facts, great cunning, unbounded suspicion, primitive passions uncontrollable when once aroused and unreasonable sense honor excellent material for able and unscrupulous leaders." America could not get to the leadership corps by influencing this peasant class, suggested Schurman; it would have to get to the peasant class by dealing with the leaders. The time was ripe because the commission's proclamation, combined with Otis's battlefield strength, had divided Aguinaldo's leadership, with some advocating acceptance of U.S. sovereignty if it included significant Filipino autonomy.

This split at the top, argued Schurman, offered an opportunity to pursue a negotiated end to the war. "Continuation of fighting," he wrote, "tends to make Filipinos consider us as conquerors rather than as liberator. . . . Believe magnanimity our safest, cheapest and best policy."

Indeed for nearly a month the Americans and Filipinos had been exploring prospects for a negotiated settlement. This gavotte of a negotiation began on April 28, when two of General Luna's officers, Colonel Manuel Arguelese and Lieutenant José Bernal, entered MacArthur's lines under a truce flag to propose a cessation of hostilities pending a peace agreement. They were promptly escorted to Manila, where they told Otis and Schurman during a three-hour conference that they came at the behest of General Luna and Aguinaldo. They asked for a two-week armistice so Aguinaldo's congress could convene and enter into negotiations with the Americans. The Filipinos wanted to avoid a humiliating battlefield surrender—and still held out for Philippine independence.

Impossible, replied the Americans. They could not negotiate with Aguinaldo's congress because America didn't recognize any such congress or any such government. The best they could do was guarantee amnesty for all insurgents. And there would be no discussion of Philippine independence. Besides, Luna's massing of 7,000 troops in front of MacArthur's army raised questions about whether the Filipinos actually desired peace or were merely "sparring for time" to rehabilitate their demoralized army. Otis refused to accept any formal armistice, though he ordered his generals to refrain from aggressive actions while the talks continued.

In the end the exchange came to naught. The insurgent negotiators conceded on May 22 that they had no authority to negotiate terms without clearing them with Aguinaldo, who already had issued a statement declaring he would never accept any U.S. autonomy plan. Otis meanwhile insisted upon an insurgent surrender without terms. He wanted to "whip the insurgents so thoroughly that they will be glad of the opportunity to surrender," as the *Post* put it. Any compromise, Otis believed, would embolden the Filipinos to prepare for another insurrection a few years hence.

Schurman disagreed. "I believe force was necessary," he told reporters, "because they thought us weaklings and cowards; but I believe also that conciliation should accompany force."

McKinley sided with Otis. Early in the gavotte, hoping for a breakthrough, he had instructed the Philippine Commission to avoid any unnecessary or humiliating conditions in order to ease the way toward a settlement. But Aguinaldo's continued insistence on independence exhausted the president's patience. Rejecting Schurman's call for conciliation after receiving his long telegram of early June, he wired the commission chief, "Those of the leaders who have willfully and for their own purposes placed us in a false position before their deluded followers cannot be relied upon to set us right."

Seeing himself outnumbered and marginalized, Schurman headed for home—leaving in place Denby and Worcester, who aligned with Otis in recommending "prosecution of war until insurgents submit," along with eventual establishment of a civil government as outlined in the president's communications.

Thus would the U.S. war effort continue—and expand. When War Secretary Root traveled to Plattsburgh, New York, to confer with McKinley during a presidential vacation there, he was accosted by an A.P. reporter asking if the Philippine war would be prosecuted with vigor. "Yes, sir," replied the secretary. ". . . All the men, all the arms, and all the supplies necessary to end the trouble in the islands will be furnished at the earliest possible moment."

How large a force?

"There will be fifty thousand men there ready for active service at the close of the rainy season . . . and more will be sent there if necessary." A 66 percent increase in military manpower, possibly more. Clearly it was dawning on official Washington that the Philippine challenge was proving far more arduous than initially thought.

BEYOND THE PHILIPPINES, a host of other issues required the president's leadership during this time. Foremost among them was urgent legislation to reorganize the military and authorize a standing army of up to 100,000 officers and men. McKinley's authorization for wartime troop levels would expire with Spain's treaty ratification. Then the army would fall from 65,000 men to 25,000, a number completely inadequate to handle the Philippines situation, not to mention Cuba and Puerto Rico. The president threatened an extra congressional session if he didn't get the authorization before Congress's early March adjournment.

But opposition was widespread and intense. Even members who favored the treaty found the idea of a 100,000-man standing army tough to swallow. It smacked of European-style militarism. "While the President . . . is hurrying the army and navy across the seas to inflict upon an alien people a government against their will," declared Indiana's Republican representative Henry Johnson, "I propose fearlessly . . . to make a plea for liberty and . . . against the perpetuation of the injustice." He compared McKinley unfavorably to Aguinaldo, whom he hailed as a statesman while the president was merely a weak reed in the winds of popular opinion, "to which he bows right or wrong."

That was too much for Charles Grosvenor, who rose on the House floor to denounce Johnson's speech as "the fiercest and most vindictive attack upon the Administration" he had heard in the House. Declaring Aguinaldo to be hardly a statesman, he accused the Philippine leader of ordering the execution of anyone who sought to print the president's proclamation on America's Philippine policy.

"Aguinaldo was our ally a few months ago," interjected Johnson.

"Why did he not remain our ally?" retorted Grosvenor, with more passion than logic. "Benedict Arnold was our ally also before he became a traitor."

The House passed the bill easily—168 to 126—on a party-line vote, but everyone knew the real test was the Senate, where opponents planned to kill it with continuous debate (called a "filibuster," after a widely used term for pirates) extending right up to adjournment. That forced a compromise in which the president got his 100,000-man army, including 65,000 regulars and 35,000 two-year recruits, as well as the organizational structure he wanted. But the authorization would expire on July 1, 1901. The revised bill passed the Senate on February 27 on a vote of 55 to 13 and quickly cleared the House with little debate. The president signed it on March 2. The permanent size and scope of America's standing army would be settled later, though few doubted that the country had entered a new era of ongoing military preparedness.

Another pressing issue was the proposed American canal across Nicaragua. In late December 1898 the president's Walker Commission issued a preliminary report based on a thorough on-site examination by some seventy engineers and scores of other workers. It pronounced such a Nicaraguan canal "entirely feasible" and added that the likely cost would be about $124 million.

America welcomed the news. "One thing is clearly indicated by the developments of the war" against Spain, a newspaper called the *Independent* had declared in May. "We must make haste and build and open the Nicaragua Canal." But a lingering problem was that nettlesome U.S.-British treaty calling for cooperation in the construction and maintenance of any isthmian canal and proscribing either nation from fortifying or exercising exclusive control over the waterway. McKinley, believing it was time to scuttle the Clayton-Bulwer Treaty, informed the British government through a private emissary that he favored a unilateral canal initiative and hoped to negotiate an abrogation of Clayton-Bulwer. Britain agreed to pursue it but wanted concessions on a lingering Canada-Alaska border dispute. As these private discussions proceeded, the president used his Annual Message of December 5, 1898, to declare an isthmian canal "indispensable" to U.S. interests and argue that America's new global standing "more imperatively than ever calls for [the canal's] control by this Government." He expressed confidence that Congress would "duly appreciate and wisely act upon" this imperative.

Congress needed no cajolery. A week after Walker's report was released, Iowa's William Hepburn, chairman of the House Interstate Commerce Committee, announced plans to expedite the matter in his committee and get "an early report to the [full] House" authorizing construction. Newspaper dispatches indicated only a single member opposed the idea. A week later the Senate also moved to limit debate and set an early vote on the issue.

On January 21 the Senate passed legislation, 48 to 6, authorizing construction of a canal large enough "for the use of the largest seagoing vessels," at a cost of no more than $115 million. It called for a negotiated abrogation of the Clayton-Bulwer Treaty. All eyes turned to the House, where Hepburn's committee cleared its own measure on February 3. Then a snag developed. Thomas Reed, who hadn't yet relinquished his speakership and who opposed the bill as another unnecessary thrust into expansionism, maneuvered to keep the measure off the House floor. To circumvent the speaker's parliamentary powers, the bill's sponsors developed a "flank movement" to get it to the floor as an amendment to a must-pass appropriations bill. But the speaker's trusty ally, Appropriations Committee chairman Joe Cannon, had that ploy ruled out of order.

An enraged Grosvenor, ever ready to fight administration battles, once again jumped into the fray, arguing that Chairman Cannon's parliamentary maneuver would kill the canal project for a generation. Then the canal's chief Senate advocate, John Morgan of Alabama, hatched a plan to have Hepburn's canal bill attached to that chamber's River and Harbor appropriation, a crucial measure, as a way of getting it onto the House floor following Senate passage. When it reached the House, though, even some pro-canal members balked at the procedural circumvention. Such momentous legislation, argued Theodore Burton of Ohio, chairman of the House River and Harbor Committee, should be "approached with due deliberation and not carried along as a rider, with perhaps only a few minutes' consideration."

In the meantime proponents of a competing canal route through Panama began to influence congressional thinking. Officials of the New Panama Canal Company, offspring of a previous French company that had failed spectacularly in a previous effort to build a canal, argued that nearly half of the excavation had been completed, the harbors at either end could accommodate the largest ships, and work was facilitated by a rail line running parallel to the canal route. Panama would be quicker, less troublesome, and cheaper, argued the new company's irrepressible lobbyist, William Nelson Cromwell.

By March 3, just before adjournment, House-Senate conferees de-cided to pull back on the Nicaraguan initiative and appropriate $1 mil-lion for the president to investigate the relative merits of the two canal routes. In response, McKinley expanded the Walker Commission and gave it the added mandate of studying the Panama route and determin-ing the most favorable waterway location. That would quiet the canal debate for the better part of a year while keeping the country moving toward eventual construction.

AT NOON ON January 1, 1899, in Havana, the Spanish flag atop the government palace was hauled down, and the U.S. flag went up. The heavy guns of nearby forts and warships fired off salutes as Americans and locals in nearby streets and plazas cheered. Spain's Cuban sover-eignty, stretching back 400 years, passed to the United States. As with the Philippines, McKinley made clear he wouldn't share sovereignty in Cuba or recognize any governmental status for the island's premier rebel leader, Máximo Gómez, and his army. Bent on avoiding the kind of hostilities he faced in the Philippines, the president installed as military governor Major General John R. Brooke and increased the U.S. troop strength on the island to 45,000 in March from 24,000 at war's end.

In a written instruction to Brooke, McKinley said America's man-date over the island was "the law of belligerent right over conquered territory," and the only lawful authority capable of administering law in Cuba was the president of the United States, "exercising . . . his constitutional function of Commander-in-Chief." This authority, he added, would continue until Congress intervened or until the Cuban people established a government sufficiently stable that the president could withdraw U.S. forces. "The people of Cuba, without regard to previous affiliations, should be invited and urged to cooperate in these objects by the exercise of moderation, conciliation, and prudent indus-try, and a quick and hearty acquiescence in the system of government which we shall maintain."

Brooke set out to repair Cuba's broken society by providing food, medical care, sanitation, and schools. In the first eleven months of 1899, he handed out 5.5 million daily rations. McKinley sent a personal envoy, Robert P. Porter, to confer with Gómez and secure his cooperation, helped along with the promise of $3 million to be distributed to Cuban rebels willing to lay down their arms and enter civilian society. On February 1, Gómez succumbed to Porter's entreaties and wired McKinley, "I am now aware of your wishes. . . . Following your advice, I willingly co-operate in the work of reconstructing Cuba." In the end, 40,000 Gómez troops received compensation.

Easing the way for this cooperation was the weighty Teller Amendment of the previous April, disclaiming any U.S. "intention to exercise sovereignty, jurisdiction, or control" over Cuba following its liberation. Not everyone in America embraced the stricture. Some prominent officials hoped Teller's disavowal would fade and that Cubans would seek U.S. annexation of the island. These included Senators Foraker and Chandler, as well as New York's Governor Theodore Roosevelt. Many of Cuba's ethnic Spaniards, about a third of the island's million inhabitants but holding two-thirds of its wealth, expressed the same hope. One prominent Havana newspaper editor suggested, according to the *New York Times*, that "between the independence of the Cubans and annexation . . . the resident Spanish would unanimously prefer annexation."

McKinley wouldn't hear of it. He viewed the Teller Amendment as an "honorable obligation" that must be "sacredly kept," as he would put it in his next Annual Message. But he also felt serious steps toward independence must wait until after April 1900, when Cubans would have to decide between Cuban and Spanish citizenship. Besides, Brooke wasn't exercising the level of civilian authority required of his position. He seemed passive and halting, reluctant to interject himself into nonmilitary matters. That situation would have to be corrected before serious actions could be taken to move Cuba toward independence. But by midyear it appeared a foundation had been laid for a smooth transition over the next two years.

On domestic policy, the president stumbled upon a hornets' nest when he sought in May to refashion Civil Service policy through executive action. Though he had won plaudits from reform-minded Republicans in June 1897 by protecting a large number of federal employees from arbitrary removal, he now felt a more balanced approach was needed to address Grover Cleveland's overly expansive policies. Specifically he wanted to exempt from Civil Service protections private secretaries and confidential clerks, among others, whose duties needed to be aligned with the particular needs and desires of their bosses. He promulgated the change on May 29, 1899.

This time the reformers went after him with a vengeance. Schurz, already livid at McKinley's foreign policy, said he "suffered immensely by that characteristic demonstration of mental and moral weakness." An official of the Civil Service Reform Association characterized the action as not only "mischievous" but also "a direct violation of the law." When Treasury Secretary Gage, defending the new policy, said it would affect no more than 4,000 federal employees, the reformers countered that the number was closer to 10,000. Succumbing to a rare bout of irritation and convinced that Cleveland's policies were unjustified and counterproductive, the president fought back. When Gage sent him the draft of an article to be published in the magazine *Forum*, the president affixed his own conclusion to the piece. "Indeed," the president wrote about himself for distribution under Gage's name, "the conduct of the public business by President McKinley and his counsellors and associates has been always characterized by freedom from partisanship and by devotion to the public interests." For further emphasis he added, "With deliberation and high purpose to benefit the Service, he has issued an order which men familiar with public administration approve, and which those who condemn will, with greater knowledge easily acquired, commend." Given his high standing with his countrymen, the president wasn't in a mood to retreat on any favored initiative.

24

Second-Term Question

"I HAVE HAD RESPONSIBILITIES
ENOUGH TO KILL ANY MAN"

However busy he might be, President McKinley never fore-closed any opportunity to educate himself on Ohio politics. And so he took delight one Sunday evening in September 1899 when a friend named James Boyle arrived at the White House. A former Ohio newspaperman and the Major's private secretary during his gubernatorial days, Boyle now was U.S. consul at Liverpool, a sinecure obtained in recompense for his longtime McKinley loyalty. He was returning to England following a home-leave visit to Ohio, and he had much to impart about the state's political condition.

The president invited Boyle into the Cabinet Room, where he was enjoying cigars and casual conversation with Charles Dawes and George Cortelyou. As Boyle digressed on Ohio's unfolding gubernatorial campaign and the attitude of various newspapers toward the president, Dawes occasionally interjected a thought or two. When Boyle's musings veered into national politics, he and Dawes dropped remarks that reflected an implicit assumption that McKinley soon would initiate a second-term campaign. As soon as the president picked up on the remarks, he straightened in his chair and spoke with quiet firmness:

If what you gentlemen are saying implies that I am a candidate for renomination next year, I want to say to you that I would be the happiest man in America if I could go out of office in 1901, of course with the feeling that I had reasonably met the expectations of the people. I have had enough of it, Heaven knows! I have had all the honor there is in the place, and have had responsibilities enough to kill any man. You [turning to Dawes] have heard me say this repeatedly, as have you [to Cortelyou]. There is only one condition upon which I would listen to such a suggestion, and that is, a perfectly clear and imperative call of duty. . . . I would be perfectly willing to have any good Republican, holding of course my views on the great questions that have come before the administration . . . to occupy this place; and I repeat that when the time comes the question of my acquiescence will be based absolutely upon whether the call of duty appears to me clear and well defined.

The younger men, sitting in rapt silence, didn't know what to make of the president's digression. They considered McKinley one of the greatest Americans of his generation and hoped to see him ascend to a hallowed place in the country's history. A successful two-term presidency likely would give him that. Boyle quickly assured McKinley that he had discovered during his travels in Ohio and elsewhere a high regard for him, even among Democrats. Citizens believed McKinley's war had transformed America into a nation that commanded world respect.

"Yes," said the president, "from the time of the Mexican War up to 1898 we had lived by ourselves in a spirit of isolation." Then he unfurled a narrative of the late war that gave full credit to himself for such crucial decisions as the refusal to recognize Cuban independence; the "exceedingly effective blockade"; the order for Dewey's destruction of Spain's Asian fleet; the decision to take the Philippines, "one of the best things we ever did," because taking just a coaling station or an island would have rendered America "the laughing stock of the world." He added, "And so it has come to pass that in a few short months we have become a world power; and I know, sitting here in this chair, with what added respect the nations of the world now deal with the United States, and it is vastly different from the conditions I found when I was inaugurated."

This was a rare immodest moment for McKinley—unabashedly crediting himself for America's transformation. But as Cortelyou and Dawes had sensed even before his second-term remarks, the president also was tired. The pressures and anxieties of 1898 had taken a toll on him—and an even greater toll on Ida, whose health recently had deteriorated. Thus it wasn't surprising that the president harbored genuine ambivalence about a second term. Some weeks before, William Osborne had written to say he had heard that McKinley's face had new lines of care and anxiety, and he hoped his cousin would give himself ample vacation time.

Osborne needn't have worried. The president's summer schedule had included five weeks of serenity at Plattsburgh, New York, situated along the western shore of Lake Champlain, surrounded by the Green Mountains of Vermont and the Adirondacks of New York. The Hotel Champlain and its expansive grounds offered walking trails and carriage routes cutting through lush forests and hugging the picturesque lakeside. Sailing excursions were readily available. So intent on escaping Washington's bustle was the president that he barred newsmen from his train and conducted only business that required immediate attention. "In view of Mrs. McKinley's ill-health," reported the *Washington Post*, "the President hopes to be able to spend his time while here in absolute rest and quiet." He devoted mornings to solitary walks through the woods and along the lake and sought to bolster Ida's strength with carriage rides on the hotel grounds. One early drive proved so taxing for the first lady that it had to be cut short. But the tranquility of the place buoyed Ida, and soon her stamina permitted two carriage rides in a single day.

From Plattsburgh the presidential entourage traveled to Long Branch, New Jersey, a "Mecca of the fashionables," as the *New York Times* described it, which never before had been "so thoroughly enlivened . . . and so awake with the roar of saluting artillery, the clatter of parading cavalry, and the music of bands." Later in Pittsburgh, helping celebrate the return of Pennsylvania volunteers from the Philippines, the president led a procession that drew 500,000 cheering citizens along a five-mile parade route. McKinley saluted the war dead by saying "There is no nobler death" and slyly interjected a polemical note into his patriotic expressions. "They did not stack arms," he said of the returning soldiers. ". . . They were not serving the insurgents in the Philippines or their sympathizers at home. They had no part or patience with the men, few in number, happily, who would have rejoiced to have seen them lay down their arms in the presence of an enemy whom they had just emancipated from Spanish rule and who should have been our firmest friends."

The speech predictably stirred reactions, pro and con. The *Brooklyn Citizen*, while noting the president's "boldness and ardor," denounced his effort to establish a Philippine government "without the consent of the governed." But Kohlsaat's *Chicago Times-Herald* praised the president's "note of leadership and defiance" and assaulted anti-imperialist agitators "who are filling the mails daily with pamphlets lauding Aguinaldo, calling our soldiers in the Philippines 'butchers' and 'murderers' and invoking the wrath of heaven on America's arms and cause."

Hardly had the president returned to Washington than he set out again on an extended tour of appearances and speeches in Chicago and other parts of the Midwest. In early November he delivered a major address at Richmond, then headed to Canton to cast his vote for governor. During August, while at Lake Champlain, he bought the McKinley home on Canton's North Market Avenue for $14,500. With its storied past—once owned by the McKinleys and more recently rented by them as a hometown retreat—it seemed ideal for retirement, whenever it might come.

THOUGH MCKINLEY ENJOYED his retreats from Washington, the imperatives of office pursued him relentlessly. In July Jacob Schurman reported to the president on his travels through the central and southern Philippine islands to assess native sentiment there. In the central Visayas, including Cebu, Panay, and Negros, he discovered that most Visayans wanted peace and seemed inclined to accept U.S. sovereignty—but studiously remained neutral pending the war's outcome. The only active insurgents in these islands, Schurman told Hay in a memo that quickly reached the president, were Tagalogs, who controlled much of the population through arms and intimidation. "Visayans are opposed to fighting," wrote Schurman. In the Mindanao islands farther south, where Muslim Moros dominated, Schurman sought to gain sway by assuring leaders there that the United States would "inviolably respect Moros customs and religion." He urged an effort "to reverse Spanish policy of distrust, non-intercourse and hostility."

Schurman concluded that the anti-American fervor came almost exclusively from the highly warlike Tagalogs, ready to kill not just Americans but other Filipinos to secure independence. Defeat the Tagalogs on Luzon and clean out their small but intimidating forces in the other islands, he said, and the rest of the archipelago would accept U.S. governance.

The question was whether Otis could do the job. The general was severely criticized in July when newspaper correspondents in Manila alleged that he had misled his superiors about the Philippine situation and used censorship to thwart reporters from filing honest stories. The correspondents accused Otis of presenting "an ultra-optimistic view that is not shared by the general officers in the field" and of ignoring the "dissention and demoralization resulting from the American campaign and the brigand character of their army." Contrary to Otis's cheery dispatches, asserted the reporters, the insurrection wouldn't likely be defeated "without a greatly increased force."

This jolted the American consciousness. McKinley's Cabinet quickly took up the issue but decided not to instruct Otis on such an internal matter, particularly since the general held two long sessions with reporters and promised "greater liberality" in letting dispatches leave Manila. But the damage was done. The *New York Times* warned, "The Administration will be seriously hampered politically by having to assume responsibility for a General whose reports will be derided as unbelievable." Numerous members of Congress urged the president to relieve the general, and the *Washington Post* reported, "The President's position against a change is less determined now than formerly."

Then newspaper accounts revealed that before his departure Secretary Alger had recommended that Otis's responsibility be limited to civil authority, with General Lawton taking the military command. The implication was that Otis's preoccupation with minutiae, particularly regarding civil matters, hampered the war effort. McKinley rejected the idea, but the *New York Times* captured Secretary Root's assessment when it reported that, while Otis would not be "shorn of any command," he was admonished to organize his priorities more effectively, break free of his "sedentary life," and recognize that "the prime object to be achieved is to crush the armed Filipinos, and afterward to attend to the minute things in civil administration that critics say might be left to subordinates."

The war debate turned nasty when McKinley supporters blamed anti-imperialists for energizing Aguinaldo's cause even in the face of repeated defeats. General Joseph Wheeler, now serving in Manila and sending the president back-channel assessments, said it was "fearful to think of American soldiers being killed by ignorant half savages who are encouraged to do so by expressions of American citizens." Thomas Platt, in a provocative statement, accused antiwar Americans of taking "immoderate satisfaction" at America's military difficulties and deceiving Aguinaldo's forces into thinking McKinley's political opponents would win the next election and grant Philippine independence. In this view, Aguinaldo's aim wasn't necessarily to win battles but merely to hold on long enough to undermine American war support.

But holding on wasn't easy given American firepower and battlefield tactics. In mid-August, MacArthur's troops dislodged an insurgent force of 2,500 troops on the outskirts of a town called Angeles, driving them north and leaving some 200 killed and wounded (compared to just two Americans killed). But the victory didn't encourage the president, who saw now that the war would require more aggressiveness and more troops. In mid-September he recalled Denby and Worcester from Manila since America's future in the islands hinged on military strength and not civilian activity. As Judge Day put it in a letter to McKinley from his Canton retirement, "There can be only one sentiment now among patriotic Americans as to our duty to put down the Aguinaldo rebellion with all the force necessary to complete the work effectually and as soon as practicable." It wasn't lost on Day, or the president, that the Philippine conflict remained McKinley's greatest impediment to a second term.

Another impediment had emerged when the anti-McKinley *Cleveland Plain Dealer* announced breathlessly, "Boom for Dewey in 1900; A Prophecy That the Admiral Is the Coming Man; A Presidential Boom

Already Launched for Him in Washington." The paper speculated that, upon his return from Asia, Admiral Dewey would be feted throughout America with military honors and parades and artillery salutes, and the frenzied enthusiasm would propel him right past McKinley and into the White House.

In the spring Dewey disavowed any interest in high office, telling a magazine reporter, "I am a sailor. A sailor has no politics." Asked if he had ever voted, he replied, "Yes, years ago."

But the frenzied enthusiasm predicted by the *Plain Dealer* did in fact sweep the country with the admiral's triumphant return, cruising up the Hudson River and into New York Harbor atop the bridge of his famous flagship, the *Olympia*. On September 29 Dewey's war vessel led the U.S. Atlantic fleet up the Hudson in a parade of giant battleships stretching, at one point, from 110th Street to 60th Street. The air was pierced by sirens and whistles, and one reporter speculated that "the ships expended more ammunition in salutes that day than had been fired at the Spanish in Manila Bay." Dewey was overwhelmed. "Even the accounts in the newspapers, the invitations from cities and corporations and civic and patriotic organizations," he wrote later, "did not fully prepare me for the splendor of the attentions awaiting me." A Fifth Avenue parade the next day boasted some 35,000 participants, and a later fireworks display somehow formed a likeness of the admiral with a pattern of colored rockets in the sky. Similar ceremonies, parades, and enthusiasm greeted the admiral a few days later in Washington, where the president organized an elaborate White House "stag" dinner for the admiral, along with the capital's top movers and shakers. Later, at an open-air ceremony that drew 50,000 citizens, Navy Secretary Long presented Dewey with a jeweled Tiffany sword from a grateful nation.

It was an open question whether this fervor would generate political energy, but some prominent Americans hoped it would. Publisher Henry Watterson of the *Louisville Courier-Journal* and the *New York World*'s influential Joseph Pulitzer both sought to generate a draft movement, and a rich financier and former navy secretary named William C. Whitney touted Dewey as a nonpolitician who could unite the country by transcending partisanship. "It is only at long intervals and special occasions," he told Pulitzer's *World*, "that Providence presents a man in whom the whole people have this unquestioning and perfect trust."

Others considered the idea ridiculous. Mark Hanna called the draft-Dewey boomlet "indecent" because the admiral "has frequently said that nothing . . . would induce him to run for President." The *Washington Post* predicted flatly, "The Dewey spasm in politics will not last." But the *Post* also suggested Dewey could rise if McKinley's political standing should somehow plummet through unforeseen developments—growing Philippine difficulties, for example, or untoward political events in Ohio. Should a Democrat win the gubernatorial battle in Ohio, said the paper, "the anti-McKinley Republicans, who are not numerous, would at once question the advisability of nominating a candidate who could not carry his own State."

The old wounds of the Ohio Republican Party remained raw, and it didn't take much of a bump to cause pain and induce bleeding. Even with all the power wielded now by the McKinley-Hanna faction, the Foraker group refused to yield. The battle was on once again, focused initially on the Cleveland mayoralty race and then, more intensely, on the state gubernatorial contest.

In Cleveland, attention focused on Mayor Robert McKisson, that stalwart of the Foraker-Bushnell-Kurtz faction, who wanted to be reelected. The year before, of course, McKisson had sought to destroy Hanna's senatorial career—with the help of Ohio Senate Democrats and after Hanna had won the state GOP endorsement. Thus McKinley-Hanna loyalists considered him a party traitor and set out to defeat his reelection bid. The lingering residues of that senatorial election obliterated party lines in the Cleveland race. Many Republicans voted for Democrat John Farley, while thousands of Democrats favored McKisson. Farley won—a small price to pay, in Hanna's view, for the luxury of kicking McKisson out of office. Better to have an opposition Democrat as mayor, thought Hanna, than a despised Republican enemy.

But Hanna and McKinley now feared a Republican enemy could grab the GOP gubernatorial nomination. With the state convention scheduled for early June, a number of Foraker-Bushnell-Kurtz men seemed bent on running, including Kurtz himself, as well as McKisson and Charles Daugherty, a journeyman politician with strong ties to Foraker and Bushnell. The nightmare scenario was a Kurtz nomination, given his vicious past attacks on Hanna and McKinley. "If Mr. Kurtz should be nominated," argued the *Washington Post*, "the anti-administration men will have Mr. Hanna on the hip," forcing him to support his most bitter intraparty adversary or risk a Democratic victory on the eve of the presidential campaign.

Kurtz bowed out, and McKisson's Cleveland defeat undercut his candidacy. That left Daugherty to challenge Hanna's favored candidate, state party chairman George Nash, a ruddy-faced former railroad lawyer who had served as Ohio's attorney general. Hanna couldn't leave anything to chance. After four years of Asa Bushnell in the governor's chair, he needed his own man there. Further, Hanna needed a GOP nominee behind whom he could galvanize his statewide organization and keep the office in Republican hands.

Known for both his deft maneuvering and his brute force in the political arena, Hanna opted now for deft maneuvering. He turned to George B. Cox, the boss of Cincinnati and longtime Foraker man. The stocky, blunt-spoken Cox ran his operation out of a dingy office over a saloon called Mecca—aptly named because anyone in town who wanted anything had to make a pilgrimage there. Cox seemed to be distancing himself a bit from Foraker, perhaps partly because the senator couldn't deliver on federal patronage as he once had. Hanna, with his White House ties, dominated that arena. Besides, Cox didn't much care for Daugherty.

Hanna told the Cincinnati boss in a letter that he would be glad to cooperate with Cox "for the best interest of the party." Though he wasn't pledged to any candidate, he added, "I am opposed to Mr. Daugherty from a party standpoint, and I understand that we agree in that position." Hanna concluded, "I admire your good sense and good management and have faith that we can work together."

When the votes were counted, Nash was the gubernatorial nominee and Cox's man John Caldwell captured the nomination for lieutenant governor. "Yes," wrote Hanna to McKinley, "the people can be trusted." It was a nicely crafted win-win outcome for both Hanna and Cox—and for McKinley. "There was an evident earnestness on the part of every one," Myron Herrick wrote to the president after the convention, "to show conclusively their loyalty to the Administration." He added that, when he encountered Bushnell for the first time since the unpleasant-ness surrounding Hanna's previous senatorial contest, the governor had extended his hand and "evinced a desire to let old matters drop." He had "substantially the same experience" with Foraker.

But when it came time to push the Nash candidacy, the intraparty wound once again began to ooze. Bushnell, the outgoing governor, refused to lift a finger in behalf of Nash, and Ohio's Western Reserve region, a Bushnell stronghold, seemed particularly apathetic about the GOP candidate. Worse, when Postmaster General Charles Emory Smith traveled to Bushnell's hometown of Springfield to talk with him about the problem, the governor suddenly discovered a pressing need to be in Columbus. It seemed that whenever Nash appeared anywhere in the state, Bushnell had a commitment elsewhere. And the hostility didn't flow merely one way. Hanna declined to invite Bushnell to the campaign's big kickoff demonstration and hardly could bring himself to utter the governor's name on the stump during his early campaign appearances.

This lingering party animus threatened to destroy Nash's candidacy, already under pressure from two serious general election opponents. One was Democrat John McLean, whose Washington-based family had made a fortune in railroads and utilities and also owned the *Cincinnati Enquirer*, a newspaper that, under McLean's leadership, became a journalistic powerhouse. The other was the nonpartisan Toledo busi-nessman and mayor, Samuel B. Jones, known as "Golden Rule" Jones for his ascetic brand of politics and extreme populism. Jones was the wild card in the deck. While he clearly would pull votes from Demo-crat McLean in several Ohio counties, he could damage Nash around Toledo and Cincinnati, where anti-Hanna sentiment was strong. A former state labor commissioner aligned with Jones predicted the gad-fly Toledo mayor would get 75 percent of his support from Republi-cans. If correct, this was ominous. It didn't help that Bushnell publicly praised Jones as "a man who practices what he preaches" while uttering nary a word in behalf of Nash.

Soon it was apparent that Nash wasn't drawing large crowds, while Jones was stirring interest in GOP areas. Newspaper accounts suggested Jones was starting to pull Republican votes also in the industrial areas around Cleveland, a threatening development. "Apathy Menaces Nash," was one *Washington Post* headline. The *New York Times* reported from Washington, "The impression is gaining ground here that if the Ohio election turns out in a way disadvantageous to the President there will be an effort to make admiral Dewey the Republican candidate for President." The paper added that reports from Vermont, where Senator Proctor seemed to be grooming Dewey for a presidential run, "are making many of the President's friends uncomfortable."

Hanna lunged into this political thicket in characteristic fashion. He got McKinley to make helpful brief remarks—nonpolitical, of course—from the rear platform of his train as he passed through Ohio during his Midwestern speaking tour. Administration officials flocked to Ohio to stump for the president's candidate. Hanna encouraged Nash to campaign on big national issues, particularly the Philippines, as a way of making the election a referendum on the president's policies, which remained popular throughout much of the country. He importuned business interests in Hamilton County and Cleveland to rally behind Nash lest the antibusiness Jones prevail. Even Hay jumped in, issuing a statement disputing reports of an emerging formal alliance between the United States and Great Britain—thus reassuring Ohio's many German American voters who were inclined to vote Republican unless the party seemed hostile to Germany.

As usual, Hanna pulled victory from the vapors of impending defeat. Nash outpolled McLean by nearly 50,000 votes, allowing the president to portray the outcome as an endorsement of his policies, rendered all the more credible by Republican victories also in Upper New York, Iowa, Pennsylvania, Kentucky, South Dakota, and elsewhere. Platt crowed, "[The voters] indorse the war policy. They repudiate the criticisms made by the so-called anti-imperialists. [The results] indicate that President McKinley will be the choice of the people for a second term." As far away as London, the *Daily News* predicted the president "will now have a free hand in the Philippines."

THE PRESIDENT MOVED aggressively to leverage this free hand into victory. He peppered Dewey with questions about the state of the archipelago and pored over back-channel letters streaming in from General Wheeler. When Dewey recommended augmenting the U.S. Philippine fleet with several warships, the president ordered them sent. He increased troop strength to 42,794 officers and men by November 5—with more ready to go if necessary. In an informal afterdinner cigar session with close associates at the White House, he emphasized his resolve to quell the rebellion and get to the job of democratizing the islands. One congressman later said the president was determined "to bend every resource to the stamping out of all opposition to our authority, the settlement of the war, and the establishment and maintenance of peace."

McKinley didn't wait for victory before moving on the civil front. In early November, America's military authority established on the island of Negros the first autonomous government of Filipinos. The island's U.S. military governor administered an oath of office to the judge of the island's top court, who in turn swore in the governor, three judges, twelve councilmen, the auditor, and the secretary of the interior, all Filipinos. Three days of feasting and an inaugural ball followed. "Negros leads in the van of civil government in the Philippines," said a U.S. colonel. "Your honor lies in adding a new star to freedom's flag." McKinley hoped this action of good faith would persuade other Filipinos to pursue America's model of autonomous government.

In mid-November, Otis unleashed a rapid movement of forces, including cavalry troops under General Samuel Young, toward Aguinaldo's suspected low-country refuge. After nearly surrounding the startled rebel leader, Otis wired to Corbin, "Indications are that insurgents will not escape to mountain capital, at Bayombong, without great difficulty and loss, if at all." But the elusive Aguinaldo managed to escape into the mountains, where his location became "a perfect enigma" to the Americans. For weeks the U.S. press peppered readers with rumors of his whereabouts, none ever confirmed. The dodgy insurgent issued a proclamation, though, declaring that his army would "not cease its efforts as long as there are any strangers in the land trying to enslave the Philippine people." He praised America's anti-imperialist opposition and invoked prayers "to God on high that the great Democratic party of the United States will win the next election, and that Imperialism will fail in its mad attempts to subjugate us."

Aguinaldo now seemed in a desperate state. "Claim to Government by Insurgents can be made no longer under any fiction," Otis wired to Corbin. U.S. forces had captured the rebel government's treasurer, interior secretary, and congressional president. Other officials had eluded the Americans by hiding away, "evidently in different central Luzon provinces," while the troops had scattered into the countryside, concealed their weapons, and blended in with society. Even Wheeler, whose letters to McKinley had deprecated Otis's military skill, agreed that "Aguinaldo's army is virtually disbanded."

And yet it couldn't be stamped out. In mid-December an American major reported he was just a few hours behind Aguinaldo, but the evasive rebel leader escaped once again. Natives said he had stolen away disguised as a Philippine peasant. On December 19, General Henry Lawton, perhaps the most skilled and savvy of the American flag officers, was killed during a skirmish as he led his troops toward a rebel stronghold. By year's end, it was clear that Aguinaldo retained an ability to assemble a mass of troops when he saw benefit in doing so. One U.S. colonel encountered a force of 1,000 insurgents near Montalban, and the *Washington Post* ended the year with the headline, "Tagalos Not Subdued; Reoccupying Districts Recently Swept by Troops." The president authorized another escalation in U.S. troop levels, soon to reach nearly 64,000.

MEANWHILE OTHER DEFINING issues and developments percolated in the country and in the president's political calculus. These included trade, a coaling station at Pago Pago in the South Pacific, the growing menace of trusts, and race. On trade, even Godkin's *Nation* smiled when McKinley said, "We have turned from academic theories to trade conditions, and are seeking our share of the world's markets." Free traders, said the magazine, generally had greeted McKinley's reciprocity initiatives with indifference—merely "as attempts to relieve the pinching of the shoe by cutting holes in it here and there." But perhaps free traders should embrace these efforts since they reflected a Republican drift "if not toward free trade . . . certainly toward freer trade." After all, McKinley's government had signed reciprocity agreements with France and six British colonies, and discussions continued with many other nations. With America pushing out into the world and

U.S. exports soaring, that old protectionist in the White House seemed bent on pushing the country—and his party—toward "freer trade."

In December 1899, McKinley acquired several islands in the Samoan chain, including Tutuila with its harbor of Pago Pago, ideal for a naval coaling station. For decades the islands had been caught in an entanglement of big power ambition and maneuvering by Britain, Germany, New Zealand, and ultimately the United States. The U.S. ability to leverage its new global position may have contributed to the U.S. acquisition—and to McKinley's comments to Boyle, Dawes, and Cortelyou that he had seen, sitting right in his Cabinet Room chair, the "added respect" now accorded the United States around the world.

Looming on the horizon in 1899 was the problem of ever larger industrial combinations, or "trusts," so powerful that they could raise prices arbitrarily and bludgeon smaller companies into doing business strictly on the trusts' terms. Even as the return of better times softened the populists' free-silver calls, the predatory practices of more and bigger monopolies generated growing calls for action. It was tricky because, following passage of the 1890 Sherman Antitrust Act, the Supreme Court had ruled that federal jurisdiction on the issue extended only to cases involving interstate commerce. McKinley's attorney general, John Griggs, interpreted that as justifying merely a "passive and minimal policy" in dealing with this troubling new economic phenomenon.

While the president preferred to delegate Justice Department management to Griggs, the attorney general's constitutional views seemed headed for a collision with the political imperatives of growing civic angers. That message came from Charles Dawes, who urged the president to get ahead of the politically dangerous trust issue. Visiting the White House on March 28, Dawes warned of the trusts' "unprecedented growth" and said the Republican Party must embrace a policy that recognized the "evil tendencies" of these corporate behemoths. The president readily accepted Dawes's admonition, assuring his friend that he would take up the matter in his next Annual Message and call for a "proper restriction" on monopolies.

But it wouldn't be easy getting ahead of such a dynamic issue. A month after Dawes's warning, twenty-one state governors appointed delegates to a national conference in Chicago to explore the problem. The title of the conference: "Trusts and Combinations, Their Uses and Abuses—Railway, Labor, Industrial, and Commercial." William Jennings Bryan, increasingly viewed as the Democrats' likely repeat standard-bearer in 1900, called for stern federal laws to regulate corporate America. He maintained that more trusts had been organized in just two years than in the country's entire previous history. "Monopoly in private hands is indefensible from any standpoint," he declared, "and intolerable."

Many Republicans believed their party should reject such radicalism. One was Ben Foraker, who said growing international commerce had spawned an imperative to seek economies of scale in order to hold down prices and compete in the global marketplace. "By consolidation of capital, plants, and management," said Foraker, "expenses of various kinds are eliminated, and it is made possible to continue the employment of our capital and . . . our labor." In this instance, Hanna agreed with his old adversary. "This formation of combines is simply an evolution in business methods," he declared.

Clearly McKinley couldn't embrace a position of defending trusts, given the gathering sentiment of the country, but neither did he wish to embrace Bryan's whole-hog attack. He would look for that comfortable middle ground in time for his Annual Message.

On the matter of race relations, the president's paternalistic attitude toward blacks seemed to be catching up with him. Always courteous to individual blacks and quick to offer praise for efforts by individuals and groups to improve the lot of African Americans, he considered North-South harmony a higher priority. Also, carefully calculating the country's willingness to address the maltreatment of blacks in the South and the effects of widespread attitudinal racism in the North, he didn't see much prospect for significant progress on this front. He accepted the racial status quo.

But some African Americans were becoming disgusted with his desultory words of protest at the mob lynchings that blighted the nation, particularly in the South and particularly against blacks. Further, as more and more Southern states moved to disenfranchise blacks, the president remained mum. At a December 1898 meeting of the Afro-

American Council, a New Jersey churchman named A. Walters said it was time for blacks to speak up:

> *Should we be silent when the President of the United States, who could not have been elected without our votes, is utterly silent in his last message to Congress concerning the outrages in [the South]?... Silent while the officials of the States of North and South Carolina admit they are powerless to protect us in our rights? Silent, while Mississippi, Louisiana, and South Carolina, by statutory enactment, have practically disfranchised their negro population...? Shall we not speak out when innocent men and women of our race are burned at the stake, hung to the limbs of trees, and shot down like dogs?*

As passionate and eloquent as were those words, and many more from many quarters of the nation, the country wasn't stirred to respond. In August, when the Afro-American Council met in Chicago and debated a resolution "denouncing" McKinley for not preventing Southern lynching, the *New York Times* dismissively asked how the president possibly could do such a thing. The proposition, stated the paper, was "intrinsically absurd."

The president did move forcefully to recruit more blacks into the armed forces and to institute programs designed to find and train black officers. He summarily rejected the view, put forth by some in the military, that black Americans wouldn't fight aggressively against colored Filipinos. "The colored regiments fight magnificently," he wrote to Root in a long memo outlining the robust recruitment program he wanted, "and I see that those in the Philippines have already shown the same splendid fighting qualities that were evidenced in Cuba." But generally he was comfortable accepting the state of racial politics that he had inherited.

ON OCTOBER 31, news reached the president that Vice President Hobart was seriously ill and deteriorating rapidly. He died at Paterson, New Jersey, on November 21. It was a huge blow to the president, not just because it left a big vacancy in his administration that he had no constitutional means to fill. Hobart had been a trusted counselor to the president, sought out for his views on nearly all major issues and problems. What's more, he had been a close and valued friend, always generous and hearty in his fellowship. Jennie Hobart had become one of Ida's closest confidantes and supporters. The president, his Cabinet, some sixty senators, and a large number of congressmen traveled to Paterson in special trains for the funeral.

"No president and vice-president have ever been so intimate as McKinley and Hobart," a journalist named W. E. Curtis wrote in the *Chicago Record*. He said the vice president was given to walking into the president's room unannounced and hailing, "Hello! What are you doing now?" And McKinley would instruct his military aide, "Tell Mr. Hobart to be ready to go driving at half-past 4." Now that camaraderie would be gone from the president's routine, and he faced the delicate political question of who should be his replacement—in the event, of course, that he decided to run again.

25

Second-Term Resolve

AN AGENDA DESIGNED TO GENERATE POLITICAL MOMENTUM

On December 5, 1899, President McKinley sent to Congress his third Annual Message, 23,000 words in length, reviewing the condition of the country as he saw it after nearly three years at the national helm. It was a government document, fulfilling the Constitution's mandate that presidents inform Congress on the state of the Union from time to time and recommend measures adjudged "necessary and expedient." But it also was a political document, crafted in recognition that the country faced a presidential campaign that would help determine McKinley's ultimate standing in history.

No doubt the president spoke sincerely that Sunday evening in September when he said he happily would renounce a second term and slip away to the tranquility of Canton if he felt the nation didn't need him. Even months later, on his fifty-seventh birthday on January 29, he would repeat that sentiment to Dawes. But this was a man who had nurtured an ambition since early manhood to intertwine his own destiny with that of his country, whose quiet reserve and equable temperament had masked an overpowering desire to leave his mark on history. Whatever he felt when beset by presidential frustrations or Ida's bouts of infirmity, his ambition burned as brightly as ever, however much he sought to shroud it with talk of "the call of duty."

After all, following Andrew Jackson's second-generation era of American politics, few presidents had managed to vie seriously for a second term. Since Jackson's reelection in 1832, nearly seventy years before, only three presidents had been elected twice: Lincoln, Grant, and Cleveland. Now McKinley also seemed poised to reach the fullest appropriate tenure established by Washington's two-term precedent. For years he had prided himself on his ability to balance political ambitions with his solicitous regard for his ailing wife, had pushed aside opportunities to get rich in the corporate world in favor of the more psychically rewarding political life, even with its difficulties and trade-offs. And to salvage his civic career and presidential hopes after a disastrous flight of financial bad judgment, he even had accepted the humiliation of letting his wealthy friends bail him out rather than pursuing private-sector opportunities that would have allowed him to bail himself out.

Now he stood at the pinnacle of American politics—not just president of the United States but a president enjoying widespread popularity. Despite his indirect methods and sometimes halting decision making, most Americans viewed him as an effective leader capable of swaying Congress and dealing adroitly with foreign nations. He had secured his hallmark tariff legislation within his first months in office and now presided over a robust economy—"a condition of unusual prosperity," as he put it in his Annual Message. In taking his country to war, he had transformed its world role and invested it with unprecedented global power and influence—all at a modest price in treasure and blood. Now his country enjoyed peace, not only abroad but also in its own streets, where just a few years before labor strife had erupted into confrontation and bloodshed.

And so it didn't figure that this president, despite his occasional private yearnings for a more quiet life, would forgo the crowning glory of a second term. In December 1899, he moved to position himself for that final political triumph with an Annual Message that catalogued the fundamentals of the country's "unusual prosperity" and established an agenda designed to generate political momentum through the coming campaign year.

The president took pains to tie the prevailing dynamic economy to recent growth trends in U.S. trade, thus demonstrating that his expansionist foreign policy directly enhanced American lives. Combined imports and exports for the year, he said, broke all previous records. Indeed exports for 1899 alone exceeded combined exports and imports twenty years earlier by more than a billion dollars. While per capita imports had declined by 20 percent in twenty years, per capita exports had increased by 58 percent, "showing," said the president, "the enlarged capacity of the United States to satisfy the wants of its own increasing population, as well as to contribute to those of the peoples of other nations."

The president acknowledged that the budget deficits he had inherited extended into the latest fiscal year, which yielded a shortfall of some $89 million. But that was about to change. With a surging economy, Treasury officials predicted a surplus in fiscal 1900 of $40 million, with even greater financial swells anticipated in subsequent years. (Within weeks Treasury Secretary Gage would revise the current-year estimate to $60 million, then quickly increase it further to $70 million.) This gave the president significant flexibility to attack problems and exploit opportunities at home and overseas.

Moreover America had emerged as the world's greatest industrial nation. In output of iron ore, coal, and coke, and in corollary iron and steel production, the United States caught up with global leader Britain in 1889, then pulled ahead in 1897, McKinley's first presidential year. "That lead can never be broken," declared an industrial expert named Charles H. Cramp. The United States stood "at the head of nations in the primary industry of modern civilization." Around the same time, steel magnate Andrew Carnegie predicted that the United States would take the global lead also in shipbuilding and other industrial manufacturing. "I see nothing to prevent this country of ours from being the chief source of supply of steel and the articles made from steel for the rest of the less-favored world," he said. It wasn't surprising that Mark Hanna, when asked to name the issues that would animate the campaign year, listed first and foremost "the prosperity of the working people of the country."

Still, the president wanted Congress to address a bit of unfinished business in economic policy. This was legislation to codify his declaration, issued in his bold speech at New York's Waldorf-Astoria Hotel nearly two years before, that the nation must place itself upon a firm gold footing in monetary policy. The president called for legislation giving Treasury the tools "to support the existing gold standard," to maintain parity between gold and silver, and establish "the equal power of every dollar at all times in the market and in the payment of debts." Though lingering free-silver sentiment posed political difficulties, congressional Republicans responded in the early months of the new year with the Gold Standard Act of 1900, which stripped away decades of ambiguity in monetary policy by defining the dollar in gold and pledging to redeem greenbacks and other federal notes in gold alone. The legislation also created a $150 million gold reserve for the redemption of notes. It cleared Congress on March 13 and was signed by the president—using a gold pen—the next day. Anyone who had predicted such a thing four years earlier, at the height of the great silver rebellion, said *The Nation*, "would have been considered a lunatic." It added, "It will be impossible in the lifetime of the present generation to revive the silver controversy."

But if the country's economic health seemed assured, it still faced ominous challenges in foreign affairs. The continuing Philippine entanglement had consumed nearly $50 million and more than 1,000 American lives between May 1 and November 1, 1898. The president displayed a defensive tone in his Annual Message as he unfurled his narrative of U.S. actions in the islands—how America had acquired sovereignty in an entirely appropriate and constitutional manner, reasonably refused to share sovereignty with insurgents, and assured Filipinos in word and deed that America would "do everything possible to advance their interests."

But, he continued, America's good intentions had been thwarted by "the sinister ambition of a few leaders of the Filipinos," and now the United States was embroiled in an "unwelcome but most righteous campaign." U.S. forces, he assured his countrymen, "have gained ground steadily in every direction, and now look forward confidently to a speedy completion of their task." Indeed in January General Otis reported significant U.S. victories in the southern reaches of Luzon—

at Taal, where some 800 insurgents were routed, and at Laguna de Bay, where U.S. forces scattered an enemy contingent described by the *Washington Post* as "probably the last considerable force of insurgents remaining in one command." Such victories, while not decisive in the field, helped blunt the anti-imperialist clamor at home and bought time—nobody knew how much—for the president's policy to succeed.

But with the election only eleven months away, McKinley needed to move the Philippines quickly toward a civilian government. In mid-January the Schurman Commission issued a voluminous report recommending a transitional approach that included a colonial governor, appointed by the president and responsible for administering the entire archipelago; an advisory council consisting of both Americans and natives; a legislative assembly, partly appointive and partly elective, whose acts would be subject in certain circumstances to a gubernatorial veto; appointive governors for the provinces; and the division of the islands into small subsections, with Americans or educated natives presiding. The concept was for a governing structure "sufficiently elastic" to allow the substitution of natives for Americans in increasingly significant positions as Filipinos acquired governing talents and skills. "No glittering promises are to be held out to the natives," explained the *Washington Post*, "but as they develop under American tuition it is proposed to gradually introduce them into positions of responsibility."

Embracing Schurman's concept, McKinley created a second Philippine Commission to serve as a budding government agency pending congressional action some months or years hence organizing a civilian government structure for the islands. Recognizing that Congress lacked the expertise to craft such a civil authority with any dispatch, lawmakers moved toward enacting legislation, sponsored by Wisconsin senator John Spooner, authorizing the president, in his capacity as commander-in-chief, to supplant military government with civilian rule. McKinley viewed his new commission as a transitional authority charged with crafting the elements of civilian governance and implementing them over time.

The president knew precisely who he wanted to lead his commission: U.S. Circuit Court Judge William Howard Taft of Cincinnati, forty-two, son of a prominent Ohio lawyer and former U.S. attorney general. Taft, who served as U.S. solicitor general under Harrison and possessed a legal mind of rare capacity, projected a corpulence that dwarfed even Tom Reed's, but with a largeness of spirit far more enveloping and cordial than the former speaker's. "One loves him at first sight," declared his friend Theodore Roosevelt. Journalist William Allen White described him as "America incarnate—sham-hating, hardworking, crackling with jokes upon himself, lacking in pomp but never in dignity . . . a great, boyish, wholesome, dauntless, shrewd, sincere, kindly gentleman."

In late January McKinley summoned Taft to Washington for "important business." Reaching the White House some days later, Taft entered the Cabinet Room to find the president with War Secretary Root and Navy Secretary Long. After pleasantries, the president explained the Philippine job and enjoined Taft to take it. The judge protested that he wasn't the right man. He had been "strongly opposed to taking the Philippines," he said, because he thought it had been "contrary to our traditions and at a time when we had quite enough to do at home."

McKinley acknowledged Taft's objection but said it was "beside the question." The Philippines belonged to America, he said, whether anyone liked it or not, and that required the United States to govern them wisely and compassionately until the people there could learn "the difficult art of governing themselves." That softened Taft's objection, and he conceded that the United States had assumed a "sacred duty to give them a good form of government." But he expressed a reluctance to give up his lifetime judicial perch.

"Well," said the president, "all I can say to you is that if you give up this judicial office at my request you shall not suffer. If I last and the opportunity comes, I shall appoint you." In case Taft didn't get the president's full meaning, Long hinted that he was talking about the Supreme Court.

"Yes," said McKinley. "If I am here, you'll be here."

Then Root weighed in. "You have had a very fortunate career," he said to Taft. "You are at the parting of the ways. Will you take the easier course, the way of least resistance . . . or will you take the more courageous course and, risking much, achieve much?"

When Taft asked for time to ponder the matter, the president assented. But hearing that Judge Day planned a trip to Cincinnati, McKinley asked him to meet with Taft and apply a bit of pressure. "I want you to appreciate, Judge," wrote McKinley to Day, "that this is a very important matter and I invoke your aid to get the consent of Judge Taft to go." The president also shared with Day some of his thinking. Given the commission's large powers and wide jurisdiction, he said, it can "accomplish great good and help me more than I can tell you in the solution of the important problem in the East." If he could recruit men "of the character of Judge Taft," it would "give repose and confidence to the country"—in other words, blunt the political influence of the anti-imperialists.

The four-man entreaty proved persuasive, and on February 6 McKinley announced Taft's new role. Taft told reporters, "The chances of failure are so many and so great that I have considered the possibility of success worth striving for." The *New York Times* wrote, "No nomination . . . made by the President has been received with more general approval here than that of Judge Taft."

Determined to ensure the commission's success, the president produced a twelve-page memorandum for Army Secretary Root, who would preside over both the Philippine military command and Taft's five-man civilian commission—to ensure, wrote McKinley, "the most perfect cooperation between the civil and military authorities." The memo explained in elaborate detail just how the president wanted his Philippine policies to be executed. Quoting from his own Annual Message, he said the military arm must remain supreme so long as the insurrection continued, but there was "no reason why steps should not be taken from time to time to inaugurate governments essentially popular in their form as fast as territory is held and controlled by our troops."

McKinley's instructions followed essentially the recommendations of the Schurman Commission—establishing civilian governments in smaller subdivisions first but working up to ever larger governmental entities as circumstances warranted. Whenever the commission concluded island conditions warranted a transfer of power from military to civilian control, said the president, it should report that judgment to Root, along with recommendations on the form of government to be established. In all instances, he instructed, municipal officers were to be selected by the native population, and "wherever officers of more extended jurisdiction are to be selected . . . natives of the islands are to be preferred, and if they can be found competent and willing to perform the duties, they are to receive the offices in preference to any others."

McKinley's letter of instruction reflected his judgment, going back to his earliest struggles over U.S. disposition of the islands, that America must embrace a stewardship role that protected the archipelago from both outside powers and internal chaos while also preparing Filipinos for as much self-government as they could undertake successfully. Though some believed this methodical approach betrayed an arrogance of power and a patronizing and invidious attitude toward Filipinos, McKinley believed his policy reflected fundamental realities of power and peoples. Of course, American naval imperatives and geopolitical interests never slipped from his consciousness, but he embraced the concept that the country could create stability and enhance the lives of Filipinos through a kind of democratic tutelage. As Judge Taft put it at a Cincinnati symposium before departing for Manila, "The high and patriotic purpose of the President . . . is to give the people of the Philippines the best civil government he can provide with the largest measure of self-government consistent with stability."

But anti-imperialists, rejecting this view of American benignity, set out to destroy McKinley's presidency at the November election. At a Philadelphia conference, delegates debated whether their antiwar resolution should invoke the president's name or merely speak more vaguely of the administration. A Philadelphia delegate named Frank Stephens bared the anger of many by declaring, "That murderer is the man who is chiefly to blame for the shame that rests upon this country, and his name should not be removed." The name remained.

Some anti-imperialist rhetoric in the Senate came close to Stephens's fevered pitch. South Dakota's Richard Pettigrew, a silver Republican and leading administration antagonist, unfurled what the *New York Times* called a "sensational speech" bitterly attacking McKinley. "The trouble with the imperialists," declared Pettigrew, "is that they have confounded the interest of the people . . . with the political desires and ambitions of their puny President, and regarded him and his success as more important than the rightful treatment of the Filipinos." Pettigrew and Massachusetts's Hoar put forth resolutions calling for the release of the administration's internal documents that they said would reveal McKinley's mendacity on his Philippine policies. They anticipated a White House refusal, which they could then attack as a demonstration of executive intransigence and disrespect for Congress. "The whole wretched business," declared Pettigrew, "was one of concealment and duplicity." But, reported the *Times*, the wily president "made known" through friendly legislators that he would accept any congressional resolutions calling for inside information and would "gratify nearly every desire on the part of such opponents as Senator Pettigrew" to demand internal documents. The president seemed confident that administration actions, even behind-the-scenes actions, would stand the test of politics.

But McKinley opponents then seized on Aguinaldo's oft-repeated declaration that U.S. officials, including Admiral Dewey, had promised Philippine independence in exchange for insurgent help in defeating the Spanish around Manila. Despite Dewey's characterization of this as "a tissue of falsehoods," it became an incendiary pivot point of the debate, with anti-imperialists blasting U.S. duplicity in dealing with Aguinaldo and McKinley supporters insisting that Aguinaldo was a liar seeking to manipulate U.S. public opinion. A fiery Republican from New Jersey, William Sewell, assaulted Pettigrew as a "traitor" and suggested his antiwar fulminations had contributed directly to the death of General Lawton. "I deprecate beyond measure," he said, "the action of the Senator from South Dakota."

Henry Cabot Lodge, whose eloquent voice in behalf of American expansion stirred national approval, sought to rise above the petty accusations and counteraccusations by placing into a global perspective the significance of America's push into the Pacific. "The possession of the Philippines made us an Eastern power," he said.

Manila, with its magnificent bay, is the prize and the pearl of the East. In our hands it will become one of the greatest distributing points, one of the richest emporiums of the world's commerce. Rich in itself, with all its fertile islands behind it, it will keep open to us the markets of China and enable American enterprise and intelligence to take a mas-

ter share in all the trade of the Orient. . . . I do not believe that this Nation was raised up for nothing. I do not believe that it is the creation of blind chance. I have faith that it has a great mission in the world—a mission of good, a mission of freedom. . . . I wish to see it master of the Pacific. . . . I know well that in the past we have committed grievous mistakes, and paid for them; done wrong, and made heavy compensation for it, stumbled and fallen and suffered. But we have always risen, bruised and grimed sometimes, yet still we have risen stronger and more erect than ever, and the march has always been forward and onward.

Thus did the debate continue into the spring, propelled in part by developments in the Philippines, where military officials received increasing reports of looming new hostilities from Aguinaldo's troops. On March 4, the *New York Times* reported that the insurgents had abandoned main force opposition in favor of greater and more sustained hit-and-run tactics. The headline: "Insurrection Not Dead; Filipinos Plan Guerrilla Warfare on a Larger Scale." Two weeks later the paper reported that Aguinaldo wanted to heighten congressional frustrations and induce lawmakers to force upon the administration an end to the war.

Responding to the more intense guerrilla tactics, Otis's killing machine exacted heavy losses upon Aguinaldo's ill-armed Filipinos. Newspaper dispatches told of actions in late April that killed 378 insurgents in a single week, 333 the next week, and 300 at another location. On May 4, Otis reported that enemy losses in killed, wounded, and captured numbered 1,721 in April. Typically he reported that locals believed "the war has terminated." Also typically his optimism was premature.

THE PHILIPPINE ENTANGLEMENT wasn't the only war-related challenge to rise up in early 1900. Pursuing his desire to help the people of Puerto Rico through the transition to U.S. sovereignty, McKinley stumbled into a treacherous patch of political brambles—and didn't escape unwounded.

With the transfer of Puerto Rico to the United States, the little island lost its longtime Spanish and Cuban markets for cattle, tobacco, coffee, and sugar. The result was a financial crisis as crops and products piled up on docks and in warehouses. McKinley sought to address this island predicament with a liberal trade policy. "Our plain duty," he said in his Annual Message, "is to abolish all customs tariffs between the United States and Puerto Rico and give her products free access to our markets." To McKinley, this policy represented nothing less than colonial obligation—mixed with a desire to avoid civic unrest on the island.

But U.S. tobacco and sugar growers fought the policy. It would devastate home producers, they said, and violate the Republicans' sacred protectionist doctrine, written into the GOP platform and reflected in the long career of President McKinley himself. Beyond these political pressures lurked a more troubling question: the status of Puerto Rico (and other U.S. possessions) within the context of the U.S. Constitution. Were these possessions U.S. territories and thus subject to constitutional protection? Or were they mere colonies, to be administered outside the framework of the Constitution? And if the former, did that put the inhabitants of these possessions on an equal footing with U.S. citizens? The fundamental question was this: Does the Constitution follow the flag?

By proposing free trade with Puerto Rico, McKinley appeared to be saying that the Constitution did indeed follow the U.S. flag, since the Constitution required uniform tax policies throughout U.S. territory. No such territory could be subject to tariffs that didn't apply to everyone else. Congressional Democrats seized upon this to argue that a tariff was unconstitutional because the acquisition of Puerto Rico had extended the Constitution *ipso facto* to the island.

McKinley had placed himself in a box. Wanting to bolster quickly the Puerto Rican economy, he hadn't considered the implications of his free-trade advocacy. If the Constitution followed the flag, he would be restricted in how he could administer those possessions—to the point, he now understood, that his ability to succeed could be seriously impaired. As Dawes wrote in his diary following a conversation with the president, "The constitutional question . . . became paramount—for upon the proposition that Congress had the right to govern the Islands by legislation with a 'free hand,' depends the success of our colonial policy—especially in the Philippines."

The president's blunder stirred Connecticut's Republican senator Orville H. Platt (no relation to the New York Platt) to argue, "We must not admit that any of our new possessions are a part of the United States in the sense that the Constitution extends itself over them, or that we must have free trade with them." Platt also feared domestic sugar and tobacco growers would savage the president's free-trade legislation. "I already hear the mutterings of the coming storm," he said.

In late January, House Ways and Means Committee chairman Sereno Payne crafted compromise legislation to levy tariffs amounting to only 25 percent of the duties imposed by the 1897 Dingley law. When the Senate Committee on Puerto Rico quickly embraced that concept, the *New York Times* editorialized, "This is not exactly free trade, but it is a near approach to it."

All eyes now fixed upon the president. Would he stand firm behind free trade for Puerto Rico? Or would he bend and weave under pressure from lobbyists and Republican legislators? After much pondering, he decided he must oppose any suggestion that the Constitution followed the flag. The stakes were too high. Therefore he would bend and weave—and take the political heat from those who would attack him as weak and vacillating. "I could ride a white horse in this situation and pass the original bill," he told a reporter privately, referring to his initial free-trade advocacy, "[but] the vital thing is to keep as many votes as possible in Congress back of the whole programme of the Administration."

But the president couldn't bring himself to state his new position boldly. When prominent House members visited him at the White House, he said he still adhered to his original free-trade view but would acquiesce should Congress enact a small tariff. "The President added," said the *Washington Post*, "that he should not be at all sorry if the [Payne] substitute was defeated." The president's pride got in the way of his political judgment. A rebellion by dissident Republicans—motivated by the free-trade principle in this instance as well as the idea that the Constitution should follow the flag—threatened to kill prospects for any legislation at all. On the very day that McKinley issued his ambiguous position, Illinois Representative William Lorimer told reporters he knew of at least seven Republicans who would join the solid Democratic opposition and vote against the Payne compromise.

The president compounded the problem in an interview with free-lance journalist Henry Loomis Nelson, who described his conversation in the *New York World*. Nelson reported that McKinley didn't believe the Constitution applied to the new possessions and that "free trade with Porto Rico is right because our protected interest will not be injured thereby." The president added that Congress possessed "plenary power" over the new islands and could impose whatever tariffs it wanted upon any of them, or none, and he would accept the outcome. As a House floor vote neared, it became clear that Republican opponents, aligned with free-trade Democrats, could defeat the bill by corralling just eight GOP votes, but between twelve and fifteen Republicans seemed ready to defy the party leadership on the issue. Many blamed McKinley for the mess. "Mr. McKinley," said *The Nation*, "is as meek as he is good. . . . His own attitude on this question confirms the worst that has been said about his moral cowardice."

Seeing a looming floor disaster, McKinley sent for three loyal congressmen—Payne, Grosvenor, and John Dalzell of Pennsylvania—and authorized them to let the word out quietly that he now favored the compromise measure. Grosvenor, often viewed as the president's House mouthpiece, speculated on the House floor that "nothing would give the President greater sorrow and regret than the defeat of this bill." But several GOP free-traders refused to yield. The president summoned four of them for quiet face-to-face entreaties—and persuaded all four to vote for the measure. He also fashioned two compromise concepts designed to unify the party: reducing the tariff to 15 percent of Dingley rates and giving the legislation an expiration date in two years. Also, all revenues from the tariff would be sent to Puerto Rico to benefit its inhabitants.

That pulled enough Republicans along to win passage for the measure in a close vote of 172 to 161. But Republicans left nothing to chance. As the *New York Times* reported, "Six men were brought from beds of sickness, two of them from hospitals." The afternoon of the vote, during a carriage ride with Ida, McKinley predicted the bill would pass with either six or eleven votes to spare. It was the latter. Though few in Washington knew it, the president had saved the bill with his last-minute maneuverings.

Then it was on to the Senate, where a similar drama played out. On March 2 the island's financial difficulties prompted McKinley to call for an immediate congressional appropriation of $2 million for the island—amounting to the duties already collected from there. The House passed the measure within two hours of getting the request. The Senate approved a similar measure some days later but loaded it up with Democratic amendments designed for election-year showboating. It took McKinley's intervention to get the conference committee to restore the bill essentially to its original form.

But the tariff measure, now commingled with legislation by Foraker to establish a civilian government in Puerto Rico, occupied the Senate for five weeks. Again free-trade Republicans balked at supporting a measure that imposed a tariff on Puerto Ricans and excluded the island's people from constitutional protection. Even Kohlsaat's *Chicago Times-Herald* blasted the president's retreat and called his performance "the first almost irreparable mistake of his Administration. "

The Senate challenge required some further presidential maneuvering, including the issuance of an "authoritative statement" from an unnamed Cabinet member outlining in detail the evolution of the president's thinking throughout the controversy and staking out his convictions on both the tariff and constitutional matters. After much pulling and hauling and some minor amendments, the Senate passed the bill on April 3 by a vote of 40 to 31. On April 11, the House concurred in the Senate's amendments, and McKinley signed the measure the next evening at seven o'clock.

The president took some hits on his handling of the nettlesome issue. The *New York Times*, normally pro-McKinley, stated, "We do not recall . . . an instance in which the President of the United States has pursued so openly a course so contradictory, involving such flagrant departure from the usually accepted standard of political good faith, with such stolid indifference to the opinion of his countrymen and such stubborn silence when candid speech was demanded." The president himself was reported to have lamented to a friend, "I made a mistake in my message." The mistake, a costly one, was in clinging to his leadership of indirection when a bold approach was needed, either in behalf of his original position or of the subsequent revision. But the ultimate outcome served Puerto Rico well, and the president's timely actions saved the legislation from a likely death.

ON FEBRUARY 4, the president got word that Secretary Hay had negotiated with British ambassador Sir Julian Pauncefote important amendments to the old Clayton-Bulwer Treaty. The revisions would terminate the requirement that the United States and Britain must cooperate in the construction and maintenance of any isthmian canal and that neither nation could fortify or exclusively control the waterway. In London, Lord Salisbury had softened his earlier effort to tie abrogation to American flexibility on a festering Alaska-Canada border dispute. Pauncefote had convinced London that the U.S. government under McKinley would never accept that linkage but might give Britain special canal access. Besides, said Pauncefote, the U.S. Congress was demonstrating a frisky resolve to proceed with a canal project even in defiance of Clayton-Bulwer. Better, he counseled, to get ahead of that wave.

McKinley thrilled at the news. He knew a canal across Central America would essentially double the U.S. Navy's global strength by assuring quick interoceanic passage of U.S. warships and would also boost U.S. trade. Musing on the development with Cortelyou, the president praised Hay's talents, modesty, and "handsome" behavior—and added with a laugh that since the time of John Sherman's tenure, when he had acted as his own secretary of state, "things have gone on beautifully." Noting a recent derisive observation that Hay had been "educated in the English school," the president suggested a good retort would be, "Yes, he was trained under Abraham Lincoln." But Hay possessed a trait that could prove problematic in Washington's give and take: he treated with disdain members of Congress, whom he considered mere grubby politicians engaged in activity far less lofty than that of diplomats. This would serve him ill after Hay and Pauncefote signed the revised treaty on February 5 at eleven, and McKinley sent the document to the Senate before noon.

Americans reacted with civic glee. The treaty, opined the *New York Press*, "adds another and crowning triumph to the series of diplomatic achievements with which Secretary Hay has dignified and rendered notable the annals of President McKinley's administration." Hay deserved "the congratulations of his friends and the thanks of his countrymen" for correcting a U.S. diplomatic "blunder" of fifty years before.

Hay's triumph came not a moment too soon, as canal enthusiasts in Congress intended to push Nicaraguan canal legislation without regard to the Clayton-Bulwer constrictions or to the competing Panamanian concept then under study by McKinley's Walker Commission. In mid-January, the House Inter-State and Foreign Commerce Committee reported a bill nearly identical to the previous Congress's Hepburn bill, and within days the corresponding Senate committee embraced the same concept. Both houses were poised to roll over Clayton-Bulwer and deliver a diplomatic insult to Britain, thus greatly embarrassing McKinley and Hay. Prompt action on the new Hay-Pauncefote Treaty could deflect that rebellion.

Then came a hitch. Senators discovered a provision in the treaty making the waterway "open, free and neutral" to all nations at all times. This meant the United States couldn't fortify the canal or keep out hostile ships even in wartime. The *Boston Daily Globe* speculated that this would "stir up a war of opinions that will prevent its final ratification by the Senate." Hearst's intemperate *New York Journal* went wild with indignation. "Has McKinley suddenly gone crazy?" asked the paper, then answered, "No, he has simply allowed a fool to make a fool of him." The *Journal* identified the first fool as Hay, "fresh from England and English flattery," more attuned to the rarefied salons of London than "this common country." The paper concluded, "It is his peanut head that accepted the treaty which poor McKinley has been gulled into laying before the American public."

Despite such fulminations, McKinley didn't immediately recognize the depth of the disaffection. Reported the *New York Times*, "There is the best authority for saying that the President believes that when the treaty comes to be considered most of the opposition to it will be removed." He was heartened when Alabama's John Morgan, the Senate's leading canal expert, expressed satisfaction with Hay's handiwork. Hay attributed the firestorm to the self-important politicians he had never liked anyway. It was, he said, an "exhibition of craven cowardice, ignorance and prejudice" by "the howling fools in the Senate." Of course those howling fools had felt the secretary's imperious scorn for months, which no doubt partially explained their own arrogant reaction to Hay's diplomatic product.

Hay derided an amendment by Senator Cushman Davis pronouncing that no treaty language could hinder U.S. actions taken for national defense or public order. Cushman, sneered Hay, was "too indolent to make a strong fight." But Cushman's action very likely saved the treaty from a Senate death. The Foreign Relations Committee reported the new treaty to the Senate floor, with the Davis amendment, on March 9.

On March 12 a disheartened Hay submitted his resignation. Lingering after the morning Cabinet meeting, he handed McKinley an envelope. "Mr. President," he said, "here are some communications which I hope you will read at your leisure." The committee action, wrote Hay in an explanatory note, "indicates views so widely divergent from mine in matters affecting . . . the national welfare and honor, that I fear my power to serve you . . . is at an end." He feared also that the newspaper attacks on him had generated so much political animosity that it could harm the president should he remain as secretary.

After clearing his desk that evening, the president pulled out a sheet of paper and wrote a reply. "Nothing could be more unfortunate than to have you retire from the Cabinet," he wrote, adding that Hay's work had had his "warm approval," and he would "cheerfully bear whatever criticism or condemnation may come." Then he offered the older man a bit of avuncular counsel: "We must bear the atmosphere of the hour. It will pass away. We must continue working on the lines of duty and honor. Conscious of high purpose and honorable effort, we cannot yield our posts however the storm may rage." The president returned Hay's resignation letter, and the secretary continued his duties. Hay wrote back, "I cannot [adequately] express my feeling of gratitude and devotion." He called the president's letter "touching and beautiful."

But the two men still faced the intertwined challenges of the treaty and the Hepburn legislation. Senators demanded at least two amendments beyond the Davis language that McKinley couldn't abide, particularly one that excised a provision inviting the participation of other powers. He called to the White House senators Lodge, Foraker, and Aldrich to meet with him and Hay and establish some common ground.

The senators said the treaty would go down without the two additional amendments; with them it would pass, and the Hepburn frenzy could be stopped. The president countered that the treaty was excellent as negotiated and should be ratified without amendment.

But he could see that that wasn't possible. In order to get Lodge to halt the Hepburn juggernaut he would have to give the Senate what it wanted on Hay-Pauncefote. When in May the House passed the Hepburn bill with an overwhelming vote of 224 to 36 and sent it to an expectant Senate, Lodge dutifully led an effort to block its progress pending disposition of the Hay-Pauncefote matter and release of the Walker Commission report. That kicked the Hepburn bill over to the next session. The *New York Times* hailed the Senate's Hepburn blockage as "a triumph for the Administration and for decency and dignity." In the meantime Hay and Pauncefote had crafted a seven-month ratification extension for the treaty, giving both nations more time to craft a compromise.

Once again the president managed to maneuver through political thickets that threatened to upend an important agenda. He didn't get things moving in his desired direction with any speed or smoothness. But Hepburn was on hold, and the treaty was still alive.

AT FIVE O'CLOCK on the afternoon of June 7, the first session of the Fifty-sixth Congress adjourned, leaving a number of important matters for subsequent sessions and subsequent Congresses: the Hay-Pauncefote treaty; the canal initiative; government structures for Cuba, Puerto Rico, Guam, and the Philippines; the issue of corporate trusts, which the president had raised to a priority in his third Annual Message; calls for a reduction in war taxes that now seemed unnecessary because the war was over and tariff revenue was soaring; and a shipping subsidy measure that was the heartthrob of Senator Hanna. Not surprisingly, Godkin's *Nation* looked at this incomplete agenda and excoriated the Republican president and Congress for their lassitude, though the magazine did acknowledge the significance of the Gold Standard Act. "On the whole," declared the magazine, "this is not a review for a great party, secure in its possession of all branches of the Government, to be proud of."

There was some truth in that. But the late war had placed before the president big burdens of governance, foreign relations, and a subsequent conflict—all of which pinned him down with matters that didn't necessarily involve Congress. Employing his studied incrementalism, he had pushed forward on many fronts with the resolve to bring them to fruition when propitious times arrived in each instance. Certainly Congress couldn't take over governance in the Philippines, for example, until the insurgency could be broken, and neither were the other new possessions ripe for congressional jurisdiction. The path ahead for the canal effort was filled with hazards and hurdles, but events seemed to be moving in the right direction. Further, though the Puerto Rican legislation had emerged only through an ugly process, it did eventually get done.

All in all, while it wasn't a particularly impressive legislative record, the president seemed well positioned for the November election, when Americans would pronounce their judgment based on such large factors as economic performance, the nation's global stature, the Philippine challenge, and their own well-being. These were the things that mattered to McKinley, which may be why he paid little heed to the reproofs of the Hearsts and the Godkins.

26

China

FIRST STIRRINGS OF NONCOLONIAL IMPERIALISM

In March 1900, Secretary of State Hay publicly released the correspondence he had solicited from major European nations and Japan regarding an "open door" to China: equal treatment for countries pursuing trade and economic development in the Middle Kingdom. Hay wanted to halt the frenzy of the industrial powers carving up China into competing spheres of dominance. The frenzy threatened not only to destroy China's ruling Qing dynasty, already struggling with rampant societal chaos, but also to heighten tensions among Western nations seeking strategic harbors, coaling stations, and economic exploitation in that Asian land. Under Hay's plan, all nations would be given an equal hand in pursuing Chinese markets and other economic opportunities.

Although some of the responses were vague, Hay hailed them as an embrace of his "open door" concept. Most observers agreed. "Secretary Hay's dexterous skill in completing his task," asserted the *London Globe*, "has left nothing to be desired." Many understood that President McKinley also contributed by thrusting America into the world as a power to be reckoned with. As Agriculture Secretary James Wilson told the *New York Times*, "A year ago no nation would have listened to a proposition of this kind, but the whole world listens to the United States now." He added with a kind of wink that, if colonialism constituted the "White Man's Burden," as poet Rudyard Kipling had suggested, Hay had eased that burden considerably through expanded trade and wealth—manifest in the rise of U.S. exports to Asia from $26 million to $73 million in ten years.

On March 31, just days after Hay's open door triumph, news dispatches from London reported that a Foreign Office official named William St. John Brodrick had informed Parliament that menacing disturbances had erupted in China against Western missionaries and Chinese Christians. The official said two British warships had been sent to Dagu, the coastal location nearest Beijing, to protect British lives and property. The United States also had sent a warship to Dagu, a response in part to an earlier attack by "secret society" mobs on an American medical mission near Chongjing. The mob "maltreated" native medical assistants, reported the *Times*, and murdered one of them.

These intertwined developments—Hay's open door breakthrough and anti-Western protests in the Chinese countryside—reflected two sides of a geopolitical reality. One was China's descent into a state of pathetic national weakness, inviting aggressive Western exploitation; the other was a seething anger among many Chinese at their accelerating national humiliation. This combustible mix was about to explode into a convulsion of mob violence throughout northern China that threatened mass slaughter of Western diplomats, missionaries, and other expatriates, including thousands of Americans.

The story of the Chinese-Western conflict goes back to the dawn of the eighteenth century and the outset of a demographic explosion in China that overpowered the Qing dynasty's ability to govern. The Chinese population, just 150 million in 1700, soared to 430 million just a century and a half later. The Qing government neglected the infrastructure—dams, canals, dikes, roads—needed to keep agricultural production apace with this demographic surge. The result was poverty, hunger, banditry, societal breakdown, and the emergence of "secret societies" aimed at seizing control of territory and restoring stability. This culminated in what was called the "White Lotus Rebellion," actually a widespread series of uprisings, which the dynasty put down only after eight years of hard fighting and national devastation.

But in the meantime it invited outside aggression. The full extent of the country's weakness was seen in the Opium War of 1839–42, when China sought to curtail Britain's lucrative Chinese opium trade. With superior firepower and warfare tactics, Britain scored successive battle-field victories, leading to the 1842 Treaty of Nanjing, which opened up five Chinese cities to British trade, including Shanghai, and imposed a robust indemnity upon the ruling dynasty. Hong Kong became a British crown colony.

Inevitably the Qing's weakness spawned further internal revolts, including the Taiping Rebellion of 1850–64, whose messianic leader, Hong Xiuquan, promised a utopian future that included "both the end of the world and its perfection, possibly at the same time," as historian David J. Silbey wryly noted. The Taipings captured Nanjing and ruled it for years before a Qing army brought them down. The struggle killed millions and further despoiled Chinese society.

During this time China's rulers also fought Britain and France in the four-year Second Opium War, as it was called (though it had little to do with opium). The hostilities, stemming from an incident in Hong Kong Harbor involving a British sea captain and local Chinese officials, easily could have been settled diplomatically. But British arrogance and Chinese defensiveness stirred animosities that precluded a quick settlement. It finally ended in 1860 after a British-French force marched on Beijing and looted it "with great gusto and no small amount of destruction," as Silbey wrote.

Shortly thereafter, China's Emperor Xianfeng died and left the government to his five-year-old son, Tongzhi. His mother, Noble Lady Yi, methodically gained power through a series of crafty and sometimes brutal maneuvers and ruled China as Empress Dowager Cixi. A sharp-edged woman with a keen sense of survival, she was once described as "the only man in China." She developed a festering anger over her country's long struggles with the West that had produced Portugal's acquisition of Macao, France's takeover of Indochina through various actions of conquest and cession, and Britain's two Opium War victories. The latest humiliation was China's defeat in the 1894–95 Sino-Japanese War, which led to Japan's acquisition of Formosa and the nearby Pescadores Islands, along with Japanese access to Chinese trading ports.

Through the early McKinley years, the Chinese exploitation gathered momentum. After Germany obtained rights to Kiao-Chau Bay, Russia demanded the same rights over Port Arthur and Ta Lien-Wan, along with permission to construct a railway in Manchuria. China complied. Britain demanded a lease for Wei-Hai-Wei, on the Shan Tung peninsula, as well as a strategically significant coastal island. France got a lease for a coaling station. When Italy demanded a coaling station at San-Mun Bay, China balked, but Western pressure soon forced a reconsideration. Former U.S. secretary of state John Foster explained the power calculus to reporters. "China," he said, "cannot withstand any assault from the sea, and Italy knows her helplessness." Italy stopped short of a military attack but hovered nearby with threatening military force.

The *Washington Post* captured the situation in a headline: "China Taken by the Throat." Many international experts predicted the eradication of China as an independent nation with its partition into Western spheres of influence. One high European official at Beijing even suggested to the *New York Times* "that the moment has now arrived for international control of China." He added that the "spheres of influence" surge likely would bring America into the fray, probably in pursuit of the province of Chi-Li.

The official was wrong. President McKinley had no interest in joining the frenzy and wanted to get Western hands off China's throat. Britain, seeing the threat to its own extensive and established interests in China, twice sought Washington's cooperation in behalf of an open trading system. The president demurred because, as Secretary Hay explained to a friend, "we think our best policy is one of vigilant protection of our commercial interests, without formal alliances with other Powers." Besides, anti-British sentiment among German and Irish Americans discouraged any overt U.S.-British partnership.

But Hay watched events in China with alarm. In London he had befriended two China experts, both widely traveled in the kingdom, who later published books on the subject. Back in America, he devoured the books when they came out and became increasingly convinced that the exploitation should be stopped. One of the authors, Charles Beresford, popularized the "open door" term and argued that the concept's strength "would lie in the fact that it would be too powerful to attack, and that it could maintain the peace while preserving the open door to all." He added the agreement would "give a new lease of life to the Chinese Empire."

When Beresford visited Washington in 1899, Hay honored him with a dinner party and introduced him to McKinley. Then came another expert, Alfred Hippisley, Britain's inspector of Chinese maritime customs, who shared Beresford's views. Hippisley enjoyed a longtime friendship with Hay's Far Eastern adviser, William Rockhill, who introduced him to the secretary and encouraged him to draft a policy statement to serve as a guide for a U.S. open door initiative. After Hippisley produced the document, Rockhill edited it and commended it to the president. He later put it into diplomatic language for Hay, who embraced it.

It contained three points: first, that all powers would recognize the other powers' vested interests, leased territory, and spheres of influence in China; second, that Chinese treaty tariffs would apply equally to all and would be collected by Chinese officials; and third, that no power would discriminate in favor of its own nationals with regard to harbor dues or railroad charges. In September 1899 Hay sent the document to Berlin, London, St. Petersburg, Tokyo, Rome, and Paris. He urged each government to endorse the open door concept and promote it to the others. By January 4 Hay had favorable responses from all governments. He pronounced the informal compact "final and definitive" and "proof of . . . the untrammeled development of commerce and industry in the Chinese Empire."

This was a brilliant diplomatic stratagem. Though McKinley didn't want America involved in the sordid China landgrab, he feared his country's diplomatic asceticism could lock it out of the vast China trade as the feeding frenzy continued. The open door policy ended that frenzy and put America on an equal footing with the other powers (leaving aside the concessions and spheres of interest already established). The high-sounding open door policy offered the industrial powers a way out of the China chaos while retaining prospects for further economic activity in East Asia. The New York Post praised the initiative's simplicity: "No treaties; just an exchange of official notes. No alliances; no playing off of one Power against another; simply a quiet inclusion of them all in a common policy. . . . It was an exceeding daring and skillful stroke of diplomacy." It also saved China from looming disintegration. Though Hay's "open door" language didn't mention China's territorial integrity, the effect was to check the geopolitical avarice that had driven the great powers' policies in China.

HAY'S HANDIWORK SOON was overtaken by the revolt that enveloped northern China when a call went forth that quickly inspired millions: "Support the Qing; exterminate the foreigners." It came from yet another secret society, Yi-He quan, translated as Righteous and Harmonious Fists and known among Westerners as "the Boxers." Like earlier Chinese secret societies, the Boxers emerged almost spontaneously among Chinese peasants, particularly in the fertile, densely populated northern province of Shandong, a strategic expanse that encompassed long stretches of the Yellow River and the Grand Canal and extended to the Chinese coastlands nearest Beijing. The Boxers of Shandong, displaying red sashes of defiance, were out for blood.

Their initial targets were Chinese Christians. Western missionaries, both Catholic and Protestant, had arrived throughout the nineteenth century to spread the Word and deliver beneficent works through the establishment of churches, schools, and hospitals. By 1900 some 850 Catholic priests and nuns, mostly French, ministered to more than 700,000 Catholic converts. Another 2,800 Protestant missionaries, largely British and American, provided religious and humanitarian service to some 85,000 converts. Well-meaning, idealistic, and naïve, these Westerners didn't comprehend how much they bruised the sensibilities of native Chinese devoted to their cultural and religious heritage. Many displayed what one Chinaman called a "patronizing impudence" toward the prevailing Chinese culture. Sir Robert Hart, British head of the Chinese Imperial Maritime Customs Service, said the missionary presence constituted "a standing insult" to many Chinese, "for does it not tell the Chinese their conduct is bad and requires change . . . their gods despicable and to be cast into the gutter, their forefathers lost and themselves only to be saved by accepting the missionary's teaching?"

Worse, the missionaries established an independent power center within Chinese society, codified in various extraterritorial treaties that exempted missionaries from local laws. They often used this power to intervene on behalf of Christian converts in legal and civic disputes, thus upending traditional power arrangements and spreading frustration and anger among local officials. Chinese Christians, relying on this intervention, flouted local customs and laws with increasing brazenness. "These Chinese Christians are the worst people in China," declared Cixi. "They rob the poor country people of their land and property, and the missionaries, of course, always protect them."

Two natural disasters heightened frustration and anger in Shandong: an 1898 Yellow River flood that destroyed vast crops and a subsequent drought that wreaked further devastation. Thus did a combination of developments, social and natural, set off an explosion of anti-Christian and anti-Western savagery. The leaderless and loosely organized Boxer movement spread through the countryside, killing Chinese Christians initially but threatening Westerners with increasing menace.

Sitting on her Beijing throne, Cixi vacillated on how to respond, then placed her own stamp upon the movement by financing it and beheading a number of anti-Boxer officials. Resolving to use the Boxers as a spearhead against the despised Westerners, she both expanded and emboldened the movement. China entered an era of officially sanctioned upheaval. That became clear on New Year's Eve, when a mob of Boxers accosted a British missionary named Sidney Brooks. They stripped him of his outer clothing, punctured his head and arms with swords, then beheaded him and threw him in a gully. This was a new development—a Boxer willingness to kill Westerners.

Most Westerners in China made a show of remaining cool in the face of the threat. These included U.S. minister Edwin Conger, a Civil War veteran and friend of McKinley who had studied at the Albany Law School when the Major was there and later served with him in Congress. He abandoned politics in 1890 for a diplomatic career that included two stints as minister to Brazil. Selected for his China post by McKinley, he arrived in Beijing with his lively wife, Sarah, in summer 1898. Conger brought to his assignment a strong conviction that the hapless kingdom should be carved up and Westernized, with America getting "at least one good port." This struck Secretary Hay and his Far

East expert, Rockhill, as so outlandish that they tended to discount Conger's warnings of looming perils to Americans in China.

But the direction of events became clear when the British minister, Sir Claude MacDonald, protested Brooks's killing and demanded a Chinese response. Cixi issued an imperial decree condemning violence against Westerners—but not always. It said that "when peaceful and law-abiding people practice their skill in mechanical arts for the self-preservation of themselves and their families" or "combine . . . for the mutual protection of the rural populations, this is in accordance with the public spirited principles of keeping mutual watch and giving mutual help." In other words, Brooks's killers were protecting society.

The Chinese ultimately offered compensation and executed two men for Brooks's murder, but it never was clear that they had executed the real killers, and Westerners remained wary of the government's true motivations. Conger protested to the Chinese Zongli Yamen, the foreign ministry, that the imperial decree bolstered the view within the secret societies that "they have the secret sympathy and endorsement of the Throne." But when Conger joined with the British, French, and German ministers to protest Boxer violence and threats, Hay administered a stern reminder that American policy was to act "singly and without the cooperation of other powers." The State Department, he said, "would have preferred if you had made separate representation on the question." Although Conger accepted the admonition, events were overtaking this studied unilateralism. The Boxer rebellion was spreading across the countryside of northern China so fast and with such force that not even Cixi or her army could contain it—and there was no evidence that they wanted to.

By May the Boxers were murdering Chinese Christians with increasing abandon, often with highly ritualistic cruelty. In one region a French bishop reported that seventy Christians had been massacred and three neophytes "cut in pieces." Villages had been pillaged and burned, and some 2,000 Christians had fled. Reports of mass slaughter of Chinese Christians—and now of more and more Western missionaries— reached Beijing with increasing frequency.

When Conger peppered the empress dowager with atrocity reports and sought protection for the missionaries, he got in return soothing words. The Zongli Yamen assured Conger that a new imperial decree would "cause peace and quiet to be restored" and he "should cease being uneasy in his mind." But in late May the first Boxers appeared in Beijing, their now-famous red sashes marking their boldness and danger. They swaggered through the streets, directing insolent looks at any Westerners who ventured forth from embassy compounds and replacing the familiar airs of Western superiority with the countenance of fear.

Fears mounted on May 28, when the Boxers destroyed the rail line between Beijing and the coast, where twenty Western warships had assembled at Dagu in April. Britain's MacDonald called a meeting of ministers to determine what to do. These representatives of what became known as the Eight-Nation Alliance (Britain, France, the United States, Italy, Japan, Germany, Russia, and Austria-Hungary) agreed to telegraph the Dagu fleet requesting troops to guard the embassies. On June 1, some 350 soldiers arrived, including fifty U.S. marines and seamen from the USS *Newark*. This brought the military contingent at the legations to 430 troops.

Undeterred, a Boxer mob burned down a racetrack outside Beijing on June 9. Two days later Chinese troops killed Japan's embassy chancellor, Sugiyama Akira, at the train station. On June 14, several hundred Boxers stormed the legation compound; Western soldiers repulsed them, killing four. The Westerners congregated at the British legation, barricaded the streets surrounding it, and pulled together enough food, water, and ammunition for an anticipated siege. On June 19, Cixi demanded that all Westerners leave Beijing and travel to Dagu under her protection. Fearing a trap, the legation people sought clarification from the Zongli Yamen. When no reply came, the German ambassador, Baron Clemens August von Ketteler, set out to get an answer—and was killed. That ended talk of Westerners leaving their protective compound. Thousands of Boxers surrounded the legations, and a mass slaughter seemed imminent if a rescue party didn't arrive soon.

In Washington, officials only slowly grasped the extent of the crisis. The idealistic China enthusiast Rockhill assured Hay on June 1 that the empress dowager wouldn't allow any mass killing of diplomats. Hay continued to admonish Conger to avoid entanglements with other powers. "We have no policy in China except to protect with energy American interests, and especially American citizens," the secretary wired Conger on June 10. "There must be no alliances."

But the next day Washington got a dose of reality from Rear Admiral Louis Kempff, commanding U.S. naval forces at Dagu. Anticipating that communication with Beijing would be cut off, he wired Secretary Long that U.S. forces could not act alone in restoring rail traffic and telegraph lines or in getting more troops to Beijing to protect Americans. The danger was too great. "If other nations go will join to relieve Americans pending instructions. Situation serious. Battalion marines from Manila has been urgently requested." Washington finally grasped the crisis. When Conger asked permission to join his colleagues in warning of Western action if the Boxers weren't suppressed, Hay answered simply "Yes."

Another jolt arrived on June 13 with news that the Boxers had destroyed the Beijing-Dagu telegraph lines, isolating the legations from outside communication. The *Washington Post* reported, "This absence of official reports has given rise to grave apprehension" in official Washington. McKinley devoted his June 15 Cabinet meeting entirely to China, and afterward ordered more ships from the Philippines to join Kempff at Dagu, despite protests from the commanding naval officer at Manila, Admiral George Remey. Notwithstanding a similar remonstrance from General MacArthur, now commanding the U.S. Philippine forces, a Philippine infantry regiment also was ordered to China.

McKinley understood that events in China contained political and global significance far beyond the fate of Beijing's beleaguered Westerners. He was responsible for the safety of American citizens everywhere around the globe, and any horrendous outcome in Beijing would undermine his leadership in an election year. Further, not even Hay's adroit diplomacy could forestall a China carve-up by the Western powers if a massacre should occur. The president's China policy would be in ruins, along with Asian stability.

China developments now centered on three theaters of operation: Beijing; Dagu and the surrounding area, including the city of Tianjin; and the rail line between Tianjin and Beijing. In Beijing, the siege continued without any end in sight short of a military rescue or a massacre. Thus did British Admiral Edward Seymour fashion a plan to assemble an Alliance force of several thousand sailors, marines, and soldiers to restore the rail line, enter the capital city, and rescue the beleaguered Westerners. Meanwhile it was imperative that Alliance forces secure Tianjin, some fifteen miles inland on the Hai River. They also needed to control the mouth of the Hai, to guarantee access to Beijing from the sea. But the Chinese had four forts protecting the Hai. Without the forts, the river would be lost; without the river, Tianjin would fall; without Tianjin and the river, Beijing would be inaccessible. The forts had to be stormed and taken.

Seymour set out on his rail mission on June 10 with a force of about 2,000, mostly British. Seymour planned to place his troops on train cars and move toward Beijing, repairing the sabotaged rail line as they went. It was hopelessly ill-conceived, since he lacked sufficient troops to garrison the line behind him. Soon the Boxers destroyed the roadbed at his rear, cutting him off from his supply train. Ahead of Seymour's troop train, meanwhile, the Boxers expanded their sabotage efforts, forcing Seymour's men into more repair work that exposed them to more ambush attacks. Worse, the Seymour expedition had enraged the empress dowager, who on June 13 ordered her imperial army to halt the Seymour incursion. Seymour and his contingent now faced not only the frenzied Boxers but well-armed and disciplined Chinese troops. He and his men were dangerously exposed, with no prospect of reaching Beijing. It would be difficult enough just getting back to Tianjin.

The job of leading the assault on China's Dagu forts fell to British Rear Admiral James Bruce, who was far more competent than Seymour. Bruce planned his operation meticulously and fostered a harmonious relationship among Alliance admirals. He crafted a plan of taking the forts with about 1,000 men who would land behind the installations and attack from the rear, with the big guns of the Western warships repressing Chinese firepower. A British naval force simultaneously would attack four Chinese destroyers moored on the riverbank. Bruce initiated his two-pronged attack at 2 a.m. on June 17, and by breakfast all four forts were in Allied hands. The British Navy captured the four Chinese destroyers. Western casualties were minimal in both operations.

U.S. Admiral Kempff, following instructions from Washington that he avoid hostilities unless subjected to a Chinese act of war, didn't participate in the operation. But he cleverly positioned the USS *Monocacy*, under Commander Frederic Wise, near the battle. When it took a shell, Kempff calculated that this was indeed the act of war he needed. Subsequent orders received from Washington read, "Act in concurrence with other powers so as to protect all American interests."

Meanwhile Seymour's contingent—haggard, hungry, and surrounded by Boxers and Chinese troops—stumbled upon a Chinese armory filled with food and ammunition. It saved them. Seymour managed to get word of his whereabouts to Western officers at Tianjin, who promptly sent out a rescue party. Still, the admiral lost 285 men, including sixty-five killed, in his ill-considered expedition. The next challenge was the mortal threat to Westerners at Tianjin, surrounded by Chinese combatants who shelled the Western enclave with such persistence that the streets at times "were simply canals of moving lead," in the words of an American mining engineer (and future U.S. president), Herbert Hoover. The British consul wrote to Admiral Bruce, "Reinforcements are *most* urgently required." It took two tries, but on June 23 the Western forces managed to cut a wide swath through Chinese forces and secure the safety of Tianjin's Westerners. They were greeted with "shouting and cheering and crying and weeping for joy."

But the Chinese still held most of the city, and Cixi ordered 20,000 Chinese troops to surround the area, shell the Western enclave, and overrun the Europeans, Japanese, and Americans. The Alliance mustered nearly 7,000 troops for an assault on the city. Storming it from two sides on July 13, the attacking forces initially failed to penetrate the twenty-foot-high perimeter walls. But the next day a brave Japanese soldier managed to blow away one of the heavy gates (dying in the effort), and Alliance soldiers stormed through to score what the *New York Times* called a "brilliant victory." Chinese troops fled, and the Alliance now possessed a secure staging area for a march to Beijing. Some 250 soldiers of the allied armies died in the fighting, with another 500 wounded. The city was essentially destroyed, with much looting and killing by allied troops.

During this time, the fate of the embassy staffs and other beleaguered foreigners in Beijing remained unknown. In Washington, McKinley fretted through the information blackout. He ordered another 1,300 officers and men dispatched to Dagu and instructed General MacArthur in the Philippines to prepare for sending more if needed. He queried Hay about the possibility of assembling all American citizens in China "in places of safety on the coast, where our ships can give them succor." Hay responded that it would be too dangerous to move Americans through China's feverish countryside. He shared McKinley's anxiety "in regard to this most trying crisis" and the "great affliction to sit apparently helpless . . . knowing what scenes of tragic horror are taking place . . . and not being able to prevent them." In mid-July, the president cut short his Canton vacation and rushed back to Washington for a hurriedly scheduled Cabinet meeting to determine if he should call a special congressional session to authorize a full complement of 10,000 troops to China. Root and Long assured him that those forces were available without any special congressional action.

Hay worked assiduously through China's ambassador to Washington, Wu Ting-fang, to open a communications channel to Conger. Wu succeeded, and Conger sent an encrypted message through Wu's channel that said, "For one month we have been besieged British Legation under continued shot and shell from Chinese troops. Quick relief only can prevent general massacre." Reaching Washington on July 20, it was authenticated and then conveyed immediately to the president, who was "much gratified by the news," particularly since British newspapers had reported for days that all foreigners in Beijing had been slaughtered. Conger later revealed to the U.S. consul at Tianjin, J. W. Ragsdale, that a cease-fire had been established with Chinese troops after five weeks of continuous assault. He said some fifty marines from all nations had been killed and many more wounded. "We have provisions for several weeks, but little ammunition," wrote Conger. "If they continue to shell us as they have done we cant hold out long. Complete massacre will follow."

With the Beijing foreigners safe but still vulnerable and with Tianjin and Dagu now secure, Alliance forces promptly began preparations for a relief expedition. The nations mustered 18,000 troops (including 2,200 Americans) for the eighty-mile trek to Beijing, with high prospects for combat against Chinese forces along the way. The contingent set out on August 4 at 3 a.m., with expectations that it would take two weeks to reach the capital.

But it wasn't clear Conger and the other legation people could hold out that long. The empress dowager and her son, increasingly frightened at prospects of losing their country, turned their government over to anti-Western hardliners while also seeking help from America and France in mediating an accord between the kingdom and the other Western countries. A communication from Emperor Zaichun to McKinley, delivered through Wu, pleaded for the president to "devise measures and take the initiative in bringing about a concert of the powers for the restoration of order and peace." McKinley replied that he couldn't accept such a mission until China gave assurance of the condition of the legation people, fostered open communication between them and their governments, removed all danger to their lives and liberty, and cooperated with the relief expedition. He chided the emperor with a reminder that U.S. troops had entered China only to protect Americans "who were sojourning in China in the enjoyment of rights guaranteed them by treaty and by international law."

The *New York Times*, reflecting widespread sentiment among increasingly apprehensive Americans, editorialized, "If the Oriental intellect in its twistings and turnings is capable of comprehending Western ideas set forth in straightforward speech the grave rebuke which President McKinley has found it necessary to administer directly to the Emperor himself ought to serve as an admonition that Chinese ways are no longer to be tolerated." The hapless emperor and his mother were in a bind, unable to rid their capital of the foreigners who were at the heart of the hostilities; unable to rein in the Boxers, whose fulminations had precipitated the crisis; and unable to stop the multinational foreign army bent on seizing their imperial city.

The rescue expedition, under a kind of makeshift command structure, encountered significant resistance during its first two days on the road to Beijing. After the foreign army routed the Chinese in both encounters, however, the opposing army and Boxer mobs simply vanished. The way to Beijing was open.

But the Western military victories near Tianjin enraged the Beijing mob, placing the legation people in ever greater danger. One Beijing escapee, a pro-Western Chinaman named Cho-Ta, said the capital bulged with 100,000 Boxers and Qing troops bent on killing any Christian converts or Westerners they could get their hands on. Some 2,000 to 3,000 converts had been killed, he said, and more than 4,000 "peaceful citizens" also had been slain. Conger reported that the Chinese had resumed firing upon the legation compound, and the Chinese government continued to insist that Westerners leave their enclave, which would mean "certain death." Washington considered the situation "very grave," reported the *Times*, adding that officials feared for the foreigners' survival prospects "if active hostilities should begin against the legationers." Washington sent to the imperial government a "sharp demand for compliance with the requirements previously formulated by President McKinley."

Alliance forces reached Beijing on August 15 and pummeled it with artillery fire, but the Chinese army held off the assault with abundant small-arms fire from the big outer walls. Japanese and Russian troops positioned themselves to the northward of the Tung-Chow Canal, while American and British forces occupied the south side. At nightfall the Japanese blew up the two eastern gates of the city, while the Americans and British entered through two southern gates. Detachments of each contingent, facing heavy resistance, forced their way through Beijing toward the legations, where the parties met and opened up communications. British troops from India entered the British legation grounds at 1 p.m. the next day, the Americans arriving at 3.

"The emaciated tenants could have lasted but little longer," reported the Associated Press; they had only three days' rations, consisting mostly of horseflesh and rice, doled out at only a pound a day, as the *New York Times* reported. Four thousand shells fell in the legation compound during the fifty-five-day siege, killing some sixty-five people and wounding 160. The Chinese government collapsed as the emperor and his mother fled the city before the Alliance arrival to avoid the inevitable despoliation of Beijing and its Forbidden City. The *Times* of London reported, "Peking is now entirely under foreign control. Looting is proceeding systematically."

ALLIANCE UNITY, REMARKABLY tight during the legation crisis, now dissipated over questions of Chinese punishment, the Chinese future, and procedures for the coming negotiation. McKinley steadfastly opposed any China dismemberment, Western territorial aggrandizement, or efforts to overthrow the Qing government. He also accepted Cixi's designated negotiator, Li Hongzhang. Hay considered Li "an unmitigated scoundrel . . . thoroughly corrupt and treacherous." But, added the secretary, "he represents China and we must deal with him." McKinley didn't want the process disrupted by such trivialities as Li's suitability to negotiate for China. The focus, he believed, should be on "indemnity for the past and security for the future," as the *New York Times* explained.

On August 28 the president convened an all-day Cabinet meeting—the longest of his presidency—to deal with Russia's embrace of McKinley's basic principles. The night before, both the president and Secretary Root had crafted ideas for an appreciative reply, and those documents now served as the basis for the discussion. When Cabinet members neared consensus, Root and the president retired to separate rooms to dictate their respective versions. Cortelyou, with his usual interest in procedure, noted that the meticulous, deliberate Root—"one might almost say labored"—took forty-five minutes to produce his beautifully fashioned argument. The straight-ahead McKinley, by contrast, rendered his version, some two or three times longer than Root's, in about ten minutes.

The final statement reiterated Hay's open door policy and leveraged the Russian position by praising it. It squared also with a July 3 statement from Hay—a kind of follow-up to his "open door" note—saying the United States opposed any actions by Alliance nations to abandon the open door compact or carve up China. Now in late August the U.S. government "receive[d] with much satisfaction the repeated and frank declaration that Russia has no designs of territorial acquisition in China; and that, equally with the other Powers now operating in China, Russia has sought the safety of her legation in Peking and to help the Chinese Government to repress the troubles."

In light of China's wanton destruction, however, the president distrusted the intentions of the other allies, particularly the rambunctious Germans, bent on expanding their presence around the world and agitated by the death of their ambassador. Japan seemed intent on taking Amoy in southeastern China, and even Britain appeared interested in territorial gains. The *New York Times* suspected these nations had been seduced by "the mighty temptations before them in the shape of land grabbing opportunities." But before the end of August, Japan had announced its withdrawal from Amoy, and France embraced a policy of restraint. On September 8 the British also bought in.

Thus did Hay's open door stratagem survive, along with the president's underlying aim. "What I want," he told a Canton friend, "is the friendship of China when the trouble is over." Tied to the question of China's fate and the harshness of the settlement was the question of whether the Alliance nations should remove most of their troops from Beijing as a sign of good faith or keep them there as bargaining leverage. The president wanted them out, partly because he didn't want to give American anti-imperialists political fodder in an election year. Besides, the troops were needed in the Philippines, and he feared the unforeseen consequences of an extended military presence. "We want to avoid being in Peking for a long time," he wrote to Hay, "and it must be a long time if we stay there for the diplomatic negotiations, and without our intending it, we may be drawn into currents that would be unfortunate."

Hay, always the realist, countered that there was no choice but to remain in place pending the diplomatic outcome. "The dilemma is clear," he said: the United States wanted out as soon as possible but didn't want to appear weak or frightened. If the country departed, leaving Germany and Britain in Beijing, those powers would dominate the negotiations, "and we shall be left out in the cold." McKinley bowed to Hay's logic.

The powers struggled with other issues involving the starkness of the terms and the severity and extent of the punishments to be meted out. Germany in particular favored a pitiless approach, while McKinley pushed for more lenient measures designed to keep the Qing regime in place. When China issued an imperial decree degrading four princes and depriving a hard-line ringleader of his official privileges, the *New York Times* heralded it as "a complete justification of the course of the Administration." On October 19, the Chinese envoys offered peace terms that recognized China's responsibility for violating international law, accepted an indemnity regimen to be worked out in coming negotiations, and promised the safety and security of foreigners. The United States promptly accepted the proposals as a basis for negotiation, and within three weeks the eight powers reached agreement on the demands to be presented at the start of the coming parlay. The State Department authorized Conger to represent his country in the negotiations. Though many details remained, the great China crisis was over.

THE CHINA EPISODE of 1900, and McKinley's role in it, represented a watershed in America's global position. Agriculture Secretary Wilson was correct, of course, in saying that the country's victory over Spain had enlarged its diplomatic profile and expanded its influence. As Wilson understood, this was seen in the impact of Hay's "open door" note on the great powers seeking aggrandizement in China. It was seen also in the aftermath of the Beijing siege, when the American president laid down his marker on the proper postsiege policies and never wavered. Eventually the other powers generally came around to McKinley's view. No previous president had exercised this kind of diplomatic sway in a matter involving all the world's greatest powers. Indeed without the Philippines and McKinley's standing army and the burgeoning U.S. Navy, America couldn't have marshaled the manpower to play a major role in the Beijing rescue. As Hay said in written musings at the height of the China crisis, "It is to Manila that we owe the ability to send troops and ships to the defence of our ministers, our missionaries, our consuls, and our merchants in China, instead of being compelled to leave our citizens to the casual protection of other powers, as would have been unavoidable had we flung the Philippines away."

But it wasn't just America's new stature that represented a turning point in global power arrangements. It was reflected also in the emerging American global philosophy. Throughout the nineteenth century, great powers had nearly all been great colonial powers. That's why Germany, now a force positioned strategically in Middle Europe, so desperately wanted colonies wherever they could be obtained. But America, also emerging as a great power, seemed at least ambivalent about colonialism and perhaps even averse to it. Under McKinley and Hay, the United States didn't rush into the China landgrab at a time when the colonial impulse threatened to gobble up that troubled kingdom and shut America out of its vast and rich markets. America had wrested Cuba from the clutches of colonial Spain and yet had demurred from acquiring it as its own colonial possession.

Of course McKinley had embraced the colonial impulse in Hawaii, Puerto Rico, and the Philippines. But Hawaii and Puerto Rico were seen primarily as isolated strategic necessities rather than elements of a general colonial push. Anti-imperialists scoffed at this distinction, of course, but to McKinley it was real. As for the Philippines, the president clung to his conviction that he simply had had no choice but to take the entire archipelago, to secure America's naval interests while preventing future turmoil in the islands. At the philosophical level, he justified it with gauzy notions about elevating uneducated and underprivileged peoples, giving them the gifts of modern economics and democratic practice, so much a part of the American ethos. His speeches during this time were replete with references to spreading humanitarian works along with American power. Again critics scoffed and tossed out suggestions of hypocrisy, but most Americans accepted the president's sincerity on the matter. And the president certainly sought to fulfill that idealistic mandate.

It would take decades for this inchoate world outlook—noncolonial imperialism based on unparalleled military and economic power and mixed with an underlying humanitarianism—to ripen into a coherent and resonant geopolitical philosophy and guide America into its coming era of global ascendancy. But when it did, it would become clear to discerning thinkers that its early stirrings emerged in the McKinley foreign policy and its underlying rationale. As the *New York Times* put it in an editorial at the height of the China drama, America was the only country to apply "anti-imperialistic . . . sentiments," not allowing the effort to go "from an alliance for rescue to an alliance for revenge." Whatever America intended to do with its burgeoning power in coming decades, that power now was indeed a global reality. Sir Robert Giffen, a well-known British statistician and expert on global trends, told the *New York Times* that America had become "the most powerful State in the world, so far as population and resources were concerned." He suggested the world now had only four global powers: Great Britain, Russia, Germany, and the United States.

27

Reelection

"I AM NOW THE PRESIDENT OF THE WHOLE PEOPLE"

At the dawn of the 1900 presidential campaign year, the *Chicago Tribune* hailed McKinley's commanding political position. So secure was the president as head of his party that he faced no opposition when Republicans gathered in Philadelphia in June to select their presidential candidate. "It is settled," announced the *Tribune*, "that he is to be nominated by acclamation." This gave the president a huge general election advantage. To get nominated, a candidate must treat with other politicians and often cut deals that voters dislike. Thus the wooing of politicians in the nomination process often complicated the wooing of voters in the fall. But no such complications confronted McKinley. "He has only the people to deal with," said the *Tribune*. "He is absolutely his own master." Further, with the economy expanding, money abundant, and the country's global stature growing, the president's prospects looked bright. "He is, indeed," stated the *Tribune*, "a happy man."

But Arkansas senator James Jones, chairman of the Democratic National Committee, planned a political ambush. He told reporters in St. Louis that the Democrats would continue the fight on bimetallism but also add two potent issues to the mix: McKinley's imperialist adventurism and those increasingly brazen monopolistic trusts grabbing more and more economic power. These issues, he said, "are demanding attention from the people of the United States."

Bimetallism didn't represent much of a threat to McKinley. The Bryanites' 1896 cry for liquidity through silver coinage lost relevance as rising gold prices and new mining technologies expanded gold extraction and brought more gold to the U.S. Mint, thus increasing the country's money stock by about 10 percent a year. And by loosening capital requirements for bank start-ups in rural areas, the president's currency legislation of early 1900 had spurred the creation of small banks in the West and South. This, explained the *New York Mail and Express*, "helped to provide currency for local needs and lessen the demand for Eastern funds." The pro-silver populists no longer mustered the kind of frenzied political energy they had unleashed in 1896.

But McKinley's foreign policy expansionism threatened his ability to maintain party unity. In Speaker Reed's valedictory speech in Maine, he expressed confidence that his beloved First District would "always be true to the principles of liberty, self-government, and the rights of man." This was interpreted by many as a slap at the president. No doubt Reed wanted to agitate those Republicans who agreed with him that McKinley's Philippine policy violated fundamental constitutional principles.

Related issues such as the Puerto Rican tariff, the isthmian canal, and the Hay-Pauncefote Treaty also threatened to divide Republicans. *The Nation* argued that the GOP "is now rent in so many different places and on so many different questions that it cannot possibly go into the coming Presidential campaign presenting a solid front to the enemy." Though clearly an overstatement, this perception reflected a political reality that the president could ill afford to ignore. Certainly any issue as emotion-laden as the Philippines presented political dangers. Illinois senator William Mason demonstrated those emotions—and dangers—when he declared, "I shall continue my opposition to the war upon the Filipinos. I would sooner resign my seat than treat a dog the way we are treating those poor people. I am ashamed of my country."

The incendiary trust issue posed further challenges, particularly since McKinley hadn't managed to stay ahead of public opinion on the matter. True to his assurance to Dawes that he would attack the trusts, the president had devoted considerable attention to the problem in his Third Annual Message of December 1899. He declared "obnoxious . . . to the public welfare" those combinations "which engross or control the market of any particular kind of merchandise or commodity necessary to the general community, by suppressing natural and ordinary competition, whereby prices are unduly enhanced to the general consumer." But he signaled his reluctance to lead on the issue when he added, "Whatever power the Congress possesses over this most important subject should be promptly ascertained and asserted."

Digressing on the Supreme Court's insistence that federal jurisdiction over trusts didn't extend beyond matters of interstate commerce, the president conceded that "the decision of our highest court . . . renders it quite doubtful whether the evils of trusts and monopolies may be adequately treated through Federal action." He urged legislation consistent with the Court's limitation and suggested state legislatures should take the lead in curbing monopolistic practices. Constitutionally he stood upon solid ground. Politically he seemed feeble. Congressional Republicans sought to buck up their position by pushing legislation in early 1900 to enhance enforcement of the 1890 Sherman Antitrust Act. It passed the House by a vote of 273 to 1, demonstrating public anger on the issue. But the measure's impact on enforcement was modest, and Democrats quickly accused Republicans of merely going through the motions "for party and political considerations and not with any real purpose of dealing with the trust subject." Some Republicans advocated a constitutional amendment to supersede Supreme Court constrictions, but nobody saw much chance of ratification. Republicans remained ill-positioned on the issue.

Then there was the Dewey question. The hero of Manila Bay, initially resistant to a presidential run, now succumbed to the adulatory pressure to go for it. In announcing his availability, however, the admiral demonstrated his own limitations in this challenging new arena. In an interview with the *New York World*, Dewey mused, "The office of the President is not such a very difficult one to fill, his duties being mainly to execute the laws of Congress." He could do that, he said, as faithfully as he had executed the orders of his superiors over a long naval career. Asked about the platform he would run on, he replied, "I think I have said enough at this time, and possibly too much."

Indeed. Many Americans felt mystified at his comment about the unchallenging duties of the presidency. Such a blithe attitude toward the office seemed to be a sign of political bewilderment. The *New York Times* suggested the admiral's cogitation had generated "a general inclination to be amused" and that Dewey's candidacy "was considered to be quite as much of a joke as his references to the simplicity of the task imposed upon the occupant of the White House."

At the White House itself, McKinley was equally amused. He told Cortelyou and Dawes that the admiral could have emerged as a formidable figure and a threat to his presidency had he taken a strong stand against retention of the Philippines immediately after his return from Manila. That would have galvanized Democrats while splitting Republicans. But he had missed that opportunity. The next day, after Dewey identified himself as a Democrat, the president dismissed his prospective candidacy with some compassion, lamenting that, while people were laughing at his stumbles, there was also "an undercurrent of pity." Although ripples of support for a Dewey presidency would continue for months, the president was correct in perceiving that he wouldn't be a factor in the race.

A bigger question was what to expect from young Theodore Roosevelt. Would the restless New York governor vie for the vice presidential position on the McKinley ticket? "The Governor is very popular all over the country," reported the *New York Times*. "The people like him for his vigor and his honesty. They like a stirring man, and he is always astir." The paper anticipated "a considerable demand that his name be on the ticket." The *Times* was right. Aside from Dewey, no war veteran from 1898 had amassed a more fervent national following than Roosevelt.

But he didn't want the job. "In view of the continued statements in the press that I may be urged as a candidate for Vice-President," he announced in February, "it is proper for me to state definitely that under no circumstances could I or would I accept the nomination for the

Vice-Presidency." He hinted at a reelection bid in New York and said, disingenuously, that he was "happy to state that Senator Platt cordially acquiesces in my views in the matter."

In fact, Platt had developed a strong antipathy toward the reform-minded governor, who predictably refused to knuckle under to Platt's demands on patronage and other matters. Since the New York boss controlled the state's legislature, and hence the power to confirm TR nominees for government jobs, Roosevelt had to work with Platt—and tried to. But Platt, accustomed to complete fealty from mere governors, demanded from Roosevelt more than he could comfortably deliver. Worse for Roosevelt, Platt dominated the state corporations that controlled the money spigot for Republican candidates. Journalist Lincoln Steffens revealed in a provocative piece that, while the corporations couldn't come out publicly against an incumbent Republican governor, "they have simply served notice on the organization that if he is renominated they will not contribute to campaign funds." Steffens said the "obvious solution" was promotion of TR to the vice presidency, and prominent GOP committeemen from the state warned the governor that he would be "tempting Providence" should he try for a second gubernatorial term.

But if Platt's dislike of Roosevelt spawned a desire to get him on the McKinley ticket, another prominent politician harbored an equal dislike that produced an opposite resolve. Mark Hanna considered Roosevelt a spoiled child of a politician, erratic, out of control, "unsafe." Now he set about to keep Roosevelt off the McKinley ticket.

Hanna also had other worries. Expecting McKinley to appoint him once again as Republican National Committee chairman—and hence manager of the presidential campaign—the senator stewed as the president remained silent on the matter well past the appropriate decision-making time. The relationship between the Major and his longtime strategist had undergone a transformation during McKinley's presidency and Hanna's years as a rising senatorial heavyweight. McKinley intimates sensed that the president chafed a bit now as Hanna expressed himself around town in ways suggesting he enjoyed a special pipeline to the White House and traded on his presidential ties in seeking special treatment from government bureaus and agencies. Later speculation centered also on a post office scandal in Havana involving a Hanna crony named Estes Rathbone. Conscious that such things could undermine his presidential image, McKinley distanced himself from Hanna with "a kind of quiet discipline," signaling that the senator should exercise greater restraint.

Ultimately Hanna got the RNC job and promptly directed to the campaign his usual energy and organizational skill (though diminished somewhat by infirmities that included heart problems and increasingly severe rheumatism). He quietly maneuvered to keep Roosevelt off the ticket and promoted instead Cornelius Bliss, the New York financier and party bigwig who had served as McKinley's Interior secretary. Other names mentioned were General Leonard Wood, serving in Cuba; Elihu Root; New York lieutenant governor Timothy Woodruff; Navy Secretary Long; and Indiana senator Charles Fairbanks. Bliss emerged as the frontrunner in the minds of many when he spent two hours with Hanna in Room 952 of the Waldorf-Astoria Hotel. Asked about it by reporters, Bliss maintained a studied coyness.

"The report is, Mr. Bliss," said a reporter, "that you had a conference to-day with Senator Hanna relative to your acceptance of the Vice Presidential nomination?"

"I always see Mr. Hanna when he comes to town," replied Bliss with a smile.

"Did you see him to-day?"

"I always see him when he is here. I would see him to-night if he were in town, but I understand he went away this afternoon."

McKinley, who seemed to share Hanna's misgivings about Roosevelt and his good feelings about Bliss, sought to nudge TR away from the vice presidency when the governor traveled to Washington to issue a frank declaration to McKinley that he didn't want the job. He was taken aback when the president readily agreed. "He did not even have a chance to launch his *nolo episcopari* at the Major," wrote Hay afterward with a certain glee. "That statesman said he did not want him on the ticket—that he would be far more valuable in New York." Then Secretary Root added, "Of course not—you're not fit for it." The ego-driven Roosevelt was more stung than relieved, and the president hoped that would settle the matter.

In the meantime McKinley took satisfaction in Hanna's dominance of the Ohio state convention in late April. The senator's favored ticket for state offices and his slate on delegates and alternates to the national convention "went through without any break," reported the *New York Times*, and his keynote address generated thunderous acclamation. "It was very much a Hanna day," said the *Times*, "without dissenting or discordant notes." After years of bitter strife, the McKinley-Hanna forces finally held complete sway over the state's Republican Party.

AS THE CAMPAIGN year progressed, the president pondered the interaction between the Philippine war and his election prospects. Much depended on Will Taft and his commission. Upon arriving in the Philippines in June, Governor-general Taft reported to the president that the military effort was succeeding, although slowly; that Arthur MacArthur was cooperating nicely; and that a steady commitment to current policy would succeed—but required, of course, McKinley's reelection. "The backbone of the revolt seems to be entirely broken," he wrote, "and its ostensible leaders are seriously contemplating a surrender relying on the work of the Commission to secure in a civil government much though not all of that which they have hoped to bring about."

That month the president promulgated an amnesty offer. Although Aguinaldo promptly declared that "the war must be continued," he didn't try to stop other rebel officers from surrendering. One top general named Aquino did so on June 30, and other officers followed suit. Meanwhile MacArthur's army continued to exact heavy losses on insurgents when opportunities emerged—200 rebels killed, for example, and 160 captured during a single June week.

After the president on August 17 requested a report from the Taft Commission on what it had discovered over ten months in country, the commission responded with a generally optimistic overview. Much of the archipelago had been pacified, the commissioners reported, and most Filipinos now perceived that U.S. designs were largely benign. The policy of leniency, marked by the amnesty program, had induced many insurgents to lay down their arms. But many others refused to surrender in hopes that a Democrat would win the U.S. presidency and withdraw from the islands. That was Aguinaldo's constant refrain. The war now was generally a guerrilla war, confined to particular regions of the various islands, and conducted mostly by Tagalogs. As soon as the rebels saw that McKinley would be in office another four years, the resistance would fade away. But a report from the islands by a *New York Herald* reporter painted a more complex picture, with Filipino commanders in districts everywhere, muster rolls maintained, some 20,000 rifles hidden away by insurgents, and guerrilla resistance lying in wait here and there in anticipation of a cue from Aguinaldo.

For McKinley's political purposes, the Taft Commission report served nicely to convey the message that the insurgency was largely under control, at least sufficiently to prevent this difficult imperial project from upending McKinley's reelection prospects. But as the *Herald* report also made clear, an end to the war wasn't likely anytime soon.

ON JUNE 11, Republican leaders began assembling in Philadelphia for a political convention that would be heavy on ceremony and light on drama. The city sparkled with bunting, evening torchlights, and enthusiasm. The only question of intrigue was the vice presidential selection, and even that didn't seem to generate much emotion. Bliss remained a favorite of many, and attention now focused also on Iowa's William Allison, a Senate graybeard and financial expert who had served in the chamber for twenty-eight years and in the House for eight years before that. A convention subcommittee, seeking to diminish disruptive maneuverings, issued a statement on June 11: "Either Mr. Allison or Mr. Bliss would be satisfactory to the President, and his wishes alone, and not the ambitions of the several other notables who have been prominently mentioned for the office, are now being consulted by the leaders."

But the president refused to name his own choice. On June 13, reporters accosted Hanna about reports the president soon would announce his favored vice presidential candidate.

"There is no truth in that report, none whatever," replied the senator. "The President will not interfere; he has no candidate."

"Then, who is your candidate?"

"I have none. My only desire is to get the best man."

"You are quoted as being opposed to Mr. Woodruff?"

"I have said when asked whether Mr. Woodruff was a candidate, that I hoped not, and I do not retract that statement. . . . As for Mr. Bliss, he is an admirable man, but he is out of the question; he cannot accept. Senator Allison? Well, I came over on the train with him, and he is absolute in his refusal. There is no doubt of his sincerity—in not wanting the place. And, as a matter of fact, we cannot spare him from his present place in the Senate."

He was asked about Iowa's young representative Jonathan Dolliver, a late entry in the mention game, favored by Grosvenor and Dawes.

"Mr. Dolliver," said Hanna, "is an avowed candidate, and he has a good following among his friends in the House, but I cannot say more as to his prospects. The truth is that there is as yet no approach to a settlement of the matter."

In fact Hanna had come to Philadelphia with two overarching aims: to get Bliss to accept the position and, barring that, to prevent Roosevelt from getting it. Although Bliss had declined the honor repeatedly in conversations with Hanna and others, the senator continued to work him in Philadelphia. But Bliss's family opposed the idea so vehemently that the New Yorker simply couldn't entertain it. Hanna was left with the task of identifying that "best man" he was looking for. But there didn't seem to be anyone available who could meet Hanna's standards and also galvanize the convention.

The only man who could galvanize the convention was the Rough Rider, who inexplicably arrived in Philadelphia wearing a hat reminiscent of his Cuban adventure. When he entered the Walton Hotel's crowded lobby at two o'clock on June 16, it caused an instant stir.

"Here comes Teddy," a man shouted, and the crowd rushed to him with cheers and chants of "Teddy, Teddy, Teddy." When the air was filled with a chorus of "There'll Be a Hot Time in the Old Town Tonight," according to one journalist, "Roosevelt blushed, doffed his hat and bowed his acknowledgements as he recognized the tune played after his charge up San Juan Hill." Similar scenes emerged through the afternoon. One political wit, noting the hat, said slyly, "Gentlemen, that's an acceptance hat." Platt, employing his most devious cunning in efforts to ignite a TR firestorm without burning his fingers, observed with quiet satisfaction that the governor was "in a state of rare excitement, even for him." Lodge, who initially had urged Roosevelt to embrace the vice presidency but later accepted his demurral, warned him to stay away from the convention if he didn't want the position. What he thought of the hat was never recorded.

The next morning the governor's hotel room was aflutter with sequential visits from state delegations imploring him to bow to the clear and powerful sentiment of the convention. First came the Western states: California, Colorado, the Dakotas, Nevada. The delegates chanted and sang to the accompaniment of "fife, drum and bugle" as they marched around the room. Then came the Eastern delegations, offering unqualified support and begging for the governor's acquiescence. Nobody could resist this phenomenon of political energy—not Roosevelt, not McKinley, not Hanna. "The town was Roosevelt mad," reported the Associated Press.

Hanna was the last to accept the inevitable. Though Roosevelt had assured the senator that he wasn't a candidate, he continued his flirtatious ways. On Sunday evening, before the start of the proceedings, Charles Dick saw disaster looming. The Roosevelt wave was becoming irresistible, and yet Hanna seemed bent on resisting it. That could embarrass the president, who was following events from far-off Washington. Dick called Cortelyou at the White House to explain the deteriorating situation. Cortelyou had the president at his side as he conversed with Dick.

"The Roosevelt boom has let loose and it has swept everything," said Dick. "The feeling is that the thing is going pell mell like a tidal wave." Although TR had opposed the wave initially, said Dick, he now seemed beguiled by it. Dick suggested the president should talk to Hanna and flag him off his anti-TR machinations. "We cannot afford to have it said that something was done in spite of ourselves," said the longtime McKinley loyalist.

At midnight the president dictated a policy statement and had Cortelyou read it to Dick and other convention officials: "The President has no choice for Vice-President. Any of the distinguished names suggested would be satisfactory to him. The choice of the Convention will be his choice; he has no advice to give. The Convention is the lawfully constituted body to make nominations, and instead of giving advice he awaits its advice, confident now as always that it will act wisely and for the highest interest of the country and the party." McKinley was never one to resist the inevitable.

But Hanna still resisted. He rushed to Roosevelt's room and demanded to know if he was a candidate. The governor waffled, then said he would issue a withdrawal statement the next morning. But the statement dripped of ambiguity. Clearly he wasn't prepared to slam the door on the vice presidency. Hanna, bewildered and irritated by McKinley's statement and the passivity it reflected, fought through the night to solidify anti-TR sentiment within various delegations. "I am not in control!" he complained to convention colleagues. "McKinley won't let me use the power of the administration to defeat Roosevelt. He is blind, or afraid, or something."

Suffering intense pain from his rheumatism and hardly able to walk, Hanna seemed genuinely out of control, in danger of placing himself (and his boss) against the convention. On Tuesday, June 19, just after Hanna slammed down the big gavel to open the convention, Roosevelt entered the hall with a well-timed flourish that touched off a raucous rally for him. The inflamed Hanna employed all his political wiles and vaunted carrot-and-stick leverage to stop the TR movement on the convention floor.

Watching Hanna with growing alarm, Dawes pleaded with him to halt his anti-Roosevelt crusade. But the irritated Hanna insisted the president supported his actions. There was "almost an altercation," Dawes recalled later, and then the young McKinley intimate retired to his hotel room and called Cortelyou. With the president listening on an extension line, Dawes said Hanna was fostering a convention split that was sure to humiliate himself and embarrass the president.

The president quickly produced yet another statement, which Cortelyou dictated to Dawes. This one could not be misinterpreted or ignored: "The President's close friends must not undertake to commit the Administration to any candidate. It has no candidate. The convention must make the nomination; the Administration would not if it could. The President's close friends should be satisfied with his unanimous renomination and not interfere with the vice-presidential nomination. The Administration wants the candidate of the convention, and the President's friends must not dictate to the convention."

Dawes rushed to Hanna with the statement, read it to him, and watched the recognition of reality slowly emerge upon his countenance. The game was up. Hanna was subdued. Dawes returned to his room to call the White House again with word that Hanna had been "a little perplexed" but would comply. Some McKinley partisans mounted a perfunctory vice presidential movement in behalf of Secretary Long, but nobody took it seriously, and it caused hardly a stir. Hanna played no role in it. He would do what he was told, he told Dawes. Indeed he got ahead of the wave by suggesting in a statement that Roosevelt, like McKinley, should be nominated by acclamation.

The convention approved a platform conforming to the president's wishes, including a plank on trusts that "condemn[ed] all conspiracies and combinations intended to restrict trade, limit production and control prices" and favored legislation to "restrain and prevent all such abuses and protect and promote competition." On foreign policy, the platform declared that "no other course was possible than to destroy Spain's sovereignty throughout the West Indies and in the Philippine Islands." That course "created our responsibility before the world . . . to provide for the maintenance of law and order, and for the establishment of good government." But U.S. authority could not be less than U.S. responsibility, and that principle justified the effort in the Philippines "to maintain [U.S.] authority, to put down armed insurrection, and to confer the blessings of liberty and civilization upon all the rescued peoples." The rest of the convention unfolded without controversy but with plenty of enthusiasm and with a robust confidence that the Republicans had the candidates, the platform, the narrative, and the popularity for another big election triumph in November.

Meanwhile the president went about his usual daily routine, spending his days at his desk in the Cabinet Room as the convention unfolded. When news flashes from Philadelphia reached the receiving room at the southeast corner of the White House, staffers rushed them to the president, who read them without emotion and returned to his paperwork. When he got word of his nomination at 12:46 p.m. on June 21, he "hastened with a light step" to the family quarters to tell Ida. But he remained only five minutes before returning to his desk. One task he took up quickly was a letter of appreciation to Hanna commending his "courage and sagacity of true leadership" and saying the senator had "added another claim to leadership and public confidence." The senator responded, "Well, it was a nice little scrap at Phila. Not exactly to my liking with my hand tied behind me. However, we got through in good shape and the ticket is all right. Your duty to the country is to live for four years from next March."

TWO WEEKS LATER, when the Democrats assembled at Kansas City, everyone knew the party once again would turn to William Jennings Bryan. But when some delegates suggested new economic circumstances justified a slight relaxation in the commitment to silver coinage at a 16-to-1 ratio, Bryan promptly threatened to appear personally, press the issue, and bolt the convention if it didn't adhere strictly to the 1896 language. That settled the matter. On foreign policy, the platform declared, "We condemn and denounce the Philippine policy of the present administration. It has involved the Republic in unnecessary war, sacrificed the lives of many of our noblest sons, and placed the United States, previously known and applauded throughout the world as the champion of freedom, in the false and un-American position of crushing with military force the efforts of our former allies to achieve liberty and self-government."

Then the delegates duly nominated Bryan and selected for vice president Adlai Stevenson of Illinois, who already had served in that role under President Cleveland. Bryan and Stevenson also captured the nomination of the populist People's Party and the Silver Republicans, both relics of the free-silver fervor of recent years.

THE 1900 GENERAL election campaign proceeded along a number of tracks—issues, campaign strategies and techniques, the roles of the two candidates, Electoral College math, and candidate personalities. The *New York Times*, forged into a major journalistic voice after Adolph Ochs's 1896 purchase, captured the candidates' personalities in a penetrating editorial in 1899. Neither politician, stated the paper, possessed "that broad and philosophic sweep of mind that marks the creative statesman." But both were "able" and displayed "gifts and capacities" for effective leadership. Bryan was "somewhat more alert" than his stolid rival but fostered mistrust among some by his call for "swift and sweeping changes in . . . substantially all of our institutions and customs," including currency, the banks, bonds, taxes, trusts, wages, and labor laws. Bryan's constituency was "the army of the discontented."

McKinley, by contrast, spoke to the sober-minded, conservative, property-owning Americans who "are afraid of overtopping talent and brilliancy." Not trusting "a man who leaps into fame by a single speech," insisted the paper with a bit of slyness, these voters shun the Clays, Websters, and Blaines in favor of "far less shining but safer men" who understand them and their concerns. McKinley's "chief and constant anxiety is not to stray from the path wherein he can command the confidence and support of this conservative majority."

The issues embraced by the two men reflected these traits of temperament and outlook. Bryan waged a campaign of anger directed against established institutions and policies of the day—banks, trusts, the gold standard, protectionism, America's new imperialism. The Nebraskan seized the issues that bubbled up as the campaign unfolded. By mid-September he had shifted his concentration from silver to imperialism and trusts, issues that seemed more resonant with his constituency. "Parties do not make issues," said the candidate in explaining the shift. "Parties meet issues." Republicans, by imposing colonial rule upon the Philippines, had struck "at the very foundation of free government."

On trusts, Bryan pounced when Hanna maladroitly uttered remarks questioning the existence of trusts. "Everybody except Mr. Hanna knows that we have trusts," retorted Bryan, adding that the senator's remarks seemed particularly strange because "there is not a man in the country who knows more about the trusts than he does." Hanna sought to clarify his remarks by saying he was speaking strictly in a legal context. But the damage was done, and McKinley found it "irksome" that his effort to neutralize the issue through platform language had been undermined.

But Hanna rebounded by cleverly reducing the campaign to a single word: *prosperity.* "There is but one issue," he intoned constantly on the stump, "only one—the issue of prosperity and the continuation of it." He said he wouldn't even discuss imperialism—a "bugaboo," a "fraud." It was a "humbug," he said, to think the American people would "resolve themselves into an empire" or that a man such as McKinley "would be an Emperor."

The president meanwhile campaigned simply by doing his job. He announced in September that he planned no public speeches or campaign tours, "despite . . . a movement to try to persuade him to take such action," reported the *Washington Post*. He wouldn't even consider another front-porch strategy. But he enjoyed plenty of adulation whenever he ventured into public.

"Major," yelled one onlooker during a presidential stop at Johnstown, "what are you going to do with us the next four years?"

"It is more important just now," replied the president with a smile, "to know what you are going to do with me the next four years."

"We are going to stand by you," yelled the man, to cheers from the crowd.

McKinley bundled his underlying campaign message into a well-crafted and widely disseminated letter acknowledging the official notification of his nomination and accepting the honor. He also took a jab at his rival in a letter sent to Alliance, Ohio, near Canton, to be read at a rally. The letter extolled "the friendly co-operation of labor and capital" and denounced "the wicked doctrine of class distinction." When 143,000 anthracite coal miners went on strike in September, the possibility of violence loomed large as a threat to the coal industry as well as to McKinley's reelection. Bryan supporters sought to exploit the strike by embracing the miners' demands, but Hanna seized the issue more effectively. He leveraged his corporate stature and contacts to mediate the dispute—largely in favor of the miners. He declared, "Any man who would put a straw in the way of a settlement . . . should be taken out to the nearest lamp-post and hanged."

Hanna revived the super-efficient organizational engine of four years earlier. By late September it produced seventy different documents (brochures, letters, pamphlets), as well as ten or more different posters and lithographs. It distributed 110 million individual items. Newspaper inserts and supplementary materials amounted to two million copies per week. McKinley speeches and utterances were translated into German, Norwegian, Swedish, French, Dutch, "and four or five other languages." The aim was to break the electorate down into discrete ethnic groups for targeted messages. The speakers bureau was revived to ensure that McKinley's message got to precisely the right location at the right time.

The key speaker turned out to be Roosevelt, who blitzed the country with his famous boundless enthusiasm in behalf of an administration he had never particularly believed in. But now he touted McKinley as one of the great presidents of U.S. history, in the process drawing huge crowds to auditoriums, sports arenas, and railroad stops. On one October day in Chicago he delivered a dozen speeches, including at the Coliseum and the First Regiment Armory, and still people had to be turned away for lack of space. He galvanized audiences with his stark and vivid expressiveness. On America's overseas mission, he said, "We have got the wolf by the ears, and we can't get away from these new duties. Now we must decide whether we are going to flinch or whether we are going to go on and finish this great work." In eight weeks of campaigning he traveled 21,209 miles in delivering 673 speeches to an estimated three million people in twenty-four states encompassing 567 towns and cities.

Hanna, itching to get into the fray, proposed late in the campaign that he go after the enemy by touring Bryan's home state of Nebraska and also South Dakota, where the outspoken silverite and anti-imperialist Richard Pettigrew, once a Republican but now a McKinley nemesis, faced a challenge to his Senate incumbency. Republican officials urged Hanna to abandon the idea, as the two states were hotbeds of populist rancor toward the administration and a dustup with Pettigrew could look like a vendetta. When Hanna persisted, McKinley sent Postmaster General Charles Emory Smith to dissuade the senator from what looked like a foolhardy mission.

"Return to Washington and tell the President that God hates a coward!" snapped Hanna to Smith. As Hanna's secretary Elmer Dover recalled, "They doubted Mr. Hanna's judgment and it irritated him." Ignoring the president's wishes, Hanna undertook the tour—and turned it into a significant success. He drew larger crowds than Roosevelt and dispelled the popular image of him as a fat, money-grubbing plutocrat with pinky rings and a smirk of self-satisfaction. "I have taken South Dakota out of the doubtful column," claimed Hanna upon returning to Chicago. "I thoroughly believe Nebraska will also go for McKinley."

HANNA WAS RIGHT. McKinley carried Nebraska and South Dakota on his way to an Electoral College victory of 292 to 155. Bryan carried the Solid South and four Western states, but the president captured the entire rest of the country. His popular vote plurality was 859,694, some 260,000 more than his 1896 margin. What's more, Republicans gained thirteen House members and three in the Senate. The GOP now would control 198 House seats to 153 for the Democrats (and five for splinter parties); the Senate margin would be 56 to 29 (with three splinter-party members). Moreover Pettigrew lost his seat in South Dakota. "It was a vendetta of politics," concluded the *New York Times*, describing an indecorous assault on Hanna by Pettigrew on the Senate floor some months before. "The radical was unhorsed and thrown out of public life, and the conservative can say with truth that it was he who did it."

McKinley not only won reelection but did it his way—by tending to his obligations and letting voters judge him on his record. Wrote Dawes after meeting with McKinley back in Washington, "The president seems more impressed with his duties than with his triumph." But the triumph contained plenty of political significance. In winning several Western states that he had lost in 1896, he finally put the silver mania to rest. And his victory clearly demonstrated the country's embrace of his overseas initiatives and management of the war's aftermath. America would not be deterred from its expansionist resolve. Further, by interpreting the race as a referendum on his policies and leadership, the president elevated his political significance as a leader with a clear popular mandate. As he told Cortelyou, "I can no longer be called the President of a party; I am now the President of the whole people."

— 28 —

Family and Nation

PERSONAL STRUGGLES AND POLITICAL AMBITIONS

Republicans throughout the land rejoiced at McKinley's second-term triumph. On election night, at the GOP's New York headquarters on Madison Avenue, teletype reports revealed around eight o'clock that the president would win big. "We carry New York by more than 110,000," yelled party official Joe Manley of Maine, once Thomas Reed's top aide but now a devoted McKinley man. Within an hour a phone update arrived from party vice chairman Henry Payne in Chicago. "Tell the boys we have carried Illinois by more than 100,000," he told Manley. Around 11:30 Payne got the South Dakota results. "We have beaten Pettigrew," he yelled, waving a telegram over his head. "Send the news to Hanna." In Washington, 20,000 residents jammed the street in front of the *Washington Post* awaiting the latest returns. The throng, reported the paper, was "so densely packed that there was hardly room to stick another human being down upon the asphalt." For nearly four hours, as *Post* officials displayed fresh bulletins on a large outdoor board, cheers and yells undulated through the multitude.

In Canton that morning, as McKinley and Day walked together down Market Street to the voting place, the president doffed his hat to acknowledge cheers here and there and offered courtly handshakes to residents along the way. In the evening, surrounded by friends and family in his cherished Market Avenue home as rain fell outside, he ripped reports off the ticker machine installed in his study. As returns came in he read them aloud with "unruffled composure" but refrained from commenting on even the most favorable developments. Around nine o'clock Manley wired from Manhattan, "Praise God from whom all blessings flow. Your triumphant re-election is conceded by Democratic managers." Soon Canton was aflutter with marching bands and cheering crowds blaring steam whistles and blasting off rockets that streaked across the night sky with flashes of light and thunderous clamor.

Surrounding the McKinley home, the crowd shouted for a presidential appearance. The Major emerged upon his famous front porch, now much expanded as part of an extensive home refurbishment. "Fellow-citizens," he said, "I thank you for the very great compliment of this call on this inclement night. . . . Of the many gratifying reports from every part of the country, none has given me more genuine and sincere gratitude than those from my own city and my own county of Stark. And I . . . thank you once more for the warm and hearty indorsement which you have to-day given my public acts." The crowd emitted a hearty roar.

There was one Cantonite that evening, however, who wasn't so sure about this second-term thing. "I did not want him to run a second time," Ida told an interviewer. "I thought he had done enough for the country . . . and when his term expires he will come home and we will settle down quietly and he will belong to me." Of course, she viewed her husband as a president for the ages. She once took umbrage when someone compared him to Daniel Webster because she thought that gave unwarranted stature to Webster. She considered him to be "the only honest man" ever to serve as president. But she was tired of sharing him with the country. She told a friend named Gertje Hamlin, as Hamlin later recalled, that "the American people did not deserve such a President as her husband." She felt he did all the work for the party. When a Republican senator complained about the need for incessant travels to his home state, she snapped, "Well, I'm glad to hear that. . . . My husband has carried the Republican Party for twenty years. Now I'd like to see somebody else do something."

She also feared assassination—and not without reason. "I am becoming somewhat anxious about your safety," the president's cousin William Osborne wrote him in early 1898. It was a time when anarchists had adopted assassination as a deadly means of political expression. In the fall of 1898 an anarchist named Luigi Lucheni stabbed to death Empress Elisabeth of Austria, and in summer 1900 an Italian American named Gaetano Bresci, from Paterson, New Jersey, killed King Umberto of Italy. The latter episode rattled Secret Service officials, who had received earlier reports of an anarchist cell in Paterson. A few months earlier a young assassin attempted to kill the Prince of Wales as he sat in a train in Brussels. Worst of all, in October newspapers reported official suspicions that two or three Italians had been dispatched from Europe to kill McKinley in Canton. The city's mayor augmented his police force and urged officers to "watch for two Italians, who will probably be accompanied by a tall man who dresses like and passes for an old soldier." Cortelyou sought to discredit the reports of a plot, but one newspaper said McKinley "was induced to refrain from taking his usual drive to-day." Generally, though, the president brushed aside warnings about his safety with fatalistic indifference and insisted on making himself accessible to the country's citizenry.

All this weighed heavily upon Ida. In July 1899, hearing from Cortelyou that matters on his desk presented no urgency, the president gladly hurried back to his wife because, as he told Cortelyou, she tended to fall apart when he was gone too long. Earlier he had been away beyond the anticipated time and returned to find her "crying like a child" with fears about his safety. McKinley attributed her behavior to "temporary weakness," but it wasn't isolated. In fact in the spring of 1899, after nearly two and a half years of relatively good health, Ida's condition turned decidedly worse—and with disturbing new symptoms. In addition to her physical deterioration, she now suffered from what Dawes called "extreme mental depression."

So severe was her neurosis that Ida's doctors urged her to relinquish her first lady duties and essentially retire. The president reportedly favored the idea, but Ida wouldn't hear of it, despite her difficulties in fulfilling the role. A presidential trip to the Midwest was postponed because of her depression. Then, during the trip, she often was unable to accompany her husband to events and speeches. Distraught, McKinley turned to a new doctor, Presley Marion Rixey, chief of the navy's Bureau of Medicine and Surgery. When the president asked Rixey to "take medical charge" of Ida, he dedicated himself to her comfort and health. "No physician had ever shown such commitment to improving Ida's condition," wrote her biographer Carl Sferrazza Anthony. Rixey gave her constant attention and eased the way for McKinley to pursue his presidential duties with less anxiety—and perhaps less guilt—than he had felt before. The doctor's ministrations to Ida's needs also encouraged the president to undertake speaking tours with her, whereas otherwise he may have avoided such outings out of deference to her infirmities.

But her symptoms continued, including her tendency toward peevishness. On the Midwest trip, when the president invited three volunteer committee members to ride in his carriage to an event, Ida raised such a fuss about not being with her husband that the three had to be disinvited. In Chicago, when the president and his wife were scheduled to attend separate events at around the same time, she refused to fulfill her obligation unless McKinley accompanied her. He cut short his own appearance and rushed to her event in order to mollify her.

She also seemed to be suffering from memory lapses. At a Missouri reception for a women's group, the delegation leader recalled a previous Kansas City meeting when she had met Ida. The first lady cut her off. "I was never there," she said.

"Oh, don't you remember?" replied the woman, intending to jog Ida's memory. "It was the time the city gave a big banquet—"

"I tell you we were never there," snapped Ida. "If my husband went, I went with him. But he never went."

Rixey became increasingly concerned about the erratic nature of Ida's health. It "fluttered constantly and rarely for a few hours remained stationary," he later wrote. By late 1899 she seemed in a downward spiral. "She does not improve at all of late," recorded Cortelyou, "and her friends are beginning to worry over her condition." Rixey brought in a noted neurologist named Frederick Peterson, a specialist in women's psychiatric health, who examined Ida at length and issued a stunning opinion: that her anticonvulsive bromides (including small amounts of potassium, sodium, and sometimes ammonium salts), administered to her over many years, could have contributed to her deterioration. He called her condition "bromism" and said that, while such bromides could control seizures temporarily if administered carefully over short periods, extended usage could damage the central nervous system, diminishing the brain's ability to control sensory and motor skills and curbing sensitivity to outside stimuli. Symptoms of bromism, said Peterson, corresponded with many of Ida's complaints and behavioral traits, including memory loss, social aggression, and depression.

McKinley's reaction to this diagnosis, after years of administering to Ida the bromides recommended by the absentee doctor in New York, Joseph Bishop, was never recorded, if indeed he was informed at all. But Ida's condition improved a bit during 1900, and the president continued to cater to her most trivial wishes in his effort to mitigate her anxieties. White House official William Crook recalled, "When she wanted a pen, or a needle, or a book to read, all she did was to say so and the President would start at once, hurrying after it as quickly as possible." He considered McKinley's devotion "beautiful" but also "pathetic when we knew the weight of affairs he was carrying."

The president never evinced any frustration or self-pity over his personal fate and seemed as much in love with his wife as ever. As Christmas approached in 1899, he shared with Cortelyou his desire to give her a special gift—consistent, though, with her admonition that he not make any expensive holiday purchases. He finally settled on a "beautiful vase" and a bejeweled picture frame, into which he placed a photo of little Katie, the daughter whose death had haunted the mother for nearly twenty-five years. Reporting to Cortelyou later that Ida was "delighted" with the gift, the president, in a contemplative mood, suggested people "should feel *holy*" during the Christmas season and embrace a "spirit of self-sacrifice." Certainly the president demonstrated his own generosity of spirit in his ongoing devotion to Ida. And yet now, nearly a year later, it was clear that one thing he never intended to sacrifice was his political ambition. During the time when he struggled with the reelection decision, Ida's condition deteriorated to its lowest point amid signs that her second-term anxieties may have contributed to her physical and emotional decline. Yet he pressed forward to fulfill his highest political aspirations.

RETURNING TO WASHINGTON from Canton after the election, the president moved quickly to maintain governmental continuity into his second term. At a November 9 Cabinet meeting, he led a three-hour discussion that yielded an ongoing commitment to his China policy in the form of maintenance of the legation guard pending a final settlement, but a transfer of some troops back to the Philippines so General MacArthur could step up his anti-insurgency efforts. Cabinet members seized upon the expectation that, with McKinley remaining in the White House, the Philippine insurgency would begin to wither more quickly.

McKinley opened the next Cabinet meeting with prepared remarks expressing his appreciation for his officials' devotion and performance and saying the election victory belonged to them as much as to him. He dispensed with any request for en masse resignations, often done in such circumstances to ease the way for personnel changes. He didn't want any personnel changes, he said; he had complete confidence in his team. His aim now was to move quickly on the most pressing challenge at hand: establishing an agenda for the coming year and crafting a strategy for executing it.

In late November the president traveled to Philadelphia for a speech before the Union League, one of the country's oldest and most influential Republican institutions. As he had with the Cabinet, he deflected credit for the election victory away from himself and toward others, including Democrats who crossed over to the GOP, silver Republicans who had abandoned the party in 1896 but "have now returned and are home again to stay," and laborers and farmers who "rejected the false doctrine of class distinction." He staked out his mandate by saying his electoral victory had established an "unquestioned indorsement of the gold standard, industrial independence, broader markets, commercial expansion, reciprocal trade, the open door in China, the inviolability of public faith, the independence and authority of the judiciary, and peace and beneficent government under American sovereignty in the Philippines"—in other words, his entire governing philosophy and record.

It was significant, though, that the president's mandate, as he described it, focused almost entirely on goals already accomplished and priorities currently established. The gold standard: in place; industrial independence: an aim of the 1897 Dingley tariff; broader markets and commercial expansion: realities; reciprocal trade: several agreements negotiated (though without any Senate ratification thus far); the open door in China: established; inviolability of public faith: uncontested; judicial independence: a constitutional principle not in dispute; beneficent American sovereignty over the Philippines: current policy, though fraught with difficulty. Left largely unsaid in this passage was what new initiatives the president planned in the forthcoming term.

McKinley's first four years had been among the most momentous presidential terms in a generation. He settled the currency issue, which for years had driven a nasty wedge through the nation. He mustered a consensus behind his tariff philosophy even as he sought to unite the country behind refinements in that philosophy. He kicked Spain out of the Caribbean and rendered that strategic body of water an American lake. He initiated the "triumphant march of imperialism," as William Osborne had called it, through the stunning military victory over Spain. He pushed America far out into the Pacific and into Asia by acquiring Hawaii and the Philippines and establishing the Chinese open door policy. He fashioned a concept of noncolonial imperialism that would guide his nation for a century or more. He developed a powerful special diplomatic relationship with Great Britain. He fostered a weighty expansion in American overseas trade. And he gave the country a level of economic growth and prosperity unseen since the early 1890s.

Few of these accomplishments had come about through any visionary thinking. As his career demonstrated, he lacked the kind of imagination that produced bold visions of national or global dimension. But he possessed that rare managerial acumen and a capacity to see how discrete events and actions, as they unfolded, could be meshed into coherent policies. Thus had he calibrated his decision making in ways that nudged events toward the outcomes he had wanted—and which ultimately defined his first-term presidency. The big question now was whether he would, or could, formulate a coherent plan for the next four years or would instead react to events and challenges as they emerged.

The first clues came with the president's Fourth Annual Message, sent to Congress on December 3. Not surprisingly he touted his record in creating prosperity, generating federal budget surpluses, and expanding foreign trade. And he put forth elaborate narratives of major episodes of the past year, including the China conflict, the Philippine challenge, the isthmian canal, the reciprocity initiative, and the effort to transition Cuba to a state of independence. Addressing Congress, he called for a standing army of 100,000 troops, ongoing support for his Philippine policy, action on monopolistic trusts, a shipping-subsidy bill, and a reduction in internal taxes imposed to fund the Spanish-American War.

It wasn't a particularly impressive agenda, though a lingering question was how much political capital he would expend in behalf of the most far-reaching of these initiatives, the emotion-laden trust issue. Even if McKinley got everything he wanted from the second session of the Fifty-sixth Congress, which began on December 3, it didn't add up to much in terms of new initiatives. On the other hand, the president and his government had their hands full with matters that had been pushed onto the national agenda during the first term.

One was the state of the army. Wartime legislation had authorized the president to maintain an army of 100,000 troops, with 65,000 regulars and 35,000 volunteers. But that legislation was set to expire in July 1901, just a few months away, and then the army's authorized manpower would drop to 27,000, roughly the prewar level. Already enlistments were expiring, and it would take time to replace the outgoing troops serving under the old legislation. With hostilities in the Philippines and global challenges such as the Boxer episode in China, not to mention ongoing troop commitments in Cuba and Puerto Rico, McKinley wanted to maintain a 100,000-troop army well into the future. But such a standing army, absent major military imperatives, was unprecedented, and anti-imperialists had pressed hard on the issue during the campaign. "If you are in favor of a large standing army," said Bryan, "you will vote the Republican ticket; if you are opposed to a large standing army, to make subjects of a people of whom we cannot make citizens, you will vote the Democratic ticket." Bryan's plan: get out of the Philippines and return to a small peacetime army.

But McKinley now argued that the American people had spoken

on the Philippine issue and favored his policy. In his view, that implied support also for the large army. When the army bill came up in the House, however, opposition arose not only from Democrats but from some maverick Republicans, most notably the independent-minded Massachusetts representative Samuel McCall, a lawyer and former journalist who had given the administration fits on the Puerto Rican tariff issue. Now he argued that the country didn't need such a large standing army and couldn't afford one in any event. Moreover he opposed giving any president that much power. Better, he said, to adopt a Philippine policy like the U.S. Cuban policy—giving the islands a promise of independence on a clear timetable: "Let us tell them that we will aid them for one year or for five if need be in setting up a Government of their own symbolized by their own flag." Democrats cheered McCall's speech.

Though the measure passed the House largely along party lines, it ran into a groundswell of opposition from a group of Senate Republicans who aligned with Democrats to put the bill in jeopardy. At one point the measure appeared so beleaguered, with the army's reduction-in-force deadline looming, that McKinley threatened to call a special session of Congress if the army bill didn't pass in the current session. Under adjournment pressure, lawmakers hastily hammered out a temporary 100,000-troop authorization, divided as the president wished between regulars and volunteers. There would be no special session.

The army legislation included two other major elements: a measure giving the president full "military, civil, and judicial powers necessary to govern the Philippine Islands" (the Spooner amendment) and a measure by Connecticut's senator Orville Platt declaring that the United States would not leave Cuba until the new government there accepted certain conditions favorable to the United States.

The Platt measure threatened to blow up into a full-scale conflict with Cuban leaders engaged in the delicate task of writing a government charter at a constitutional convention in Havana. Convention delegates naturally didn't like having conditions imposed upon their efforts. The requirements included a proscription against any treaties or engagements with other powers that could threaten Cuban independence; a recognized right of the United States to intervene in Cuban affairs if necessary to preserve the island's independence and societal stability; a requirement that the new Cuban government refrain from assuming debt that could swamp its public finances; and a U.S. prerogative to acquire land for naval stations.

For many Cuban officials laboring to form an independent government and create a new society, this didn't seem like full independence at all. But it wasn't difficult to see why the McKinley administration and Congress considered the Platt conditions necessary to hedge against island chaos that could threaten stability in the Caribbean and undermine U.S. regional interests. America certainly couldn't ignore the reality that, if Cuba fell into hostile hands, not only would U.S. Caribbean hegemony be at risk but so would the country's isthmian canal project. The imperatives that Washington sought to impose on the emergent Cuban government, constituting a kind of big brother status, represented another foray into the realm of noncolonial imperialism, applying military, economic, and diplomatic power to get other nations to bend to U.S. desires. Ultimately it was about America's perceived imperative of protecting and maintaining its sphere of influence, codified in the 1823 Monroe Doctrine and expanded with the Spanish-American War.

The Cuban constitutional convention delegates served notice on February 16 that they would not allow the United States to establish a naval station on the island. Some days later, when the final document was ready for signature, one top delegate, Salvador Cisneros Betancourt, refused to sign because a copy was to be sent to U.S. military governor Leonard Wood for U.S. review. "Cuba is now independent, and I can see no reason for sending this Constitution to the United States for acceptance," declared Cisneros. As colleagues sought to persuade him to sign, one reminded him, "We are all Cubans, Senor."

"Yes," shot back Cisneros, "when the time comes to fight the Americans, we will fight them together."

The last thing McKinley needed was another war in Cuba like the one he was fighting on Luzon. Even if he were inclined to compromise on the matter, which he wasn't, the Platt Amendment precluded any U.S. military withdrawal from Cuba before the congressional conditions were met. Still, McKinley wanted to avoid any incendiary action that could generate civic anger in Cuba. On March 2, Navy Secretary Long called Cortelyou to say three U.S. warships were scheduled to stop in Havana on a routine visit. Should they proceed? McKinley responded, "Tell the Secretary of the Navy not to have the battleships stop at Havana now."

On February 27, the constitutional delegates in Havana approved a series of amendments that generally acceded to most of the U.S. conditions, while adding a call for reciprocal trade relations between the two countries. But they pointedly refused to accept any U.S. naval base. The convention president told General Wood on March 1 that the delegates might simply dissolve rather than accept such an assault on Cuban sovereignty. But when the U.S. Congress adjourned on March 3, the Platt Amendment stood as the law of the land and couldn't be changed until Congress reconvened the following December. "Briefly stated," explained the *Washington Post*, "the expectation in Washington is that the Cuban convention will accept the conditions laid down by the American Congress eventually, if not in the immediate future, and that the Cuban delegates will be given to understand that the action of Congress was final." With Congress recessed and the Cuban commission continuing its work, the issue was kicked over till later in the year.

The Philippine issue remained very much alive, however. Days after the election, MacArthur issued a status report that "cannot be called highly encouraging," as the *New York Times* described it. MacArthur said that Aguinaldo's bedraggled army had been replaced by guerrilla units; that this had compelled the distribution of American forces to numerous locations over a wide territory; that the antiguerrilla effort remained difficult and dangerous; and that he hadn't made substantial progress in suppressing the guerrillas, though their losses had been heavy. Clearly the military operation was far from over. The news wasn't all bad, however. On December 3, some 2,200 rebels relinquished their arms and swore allegiance to the United States. The first political party to organize under the American flag recognized U.S. sovereignty over the islands. By mid-January, several insurgent leaders had surrendered, and Taft, from his perch as head of McKinley's Philippine Commission, filed a favorable report. "Conditions rapidly improving," he told

Root. "Rifles, officers, privates are being captured or surrendered daily in considerable numbers in North and South Luzon. Same condition in Panay, where more than 35,000 have taken oath of allegiance. Insurgent forces completely scattered."

It was a paradox. Taft was right that things were improving. And the *Times's* interpretation of the MacArthur report also was right: the guerrilla forces, while beleaguered, were far from being wiped out. There were too many of them, fueled by too much civic passion. The Taft Commission sought to explain this paradox in a voluminous January report revising its earlier prediction that the insurgency would collapse within sixty days of the U.S. election. Clearly, said the commissioners, it would take longer. It also would take a greater U.S. effort at encouraging the native population through civic enlightenment, for the vast majority of Filipinos lacked sufficient education to participate meaningfully in any transition to self-government. But most of them wanted peace "and are entirely willing to accept the establishment of a Government under the supremacy of the United States," particularly with the "policy of conciliation" that was emerging under Taft's leadership. A lingering problem, though, was insurgency intimidation. Anyone suspected of collaborating with the Americans was "immediately marked for assassination." It was, said the commission, "a Mafia on a very large scale."

Reading this, McKinley concluded he needed, along with MacArthur's military operation, a greater civilian effort to foster education, self-government, and economic progress. On January 25 he sent the commission's report to the Senate, along with accompanying documents and a cover memorandum from Root recommending creation of a civil government capable of fostering "peaceful industrial progress" on the islands. Endorsing the concept, the president asked for legislation "under which the government of the islands may have authority to assist in their peaceful industrial development in the directions indicated by the Secretary of War." When Congress passed the army bill, with the Spooner Amendment, he had the authority he needed. The key person in his plan was Judge Taft, whose managerial talents and compassionate approach to civilian rule, the president believed, would accelerate the pacification program. The imperious MacArthur didn't like the compassionate approach any more than he liked sharing power with a civilian authority. But Taft enjoyed the president's confidence and support, and his philosophy ultimately prevailed.

IN EARLY DECEMBER, a month after the election, the Isthmian Canal Commission, known as the Walker Commission, issued a 17,000-word report stating its unanimous opinion that "the most practicable and feasible route for an isthmian canal, under the control, management, and ownership of the United States, is that known as the Nicaragua route." The price tag was huge, $200,540,000, far more than any previous estimate and some $50 million more than the proposed Panama route, which already had been partially excavated by the failed French project. But those advantages were offset, declared the commission, by shorter distances between major ports via the Nicaragua route and also the fact that the Nicaraguans were far more willing to grant U.S. ownership over the canal and contiguous land than Colombia would grant within its Panama territory. If the canal was to be owned and controlled by America, Nicaragua represented the best bet.

Release of the Walker Commission report removed one obstacle thwarting U.S. lawmakers from moving forward on the project via the highly popular Hepburn bill. The other was disposition of the Hay-Pauncefote Treaty designed to terminate the old Clayton-Bulwer requirement that the United States and Britain cooperate in the construction and maintenance of any isthmian canal and that neither could exclusively control it. Hay still chafed at the action of the Senate Foreign Relations Committee and his friend Henry Cabot Lodge in stripping out language that prohibited the United States from fortifying the canal and keeping out hostile ships in wartime. But Hay and McKinley reluctantly had conceded defeat on that matter.

The two Senate floor amendments continued to rankle the two men, however. The amendments declared that the new treaty superseded the old Clayton-Bulwer language and the United States would proceed without inviting involvement from other nations. Even senators who favored such language, reported the *New York Times*, conceded that it would render the Hay-Pauncefote negotiations "absurd, void, and of no effect." Hay was aghast. "If Great Britain should now reject the

Treaty," he wrote to his ambassador in London, Joseph Choate, "the general opinion of mankind should justify her in it." Even before the Senate's treaty mutilation, he complained to McKinley about the congressional frenzy for action on the Hepburn bill while Clayton-Bulwer remained in effect—"that is, to repudiate and violate a solemn obligation to a friendly power when that power is perfectly ready and willing to release us from it."

On December 20, the Senate ratified the treaty, with the three amendments, by a vote of 55 to 18. In receiving it, McKinley felt his only appropriate action was to send it to Britain via Ambassador Pauncefote for London's reaction. The *Times* of London viewed that approach as cowardly, as "shifting a dangerous responsibility on the British Government": "If the Hay-Pauncefote treaty is not adopted in a form acceptable to us, we shall stand quietly upon our indubitable rights under the Clayton-Bulwer treaty, rights which cannot be affected by any action the American Senate may choose to take." The British government agreed. Without rejecting the revised treaty outright, it simply allowed the time for ratification to expire, thus keeping in place the old Clayton-Bulwer language. But when Ambassador Choate asked Lord Salisbury about prospects for reopening the negotiations with an aim of somehow reconciling the differences, the prime minister readily agreed. He signaled his flexibility by stipulating only that all nations must be charged equally for canal access.

Thus did Secretary Hay get a second chance to apply his famous diplomatic skills to the even greater challenge of picking up the pieces from the initial failed effort. But now the autocratic and fastidious secretary would have to apply those skills to bringing those pesky senators along as he proceeded with his delicate negotiations with the British.

AS CONGRESS RUSHED to adjournment, the president won a small victory with passage of legislation to reduce, by some $40 million, internal taxes enacted in 1898 to pay for the war. These were largely excise taxes on tobacco, cigars, cigarettes, and beer, as well as on various financial transactions. But now the war was over and, as Secretary Gage reported on November 17, the government's budget surplus for the current fiscal year would be $80 million. McKinley was thwarted, however, in his effort to get a controversial measure to provide federal subsidies to the shipping industry. A favorite hobbyhorse of Hanna, the bill died in the late-session legislative crunch.

AT 9:29 P.M. on January 22, Queen Victoria died after sixty-three years on the throne. The president sent a wreath that a *Times* of London correspondent said "would have compelled the attention of the least observant" because of its "magnificence and superb beauty." The *Times* writer added that the wreath, combined with a "lovely cross" presented by Ambassador Choate on behalf of the American people, represented "one of the most beautiful sights that even the Queen's funeral produced, for, here at the very side of the spot reserved for the coffin, were the tributes of those who represent the nation to which we are more nearly allied by origin, language, and sentiment than any other in the wide world."

Such sentiments from a writer representing a newspaper that never hesitated to criticize U.S. policy in the most rancorous terms whenever it diverged from British interests, signified an important development of the new century: the maturing relationship between the two Anglo-Saxon nations, one an established global power, the other a frisky newcomer on the international scene. In circumstances that easily could have produced competitive anxieties and frictions, the two nations were moving into a period of growing amity and collaboration. Britain indeed welcomed America's global emergence, as Lord Salisbury made clear at a London banquet a day after McKinley's reelection triumph. Rising from his seat next to Ambassador Choate, the prime minister said, "We believe that the cause which has won is the cause of civilization and commercial honor. . . . Therefore we claim that we have as much right to rejoice in what has taken place as the distinguished gentleman who sits at my side." Then, recognizing he had transgressed protocol in commenting on the internal politics of another nation, he expressed the hope that the ambassador would forgive him "for expressing the supreme satisfaction with which all of us have heard of what has recently taken place in the United States."

But of course not all Americans embraced His Lordship's view. Senator Pettigrew, with his usual satiric jocularity, proposed an amendment to the army appropriations bill to read, "And the title of the President shall hereafter be the President of the so-called republic of the United States and the Emperor of the Islands of the Sea." Marion Butler of North Carolina asked with similar droll intent if the coming inaugural ceremonies would reflect this imperial stature.

"Yes," replied Pettigrew, "everything will be conducted with due pomp."

Chandler of Vermont, more of a McKinley man than his two colleagues, suggested that the three of them "should not feel concerned about such matters" inasmuch as all three had lost their seats in the November elections, while the subject of their badinage had scored a definitive political victory.

Buffalo

"HIS WILL, NOT OURS, BE DONE"

A s McKinley's second inauguration approached, Washington swelled with people and patriotic enthusiasm. By March 2, two days before the celebration, brass bands and military units began converging upon the festively decorated capital, filling the air with martial sounds and marching commands. The growing crowds discovered that restaurant meals now cost up to 50 percent more than usual, and window seats along the parade route fetched $15 to $20 "for the cheaper windows, and out of all reason for the higher-priced and most comfortable places of observation," reported the *New York Times*. Volunteers with the Committee on Public Comfort, readily identifiable by their red badges, met arrivals at train stations and guided them to rooming houses. A bed in a sleeping hall could be obtained for fifty cents a night, room and board for $1.50.

"Is 50 cents a night the cheapest?" one wayworn traveler asked a Public Comfort volunteer, noting that twenty-five cents was a reasonable expectation in his hometown.

"That's about the cheapest on the list," was the reply.

Some 12,000 people sought tickets to the swearing-in ceremony, although the area nearest the temporary platform at the east front of the Capitol contained only 7,000 seats. But the surrounding grounds offered abundant standing room, and the day's festivities also would feature the parade, fireworks, hotel receptions, and general civic excitement. Theodore Roosevelt stepped off the *Congressional Limited* at Pennsylvania Station at 4:50 the afternoon of March 2 and in a rare display of restraint avoided attention. He quietly ushered his family into waiting carriages for the short drive to the home of his sister, Anna Cowles, on N Street. He paid a brief courtesy call to the president on March 3.

When inauguration day arrived, the president rose a bit earlier than usual and discovered opaque skies threatening rain. He ate breakfast with family and guests, then signed a large stack of bills that Congress had enacted during its late-session crunch. The congressional escort committee arrived just before eleven to take the president to the Capitol. On the ceremonial drive, the president sat with his closest political ally, Mark Hanna, designated escort committee chairman. As cheers greeted the presidential carriage along the procession route, Hanna maintained a stoic demeanor, refusing to acknowledge any crowd adulation that he thought belonged exclusively to the president. Prominently positioned ahead of the presidential carriage were Civil War veterans, drawing enthusiastic applause, followed by the soldiers of the Ohio National Guard's Cavalry Troop A, atop their famous coal-black mounts and resplendent in flashy uniforms.

Ida, "magnificently costumed," was escorted to her Senate gallery seat by White House military aides Henry Corbin and Theodore Bingham. The president, knowing her comfort was well in hand, showed less anxiety than when he entered the Capitol Building in similar circumstances four years earlier.

As usual, the vice president was sworn in at a smaller Senate chamber ceremony attended by governmental dignitaries and diplomats. Roosevelt's speech, appropriately brief, reflected his vision of a nation with growing responsibilities attending its growing power. "We belong to a young nation," said the New Yorker, "already of giant strength, yet whose political strength is but a forecast of the power that is to come." Echoing McKinley, he emphasized America's responsibility to humanity. "Accordingly as we do well or ill, so shall mankind in the future be raised or cast down."

Then those within the Senate chamber filed outside to the platform, filled with "high-hatted, long-coated, cane-carrying" gentlemen and their well-dressed ladies. As he walked down the steps to his designated chair, the president could see an ocean of citizenry, 40,000 strong, stretching into the distance, some spectators perched in trees and upon rooftops. Then came the rains, an "unwelcome freight of moisture," stirring many to abandon their open-air platform seats and rush to shelter under the Capitol's eaves and in doorways. A sea of umbrellas emerged, providing only partial shelter under such an onslaught. It was in this chaos of discomfort that William McKinley took the oath of office and delivered his second inaugural address. The rains ceased shortly thereafter.

Not surprisingly, the president compared the state of the Union on this celebratory day with the national circumstance four years earlier—anxiety over the currency and credit then, but little foreboding now; Treasury receipts inadequate then, but robust today; a deep and lingering economic depression then, but solid prosperity now; ever expanding foreign trade, with more to come under his reciprocity program. "The national verdict of 1896 has for the most part been executed," he said, adding a stout defense of his policies, particularly in foreign relations. "The American people, entrenched in freedom at home, take their love for it with them wherever they go, and they reject . . . the doctrine that we lose our own liberties by securing the enduring foundations of liberty to others."

As for his most troublesome challenge, the president declared, "Our country should not be deceived. We are not waging war against the inhabitants of the Philippine Islands. A portion of them are making war against the United States." He insisted that "the greater part of the inhabitants" accepted American sovereignty and welcomed the protections of the American democratic tradition.

Following the ceremonies at the Capitol, the president and his wife held a White House luncheon for presidential houseguests, members of the Cabinet and their wives, congressional bigwigs, Mr. and Mrs. Roosevelt, and various Roosevelt relatives. Ida managed to hold up through the Capitol ceremonies and the luncheon but bowed to the Major's suggestion that she forgo the parade and rest up for the evening ball. The president occupied the enclosed and heated reviewing stand for nearly three hours as regular troops, militias, and civic organizations marched by in a heady display of American might, music, and patriotism.

The evening ball, held once again in the gigantic redbrick Pension Building, with its huge internal columns and impressive friezes reminiscent of ancient Greece and Rome, was described by the *Washington Post* as "a gathering of well-bred people who showed in their bearing and demeanor that they were accustomed to the graces of good society." Ida wore a white satin gown, "high in the neck and long in the sleeves," with an overlay of lace and an immense train. She and the president arrived just before ten and spent most of the evening in a private reception and dining area that accommodated about sixty presidential guests. The party enjoyed a meal that included lobster Newburg, mushrooms, croquettes exquises, French peas, salmon à la Bayadère, boned capon, tongue in jelly, ham, mayonnaise of chicken à la Reine, and assorted rolls. "It is noticeable," observed the *Post*, "that no wines appear, the only beverage being Apollinaris water."

THE PRESIDENT DEVOTED March 5 to meeting with Washington visitors, prominent and otherwise, who came for the inauguration, including many of the dozen or so Republican governors in town, other GOP notables, members of Ohio's Troop A that acted as his inauguration escort, schoolchildren from Chicago, and various GOP clubs. Ohio's Governor Nash called, along with the Columbus Glee Club, which sang a number of tunes in the East Room, much to Ida's delight. Meanwhile Republicans basked in the glow of public support. The *Baltimore American* called the president's contrast of 1897 with 1901 "particularly striking" and a key to understanding "why the people again intrusted him with power." Whitelaw Reid's *Tribune* said the president spoke "with more than ordinary authority," given his electoral mandate. But the anti-McKinley *Philadelphia Record* described the speech as "smooth and dulcet to the point of oiliness" and decried the president's habitual "benevolent optimism."

In late March McKinley received stunning news from Manila. General Frederick Funston, a slightly built Kansan with a zest for combat and a streak of cruelty toward the enemy, had captured the elusive

Emilio Aguinaldo in his remote hiding place at Palanan, in the northeast section of Luzon. Though the American anti-insurgency campaign had constricted the rebel leader's range of maneuver and destroyed his main-force military capacity, the wily guerrilla fighter had remained a nettlesome adversary and influential personification of the Philippine independence movement. Funston, learning of Aguinaldo's location from a captured courier, crafted a plan to seize the rebel leader in a clever ruse. He organized an expedition consisting of four U.S. officers, the captured messenger, four ex-insurgent officers, and seventy-eight friendly, Tagalog-speaking Filipino scouts from the town of Macabebe. The Filipinos, disguised as guerrilla fighters with U.S. soldiers as prisoners, managed to march through the countryside for three days without alerting natives. Once near Aguinaldo's compound, they discarded the disguises and attacked, killing two insurgents, capturing eighteen rifles and a thousand rounds of ammunition, and taking Aguinaldo into custody. "No casualties our side," MacArthur reported to Washington.

MacArthur had told the mission leader in approving his plan, "Funston, this is a desperate undertaking. I fear I shall never see you again." But its success became a turning point in the war. With many of Aguinaldo's generals already having surrendered and his troops fading back into their regular lives, it seemed now merely a matter of time before the United States would snuff out the insurgency. More significant, it gave McKinley impetus to accelerate his plan to bring the Philippines under the civilian jurisdiction of Will Taft. Even MacArthur, who guarded his authority with tiger-like ferocity, understood the need for the transfer. With Taft and Secretary Root he helped fashion a plan for a July hand-off, when MacArthur would relinquish his command to General Adna Chaffee, a through-the-ranks officer with extensive combat experience in the Civil War, the Indian campaigns, and most recently in China. Root emphasized to Chaffee that the army would be subordinate to Taft except where lingering military threats necessitated otherwise.

Even Aguinaldo understood that the game was up. In April he issued a statement that constituted his own surrender: "The complete termination of hostilities and a lasting peace are not only desirable but absolutely essential to the welfare of the Philippines." Employing his hallmark eloquence, he added, "Enough of blood, enough of tears and desolation. . . . By acknowledging and accepting the sovereignty of the United States throughout the entire archipelago, as I now do without any reservation whatsoever, I believe that I am serving thee, my beloved country." Thus did this much-misunderstood man give up the dream that had animated him throughout his brief life. Murat Halstead, the Cincinnati editor and McKinley intimate, warned the president to be wary of the captured warrior. Use him for pacification, advised Halstead. "But he will promise all things to all and betray all. . . . It is in his blood and brain to do it again." Mark Twain, on the other hand, likened Aguinaldo's ambition to that of "Washington, Tell, Joan of Arc, the Boers, and certain other persons whose names are written large in honorable history." Neither caricature captured the complexity or contradictions of this driven, vain, eloquent, paranoid, ambitious, at times brutal patriot of Philippine independence. In any event, with his military vocation destroyed, he settled into a life of resigned quietude under U.S. confinement.

IN SPRING THE president formulated plans for an extensive cross-country trip, with the purpose of pushing the twin initiatives that were his second-term priorities: reining in the trusts and pushing his trade-reciprocity program. The idea was to traverse the continent through the South and Southwest to Los Angeles, then up the West Coast to the Northwest and back across the nation's northern tier. It would culminate at the Pan-American Exposition in Buffalo, where the president would crystallize the reciprocity views he intended to tout during the journey. The tour would begin in late April and extend to mid-June—six weeks on the rails with an entourage of forty-three, including friends, family, servants, reporters, Cabinet secretaries, and other officials.

The American people seemed to embrace the president's views on both the trusts and reciprocity, but that sentiment hadn't congealed sufficiently within the electorate to force old-line congressional Republicans to alter their traditional attitudes. On the trusts, the president was still pondering how he would accomplish two fundamental goals:

getting the GOP establishment to embrace the antitrust imperative by galvanizing popular sentiment throughout the country and getting around the Supreme Court's ruling that federal jurisdiction applied only to interstate matters. In the meantime he would concentrate on reciprocity, which he intended to push most aggressively during the tour.

His immediate problem was that Senate Republicans, even including Hanna, had thwarted his efforts to get ratification of the seven trade treaties negotiated by special envoy John Kasson. The weary Kasson, resigning his post in April, told the president he was "unwilling to proceed with a work which promised to be without result." But McKinley refused to give up and told Kasson he intended to "seize all occasions that would present themselves to defend the policy of commercial reciprocity and change opinion on it." He went further in a conversation with a visiting French statesman, Jules Siegfried, telling him that he no longer was an "ultra-protectionist," as the *New York Times* called him, and believed the country had reached a time when the necessity to secure global markets had obviated any rationale for heavy protection.

But congressional Republicans chafed at the president's newfound sentiments. Senate Finance Committee chairman Nelson Aldrich planned a Washington trip during the congressional recess to implore the president to abandon such heterodox nonsense. "It is asserted," reported the *New York Times*, "that under Mr. Adrich's direction a propaganda is to be begun and maintained for a continuance of all the tariff duties of the Dingley law without any modification whatever."

The president's tour was designed as his own propaganda counter-campaign, with a particularly relentless drumbeat during the return leg and in Buffalo, as well as in his San Francisco remarks at the launch and dedication of the country's latest battleship, the *Ohio*. His intention was to exploit popular sentiment for America's military and economic push into the world by bundling the issue of lower tariffs into the broader vision of American expansionism. He also eyed policy imperatives attending Cuba's ultimate independence—when propriety and sound thinking, in his view, dictated a generous trade policy toward the island. Already the president had assured visiting commissioners from the Havana constitutional convention that America wouldn't saddle the new nation with onerous tariffs. But that of course would put him at odds with domestic sugar and tobacco interests—further necessitating that he invigorate free-trade thinking within the electorate.

The presidential train that left Washington on April 29 was a virtual "home on the rails," with a drawing-room car featuring fresh roses delivered regularly; a dining car with the finest in silver, linens, china, and stemware; a parlor car (cigars, wine); and a presidential bedroom with a marble-tiled bathtub. Ida, as always, looked forward to the stimulation of travel, as well as the popular adulation and the opportunity to spend abundant time with the Major. Attending her would be her maid, Clara, and her favorite niece, Mary Barber, as well as the attentive and well-tempered Dr. Rixey, who had won McKinley's respect by curbing Dr. Bishop's bromides and bringing about a noticeable improvement in Ida's condition. So appreciative was the president that he called the doctor into the Cabinet Room to pose a question: "Do you know that you have been taking care of us for over a year and you have not asked me to do anything for you? Isn't there something that you want that I can do for you?"

"Mr. President," replied the doctor, "when I came on duty here I made up my mind not to add to your cares but to do all in my power to make them as light as possible."

"I am sure that there is something I can do for you," insisted the president, "and it will do me good to do it."

Rixey finally revealed that his nephew wished to join the Marine Corps but was languishing on a wait list. The president promptly assigned the next vacancy to the young man, "subject to examination." Thus did the president get satisfaction in providing a small recompense to the doctor while indulging his own enjoyment of patronage prerogatives.

As the presidential train moved south, Cortelyou sought to maintain for Ida a modest schedule of events mixed with plenty of rest time. But he went too far when he sent regrets, on his own, to a group of Memphis women planning a luncheon for the first lady. When Ida heard about it, she insisted on going and impressed the local ladies with her sprightly demeanor. The president added luster by showing up unannounced and displaying his characteristic graciousness. In New Orleans, Ida experienced a bout of depression, but it passed quickly, and she felt particularly strong and lighthearted as the train passed through Texas.

At El Paso she developed a bone felon on her index finger that became inflamed and quite painful. Rixey lanced it, but the swelling remained, and she also developed a serious case of dysentery. Despite the pain and discomfort, she insisted on fulfilling the social and political schedule in Los Angeles, which further sapped her strength. On the trip north, near Santa Cruz, Rixey lanced the finger again, to little effect. The dysentery also resisted treatment. Despite her pain and the onset of fever, Ida gamely accompanied the president to speaking engagements in the vicinity of Del Monte, where the party had planned to stop for a weekend respite. By Sunday she was in an almost complete state of collapse. So alarmed was the president that he abandoned his personal stricture against travel on the Sabbath and rushed Ida to San Francisco, where she was placed in the spacious Lafayette Park home of industrialist Henry T. Scott, head of the iron works company that had constructed the battleship *Ohio*. Trained nurses were summoned, along with consulting physicians, as Ida descended into a state of semiconsciousness.

Statements to the press, crafted by Rixey and delivered by Cortelyou, dissembled about the true state of Ida's health, which was far more serious than reported. Leaks to the press from members of the entourage gave a truer picture of the situation while hinting at the official misrepresentation. The president's concern turned to distraught fear when the consulting physician Joseph Hirshfelder told him on Monday that Ida wasn't responding to treatment. She was too weak to speak and languished in long periods of sleep interrupted by restlessness. When doctors counseled against his leaving the house for a brief speech nearby for fear that Ida might die in the meantime, the president became "completely unnerved."

On Wednesday McKinley canceled the remainder of the tour, and the next morning the *Washington Star* reported, "Mrs. McKinley is slowly dying. . . . There is not one chance in a hundred that she will recover and be taken back to Washington alive." In desperation, doctors applied heart stimulants, then injected a saline solution into her bloodstream. The dual treatment slowly took effect. By noon on Thursday, Ida was stirring. She opened her eyes and said, "I am tired of the food the doctors have been giving me!" She wanted "a piece of chicken and a cup of coffee."

The worst was over, though Ida certainly wasn't out of danger. While never straying from the Scott home for long, the president fulfilled a smattering of speaking commitments in the San Francisco area. On May 25 the presidential entourage was back on the train for the five-day trip to Washington, with well-wishing Americans lining the tracks at various points along the way. Although the trip proved burdensome for the infirm first lady and she seemed to relapse a bit upon arriving in Washington, doctors managed to keep her stable and effect a slow but steady revival. By June 20, some five weeks after she fell ill, Ida was able to see visitors and five days later managed to leave her bed and descend the stairs for lunch with her husband. From there her recuperation gained momentum.

BACK IN WASHINGTON, with Ida improving, McKinley threw himself into his duties, with a primary aim of closing out a number of lingering matters. But first he faced the need to deal with a messy situation that emerged when New York senator Chauncey Depew and Ohio congressman Charles Grosvenor, both intensely loyal to the president, unwisely touted prospects for a McKinley third term. On June 9, a Sunday, the president drafted a statement renouncing any such ambition. When he showed it to Hay the next afternoon, the secretary questioned the wisdom or necessity of such a renunciation so early in the current term. Secretary Long, however, when shown the statement during an afternoon drive with the president, heartily embraced it. That evening the president summoned the remaining Cabinet members to inform them of his plan.

Later that night, McKinley told Cortelyou that he harbored a lingering concern that the statement might appear "strange or ridiculous," given that there was no evidence of any popular groundswell favoring a third term. But he concluded it was "better, from every point of view," to settle the matter. Accordingly the next morning he issued the statement:

I regret that the suggestion of a third term has been made. I doubt whether I am called upon to give it notice. But there are now questions of the gravest importance before the Administration and the country, and their just consideration should not be prejudiced in the public mind by even the suspicion of the thought of a third term. . . . I will say now, once for all, expressing a long settled conviction that I not only am not and will not be a candidate for a third term, but would not accept a nomination for it if it were tendered me. My only ambition is to serve through my second term to the acceptance of my countrymen, whose generous confidence I so deeply appreciate, and then, with them, to do my duty in the ranks of private citizenship.

That ended all speculation, allowing the president to direct his attention to lingering matters, some of which seemed close to resolution.

One was the Cuban constitutional convention, which could demolish U.S.-Cuban relations if it refused to accept the Platt Amendment outlining conditions for U.S. withdrawal from the island, including U.S. acquisition of a naval base there. On May 28 the convention voted 15 to 14 to accept the amendment—but pointedly interpreted it in such a way as to rebuff elements of Platt's language. McKinley hurriedly called an emergency meeting at the White House with top administration officials and key lawmakers to determine if the United States could accept the Cuban action. The answer was no. After Platt drafted a letter, at the administration's request, clarifying his intent, the Cuban convention accepted his amendment as written. Thus did the saga of U.S. direct involvement in Cuba move toward its conclusion.

In Beijing, one of Hay's favorite diplomats, William Rockhill, worked with Edwin Conger on final details of the settlement with China's Qing government. The big issue among the representatives of the foreign powers—or "the Ministers," as they were known—was the level of indemnity to be imposed and the punishments to be demanded for leaders of the rebellion. In May, McKinley objected to the "exorbitant" indemnity demands pushed by other powers and also the call for death sentences for too many people based on too little evidence. By June the negotiators agreed on a reasonable indemnity formula, and McKinley's more lenient attitude on death sentences also prevailed.

The powers promptly evacuated their troops from Beijing, leaving only legation guards. In a July 18 letter to the president, Hay reported that the Ministers had acquired "indubitable evidence that a considerable proportion of these officials for whom the other powers were demanding a death sentence are entirely innocent of any wrong doing." If the United States had not halted the pursuit of vengeance, continued Hay, "the blood of innocent men would have now been on the hands of the Christian world."

In late May, as McKinley's presidential train sped across the country toward Washington, the U.S. Supreme Court delivered to the administration a hallmark legal victory. At issue was the status of Puerto Rico in relation to the United States following the peace treaty with Spain. More specifically, did the Constitution follow the flag there, thus conferring U.S. citizenship upon Puerto Ricans now under American jurisdiction? Or could Congress govern the new possession as a domestic territory, conferring what rights it saw fit under its own constitutional authority? McKinley embraced the latter position, while plaintiffs in the case argued that the tariff that had generated so much political conflict in 1900 was unconstitutional because Puerto Rico belonged to the United States in the same way the various states did. The Court agreed with the president. As Senator Foraker explained to reporters, Puerto Rico was not a part of the United States but rather a U.S. territory: "It is, therefore, within the constitutional power of Congress to so legislate with respect to it, including the imposition of tariff duties, as it may see fit." Foraker called the decision "a complete vindication of the position held by the Republican Party with respect to the power of Congress to legislate for Porto Rico and the Philippines." Indeed a contrary ruling would have halted America's global expansionism in its tracks and severely attenuated McKinley's entire overseas policy.

That other big element of the McKinley foreign policy, the isthmian canal, also came closer to fruition in the summer, when Britain signaled it was prepared to accept revised Hay-Pauncefote language that Hay had crafted in the spring. Hay had learned his lesson well. This time he didn't ignore key senators but rather worked closely with them on fine calibrations in the language, designed to mollify the British while also capturing a two-thirds Senate vote. The new language formally abro-

gated the Clayton-Bulwer Treaty, excised the offending Davis amendment while retaining a U.S. right to defend the canal during wartime,
eliminated Britain as a guarantor of canal neutrality, and conferred that
guarantor status solely upon the United States. The new language better served U.S. interests than Hay had thought possible during the first
go-round, but Britain's Boer War difficulties and concerns about a rising Germany contributed to London's flexibility.

When Ambassador Pauncefote signaled his government's recep-
tivity to the Hay handiwork, the secretary rushed to Canton in late
August to get the president's final approval. McKinley gave his hearty
assent, and Hay returned to Washington confident that this remaining obstacle to the canal project would be speedily disposed of. "I am
profoundly gratified at the way the matter now presents itself," the
secretary wrote to Ambassador Choate at London. The *London Daily
News* agreed: "A wise diplomacy would make the Nicaragua question
a golden opportunity for strengthening the ties between the British
people and their kinsfolk in the United States. The special nature of
America's own claim to predominance cannot be overlooked."

The president meanwhile quietly formulated plans to press ahead
on the trusts and reciprocity. The trust question gained force almost
by the week as new corporate combinations emerged or were hinted
at during the summer of 1901. In June the *New York Times* offered
this headline: "United States Steel Corporation Said to be Moving
to Control Its Four Big Competitors." Salt producers were developing plans for the first global trust. In July, the *Washington Post*
reported plans for a consolidation of the bituminous coal industry.
Wall Street share prices swooned briefly at the news that industrialists J. P. Morgan, James J. Hill, and E. H. Harriman were collaborating on plans to control the Northern Pacific Railroad. During his
Canton vacation that summer, McKinley watched these developments with mounting doggedness. "This trust question has got to
be taken up in earnest, and soon," he told Cortelyou. The president
asked his secretary for "a collection of data on the subject of trusts,"
recalled Cortelyou later, adding, "I never saw him more determined
on anything than on this."

While the president seemed resolved to lead his party and the nation into new territory on the trust issue, reciprocity came first. He had been thwarted, of course, in his plan to hammer away on his revised trade-policy views during his Western-tour return, but he would renew that priority campaign with his Buffalo address, coming up in early September. As he crafted the speech during the Canton respite, he seemed particularly relaxed about the state of the nation and his political standing. Charles and Caro Dawes arrived on August 12 to find Ida in particularly good health and the president "in his best mood." The day unfolded with carriage rides, a relaxed luncheon with Mary Barber and Dr. Rixey in attendance, "a jolly evening" with pleasant dinner conversation, afterdinner euchre, and Cortelyou playing lively tunes on his "Caecilian," a kind of piano. The president and Ida, noted Dawes, were "passing a quiet and pleasant summer. The callers are many but are not so pestiferous as when they came bent on getting office."

AS THE PRESIDENT enjoyed his summer interlude at Canton, Leon Czolgosz made plans to travel to Buffalo to kill him during his visit to the Pan-American Exposition. Born in Detroit twenty-eight years before, the son of Polish immigrants, he was educated in Detroit public schools, then traveled to Cleveland to pursue factory jobs. He hung out in a working-class saloon called Dryers on Third Avenue and Tod, ate his meals there, slept intermittently in his chair, read the newspapers, kept to himself. Slight of build and sallow of skin, with a bland face accentuated by pale blue eyes, he struck others at the pub as bitter and jittery. "I never had much luck at anything," he would recall, "and this preyed upon me. It made me morose and envious." He fell in with a group of anarchists.

Then he went to hear a lecture by Emma Goldman, the well-known and brutal-minded writer, thinker, and lecturer, dubbed by Murat Halstead "the queen of anarchy," advocate of the assassination of all rulers everywhere. "She set me on fire," recalled Czolgosz. "Miss Goldman's words went right through me, and when I left the lecture I had made up my mind that I would have to do something heroic for the cause I loved."

In Buffalo he studied the exposition grounds carefully and pursued his deadly purpose methodically. He attended the president's big trade speech at the Esplanade and sought to get close to him, but a big police guard stepped in front of him, cooling his ardor for the kill. Afterward he moved toward the president's departing carriage but was herded back with the rest of the crowd. He showed up at subsequent presidential events but couldn't get close enough. He finally concluded his best chance would be the president's reception at four the next afternoon. He went to the Temple of Music well before McKinley's scheduled arrival and positioned himself near where the president would stand for the receiving line. When McKinley entered through a side door, he pushed toward the front. In his right hand he held a .32 caliber pistol, wrapped in a handkerchief and pressed against his chest to simulate an injury.

When a small girl, led by her father, was presented to the president, McKinley leaned down and shook her hand, then guided her on to the right, smiling and waving after her. Next in line was a short, dark, mustachioed man who displayed a look of possible menace. Though he drew the attention of Secret Service agents, he passed by the president cordially. Then came Czolgosz. As the president thoughtfully reached for his unbandaged left hand, the anarchist pressed his revolver against the president's chest and fired twice. At the first shot, McKinley gasped and moved back upon his toes, positioning himself to take the second round to the abdomen, just below the navel. He reeled backward, into the arms of Detective John Geary.

"Am I shot?" asked the president in a steady voice.

Geary unbuttoned McKinley's vest, saw blood, and replied, "I fear you are, Mr. President."

Immediately Secret Service Agent S. R. Ireland thrust Czolgosz to the ground as a black waiter named James Parker leaped upon him. Secret Service Agent Albert Gallagher grabbed the assassin's hand, ripped away the handkerchief, and seized the revolver. Within seconds he was being jostled by law enforcement officials bent on subduing him completely. Meanwhile Cortelyou, Geary, and exposition chairman John Milburn helped the president to a chair. White-faced and stoic, he displayed no anxiety for himself but serious concern for Ida.

"My wife," said the president to his secretary as Cortelyou leaned over him, "—be careful, Cortelyou, how you tell her—oh, be careful."

Then he saw Czolgosz bleeding upon the floor, beset by angry law enforcement officials, with an angry crowd gathering around. He raised his right hand, red with his own blood, and placed it upon Cortelyou's shoulder. "Let no one hurt him," he gasped as guards dragged the malefactor away.

When the president arrived by ambulance at the exposition emergency hospital at eighteen minutes after four, he was in shock but seemingly calm. Attendants, placing him on a table and removing his clothing, discovered a bullet that barely had penetrated his body at the rib cage. But hurriedly summoned Buffalo surgeons, led by Dr. Matthew Mann, discovered the entry wound of the second bullet, with no exit wound. Seeing a potentially ominous situation, they initiated exploratory surgery that quickly revealed the bullet had pierced both the front and rear walls of the stomach, lodging somewhere in tissue beyond the pancreas, which had not been penetrated. They cleaned up the area surrounding the stomach lacerations and sutured the two stomach holes to prevent escaped gastric or intestinal contents from getting into the peritoneal cavity. The president readily consented to the surgery and whispered the Lord's Prayer as he received the ether.

The surgeons failed to locate the bullet but concluded it hadn't done any further damage to vital organs and abandoned the search in fear that the probing was more dangerous than the bullet. Besides, the president's pulse was weakening, and sunlight soon would be fading. They removed any blood clots, closed the flesh wound, washed it with hydrogen dioxide, and applied dressing. The operation, lasting about an hour and a half, was completed by 6:50 p.m. Within half an hour, the president was taken by ambulance to the Milburn house, where he would recuperate in an upstairs bedroom under the care of a cadre of doctors and attendants.

When Rixey informed the first lady of what had happened, she didn't respond as he had expected. Though she fainted briefly, she soon became self-possessed and assertive.

"Tell me all," she demanded, "keep nothing from me! I will be brave—yes, I will be brave for his sake!" She insisted that the president be brought to her, which already was in progress. That night she wrote in her diary, "Went to visit Niagra [*sic*] Falls this morning. My Dearest was received in a public hall on our return, when he was shot by a . . ." It seems she may have been stumped by the word *anarchist*. She confided to her diary just how shattered she felt.

Friends and associates rushed to Buffalo when they heard the news, including Cabinet officials, Vice President Roosevelt, the ever-loyal Hanna, and the president's favorite protégé, Dawes. The nation settled into a stunned news vigil in recognition that, while doctors said the president's condition was "somewhat encouraging," the danger of peritonitis, blood poisoning, and sepsis remained high.

By the second day, Sunday, September 8, doctors still detected no indication of peritonitis, and the president was resting comfortably. Reports to the press were uplifting. By the fourth day "his mind was clear and cheerful." On Wednesday, he was given beef broth, the first food taken by the damaged stomach, and on Thursday he added a few bites of toast to the broth. He seemed to be out of serious danger. What the doctors could not know, though, was that Czolgosz's second bullet, while it bypassed the pancreas, had nonetheless caused a kind of ballistic trauma to the organ through heat and vibration. McKinley's pancreas began to shut down, leaking dangerous enzymes that caused severe inflammation in the area between the stomach and pancreas. This was a dangerous but unseen development. On Friday it became evident that something was wrong, as the president's condition suddenly worsened. At 2:50 a.m. his doctors wrote in their log, "The President's condition is very serious, and gives rise to the gravest apprehension." That afternoon he revived from a stupor and said to his doctors, "It is useless, gentlemen. I think I ought to have prayer." He asked for Ida, and Cortelyou led her into the room. As family and friends stepped back against the walls, she took his hand and leaned down to kiss him.

"Good-bye—good-bye, all," said the president in a weak voice. Moments later he whispered in Ida's ear, "It is God's way. His will, not ours, be done."

"I want to go with you," she whispered back.

"We are all going, my dear," he said, then slipped back into a stupor as he whispered the words to a favorite hymn, "Nearer, My God, to Thee." Ida was escorted back to her room for the rest that her doctors deemed imperative to her fragile health. She later returned for a brief visit as the president faded into oblivion.

He died at 2:15 on the morning of September 14, 1901.

Where He Stands

A s the nation mourned the loss of its leader and grappled with its third presidential murder in just thirty-six years, young Theodore Roosevelt took hold of the government with unbridled self-assurance. He promptly issued what one biographer called "a solemn pledge" to be "one in purpose" with his predecessor. "In this hour of deep and terrible bereavement," said the new president, "I wish to state that I shall continue absolutely unbroken the policy of President McKinley for the peace, prosperity, and the honor of the country." Within twenty-four hours, however, Roosevelt demonstrated that his pledge wasn't so solemnly given after all. It seems fears of a stock market swoon contributed more to his expression than any sincere regard for the dead leader or the mandate he had extracted from voters. "I am President," he declared to a group of reporters on his first day in the White House, "and shall act in every word and deed precisely as if I and not McKinley had been the candidate for whom the electors cast the vote for President."

This was a remarkable public utterance issued as the nation struggled with its loss and as the fallen president's body was en route to Washington, thence to Canton for a final memorial service and burial. As his open casket lay in state in the Capitol Rotunda, 100,000 people filed by after standing for hours in the rain. In Canton, another 100,000 passed by as McKinley lay in the Stark County Courthouse. He was buried at the West Lawn Cemetery in an elaborate tomb paid for in part by donations from more than a million schoolchildren. Other memorials emerged throughout Ohio, including in front of the State-house Building, at his birthplace town of Niles, and elsewhere—most of them funded by citizen donations. Twenty Ohio schools bear his name. Writer Kevin Phillips has suggested this outpouring of commemoration indicates Ohioans believed McKinley would loom large in history.

It wasn't to be. Generally lost to the country's historical conscious-ness, McKinley today languishes at a middling level in the periodic academic polls on presidential standing that are viewed collectively as history's judgment on White House performance. In seven of the most prominent of these polls conducted since Arthur M. Schlesinger Sr. pioneered the concept in 1948, the Ohioan is ranked variously at 15th, 16th, and 14th. Only in one, a 1982 *Chicago Tribune* survey, does he reach as high as 11th. Often he ranks below such undistinguished or failed presidents as Chester Arthur, Martin Van Buren, Rutherford Hayes, Grover Cleveland, and John Quincy Adams.

And yet it can't be denied that momentous events occurred during the McKinley presidency or that the country moved into a bold new era of economic growth and global stature—and also of Republican political dominance that lasted for most of the next thirty-six years. Indeed few chief executives have presided over so many pivotal de-velopments in so many civic areas: the definitive embrace of the gold standard, annexation of Hawaii, destruction of the Spanish Empire and consolidation of America's Caribbean sphere of influence, the res-cue of Cuba, the push into the Pacific with the Philippines and Guam, the open door policy in China, the doctrine of noncolonial imperial-ism, the emergence of reciprocity as a trade policy synthesis (called "fair trade" in later decades), growing momentum toward an isthmian canal, the forging of a "special relationship" with Great Britain. Many of these accomplishments would become essential elements of what publisher Henry R. Luce later famously called the "American Cen-tury." As Alan J. Lichtman and Ken DeCell write, McKinley enjoyed "one of the more successful incumbencies in American history." They add, however, that he found himself "benefitting in part from circumstances beyond his control."

And there's the rub. Those inclined to discount or denigrate the McKinley presidency often acknowledge that, yes, big events occurred during his White House years, but little of it can be attributable to him. He was merely the passive occupant of the executive mansion as the country pursued its destiny. Thus do we return to the mystery of William McKinley, the persistent question of how this man, so lacking in dramatic flair or charismatic force, managed to bring about so much significant national change—or whether in fact he brought it about at all. The McKinley detractors argue that he didn't. He was simply there.

A case in point is a book called *First Great Triumph* by the late Warren Zimmermann, profiling five Americans who "made their country a world power": Roosevelt, Hay, Lodge, Mahan, and Root. It's an excellent work on its own terms, but Zimmermann falters in explaining why he left out other powerful figures of the era, including McKinley. Historians differ, wrote Zimmermann, on whether McKinley "consciously masterminded America's war with Spain or was dragged unwillingly into it." He says the evidence "seems to support the latter interpretation, thus reducing McKinley's importance as a force behind imperialism."

This represents a false dichotomy. The president certainly didn't set out to maneuver America into war with Spain, as Polk did with Mexico or Lincoln did with the errant South (or as Wilson later would do during the Great War in Europe). But neither was he dragged unwillingly into it. A close reading of the historical record shows that he consciously took a series of steps that rendered war increasingly inevitable. He abandoned Cleveland's tilt toward Spain and away from the Cuban insurgents, audaciously placed difficult demands on the Iberian nation, refused to bend when Madrid pushed back, and ultimately embraced the position that Spain must leave the Caribbean, either peacefully or under military pressure. In the meantime he prepared his navy for war. True, he refused to recognize the insurgent movement as Cuba's government, and his final actions leading to war could be described as ragged, but he understood fully where his actions were leading.

Further, it is difficult to argue that McKinley lacked importance as a force behind imperialism when he personally initiated Hawaiian annexation (after Cleveland had essentially killed it), took Puerto Rico and Guam, absorbed the Philippines, and applied all the military means at his disposal—in the face of serious domestic opposition—to pacify the Philippine archipelago as a U.S. possession.

Most of those close to McKinley, including at least four of the five men portrayed by Zimmermann, never questioned whose hand was on the tiller of the national destiny or whose judgment would prevail as government officials grappled with the challenge of molding unfolding events into American greatness. It was McKinley. As Root said, he always got his way, in part because he never cared who got the credit. With his inevitable commissions, constant overtures to members of Congress, openness toward the press, widespread public advocacy of his policies, leadership of indirection, and affable persona, he always managed to shepherd the flock where he wanted it to go. He seldom failed to get all the apples from the orchard.

And consider those who set themselves against him. While studiously avoiding overt political showdowns, McKinley always seemed to outmaneuver his rivals. Thomas Reed quit the field in frustration when he saw he couldn't beat a man he had underestimated for years. Ben Foraker struggled manfully to gain dominance over the Ohio Republican Party so he could parlay it into a presidential run—and saw his rival get to the White House ahead of him and then gain total sway over the state party. Eastern bosses Tom Platt and Matthew Quay, full of wiles and resolve, were outmaneuvered in 1896. William Jennings Bryan rode to national prominence on the silver issue—and discovered four years later that McKinley had shorn it of its sting.

These things didn't just happen. They happened because McKinley wanted them to happen and because he possessed the political tools to nudge events where he wanted them to go. There were missteps along the way, of course, and occasionally his tactics of patience and attrition were overwhelmed by political forces that had gained greater magnitude than he had anticipated. One could argue that his methodical ways and roundabout decision making robbed him of opportunities to have an even bigger impact on the history of his time than he actually did.

Certainly on the issue that helped define Roosevelt's subsequent presidency, the trusts, he held back and sought to clear the decks on trade reciprocity before plunging into that thicket. But the record shows that he perceived clearly the necessity for reining in the monopolistic combinations that were grafting themselves upon industrial America with such menace. McKinley emphasized particularly to Dawes, who never ceased pounding away on the issue in conversations with the president, that this was something he would address—in his usual methodical, step-by-step way and when he perceived the time to be right.

But that methodical, step-by-step style contributed to the durability of the McKinley mystery through the decades. We have come to regard true presidential greatness as consisting of boldness, brashness, directness, and flamboyance. It is difficult for many in the television era to see anything approaching greatness in a man lacking in those traits, a man whose leadership was more of the hidden hand variety.

But the biggest contributor to McKinley's standing in history was Theodore Roosevelt, whose leadership style could not have been further removed from that of McKinley. Impetuous, voluble, amusing, grandiose, prone to marking his territory with political defiance, Roosevelt stirred the imagination of the American people as McKinley never had. To the Major's solidity, safety, and caution, the Rough Rider offered a mind that moved "by flashes or whims or sudden impulses," as William Allen White described it. He took the American people on a political roller-coaster ride, and to many it was thrilling.

But the New Yorker was never one to share the credit with others. His theatrical self-importance led even his children to acknowledge that he wanted to be "the bride at every wedding and the corpse at every funeral." It wasn't surprising that soon he was denigrating the man whose presidency he had extolled through thousands of miles of political campaigning on his way to national power. Years later, after his own White House tenure, when he set about to destroy the presidency of his chosen successor and erstwhile close friend, William Taft, he described Taft as "a flubdub with a streak of the second rate and the common in him." But he allowed as how he considered Taft "a better president than McKinley or Harrison."

That view was picked up by Roosevelt biographers inclined to view the New Yorker's piquant style as a requisite for presidential distinction. Thus did McKinley's reputation fade through the decades as the Roosevelt story, heightened to accommodate the man's sense of his own glory, dominated the country's view of that historical period.

It's interesting, though, that a different outlook has emerged from the research of the few McKinley biographers who have stepped forward since the late 1950s, when Margaret Leech published her splendid work, *In the Days of McKinley*. While implicitly acknowledging elements of the McKinley mystery, Leech pulled together the complexities of the time into a coherent picture of how this purposeful, deliberate, self-effacing politician moved men and events stealthily but effectively through tumultuous times. Since then subsequent works by Lewis L. Gould and H. Wayne Morgan have further illuminated the mystery. Gould calls McKinley "the first modern president" based on his embrace of the tools of executive power, his agenda-setting resolve, his foreign policy expansionism, and his success in positioning the Republican Party for ongoing political dominance. Morgan, noting that McKinley lacked the "grand manner" that would have highlighted his philosophy of government and politics, offers a poignant insight. "His reliance on manipulation and conciliation," writes the biographer, "required unwritten understandings and personal agreements that kept him from history's limelight, for he could not advertise his methods without destroying them."

Just so. And that reality likely will continue to influence the nation's view of William McKinley, a man of prudence, character, compassion, competence, patriotism, and subtle force who presided over momentous times in American history but whose true contributions to his country no doubt will remain a point of contention.

— ACKNOWLEDGMENTS —

T he impetus for this book came from Jonathan Karp, head of editorial and publishing activities at Simon & Schuster, who deflected me from a different historical exploration and kept me focused on presidents and the presidency after two previous books in that realm. Given the richness of the McKinley story—and the American story of that era—I begin this expression of acknowledgment and appreciation by noting Jonathan's contribution and thanking him for it.

I was blessed on this project, as with three previous ones with Simon & Schuster, in having the penetrating editorial guidance and extensive historical judgment of the well-known and highly regarded Alice Mayhew, whose contribution to my literary pursuits has been incalculable. It would be impossible to give adequate expression to my gratitude. Stuart Roberts, assistant editor under Alice, performed invaluable service in keeping all aspects of the project on track. The vaunted Simon & Schuster copyediting team provided its usual meticulous ministrations.

As always I express appreciation to my agent, Philippa ("Flip") Brophy of Sterling Lord Literistic Inc., who secured the contract for this work with her usual smooth efficiency and guided me through the change of topics suggested by Jonathan Karp.

I extend my gratitude to three valued friends who read the manuscript and provided good counsel on words, facts, and interpretations. David Ignatius of the *Washington Post*, whose own ten books testify to his credentials for the task, perceived how elements of the story meshed into what became one of its underlying themes—the mystery of William McKinley. David Brewster, whose Seattle civic and journalistic career has inspired many in and around that city, was particularly adept in identifying unanswered questions and gaps in the narrative. And the late James M. Perry, longtime friend and once a colleague in the game of political reporting, brought an invaluable historical perspective, derived in part through his own sterling book on the five Civil War veterans who became president.

Dr. John Ryan of Seattle, medical historian and former surgeon, generously provided expertise on the medical activities that ensued after William McKinley was shot in Buffalo.

Research assistance came in many forms from many quarters, starting with Kaity Bergert of Canton, Ohio, who performed research duties at McKinley's hometown. I thank also Mark Holland and his colleagues at the McKinley Presidential Library and Museum at Canton; the good folks at the Documents Room at the Library of Congress; and the helpful people at the Rutherford B. Hayes Presidential Center at Fremont, Ohio.

I was the beneficiary of the usual abundant encouragement and rah-rah spirit from the extended Merry family, including children Rob Merry, Johanna Derlega, and Stephanie Merry, along with their spouses, Kristin Merry, John Derlega, and Matt McFarland. Maisie, Elliott, Genevieve, and Colton contributed what they could, which mostly amounted to perspective on what's important in life.

Finally, a reiteration of previous expressions of appreciation and affection to Susan Pennington Merry, best friend through triumphs and tribulations, who read chapters (or submitted to having them read to her), offered advice, criticism, and occasional praise; relieved me of household duties; and generally buoyed my life through the project, as she has done in general for forty-eight years.

— BIBLIOGRAPHY —

BOOKS

Adams, Henry. *The Education of Henry Adams.* Boston: Houghton, Mifflin, 1974. (Originally published by the Massachusetts Historical Society, 1918.)

Allen, Garner Weld, ed. *Papers of John Davis Long 1897–1904.* Boston: Massachusetts Historical Society, 1939.

Anthony, Carl Sferrazza. *Ida McKinley: The Turn-of-the-Century First Lady through War, Assassination, and Secret Disability.* Kent, Ohio: Kent State University Press, 2013.

Armstrong, William. *Major McKinley: William McKinley and the Civil War.* Kent, Ohio: Kent State University Press, 2000.

Bacevich, Andrew J. *American Empire: The Realities and Consequences of U.S. Diplomacy.* Cambridge, Massachusetts: Harvard University Press, 2002.

Bailey, Thomas A. *A Diplomatic History of the American People.* New York: Appleton-Century-Crofts, 1958.

Beer, Thomas. *Hanna.* New York: Octagon Books, 1973.

Beisner, Robert L. *Twelve against Empire: The Anti-Imperialists 1898–1900.* New York: McGraw-Hill, 1968.

Belden, Henry S., III, ed. *Grand Tour of Ida Saxton McKinley and Sister Mary Saxton Barber 1869.* Canton, Ohio: Henry S. Belden III, 1985.

Beveridge, Albert J., III, and Susan Radomsky. *The Chronicle of Catherine Eddy Beveridge.* Lanham, Maryland: Hamilton Books, 2005.

Blow, Michael. *A Ship to Remember: The Maine and the Spanish-American War.* New York: Morrow, 1992.

Brands, H. W. *American Colossus: The Triumph of Capitalism, 1865–1900.* New York: Anchor, 2011.

————. *Bound to Empire: The United States and the Philippines.* New York: Oxford University Press, 1992.

————. *The Reckless Decade: America in the 1890s.* Chicago: University of Chicago Press, 2002.

————, ed. *The Selected Letters of Theodore Roosevelt.* New York: Cooper Square Press, 2001.

Brinkley, Alan, and David Dyer, eds. *The American Presidency*. Boston: Houghton Mifflin, 2004.

Bryan, William Jennings. *The First Battle: A Story of the Campaign*. Chicago: W. B. Conkey, 1896.

Buchanan, Patrick J. *The Great Betrayal: How American Sovereignty and Social Justice Are Being Sacrificed to the Gods of the Global Economy*. Boston: Little, Brown, 1998.

————. *A Republic, Not an Empire: Reclaiming America's Destiny*. Washington, D.C.: Regnery, 1999.

Burton, Theodore E. *John Sherman*. Boston: Houghton, Mifflin, 1906.

Byars, William Vincent. *An American Commoner: The Life and Times of Richard Parks Bland*. St. Louis: H. L. Conard, 1900.

Cayton, Andrew R. L. *Ohio: The History of a People*. Columbus: Ohio State University Press, 2002.

Cayton, Andrew R. L., and Stuart D. Hobbs, eds. *The Center of a Great Empire: The Ohio Country in the Early Republic*. Athens: Ohio University Press, 2005.

"Coe." *Canton's Great Tragedy: The Murder of George D. Saxton, Together with a History of the Arrest and Trial of Annie E. George, Charged with the Murder*. Wooster, Ohio: Press of Clapper Printing, 1899.

Coit, Margaret L. *Mr. Baruch: The Man, the Myth, the Eighty Years*. Boston: Houghton, Mifflin, 1957.

Correspondence Relating to the War with Spain and Conditions Growing Out of the Same . . . from April 15, 1898, to July 30, 1902. Official military correspondence, in two volumes. Washington, D.C.: Government Printing Office, 1902.

Cortissoz, Royal. *The Life of Whitelaw Reid*. Vol. 1: *Journalism—War—Politics*. London: Thornton Butterworth, 1921.

Cosmas, Graham A. *An Army for Empire: The United States Army in the Spanish-American War*. College Station: Texas A&M University Press, 1994.

Cowan, Geoffrey. *Let the People Rule: Theodore Roosevelt and the Birth of the Presidential Primary*. New York: Norton, 2016.

Croly, Herbert David. *Marcus Alonzo Hanna: His Life and Work*. New York: Macmillan, 1912.

Dalton, Kathleen. *Theodore Roosevelt: A Strenuous Life*. New York: Knopf, 2002.

Dawes, Charles Gates. *A Journal of the McKinley Years*. Edited by Bascom Nolly Timmons. Chicago: Lakeside Press, 1950.

DeConde, Alexander. *A History of American Foreign Policy*. Vol. 2: *Global Power (1900 to the Present)*. New York: Scribner's, 1978.

Depew, Chauncey Mitchell, and Murat Halstead. *Life and Distinguished Services of Hon. William McKinley and the Great Issues of 1896: Containing Also a Sketch of the Life of Garret A. Hobart*. Philadelphia: Edgewood, 1896.

Dewey, George. *Autobiography of George Dewey, Admiral of the Navy*. New York: Scribner's, 1913.

DiNunzio, Mario R., ed. *Theodore Roosevelt: An American Mind*. New York: St. Martin's Press, 1994.

Dobson, John. *Reticent Expansionism: The Foreign Policy of William McKinley*. Pittsburgh: Duquesne University Press, 1988.

Duncan, Bingham. *Whitelaw Reid: Journalist, Politician, Diplomat*. Athens: University of Georgia Press, 1975.

Faulkner, Harold Underwood. *American Economic History*. New York: Harper & Brothers, 1924.

———. *The Quest for Social Justice 1898–1914*. New York: Macmillan, 1931.

Ferrell, Robert H. *American Diplomacy: A History*. New York: Norton, 1959.

Foraker, Joseph Benson. *Notes of a Busy Life*. Vol. 1. Cincinnati: Stewart & Kidd, 1916.

———. *Notes of a Busy Life*. Vol. 2. Cincinnati: Stewart & Kidd, 1916.

Garraty, John A. *Henry Cabot Lodge: A Biography*. New York: Knopf, 1968.

Gold, David M. *Democracy in Session: A History of the Ohio General Assembly*. Athens: Ohio University Press, 2009.

Goodwin, Doris Kearns. *The Bully Pulpit: Theodore Roosevelt, William Howard Taft, and the Golden Age of Journalism*. New York: Simon & Schuster, 2013.

Gould, Lewis L. *The Presidency of William McKinley*. Lawrence: University Press of Kansas, 1980.

———. *The Spanish-American War and President McKinley*. Lawrence: University Press of Kansas, 1980.

Graff, Henry F. *Grover Cleveland*. New York: Times Books, 2002.

Grant, James. *Mr. Speaker! The Life and Times of Thomas B. Reed*. New York: Simon & Schuster, 2011.

Halstead, Murat. *Full Official History of the War with Spain*. New Haven, Connecticut: Butler & Alger, 1899.

———. *The Illustrious Life of William McKinley: Our Martyred President*. Published by Murat Halstead, 1901.

Harbaugh, William Henry. *Power and Responsibility: The Life and Times of Theodore Roosevelt*. New York: Farrar, Straus and Cudahy, 1961.

Heald, Edward T. *Brief History of Stark County, Ohio*. Canton, Ohio: Klingstedt Bros., 1963.

Healy, Laurin Hall, and Luis Kutner. *The Admiral*. Chicago: Ziff-Davis, 1944.

Horner, William T. *Ohio's Kingmaker: Mark Hanna, Man and Myth*. Athens: Ohio University Press, 2010.

Jones, Gregg. *Honor in the Dust: Theodore Roosevelt, War in the Philippines, and the Rise and Fall of America's Imperial Dream*. New York: New American Library, 2012.

Josephson, Matthew. *The Robber Barons: The Great American Capitalists 1861–1901*. New York: Harcourt, Brace, 1934.

Kaplan, Justin. *Lincoln Steffens: A Biography*. New York: Simon & Schuster, 1974.

Karnow, Stanley. *In Our Image: America's Empire in the Philippines*. New York: Random House, 1989.

Koenig, Louis W. *Bryan: A Political Biography of William Jennings Bryan*. New York: Putnam's, 1971.

Kohlsaat, Herman Henry. *From McKinley to Harding: Personal Recollections of Our Presidents*. New York: Scribner's, 1923.

Lachman, Charles. *A Secret Life: The Lies and Scandals of President Grover Cleveland*. New York: Skyhorse, 2012.

Leech, Margaret. *In the Days of McKinley*. New York: Harper & Brothers, 1959.

Lichtman, Allan J., and Ken DeCell. *The 13 Keys to the Presidency: Prediction without Polls*. Lanham, Maryland: Madison Books, 1990.

Long, John D. *America of Yesterday: As Reflected in the Journal of John Davis Long*. Edited by Lawrence Shaw Mayo. Boston: Atlantic Monthly Press, 1923.

Lukas, J. Anthony. *Big Trouble: A Murder in a Small Western Town Sets Off a Struggle for the Soul of America*. New York: Simon & Schuster, 1997.

MacDonald, Claude. *The Siege of the Peking Embassy, 1900*. (MacDonald's official report on the Boxer Rebellion.) London: Stationery Office, 2000.

Mahan, Alfred Thayer. *The Influence of Sea Power upon History 1660–1805*. New York: Gallery Books, 1980.

———. *Mahan on Naval Strategy: Selections from the Writings of Rear Admiral Alfred Thayer Mahan*. Edited by John B. Hattendorf. Annapolis, Maryland: Naval Institute Press, 1991.

May, Ernest R. *Imperial Democracy: The Emergence of America as a Great Power*. New York: Harcourt, Brace & World, 1961.

McCullough, David. *Mornings on Horseback*. New York: Simon & Schuster, 1981.

———. *The Path Between the Seas: The Creation of the Panama Canal 1870–1914*. New York: Touchstone, 1977.

McFarland, Philip. *Mark Twain and the Colonel: Samuel L. Clemens, Theodore Roosevelt, and the Arrival of a New Century*. Lanham, Maryland: Rowman & Littlefield, 2012.

McKinley, William. *Speeches and Addresses of William McKinley: From His Election to Congress to the Present Time*. New York: D. Appleton, 1893.

———. *Speeches and Addresses of William McKinley, from March 1, 1897 to May 30, 1900*. New York: Doubleday, 1900.

Robert W. Merry. *A Country of Vast Designs: James K. Polk, the Mexican War and the Conquest of the American Continent*. New York: Simon & Schuster, 2009.

———. *Sands of Empire: Missionary Zeal, American Foreign Policy, and the Hazards of Global Ambition*. New York: Simon & Schuster, 2005.

————. *Where They Stand: The American Presidents in the Eyes of Voters and Historians*. New York: Simon & Schuster, 2012.

Miller, Scott. *The President and the Assassin: McKinley, Terror, and Empire at the Dawn of the American Century*. New York: Random House, 2011.

Miller, Stuart Creighton. *"Benevolent Assimilation": The American Conquest of the Philippines, 1899–1903*. New Haven, Connecticut: Yale University Press, 1982.

Moore, John L., Jon P. Preimesberger, and David R. Tarr. *Congressional Quarterly's Guide to U.S. Elections*. 2 vols. Washington, D.C.: CQ Press, 2001.

Morgan, H. Wayne. *William McKinley and His America*. Kent, Ohio: Kent State University Press, 2003.

Morgan, William Michael. *Pacific Gibraltar: U.S.-Japanese Rivalry over the Annexation of Hawai'i, 1885–1898*. Annapolis, Maryland: Naval Institute Press, 2011.

Morris, Edmund. *The Rise of Theodore Roosevelt*. New York: Coward, McCann & Geoghegan, 1979.

————. *Theodore Rex*. New York: Random House, 2001.

Mott, T. Bentley. *Myron T. Herrick: Friend of France*. Garden City, New York: Doubleday, Doran, 1929.

Mowat, R. B. *The Life of Lord Pauncefote: The First Ambassador to the United States*. Boston: Houghton Mifflin, 1929.

Musicant, Ivan. *Empire by Default: The Spanish-American War and the Dawn of the American Century*. New York: Holt, 1998.

Nasaw, David. *The Chief: The Life of William Randolph Hearst*. Boston: Houghton Mifflin, 2000.

Nelson, Scott Reynolds. *A Nation of Deadbeats: An Uncommon History of America's Financial Disasters*. New York: Vantage, 2013.

Nevins, Allan. *Grover Cleveland: A Study in Courage*. Vol. 1. Norwalk, Connecticut: Easton Press, 1932.

————. *Grover Cleveland: A Study in Courage*. Vol. 2. Norwalk, Connecticut: Easton Press, 1932.

Nugent, Walter. *The Tolerant Populists: Kansas Populism and Nativism*. Chicago: University of Chicago Press, 1963.

Offner, John L. *An Unwanted War: The Diplomacy of the United States and Spain over Cuba, 1895–1898*. Chapel Hill: University of North Carolina Press, 1992.

Olcott, Charles Sumner. *The Life of William McKinley*. Vol. 1. Boston: Houghton Mifflin, 1916.

————. *The Life of William McKinley*. Vol. 2. Boston: Houghton Mifflin, 1916.

O'Toole, Patricia. *The Five of Hearts: An Intimate Portrait of Henry Adams and His Friends 1880–1918*. New York: Clarkson Potter, 1990.

Penrose, Charles. *George B. Cortelyou (1862–1940): Briefest Biography of a Great American*. New York: Newcomen Society, 1955.

Perez, Louis A. *The War of 1898: The United States and Cuba in History and Historiography*. Chapel Hill: University of North Carolina Press, 1998.

Perry, James M. *Touched with Fire: Five Presidents and the Civil War Battles That Made Them*. New York: Public Affairs, 2003.

Phillips, Kevin. *William McKinley*. New York: Times Books, 2003.

Porter, Robert P. *Life of William McKinley: Soldier, Lawyer, Statesman*. Cleveland, Ohio: N. G. Hamilton, 1896.

Powers, Ron. *Mark Twain: A Life*. New York: Free Press, 2005.

Preston, Diana. *The Boxer Rebellion: The Dramatic Story of China's War on Foreigners That Shook the World in the Summer of 1900*. New York: Berkley, 1999.

Puleston, W. D. *Mahan: The Life and Work of Captain Alfred Thayer Mahan, U.S.N.* New Haven, Connecticut: Yale University Press, 1939.

Ratcliffe, Donald J. *Party Spirit in a Frontier Republic: Democratic Politics in Ohio 1793–1821*. Columbus: Ohio State University Press, 1998.

Reid, Whitelaw. *Making Peace with Spain: The Diary of Whitelaw Reid September–December, 1898*. Edited by H. Wayne Morgan. Austin: University of Texas Press, 1965.

———. *Problems of Expansion—As Considered in Papers and Addresses*. New York: Century, 1900.

Renehan, Edward J., Jr. *The Lion's Pride: Theodore Roosevelt and His Family in Peace and War*. New York: Oxford University Press, 1998.

Rixey, Presley Marion, and William C. Braisted. *The Life Story of Presley Marion Rixey, Surgeon General, U.S. Navy 1902–1910: Biography and Autobiography*. Strasburg, Virginia: Shenandoah Publishing House, 1930.

Rove, Karl. *The Triumph of William McKinley: Why the Election of 1896 Still Matters*. New York: Simon & Schuster, 2015.

Schlesinger, Arthur Meier. *The Rise of the City, 1878–1898*. New York: Macmillan, 1933.

Sears, Lorenzo. *John Hay: Author and Statesman*. New York: Dodd, Mead, 1915.

Silbey, David J. *The Boxer Rebellion and the Great Game in China*. New York: Hill and Wang, 2012.

———. *A War of Frontier and Empire: The Philippine-American War, 1899–1902*. New York: Hill & Wang, 2007.

Siler, Julia Flynn. *Lost Kingdom: Hawaii's Last Queen, the Sugar Kings, and America's First Imperial Adventure*. New York: Atlantic Monthly Press, 2012.

Spector, Ronald. *Admiral of the New Empire: The Life and Career of George Dewey*. Columbia: University of South Carolina Press, 1988.

Steffens, Lincoln: *The Autobiography of Lincoln Steffens*. New York: Harcourt, Brace, 1931.

Sternlicht, Sanford. *McKinley's Bulldog: The Battleship Oregon*. Chicago: Nelson-Hall, 1977.

Stevenson, Elizabeth. *Henry Adams: A Biography*. New York: Macmillan, 1956.

Swanberg, W. A. *Pulitzer*. New York: Scribner's, 1967.

Taliaferro, John. *All the Great Prizes: The Life of John Hay, from Lincoln to Roosevelt*. New York: Simon & Schuster, 2013.

Tarbell, Ida Minerva. *The Tariff in Our Times*. New York: Macmillan, 1911.

Thayer, William Roscoe. *The Life and Letters of John Hay*. 2 vols. Boston: Houghton, Mifflin, 1908.

Thomas, Evan. *The War Lovers: Roosevelt, Lodge, Hearst, and the Rush to Empire, 1898*. New York: Little, Brown, 2010.

Timmons, Bascom N. *Portrait of an American: Charles G. Dawes*. New York: Henry Holt, 1953.

Trask, David F. *The War with Spain in 1898*. Lincoln: University of Nebraska Press, 1981.

Treese, Joel D., ed. *Biographical Directory of the American Congress*. Alexandria, Virginia: CQ Staff Directories, 1997.

Trefousse, Hans L. *Rutherford B. Hayes*. New York: Times Books, 2002.

Tuchman, Barbara W. *The Proud Tower: A Portrait of the World before the War 1890–1914*. New York: Macmillan, 1966.

Turner, Frederick Jackson. *The Frontier in American History*. New York: Holt, 1921.

Walters, Everett. *Joseph Benson Foraker: An Uncompromising Republican*. Columbus: Ohio History Press, 1948.

White, Trumbull. *United States in War with Spain and the History of Cuba*. Chicago: International, 1898.

White, William Allen. *The Autobiography of William Allen White*. New York: Macmillan, 1946.

Williams, R. Hal. *Realigning America: McKinley, Bryan, and the Remarkable Election of 1896*. Lawrence: University Press of Kansas, 2010.

Wilson, Charles Morrow. *The Commoner: William Jennings Bryan*. Garden City, New York: Doubleday, 1970.

Woodward, C. Vann. *Tom Watson: Agrarian Rebel*. London: Oxford University Press, 1938.

Zimmermann, Warren. *First Great Triumph: How Five Americans Made Their Country a World Power*. New York: Farrar, Straus and Giroux, 2002.

NEWSPAPERS

Boston Daily Globe
Brooklyn Citizen
Brooklyn Daily Eagle
Canton Repository (also variously *Canton Repository and Republic* and *Evening Repository*)

Chicago Evening Press
Chicago Times Herald
Chicago Tribune
Cleveland Plain Dealer
Columbus Dispatch
Louisville Courier-Journal
McKeesport (Pennsylvania) Daily News
New York Daily Tribune
New York Herald
New York Journal
New York Mail and Express
New York Press
New York Times
Philadelphia Inquirer
Louisville Commercial
St. Louis Globe-Democrat
St. Louis Republic
Times of London
Topeka Daily Capitol
Washington Evening Star
Washington Post
Washington Times

ARCHIVES

Library of Congress, Washington, DC
    George B. Cortelyou Papers
    William Day Papers
    Hanna-McCormick Papers
    John Hay Papers
    William McKinley Papers
    John Bassett Moore Papers
    Elihu Root Papers
Rutherford B. Hayes Presidential Center, Fremont, Ohio
    Gilded Age Collections
    Rutherford B. Hayes and Hayes Family Papers
William McKinley Presidential Library, Canton, Ohio
    Letters about McKinley
    McKinley Family Letters and Saxton
    McKinley Letters 1864–1901

Theodore Roosevelt Center, Dickinson State University, Dickinson, North Dakota, Theodore Roosevelt Diary, http://www.theodorerooseveltcenter.org

ARTICLES AND PAPERS

Deibel, Mary Aldora. "William McKinley as Governor of Ohio, 1892–1896." Master's thesis, Ohio State University, 1939.

Gould, Lewis L. "William McKinley and the Expansion of Presidential Power." *Ohio History*, Winter 1978.

Halstead, Murat. "Mrs. McKinley." *Saturday Evening Post*, September 6, 1902.

Hunter, Cathy. "Winfield Scott Schley: A Hero, but Not without Controversy." *National Geographic*, December 20, 2012. Online.

Leech, Margaret. "The Front Porch." *American Heritage*, December 1956.

Mahan, Alfred Thayer. "Hawaii and Our Future Sea Power." *Forum*, 1893.

McKinley, William. Civil War Diary, June 12, 1861–November 1, 1861. *Ohio Memory*, http://www.ohiomemory.org/cdm/compoundobject/collection/p26 7401coll32/id/5569/rec/1.

Merry, Robert W. "Lord Salisbury's Lessons for Great Powers." *The National Interest*, March 14, 2014. Online.

———. "The Odd Couple." *The National Interest*, January–February 2014.

The Nation:

"The De Lome Letter," February 17, 1898.

" 'Dignified' Diplomacy," July 22, 1897.

"A Free-Coinage Catechism," July 9, 1896.

"Governing at a Distance," May 19, 1898.

"The Morals of the Porto Rico Question," February 22, 1900.

"Mr. Sherman's Reply to Japan," July 8, 1897.

"The Nicaragua Canal," May 26, 1898.

"Passage of the Gold Bill," February 22, 1900.

"The President in Boston," February 23, 1899.

"The President's Speech," February 3, 1898.

"Prosperity's Advance Orator," June 18, 1896.

"Record of Congress," June 14, 1900.

"The Reform Victory," August 5, 1897.

"The Republican Imbroglio," March 15, 1900.

"The Republican Nominee," June 25, 1896.

"The Situation in Spain," March 3, 1898.

"The Situation in the Philippines," August 16, 1900.

"The Week," June 18, 1896.

"The Week," April 29, 1897.
"The Week," February 23, 1899.
"The Week," December 14, 1899.
Quigg, Lemuel Ely. "Thomas Platt." *North American Review*, May 1910.
Smith, Charles Emory. "McKinley in the Cabinet Room." *Saturday Evening Post*, October 11, 1902.

WEBSITES

The Almanac of Theodore Roosevelt. www.theodore-roosevelt.com.
The American Presidency Project. University of California, Santa Barbara. http://www.presidency.ucsb.edu.
The Avalon Project: Documents in Law, History, and Diplomacy. Lillian Goldman Law Library, Yale School of Law. http://avalon.law.yale.edu.
Bartleby: Great Books Online. http://www.bartleby.com.
History Central. http://www.historycentral.com.
Miller Center: History, Policy, Impact. University of Virginia. http://www.miller center.org.
Mining Artifacts and History. http://www.miningartifacts.org.
Mount Holyoke. http://www.mtholyoke.edu.
National Humanities Center. http://nationalhumanitiescenter.org.
Project Gutenberg. http://www.gutenberg.org/15749/15749-h/15749-h.htm.
The Spanish-American War Centennial Website. http://www.spanamwar.com.
State of New Jersey, Department of Labor and Workforce Development. http://lwd.dol.state.nj.us.
Theodore Roosevelt Center. Dickinson State University. http://www.theodoreroo seveltcenter.org.
University District History: Columbus, Ohio. http://www.univdistcol.com.
Wikipedia. http://en.wikipedia.org.

— NOTES —

ABBREVIATIONS AND SHORT CITES

GBC, George B. Cortelyou

GBCD, George B. Cortelyou Diary, in George B. Cortelyou Papers

GBCP, George B. Cortelyou Papers

HMcCP, Hanna-McCormick Papers

ISM, Ida Saxton McKinley

JBF, Joseph B. Foraker

JBMP, John Bassett Moore Papers

LoC, Library of Congress

MAH, Marcus Alonzo Hanna

RBH, Rutherford B. Hayes

WMcK, William McKinley

WMcKP, William McKinley Papers

WMPL, William McKinley Presidential Library

INTRODUCTION

1 *at six-thirty that evening*: "President in Buffalo," *Washington Post*, September 5, 1901.

2 *an estimated eight million*: "Pan-American Exposition," *Wikipedia*.

2 *"a splendid little war"*: quoted in Thomas, *The War Lovers*, p. 364.

2 *"Brotherhood of the Nations"*: quoted in "Our American Friends," *New York Times*, June 15, 1901.

3 *"unconcealed haughtiness"*: Ibid.

3 *"this grand and beautiful spectacle"*: quoted in ibid.

3 *"the masks that he wore"*: quoted in Gould, *The Spanish-American War and President McKinley*, p. 2.

3 *"a tantalizing enigma"*: Zimmermann, p. 10.

4 *"Here, you put on this overcoat"*: quoted in Olcott, p. 2:359.

5 *She swooned briefly*: Anthony, p. 241.

5 *"sensory overload"*: Ibid.

5 *The solicitous husband*: Ibid.

5 *"smiled happily"*: "President in Buffalo."

5 *350-acre fairground*: Miller, *The President and the Assassin*, p. 4.

5 *389-foot-high Electric Tower*: Ibid., p. 3.

5 *green-brick mansion*: "The Milburn Home," *New York Times*, September 7, 1901.

6 *at around ten*: "President M'Kinley Favors Reciprocity," *New York Times*, September 6, 1901.

6 *"probably the greatest crowd"*: Ibid.

6 *116,000 people flocked*: Miller, *The President and the Assassin*, p. 4.

6 *"the timekeepers of progress"*: WMcK, "Last Speech of William McKinley," U.S. Senate, 58th Congress, 2nd Session, Document No. 268 (Washington, DC: Government Printing Office, 1904).

8 *"It is the utterance of a man"*: quoted in "Comment on President's Speech," *New York Times*, September 6, 1901.

8 *particularly hearty applause*: "President M'Kinley Favors Reciprocity."

8 *people broke through*: "M'Kinley Points Way," *Washington Post*, September 6, 1901.

8 *"I warned him against this"*: quoted in "Mr. Griggs Warned Mr. M'Kinley," *New York Times*, September 7, 1901.

8 *enjoy a solitary walk*: Miller, *The President and the Assassin*, p. 8.

8 *"Why should I?"*: Olcott, p. 1:314.

9 *fifty hands a minute*: Halstead, *The Illustrious Life of William McKinley*, p. 428.

9 *shook hands for twenty minutes*: "M'Kinley Points Way."

9 *Lurking in the shadows*: Miller, *The President and the Assassin*, pp. 5-6.

1. OHIO ROOTS

11 *"the garden of the world"*: quoted in Andrew R. L. Cayton, "The Significance of Ohio in the Early American Republic," in Cayton and Hobbs, *The Center of a Great Empire*, p. 1.

11 *died in Massachusetts in 1823*: Ibid., p. 3.

11 *fifth largest population*: Ibid.

12 *by 1830 they had subdued*: Cayton, *Ohio*, p. 16.

12 *production of corn*: Ibid., p. 22.

12 *population of 2,339,502*: Cayton, "The Significance of Ohio in the Early American Republic."

12 *"Ohio recapitulated"*: quoted in ibid., p. 2.

12 *"fully competent to govern"*: quoted in ibid., p. 5.

12 *"in a Country"*: quoted in ibid.

13 *320,000 men into blue uniforms*: "Ohio in the American Civil War," *Wikipedia*.

13 *"David the Weaver"*: Olcott, p. 1:3.

13 *Scottish chieftain named Fionn laoch*: S. S. Knabenshue, "The McKinleys of County Antrim," unpublished manuscript, enclosed with letter to George B. Cortelyou, December 4, 1908, GBCP, Box 41.

14 *316 acres*: Olcott, p. 1:3.

14 *fought in the American Revolution*: Ibid.

14 *William, born in 1807*: Ibid., p. 4.

14 *the Bible, Shakespeare, and Dante*: Ibid., p. 5.

14 *In 1829 William McKinley married*: Porter, p. 40.

14 *"a born gentlewoman"*: Olcott, p. 1:6.

15 *Hume's* History of England: Morgan, *William McKinley and His America*, p. 5.

15 *"3 churches, 3 stores"*: quoted in Olcott, p. 1:10.

15 *"There wasn't much of a town"*: quoted in Morgan, *William McKinley and His America*, p. 5.

15 *nine children*: Porter, p. 41.

15 *born January 29, 1843*: Ibid., p. 42.

15 *teacher named Alva Sanford*: Olcott, p. 1:8.

15 *"pure luxury"*: quoted in Leech, *In the Days of McKinley*, p. 4.

16 *founded in 1849*: Olcott, p. 1:15.

16 *"Will is good at anything"*: quoted in ibid., p. 14.

16 *never indulged in swear words*: Ibid., p. 15.

16 *"torrents of eloquence"*: Ibid., p. 18.

16 *"profess conversion"*: Ibid., p. 19.

16 *"It was seldom"*: quoted in Morgan, *William McKinley and His America*, p. 8.

17 *"speaking pieces"*: Olcott, p. 1:19.

17 *Everett Literary and Debating Society*: Ibid., p. 20.

17 *"very strong abolitionists"*: quoted in Morgan, *William McKinley and His America*, p. 10.

17 *liked to linger and discuss politics*: Ibid.

17 *money from their savings*: Ibid., p. 11.

17 *venturing toward treason*: Ibid.

18 *"boarding around"*: Olcott, p. 1:21.

18 *scrambling over fences*: Morgan, *William McKinley and His America*, p. 12.

18 *"Six miles would be a long walk"*: quoted in ibid.

18 *$25 a month*: Ibid.

18 *"They've fired on her!"*: quoted in ibid., p. 13.

18 *Sparrow House tavern*: Olcott, p. 1:22.

19 *"we can't stay out of this war"*: quoted in Morgan, *William McKinley and His America*, p. 13.

19 *"Well, boys"*: quoted in ibid., p. 14.

19 *"into the hands of the good Lord"*: quoted in Olcott, p. 1:24.

19 *"I came to a deliberative conclusion"*: quoted in Perry, p. 12.

2. THE FORGE OF WAR

20 *"paltry pittance of pay"*: WMcK, "The American Volunteer Soldier," address at the Metropolitan Opera House, New York City, May 30, 1889, reprinted in McKinley, *Speeches and Addresses of William McKinley: From His Election to Congress to the Present Time*, p. 358.

20 *sworn into the army*: Volunteer Descriptive List and Account of Pay and Clothing, Army official document, Gilded Age Collections, GA-29.

21 *five feet, seven inches*: Ibid.

21 *listed as "student"*: Ibid.

21 *"a great man to me"*: quoted in Perry, p. 131.

21 *"Depend on it"*: quoted in ibid., p. 132.

22 *"From that very moment"*: WMcK, "Rutherford B. Hayes," address before the Ohio Wesleyan University at Delaware, Ohio, June 20, 1893, in McKinley, *Speeches and Addresses of William McKinley: From His Election to the Present Time*, p. 639.

22 *3,000 troops sleeping*: Morgan, *William McKinley and His America*, p. 15.

22 *"a good effect"*: quoted in ibid., p. 16.

22 *"It seems to be the determination"*: quoted in ibid.

22 *poems by Lord Byron*: WMcK diary, July 3, 1861, Ohio History Connection Selections, http://cdm267401.cdmhost.com/cdm/ref/collection/p267401coll32/id/5569. All diary references were obtained from this online source.

22 *"I enjoyed sleeping"*: Ibid., June 20, 1861.

22 *"our Revolutionary fathers"*: quoted in Morgan, *William McKinley and His America*, p. 16.

22 *"to hand down to posterity"*: quoted in ibid.

22 *"hills, high"*: WMcK diary, August 16, 1861.

23 *"Tomorrow morning's sun"*: Ibid., June 12, 1861.

23 *"venomous smell"*: WMcK to W. K. Miller, reprinted in Olcott, p. 1:29.

24 *"With no blankets for a covering"*: WMcK diary, September 10, 1861.

24 *"It gave us confidence"*: quoted in Olcott, p. 1:33.

24 *"We soon found"*: quoted in Porter, p. 61.

25 *"a lovely September day"*: WMcK, "Rutherford B. Hayes."

25 *"made one more appeal"*: quoted in Perry, p. 174.

25 *"God bless the lad"*: quoted in ibid.

26 *"Our young friend"*: quoted in Morgan, *William McKinley and His America*, p. 22.

26 *"proudest and happiest moment"*: WMcK to RBH, July 2, 1888, Hayes Papers.

26 *"how would you like to go home"*: quoted in Perry, p. 175.

26 *"bubbling over with enthusiasm"*: quoted in Olcott, p. 1:38.

26 *had a photograph made*: "M'Kinley as First Lieutenant," taken at Gallipolis, Ohio, December 1862, photograph, reprinted in Porter between pp. 58 and 59.

26 *"Our new second lieutenant"*: quoted in Olcott, p. 1:38.

27 *"generals of the next war"*: quoted in Perry, p. 175.

27 *the "carnage" he witnessed*: WMcK, "The American Volunteer Soldier."

27 *"William, I shall never see you again"*: quoted in Morgan, *William McKinley and His America*, p. 14.

27 *"a formative period of my life"*: quoted in Depew and Halstead, *Life and Distinguished Services of Hon. William McKinley and the Great Issues of 1896*, p. 42.

28 *so thin and scraggly*: Morgan, *William McKinley and His America*, p. 23.

28 *"There is nothing new in camp"*: quoted in ibid.

28 *"We penetrated a country"*: quoted in Olcott, p. 1:40.

28 *"Out of grub"*: quoted in Perry, p. 188.

28 *"Stopped and ate"*: quoted in Olcott, p. 1:42.

29 *"None of us expected to see him"*: quoted in Porter, p. 96. This and the following quotations about the incident come from a long exposition from Russell Hastings, given to Porter.

30 *"Don't worry, my dear madam"*: quoted in ibid., p. 98.

30 *"Well, McKinley"*: quoted in ibid., p. 101.

30 *"cried like a baby"*: Ibid.

30 *"We whipped them"*: quoted in Perry, p. 198.

31 *"Away went McKinley"*: quoted in ibid., p. 204.

31 *"By what route"*: quoted in Porter, p. 105. Further quotations from this incident come from the same source.

31 *"brown October"*: quoted in Perry, p. 206.

31 *"This valley will feed"*: quoted in ibid.

32 *"Then it was suggested"*: Ibid., p. 209.

32 *"gallant and meritorious service"*: quoted in ibid., p. 211.

32 *"colder than any huckleberry pudding"*: quoted in ibid.

33 *"I did literally"*: quoted in Porter, p. 62.

33 *"Now, William"*: quoted in Morgan, *William McKinley and His America*, p. 20.

34 *"Call me Major"*: quoted in Armstrong, p. 103.

3. LIFE AND WORK

35 *"How are my old fellows"*: WMcK to Russell Hastings, August 28, 1865, McKinley Letters 1864–1901.

36 *Walker, loaned him money*: Mott, p. 48.

36 *a "jolly" companion*: Olcott, p. 1:57.

36 *"A man in any of our western towns"*: RBH to WMcK, November 6, 1866, Hayes Papers, GA-29.

36 *hit 5,000 by war's end*: Olcott, p. 1:58.

36 *"Do you know a young man"*: George W. Belden to Joseph Frease, Letters about McKinley.

37 *"If you don't try this case"*: quoted in Olcott, p. 1:59.

37 *"I can't take so much"*: quoted in ibid., p. 60.

37 *"the same power of epigrammatic expression"*: Ibid., p. 61.

37 *the look of a statesman*: Ibid., p. 63.

37 *civic and fraternal activities*: Leech, *In the Days of McKinley*, p. 11.

38 *"a good lawyer"*: quoted in Morgan, *William McKinley and His America*, p. 34.

38 *went after illicit liquor sales*: Leech, *In the Days of McKinley*, p. 13.

38 *just 143 votes*: Olcott, p. 1:76.

39 *nearly $10,000 a year*: Leech, *In the Days of McKinley*, p. 17.

39 *equal to his annual income*: Ibid., p. 21.

39 *"I am pleased to hear"*: quoted in Morgan, *William McKinley and His America*, p. 32.

39 *"I was a simple country boy"*: quoted in Leech, *In the Days of McKinley*, p. 10.

40 *"Mother McKinley"*: Ibid., p. 14.

40 *transported a printing press*: Anthony, p. 1.

40 *Joseph Medill*: Ibid., p. 2.

40 *three live-in servants*: Ibid., p. 4.

40 *"more practical than ornamental"*: quoted in ibid., p. 5.

41 *"mischievous" directions*: quoted in ibid., p. 7.

41 *"left the stamp of her personality"*: quoted in ibid.

41 *"Through all the flutter"*: quoted in ibid., p. 8.

41 *Anna McKinley approached*: Ibid., p. 10.

41 *arriving at Geneva*: Belden, p. 313.

42 *"Ida looked pale"*: quoted in ibid.

42 *"How different things [will] look,"*: quoted in ibid., p. 325.

42 *"You are the only man"*: quoted in Anthony, p. 21.

42 *"It is now settled"*: WMcK to RBH, December 12, 1870, McKinley Letters 1864–1901.

42 *Nearly 1,000 guests*: "Marriage of Major Wm. McKinley and Miss Ida Saxton," *Canton Repository and Republic,* January 27, 1871.

43 *ring of California gold*: Anthony, p. 21.

43 *Ida became convinced*: Ibid., p. 22.

43 *for $7,800*: Ibid., p. 23.

43 *"nervous system was nearly wrecked"*: Olcott, p. 1:71. (These are Olcott's words based on interviews with Mary ["Pina"] Barber, Ida McKinley's sister.)

43 *"sickly" from birth*: quoted in Anthony, p. 25.

43 *"paroxysms" or "convulsions"*: Ibid., p. 26.

44 *"never entirely recovered"*: quoted in ibid., p. 28.

44 *real estate ventures*: described in ibid.

44 *"She would sit for hours"*: quoted in ibid., p. 29.

44 *"the black pall of grief"*: quoted in ibid., p. 30.

44 *"Ida would have died"*: quoted in ibid.

44 *"interest in existence"*: quoted in ibid., p. 31.

44 *"If you would suffer"*: quoted in ibid., p. 32.

45 *"spotless record"*: "The Congressional Contest," *Alliance Mirror*, reprinted in *Canton Repository and Republic*, August 11, 1876.

45 *Coal miners in the Tuscarawas Valley*: Olcott, p. 1:78.

46 *3,300 votes*: Olcott, political map, between pp. 1:82 and 83.

46 *51 percent of the popular vote*: Merry, *Where They Stand*, p. 82.

46 *184 to 165*: Ibid., p. 83.

47 *under the care of a leading neurologist*: Anthony, p. 35.

47 *three letters a day*: Halstead, "Mrs. McKinley," pp. 6–7.

47 *"one of the best political stumpers"*: "Maj. McKinley," *Warren Chronicle*, reprinted in *Canton Repository and Republic*, November 10, 1876.

48 *just 1,234 votes*: Olcott, vol. 1, political map.

48 *"The Victory in the District"*: WMcK to RBH, October 10, 1878, Hayes Papers, GA-29.

48 *outnumbered Republicans by 19,000 votes*: Olcott, p. 1:84.

48 *gained seventy House seats*: Moore, Preimesberger, and Tarr, p. 2:1569.

48 *"The trouble with McKinley"*: quoted in "Mahoning Co. Man Not in Either Camp," *New York Times*, January 9, 1882.

49 *"I was disposed"*: WMcK to Abner McKinley, March 8, 1882, McKinley Family Letters and Saxton.

49 *advantage of some 900 votes*: Olcott, political map following p. 1:82.

49 *"I believe we can carry it"*: WMcK to Allan Carnes, February 18, 1844, McKinley Letters 1864–1901.

49 *"There will be nothing"*: WMcK to John Pollock, March 24, 1884, McKinley Letters 1864–1901.

49 *2,000 votes*: Olcott, political map following p. 1:82.

49 *"Ida is growing stronger"*: WMcK to Abner McKinley, January 13, 1882, McKinley Letters 1864–1901.

49 *"My own precious darling"*: WMcK to ISM, August 23, March 22, March 17, 1880, McKinley Family Letters and Saxton.

4. THE OHIO REPUBLICANS

51 *"I am neither 'an active friend'"*: WMcK to Robert P. Kennedy, McKinley Letters 1864–1901.

52 *thirty-two eastern and southern counties*: "Ohio Mines," *Mining Artifacts and History*, http://www.miningartifacts.org/Ohio-Mines.html.

52 *five million tons of coal*: Ibid.

52 *Ohio ranked second*: "History of Ohio," *Wikipedia*.

52 *"Buggy Capital of the World"*: Ibid.

52 *3,672,329*: Table 1. United States Resident Population by State: 1790–1850, State of New Jersey, Department of Labor and Workforce Development, http://lwd.dol.state.nj.us/labor/lpa/census/1990/poptrd1.htm.

52 *half of all foreign-born*: Cayton, *Ohio*, p. 143.

53 *"Lemonade Lucy"*: quoted in ibid., p. 198.

53 *"inconceivable that any self-respecting"*: quoted in ibid., p. 197.

54 *Born in 1823*: Burton, p. 1.

54 *six years in the House*: Treese, p. 1815.

55 *"the Ohio icicle"*: Grant, p. 233.

55 *"bad grace"*: Tarbell, p. 111.

55 *born three years after McKinley*: Walters, p. 6.

55 *"aptitude for declamation"*: quoted in ibid., p. 7.

55 *"a voice like a fire-alarm"*: "Capitol Chat," *Washington Post*, May 26, 1896.

56 *"The Republicans are demoralized"*: quoted in Walters, p. 23.

56 *"No candidate for Governor"*: WMcK to JBF, October 12, 1883, McKinley Letters 1864–1901.

56 *farmer and grocer in 1814*: Croly, p. 8.

56 *"The table was abundant"*: Ibid., p. 18.

56 *"a pleasant, wholesome fellow"*: quoted in ibid., p. 22.

56 *invested $200,000 in a canal*: Horner, p. 31.

56 *"It's all over now, Mark"*: quoted in Mrs. Marcus A. Hanna, dictated statement to J. B. Morrow, May 18, 1905, HMcCP, Box 4.

57 *"Your money is gone now"*: quoted in ibid.

57 *"absolute accuracy"*: Andrew Squire, dictated statement to J. B. Morrow, May 23, 1905, HMcCP, Box 4.

58 *"Mr. Hanna wanted company"*: Elmer Dover, dictated statement to J. B. Morrow, September 1905, HMcCP, Box 4.

59 *"A place on [Ways and Means]"*: WMcK to Allan Carnes, December 14, 1881, McKinley Letters 1864–1901.

59 *"an advantage"*: Tarbell, p. 186.

59 *"The difference between"*: quoted in Porter, p. 134.

60 *deft parliamentary maneuver*: Ibid., p. 138.

60 *"Among the few pleasures"*: MAH to JBF, June 11, 1884, HMcCP, Box 2.

60 *"I assure you, my dear fellow"*: MAH to JBF, June 19, 1884, HMcCP, Box 2.

61 *"The Major is never behind"*: MAH to JBF, November 28, 1885, HMcCP, Box2.

61 *"I tell you my dear friend"*: MAH to JBF, January 14, 1886, HMcCP, Box 2.

61 *"I am keeping out of the fight"*: JBF to MAH, July 20, 1887, HMcCP, Box 2.

62 *a "strain" upon their friendship*: quoted in Walters, p. 55.

62 *"very mad"*: quoted in ibid., p. 56.

62 *"No one will make any headway"*: JBF to MAH, January 19, 1888, HMcCP, Box 2.

62 *"How glad I am"*: MAH to JBF, January 17, 1888, HMcCP, Box 2.

63 *"I am wholly ignorant"*: JBF to MAH, May 10, 1888, HMcCP, Box 2.

63 *"seems to be developing"*: quoted in Walters, p. 65.

63 *"With these letters before me"*: JBF to MAH, May 25, 1888, HMcCP, Box 2.

63 *"They will be left"*: MAH to JBF, undated but referenced as May 29, 1888, HMcCP, Box 2.

63 *Foraker then said no*: JBF to MAH, June 4, 1888, HMcCP, Box 2.

64 *Hanna patiently replied*: MAH to JBF, June 10, 1888, HMcCP, Box 2.

64 *would garner 300 delegates*: Croly, p. 134.

64 *"The Sherman men"*: "At Chicago: 'Blaine and Protection' Is the Cry," *Evening Repository* (Canton, Ohio), June 16, 1888.

64 *"Sherman won't do"*: quoted in Grant, p. 235.

64 *"more of a Foraker boom"*: "Mixed: Sherman Loses, after the Second Ballot," *Evening Repository* (Canton, Ohio), June 22, 1888.

64 *229 votes*: "More Mix: A Splendid Speech," *Evening Repository* (Canton, Ohio), June 23, 1888. Subsequent vote counts in this paragraph are taken from this source.

65 *"Everything is arranged"*: quoted in "Seen by a Kansan: J. Ware Butterfield Tells of the Attempt to Nominate McKinley in 1888," *Topeka Daily Capitol*, September 26, 1901.

65 "Mr. President and Gentlemen": WMcK, "Not a Candidate: Speech at the Republican National Convention at Chicago, Illinois, June 23, 1888," reprinted in McKinley, *Speeches and Addresses of William McKinley: From His Election to Congress to the Present Time*, p. 236.

66 *224 on the fifth ballot*: "More Mix: A Splendid Speech."

66 *"Many of your best friends"*: quoted in Horner, p. 73.

66 *"The Blaine move"*: Ibid., p. 74.

66 *"To accept a nomination"*: quoted in Porter, p. 147.

67 *"faithful and true"*: quoted in Walters, p. 73.

67 *"The Ohio delegation"*: Ibid., p. 74.

67 *"Let my name stand"*: quoted in ibid.

67 *Harrison crept up to 231*: Ibid., p. 76.

68 *"Guided by a fine sense"*: Murat Halstead, commentary reprinted in *Evening Repository* (Canton, Ohio), June 25, 1888.

68 *"Mr. Hanna despised treachery"*: James H. Dempsey, dictated statement to J. B. Morrow, May 22, 1905, HMcCP, Box 4.

68 *"I stand by my friends"*: quoted in Charles F. Leach, dictated statement to J. B. Morrow, May 16, 1905, HMcCP, Box 4.

68 *never again had a political ally*: Croly, p. 138.

69 *"You gained gloriously"*: RBH to WMcK, June 27, 1888, Hayes Papers.

5. STEADFAST PROTECTIONIST

70 *"To achieve success"*: quoted in "M'Kinleys of Antrim," *Washington Post*, December 21, 1896.

71 *"without a superior"*: WMcK, speech in the House of Representatives, April 6, 1882, reprinted in McKinley, *Speeches and Addresses of William McKinley: From His Election to Congress to the Present Time*, p. 105.

71 *1,524 separate tariffs*: Tarbell, p. 87.

71 *two trips to California*: Leech, *In the Days of McKinley*, p. 22.

71 *allowed to travel alone*: Anthony, p. 48.

72 *"I hope you will not worry"*: WMcK to ISM, April 4, 1888, McKinley Letters and Saxton.

72 *"I am quite solicitous"*: WMcK to ISM, March 17, 1888, McKinley Letters and Saxton.

72 *arrival time of telegrams*: *Washington Post* article cited in Anthony, p. 48.

72 *"He can say he loves me"*: quoted in ibid.

72 *retreat to her tent*: Leech, *In the Days of McKinley*, p. 22.

72 *a fit of jealousy so intense*: Ibid.

72 *"the most beautiful girl"*: quoted in ibid., p. 30.

73 *"Ida, it is I"*: quoted in Olcott, p. 2:362.

73 *leave of absence*: Anthony, p. 50.

73 *glued to the Ebbitt House*: Ibid., p. 51.

73 *"his entire consecration"*: quoted in ibid.

73 *annual salary of $25,000*: Leech, *In the Days of McKinley*, p. 22.

73 *"serving the country a little"*: quoted in ibid.

74 *"I am doing no soliciting"*: WMcK to RBH, December 31, 1888, Hayes Papers.

74 *discerned his seriousness in Hanna's Washington presence*: Horner, p. 82.

74 *"No one except those"*: Theodore Burton, dictated statement to J. B. Morrow, April 16, 1906, HMcCP, Box 4.

74 *"read heavily and happily in French"*: Grant, p. 214.

74 *"for practice"*: quoted in Tuchman, p. 123.

75 *"Having embedded that fly"*: quoted in Morgan, *William McKinley and His America*, p. 97.

75 *"Everybody enjoys Reed's"*: quoted in Leech, *In the Days of McKinley*, p. 43.

75 *"a man of little scope"*: quoted in Grant, p. 251.

75 *about 8.5 percent*: Tarbell, p. 1.

75 *Hamilton argued*: Ibid.

76 *between 16 and 26 percent*: Daniel Kerr of Iowa, table on tariff rates presented to House of Representatives, May 9, 1890, *Congressional Record*, p. 4408.

76 *Polk proposed legislation*: Merry, *A Country of Vast Designs*, p. 99.

76 *between 20 and 28 percent*: Kerr table on tariff rates.

77 *"a booby of a bill"*: quoted in Tarbell, p. 10.

77 *well over 40 percent*: Kerr table on tariff rates.

78 *"The people have spoken"*: WMcK, speech before the House of Representatives, May 7, 1890, *Congressional Record*, p. 4246.

78 *about $10 million*: Tarbell, p. 190.

78 *"you diminish importations"*: WMcK, House speech, May 7, 1890, *Congressional Record*, p. 4408.

79 *"bounty" of two cents*: Hilary Abner Herbert, House of Representatives speech, May 20, 1890, *Congressional Record*, p. 5039.

79 *seven eighths of the sugar*: Ibid.

79 *nearly $56 million*: Ibid.

79 *bounty cost of $8 million*: Ibid.

79 *"that the whole [tariff] system"*: Ways and Means Committee minority report, read into the *Congressional Record* by James Allison Hayes, May 10, 1890, p. 4530.

79 *"We place no tax or burden"*: WMcK, House speech, May 7, 1890, *Congressional Record*, p. 4408.

80 *"in all branches of our industries"*: Roger Q. Mills, House of Representatives speech, May 7, 1890, *Congressional Record*, p. 4257.

80 *4,000 separate items*: Olcott, p. 1:179.

80 *164–142 tally*: Ibid., p. 177.

80 *some 496 amendments*: Ibid., p. 179.

80 *"I think the bill is an infamy"*: quoted in "Blaine's Angry Blow," *Washington Post*, April 6, 1896.

81 *"smash it flatter than a pancake"*: Ibid.

81 *"reciprocity," the Blaine concept*: Tarbell, p. 206.

81 *distinctive in four particulars*: Morgan, *William McKinley and His America*, p. 114. The analytical framework was put forth by Morgan.

81 *A pleased President Harrison*: Olcott, p. 1:179.

81 *value of U.S. imports and exports*: WMcK, House floor speech, May 7, 1890, *Congressional Record*, p. 4408.

82 *"prosperity and adversity"*: John B. Allen, Senate speech, March 30, 1897, *Congressional Record*, p. 468.

82 *Democratic Holmes County*: Olcott, vol. 1, redistricting chart.

83 *303 votes*: Ibid.

83 *eighty-five House seats*: Moore, Preimesberger, and Tarr, p. 2:1569.

83 *"It's all over"*: quoted in Olcott, p. 1:186. The rest of the exchange comes from the same source.

83 *"Protection was never stronger"*: quoted in ibid., p. 187.

83 *"I agree with you that defeat"*: WMcK to MAH, November 12, 1890, HMcCP, Box 2.

83 *"Reason will be enthroned"*: Olcott, p. 1:187.

6. FOUR YEARS IN COLUMBUS

84 *"cheap goods from abroad"*: WMcK, "A Reply to Mr. Cleveland," address at the Lincoln Banquet of the Ohio Republican League at Toledo, Ohio, February 12, 1891, reprinted in McKinley, *Speeches and Addresses of William McKinley: From His Election to the Present Time*, p. 487.

85 *"I should be quite content"*: quoted in Deibel, p. 6.

85 *He listened respectfully*: Olcott, p. 1:270.

85 *showed up unannounced*: Morgan, *William McKinley and His America*, p. 118.

85 *every Democrat "fears him"*: quoted in Olcott, p. 1:271.

85 *"Protection is Prosperity"*: Morgan, *William McKinley and His America*, p. 119.

85 *flirted with inflationist sentiments*: Ibid.

85 *Silver Purchase Act*: Burton, p. 368.

86 *"We cannot gamble"*: WMcK, "The Ohio Campaign of 1891," Opening Speech of Mr. McKinley's Gubernatorial Campaign at Niles, Ohio, August 22, 1891, reprinted in McKinley, *Speeches and Addresses of William McKinley: From His Election to the Present Time*, p. 539.

86 *"I am a thousand times obliged"*: WMcK to MAH, August 30, 1891, HMcCP, Box 2.

86 *"I have sufficient"*: WMcK to MAH, September 13, 1891, HMcCP, Box 2.

86 *"Foraker has been a very heavy load"*: quoted in Walters, p. 98.

86 *"The situation was bad"*: James C. Donaldson, dictated statement to J. B. Morrow, undated, HMcCP, Box 4.

87 *"I feel that without you"*: John Sherman to MAH, January 9, 1892, HMcCP, Box 2.

87 *by 21,511 votes*: Olcott, p. 1:272.

87 *"I am much rejoiced"*: Thomas Reed to WMcK, November 4, 1891, WMcKP, Reel 1.

87 *When the Chittenden burned down*: University District History: Columbus, Ohio, http://www.univdistcol.com/htc3.html.

87 *spacious apartment*: Leech, *In the Days of McKinley*, p. 27.

87 *serious initiatives*: Deibel, p. 20.

87 *During the evenings*: Anthony, p. 56. Anthony quotes from Charles Bawsel manuscript, "New Slants on William McKinley," WMPL.

88 *"But a conference must be"*: Ibid.

88 *morning and afternoon ritual*: described in ibid., p. 55.

88 *to express suspicions*: Anthony, p. 65.

88 *she became quite "huffy"*: quoted in ibid., p. 58.

88 *became indignant*: Ibid., p. 58.

88 *"the greatest exhibition"*: Ibid., p. 57.

89 *182 first-ballot votes*: Porter, p. 181.

89 *thirty-eight House seats*: Moore, Preimesberger, and Tarr, p. 2:1569.

89 *Dunkirk, New York*: Anthony, p. 59.

89 *amounting to $17,000*: Kohlsaat, p. 11.

90 *might be $100,000*: Mott, p. 48.

90 *"Have courage, Robert"*: quoted in ibid., p. 49.

90 *"I will pay every note"*: quoted in Anthony, p. 60.

90 *"Do not worry"*: quoted in ibid.

91 *"Have just read"*: quoted in Kohlsaat, p. 11.

91 *"pale and wan"*: Ibid., p. 12.

91 *"in excess of anything"*: quoted in Anthony, p. 61.

91 *an estimated $75,000*: Ibid.

91 *"My husband has done everything"*: quoted in ibid.

92 *"Because McKinley has made a fool of himself"*: quoted in Kohlsaat, p. 13.

92 *session in Cleveland yielded an agreement*: Morgan, *William McKinley and His America*, p. 131.

92 *"shall never forget"*: WMcK to Myron Herrick, reprinted in Mott, p. 50.

92 *"The pen will not"*: WMcK to H. H. Kohlsaat, reprinted in Kohlsaat, p. 17.

92 *"I cannot for a moment entertain"*: WMcK to Messrs. Kohlsaat, Herrick, Hanna, Day, and McDougal, reprinted in Mott, p. 51.

93 *The money flowed in*: contribution amounts are taken from Morgan, *William McKinley and His America*, p. 133; Anthony, p. 64.

93 *by 10 percent*: Kohlsaat, p. 16.

93 *Some 5,000 donations*: Ibid.

93 *"stem the flood"*: Leech, *In the Days of McKinley*, p. 60.

94 *A $200 investment*: Grant, p. 236.

94 *"Small wonder"*: quoted in ibid., p. 238.

94 *dropped below $100 million*: Lichtman and DeCell, p. 174.

94 *81,000 votes*: Deibel, p. 41.

94 *111 legislative seats*: Ibid.

94 *"The best government"*: quoted in ibid., p. 43.

95 *"one of the greatest strikes"*: quoted in ibid., p. 59.

95 *200,000 miners*: Ibid., p. 60.

95 *3,000 in all*: Ibid., p. 63.

95 *"I do not care"*: quoted in ibid., p. 68.

95 *"Praise for the prompt action"*: "Praise for the Governor," *Evening Repository*, November 2, 1895, reprinted from the *Cincinnati Enquirer.*

95 *forty-six set speeches:* Porter, p. 219. McKinley's campaign tours are described in Porter, pp. 217–29.

95 *he "seemed tireless"*: quoted in Porter, p. 219.

96 *They arrived in Canton on January 24, 1896*: Anthony, p. 72.

96 *1,000 invitations*: Ibid., p. 78.

96 *"which we prize very much"*: Ibid.

96 *always set for twelve*: Ibid.

96 *"Mrs. McKinley is not getting on"*: quoted in ibid., p. 75.

97 *"a dropsical trouble"*: quoted in ibid.

97 *"The recent elections"*: "Sherman Says the Recent Elections Have Cleared the Political Sky," *Evening Repository*, November 14, 1895.

7. THE MAJOR VERSUS THE BOSSES

98 *"Almost a full score"*: Quigg, "Thomas Platt."

98 *"there is little else he can not do"*: quoted in Williams, p. 49.

99 *willing "to approach the gates"*: quoted in Grant, p. 287.

99 *called his "den"*: Kohlsaat, p. 30.

99 *"as keen as a razor blade"*: quoted in Mott, p. 60.

99 *"Now, Major, it's all over"*: quoted in ibid. This conversation is constructed from the reports of the only two witnesses to the exchange to give renditions: Myron Herrick, quoted extensively in Mott, beginning on p. 60; and Kohlsaat, p. 30. I pieced together the conversation from the two sources to give the exchange as much realism as possible.

100 *resigned his position as head of Hanna & Co.*: Croly, p. 174.

101 *"the John the Baptist"*: "Clever as the Bosses," *Washington Post*, March 21, 1896.

101 *"he loved to be a leader"*: Andrew Squire, dictated statement to J. B. Morrow, May 23, 1905, HMcCP, Box 4.

101 *"Whatever he went into"*: A. B. Hough, dictated statement to J. B. Morrow, May 18, 1905, HMcCP, Box 4.

101 *knew most of them by name*: George G. Mulhern, dictated statement to J. B. Morrow, May 17, 1905, HMcCP, Box 4.

101 *"Boys," he said*: quoted in ibid.

102 *"It looks pretty blue"*: quoted in Dan F. Reynolds, dictated statement to J. B. Morrow, August 1905, HMcCP, Box 4.

102 *"You can't serve two masters"*: quoted in David H. Kimberly, dictated statement to J. B. Morrow, May 15, 1905, HMcCP, Box 4.

102 *"He was the biggest hearted man"*: Ibid.

103 *"He had the South"*: quoted in Williams, p. 57.

103 *"never wrinkled"*: White, *The Autobiography of William Allen White*, p. 251.

103 *"Whether you plunge into it"*: "Prosperity's Advance Orator," *Nation*, June 18, 1896.

103 *"unusual qualities"*: quoted in ibid.

104 *"I wish that fellow"*: quoted in Leech, *In the Days of McKinley*, p. 25.

104 *"angry and astounded"*: "He Declined to Deal," *Washington Post*, March 26, 1896.

104 *"I am afraid we must count on"*: John Hay to MAH, January 27, 1896, WMcKP, Reel 1.

105 *Harrison, now approaching sixty-two*: Treese, p. 1169.

105 *"shocked us a good deal"*: Charles Dick, dictated statement to J. B. Morrow, February 10, 1906, HMcCP, Box 4.

106 *"Progress is the essence"*: quoted in Williams, p. 11.

106 *"The Democratic party can not"*: John Logan Chipman, U.S. House floor speech, May 10, 1890, *Congressional Record*, p. 4509.

106 *seventy-four railroads*: "Panic of 1893," *History Central*, http://www.historycentral.com.

106 *"The farmers of the West"*: Henry G. Turner, speech on the U.S. House floor, May 19, 1890, *Congressional Record*, p. 4932.

107 *at Hanna's Cleveland home*: William B. Merriam, transcribed interview with J. B. Morrow, undated, HMcCP, Box 4.

107 *"and he was anxious"*: Ibid.

107 *"The Advance Agent of Prosperity"*: Williams, p. 55.

107 *fourteen and a half delegates*: Croly, p. 180. All delegate numbers come from the same passage.

108 *"Can you come down"*: Charles Dick, transcribed interview with J. B. Morrow, February 10, 1906, HMcCP, Box 4.

108 *"No," said Hanna*: quoted in ibid.

109 *three of the state's five district conventions*: "Yielded to M'Kinley," *Washington Post*, March 25, 1896.

109 *"If they can capture the State"*: "Cullom's Hard Fight," *Washington Post*, March 16, 1896.

109 *"He doesn't* look *much"*: quoted in Kohlsaat, p. 21.

109 *"McKinley seems to be the coming man"*: Dawes, p. 51.

110 *"Cullom is furious"*: Ibid., p. 65.

110 *"It is McKinley against the field"*: Ibid., p. 66.

110 *"It is not fighting fair"*: Ibid., p. 67.

110 *"indignation meeting"*: Ibid., p. 68.

110 *"We have them beaten"*: Dawes to WMcK, March 19, 1896, WMcKP, Reel 1.

110 *"I have not withdrawn"*: quoted in "Cullom Will Not Withdraw," *Washington Post*, April 14, 1896.

110 *"I do not hesitate"*: Shelby Cullom to Peter Grosscup, April 4, 1896, WMcKP, Reel 1.

111 *after April 23, when three district conventions*: "Cullom Loses Eight Delegates," *Washington Post*, April 24, 1896.

111 *Swift attacked Dawes*: Dawes, p. 77.

111 *"It was a question of my life or death"*: Ibid.

111 *"in a perfect furor"*: "They Prefer M'Kinley," *Washington Post*, April 30, 1896.

111 *"a tidal wave"*: quoted in "Mr. Proctor Explains," *Washington Post*, May 3, 1896.

112 *"My Dear Mr. Dawes"*: WMcK to Dawes, April 30, 1896, reprinted in Dawes, p. 81.

112 *488 committed delegates*: "All but the Shouting," *Washington Post*, May 11, 1896.

112 *456 convention votes*: "Reed and M'Kinley," *Washington Post*, April 27, 1896.

113 *"Everybody who has knowledge"*: quoted in "All but the Shouting."

113 *"set the tongues of statesmen"*: "Quay to See M'Kinley," *Washington Post*, May 20, 1896.

113 *"Well, you see"*: quoted in ibid.

113 *"Maj. McKinley is sound on the money question"*: quoted in "Capitol Chat," *Washington Post*, May 27, 1896.

114 *"that the big three of the Republican Party"*: "He Declined to Deal," *Washington Post*, March 26, 1896.

8. ST. LOUIS TRIUMPH

115 *lingered for eight hours at the McKinleys'*: Kohlsaat, p. 33.

115 *"Kohlsaat is a crank"*: quoted in ibid.

116 *90 percent of his correspondence*: Ibid., p. 33.

116 *"If a gold plank is adopted"*: quoted in ibid.

116 *"There is no occasion"*: quoted in ibid., p. 34.

116 *"silverish man"*: "The Week," *Nation*, June 18, 1896.

117 *"If you want to see the word 'gold'"*: quoted in Kohlsaat, p. 34.

118 *"Mr. Speaker; if metallic money"*: William Jennings Bryan, U.S. House floor speech, February 9, 1893, reprinted in Bryan, p. 106.

118 *increased by 240 percent since 1860*: "A Free-Coinage Catechism," *Nation*, July 9, 1896.

119 *favored sound money "unreservedly"*: quoted in Croly, p. 197.

119 *"the drift at present"*: "What Will the Platform Say?," *Washington Post*, June 12, 1896, reprinted from the *New York Sun*.

120 *between* existing *and* standard: Kohlsaat, p. 36.

120 *avoiding the word was "cowardice"*: Ibid., p. 35.

121 *"dauntless intolerance"*: quoted in Zimmermann, p. 187.

121 *"Mr. Hanna, I insist"*: quoted in Kohlsaat, p. 37.

122 *"Why, that plank is all right"*: quoted in ibid., p. 38.

122 *"Hanna Yields to Lodge"*: subheadline, "Gold Men Are Ahead," *Washington Post*, June 16, 1896.

122 *"The whole thing was managed"*: quoted in Croly, p. 199.

123 *"There's no use"*: quoted in "Capitol Chat," *Washington Post*, June 9, 1896.

123 *"is in a somewhat embarrassing"*: "Quay Is Embarrassed," *Washington Post*, June 15, 1896.

123 *"In my judgment"*: quoted in "Mr. Reed's Battle Is Lost," *Washington Post*, June 11, 1896.

123 *"No, sir; it is not true"*: quoted in "His Boom Went Awry," *Washington Post*, June 13, 1896.

124 *sixty-two in McKinley's favor*: "The Committee on Credentials," *Washington Post*, June 12, 1896.

124 *"This is a riot of excess"*: quoted in "Platt Makes a Bluff," *Washington Post*, June 13, 1896.

124 *"I cannot sacrifice"*: quoted in ibid.

124 *seventeen New York delegates*: "Miller versus Platt," *Washington Post*, June 16, 1896.

124 *a cost of $70,000*: "Built to Hold Hosts," *Washington Post*, June 7, 1896.

125 *"honest currency laws"*: "No M'Kinley Cheers," *Washington Post*, June 17, 1896.

125 *"There will be enthusiasm"*: quoted in ibid.

125 *568½ votes*: "M'Kinley's Vote 568," *Washington Post*, June 18, 1896.

125 *40–11 vote*: "Silver Men in Tears," *Washington Post*, June 18, 1896.

125 *"Utah Maverick"*: Treese, p. 777.

126 *nearly forty minutes*: "Bolted amid Hisses," *Washington Post*, June 19, 1896.

126 *"without heart burnings"*: Henry Teller, speech before the Republican National Convention, June 18, 1896, reprinted in Bryan, p. 176.

126 *105½ to 818½*: "Bolted amid Hisses."

126 *"once the redeemer"*: quoted in Morgan, *William McKinley and His America*, p. 165.

126 *"Go! Go!"*: quoted in ibid.

126 *"Had it not been for the personality and prominence"*: "Bolted amid Hisses."

126 *"Bannockburn"*: Anthony, p. 84.

127 *"pensive" element*: Depew and Halstead, p. 421.

127 *"He does, indeed, know"*: quoted in ibid., p. 422.

127 *"Are you young ladies getting anxious"*: quoted in ibid., p. 424.

128 *"veritable Niagara"*: "Easy for M'Kinley," *Washington Post*, June 19, 1896.

128 *"like a storm at sea"*: Depew and Halstead, p. 425.

128 *"You seem to have heard"*: quoted in "Easy for M'Kinley."

128 *"No, no!"*: quoted in Depew and Halstead, p. 427.

128 *Ohio's forty-six votes*: Ibid., p. 429.

128 *"stark, gloriously mad"*: quoted in ibid., p. 430.

128 *15,000 happy citizens*: "Ovation to M'Kinley," *Washington Post*, June 19, 1896.

128 *"There is nothing more gratifying"*: quoted in ibid.

129 *final total of 661½*: "Easy for M'Kinley."

129 *"Under no circumstances"*: "Mr. Manley and the Reed Boom," *Washington Post*, June 10, 1896.

129 *"I knew from the first"*: "Mr. Hobart Not Surprised," *Washington Post*, June 24, 1896.

9. THE VICTOR

130 *$30-a-week*: Wilson, p. 195.

130 *"It will be Dick Bland"*: Timmons, p. 48.

131 *Carlisle's name went forward*: "Carlisle a Candidate," *Washington Post*, March 17, 1896.

131 *"would be the weakest nominee"*: "Carlisle's Candidacy," *Washington Post*, March 18, 1896.

131 *Carlisle quietly departed the race*: "Mr. Carlisle Declines," *Washington Post*, April 6, 1896.

131 *gone to the same church*: Timmons, foreword to Dawes, p. vii.

132 *"train robber"*: quoted in Williams, p. 81.

132 *"old Democrats . . . who have grown gray"*: quoted in ibid., p. 82.

133 *sucking on a lemon*: Williams, p. 81.

133 *"The man who is employed"*: Bryan, speech before the Democratic National Convention, July 9, 1896, reprinted in Bryan, p. 199.

133 *"Go after them, Willie!"*: quoted in Williams, p. 84.

134 *didn't mention the currency*: "Talks Only of Tariff," *Washington Post*, June 21, 1896.

134 *"McKinley's character"*: "The Republican Nominee," *Nation*, June 25, 1896.

134 *"I am a Tariff man"*: quoted in Olcott, p. 1:321.

134 *"The Chicago convention has changed everything"*: quoted in Williams, p. 129.

135 *"the free silver craze"*: quoted in ibid., p. 130.

135 *"in the saddle"*: quoted in Morgan, *William McKinley and His America*, p. 170.

135 *"No contract is made"*: Dawes to WMcK, August 1, 1896, reprinted in Dawes, pp. 92–93.

136 *100 million pieces*: Elmer Dover, dictated statement to J. B. Morrow, September 1905 (date not given), HMcCP, Box 4.

136 *20 million more*: Croly, p. 217.

136 *100 employees*: Williams, p. 138.

136 *275 separate messages*: Croly, p. 217.

136 *nearly 3 million people*: Williams, p. 139.

136 *close to half a million dollars*: Dawes, "Statement to November 21, 1896," reprinted in Dawes, p. 106.

137 *"scared . . . so blue"*: quoted in Leech, "The Front Porch Campaign."

137 *"that we are mistaken"*: Dawes to WMcK, August 1, 1896, reprinted in Dawes, p. 92.

137 *Standard Oil Company*: Croly, p. 220.

137 *Rockefeller himself contributed another $2,500*: Williams, p. 137. Subsequent contribution numbers come from the same source.

138 *a tenth of McKinley's*: Ibid.

138 *Lincoln to Chicago*: Wilson, p. 221.

138 *"high character and personal worth"*: "Mr. Bryan at Canton," *Washington Post*, August 11, 1896.

138 *570 speeches*: Williams, p. 98.

138 *18,000 miles*: Koenig, p. 250.

138 *twenty-nine states*: Williams, p. 98.

138 *twenty-three speeches*: "Broke His Own Record," *Washington Post*, October 17, 1896.

138 *placing "himself"*: "Bryan's Chicago Programme," *Washington Post*, October 24, 1896.

138 *"You've got to stump"*: quoted in Williams, p. 130.

138 *"scared to death"*: quoted in Mott, p. 64.

139 *"If I took a whole train"*: quoted in Timmons, p. 56.

139 *"That will hardly do"*: quoted in Charles Dick, dictated statement to J. B. Morrow, September 1905, HMcCP, Box 4.

140 *"Just read it to me"*: quoted in ibid.

140 *two glasses of beer*: Williams, p. 131.

140 *"like a child"*: quoted in Leech, "The Front Porch Campaign."

140 *750,000 Americans*: Williams, p. 134.

141 *"new experiment"*: quoted in "Toilers Visit Canton," *Washington Post*, July 26, 1896.

141 *"That which we call money"*: quoted in "Tariff and Revenue," *Washington Post*, July 31, 1896.

141 *"a somewhat furtive way"*: quoted in Leech, "The Front Porch Campaign."

141 *"Having diminished our business"*: quoted in "Tariff Still His Text," *Washington Post*, August 23, 1896.

141 *"My countrymen"*: quoted in "Hard for Men to Get," *Washington Post*, August 19, 1896.

142 *"Lunacy having dictated"*: quoted in "Bolting the Nominee," *Washington Post*, July 11, 1896, reprinted from the *New York World*.

142 *slipped increments of cash*: Williams, p. 123.

143 *"I promise you"*: quoted in ibid., p. 124.

143 *"minced no words"*: "Roosevelt Scores Altgeld," *Washington Post*, October 16, 1896.

144 *identified fifteen states as "doubtful"*: "States Yet Doubtful," *Washington Post*, November 2, 1896.

144 *"I want people to feel apprehensive"*: quoted in "Hanna Glad Republicans Are Scared," *Washington Post*, October 21, 1896.

144 *"The outlook is generally encouraging"*: quoted in Williams, p. 143.

144 *80 cents a bushel*: Ibid., p. 142.

144 *"What has happened to this 'law'"*: quoted in ibid.

145 *"Glorious old banner"*: quoted in ibid., p. 145.

145 *"I never saw him look better"*: quoted in "Confidence in Canton," *Washington Post*, November 3, 1896.

145 *"The feeling here"*: quoted in Morgan, *William McKinley and His America*, p. 185.

145 *271 electoral votes*: Moore, Preimesberger, and Tarr, p. 1:745.

145 *plurality of 464,000*: Williams, p. 152.

145 *7,107,822 popular votes*: Koenig, p. 251.

145 *"Oh, God, keep him humble"*: quoted in Kohlsaat, p. 54.

146 *an "attempt"*: Croly, p. 226.

10. BUILDING A CABINET

147 *"Your unfaltering and increasing friendship"*: WMcK to MAH, November 12, 1896, HMcCP, Box 2.

148 *circulation ploy*: Nasaw, p. 118.

148 *his pro-gold convictions*: Koenig, p. 204.

148 *"That hurts"*: quoted in Horner, p. 114.

148 *"Jim," said Hanna*: James M. Dempsey, transcribed statement to J. B. Morrow, May 22, 1905, HMcCP, Box 4.

149 *"I guess that is about the only thing"*: quoted in "Conference at Cleveland," *Washington Post*, November 15, 1896.

149 *"unsafe and erratic"*: quoted in Whitelaw Reid to WMcK, December 5, 1896, WMcKP, Reel 1.

150 *"They must not dictate"*: quoted in Morgan, *William McKinley and His America*, p. 203.

150 *invited Dingley to Canton*: "Dingley at Canton," *Washington Post*, December 4, 1896.

150 *serious health problems*: Nelson Dingley to WMcK, December 22, 1896, WMcKP, Reel 1.

150 *"a close friend of Chairman Hanna"*: "Depends on Sherman," *Washington Post*, Nov. 24, 1896.

150 *"a gentleman who is as much"*: "Sherman and Hanna's Ambition," *Washington Post*, November 25, 1896.

150 *"He is not ready yet"*: quoted in "His Goal the Senate," *Washington Post*, November 26, 1896.

151 *"Mr. Hanna has his heart set"*: William Osborne to WMcK, December 11, 1896, WMcKP, Reel 1.

151 *authorized to ask*: John Sherman to MAH, December 15, 1896, WMcKP, Reel 1.

151 *"After full reflection"*: Ibid.

151 *"the sage old pilot"*: quoted in "William B. Allison," *Wikipedia*.

151 *Allison signaled*: A. B. Cummins to Charles Dawes, December 24, 1896, WMcKP, Reel 1; H. M. McFarland to WMcK, December 29, 1896, WMcKP, Reel 1.

151 *outlined the plan to Foraker*: Foraker, p. 1:496.

151 *"very well endowed"*: Ibid., p. 497.

152 *"The stories regarding Senator Sherman's 'mental decay'"*: WMcK to Joseph Medill, February 8, 1897, WMcKP, Reel 1.

152 *McKinley offered the job to Sherman*: John Sherman to WMcK, January 7, 1896, WMcKP, Reel 1.

152 *"I have concluded"*: Ibid.

152 *Hanna didn't take any chances*: MAH to WMcK, January 13, 1897, WMcKP, Reel 1.

152 *"serious and favorable consideration"*: John Sherman to Asa Bushnell, January 16, 1897, WMcKP, Reel 1.

152 *"from a good source"*: quoted in "Will Foraker Oppose Hanna?," *Washington Post*, January 14, 1897.

152 *attorney general Asa Jones*: "Will Not Name Hanna," *Washington Post*, January 25, 1897.

153 *announced he would appoint Hanna*: Asa Bushnell to WMcK, February 21, 1897, WMcKP, Reel 1.

153 *"So strong was the storm"*: "Hanna to Be Senator," *Washington Post*, February 22, 1897.

153 *"I have a Secretary of the Treasury"*: Kohlsaat, p. 58.

153 *the young entrepreneur reported back:* Dawes, p. 113.

153 *"no sense of disappointment":* Ibid.

154 *His relations with Sherman*: "Alger Makes a Reply," *Washington Post*, November 22, 1896.

154 *dogged by accusations*: H. V. Boynton to WMcK, January 18, 1897, WMcKP, Reel 1.

154 *"it would be very gratifying"*: Russell Alger to WMcK, January 11, 1897, WMcKP, Reel 1.

154 *"Oh, there is nothing in that"*: quoted in "Alger Put On the List," *Washington Post*, January 30, 1897.

154 *Alger got other friends*: William Chandler to WMcK, January 12, 1897, WMcKP, Reel 1; Redfield Proctor to WMcK, January 12, 1897, WMcKP, Reel 1.

154 *"There is nothing in the files"*: H. V. Boynton to WMcK, January 18, 1897, WMcKP, Reel 1.

154 *to overcome McKenna's concern*: Joseph McKenna to WMcK, December 29, 1896, WMcKP, Reel 1.

154 *He sent Melville Stone*: Melville Stone to WMcK, December 29, 1896, WMcKP, Reel 1.

154 *Otis to press further*: Morgan, *William McKinley and His America*, p. 201.

154 *"Well, judge"*: quoted in Kohlsaat, p. 59.

155 *Hanna disliked McCook*: Ibid., p. 60.

155 *"probably the most popular man"*: quoted in Morgan, *William McKinley and His America*, p. 199.

155 *intermittent emotional strains*: Leech, *In the Days of McKinley*, p. 106.

155 *It has been my dearest wish*: WMcK to MAH, February 18, 1897, WMcKP, Reel 1.

156 *preferably the State Department*: Morgan, *William McKinley and His America*, p. 202.

156 *Hay had encouraged Reid's ambitions*: Taliaferro, p. 312. A full treatment of the Hay-McKinley intrigue is contained in Taliaferro's chapter 13.

156 *"I have ceased thinking of Reid"*: Ibid., p. 314.

156 *"I feel that I must reluctantly forego"*: WMcK to Whitelaw Reid, February 19, 1897, WMcKP, Reel 1.

157 *health was "certainly better than"*: Whitelaw Reid to WMcK, March 3, 1897, WMcKP, Reel 2.

157 *McCook announced that the only job he wanted*: John McCook to WMcK, February 27, 1897, WMcKP, Reel 2.

157 *Platt now demanded*: Morgan, *William McKinley and His America*, p. 203.

157 *"I need your sympathy"*: quoted in "Bliss Yields at Last," *Washington Post*, March 4, 1897.

158 *master at tossing out names*: Kohlsaat, p. 59.

158 *"[You may] wipe out every obligation"*: quoted in Leech, *In the Days of McKinley*, p. 105.

158 *"I never met a man"*: quoted in Gould, *The Presidency of William McKinley*, p. 15.

158 *"But he met me"*: John Hay to Henry Adams, October 20, 1896, reprinted in Thayer, p. 2:153.

159 *"My real trouble"*: quoted in Garraty, p. 104.

159 *"I want peace"*: quoted in Goodwin, p. 221.

159 *"The truth is, Will"*: quoted in ibid.

159 *"a chance to prove"*: quoted in ibid., p. 222.

159 *"Everything is going on pleasantly"*: WMcK to ISM, December 11, 1896, McKinley Family Letters and Saxton.

159 *"since Mrs. McKinley is in Chicago"*: "President-Elect McKinley," *Washington Post*, December 14, 1896.

159 *"to find rest and change"*: "M'Kinley Goes to Chicago," *Washington Post*, December 17, 1896.

159 *crowd of 4,000*: "Maj. McKinley Goes Shopping," *Washington Post*, December 23, 1896.

160 *the couple dined*: "Merry Christmas at Canton," *Washington Post*, December 25, 1896.

160 *she organized a dinner dance*: Anthony, p. 100.

160 *"an old-fashioned cotillion"*: quoted in ibid., p. 101.

160 *leaden skies brought rain*: "Farewell at Canton," *Washington Post*, March 2, 1897.

160 *McKinley arrived at 7:30*: "White House Dinner," *Washington Post*, March 3, 1897.

161 *"I have not seen you"*: quoted in "Washington's Busy Day," *Washington Post*, March 4, 1897.

161 *exchange of courtesy visits*: Ibid.

11. INAUGURATION DAY

162 *President-elect McKinley rose from bed at six*: "A Day with M'Kinley," *Washington Post*, March 5, 1897. Details of McKinley's morning are from this source.

162 *"Not a cloud"*: "M'Kinley Is Now the President," *New York Times*, March 5, 1897.

163 *225,000 visitors*: "Crowd of Vast Size," *Washington Post*, March 2, 1897.

163 *hotels were filled to capacity*: "Hotels to Be Jammed," *Washington Post*, November 23, 1897.

163 *"in the most affectionate terms"*: "A Day with M'Kinley."

163 *Clarence Chaplin arrived*: Ibid.

163 *American-grown wool*: "McKinley's Inaugural Suit," *Washington Post*, December 28, 1897.

163 *eighty men atop coal-black chargers*: "Maj. M'Kinley's Mounted Escort," *Washington Post*, March 1, 1897.

163 *four-in-hand team*: "March Down the Avenue," *New York Times*, March 5, 1897.

163 *"The ring of nearly 2,000 iron hoofs"*: "A Day with M'Kinley."

163 *"Major McKinley kept removing his hat"*: "March Down the Avenue."

163 *McKinley asked if Ida*: "A Day with M'Kinley."

164 *At 12:18*: "President M'Kinley," *Washington Post*, March 5, 1897.

164 *She wore a purple gown*: "Nation's First Lady," *Washington Post*, March 5, 1897.

164 *More than 40,000 spectators*: "M'Kinley Is Now the President."

164 *kissed the Bible*: "Oath of Office Taken," *Washington Post*, March 5, 1897.

164 *"depression in business"*: WMcK, Inaugural Address, March 4, 1897, reprinted in McKinley, *Speeches and Addresses of William McKinley, from March 1, 1897 to May 30, 1900*, p. 2.

165 *"one of the biggest displays"*: "The Pyrotechnic Display," *New York Times*, March 5, 1897.

165 *a gown of silver and white brocade*: "Mrs. M'Kinley's Inaugural Gown," *Washington Post*, January 28, 1897.

165 *The McKinleys reached the Pension Building at 8:40*: "The Inaugural Ball," *New York Times*, March 5, 1897. The *Times* reports a later arrival time, but it doesn't square with the schedule of evening events reported in the same article. My arrival time is calculated by adding time segments reported by the *Times*.

165 *"Shortly after"*: Ibid.

165 *to 75 million*: "Demographic History of the United States," *Wikipedia*.

165 *from native births*: "Immigration to the United States by decades, 1820–1930," National Humanities Center, nationalhumanitiescenter.org/ows/seminarsflus/BecomingAmerican.pdf.

166 *"Yes," he said, "but this is a billion dollar country!"*: quoted in Musicant, p. 10.

166 *outpaced all others*: Zimmermann, p. 25.

166 *"For nearly three centuries"*: Turner, p. 219.

166 *"industrial distress"*: "The New Administration," *Washington Post*, March 5, 1897.

166 *nearly 50 percent*: "Gorman's Triumph—A Humiliating Spectacle," *Harper's Weekly*, September 8, 1894, reprinted on *On This Day*, www.nytimes.com /learning/general/onthisday/harp/0908.html.

167 *70 million dollars*: Tarbell, p. 240.

167 *Republicans held forty-six seats*: Moore, Preimesberger, and Tarr, p. 2:1569.

167 *"doing something for silver"*: "The Republican Nominee," *Nation*, June 25, 1896.

167 *"The victory for gold"*: quoted in "Will Keep Up the Fight," *Washington Post*, November 9, 1896.

167 *significant cargo increases*: "Better Times at Hand," *Washington Post*, November 6, 1896.

167 *large amounts of gold*: "Business Gets Brisk," *Washington Post*, November 8, 1896.

167 *global gold production*: "The Increase of Gold," *Washington Post*, January 3, 1897.

167 *"No one now doubts"*: quoted in "Trade Grows Better," *Washington Post*, November 14, 1896.

168 *pig iron output*: "Our Expanding Trade," *Washington Post*, January 16, 1897.

168 *"Money markets"*: quoted in ibid.

168 *Even before his inauguration*: "The Monetary Conference," *Washington Post*, December 31, 1896.

168 *McKinley's approach constituted a shrewd political maneuver*: "Mr. Wolcott's Report," *Washington Post*, January 4, 1897.

169 *"ever faithful isle"*: quoted in Musicant, p. 38.

169 *almost 260,000 lives*: Zimmermann, p. 246.

169 *"scorched earth" strategy*: Bailey, p. 451.

169 *Spain had nearly 200,000 troops*: Offner, p. 12.

169 *the insurgency's 40,000*: Ibid., p. 6.

169 *another 50,000 troops*: Ibid., p. 12.

170 *400,000 rural peasants*: Ibid., p. 13.

170 *tens of thousands had died*: Ibid.

170 *U.S. imports from Cuba*: Zimmermann, p. 250.

171 *Of seventy-one missions launched*: Offner, p. 6.

171 *"rascally Cubans"*: quoted in Ferrell, p. 350.

171 *"the independence of Cuba"*: quoted in Offner, p. 18.

171 *"The only action now proper"*: quoted in "President and Cuba," *Washington Post*, March 4, 1896.

171 *Secretary of State Richard Olney warned*: Offner, p. 33.

171 *a plan for Cuban autonomy*: Ibid.
172 *"I have been through one war"*: quoted in Zimmermann, p. 252.
172 *He let congressional leaders know*: Musicant, p. 96.
172 *"create an immediate ugly situation"*: quoted in ibid.
172 *"Mr. President, if I can only"*: quoted in ibid.
172 *five-sixths of all ships*: Bailey, p. 428.
173 *"port, harbor, or territory"*: quoted in Morgan, *Pacific Gibraltar*, p. 23.
173 *"the intimacy of our relations"*: quoted in ibid., p. 24.
173 *Soon nearly all Hawaiian sugar*: Ibid., p. 29.
173 *jumped 50 percent*: Ibid., p. 32. The same citation covers subsequent production numbers.
173 *"Plantations became so mechanized"*: Ibid., p. 33.
173 *50 percent in good years*: Ibid., p. 35.
173 *nearly 30,000 immigrants*: Ibid., p. 48.
174 *about 109,000*: Ibid., p. 18.
174 *thus ending the 1,600-year-old kingdom*: Ibid., p. 109.
175 *It arrived on February 3*: Ibid., p. 111.
175 *the Senate, where an informal poll*: Ibid., p. 114.
175 *for "the purpose of reexamination"*: quoted in Ferrell, p. 331.
175 *"stop and look and think"*: quoted in Morgan, *Pacific Gibraltar*, p. 118.
176 *"growing Japanese trouble"*: "Annexation Feeling in Hawaii," *Washington Post*, September 5, 1896.
176 *Japanese residents now numbered 25,000*: Ibid.
176 *"the ultimate fate of the islands"*: "Hawaii to Seek Annexation," *Washington Post*, November 29, 1896.
176 *"probably the most influential work"*: Zimmermann, p. 94.
178 *"a position powerfully influencing"*: Mahan, "Hawaii and Our Future Sea Power."
178 *"peace is preferable to war"*: WMcK, Inaugural Address, March 4, 1897, *Avalon Project*, http://avalon.law.yale.edu.

12. TAKING CHARGE

179 *"Never keep books"*: quoted in Gould, *The Spanish American War and President McKinley*, p. 4.
179 *"with all his equanimity"*: Charles Emory Smith, "McKinley in the Cabinet Room," *Saturday Evening Post*, October 11, 1902.
179 *"He is hunting for men"*: quoted in Morgan, *William McKinley and His America*, notes elaboration, p. 435.
180 *"jackass"*: quoted in Leech, *In the Days of McKinley*, p. 136.
180 *"The quarrel ended"*: Ibid., p. 136.

180 *"I always yielded"*: quoted in ibid.

180 *always with a carnation*: "A White House Souvenir," *Chicago Times Herald*, October 9, 1897. McKinley's well-known penchant for boutonnieres and for giving them to children is described in detail here.

180 *"I don't think that McKinley"*: Charles Dick, transcribed statement to J. B. Morrow, February 10, 1906, HMcCP.

181 *"Why, if McKinley and I were walking"*: quoted in "White House Humor," *Washington Post*, July 5, 1897.

181 *"the masks that he wore"*: quoted in Gould, *The Spanish American War and President McKinley*, p. 2.

181 *"He had a way of handling men"*: quoted in ibid.

181 *Tuesdays and Fridays at eleven*: "Office-Seeking Hosts," *Washington Post*, March 11, 1897.

181 *anecdote or story*: Smith, "McKinley in the Cabinet Room."

181 *"His pre-eminence in the council"*: Ibid. Other observations about McKinley's approach to Cabinet meetings are taken from this source.

182 *"This is the first time in eight years"*: "Policy of Good Will," *Washington Post*, March 6, 1897.

182 *vetoed only fourteen bills*: Morgan, *William McKinley and His America*, p. 210.

182 *"We have never had a president"*: quoted in ibid.

183 *"the fashion in which highwaymen"*: quoted in Gould, "William McKinley and the Expansion of Presidential Power."

183 *"Newspaper Row"*: quoted in ibid.

183 *"While apparently not courting publicity"*: quoted in ibid.

183 *"to carry out what he considered"*: quoted in ibid.

183 *thirty-seven public addresses*: Ibid. The number of speeches noted for 1898 and 1899 also come from this source.

183 *"No President . . . ever did"*: quoted in ibid.

183 *a penchant for naming prominent members*: Ibid.

184 *liked to place prominent academics*: Ibid.

184 *peeling paint and wallpaper*: Morgan, *William McKinley and His America*, p. 231.

184 *some modern amenities*: Leech, *In the Days of McKinley*, p. 121. Other details of the White House setup come from the same source.

184 *just six*: Morgan, *William McKinley and His America*, p. 231.

184 *carved-oak swivel chair*: James Creelman, "Mr. Cortelyou Explains President McKinley," *Pearson's Magazine*, June 1908.

185 *"he would impress you"*: John Russell Young, "Washington after Political Honeymoon," *New York Herald*, April 11, 1897.

185 *A stern-looking man*: photo, Creelman, "Mr. Cortelyou Explains President McKinley."

185 *"I want to tell you"*: J. E. Niles to George Cortelyou, July 18, 1898, WMcKP, Reel 4.

186 *"an explosion of bad manners"*: quoted in "'Dignified' Diplomacy," *Nation*, July 22, 1897.

186 *"a mixture of deceit"*: Ibid.

186 *"The chaotic condition"*: "John Sherman Makes Chaos of State Affairs," *Columbus Dispatch*, August 11, 1897.

186 *"This is a heavy price"*: "The Case of Secretary Sherman," *New York Journal*, August 12, 1897.

186 *"Judge Day will become Secretary"*: "John Sherman Makes Chaos of State Affairs."

187 *"We tremble to contemplate"*: quoted in Gould, *The Presidency of William McKinley*, p. 17.

187 *"He is so enthusiastic"*: Long, p. 168.

187 *Among the president's frequent guests*: GBCD, November 16, 1897.

187 *"perfect . . . exactly right"*: Hay to WMcK, March 6, 1897, WMcKP, Reel 2.

188 *"It is my confident hope"*: quoted in Leech, *In the Days of McKinley*, p. 110.

188 *He neglected to mention*: Taliaferro, p. 311.

188 *"I know the place"*: Hay to WMcK, April 13, 1897, WMcKP, Reel 2.

188 *"as unprotected as a jellyfish"*: quoted in Merry, *Sands of Empire*, p. 76.

189 *"extra session"*: WMcK, proclamation, "By the President of the United States," March 6, 1897, *Congressional Record*, March 15, 1897, p. 11.

189 *"the remarkable spectacle"*: WMcK, "Special Message of the President," *Congressional Record*, March 19, 1897, p. 19.

189 *"the opening up of new markets"*: WMcK, Inaugural Address, March 4, 1897, *Avalon Project*, http://avalon.law.yale.edu/19thcentury/mckin1.asp.

190 *"We expect to cut"*: quoted in Tarbell, p. 242.

190 *Dingley took his bill to the House floor*: "Tariff Bill," *Congressional Record*, March 19, 1897, p. 19.

190 *a floor debate lasting only nine legislative days*: Tarbell, p. 245.

190 *"Free-trade tariffs have always brought calamity"*: Henry Gibson, House floor speech, March 23, 1897, *Congressional Record*, p. 175.

190 *"I warn you now"*: Joseph W. Bailey, House floor speech, March 19, 1897, *Congressional Record*, p. 75.

190 *"was a fairly good protectionist measure"*: Tarbell, p. 243.

191 *"Industrial conditions in this country"*: quoted in ibid., p. 244.

191 *particularly for chemicals*: Ibid., p. 244.

191 *reached unprecedented levels*: Ibid., p. 248.

191 *some 872 amendments*: Ibid., p. 251.

191 *"more oppressive"*: Ibid., p. 252.

192 *Just before four on the afternoon of July 24*: "The Law of the Land," *Washington Post*, July 25, 1897. All details of this White House episode are taken from the same source.

192 *three avenues of reciprocal negotiation*: "The Reciprocity Clause," *Washington Post*, July 20, 1897.

193 *respected diplomat, John A. Kasson*: "Reciprocity in Trade," *Washington Post*, October 15, 1897.

193 *the legislation's "ultra-protectionism"*: "M'Kinley Redeems His Pledge," *Washington Post*, July 21, 1897, reprinted from the *London Standard*.

193 *lowest point in 1896*: Tarbell, p. 252.

193 *"Wealth of all descriptions"*: Ibid., p. 253.

193 *"business men of both parties"*: John McCook to WMcK, August 2, 1897, WMcKP, Reel 2.

13. WHITE HOUSE LIFE

194 *"Madam, your party"*: Anthony, p. 120.

194 *"no end of pains"*: Ibid.

195 *to visit Russell Hastings*: Ibid., p. 107.

195 *At a New York dinner*: "Dinner to Mrs. McKinley," *Washington Post*, April 28, 1897.

195 *Corrections followed*: "Mrs. McKinley at the Theater," *Washington Post*, April 29, 1897.

195 *"Mrs. McKinley had one of her headaches"*: quoted in Anthony, p. 122. Except where documented otherwise, the following quotes and anecdotes relating to Ida McKinley are from this source.

198 *"jealous suspicions"*: Leech, *In the Days of McKinley*, p. 435.

199 *"I have decided to make a change"*: J. N. Bishop to WMcK, September 22, 1896, WMcKP, Reel 1.

199 *"Pardon me for saying"*: Bishop to WMcK, November 27, 1897, WMcKP, Reel 1.

199 *"Bottle of medicine just received"*: quoted in M. E. F. Smith to WMcK, July 15, 1897, WMcKP, Reel 2.

199 *"The president has taken a notion"*: "Took a Half Holiday," *Washington Post*, March 27, 1897.

200 *"was a very good game"*: "As Seen by a Woman," *Washington Post*, August 23, 1897.

200 *Ulysses Grant's old pew*: "President at Church," *Washington Post*, March 8, 1897.

200 *"who likes his cigars"*: "Cigars That Cost $2 Each," *Washington Post*, March 30, 1897.

200 *"The distrust of the present"*: WMcK, speech at a banquet given by the Philadelphia Museums and the Manufacturers' Club, June 2, 1897, in McKinley, *Speeches and Addresses of William McKinley, from March 1, 1897 to May 30, 1900*, p. 29.

201 *grave of abolitionist John Brown*: "President at Brown's Tomb," *Washington Post*, August 12, 1897.

201 *within ten days were off again*: "President Is Gone Again," *Washington Post*, September 22, 1897.

201 *"a fixity of relative value"*: John Hay, diplomatic dispatch, May 20, 1897, WMcKP, Reel 2.

201 *"an almost religious view"*: "Clipping from *Times* (London), April 13, 1897," transcription for WMcK file, WMcKP, Reel 2.

201 *"mistaken personal courtesies"*: Ibid.

202 *"entirely separable and distinct"*: quoted in Morgan, *William McKinley and His America*, p. 215.

202 *a conditional understanding by mid-June*: Gould, *The Presidency of William McKinley*, p. 45.

202 *"He answered," Hay reported*: Hay, diplomatic dispatch, May 20, 1897, WMcKP, Reel 2.

202 *"a considerable division"*: Ibid.

202 *"absolutely no possibility"*: Ibid.

203 *the British now seemed to understand*: Hay to WMcK, July 16, 1897, WMcKP, Reel 2.

203 *"an admirable impression"*: Ibid.

203 *"The whole situation"*: Edward Wolcott to WMcK, June 18, 1897, WMcKP, Reel 2.

203 *the British announced an extended delay*: Hay, diplomatic dispatch, August 7, 1897, WMcKP, Reel 2.

203 *"dead against"*: Hay to WMcK, October 11, 1897, WMcKP, Reel 2.

203 *Already he had urged Congress*: Gould, *The Presidency of William McKinley*, p. 47.

204 *"It should be our settled purpose"*: WMcK, remarks at the Chamber of Commerce, Cincinnati, October 29, 1897, in McKinley, *Speeches and Addresses of William McKinley, from March 1, 1897 to May 30, 1900*, p. 54.

204 *spike in global gold production*: "World's Gold Production," *Washington Post*, August 8, 1897.

204 *"Of course I have my ideas"*: quoted in Gould, *The Presidency of William McKinley*, p. 48.

204 *leading diplomatic "handyman"*: quoted in Morgan, *Pacific Gibraltar*, p. 110.

204 *"We ought not to take"*: quoted in ibid., p. 186.

204 *McKinley showed up*: Ibid.

205 *"a great interest" in Hawaii*: quoted in ibid.

205 *"unfortunately, he is going to be the judge"*: quoted in ibid., p. 187.

206 *now numbered 18,156*: Ibid., p. 196.

206 *"the Japanese are still piling in"*: quoted in ibid., p. 195.

206 *"A stand must be taken"*: quoted in ibid., p. 200.

206 *rejected hundreds of migrants*: Ibid.

206 *armored cruiser* Philadelphia: "Is Ordered to Honolulu," *Washington Post*, April 2, 1897.

206 *"peaceful invasion" of Hawaii*: quoted in "Disquieting News from Hawaii," *Washington Post*, April 11, 1897.

206 *Okuma ordered Japan's ambassador*: Morgan, *Pacific Gibraltar*, p. 201.

207 *"invasion of the Asiatics"*: quoted in ibid., p. 203.

207 *McKinley asked Roosevelt to identify all warships*: Ibid., p. 204.

207 *"a Jingo and annexationist"*: "The Week," *Nation*, April 29, 1897.

207 *"a full avowal to the President"*: quoted in Morgan, *Pacific Gibraltar*, p. 204.

207 *The president asked Sewall*: Ibid., p. 206.

207 *He vowed to investigate*: Ibid., p. 205.

207 *"And that little roll"*: quoted in Morgan, *William McKinley and His America*, p. 223.

208 war *sixty-two times*: Morris, *The Rise of Theodore Roosevelt*, p. 570.

208 *"All the great masterful races"*: quoted in ibid., p. 569.

208 *"if I had my way"*: quoted in ibid., p. 573.

208 *"I suspect that Roosevelt is right"*: quoted in ibid., p. 572.

208 *three disturbing dispatches from Honolulu*: Morgan, *Pacific Gibraltar*, p. 206.

208 *"Respectfully submitted"*: quoted in ibid., p. 207.

208 *decided to get the treaty signed*: "To Annex Hawaii," *Washington Post*, June 16, 1897.

208 *"Watch carefully the situation"*: Morgan, *Pacific Gibraltar*, p. 209.

209 *"despite successive denials"*: "Its Text Made Public," *Washington Post*, June 18, 1897.

209 *abrogated terms of past treaties*: "Mr. Sherman's Reply to Japan," *Nation*, July 8, 1897.

209 *"for the purpose of occupying the islands"*: Morgan, *Pacific Gibraltar*, p. 211.

209 *"It is too late"*: quoted in ibid., p. 212.

209 *"The sum and substance"*: "Mr. Sherman's Reply to Japan."

209 *"TO HOIST OUR FLAG"*: *Washington Post*, July 13, 1897.

209 *The vote was 6 to 2*: "The Annexation of Hawaii," *Washington Post*, July 15, 1897.

209 *annexation through legislation*: "Hawaiian Annexation," *Washington Post*, July 22, 1897; "The Annexation of Hawaii," *Washington Post*, July 29, 1897.

210 *Japan accepted an offer:* "Japan Will Arbitrate," *Washington Post,* July 31, 1897.
210 *withdrawn its protests:* Morgan, *Pacific Gibraltar,* p. 216.
210 *"Will America pursue":* "Severe Check to Japanese," *Washington Post,* June 17, 1897.
211 *"The most important act":* quoted in Morgan, *Pacific Gibraltar,* p. 217.

14. CUBA

212 *"wonderful land pirate":* quoted in Beisner, p. 19.
212 *"Ah, you may be sure":* quoted in ibid., p. 24.
213 *"Yes, yes, I remember now":* quoted in ibid.
213 *Schurz wasn't assuaged:* Beisner, p. 24.
214 *"crowded" with Americans:* John Morgan, Senate floor speech, April 6, 1897, *Congressional Record,* p. 621.
215 *only twelve U.S. citizens:* Eugene Hale, Senate floor speech, April 7, 1897, *Congressional Record,* p. 644.
215 *Ruiz's widow arrived:* "Mrs. Ruiz in the City," *Washington Post,* March 10, 1897.
215 *"pursuing lawful occupations":* "No Aid for Such Men," *Washington Post,* April 3, 1897.
215 *"make a very comprehensive inquiry":* "The New Cuban Commissioner," *Washington Post,* April 29, 1897.
216 *He left Washington on May 8:* "Calhoun Leaves for Cuba," *Washington Post,* May 9, 1897.
216 *"It is time":* quoted in "A Protest to Spain," *Washington Post,* April 6, 1897.
216 *"Now, what have we here?":* George F. Hoar, Senate floor speech, April 5, 1897, *Congressional Record,* p. 575.
216 *"It is a fact":* William Allen, Senate floor remark, April 5, 1897, *Congressional Record,* p. 576.
217 *passed Gallinger's resolution:* "A Protest to Spain."
217 *"a condition of public war":* "Great Day for Cuba," *Washington Post,* May 21, 1897.
217 *"A 'recognition of belligerency'":* Alvey A. Adee to John Sherman, August 19, 1897, WMcKP, Reel 2.
217 *approved Morgan's resolution, 41–14:* "Great Day for Cuba."
217 *"their failure":* Ibid.
218 *to solicit telegraphic reports:* "Again Talked of Cuba," *Washington Post,* May 15, 1897.
218 *between 600 and 800 American citizens:* WMcK, "Message to Congress on the Condition of American Citizens in Cuba," May 17, 1897, *American Presidency Project,* http://www.presidency.ucsb.edu/ws/index.php?pid=69294.

218 *within eighteen minutes*: "Relief for Cuba," *Washington Post*, May 18, 1897.

218 *"The policy of the Administration"*: quoted in Gould, *The Presidency of William McKinley*, p. 66.

218 *On June 8, Calhoun returned*: "What He Saw in Cuba," *Washington Post*, June 9, 1897.

218 *"Every house had been burned"*: quoted in Offner, p. 47.

218 *"wrapped in the stillness of death"*: quoted in Gould, *The Presidency of William McKinley*, p. 67.

219 *"uncivilized and inhumane"*: quoted in Offner, p. 48.

219 *Cleveland urged McKinley to fire*: Ibid., p. 40.

219 *"What am I going to do"*: quoted in Morgan, *William McKinley and His America*, p. 256.

219 *he was "desirous to adopt"*: quoted in Gould, *The Presidency of William McKinley*, p. 68.

220 *"You have done me great honor"*: Stewart Woodford, telegram to WMcK, June 16, 1897, WMcKP, Reel 2.

220 *"I remember your personal injunctions"*: Woodford to WMcK, September 6, 1897, JBMP, Box 185.

221 *a brusque response to McKinley's diplomatic note*: Offner, p. 50.

221 *"popular feeling"*: Woodford to WMcK, August 23, 1897, JBMP, Box 185.

221 *"I read it in her face"*: Woodford to WMcK, September 22, 1897, JBMP, Box 185.

221 *"a degree of injury and suffering"*: quoted in Gould, *The Presidency of William McKinley*, p. 69.

222 *the duke was "courteous and temperate"*: Woodford to WMcK, September 22, 1897, JBMP, Box 185.

222 *"I felt compelled"*: Woodford to WMcK, October 10, 1897, JBMC, Box 185.

222 *soothe the diplomatic situation*: Woodford to WMcK, October 17, 1897, JBMP, Box 185.

222 *McKinley wasn't pleased*: Offner, p. 64.

222 *threatened to expel the* Journal *reporter*: Woodford to WMcK, October 17, 1897, JBMP, Box 185.

223 *outlined the American position*: Woodford to John Sherman, September 13, 1897, JBMP, Box 185. This memo describes a meeting with the British ambassador; similar memos relating sessions with the Russian, German, and French ambassadors can be found in the same box.

223 *"Spain," contended the* Post: "Spain Has No Allies," *Washington Post*, September 23, 1897.

223 *"except commercial ones"*: quoted in Merry, "Lord Salisbury's Lessons for Great Powers."

223 *Liberal manifesto advocating a division*: Práxedes M. Sagasta, "Manifesto of the Liberal Party," June 24, 1897, WMcKP, Reel 2.

224 *"Senor Sagasta is a very shrewd politician"*: Woodford to WMcK, November 7, 1897, JBMP, Box 185.

224 *"honest and earnest"*: Ibid.

224 *advocated Cuban autonomy since 1891*: Offner, p. 65.

224 *"would have averted the disasters"*: "Manifesto of the Liberal Party," June 24, 1897, WMcKP, Reel 2.

224 *"I have reason to know"*: Woodford to WMcK, October 17, 1897, JBMP, Box 185.

224 *"President McKinley will endeavor"*: "Queen Regent Cordial," *Washington Post*, October 13, 1897.

224 *"Senor Sagasta . . . must be controlled"*: "The Spanish Crisis," *Washington Post*, October 1, 1897.

225 *some 350,000 islanders*: "As the Matter Stands in Cuba," *Washington Post*, January 15, 1898.

225 *"They believe," reported the* Post: Ibid.

225 *Riots in the streets of Havana*: "Will Punish Leaders," *Washington Post*, January 16, 1898.

225 *"energetic action"*: quoted in "Cuba Fails to Accept," *Washington Post*, October 18, 1897.

225 *a 1,000-word statement*: "The Reply of Spain," *Washington Post*, October 28, 1897.

225 *"a great moral victory"*: Woodford to WMcK, November 7, 1897, JBMP, Box 185.

225 *the minister expressed satisfaction*: Woodford to WMcK, November 14, 1897, JBMP, Box 185.

225 *"acquiescent, but not enthusiastic"*: Woodford to WMcK, December 4, 1897, JBMP, Box 185.

225 *"still acquiescent, but even less cordial"*: Woodford to WMcK, December 11, 1897, JBMP, Box 185.

225 *"to grow less and less cordial"*: Woodford to WMcK, December 18, 1897, JBMP, Box 185.

225 *"elements now in opposition"*: Ibid.

226 *asked anxiously about McKinley's view*: Woodford to WMcK, November 27, 1897, JBMP, Box 185.

226 *"Not an autonomist"*: Fitzhugh Lee, letter to William Day, December 15, 1897, William Day Papers, Box 35.

226 *"My scouts . . . report"*: Fitzhugh Lee, letter to William Day, December 22, 1897, William Day Papers, Box 35.

226 *"the success or failure"*: Woodford to WMcK, December 11, 1897, JBMP, Box 185.

227 *"I know that the people"*: "The President Unduly Alarmed," *Chicago Tribune*, September 29, 1897.

227 *"tantamount to saying"*: "Questions before the McKinley Administration," *Collier's Weekly*, October 7, 1897.

15. YEAR-END ASSESSMENT

228 *a reunion of old soldiers*: "President a Comrade," *Washington Post*, September 3, 1897. All descriptions of the day come from the same source.

228 *"My comrades"*: WMcK, "Speech at the Reunion of the Twenty-Third Ohio Regiment, at Fremont, Ohio, September 2, 1897," in McKinley, *Speeches and Addresses of William McKinley, from March 1, 1897 to May 30, 1900*, p. 42.

229 *"the growing feeling of fraternal regard"*: WMcK, First Annual Message, December 6, 1897, Miller Center.

231 *"Any doubts which might have existed"*: "Praise for McKinley," *Chicago Tribune*, June 10, 1897.

231 *"President McKinley deserves"*: "The Reform Victory," *Nation*, August 5, 1897.

231 *"with a degree of confidence"*: "In Iron and Steel," *Washington Post*, August 16, 1897, reprinted from *Pittsburgh Dispatch*.

232 *"permanent, and everything points"*: *Pall Mall Gazette*, quoted in "Britain's Lost Supremacy in Iron," *Washington Post*, October 25, 1897, reprinted from *Springfield Republican*.

232 *started reopening mills*: "Prosperity Is Coming," *Washington Post*, August 17, 1897.

232 *a dollar a bushel*: "Dollar Wheat at Last," *Washington Post*, August 21, 1897.

232 *"will reach figures"*: "Another Boost for Wheat," *Washington Post*, August 23, 1897.

232 *issuing business loans*: "Heavy Loans by Banks," *Washington Post*, August 1, 1897.

232 *"general condition to-day"*: "1897," *Philadelphia Inquirer*, January 1, 1898.

232 *"one of the weakest characters"*: "Disgraceful Weakness," *St. Louis Republic*, October 21, 1897.

232 *she couldn't speak*: "Her Life Near Its End," *Washington Post*, December 3, 1897.

232 *"Tell mother I will be there"*: quoted in ibid.

232 *ten o'clock the next morning*: Ibid.

233 *his mother still alive*: "Back to Canton in Time," *Washington Post*, December 8, 1897.

233 *"The President is almost constantly"*: "Mrs. McKinley Still Alive," *New York Times*, December 9, 1897.

233 *just after two o'clock*: "President's Mother Dead," *New York Times*, December 11, 1897.

233 *"gave no outward evidence"*: "Mrs. M'Kinley's Funeral," *New York Times*, December 15, 1897.

233 *"Still, Still with Thee"*: Ibid.

233 *"It is not given"*: quoted in ibid.

233 *a crowd of 3,000*: Ibid.

233 *"very short and simple"*: "Last Rites at Canton," *Washington Post*, December 15, 1897.

233 *boarded an overnight train*: Ibid.

234 *thwart any endorsement*: "War Begun on Hanna," *Washington Post*, April 8, 1897.

234 *"Mark Hanna is in grave danger"*: "Warns the Hanna Men," *Washington Post*, April 30, 1897.

234 *"This means the overthrow"*: "M'Kisson Loses Control," *Washington Post*, June 19, 1897.

234 *"I suppose they need"*: quoted in "Senator Hanna Is Grateful," *Washington Post*, June 21, 1897.

234 *But Bushnell argued*: "Party Strife in Ohio," *Washington Post*, June 22, 1897.

235 *"freely quoted"*: Ibid.

235 *sought to ease tensions*: "Dick Defeats Kurtz," *Washington Post*, June 23, 1897.

235 *Dick won 2 to 1*: Ibid.

235 *Foraker even praised*: "Hanna Talks of Isms," *Washington Post*, September 12, 1897.

235 *30,000-vote edge*: "Hanna's Fate in Ohio," *Washington Post*, October 31, 1897.

235 *"Our position has greatly improved"*: quoted in ibid.

235 *"I sympathize with you"*: WMcK to MAH, October 14, 1897, McKinley Letters 1864–1901.

235 *"There was quite a smile"*: "Hanna's Fate in Ohio."

236 *drubbing in Hamilton County*: "Hanna's Fate in Doubt," *Washington Post*, November 3, 1897.

236 *five-vote legislative majority*: "Five Majority in Ohio," *Washington Post*, November 4, 1897.

236 *"Am just home"*: WMcK to MAH, November 4, 1897, HMcCP.

236 *"The Foraker men have knives"*: "Hanna's Fate in Ohio."

236 *thirty of them wouldn't pledge*: "Deal to Down Hanna," *Washington Post*, November 9, 1897.

236 *"We have decided"*: quoted in ibid.

236 *"The days of Hanna's bossism"*: quoted in "Hanna to Be Retired," *Washington Post*, November 11, 1897.

237 *"So far as I can now foresee"*: quoted in "Will Keep His Hands Off," *Washington Post*, November 11, 1897.

237 *"I do not care to talk"*: quoted in "Bushnell for Senate," *Washington Post*, November 8, 1897.

237 *McKinley became alarmed*: "Mr. M'Kinley Is Concerned," *Washington Post*, November 12, 1897.

237 *until after three o'clock*: "Grosvenor His Guest," *Washington Post*, November 12, 1897.

237 *"Along the whole line"*: "He Will Fight Hanna," *Washington Post*, November 13, 1897.

238 *"I have had an extensive correspondence"*: quoted in "More Troubles for Hanna," *Washington Post*, December 2, 1897.

238 *"Senator Foraker, Mr. Hanna"*: quoted in "Hobart and Foraker Exchanged Threats," *St. Louis Republic*, December 19, 1897, reprinted from *New York Journal*.

238 *J. L. Carpenter might bolt*: Charles Grosvenor to J. L. Carpenter, December 24, 1897, WMcKP, Reel 3.

238 *a testy letter to McKinley*: J. L Carpenter to WMcK, December 28, 1897, WMcKP, Reel 3.

239 *A similar letter*: O. P. Austin to WMcK, December 30, 1897, WMcKP, Reel 3.

239 *seventy-five Republicans*: "Hanna Short 4 Votes," *Washington Post*, January 2, 1898.

239 *ten Republicans and Fusionists*: "Defeat for Hanna," *Washington Post*, January 4, 1898.

239 *"Unless there is a material change"*: Ibid.

239 *Hanna needed at least three*: "Where Hanna Now Stands," *Washington Post*, January 5, 1898.

239 *"is wearing on him"*: J. G. Schmidlapp to WMcK, January 5, 1898, WMcKP, Reel 3.

239 *"I cannot tell you"*: WMcK to MAH, January 7, 1898, McKinley's Letters 1864–1901.

240 *"voters of Ohio arose"*: "His Title in the People's Will," *New York Press*, January 13, 1898.

240 *"frost"*: "Frost for Bushnell," *Washington Post*, January 11, 1898. Other details on the inauguration come from the same source.

240 *promised if elected*: "Hanna Gets 73 Votes," *Washington Post*, January 12, 1898.

240 *seven Republicans who ultimately bolted*: Ibid.

240 *one-vote victory*: Ibid.

240 *"God reigns"*: quoted in "They Stood by Hanna," *Washington Post*, January 13, 1898.

241 *"one of the most sensational"*: "The Ohio Victory," *St. Louis Globe-Democrat*, January 12, 1898.

241 *"Believers in fair play"*: "Hanna and Popular Choice of Senators," *Brooklyn Daily Eagle*, January 12, 1898.

241 *"There has never been"*: "Senator Hanna's Victory," *New York Mail and Express*, January 12, 1898.

241 *"in a maimed and enfeebled condition"*: "Mr. Hanna's Victory," *New York Daily Tribune*, January 13, 1898.

241 *"The difficult task"*: Ibid.

16. AMERICA AND SPAIN

242 *"I have done all"*: quoted in Woodford to WMcK, January 17, 1896, JBMP, Box 185. All quotes from Woodford's report come from the same source.

244 *They smashed windows*: "Army Riot in Havana," *Washington Post*, January 13, 1898.

244 *part of a broader plot*: Offner, p. 94.

245 *"pretext . . . to interfere"*: "Spaniards Angered by Aid," *Washington Post*, January 12, 1898.

245 *"that U.S. intermediation"*: Fitzhugh Lee to William Day, January 15, 1895, William Day Papers, Box 35.

245 *"Those persons who have presumed"*: "The McKinley Patience," *St. Louis Globe-Democrat*, February 6, 1898.

245 *When Russell Hastings sought consideration*: Russell Hastings to WMcK, March 2, 1898, WMcKP, Reel 3.

245 *"I desire to thank you"*: Russell Hastings to WMcK, March 27, 1898, WMcKP, Reel 3.

246 *"For the first time"*: "A Scene of Splendor," *Washington Post*, January 20, 1898.

246 *"vulgar mobs"*: quoted in Leech, *In the Days of McKinley*, pp. 130–31.

246 *shut down Bingham's program*: Ibid., p. 131.

246 *"There is enough trouble"*: quoted in Anthony, p. 140.

246 *a stream of actors*: Ibid.

246 *character monologues*: Ibid., p. 141.

246 *throne-like blue velvet chair*: "A Scene of Splendor," *Washington Post*, January 20, 1898.

246 *"elixir of ambition"*: quoted in Anthony, notes, p. 320.

246 *"tenderness toward his patient"*: "How Leonard Wood Rose," *New York Times*, August 23, 1903.

247 *a $250 check*: Anthony, p. 139.

247 *"not more devoted"*: "How Leonard Wood Rose."

247 *Speaking before 1,000*: "To Pay Bonds in Gold," *Washington Post*, January 28, 1898.

247 *would not violate the public faith*: Ibid.

247 *The money of the United States*: WMcK, speech before the National Association of Manufacturers, New York, January 27, 1898, in McKinley, *Speeches and Addresses of William McKinley, from March 1, 1897 to May 30, 1900*, p. 60.

248 *"rent in the same manner"*: "The President's Speech," *The Nation*, February 3, 1898.

248 *"step-by-step" acquisition*: quoted in Morgan, *Pacific Gibraltar*, p. 178.

248 *sixty Senate votes needed*: "The Hawaiian Treaty," *Washington Post*, January 6, 1898.

248 *eighty-eight-seat chamber*: Morgan, *Pacific Gibraltar*, p. 179.

249 *three Republicans from beet sugar states*: "Have Lost Two Votes," *Washington Post*, January 12, 1898.

249 *"that the opening of the new century"*: quoted in ibid.

249 *"In case the islands"*: quoted in ibid.

249 *"the President has been appealed to"*: "Still Lacks Enough Votes," *Washington Post*, January 15, 1898.

250 *He debarked in San Francisco*: "Mr. Dole Is Coming at Once," *Washington Post*, January 19, 1898.

250 *Chicago on January 22*: "Dole Has No Special Power," *Washington Post*, January 23, 1898.

250 *occasional mood swings*: Morgan, *Pacific Gibraltar*, p. 95.

250 *"I welcome you"*: quoted in "President Dole Here," *Washington Post*, January 27, 1898.

250 *nearly 3,000 guests*: "The Social World," *Washington Evening Star*, February 3, 1898.

250 *"to awe their way"*: Ibid.

250 *"profusion of ferns"*: "White House Crowded," *Washington Post*, February 3, 1898.

251 *"extremely favorable"*: quoted in "President Dole at Home," *Washington Post*, March 14, 1898.

251 *circumvent his opposition*: "To Checkmate Reed," *Washington Post*, January 22, 1898.

251 *the speaker announced his support*: "Reed and the Treaty," *Washington Post*, February 7, 1898.

251 *Senate leaders decided to abandon the treaty*: "Will Abandon the Treaty," *Washington Post*, February 24, 1898.

251 *approved resolution language*: "Treaty Abandoned," *Washington Post*, March 17, 1898.

251 *"The President is anxious"*: GBCD, June 8, 1898, Box 52.

251 *Under congressional authority*: WMcK, Second Annual Message, December 5, 1897, Miller Center.

252 *the commission traveled to Nicaragua*: "Nicaragua Canal Commission," *Washington Post*, January 16, 1898.

252 *Godkin saw no problem*: "The Nicaragua Canal," *Nation*, May 26, 1898.

252 *a brazen challenge*: William Day memo, January 20, 1898, William Day Papers, Box 35.

253 *"a fair opportunity"*: William Day, "Memorandum," undated, William Day Papers, Box 35.

253 *After the session*: Ibid.

254 *324-foot, 6,682-ton Maine*: Blow, pp. 73, 75.

254 *"came gliding into [Havana] harbor"*: Fitzhugh Lee to William Day, January 26, 1898, William Day Papers, Box 35.

254 *cordial welcoming visit*: "Maine Now at Havana," *Washington Post*, January 26, 1898.

254 *"and all the ceremonies"*: Ibid.

254 *"rattled" by the arrival*: Fitzhugh Lee to William Day, January 26, 1898, William Day Papers, Box 35.

254 *reinforced police protection*: "Increased the Guard," *Washington Post*, January 27, 1898.

254 *"I see that we have only good news"*: quoted in Musicant, p. 130.

254 *"sincere declaration"*: quoted in ibid.

255 *"still very much excited"*: Woodford to WMcK, January 28, 1898, JBMP, Box 185.

255 *"hints of a change"*: quoted in Musicant, p. 131.

255 *Spanish authorities had become pessimistic*: Woodford to WMcK, February 7, 1898, JBMP, Box 185.

255 *"They will do no more"*: Ibid.

255 *"expressions humiliating to the President"*: quoted in Musicant, p. 132.

255 *clerk at the Spanish embassy*: "Cubans on Its Track," *Washington Post*, February 14, 1898.

256 *"natural and inevitable coarseness"*: quoted in "Branded as Forgery," *Washington Post*, February 9, 1898. The full Dupuy de Lôme letter is reprinted here.

256 *"asked and accepted"*: Woodford to John Sherman, February 11, 1898, JBMP, Box 185.

257 *"The Spanish government"*: quoted in "Wants Spain to Reply," *Washington Post*, February 12, 1898.

257 *in a letter to Gullón*: Woodford to WMcK, February 15, 1898, JBMP, Box 185.

257 *"an open door"*: quoted in ibid.

257 *"was not all that I could have wished"*: Woodford to WMcK, February 19, 1898, JBMP, Box 185.

257 *"the best comment one can make"*: "The De Lome Letter," *Nation*, February 17, 1898.

<h3 style="text-align:center">17. PATH TO WAR</h3>

258 *bugler C. H. Newton*: Blow, p. 38.

258 *"No," replied Blandin*: quoted in ibid., p. 96.

258 *"terrible roar"*: quoted in "Saw Maine Blown Up," *Washington Post*, February 22, 1898.

259 *"bursting, rending"*: quoted in Blow, p. 96.

259 *"white forms"*: quoted in ibid., p. 97.

259 *"Maine blown up"*: Charles Sigsbee to John D. Long, cable message, reprinted in Blow, p. 101.

259 *It was approaching 1 a.m.*: Blow, p. 102.

259 *"The Maine blown up!"*: quoted in ibid., p. 105.

259 *chided him for being late*: GBCD, January 22, 1899, Box 52.

260 *eventually hit 266*: "266 the Total Loss," *Washington Post*, March 23, 1898.

260 *"My duty is plain"*: quoted in Olcott, p. 2:12.

260 *"semi-official statement"*: "Administration Is Mystified," *Washington Post*, February 17, 1898.

260 *"Every representative"*: Ibid.

260 *"Being a Jingo"*: quoted in Blow, p. 110.

260 *"other big news"*: quoted in Nasaw, p. 131.

260 *"WAR! SURE!"*: quoted in Blow, p. 111.

261 *the facts were "being concealed"*: quoted in "Some Rash Talk," *Washington Post*, February 19, 1898.

261 *Five days later*: "War Talk in Senate," *Washington Post*, February 24, 1898.

261 *"Calmness, silence"*: quoted in ibid.

261 *"will not be jingoed"*: quoted in "Will Not Be Jingoed into War," *Washington Post*, February 27, 1898.

261 *"seek to delay"*: "Memorandum of Feb. 26th, 1898," unsigned but presumably written by William Day, William Day Papers, Box 35.

261 *once again pleaded*: Woodford to WMcK, February 23, 1898, JBMP, Box 185.

261 *The same entreaty*: Woodford to WMcK, February 26, 1898, JBMP, Box 185.

262 *But in a gesture of friendship*: Ibid.

262 *a U.S. naval officer named "Brownsfield"*: Woodford to WMcK, March 2, 1898, JBMP, Box 185.

262 *"The President will not consider"*: "Supports Lee," *Washington Post*, March 7, 1898.

262 *"There was not, of course"*: "Crowninshield Suspected," *Washington Post*, March 9, 1898.

263 *"Moret is sincerely grateful"*: Woodford to WMcK, March 4, 1898, JBMP, Box 185.

263 On March 7 *the president summoned*: "If War Comes," *Washington Post*, March 8, 1898.

263 *passed the bill unanimously*: "Moved by Patriotism," *Washington Post*, March 9, 1898.

263 *"We now propose"*: quoted in "If War Comes."

263 *"simply stunned"*: Woodford to WMcK, March 9, 1898, JBMP, Box 185.

264 *two Brazilian cruisers*: Gould, *The Presidency of William McKinley*, p. 76.

264 *exceeded $400 million*: "The Situation in Spain," *Nation*, March 3, 1898.

264 *"There can be no question"*: Ibid.

264 *up to $200 million*: "What Gomez Will Accept," *Washington Post*, March 27, 1898.

264 *"The Spanish people are as patriotic"*: "The Situation in Spain."

264 *until eleven o'clock or later*: GBCD, March 16, 1898.

264 *"careworn" and "haggard"*: Ibid.

264 *"gentle and considerate"*: GBCD, March 20, 1898, Box 52.

265 *"one of the plainest dictates"*: quoted in "Senator Chandler for War," *Washington Post*, March 8, 1898.

265 *"Torn from their homes"*: quoted in "What He Saw in Cuba," *Washington Post*, March 18, 1898.

265 *"The speech will undoubtedly"*: quoted in "It Should Make Cuba Free," *Washington Post*, March 18, 1898.

265 *coincided with a White House briefing*: Gould, *The Presidency of William McKinley*, p. 78.

265 *"within a very few days"*: Woodford to WMcK, March 22, 1898, JBMP, Box 185.

266 *"The President approves"*: William Day to Woodford, March 23, 1898, Day Papers, Box 35.

266 *Woodford repeated the warning*: Woodford to WMcK, March 24, 1898, JBMP, Box 185.

266 *Spanish officials would consider further concessions*: Woodford to WMcK, March 25, 1898, JBMP, Box 185.

266 *The President's desire*: Day to Woodford, March 25, 1895, Day Papers, Box 35.

267 *"Do the words"*: Woodford to Day, March 27, 1898, Day Papers, Box 35.

267 *"Full self Government"*: Day to Woodford, March 28, 1898, Day Papers, Box 35.

267 *a fuller rendition*: Day to Woodford, March 27, 1898, Day Papers, Box 35.

267 *"It is of the utmost importance"*: Day to Woodford, March 29, 1898, Day Papers, Box 35.

268 *discipline aboard ship had been "excellent"*: "Summary of the report made March 21 by United States board of inquiry in case of the Maine," unsigned, JBMP, Box 185.

268 *The president brought in Day and Long*: GBC, transcript of shorthand notes, March 25, 1898, GBCP, Box 52.

268 *He spent most of Saturday*: GBC, transcript of shorthand notes, March 26, 1898, GBCP, Box 52.

268 *"appalling calamity"*: "The President's Message," *Washington Post*, March 29, 1898.

269 *"It is to speak moderately"*: "Impatience in Congress," *New York Times*, March 29, 1898.

269 *Joseph Bailey of Texas introduced a resolution*: "Stood by the Speaker," *Washington Post*, March 31, 1898.

269 *"the succession of events"*: "Senate in a Ferment," *Washington Post*, March 29, 1898.

269 *"Say no more"*: quoted in Morgan, *William McKinley and His America*, p. 280.

269 *a day of "grave anxiety"*: GBCD, March 31, 1898, Box 52.

269 *Sagasta said he would submit*: Woodford to WMcK, March 31, 1898, JBMP, Box 185.

269 *"was a sorrow to me"*: Woodford to WMcK, April 1, 1898, JBMP, Box 185.

269 *"Spain's only hope"*: "War Now Seems Inevitable," *Washington Post*, April 1, 1898.

270 *"Anxiety for prompt action"*: "Action Is Delayed," *Washington Post*, April 1, 1898.

270 *the president had "risen above politics"*: "The President's Due," *Washington Post*, April 1, 1898, reprinted from *Louisville Courier-Journal*.

270 *"a patient and forbearing nation"*: "President McKinley Is Right," *Washington Post*, April 3, 1898, reprinted from *Baltimore Sun*.

270 *burning the president in effigy*: "Enraged at McKinley," *Washington Post*, March 31, 1898.

271 *"The Spanish fleet"*: quoted in Kohlsaat, p. 66. Kohlsaat's full rendition of the episode has McKinley breaking down in tears and expressing worry about whether his reddened eyes would be evident when he returned to his other guests in the Blue Room. Lewis L. Gould, doubting the veracity of this and

other reports of such visible despair on the president's part, writes, "Memoir accounts that have him in tears and despair seem, aside from the factual errors that they contain, to be unreliable in substance" (Gould, *The Presidency of William McKinley*, p. 78).

271 *"has shown a good deal"*: Long, p. 175.

271 *Pope Leo XIII serve as a mediator*: "Leo XIII as Mediator," *Washington Post*, April 4, 1898.

271 *"If conditions at Washington"*: Woodford to WMcK, April 3, 1898, JBMP, Box 185.

271 *"is not armistice"*: Day to Woodford, April 4, 1898, Day Papers, Box 35.

271 *A crowd of 10,000 gathered*: GBC, transcript of shorthand notes, April 6, 1898, GBCP, Box 52.

271 *"History is being made"*: Ibid.

272 *"I will not do it"*: quoted in ibid.

272 *"as soft as a chocolate éclair"*: quoted in Buchanan, *A Republic, Not an Empire*, p. 155.

272 *"Does the Senator"*: "Lee Advised Delay," *Washington Post*, April 7, 1898.

272 *Washington recognized "the good will"*: WMcK, reply to six European powers, April 7, 1898, WMcKP.

272 *The queen regent on April 9*: Woodford to Day, April 9, 1898, Day Papers, Box 35.

273 *he obligingly praised the decision*: "For Peace in Cuba," *Washington Post*, April 6, 1898.

273 *The Cabinet drew up a memorandum*: "Memorandum, Department of State, April 10, 1898," Day Papers, Box 35.

273 *Lee left Havana*: "Lee Leaves Havana," *Washington Post*, April 10, 1898.

273 *a 7,000-word "war message"*: "William McKinley: War Message," https://www.mtholyoke.edu/acad/intrel/mkinly2.htm.

274 *"somewhat indefinite"*: Long, p. 178.

274 *"The message has caused great discontent"*: "An Angry Congress," *New York Times*, April 12, 1898.

274 *"I have no patience"*: quoted in "Comment on the Message," *New York Times*, April 12, 1898.

274 *"anemic"*: quoted in ibid.

274 *"I have some communications"*: quoted in GBCD, April 12, 1898, Box 52.

275 *a vote of 150 to 190*: Gould, *The Presidency of William McKinley*, p. 87.

275 *"at once relinquish"*: quoted in "Cuba Must Be Free," *New York Times*, April 19, 1898.

275 *"as the true and lawful"*: quoted in Gould, *The Presidency of William McKinley*, p. 87.

275 *disavowed any U.S. domination*: Leech, *In the Days of McKinley*, p. 188.

275 *"Until Saturday"*: quoted in GBCD, April 20, 1898, Box 52.

276 *"This is a historic occasion"*: Ibid.

18. VICTORY AT SEA

277 *a blockade of Cuba*: WMcK, "Proclamation 411. Blockade of Cuba," April 22, 1898, *American Presidency Project*, http://www.presidency.ucsb.edu/ws/inex.php?pid=69195.

277 *"remarkable for terseness"*: "Long's War Orders to Dewey," *New York Times*, May 10, 1898.

277 *"Dewey, Hongkong, China"*: William Long telegram, April 24, 1898, WMcKP, Reel 3.

278 *"the best fellow in the world"*: Long, p. 170.

278 *"great inventive capacity"*: quoted in Spector, p. 37.

278 *When Chandler rebuffed Roosevelt's entreaty*: Musicant, p. 113.

278 *"Do you know any senators?"*: Dewey, p. 168.

278 *the senator seemed "delighted"*: quoted in ibid., p. 169.

278 *"is the man you want"*: quoted in Healy and Kutner, p. 137.

279 *"I am glad to appoint you"*: quoted in ibid., p. 138.

279 *"You are in error"*: quoted in Dewey, p. 169.

279 *"little pinpricking slight"*: quoted in Spector, p. 38.

279 *"little opportunity"*: quoted in Musicant, p. 111.

280 *"to carry the heaviest armor"*: "Millions for the Navy," *Washington Post*, March 25, 1896.

280 *"torpedo boat catchers"*: "Strengthening the Navy," *Washington Post*, April 8, 1896.

281 *the U.S. naval fleet consisted of*: Leech, *In the Days of McKinley*, p. 157.

281 *"I have all Navy"*: Theodore Roosevelt Diary, April 16, 1898.

281 *top speed of seventeen knots*: "Iowa Capable of 17 Knots," *Washington Post*, November 14, 1896.

281 *to prepare its fleets*: Citations include *Washington Post* articles, "Will Not Be Derelict," March 5, 1898; "Putting On War Paint," March 30, 1898; "Preparations at Key West," April 5, 1898; and "Battleships Taking On Coal," January 14, 1898.

281 *Washington naval officials ordered Dewey*: Gould, *The Spanish-American War and President McKinley*, p. 60.

281 *Long organized his Atlantic fleet*: "Two New Squadrons," *Washington Post*, March 26, 1898.

282 *"hysterical anxiety"*: quoted in Musicant, p. 298.

282 *"calm and scholarly"*: quoted in ibid., p. 299.

282 *son of a day laborer*: "The Rise of Sampson," *Washington Post*, July 5, 1898.

282 *"pleasure and holidays"*: quoted in Cathy Hunter, "Winfield Scott Schley: A Hero, but Not without Controversy," *National Geographic*, December 20, 2012, http://voices.nationalgeographic.com/search/Winfield+Scott+Schley.

282 *two sailors killed*: "Real Admiral Winfield Scott Schley," Spanish-American War Centennial Website, http://www.spanamwar.com/schley/htm.

282 *"If the Army were one-tenth as ready"*: TR to Robley D. Evans, April 20, 1898, Theodore Roosevelt Center.

282 *"unguarded condition"*: "Be Prepared for War," *Washington Post*, November 12, 1895.

283 *"entire Gulf coast"*: Ibid.

283 *one soldier for every 2,000 citizens*: "Urges a Larger Army," *Washington Post*, November 12, 1896.

283 *"brave peacock"*: quoted in "Nelson A. Miles," *Wikipedia*.

283 *converted into a "War Room"*: GBCD, May 3, 1898, Box 52.

283 *fifteen telephone lines*: Jones, p. 79.

283 *"an expert Western Union operator"*: GBCD, May 3, 1898, Box 52.

283 *thousands of secret cables*: "Telegraphy and War," *Washington Post*, August 14, 1898.

283 *"The President appears to be cheerful"*: GBCD, May 3, 1898, Box 52.

284 *the longest walk*: Long, p. 184.

284 *"It's a good plan"*: GBCD, May 3, 1898, Box 52.

284 *"a good working Cabinet"*: GBCD, April 16, 1898, Box 52.

284 *"made a mistake"*: Long, p. 194.

284 *"of little use in the Cabinet"*: Ibid., p. 186.

284 *"crisis was precipitated"*: quoted in Leech, *In the Days of McKinley*, p. 191.

284 *McKinley sat down with Sherman*: Ibid.

285 *"Judge Day," declared the* Louisville Commercial: "The State Portfolio," *Louisville Commercial*, April 24, 1898.

285 *"endangering his position"*: Dawes, p. 158.

285 *"At present it seems as if"*: Long, p. 183.

285 *increase the regular forces to 62,527*: Musicant, p. 245.

285 *volunteer force of 60,000*: Ibid., p. 244.

285 *125,000 volunteers*: "By the President of the United States: A Proclamation," *Washington Post*, April 24, 1898.

285 *"to last an army"*: quoted in Musicant, p. 254.

285 *force of 5,000*: Gould, *The Presidency of William McKinley*, p. 107.

286 *some 17,000 troops*: Ibid.

286 *specially made by Brooks Brothers*: Morris, *The Rise of Theodore Roosevelt*, p. 615.

286 *"No words could describe"*: quoted in Gould, *The Presidency of William McKinley*, p. 107.

286 *"The place was overestimated"*: quoted in ibid.

286 *some $100 million*: "Support of the Army," *Washington Post*, May 3, 1898.

287 *"While it is quite clear that the Spanish squadron"*: "The News in London," *New York Times*, May 2, 1898.

287 *"wild rejoicing"*: "Rejoicing in Washington," *New York Times*, May 2, 1898.

287 *Newsboys rushed*: Ibid.

287 *"was a source of the greatest satisfaction"*: GBCD, May 3, 1898, Box 52.

287 *Dewey had set out for the Philippines*: Details of the Battle of Manila come largely from Dewey, *The Autobiography of George Dewey*; Trask, *The War with Spain in 1898*, p. 95.

288 *"Now we have them!"*: quoted in Trask, p. 98.

288 *"You may fire"*: quoted in Dewey, p. 214.

288 *"It was a most anxious moment"*: Ibid., p. 218.

288 *sunk or disabled*: Ibid., p. 223.

288 *161 Spaniards*: Trask, p. 104.

288 *nine men had been wounded*: Ibid.

288 *"From the moment"*: quoted in Dewey, p. 224.

288 *"Dewey Chewies"*: quoted in Leech, *In the Days of McKinley*, p. 209.

290 *"badges, banners"*: Ibid., p. 208.

290 *"Every American"*: quoted in Dewey, p. 227.

290 *"mingled wisdom and daring"*: quoted in ibid.

290 *"It is these quiet, gentlemanly Americans"*: quoted in "All Talked of Dewey," *Washington Post*, May 3, 1898.

290 *"We may run him"*: quoted in Dewey, p. 228.

290 *"The magnitude of this victory"*: WMcK, "Message on Manila," May 9, 1898, Spanish American War file, WMPL.

290 *"the Department of the Pacific"*: Musicant, p. 260.

290 *ballooned to 15,000*: Leech, *In the Days of McKinley*, p. 211.

290 *"conquering a territory"*: quoted in Musicant, p. 261.

291 *"The force ordered"*: quoted in ibid.

291 *troop strength to 20,000*: Leech, *In the Days of McKinley*, p. 211.

291 *"acquisition and control"*: quoted in ibid.

291 *began his education*: Morgan, *William McKinley and His America*, p. 294.

291 *"It is evident"*: quoted in ibid.

292 *"Unless I am utterly"*: quoted in Musicant, p. 262.

19. THE CARIBBEAN WAR

293 *he needed three weeks*: Gould, *The Spanish American War and President McKinley*, p. 74.

294 *"stating that the Navy is ready"*: Long, p. 188.

294 *"that there is any delay"*: Ibid.

294 *"the most active"*: Ibid.

294 *"whereas, in fact"*: Ibid.

294 *"To invade Cuba"*: quoted in Musicant, p. 258.

295 *"a short, sharp, conclusive"*: "Advance on Cuba," *Washington Post*, May 10, 1898.

295 *"seize and hold"*: J. C. Gilmore, "Confidential Memorandum for the Adjutant General," May 9, 1898, WMcKP, Reel 3.

295 *"without delay"*: "Ordered to Tampa," *Washington Post*, May 11, 1898.

295 *"Our ships are all ready"*: Long, p. 192.

296 *"The blunders [and] delays"*: Theodore Roosevelt Diary, May 21, 1898.

296 *Miles urged McKinley to put off the Cuba attack*: Gould, *The Spanish-American War and President McKinley*, p. 74.

296 *defended by 10,000 or so Spanish regulars*: Trask, p. 199.

296 *added new initiatives*: Musicant, p. 264.

297 *"the color having faded"*: GBCD, May 15, 1898, Box 52.

297 *"The President looked exceedingly well"*: GBCD, May 22, 1898, Box 52.

297 *"Now she can almost walk alone"*: GBCD, June 17, 1898, Box 52.

297 *"very tired and worn out"*: quoted in Anthony, p. 145.

297 *She demanded a direct telephone connection*: Ibid.

297 *his usual telegram*: Ibid.

297 *"No matter how busy"*: quoted in ibid., p. 147.

297 *usually well past eleven*: GBCD, May 15, May 17, May 22, 1898, Box 52.

298 *"capture or destroy"*: quoted in Gould, *The Spanish-American War and President McKinley*, p. 74.

298 *"confusion, confusion"*: quoted in Trask, p. 184.

298 *300 railroad cars*: Musicant, p. 268.

298 *"a perfect welter of confusion"*: quoted in ibid., p. 269.

298 *His troops were forced to buy food*: Ibid., p. 269.

298 *"most earnestly"*: GBCD, June 17, 1898, Box 52.

299 *At 7:50 p.m. Corbin wired Shafter*: Trask, p. 180.

299 *"Since telegraphing you"*: quoted in ibid.

299 *17,000-man advance force*: Musicant, p. 354.

299 *"Wait until you get further orders"*: quoted in Trask, p. 186.

299 *"We mean to start"*: quoted in ibid., p. 187.

299 *"the interminable delays"*: Theodore Roosevelt to Douglas Robinson Jr., June 12, 1898, Theodore Roosevelt Center.

300 *"a regular gamecock"*: quoted in Trask, p. 219.

300 *"We've got the damn Yankees"*: quoted in ibid., p. 221.

300 *sixteen killed and fifty-two wounded*: Ibid., p. 222.

301 *"The situation was desperate"*: quoted in Jones, p. 75.

301 *"someone had made an awful"*: quoted in ibid., p. 76.

301 *"very gallant"*: quoted in ibid.

302 *"Had a very heavy engagement"*: William Shafter to War Department, "Heavy Battle at Santiago," *Washington Post*, July 2, 1898.

302 *225 Americans killed*: Musicant, p. 425.

302 *"I fear I have underestimated"*: quoted in ibid., p. 429.

302 *"We are awaiting with intense anxiety"*: quoted in ibid., p. 430.

304 *"The fleet under my command"*: William Sampson, dispatch to Secretary of the Navy, reprinted in "Naval Victory Is Complete," *New York Times*, July 5, 1898.

304 *"like splendid sunlight"*: "Apprehension Turned into Great Rejoicing," *New York Times*, July 4, 1898.

304 *"You have the gratitude"*: WMcK to William Sampson, reprinted in "Naval Victory Is Complete."

304 *"discouraged tone"*: "Apprehension Turned into Great Rejoicing."

305 *"I shall hold"*: quoted in Leech, *In the Days of McKinley*, p. 254.

305 *"sorrow and anxiety"*: quoted in Gould, *The Spanish-American War and President McKinley*, p. 79.

305 *"Under these circumstances"*: quoted in ibid.

305 *"What you went to Santiago for"*: quoted in Olcott, p. 2:50.

306 *"and the opinion of the surgeon"*: quoted in Gould, *The Spanish-American War and President McKinley*, p. 79.

306 *"unless in your judgment"*: quoted in ibid., p. 80.

306 *They gave Toral twenty-four hours*: Ibid., p. 80.

307 *"He is the strong man"*: GBCD, June 17, 1898.

307 *"No orders of importance"*: Olcott, p. 2:49.

308 *"ceases to be the compass"*: Henry Norman, "America of the Future: The Policy of Expansion," *Washington Post*, July 3, 1898, reprinted from *London Chronicle*.

308 *"While we are conducting war"*: quoted in Leech, *In the Days of McKinley*, p. 238.

20. END OF HOSTILITIES

309 *meeting for three-thirty*: William Day, "Memorandum of interviews with the French Ambassador," JBMP, Box 185. All quotations and descriptions of the various meetings between Cambon and McKinley come from this source unless otherwise noted.

309 *"the vindication of her prestige"*: "Message of the Government of H. M. the Queen Regent of Spain," submitted to WMcK on July 26, 1898 by Jules Cambon, WMcKP, Reel 4.

310 *the president scribbled out his terms*: WMcK, handwritten note describing terms, July 26, 1898, WMcKP, Reel 4.

310 *back from vacation*: Leech, *In the Days of McKinley*, p. 282.

310 *the thoughts of John Hay*: John Hay to William Day, telegram, July 28, 1898, WMcKP, Reel 4.

310 *Griggs, Bliss, and Wilson favored*: Leech, *In the Days of McKinley*, p. 285.

310 *"Judge Day only wants"*: quoted in Olcott, pp. 2:62–63.

311 *Thus the final version*: William Day, statement to be delivered to the Duke of Almodovar del Rio via Jules Cambon, July 30, 1898, WMcKP, Reel 4.

311 *pulled from his pocket*: GBCD, July 31, 1898, Box 52.

311 *"The final changes"*: GBCD, July 30, 1898, Box 52.

311 *"The President has had his way"*: Dawes, p. 166.

311 *McKinley asked Day to read:* Day, "Memorandum of interviews with the French Ambassador."

312 *Four days later:* Ibid.

313 *Santiago de Cuba, August 3*: Associated Press dispatch, printed in "Return or Perish," *Washington Evening Star*, August 4, 1898.

314 *devoting more attention to the disposition*: Leech, *In the Days of McKinley*, p. 271.

314 *"somewhat improving"*: quoted in ibid.

315 *On August 2 he cabled Washington*: William Shafter, cable to Henry Corbin, August 2, 1898, in *Correspondence Relating to the War with Spain*, p. 1:194.

315 *Surgeon General George Sternberg*: Leech, *In the Days of McKinley*, p. 275.

315 *a stern order to Shafter*: Russell Alger, cable to William Shafter, August 2, 1898, in *Correspondence Relating to the War with Spain*, p. 1:196.

315 *"very much agitated"*: quoted in Leech, *In the Days of McKinley*, p. 276.

315 *"to kill off our sick"*: "The Medical Department Scandals," *New York Times*, August 4, 1898.

315 *"many searching questions"*: GBCD, August 3, 1898, Box 52.

315 *Secretary Alger sought to explain*: "War Secretary Explains," *New York Times*, August 4, 1898.

316 *Cortelyou considered Alger's statement "lame"*: GBCD, August 4, 1898, Box 52.

316 *"the impression"*: Ibid.

316 *"makes the situation"*: quoted in Gould, *The Presidency of William McKinley*, p. 120.

316 *"I demanded of Spain"*: Day, memo to Alvey Adee, "SPECIAL. For the President," November 18, 1898, WMcKP, Reel 5.

316 *"full and unqualified"*: quoted in Day, "Memorandum of interviews with the French Ambassador," JBMP, Box 185.

317 *"Spain will have nothing more"*: quoted in Gould, *The Presidency of William McKinley*, p. 121.

317 *"Mr. Ambassador"*: quoted in GBCD, August 12, 1898, Box 52.

317 *"Let's see what we get"*: quoted in ibid.

318 *"Speaker Reed"*: "Reed Still Fights Hawaii," *Washington Post*, May 12, 1898.

318 *On May 11 he summoned*: Ibid.

318 *cleared the annexation measure*: "Enemy Might Drub Us," *Washington Post*, May 13, 1898.

318 *a dismissive coyness*: "Anxiety over Hawaii," *Washington Post*, May 18, 1898.

318 *Reed announced*: "Speaker Reed Gives It Up," *Washington Post*, May 24, 1898.

318 *the resolutions fell behind*: "To Let Hawaii Alone," *Washington Post*, May 26, 1898.

318 *crowd the calendar*: "More Delay about Hawaii," *Washington Post*, June 8, 1898.

318 *"Just where the friends"*: Ibid.

319 *"a continuing order"*: quoted in "A Clash with Mr. Reed," *Washington Post*, June 9, 1898.

319 *"much vigor"*: Ibid.

319 *a military necessity*: "Hawaii's Chance Today," *Washington Post*, June 10, 1898.

319 *passed the resolutions*: "Big Vote for Hawaii," *Washington Post*, June 16, 1898.

319 *a test vote*: "Test Vote on Hawaii," *Washington Post*, June 21, 1898.

319 *"If we consummate this scheme"*: quoted in "Attack by the Pacific," *Washington Post*, June 23, 1898.

319 *"if we come out of this war"*: quoted in "No Flag of Dominion," *Washington Post*, July 6, 1898.

319 *it passed 42–21*: "Hawaii to Come In," *Washington Post*, July 7, 1898.

320 *"a new era"*: quoted in "Signed by the President," *Washington Post*, July 8, 1898.

320 *"genial and pleasant"*: GBCD, August 12, 1898.

320 *2,500 officers and men*: Gould, *The Presidency of William McKinley*, p. 125.

321 *"Forty of our men"*: quoted in "Trials of the Regiment," *New York Times*, August 30, 1898.

321 *"The general opinion"*: "Alger's Apologists Turn," *New York Times*, August 27, 1898.

321 *"The Secretary of War"*: quoted in "Alger Talks of His Work," *New York Times*, August 27, 1898.

321 *"unreasonable and unwarranted"*: quoted in GBCD, August 23, 1898, Box 52.

321 *"Alger is responsible"*: quoted in Gould, *The Presidency of William McKinley*, p. 123.

322 *"I'm sorry to see you so sick"*: quoted in "Mr. M'Kinley at Montauk," *New York Times*, September 4, 1898.

322 *Wilson as an intermediary*: Gould, *The Presidency of William McKinley*, p. 126.

322 *"He told me he is having"*: James Wilson to WMcK, September 7, 1898, GBCP, Box 69.

322 *Wilson "pointed out the weight"*: Ibid.

322 *"If there have been wrongs"*: quoted in Leech, *In the Days of McKinley*, p. 315.

323 *"The place is beyond my ambition"*: John Hay to WMcK, August 15, 1898, WMcKP, Reel 4.

323 *"This is—I am told"*: John Hay to WMcK, August 22, 1898, WMcKP, Reel 4.

323 *"between English-speaking peoples"*: quoted in Buchanan, *A Republic, Not an Empire*, p. 150.

323 *"There is a powerful"*: quoted in "Anglo-Saxon Allies," *Washington Post*, May 14, 1898.

323 *"a peace between us"*: quoted in "Cementing the Bond," *Washington Post*, April 21, 1898.

324 *But Hoar declined*: George Hoar to WMcK, September 14, 1898, WMcKP, Reel 4.

324 *twenty-two-page letter*: Thomas Platt to WMcK, August 14, 1898, WMcKP, Reel 4.

324 *"Permit me to respectfully"*: William Chandler to WMcK, August 17, 1898, WMcKP, Reel 4.

324 *Prices were solid*: "Outlook for the Fall," *Washington Post*, July 9, 1898.

324 *total exports were double*: "Great Import Trade," *Washington Post*, July 18, 1898.

325 *"not making political speeches"*: quoted in Gould, *The Presidency of William McKinley*, p. 127.

325 *"a significant departure"*: Ibid., p. 127.

325 *Democrats gained twenty-nine seats*: Moore, Preimesberger, and Tarr, p. 2:1569.

21. EMPIRE

326 *sixteen-year army career*: "Francis Vinton Greene," *Wikipedia*.

326 *3,550 troops*: Silbey, *A War of Frontier and Empire*, p. 44.

327 *Bradford warned*: Leech, *In the Days of McKinley*, p. 327.

327 *Dewey selected Luzon*: Ibid., p. 334.

327 *"a few random bits"*: Ibid.

328 *Greene estimated the Philippine population*: Francis V. Greene, "Memoranda concerning the situation in The Philippines, on Aug. 30, 1898," GBCP, Box 69. All descriptions of Philippines in this passage are from the same source unless otherwise noted.

328 *Philippine raw materials*: Silbey, *A War of Frontier and Empire*, p. 10.

328 *Spain first opened up society*: Ibid., p. 11.

329 *"Grandson of a Chinaman"*: Mark Twain, "Thirty Thousand Killed a Million,"

manuscript written in 1902 but unpublished until printed in *The Atlantic*, April 1992.

329 *"short but well-knit"*: "Aguinaldo the Insurgent," *Washington Post*, August 1, 1898, reprinted from *New York Tribune*.

330 *He was executed on May 10:* Silbey, *A War of Frontier and Empire*, p. 14.

331 *"honeyed phrases"*: quoted in ibid., p. 36.

331 *Pratt denied*: Ibid.

331 *U.S. naval officials transported Aguinaldo*: Healy and Kutner, p. 224.

331 *Aguinaldo once again insisted*: Ibid.

331 *Dewey denied it*: Ibid.

331 *"The situation is very grave"*: quoted in "Must Soon Give In," *Washington Post*, June 9, 1898.

331 the *"white population of the suburbs"*: quoted in "Manila's Situation Is Critical," *Washington Post*, June 16, 1898.

332 *11,000 troops at Cavite*: Silbey, *A War of Frontier and Empire*, pp. 43–44, 46.

332 *General Greene entered into a negotiation*: Ibid., p. 47.

332 *if the Americans attacked*: "Ready to Surrender," *Washington Post*, August 2, 1898.

334 *"uplift and civilize"*: quoted in Gould, *The Presidency of William McKinley*, p. 141. Historians have been amused by James F. Rusling's 1903 description of this meeting with the Methodists. According to Rusling, McKinley said he had been mystified by the Philippine conundrum until, pacing the floor late one night, "I went down on my knees and prayed Almighty God for light and guidance. It came to me this way—I don't know how it was, but it came" (quoted in Olcott, 2:109). The Rusling version had been credited by historians for decades until Lewis L. Gould noted that Rusling had rendered a similar portrait of President Lincoln revealing that he had gone to his knees to pray for divine assistance before the Battle of Gettysburg. A bit of a coincidence that this man would be positioned to hear two presidents tell of having successfully summoned divine intervention by going to their knees. Also, it is noteworthy that no one else among the many people at the meeting thought to recount the president's remarkable revelation during the four years between the meeting and Rusling's rendition. I left it out of the narrative with a view that it lacked credibility.

334 *"Is Government willing"*: cable, Wesley Merritt and Dewey to Corbin, August 13, 1898 (received August 17), in *Correspondence Relating to the War with Spain*, p. 2:754.

334 *"The President directs"*: cable, Corbin to Merritt and Dewey, August 17, 1898, in ibid.

335 *On September 15 he met with his peace commissioners*: GBCD, September 15, 1898, Box 52.

335 *memorandum of instruction*: GBCD, September 16, 1898.

335 *"imperative necessity"*: WMcK, memorandum of instruction to Peace Commission, September 16, 1898, reprinted in Olcott, p. 2:95.

335 *The president emphasized to Day*: Day, cable to WMcK, September 30, 1898, WMcKP, Reel 4.

335 *McKinley dropped a "hint"*: Whitelaw Reid to WMcK, October 4, 1898, WMcKP, Reel 4.

336 *"valuable notes and memoranda"*: John Hay, memorandum to Day, October 4, 1898, WMcKP, Reel 4.

336 *incident at the White House*: Memorandum, for the record, Alvey Adee, October 1, 1898, WMcKP, Reel 4.

336 *"Following his purpose"*: John Hay, memorandum to Day, October 4, 1898, WMcKP, Reel 4.

337 *"directly and openly"*: Joseph Medill to WMcK, October 17, 1898, WMcKP, Reel 4.

337 *"You would be astounded"*: Day to WMcK, October 23, 1898, WMcKP, Reel 4.

337 *"status quo" in the Philippines*: Day to WMcK, October 5, 1898, WMcKP, Reel 4.

337 *acquiesced with a "conciliatory" tone*: Ibid.

337 *"the expense," Day wrote*: Day to WMcK, October 23, 1898, WMcKP, Reel 4.

337 *"We are still free to regard it"*: John Hay to Day, October 13, 1898, WMcKP, Reel 4.

337 *"I hope we shall be able"*: Day to WMcK, October 23, 1898, WMcKP, Reel 4.

337 *"The President directs me"*: John Hay to Day, October 25, 1898, reprinted in Olcott, p. 2:102.

338 *"he seemed almost to break down"*: Whitelaw Reid to WMcK, October 28, 1898, WMcKP, Reel 4.

338 *"Spanish authority has been completely destroyed"*: George Dewey to John D. Long, October 18, 1898, WMcKP, Reel 4.

338 *"I am greatly pleased"*: WMcK to Day, October 25, 1898, WMcKP, Reel 4.

338 *"shall be embarrassed"*: Day to WMcK, October 28, 1898, WMcKP, Reel 4.

339 *favored taking the full archipelago*: Peace Commissioners, memorandum to John Hay, November 11, 1898, WMcKP, Reel 5.

339 *"moderation, restraint"*: George Gray to John Hay, November 11, 1898, WMcKP, Reel 5.

339 *"Grave as are the responsibilities"*: quoted in Gould, *The Spanish-American War and President McKinley*, p. 109.

339 *"I wish to submit"*: Day to WMcK, November 2, 1898, WMcKP, Reel 4.

339 *"a reasonable sum of money"*: quoted in Gould, *The Spanish-American War and President McKinley*, p. 110.

340 *"Yesterday everybody was predicting"*: Whitelaw Reid to WMcK, November 15, 1898, WMcKP, Reel 5.

340 *"I think & know"*: Ibid.

340 *"benevolent assimilation"*: WMcK, Benevolent Assimilation Proclamation, December 21, 1898, sent to Russell Alger, in *Correspondence Relating to the War with Spain*, p. 2:858.

340 *"Our concern was not for territory"*: WMcK, speech before the Home Market Club, Boston, February 16, 1899, in McKinley, *Speeches and Addresses of William McKinley from March 1, 1897 to May 30, 1900*, p. 185.

341 *"Sea power counts"*: "How Sea Power Counts," *Washington Post*, May 17, 1898, reprinted from *Philadelphia Press*.

341 *"a triumphant march"*: William Osborne to WMcK, November 11, 1898, WMcKP, Reel 5.

341 *"initiates the first experiment"*: "Governing at a Distance," *Nation*, May 19, 1898.

341 *"I . . . predict"*: Carl Schurz to WMcK, September 22, 1898, WMcKP, Reel 4.

22. WAR'S AFTERMATH

342 *"a perfect "Dodworth curtsy"*: Anthony, p. xii. This entire episode comes from the same source.

344 *eleven public appearances*: speeches enumerated in McKinley, *Speeches and Addresses of William McKinley, from March 1, 1897 to May 30, 1900*, p. 158.

344 *"Sectional lines no longer"*: WMcK, "Speech before the Legislature in Joint Assembly at the State Capitol, Atlanta, Georgia, December 14, 1898," ibid., p. 158.

344 *singing Methodist hymns*: Dawes, p. 180.

344 *five evening receptions*: "White House Guests," *Washington Post*, January 19, 1899.

344 *nearly 8,000 visitors*: "The President's Reception," *New York Times*, January 23, 1899.

344 *lavish White House dinner*: "A Dinner at the White House," *New York Times*, January 14, 1899.

344 *"one of the most beautifully appointed"*: "Social and Personal: President and Mrs. McKinley Entertained at Dinner," *Washington Post*, January 17, 1899.

344 *"How these men try"*: quoted in GBCD, January 22, 1899, Box 52.

345 *perhaps seventy*: "Treaty in the Senate," *Washington Post*, January 5, 1899.

345 *"a locomotive bottomside up"*: quoted in Jones, p. 98.

345 *U.S. forces organized police and garbage collection*: Ibid.

345 *to issue an order forbidding his troops*: Miller, *"Benevolent Assimilation,"* p. 58.

346 *(approved by the president)*: Corbin to Otis, September 7, 1898, in *Correspondence Relating to the War with Spain*, p. 2:789.

346 *"I shall be obliged"*: Elwell Otis, message to Emilio Aguinaldo, sent in dispatch to Corbin, September 7, 1898, ibid., p. 788.

346 *Otis toned down the wording*: Miller, *"Benevolent Assimilation,"* p. 47.

346 *"Affairs much more satisfactory"*: Otis to Corbin, September 15, 1898, in *Correspondence Relating to the War with Spain*, p. 2:790.

346 *Permission was granted*: Corbin to Otis, December 21, 1898, ibid., p. 2:857.

346 *"It is most important"*: Ibid.

346 *"The President considers it"*: Corbin to Otis, January 1, 1899, ibid., p. 2:866.

347 *"is to be extended"*: WMcK, "Benevolent Assimilation Proclamation," sent to Russell Alger, December 21, 1898, ibid., p. 2:858.

347 *30,000-strong force*: "Filipino Army 30,000 Strong," *New York Times*, January 25, 1899.

347 *"I believe it only a matter of time"*: quoted in Silbey, *A War of Frontier and Empire*, p. 61.

348 *"to exercise sovereignty"*: Senate resolution, quoted in "Filipinos Will Be Free," *New York Times*, January 12, 1899.

348 *"an act of war"*: Ibid.

348 *"Among the powers of nationality"*: quoted in ibid.

348 *"continued uncertainty"*: quoted in "To Vote on the Treaty," *New York Times*, January 26, 1899.

348 *"the lack of sufficient votes"*: "Still Lack Two Votes," *Washington Post*, February 1, 1899.

349 *would let the treaty die*: Ibid.

349 *dangling patronage and other favors*: Karnow, p. 138.

349 *"Oh . . . that need not trouble you"*: quoted in Gould, *The Presidency of William McKinley*, p. 149.

349 *McKinley sat at his Cabinet Room table*: GBCD, February 4, 1899, Box 52.

349 *"It is always the unexpected"*: quoted in ibid.

349 *At 8:05 the next morning*: Dewey to Long, February 5, 1899, in *Correspondence Relating to the War with Spain*, p. 2:894.

350 *"We are still driving enemy"*: Otis to Corbin, February 5, 1899, ibid.

350 *fifty-nine U.S. servicemen had died*: Karnow, p. 144.

350 *the first shot likely had been fired*: Ibid., p. 140.

350 *"Hangs Upon a Thread"*: "Hangs upon a Thread," *Washington Post*, February 5, 1899.

350 *the final two votes*: "Should Help Treaty," *Washington Post*, February 6, 1899.

350 *The Senate revealed its sentiment*: "Senate Ratifies the Peace Treaty," *New York Times*, February 7, 1899.

350 *McLaurin announced his support*: Ibid.

350 *"not intended to incorporate"*: quoted in "The McEnery Amendment," *New York Times*, February 7, 1899.

350 *died in the House*: Gould, *The Spanish-American War and President McKinley*, p. 118.

350 *Jones of Nevada switched*: "How the Vote Was Taken," *New York Times*, February 7, 1899.

351 *fifty-seven votes for ratification*: Ibid.

351 *"It was the closest, hardest fight"*: quoted in Leech, *In the Days of McKinley*, p. 358.

351 *"with a beaming smile"*: Ibid.

351 *"Only a few hours before"*: quoted in ibid.

351 *"Pretty pugnacious"*: Beisner, p. 152.

351 *109 meetings*: "The Spanish-American War: Tropical Preventive Medicine (1898–1914), The Spanish-American War (1898), Part VII," U.S. Army Medical Department, Office of Medical History, http://history.amedd.army.mil/booksdocs/misc/evprev/ch7.htm.

351 *Chicago, Detroit, Harrisburg*: Cosmas, p. 285. Subsequent details about the commission and related quotes are from this source.

353 *Miles took umbrage at a cable*: Ibid., p. 286.

353 *The general again took umbrage*: Ibid., p. 287.

353 *Miles went public with his animosities*: Ibid.

353 *"Gen. Nelson A. Miles"*: headline, *Washington Post*, February 12, 1899.

354 *parade through New York*: Cosmas, p. 288.

354 *"wild with suppressed rage"*: quoted in ibid., p. 289.

354 *tasted of boric and salicylic acids*: Ibid., p. 290.

354 *"At the best"*: "Roosevelt on Army Beef," *New York Times*, January 14, 1899.

354 *liquefaction of the meat's fat*: Associated Press, "Report of War Board," *Washington Post*, February 9, 1899.

354 *found it "in perfect condition"*: "Cabinet Tests the Beef," *Washington Post*, February 11, 1899.

354 *"not borne out"*: Associated Press, "Report of War Board."

355 *"with as black a heart"*: quoted in Cosmas, p. 292.

355 *"the words of violence and heat"*: quoted in "Gen. Eagan Is Denounced," *New York Times*, January 14, 1899, reprinted from *Washington Times*.

355 *"long in duration"*: "Gen. Eagan to Be Tried," *Washington Post*, January 18, 1899.

355 *"unbecoming of an officer"*: quoted in ibid.

355 *Miles quickly retreated*: Cosmas, p. 294.

355 *"colossal error"*: quoted in ibid.

355 *Eagan was found guilty*: "Gen. Eagan Found Guilty," *New York Times*, January 29, 1899.

356 *McKinley commuted that sentence*: "General Eagan's Sentence," *Washington Post*, February 8, 1899.

356 *"The honor of the army"*: "The President and Algerism," *New York Times*, January 31, 1899.

356 *his name elicited hisses*: "Alger in Boston," *New York Times*, February 18, 1899.

356 *"clear the atmosphere"*: William Osborne to WMcK, March 3, 1899, WMcKP, Reel 6.

356 *Alger traveled to Cuba*: "Alger Back from Cuba," *Washington Post*, April 15, 1899.

356 *announced plans to run for senator*: "Alger Aims for the Senate," *New York Times*, May 1, 1899.

356 *"Gov. Pingree is for President McKinley"*: quoted in "Pingree's True Position," *New York Times*, June 27, 1899.

356 *The question whether I am for McKinley*: quoted in ibid.

356 *Gage did the same*: "Blame Secretary Alger," *New York Times*, June 28, 1899.

357 *"Why,"* asked the New York Times: "The President and Algerism," *New York Times*, January 31, 1899.

357 *"Mr. Alger is a burden"*: quoted in "Algerism," *Times* (London), June 30, 1899.

357 *"kindliness of [McKinley's] heart"*: quoted in "New Report about Alger," *New York Times*, February 26, 1899.

357 *"demand for a change"*: GBCD, July 13, 1899, Box 52.

357 *"with every courtesy"*: Ibid.

357 *"several rather trying interviews"*: GBCD, July 19, 1899, Box 52.

357 *"Something will come to a head"*: WMcK, quoted in GBCD, July 18, 1899, Box 52.

357 *"Well," said the president*: WMcK, quoted in GBCD, July 19, 1899, Box 52.

358 *"I'll leave that there to-night"*: WMcK, quoted in ibid.

358 *"frank and murderous smile"*: quoted in Leech, *In the Days of McKinley*, p. 380.

358 *presidential messenger, Congressman Lemuel Quigg*: Ibid., p. 379.

358 *"The President directs me"*: quoted in Zimmermann, p. 147.

358 *"great satisfaction"*: WMcK, quoted in GBCD, July 22, 1899.

23. AGUINALDO

359 *$50,000-a-year position*: "Speaker Reed Retires," *Washington Post*, April 20, 1899.

359 *"Speaker Reed's withdrawal"*: Ibid.

360 *"This seems like a great waste"*: quoted in Grant, p. 362.

360 *"Had I stayed"*: quoted in ibid., p. 363.

360 *"a man of little scope"*: quoted in ibid., p. 251.

360 *he had set foot in the White House*: "Speaker Reed Retires."

361 *Carl Schurz and Mark Twain*: Beisner, p. 180.

361 *"Your friend personally"*: quoted in ibid., p. 181.

361 *"half a dozen bloody wars"*: quoted in ibid., p. 27.

361 *a robust opposition movement*: Ibid., p. x.

361 *"It would be no mean task"*: Ibid., p. xii.

361 *feared a massive influx of "Spanish-Americans"*: quoted in ibid., p. 27.

361 *"There has never been a republic"*: "Mr. Hoar on Imperialism," *Washington Post*, January 10, 1899.

362 *"disastrous to the republic"*: "Disastrous to Republic," *Washington Post*, December 30, 1898.

362 *"much troubled"*: Dawes, p. 182.

362 *"enormous responsibilities"*: Ibid., p. 183.

362 *"in the name of human progress"*: WMcK, speech at dinner of the Home Market Club, Boston, February 16, 1899, in McKinley, *Speeches and Addresses of William McKinley, from March 1, 1897 to May 30, 1900*, p. 185.

362 *5:25 p.m. on February 15*: "President Starts for Boston," *New York Times*, February 16, 1899.

362 *The party reached Boston at 10:02*: "The Arrival in Boston," *New York Times*, February 17, 1899.

362 *"Yah, yah, yah"*: quoted in ibid.

363 *"in quietude"*: quoted in "Our Duty as We See It," *Washington Post*, February 17, 1899.

363 *"the largest banquet"*: Ibid.

363 *"Liberator"*: quoted in ibid.

363 *"universal and hearty commendation"*: Home Market Club speech.

365 *"There was not a spark"*: "The President in Boston," *Nation*, February 23, 1899.

366 *"If Regular troops enroute"*: Otis to Corbin, February 12, 1899, in *Correspondence Relating to the War with Spain*, p. 2:902.

366 *"Situation in Manila critical"*: Otis to Henry Lawton, February 24, 1899, ibid., p. 2:916.

366 *"completely routed"*: "Rebels Cleared Out," *Washington Post*, March 8, 1899.

366 *"skulked back to their homes"*: quoted in Miller, *"Benevolent Assimilation,"* p. 69.

366 *"desperate resistance"*: quoted in Silbey, *A War of Frontier and Empire*, p. 85.

367 *"Present indications denote"*: Otis to Corbin, April 3, 1899, in *Correspondence Relating to the War with Spain*, p. 2:957.

367 *most Washington officials, including McKinley*: Gould, *The Presidency of William McKinley*, p. 180.

367 *"an enlightened system"*: quoted in ibid., p. 181.

367 *"Filipinos in general incapable"*: Jacob Schurman to John Hay, April 13, 1899, WMcKP, Reel 6.

368 *In four hours of fighting*: "MacArthur Routs Aguinaldo's Army," *New York Times*, April 28, 1899.

368 *7,000 regulars*: "Our Philippine Army," *Washington Post*, April 20, 1899.

368 *"This is believed"*: Ibid.

368 *insurgent force of 7,000*: "New Army in His Front," *Washington Post*, May 8, 1899.

368 *At a June 2 Cabinet meeting*: "No Volunteers for Otis," *New York Times*, June 3, 1899.

368 *Hay wryly suggested*: Hay to WMcK, June 3, 1899, WMcKP, Reel 7.

368 *"and win by dividing"*: Schurman to Hay, June 3, 1899, WMcKP, Reel 7.

369 *began on April 28*: "Filipinos Come to Plead for Peace," *New York Times*, April 29, 1899.

369 *The best they could do*: "Conference with Rebels," *New York Times*, April 30, 1899.

369 *"sparring for time"*: quoted in ibid.

369 *The insurgent negotiators conceded*: "Just a Filipino Trick," *Washington Post*, May 22, 1899.

370 *declaring he would never accept*: "Filipinos Issue a Manifesto," *Washington Post*, May 15, 1899.

370 *"whip the insurgents"*: "No Headway at Manila," *Washington Post*, May 24, 1899.

370 *"I believe force was necessary"*: quoted in ibid.

370 *he had instructed the Philippine Commission*: "Fair Terms for Peace," *Washington Post*, May 6, 1899.

370 *"Those of the leaders"*: WMcK, quoted in Gould, *The Presidency of William McKinley*, p. 182.

370 *"prosecution of war until"*: Charles Denby, Dean Worcester, and Otis to Hay, June 7, 1899, WMcKP, Reel 7.

370 *"Yes, sir," replied the secretary*: quoted in "Vigorous War Policy," *Washington Post*, August 9, 1899.

371 *65,000 men to 25,000*: "Army Bill Must Pass," *Washington Post*, February 10, 1899.

371 *threatened an extra congressional session*: "Extra Session Probable," *New York Times*, January 11, 1899.

371 *"While the President"*: quoted in "Attack on Army Increase," *New York Times*, January 26, 1899.

371 *"the fiercest and most vindictive attack"*: quoted in "Debate on the Army Bill," *New York Times*, January 27, 1899.

371 *168 to 126*: Gould, *The Presidency of William McKinley*, p. 173.

372 *would expire on July 1*: "Senate for Army Increase," *New York Times*, February 28, 1899.

372 *vote of 55 to 13*: Ibid.

372 *"entirely feasible"*: "Nicaragua Canal Report," *New York Times*, December 30, 1898.

372 *"One thing is clearly indicated"*: "Need of the Canal," *Washington Post*, May 23, 1898, reprinted from *The Independent*.

372 *time to scuttle the Clayton-Bulwer Treaty*: Gould, *The Presidency of William McKinley*, p. 197.

372 *"indispensable" to U.S. interests*: WMcK, Second Annual Message, December 5, 1898, Miller Center.

372 *"an early report"*: "Eager to Build Canal," *Washington Post*, January 4, 1899.

373 *Senate also moved*: "The Nicaragua Canal Bill," *New York Times*, January 10, 1899.

373 *48 to 6*: "The Nicaraguan Canal Bill," *New York Times*, January 22, 1899.

373 *"for the use of the largest"*: quoted in ibid.

373 *"flank movement"*: quoted in "Canal May Be Built," *Washington Post*, February 9, 1899.

373 *would kill the canal project*: "No Nicaragua Canal Now," *New York Times*, February 16, 1899.

373 *hatched a plan*: "The Nicaragua Canal," *New York Times*, February 17, 1899.

373 *"approached with due deliberation"*: quoted in "River and Harbor Funds," *New York Times*, February 19, 1899.

373 *the New Panama Canal Company*: "Canal by the Isthmus," *Washington Post*, January 18, 1899.

374 *$1 million for the president*: "River and Harbor Bill," *New York Times*, March 4, 1899.

374 *McKinley expanded the Walker Commission*: "Isthmian Canal Commission," *New York Times*, June 10, 1899.

374 *At noon on January 1*: "Havana Now Ours," *Washington Post*, January 2, 1899.

374 *to 45,000 in March*: Gould, *The Presidency of William McKinley*, p. 190.

374 *"the law of belligerent right"*: WMcK, instruction to John Brooke, December 22, 1898, reprinted in Olcott, p. 2:196.

374 *5.5 million daily rations*: Gould, *The Presidency of William McKinley*, p. 190.

375 *promise of $3 million*: "40,000 Cubans Get It," *Washington Post*, May 7, 1899.

375 *"I am now aware"*: quoted in "Gen. Gomez Won Over," *Washington Post*, February 3, 1899.

375 *40,000 Gómez troops*: "40,000 Cubans Get It."

375 *Many of Cuba's ethnic Spaniards*: "America's Stay in Cuba," *New York Times*, April 25, 1899.

375 *"between the independence"*: quoted in ibid.

375 *"honorable obligation"*: WMcK, Third Annual Message, December 5, 1899, Miller Center.

376 *"suffered immensely"*: quoted in Gould, *The Presidency of William McKinley*, p. 167.

376 *not only "mischievous"*: quoted in "On Civil Service Rules," *New York Times*, June 13, 1899.

376 *"Indeed," the president wrote about himself*: quoted in Gould, *The Presidency of William McKinley*, p. 167.

24. SECOND-TERM QUESTION

377 *U.S. consul at Liverpool*: Leech, *In the Days of McKinley*, p. 462.

378 *"If what you gentlemen are saying"*: WMcK, quoted in GBCD, September 17, 1899, Box 52.

379 *greater toll on Ida*: Osborne to WMcK, July 10, 1899, WMcKP, Reel 7.

379 *McKinley's face had new lines*: Ibid.

379 *he barred newsmen*: "President Seeking Rest," *Washington Post*, July 24, 1899.

379 *"In view of Mrs. McKinley's ill-health"*: Ibid.

379 *One early drive*: "Mrs. McKinley Gains Strength," *Washington Post*, July 30, 1899.

379 *two carriage rides*: "Mr. McKinley Sees Visitors," *New York Times*, August 4, 1899.

379 *"Mecca of the fashionables"*: "Mr. M'Kinley by the Sea," *New York Times*, August 26, 1899.

379 *500,000 cheering citizens*: "President Justifies Otis," *New York Times*, August 29, 1899.

379 *"There is no nobler death"*: WMcK, speech in Pittsburgh, August 28, 1899, reprinted in ibid.

380 *"boldness and ardor"*: "The President on the Philippine Question," *Brooklyn Citizen*, August 29, 1899.

380 *"note of leadership"*: "The President's Weighty Words at Pittsburg," *Chicago Times/Chicago Herald*, August 30, 1899.

380 *an extended tour of appearances*: "Trip to Chicago and the Northwest, October 1899," White House memo, unsigned and undated, WMcKP, Reel 8.

380 *North Market Avenue*: "The President's Canton Home," *New York Times*, August 7, 1899.

380 *"Visayans are opposed"*: Jacob Schurman to Hay, July 4, 1899, WMcKP, Reel 7.

381 *"an ultra-optimistic view"*: "An Agreed Statement of Facts," statement of Manila reporters, reprinted in "War News Kept Back," *Washington Post,* July 18, 1899.

381 *McKinley's Cabinet quickly took up*: "Dropped by Cabinet," *Washington Post,* July 19, 1899.

381 *"greater liberality"*: "War News Kept Back."

381 *"The Administration will be"*: "The Philippine Censorship," *New York Times,* September 10, 1899.

381 *Numerous members of Congress urged*: "Want Gen. Otis Removed," *Washington Post,* September 14, 1899.

381 *"The President's position"*: Ibid.

381 *McKinley rejected the idea*: "Suggested a Change," *Washington Post,* August 11, 1899.

382 *"shorn of any command"*: "Mr. Root Is Determined," *New York Times,* August 24, 1899.

382 *"fearful to think"*: Joseph Wheeler to WMcK, August 23, 1899, WMcKP, Reel 7.

382 *"immoderate satisfaction"*: "In Defence of McKinley," *New York Tribune,* July 20, 1899.

382 *2,500 troops on the outskirts*: "Filipinos Lose Angeles," *New York Times,* April 17, 1899.

382 *he recalled Denby and Worcester*: "President in Doubt," *Washington Post,* September 16, 1899.

382 *"There can be only one sentiment"*: Day to WMcK, September 26, 1899, WMcKP, Reel 8.

382 *"Boom for Dewey in 1900"*: *Cleveland Plain Dealer,* December 1, 1898.

383 *"I am a sailor"*: quoted in "Dewey and the Presidency," *Washington Post,* April 10, 1899.

383 *110th Street to 60th Street*: Spector, p. 105.

383 *"the ships expended more ammunition"*: Ibid.

383 *"Even the accounts"*: Dewey, p. 289.

383 *some 35,000 participants*: Spector, p. 105.

383 *White House "stag" dinner*: "M'Kinley as His Host," *Washington Post,* October 2, 1899.

383 *50,000 citizens*: Spector, p. 106.

383 *to generate a draft movement*: Ibid., p. 110.

383 *"It is only at long intervals"*: quoted in "Whitney Nominates Dewey," *Washington Post,* October 1, 1899.

384 *"indecent"*: quoted in "Indecent, Says Mr. Hanna," *Washington Post,* October 2, 1899.

384 *"The Dewey spasm"*: "Dewey Spasm in Politics," *Washington Post,* September 29, 1899.

384 *thousands of Democrats*: "Mayor M'Kisson's Defeat," *Washington Post*, April 4, 1899.

385 *"If Mr. Kurtz should be nominated"*: "Hanna's New Dilemma," *Washington Post*, March 17, 1899.

385 *saloon called Mecca*: Walters, p. 118.

385 *distancing himself a bit*: Ibid., p. 174.

385 *senator couldn't deliver*: Ibid.

385 *"for the best interest"*: MAH to George B. Cox, reprinted in Croly, p. 294.

385 *"Yes," wrote Hanna*: MAH to WMcK, June 6, 1899, WMcKP, Reel 7.

385 *"There was an evident earnestness"*: Herrick to WMcK, June 3, 1899, WMcKP, Reel 7.

386 *refused to lift a finger*: "High Praise for Jones," *Washington Post*, October 25, 1899.

386 *particularly apathetic*: "Apathy Menaces Nash," *Washington Post*, October 27, 1899.

386 *a pressing need*: "High Praise for Jones."

386 *Hanna declined to invite Bushnell*: Ibid.

386 *hardly could bring himself*: Ibid.

386 *75 percent of his support*: "Hanna Turns His Guns," *Washington Post*, November 1, 1899.

386 *"a man who practices"*: quoted in "High Praise for Jones."

387 *"Apathy Menaces Nash."*: headline, *Washington Post*, October 27, 1899.

387 *"The impression is gaining ground"*: "Ohio and the Presidency," *New York Times*, October 14, 1899.

387 *from the rear platform*: "Dick Confers with Hanna," *Washington Post*, September 22, 1899.

387 *German American voters*: "Led to Much Comment," *Washington Post*, September 14, 1899.

387 *nearly 50,000 votes*: "Victory for the President," *Washington Post*, November 14, 1899.

387 *Republican victories also*: "Senator Platt Sums Up," *Washington Post*, November 10, 1899.

387 *"[The voters] indorse"*: quoted in ibid.

387 *"will now have a free hand"*: quoted in "Second Term for M'Kinley," *Washington Post*, November 9, 1899.

388 *the president ordered them sent*: "Warships for Manila," *Washington Post*, October 5, 1899.

388 *42,794 officers and men*: "Troops in the Philippines," internal memo, War Department, Adjutant General's Office, October 30, 1899, WMcKP, Reel 8.

388 *he emphasized his resolve*: "Dewey to State His Views," *Washington Post*, October 4, 1899.

388 *"to bend every resource"*: quoted in ibid.

388 *"Negros leads in the van"*: quoted in "Local Rule in Negros," *Washington Post*, November 7, 1899.

388 *"Indications are"*: Otis dispatch, reprinted in "May Catch Aguinaldo," *Washington Post*, November 14, 1899.

388 *"a perfect enigma"*: "Aguinaldo Mystifies Otis," *Washington Post*, November 15, 1899.

388 *"not cease its efforts"*: "Aguinaldo's Latest Proclamation," WMcKP, Reel 9.

389 *"Claim to Government"*: Otis to Corbin, November 24, 1899, WMcKP, Reel 9.

389 *"Aguinaldo's army is virtually disbanded"*: Wheeler to WMcK, November 27, 1899, summary in WMcKP, Reel 9.

389 *disguised as a Philippine peasant*: "Pursuit of Aguinaldo," *Washington Post*, December 18, 1899.

389 *On December 19, General Henry Lawton*: "Gen. Lawton Slain," *Washington Post*, December 20, 1899.

389 *1,000 insurgents near Montalban*: "Rebels Still in Force," *Washington Post*, December 28, 1899.

389 *"Tagalos Not Subdued"*: Ibid.

389 *nearly 64,000*: "Memorandum, Report of Sec. of War," December 1, 1899, WMcKP, Reel 9.

389 *"We have turned"*: WMcK, quoted in "The Week," *Nation*, February 23, 1899.

389 *"as attempts to relieve"*: "The Week," *Nation*, December 14, 1899.

390 *Pago Pago, ideal*: Ferrell, p. 326.

390 *"passive and minimal policy"*: Gould, *The Presidency of William McKinley*, p. 160.

390 *"unprecedented growth"*: Dawes, p. 185.

391 *"Trusts and Combinations"*: "The Conference on Trusts," *New York Times*, August 28, 1899.

391 *"Monopoly in private hands"*: quoted in "Bryan on Monopoly," *Washington Post*, September 17, 1899.

391 *"By consolidation of capital"*: quoted in "Foraker Has Spoken," *Washington Post*, September 23, 1899.

391 *"This formation of combines"*: quoted in "Hanna Speaks of Trusts," *New York Times*, October 20, 1899.

392 *"Should we be silent"*: quoted in "Aims to Help Negros," *Washington Post*, December 30, 1898.

392 *"denouncing" McKinley*: "Lynching as an Issue," *Washington Post*, August 14, 1899.

392 *"intrinsically absurd"*: "Lynchings and the President," *New York Times*, August 16, 1899.

392 *"The colored regiments"*: WMcK to Root, August 19, 1899, WMcKP, Reel 7.

393 *special trains for the funeral*: "Hobart Funeral Train," *Washington Post*, November 24, 1899.

393 *"No president and vice-president"*: quoted in "McKinley and Hobart," *McKeesport* (Pennsylvania) *Daily News*, June 12, 1899, taken from *Chicago Record*.

25. SECOND-TERM RESOLVE

394 *he would repeat that sentiment*: Dawes, p. 214.

395 *"a condition of unusual prosperity"*: WMcK, Third Annual Message, December 5, 1899, Miller Center.

396 *Within weeks Treasury Secretary Gage would revise*: "Big Surplus This Year," *New York Times*, March 31, 1900; "Mr. Gage's Estimates," *New York Times*, April 11, 1900.

396 *In output of iron ore*: "United States Leads," *Washington Post*, January 18, 1900.

396 *"That lead can never"*: Ibid.

396 *"I see nothing to prevent"*: quoted in "Will Build for the World," *Washington Post*, January 28, 1900.

396 *"the prosperity of the working people"*: quoted in "Mr. Hanna States the Issues," *New York Times*, January 14, 1900.

397 *"to support the existing gold standard"*: WMcK, Third Annual Message.

397 *$150 million gold reserve*: Gould, *The Presidency of William McKinley*, p. 171.

397 *using a gold pen*: Ibid.

397 *"would have been considered a lunatic"*: "Passage of the Gold Bill," *Nation*, February 22, 1900.

397 *nearly $50 million*: "Cost of the Philippine War," *New York Times*, March 7, 1900.

397 *more than 1,000 American lives*: estimated from overall casualty statistics in "Philippine-American War," *Wikipedia*.

398 *800 insurgents were routed*: "By the Army and Navy," *Washington Post*, January 23, 1900.

398 *"probably the last considerable force"*: "Flanked and Routed," *Washington Post*, January 26, 1900.

398 *issued a voluminous report*: "Ruler for Filipinos," *Washington Post*, January 17, 1900.

398 *"sufficiently elastic"*: Ibid.

398 *"No glittering promises"*: Ibid.

398 *supplant military government*: Karnow, p. 166.

399 *"One loves him"*: quoted in Merry, "The Odd Couple."

399 *"America incarnate"*: quoted in ibid.

399 *"important business"*: quoted in Goodwin, pp. 264–65. Quotes from McKinley's meeting with Taft are from this source.

400 *"I want you to appreciate"*: WMcK to Day, January 30, 1899, WMcKP, Reel 9.

400 *"The chances of failure"*: quoted in "Judge Taft on His Mission," *New York Times*, February 8, 1900.

400 *"No nomination"*: Ibid.

400 *"the most perfect cooperation"*: WMcK, Memorandum to Secretary of War, April 7, 1900, WMcKP, Reel 9.

401 *"The high and patriotic purpose"*: quoted in "Taft Outlines the Philippine Policy," *New York Times*, March 6, 1900.

401 *"That murderer is the man"*: quoted in "To Vote as They Talk," *Washington Post*, February 24, 1900.

401 *"sensational speech"*: "The President Assailed," *New York Times*, January 12, 1900.

402 *"gratify nearly every desire"*: "Light on the Philippines," *New York Times*, January 9, 1900.

402 *"a tissue of falsehoods"*: George Dewey to Henry Cabot Lodge, reprinted in "Dewey's Letter Read," *New York Times*, February 1, 1900.

402 assaulted Pettigrew as a *"traitor"*: quoted in "Philippine Debate Embitters Senators," *New York Times*, February 1, 1900.

402 *"The possession of the Philippines"*: Henry Cabot Lodge, Senate speech, March 7, 1900, reprinted in "Senator Lodge on the Philippines," *New York Times*, March 8, 1900.

403 *hit-and-run tactics*: "Insurrection Not Dead," *New York Times*, March 4, 1900.

403 *Aguinaldo wanted to heighten*: "Filipinos Prepare for More Warfare," *New York Times*, March 19, 1900.

403 *killed 378 insurgents*: "Filipinos Lose 1,000 Men," *New York Times*, April 23, 1900.

403 *333 the next week*: "Otis Reports Fighting," *New York Times*, April 25, 1900.

403 *300 at another location*: "300 Filipinos Killed," *New York Times*, April 27, 1900.

403 *"the war has terminated"*: quoted in "Otis Sends His Last Report," *Washington Post*, May 5, 1900.

404 *"Our plain duty"*: WMcK, Third Annual Message.

404 *Does the Constitution follow the flag?*: "The President and the Philippines," *Washington Post*, February 12, 1900; "Held by Mr. M'Kinley," *Washington Post*, February 18, 1900.

404 *"The constitutional question"*: Dawes, p. 217.

405 *"We must not admit"*: quoted in Gould, *The Presidency of William McKinley*, p. 209.

405 *"This is not exactly free trade"*: "Legislating for Puerto Rico," *New York Times*, February 2, 1900.

405 *"I could ride a white horse"*: quoted in Gould, *The Presidency of William McKinley*, p. 209.

405 *"The President added"*: "Rebel over the Bill," *Washington Post*, February 15, 1900.

405 *at least seven Republicans*: Ibid.

406 *"free trade with Porto Rico"*: Henry Loomis Nelson, "Held by Mr. M'Kinley," *Washington Post*, February 18, 1900, originally published in *New York World*.

406 *just eight GOP votes*: "Injustice of a Tariff," *Washington Post*, February 21, 1900.

406 *"Mr. McKinley," said* The Nation: "The Morals of the Porto Rico Question," *Nation*, February 22, 1900.

406 *"nothing would give"*: quoted in Leech, *In the Days of McKinley*, p. 491.

406 *persuaded all four*: Ibid., p. 491.

406 *15 percent of Dingley rates*: Ibid.

406 *vote of 172 to 161*: "Puerto Rico Bill Passes the House," *New York Times*, March 1, 1900.

406 *"Six men were brought"*: Ibid.

406 *either six or eleven votes*: Leech, *In the Days of McKinley*, p. 491.

407 *appropriation of $2 million*: "Millions Voted to Aid Puerto Ricans," *New York Times*, March 3, 1900.

407 *House passed the measure*: Ibid.

407 *Democratic amendments*: Leech, *In the Days of McKinley*, p. 492.

407 *"the first almost irreparable mistake"*: quoted in "Condemns the President," *New York Times*, March 4, 1900, reprinted from "The President's Momentous Mistake," *Chicago Times-Herald*, March 3, 1900.

407 *"authoritative statement"*: "Administration on Puerto Rico Tariff," *New York Times*, March 9, 1900.

407 *vote of 40 to 31*: "Senate Passes the Puerto Rican Bill," *New York Times*, April 4, 1900.

407 *at seven o'clock*: "President Signs the Puerto Rico Bill," *New York Times*, April 13, 1900.

407 *"We do not recall"*: "The Republican Situation," *New York Times*, April 9, 1900.

407 *"I made a mistake"*: quoted in ibid.

408 *Lord Salisbury had softened*: Mowat, p. 278.

408 *U.S. Navy's global strength*: Ibid., p. 277.

408 *"handsome" behavior*: GBCD, February 4, 1900, Box 53.

408 *"adds another and crowning triumph"*: "The Great Diplomatic Triumph," *New York Press*, February 6, 1900.

409 *"the congratulations of his friends"*: "The Amended Clayton-Bulwar Treaty," *New York Times*, February 6, 1900.

409 *a bill nearly identical*: "To Build an Isthmian Canal," *New York Times*, January 13, 1900.

409 *embraced the same concept*: "To Build the Canal," *Washington Post*, January 16, 1900.

409 *"open, free and neutral"*: quoted in "Canal Pact Doomed to Rejection," *Chicago Evening Post*, February 6, 1900.

409 *"stir up a war of opinions"*: "The New Canal Treaty," *Boston Daily Globe*, February 8, 1900.

409 *"Has McKinley suddenly gone crazy?"*: Untitled, *New York Evening Journal*, February 14, 1900.

409 *"There is the best authority"*: "New Treaty Likely to Be Ratified," *New York Times*, February 9, 1900.

409 *satisfaction with Hay's handiwork*: "Canal Treaty Discussed," *New York Times*, February 8, 1900.

409 *"exhibition of craven cowardice"*: quoted in Leech, *In the Days of McKinley*, p. 510.

410 *no treaty language could hinder*: Davis Amendment, reprinted in "Committee Reports the Canal Bill," *New York Times*, March 10, 1900.

410 *"too indolent to make a strong fight"*: quoted in Leech, *In the Days of McKinley*, p. 509.

410 *Committee reported the new treaty*: "Committee Reports the Canal Bill."

410 *Hay submitted his resignation*: GBCD, March 13, 1900, Box 53.

410 *"indicates views so widely divergent"*: Hay to WMcK, March 13, 1900, reprinted in Thayer, p. 2:226.

410 *"Nothing could be more unfortunate"*: WMcK to Hay, March 13, 1900, reprinted in ibid.

410 *"I cannot [adequately] express"*: quoted in Leech, *In the Days of McKinley*, p. 511.

410 *to meet with him and Hay*: Ibid., p. 512.

411 *vote of 224 to 36*: Gould, *The Presidency of William McKinley*, p. 232.

411 *Lodge dutifully led an effort*: Leech, *In the Days of McKinley*, p. 513.

411 *"a triumph for the Administration"*: "The Senate," *New York Times*, May 23, 1900.

411 *ratification extension*: "Hay-Pauncefote Treaty Extended," *Washington Post*, May 6, 1900.

411 *At five o'clock*: "The House Yields; Congress Adjourns," *New York Times*, June 8, 1900.

411 *"On the whole"*: "The Record of Congress," *Nation*, June 14, 1900.

26. CHINA

413 *"Secretary Hay's dexterous skill"*: quoted in "Praise for Secretary Hay," *New York Times*, March 29, 1900.

413 *"A year ago no nation"*: quoted in "The Open Door Agreement," *New York Times*, January 6, 1900.

414 *news dispatches from London*: "Difficulties in China," *New York Times*, March 31, 1900.

414 *also had sent a warship*: "The Wheeling Goes to Taku," *New York Times*, March 21, 1900.

414 *The mob "maltreated"*: "American Mission Attacked," *Washington Post*, March 17, 1898.

414 *The Chinese population*: Silbey, *The Boxer Rebellion and the Great Game in China*, pp. 22–29. This work is the source of the following history and quotes.

416 *After Germany obtained rights*: "German Eyes on China," *Washington Post*, May 2, 1900.

416 *Russia demanded the same*: "New Demand on China," *Washington Post*, March 7, 1898.

416 *lease for Wei-Hai-Wei*: "England Gets Wei-Hai-Wei," *Washington Post*, April 4, 1898.

416 *France got a lease*: "China Yields to France," *Washington Post*, April 6, 1898.

416 *Western pressure soon forced a reconsideration*: "China Close Pressed," *Washington Post*, March 9, 1899.

416 *"China," he said*: quoted in "Italy's Hold on China," *Washington Post*, March 10, 1899.

416 *"China Taken by the Throat"*: headline, *Washington Post*, March 12, 1900.

416 *"that the moment has now arrived"*: quoted in "Partition of China Near," *New York Times*, March 4, 1899.

416 *sought Washington's cooperation*: "For Joint Action in China," *Washington Post*, April 23, 1900.

416 *"we think our best policy"*: quoted in Thayer, p. 2:241.

416 *"would lie in the fact"*: quoted in Taliaferro, p. 357.

417 *Hay honored him*: Ibid.

417 *encouraged him to draft a policy statement*: Ibid., p. 358.

417 *It contained three points*: Bailey, p. 480.

417 *"final and definitive"*: quoted in Thayer, p. 2:242.

417 *"No treaties"*: quoted in Taliaferro, p. 366.

418 *"Support the Qing"*: quoted in Silbey, *The Boxer Rebellion and the Great Game in China*, p. 36.

418 *850 Catholic priests*: Preston, p. 27.

418 *2,800 Protestant missionaries*: Ibid.

418 *"patronizing impudence"*: quoted in ibid.

418 *"a standing insult"*: quoted in Silbey, *The Boxer Rebellion and the Great Game in China*, p. 42.

419 *"These Chinese Christians"*: quoted in Preston, p. 26.

419 *U.S. minister Edwin Conger*: biographical description in "Minister Conger's Career," *New York Times*, July 6, 1900.

419 *"at least one good port"*: quoted in Leech, *In the Days of McKinley*, p. 518.

420 *"when peaceful and law-abiding"*: quoted in Silbey, *The Boxer Rebellion and the Great Game in China*, p. 58.

420 *"they have the secret sympathy"*: quoted in ibid., p. 59.

420 *"singly and without the cooperation"*: quoted in ibid., p. 60.

420 *"cut in pieces"*: quoted in ibid., p. 74.

420 *When Conger peppered the empress*: Conger to Empress Dowager Cixi, May 31, June 2, June 4, June 7, June 8, 1900, WMcKP, Reel 10.

421 *"cause peace and quiet"*: Zongli Yamen to Conger, June 6, 1900, WMcKP, Reel 10.

421 *"should cease being uneasy"*: Zongli Yamen to Conger, June 10, 1900, WMcKP, Reel 10.

421 *destroyed the rail line*: "Chinese Capital Menaced," *New York Times*, May 29, 1900.

421 *twenty Western warships*: Louis Kempff to Long, received June 8, 1900, in *Correspondence Relating to the War with Spain*, p. 1:410.

421 *350 soldiers arrived*: Conger to Hay, June 1, 1900, WMcKP, Reel 10.

421 *430 troops*: Long to Kempff, June 23, 1900, WMcKP, Reel 10.

421 *On June 19, Cixi demanded*: "Envoys Were Told to Leave China," *New York Times*, July 1, 1900.

421 *Rockhill assured Hay*: Leech, *In the Days of McKinley*, p. 519.

422 *"We have no policy in China"*: Hay to Conger, June 10, 1900, WMcKP, Reel 10.

422 *"If other nations go"*: Kempff to Long, June 11, 1900, WMcKP, Reel 10.

422 *Hay answered simply "Yes"*: Hay to Conger, June 9, 1900, WMcKP, Reel 10.

422 *isolating the legations*: Silbey, *The Boxer Rebellion and the Great Game in China*, p. 78.

422 *"This absence of official reports"*: "Troops Will Be Sent," *Washington Post*, June 17, 1900.

422 *June 15 Cabinet meeting*: Leech, *In the Days of McKinley*, p. 519.

423 *a force of about 2,000*: Silbey, *The Boxer Rebellion and the Great Game in China*, p. 83.

423 *about 1,000 men who would land*: Ibid., p. 94.

424 *"Act in concurrence"*: Frank W. Hackett to Kempff, June 18, 1900, in *Correspondence Relating to the War with Spain*, p. 1:414.

424 *lost 285 men*: Silbey, *The Boxer Rebellion and the Great Game in China*, p. 135.

424 *"were simply canals"*: quoted in ibid., p. 112.

424 *"Reinforcements are* most *urgently required"*: quoted in ibid.

424 *"shouting and cheering"*: quoted in ibid., p. 116.

424 *Cixi ordered 20,000 Chinese troops*: Ibid., p. 138.

424 *nearly 7,000 troops*: "Battle of Tientsin," *Wikipedia*.

424 *"brilliant victory"*: "Allies Victorious: Tien-Tsin Captured," *New York Times*, July 18, 1900.

424 *Some 250 soldiers of the allied armies*: "Battle of Tientsin."

425 *1,300 officers and men*: MacArthur to Corbin, June 28, 1900, in *Correspondence Relating to the War with Spain*, p. 1:419.

425 *instructed General MacArthur*: Corbin to MacArthur, July 7, 1900, in ibid., p. 1:422.

425 *"in places of safety"*: WMcK to Hay, July 5, 1900, WMcKP, Reel 10.

425 *"in regard to this most trying crisis"*: Hay to WMcK, July 6, 1900, WMcKP, Reel 11.

425 *rushed back to Washington*: "President Leaves for Washington," *New York Times*, July 17, 1900.

425 *Root and Long assured him*: "Cabinet Discusses China," *New York Times*, July 18, 1900.

425 *"For one month"*: Conger, message to State Department, undated, sent through Chinese minister to Washington, D.C., WMcKP, Reel 11.

425 *"much gratified by the news"*: "President Hears the News," *New York Times*, July 21, 1900.

425 *British newspapers had reported*: Preston, p. 172.

425 *"We have provisions"*: Conger to J. W. Ragsdale, July 21, 1900, WMcKP, Reel 11.

425 *18,000 troops*: Silbey, *The Boxer Rebellion and the Great Game in China*, p. 172.

426 *"devise measures"*: Emperor Zaichun to WMcK, reprinted in "Kwang-Su's Appeal; Mr. M'Kinley's Reply," *New York Times*, July 25, 1900.

426 *"who were sojourning"*: WMcK to Emperor Zaichun, reprinted in ibid.

426 *"If the Oriental intellect"*: "Mr. M'Kinley's Good Counsel," *New York Times*, July 25, 1900.

427 *the capital bulged with 100,000 Boxers*: quoted in "Anarchy in Peking," *New York Times*, August 4, 1900.

427 *"certain death"*: quoted in "Ministers Again in Great Danger," *New York Times*, August 8, 1900.

427 *"very grave"*: "Alarm in Washington," *New York Times*, August 9, 1900.

427 *"sharp demand for compliance"*: "Sharp Demand Sent to China," *New York Times*, August 9, 1900.

427 *legation grounds at 1 p.m.*: Associated Press, "How Peking Was Taken," *New York Times*, August 22, 1900.

427 *"The emaciated tenants"*: Ibid.

427 *only a pound a day*: "Envoys Relieved Just in Time," *New York Times*, August 25, 1900.

427 *Four thousand shells*: Associated Press, "How Peking Was Taken."

427 *killing some sixty-five people*: Ibid.

427 *"Peking is now"*: "The Despoiling of Peking," *New York Times*, August 25, 1900, reprinted from *Times* of London.

428 *"an unmitigated scoundrel"*: Hay to Alvey Adee, September 14, 1900, WMcKP, Reel 12.

428 *"indemnity for the past"*: "The Problem before the Allies," *New York Times*, August 30, 1900.

428 *"one might almost say labored"*: GBCD, August 29, 1900, Box 53.

428 *"receive[d] with much satisfaction"*: Memorandum, Alvey Adee, "in response to the Russian charge's oral communication," August 28, 1900, WMcKP, Reel 12.

429 *"the mighty temptations"*: "Russo-American Combination," *New York Times*, August 31, 1900.

429 *"What I want"*: quoted in Morgan, *William McKinley and His America*, p. 359.

429 *"We want to avoid"*: quoted in ibid., p. 360.

429 *"The dilemma is clear"*: Hay to Alvey Adee, September 14, 1900, WMcKP, Reel 12.

429 *"a complete justification"*: "The Change in the China Situation," *New York Times*, October 1, 1900.

430 *"It is to Manila that we owe"*: Hay, "suggested remarks," July 8, 1900, WMcKP, Reel 11.

431 *"anti-imperialistic . . . sentiments"*: "Our Imperialism in China," *New York Times*, November 6, 1900.

431 *"the most powerful State"*: "America as a World Power," *New York Times*, October 21, 1900.

27. REELECTION

432 *"It is settled"*: "M'Kinley's Happy Future," *Washington Post*, December 24, 1899, reprinted from *Chicago Tribune*.

433 *"are demanding attention"*: "The Issues of 1900," *New York Times*, October 16, 1899.

433 *about 10 percent a year*: Lichtman and DeCell, p. 185.

433 *"helped to provide currency"*: "The Currency Act," *Washington Post*, September 16, 1900, reprinted from *New York Mail and Express*.

433 *"always be true to"*: quoted in "Mr. Reed's Valedictory," *Washington Post*, September 20, 1899.

433 *"is now rent"*: "The Republican Imbroglio," *Nation*, March 15, 1900.

433 *"I shall continue my opposition"*: quoted in "Will Fight in the Senate," *Washington Post*, September 21, 1899.

434 *"obnoxious . . . to the public welfare"*: WMcK, Third Annual Message.

434 *a vote of 273 to 1*: "House Passes Trust Bill," *New York Times*, January 3, 1900.

434 *"for party and political considerations"*: quoted in "Democrats on Trusts," *New York Times*, May 22, 1900.

434 *"The office of the President"*: quoted in "Dewey's Eyes on the White House," *New York Times*, April 5, 1900.

435 *"a general inclination"*: Ibid.

435 *He told Cortelyou and Dawes*: GBCD, April 5, 1900, Box 53.

435 *"an undercurrent of pity"*: quoted in GBCD, April 7, 1900, Box 53.

435 *"The Governor is very popular"*: "Governor or Vice President?," *New York Times*, February 2, 1900.

435 *"In view of the continued statements"*: quoted in "Roosevelt Says No," *Brooklyn Daily Eagle*, February 13, 1900.

436 *"they have simply served notice"*: quoted in Goodwin, p. 258.

436 *"tempting Providence"*: quoted in ibid., p. 259.

436 *"unsafe"*: quoted in Croly, p. 310.

436 *president chafed a bit*: Gould, *The Presidency of William McKinley*, p. 215.

437 *crony named Estes Rathbone*: Horner, p. 260.

437 *"a kind of quiet discipline"*: Gould, *The Presidency of William McKinley*, p. 215.

437 *diminished somewhat by infirmities*: Leech, *In the Days of McKinley*, p. 533.

437 *"The report is, Mr. Bliss"*: quoted in "Bliss Now the Favorite," *New York Times*, April 10, 1900.

437 *"He did not even have a chance"*: Hay to Henry White, June 15, 1900, reprinted in Thayer, p. 2:342.

437 *"you're not fit for it"*: quoted in ibid.

438 *"went through without any break"*: "Mr. Hanna Wins in Ohio," *New York Times*, April 26, 1900.

438 *"It was very much a Hanna day"*: "Hanna's Speech Rouses Enthusiasm in Ohio," *New York Times*, April 25, 1900.

438 *"The backbone of the revolt"*: Taft to WMcK, June 15, 1900, WMcKP, Reel 10.

438 *"the war must be continued"*: Memorandum of conversation between Arthur MacArthur and Jose Ner, untitled, August 8, 1900, WMcKP, Reel 11.

438 *One top general named Aquino*: "Gen. Aquino Surrenders," *New York Times*, July 1, 1900.

438 *200 rebels killed*: "Over 200 Filipinos Killed," *New York Times*, June 11, 1900.

438 *requested a report from the Taft Commission*: "Report by Taft et al," *Washington Post*, September 20, 1900.

438 *a generally optimistic overview*: Taft and Philippine Commission to Root, August 21, 1900, WMcKP, Reel 11.

439 *a more complex picture*: article in *New York Herald*, described in "The Situation in the Philippines," *Nation*, August 16, 1900.

439 *"Either Mr. Allison or Mr. Bliss"*: quoted in "Republican Leaders on Vice President," *New York Times*, June 12, 1900.

439 *"There is no truth"*: quoted in "No 'President's Candidate,'" *New York Times*, June 14, 1900.

440 *at two o'clock on June 16*: "Delegations Arriving," *Washington Post*, June 17, 1900.

440 *"Here comes Teddy"*: quoted in ibid.

440 *"Roosevelt blushed"*: quoted in Goodwin, p. 262.

440 *"Gentlemen, that's an acceptance hat"*: quoted in Morgan, *William McKinley and His America*, p. 376.

440 *"in a state of rare excitement"*: quoted in ibid.

441 *warned him to stay away*: Goodwin, p. 261.

441 *"fife, drum, and bugle"*: quoted in ibid., p. 263.

441 *"The town was Roosevelt mad"*: "First of All, M'Kinley," *Washington Post*, June 19, 1900.

441 *"The Roosevelt boom"*: Memo, Charles Dick conversation with GBC, June 17, 1900, WMcKP, Reel 10.

441 *"The President has no choice"*: "Message dictated by President McKinley to be communicated to Hon. Charles Dick," June 17, 1900, WMcKP, Reel 10.

442 *"I am not in control!"*: quoted in Morgan, *William McKinley and His America*, p. 377.

442 *"almost an altercation"*: Dawes, p. 232.

442 *"The President's close friends"*: WMcK, message dictated to GBC, June 19, 1900, WMcKP, Reel 10.

443 *"a little perplexed"*: memo recounting Dawes conversation with GBC, June 20, 1900, WMcKP, Reel 10.

443 *He would do what*: quoted in ibid.

443 *"condemn[ed] all conspiracies"*: Republican platform, reprinted in *Washington Post*, June 21, 1900.

443 *spending his days at his desk*: "Flashed to M'Kinley," *Washington Post*, June 22, 1900.

443 *"hastened with a light step"*: Ibid.

443 *But he remained only five minutes*: Ibid.

443 *"courage and sagacity"*: WMcK to MAH, June 22, 1900, HMcCP, Box 3.

444 *"Well, it was a nice little scrap"*: MAH to WMcK, June 23, 1900, WMcKP, Reel 10.

444 *Bryan promptly threatened*: "Bryan to Rest All on Silver?," *New York Times*, July 3, 1900.

444 *"We condemn and denounce"*: Democratic national platform, printed in *New York Times*, July 6, 1900.

444 *"that broad and philosophic sweep"*: "The Way of M'Kinley and the Way of Bryan," *New York Times*, July 29, 1899.

445 *"Parties do not make issues"*: quoted in "Mr. Bryan Explains Change of Issues," *New York Times*, August 17, 1900.

445 *Hanna maladroitly uttered*: Horner, p. 281.

445 *"Everybody except Mr. Hanna"*: quoted in "Bryan Retort to Hanna," *Washington Post*, September 22, 1900.

445 *Hanna sought to clarify*: "Hanna Explains His Speech," *Washington Post*, September 24, 1900.

445 *"irksome"*: Leech, *In the Days of McKinley*, p. 556.

445 *"There is but one issue"*: quoted in "Hanna on the 'One Issue,'" *New York Times*, October 3, 1900.

446 *"despite . . . a movement"*: "No Speeches by M'Kinley," *Washington Post*, September 22, 1900.

446 *"Major," yelled one onlooker*: quoted in "President Returns to Canton," *Washington Post*, September 14, 1900.

446 *"the friendly co-operation"*: quoted in "Mr. M'Kinley on Bryanism," *New York Times*, October 30, 1900.

446 *143,000 anthracite coal miners*: "A Strike Is Declared," *Washington Post*, September 13, 1900.

446 *He leveraged his corporate stature*: "Hanna's Part in Settlement," *New York Times*, October 19, 1900.

446 *"Any man who would put a straw"*: quoted in "Mr. Hanna on the Strike," *New York Times*, October 2, 1900.

446 *seventy different documents*: Perry Heath to GBC, September 27, 1900, WMcKP, Reel 13.

446 *"four or five other languages"*: Perry Heath to GBC, October 1, 1900, WMcKP, Reel 13.

447 *delivered a dozen speeches*: "Chicago Hears Roosevelt," *New York Times*, October 7, 1900.

447 *"We have got the wolf"*: quoted in "Gov. Roosevelt's Ride across Kansas," *New York Times*, July 3, 1900.

447 *he traveled 21,209 miles*: "Roosevelt Ends His Tour," *New York Times*, November 3, 1900.

447 *"Return to Washington"*: quoted in Elmer Dover, dictated statement to J. B. Morrow, September 1905, HMcCP, Box 4.

447 *"They doubted"*: Ibid.

447 *"I have taken South Dakota"*: quoted in "Hanna Back in Chicago," *New York Times*, October 22, 1900.

448 *victory of 292 to 155*: Moore, Preimesberger, and Tarr, p. 1:746.

448 *plurality was 859,694*: Ibid., p. 2:1569.

448 *gained thirteen House members*: Ibid. Other congressional statistics come from the same source.

448 *"It was a vendetta of politics"*: "Hanna-Pettigrew Feud," *New York Times*, November 18, 1900.

448 *"The president seems more impressed"*: Dawes, p. 253.

448 *"I can no longer be called"*: quoted in Olcott, p. 2:296.

28. FAMILY AND NATION

449 *"We carry New York"*: quoted in "Joy among Republicans," *New York Times*, November 7, 1900.

449 *"Tell the boys"*: quoted in ibid.

449 *"We have beaten Pettigrew"*: quoted in " 'Send the News to Hanna,' " *Washington Post*, November 7, 1900.

449 *20,000 residents jammed*: "Throng in the Street," *Washington Post*, November 7, 1900.

449 *"so densely packed"*: Ibid.

449 *the president doffed his hat*: "M'Kinley at the Polls," *Washington Post*, November 7, 1900.

450 *"unruffled composure"*: "The President Unruffled," *Washington Post*, November 7, 1900.

450 *"Praise God"*: quoted in ibid.

450 *"Fellow-citizens"*: quoted in ibid.

450 *"I did not want him to run"*: quoted in Anthony, p. 191.

450 *She once took umbrage*: Ibid., p. 207.

450 *"the only honest man"*: quoted in ibid.

450 *"the American people did not deserve"*: quoted in ibid., p. 208.

450 *"Well, I'm glad to hear that"*: quoted in ibid.

451 *"I am becoming somewhat anxious"*: William Osborne to WMcK, March 22, 1898, WMcKP, Reel 3.

451 *"watch for two Italians"*: "Reported Plot to Kill the President," newspaper clipping, unidentified newspaper, October 3, 1900, WMcKP, Reel 13.

451 *Cortelyou sought to discredit*: "The President Goes Driving," *New York Times*, October 4, 1900.

451 *"was induced to refrain"*: "Reported Plot to Kill the President," newspaper clipping, unidentified newspaper, October 3, 1900, WMcKP, Reel 13.

451 *"crying like a child"*: quoted in GBCD, July 1, 1899.

451 *"temporary weakness"*: quoted in ibid.

451 *"extreme mental depression"*: Dawes, p. 197.

451 *Ida's doctors urged her*: "Anxiety in Washington," *New York Times*, May 16, 1901.

451 *Then, during the trip*: Anthony, p. 194.

452 *"take medical charge"*: quoted in ibid., p. 187.

452 *"No physician had ever shown"*: Ibid., p. 194.

452 *Ida raised such a fuss*: Ibid., p. 195.

452 *she refused to fulfill her obligation*: Ibid.

452 *"I was never there"*: quoted in ibid., p. 201.

452 *"fluttered constantly"*: quoted in ibid., p. 199.

452 *"She does not improve"*: GBCD, December 19, 1899, Box 52.

452 *issued a stunning opinion*: Anthony, p. 200.

453 *"When she wanted a pen"*: quoted in ibid., p. 205.

453 *As Christmas approached*: GBCD, December 23, 1899, Box 52.

453 *"beautiful vase"*: Ibid.

453 *Ida was "delighted"*: quoted in ibid.

454 *November 9 Cabinet meeting*: "American Foreign Policy," *New York Times*, November 10, 1900.

454 *the next Cabinet meeting*: "No Change in the Cabinet," *New York Times*, November 14, 1900.

454 *"have now returned"*: WMcK, speech before Union League, Philadelphia, reprinted in "The President on Election Results," *New York Times*, November 25, 1900.

456 *he touted his record*: WMcK, Fourth Annual Message, Miller Center.

456 *Wartime legislation had authorized*: "To Continue the Present Army," *New York Times*, November 23, 1900.

456 *"If you are in favor"*: quoted in ibid.

457 *"Let us tell them"*: quoted in "Debate on the Army Bill," *New York Times*, December 6, 1900.

457 *"military, civil, and judicial powers"*: quoted in "The Army Bill Passed," *Washington Post*, February 28, 1901.

457 *The requirements included*: "Cubans Must Assent," *Washington Post*, February 26, 1901.

458 *"Cuba is now independent"*: quoted in "Cubans Submit Their Constitution To-Day," *New York Times*, February 22, 1901.

459 *"Tell the Secretary"*: WMcK, quoted in "Memorandum," March 2, 1901, unsigned, GBCP, Box 53.

459 *On February 27, the constitutional delegates*: "Terms Fixed by Cuba," *Washington Post*, February 28, 1901.

459 *might simply dissolve*: "Cubans Show Temper," *Washington Post*, March 2, 1901.

459 *"Briefly stated"*: "Cubans Cannot Shirk," *Washington Post*, March 6, 1901.

459 *"cannot be called"*: "Gen. MacArthur's Report," *New York Times*, November 12, 1900.

459 *some 2,200 rebels relinquished*: "Filipinos Take the Oath," *New York Times*, December 4, 1900.

459 *recognized U.S. sovereignty*: "Politics in Philippines," *New York Times*, December 18, 1900.

459 *insurgent leaders had surrendered*: "Filipinos Lay Down Arms," *New York Times*, January 15, 1901.

459 *"Conditions rapidly improving"*: William Howard Taft to Root, January 9, 1901, WMcKP, Reel 14.

460 *"and are entirely willing to accept"*: quoted in "Civil Government for the Philippines," *New York Times*, January 26, 1901.

460 *"policy of conciliation"*: quoted in Goodwin, p. 269.

460 *"immediately marked for assassination"*: quoted in "Civil Government for the Philippines."

460 *"peaceful industrial progress"*: quoted in ibid.

461 *"the most practicable and feasible"*: quoted in "Isthmian Canal Report," *New York Times*, December 5, 1900.

461 *The two Senate floor amendments*: Taliaferro, p. 391.

461 *"absurd, void"*: "The Canal Treaty Still Under Fire," *New York Times*, December 16, 1900.

461 *"If Great Britain should now reject"*: quoted in Taliaferro, p. 391.

462 *"that is, to repudiate"*: Hay to WMcK, September 23, 1900, WMcKP, Reel 12.

462 *by a vote of 55 to 18*: "Canal Treaty Ratified," *New York Times*, December 21, 1900.

462 *"shifting a dangerous responsibility"*: quoted in "Comment on Canal Treaty," *New York Times*, December 24, 1900.

462 *He signaled his flexibility*: Thayer, p. 2:258.

462 *would be $80 million*: "Surplus Will Be $80,000,000," *New York Times*, November 17, 1900.

463 *At 9:20 p.m. on January 22*: Joseph Choate to WMcK, WMcKP, Reel 14.

463 *"would have compelled"*: "M'Kinley's Tribute to Queen," *Washington Post*, February 7, 1901.

463 *"We believe that the cause"*: quoted in "Salisbury Comments on American Election," *New York Times*, November 10, 1900.

464 *"And the title"*: quoted in "A New Title for M'Kinley," *Washington Post*, February 24, 1901.

464 *"should not feel concerned"*: quoted in ibid.

29. BUFFALO

465 *50 percent more*: "Ready for Inauguration," *New York Times*, March 3, 1901.

465 *"for the cheaper windows"*: Ibid.

465 *A bed in a sleeping hall*: Ibid.

465 *"Is 50 cents a night"*: quoted in ibid.

465 *Some 12,000 people sought tickets*: Ibid.

466 *Pennsylvania Station at 4:50*: "Mr. Roosevelt's Quiet Entry," *New York Times*, March 3, 1901.

466 *He paid a brief courtesy call*: "Men of the Day Meet," *Washington Post*, March 4, 1901.

466 *Hanna maintained a stoic demeanor*: "Escorted to Capitol," *Washington Post*, March 5, 1901.

466 *"magnificently costumed"*: "Inauguration: McKinley and Roosevelt Installed with Fitting Honors," *Washington Post*, March 5, 1901.

466 *"We belong to a young nation"*: Theodore Roosevelt, inaugural address as vice president, March 4, 1901, www.theodore-roosevelt.com/images/research /speeches/trinauguralvicepresident.pdf.

467 *"high-hatted, long-coated"*: "Inauguration: McKinley and Roosevelt Installed with Fitting Honors."

467 *40,000 strong*: Ibid.

467 *"unwelcome freight of moisture"*: Ibid.

467 *"The national verdict of 1896"*: WMcK, inaugural address, March 4, 1901, *Bartleby*, http://www.bartleby.com/124/pres41.html.

468 *"a gathering of well-bred people"*: "In Fairyland," *Washington Post*, March 5, 1901.

468 *"high in the neck"*: Ibid.

468 *"It is noticeable"*: Ibid.

468 *The president devoted March 5*: "First of His New Term," *Washington Post*, March 6, 1901.

468 *"particularly striking"*: "From the Baltimore American," *Washington Post*, March 6, 1901, reprint of *Baltimore American* editorial, "Mr. M'Kinley's Inaugural."

468 *"with more than ordinary authority"*: "From the New York Tribune," *Washington Post*, March 6, 1901, reprint of *New York Tribune* editorial.

468 *"smooth and dulcet"*: "From the Philadelphia Record," *Washington Post*, March 6, 1901, reprint of *Philadelphia Record* editorial.

469 *"No casualties our side"*: MacArthur to Corbin, received March 28, 1901, in *Correspondence Relating to the War with Spain*, p. 2:1262.

469 *"Funston, this is a desperate undertaking"*: quoted in Silbey, *A War of Frontier and Empire*, p. 176.

469 *"The complete termination"*: Emilio Aguinaldo, "To the Philippine People," reprinted in MacArthur to Corbin, received April 10, 1901, in *Correspondence Relating to the War with Spain*, p. 2:1267.

470 *"But he will promise"*: Murat Halstead to WMcK, April 5, 1901, WMcKP, Reel 15.

470 *"Washington, Tell, Joan of Arc"*: Twain, "Thirty Thousand Killed a Million."

471 *"unwilling to proceed"*: quoted in Gould, *The Presidency of William McKinley*, p. 247.

471 *"seize all occasions"*: quoted in ibid.

471 *"ultra-protectionist"*: "President's Tariff Views," *New York Times*, May 31, 1901.

471 *"It is asserted"*: "Uneasy about Tariff," *New York Times*, June 16, 1901.

472 *"home on the rails"*: Anthony, p. 225.

472 *"Do you know that you"*: quoted in Rixey and Braisted, p. 239.

472 *When Ida heard about it*: Anthony, p. 226. The following descriptions and quotes regarding Ida on this trip are from this source.

474 *drafted a statement renouncing*: GBCD, June 10, 1901, Box 53.

474 *"strange or ridiculous"*: quoted in ibid.

475 *I regret that the suggestion*: WMcK, statement issued June 11, 1901, reprinted in "President Does Not Want a Third Term," *New York Times*, June 12, 1901.

475 *convention voted 15 to 14*: "Accept Platt Amendment," *New York Times*, May 29, 1901.

475 *McKinley hurriedly called an emergency meeting*: "Cuban Problems Serious," *New York Times*, May 31, 1901.

475 *"exorbitant" indemnity demands*: Hay to William Rockhill, May 9, 1901, WMcKP, Reel 15.

476 *"indubitable evidence"*: Hay to WMcK, July 18, 1901, WMcKP, Reel 16.

476 *"It is, therefore, within the constitutional power"*: quoted in "Senator Foraker's View," *New York Times*, May 28, 1901.

476 *The new language formally abrogated*: Leech, *In the Days of McKinley*, p. 514.

477 *"I am profoundly gratified"*: quoted in Taliaferro, p. 405.

477 *"A wise diplomacy"*: quoted in "Pauncefote's Diplomacy," *Washington Post*, July 19, 1901.

477 *"United States Steel Corporation"*: "Gigantic Steel Monopoly," *New York Times*, June 15, 1901.

477 *Salt producers were developing*: "First International Trust Forming," *New York Times*, June 25, 1901.

477 *bituminous coal industry*: "Morgan's Coal Trust," *Washington Post*, July 2, 1901.

477 *Wall Street share prices*: Gould, *The Presidency of William McKinley*, p. 248.

477 *"This trust question"*: quoted in ibid., p. 249.

477 *"a collection of data"*: quoted in ibid.

478 *"in his best mood"*: Dawes, p. 274. This diary entry captures the full description of the Canton visit.

478 *He hung out in a working-class saloon*: Miller, *The President and the Assassin*, p. 32.

478 *"I never had much luck"*: "Career of Assassin," *Washington Post*, September 8, 1901.

478 *"the queen of anarchy"*: Halstead, *The Illustrious Life of William McKinley*, p. 36.

478 *"She set me on fire"*: quoted in "Career of Assassin."

478 *pursued his deadly purpose*: Halstead, *The Illustrious Life of William McKinley*, p. 36.

479 *.32 caliber pistol*: "Official Report of the Case of President McKinley," *American Journal of the Medical Sciences*, October 19, 1901, p. 505.

479 *When a small girl*: Halstead, *The Illustrious Life of William McKinley*, p. 36.

479 *"Am I shot?"*: quoted in ibid., p. 38.

479 *"I fear you are"*: quoted in ibid.

479 *"My wife"*: quoted in Olcott, p. 2:316.

480 *"Let no one hurt him"*: quoted in ibid.

480 *eighteen minutes after four*: "Official Report of the Case of President McKinley," p. 503.

480 *whispered the Lord's Prayer*: Leech, *In the Days of McKinley*, p. 596.

480 *completed by 6:50 p.m.*: "Official Report of the Case of President McKinley," p. 507.

480 *"Tell me all"*: quoted in Anthony, p. 245.

480 *"Went to Niagra* [sic] *Falls"*: quoted in ibid.

481 *"somewhat encouraging"*: "Feared by Doctors," *Washington Post*, September 8, 1901.

481 *"his mind was clear"*: "Official Report of the Case of President McKinley," p. 512.

481 *"The President's condition"*: Ibid., p. 516.

481 *"It is useless, gentlemen"*: quoted in Leech, *In the Days of McKinley*, p. 600.

481 *"Good-bye"*: quoted in ibid., p. 601.

481 *"It is God's way"*: quoted in ibid.

481 *"I want to go with you"*: quoted in Anthony, p. 250.

481 *"We are all going"*: quoted in ibid.

481 *He died at 2:15*: "Official Report of the Case of President McKinley," p. 517.

EPILOGUE

483 *"a solemn pledge"*: Goodwin, p. 280.

483 *"In this hour of deep"*: quoted in ibid.

483 *"I am President"*: quoted in ibid., p. 281.

484 *100,000 people filed by*: "William McKinley," *Wikipedia*.

484 *In Canton, another 100,000*: Ibid.

484 *a million schoolchildren*: Ibid.

484 *Twenty Ohio schools*: Ibid.

484 *believed McKinley would loom large*: Phillips, p. 161.

484 *ranked variously at 15th, 16th*: Merry, *Where They Stand*, p. 244.

485 *"one of the more successful"*: Lichtman and DeCell, p. 185.

485 *"made their country a world power"*: Zimmermann, part of book subtitle.

485 *"consciously masterminded"*: Ibid., p. 10.

487 *"by flashes or whims"*: quoted in Merry, "The Odd Couple."

487 *"the bride at every wedding"*: quoted in ibid.

487 *"a flubdub with a streak"*: quoted in Cowan, p. 20.

487 *"a better president than McKinley"*: quoted in ibid.

488 *"the first modern president"*: Gould, *The Presidency of William McKinley*, chapter heading, p. 231.

488 *"His reliance on manipulation"*: Morgan, *William McKinley and His America*, p. 405.

— INDEX —

— ILLUSTRATION CREDITS —

1. Library of Congress
2. Library of Congress
3. Library of Congress
4. McKinley Presidential Library & Museum
5. McKinley Presidential Library & Museum
6. McKinley Presidential Library & Museum
7. Library of Congress
8. Library of Congress
9. McKinley Presidential Library & Museum
10. First Ladies Museum
11. McKinley Presidential Library & Museum
12. First Ladies Museum
13. Library of Congress
14. Library of Congress
15. Library of Congress
16. Library of Congress
17. McKinley Presidential Library & Museum
18. Library of Congress
19. Library of Congress
20. Library of Congress
21. Library of Congress
22. Library of Congress
23. Library of Congress
24. Library of Congress
25. Library of Congress
26. Library of Congress
27. Library of Congress
28. Library of Congress
29. Library of Congress
30. Library of Congress
31. Library of Congress
32. Getty Images
33. Library of Congress
34. Library of Congress
35. McKinley Presidential Library & Museum

— ABOUT THE AUTHOR —

ROBERT W. MERRY has spent nearly forty-five years as a Washington, D.C., journalist and publishing executive, including *Wall Street Journal* correspondent and CEO of Congressional Quarterly Inc. He is the author of the *New York Times* bestseller and Notable Book *A Country of Vast Designs*, a biography of James K. Polk; *Where They Stand*, on presidential rankings; *Sands of Empire*, a foreign policy treatise; and *Taking on the World*, about prominent twentieth-century journalists Joseph and Stewart Alsop. He lives with his wife, Susan P. Merry, in Langley, Washington, and Washington, D.C.